9780331623406

UNDER THE GENERAL EDITORSHIP OF

Gordon N. Ray

REALISM

NATURALISM

SYMBOLISM

EXPRESSIONISM

Landmarks in

DRAMA OF DISCUSSION

VERSE DRAMA

FOLK DRAMA

THEATER OF THE GROTESQUE

EPIC THEATER

ECLECTICISM

THEATER OF THE ABSURD

Edited by

Modern Drama

FROM IBSEN TO IONESCO

Charles Edward Aughtry · WHEATON COLLEGE

HOUGHTON MIFFLIN COMPANY · BOSTON
New York · Atlanta · Geneva, Ill. · Dallas · Palo Alto

Copyright © 1963 by Charles Edward Aughtry. All rights reserved. The selections in this collection are used by permission of and special arrangement with the proprietors of their respective copyrights. Printed in the U.S.A.

Ibsen's notes and scenario for "A Doll's House," reprinted with the permission of Charles Scribner's Sons from *The Collected Works of Henrik Ibsen*, Volume 12. From Ibsen's Workshop. Translated by A. G. Chater. Copyright 1911 Charles Scribner's Sons; renewal copyright 1939 Frank Archer.

"A Doll's House," by Henrik Ibsen; translated by Eva Le Gallienne. From *Six Plays by Henrik Ibsen*. © Copyright 1957 by Eva Le Gallienne. Reprinted by permission of Random House, Inc.

"Miss Julie," by August Strindberg, with Author's Foreword to same; translated by Elizabeth Sprigge. Reprinted by permission of Willis Kingsley Wing. Copyright © 1955, by Elizabeth Sprigge.

"A Dream Play," by August Strindberg, with Author's Note to same; translated by Elizabeth Sprigge. Reprinted by permission of Willis Kingsley Wing. Copyright © 1955, by Elizabeth Sprigge.

"Man and Superman," by George Bernard Shaw. Used by permission of the Public Trustee, The Society of Authors, and Dodd, Mead & Company, Inc.

"The Reform of the Theatre" and "The Play, the Player, and the Scene," by W. B. Yeats. Reprinted with the permission of the publisher from *Plays and Controversies* by W. B. Yeats. Copyright 1907, 1912, 1921, 1924 by The Macmillan Company.

"On Baile's Strand," by W. B. Yeats. Reprinted with the permission of the publisher from *Collected Plays* by W. B. Yeats. Copyright 1934, 1952 by The Macmilllan Co.

"The Playboy of the Western World," by John M. Synge. Copyright 1907 and renewed 1934 by The Executors of the Estate of John M. Synge. Reprinted by permission of Random House, Inc.

"Six Characters in Search of an Author," by Luigi Pirandello, with Preface to same. From the book *Naked Masks: Five Plays* by Luigi Pirandello. Copyright, 1922, by E. P. Dutton & Co., Inc. Renewal, 1950, by Stefano, Fausto and Lietta Pirandello. Reprinted by permission of the publishers.

"The Alienation Effect in Chinese Acting," by Bertolt Brecht; translated by Eric Bentley. Copyright 1949 by *Furioso*. Reprinted by permission.

"The Good Woman of Setzuan," by Bertolt Brecht; translated by Eric Bentley. Copyright © 1947, 1948, 1961 by Eric Bentley. Originally published in the volume *Parables for the Theater* by the University of Minnesota Press, Minneapolis.

From the Introduction to Arthur Miller's *Collected Plays*. Copyright © 1957 by Arthur Miller. Reprinted by permission of The Viking Press, Inc.

"Death of a Salesman," by Arthur Miller. Copyright © 1949 by Arthur Miller. This play in its printed form is designed for the reading public only. All dramatic rights in it are fully protected by copyrights and no public or private performance — professional or amateur — and no public readings for profit may be given without the written permission of the author and the payment of royalty. Anyone disregarding the author's rights renders himself liable to prosecution. Communications should be addressed to the author's representatives, MCA Artists, Ltd., 598 Madison Ave., New York 22, N.Y.

"The Tragedy of Language," by Eugene Ionesco; translated by Jack Undank. Reprinted from *The Tulane Drama Review*, by permission of M. Ionesco, Mr. Undank, and *The Tulane Drama Review*.

"The Bald Soprano," by Eugene Ionesco. Reprinted from *Four Plays* by Eugene Ionesco, translated by Donald M. Allen, published by Grove Press, Inc., copyright © 1958 by Grove Press, Inc. (A shortened version of the translation of "The Bald Soprano" was published in *New World Writing, Ninth Mentor Selection:* © 1956 by Eugene Ionesco.)

Contents

PREFACE	ix
REALISM · *Henrik Ibsen*	1
Notes and Scenario for *A Doll's House*	5
A Doll's House (1879). Translated by Eva Le Gallienne	8
NATURALISM · *August Strindberg*	65
Author's Foreword to *Miss Julie*	69
Miss Julie (1888). Translated by Elizabeth Sprigge	78
SYMBOLISM · *Maurice Maeterlinck*	107
The Tragical in Daily Life	111
Pelléas and Mélisande (1893). Translated by Richard Hovey	118
EXPRESSIONISM · *August Strindberg*	153
Author's Note to *A Dream Play*	158
A Dream Play (1902). Translated by Elizabeth Sprigge	159
THE DRAMA OF DISCUSSION · *George Bernard Shaw*	207
Epistle Dedicatory to *Man and Superman*	211
Man and Superman (1903)	232
The Revolutionist's Handbook	350
VERSE DRAMA · *William Butler Yeats*	385
The Reform of the Theatre	390
FROM The Play, the Player, and the Scene	392
On Baile's Strand (1903)	396

FOLK DRAMA · *John Millington Synge*	417
Preface to *The Playboy of the Western World*	420
The Playboy of the Western World (1907)	422
THE THEATER OF THE GROTESQUE · *Luigi Pirandello*	465
Preface to *Six Characters in Search of an Author*	469
Six Characters in Search of an Author (1921). Translated by Edward Storer	479
EPIC THEATER · *Bertolt Brecht*	521
The Alienation Effect in Chinese Acting	525
The Good Woman of Setzuan (1941). Translated by Eric Bentley	533
ECLECTICISM · *Arthur Miller*	595
FROM THE Introduction to Arthur Miller's *Collected Plays*	598
Death of a Salesman (1949)	612
THE THEATER OF THE ABSURD · *Eugene Ionesco*	687
The Tragedy of Language	692
The Bald Soprano (1950). Translated by Donald M. Allen	696
SELECTED GENERAL READING LIST	721
SELECTED CRITICISM	722
GLOSSARY OF TERMS	724

Preface

The chief originality of this volume is that for the first time it makes readily available to students some relevant documents by major modern playwrights and juxtaposes these documents with plays which have proved to be milestones in the development of the modern drama. Each play is preceded by notes or other commentary in which the dramatist throws light on his purpose, and this the reader may use as a touchstone in evaluating the aim, method, and achievement of the play.

The plays themselves have been chosen as representative of the major tempers and trends of modern drama, each being an example of an innovation which has shown staying power and has exerted influence over the years. The major considerations behind the selection of plays were the following: (1) intrinsic worth as dramatic literature; (2) originality and priority in time; (3) representative quality; and (4) subsequent influence or historical importance. Thus this anthology is predicated on the belief that a limited number of significant plays exemplifying innovations in style and technique, together with well-chosen comments by their authors, provides the best introduction to the modern drama and theater. These eleven plays, without exception, are truly landmarks: even the more recent ones have established themselves in the canon of the modern drama. The plays, with accompanying documents, are presented in chronological order to constitute a short history of the main currents of modern drama.

Editorial interpretation has been deliberately held to a minimum. The introductions comment briefly on the playwright, play, and dramatic mode or style exemplified, but make no direct allusions to the prefatory documents, leaving these to speak for themselves. It has been the editor's intent that his brief remarks should serve merely to enlighten and to introduce, but not to intrude between the play and the reader. Rather, let the two — reader and play — develop their own special relationship, without too much attendance or chaperonage.

CHARLES EDWARD AUGHTRY

Wheaton College
Norton, Massachusetts

REALISM

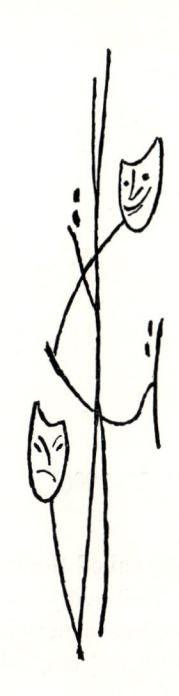

Henrik Ibsen

A DOLL'S HOUSE

[1879]

Henrik Ibsen [1828–1906]

Henrik Ibsen is often called the father of modern drama. By this, one usually means that with his emergence into his "modern" period, Ibsen established a new basis in both form and idea for the drama of his time and later. Prior to the late 1870's the contemporary drama of Europe was essentially romantic or comic entertainment. Plays hinged upon the unfolding of intricate plots in which an artificial view of human experience was presented. With Ibsen, however, a new age was born.

Ibsen took the drama seriously, which is to say that he took life seriously (and very soberly too). His career as director and writer in Bergen and Christiania (Oslo) introduced him to the drama of his day, and made him aware that the theater could serve a more valuable use. Ibsen himself moved from plays which celebrated figures from Norwegian history and mythology, and from the great romantic odyssey, *Peer Gynt*, to plays which dealt authentically and candidly with typical figures in contemporary life. He established what was to be the norm of modern drama: realism in both content and method. *Pillars of Society* (1877), *A Doll's House* (1879), and *Ghosts* (1881) announce dramatically a new idea of the theater. Though Ibsen veered off into somewhat misty regions in some of his last plays (of the 1890's), he is remembered as an innovator of realism; and it was as a realist that he was influential in determining the pattern of modern drama.

It is relatively easy to define realism in the drama, though not so easy to separate it from its extreme form, naturalism (see Strindberg's *Miss Julie*). Realism is the artistic presentation of selected facts of human experience as they might actually happen in the lives of real people. In its selectivity it usually criticizes; that is, it presents an action and makes some comment on it. In realistic plays one can often see characters who are familiar to him involved in circumstances which he may know at first hand. Realism is, in a very literal sense, believable (once we have accepted certain dramatic conventions which are by now so familiar to us that we are not even aware of them). Realism does not require the same degree of "suspension of disbelief" that, say, a poetic drama ordinarily does. In the realistic play the characters dress, speak, and act as you would expect them to in the circumstances in which you see them. Ordinarily the realistic theater is no place for wonderment, but essentially a place in which to see "real-life" situations acted out with fidelity to the observable facts.

When Nora Helmer slammed the door near the final curtain in *A Doll's House*, it may be said that the modern drama was announced. Here was a realistic, candid presentation, in a believable context, of some of the real problems of real men and women. The citadel of the family was no longer sacrosanct. In 1879, when Ibsen was writing the play, women's emancipation was a controversial issue. Ibsen was not a feminist or a proponent of women's rights as such. Rather, he was a devotee of truth and freedom: if

Ibsen and Realism

women were subordinate to men, they were not free human agents. If they were slaves to duty (an abominable word to Ibsen), they should cast off their bonds and declare themselves free. Understandably, suffragettes took Ibsen as their champion, though Ibsen was of no party. In some ways one can say that he missed his target: he spoke for freedom using a specific abridgment of freedom as an example, and was thought to be a party man with a platform. He did not mean to be a reformer in any narrow sense, and yet seemed to many to be one. The realism of his presentation was overwhelming.

Some may say, with Halvdan Koht, that Ibsen's view of women was romantic. But he was on the side of pure, natural feelings unhampered by the platitudes of duty and "idealism" (see Shaw's *The Quintessence of Ibsenism*), and seemed to feel that a natural instinct for right inhered in women. As a result of Ibsen's portrayal of Nora, one of the major difficulties in A *Doll's House* is to see Torvald not as a conventional tyrannical husband from the melodrama, but as someone whom Nora could genuinely love. (If Torvald is *merely* an obtuse, domineering husband, why would such a one as Nora have married him in the first place; and why would she cheerfully continue to make sacrifices for him?) As the play progresses toward its final face-to-face discussion between Nora and Torvald, one has to decide just what issues are at stake. What, essentially, is the play about? What is the theme?

NOTES AND SCENARIO FOR A DOLL'S HOUSE*

Notes for the modern tragedy Rome, 19. 10, 78.

There are two kinds of spiritual law, two kinds of conscience, one in man and another, altogether different, in woman. They do not understand each other; but in practical life the woman is judged by man's law, as though she were not a woman but a man.

The wife in the play ends by having no idea of what is right or wrong; natural feeling on the one hand and belief in authority on the other have altogether bewildered her.

A woman cannot be herself in the society of the present day, which is an exclusively masculine society, with laws framed by men and with a judicial system that judges feminine conduct from a masculine point of view.

She has committed forgery, and she is proud of it; for she did it out of love for her husband, to save his life. But this husband with his commonplace principles of honor is on the side of the law and regards the question with masculine eyes.

Spiritual conflicts. Oppressed and bewildered by the belief in authority, she loses faith in her moral right and ability to bring up her children. Bitterness. A mother in modern society, like certain insects who go away and die when she has done her duty in the propagation of the race. [sic] Love of life, of home, of husband and children and family. Here and there a womanly shaking-off of her thoughts. Sudden return of anxiety and terror. She must bear it all alone. The catastrophe approaches, inexorably, inevitably. Despair, conflict and destruction.

(Krogstad has acted dishonorably and thereby become well-to-do; now his prosperity does not help him, he cannot recover his honor.)

* From *The Collected Works of Henrik Ibsen:* Vol. XII, *From Ibsen's Workshop,* trans. A. G. Chater (New York: Charles Scribner's Sons, 1912), pp. 91–95.

SCENARIO

First Act

A room comfortably, but not showily, furnished. In the back, on the right, a door leads to the hall; on the left another door leads to the room or office of the master of the house, which can be seen when the door is opened. A fire in the stove. Winter day.

She enters from the back, humming gaily; she is in outdoor dress and carries several parcels, has been shopping. As she opens the door, a Porter is seen in the hall, carrying a Christmas tree. She: Put it down there for the present. (Taking out her purse) How much? Porter: Fifty öre. She: Here is a crown. No, keep the change. The Porter thanks her and goes. She continues humming and smiling with quiet glee as she opens several of the parcels she has brought. Calls off, is he at home? Yes! At first, conversation through the closed door; then he opens it and goes on talking to her while continuing to work most of the time, standing at his desk. There is a ring at the hall door; he does not want to be disturbed; shuts himself in. The maid opens the door to her mistress's friend, just arrived in town. Happy surprise. Mutual explanation of the position of affairs. He has received the post of manager in the new joint-stock bank and is to enter on his duties at the New Year; all financial worries are at an end. The friend has come to town to look for some small employment in an office or whatever may present itself. Mrs. Stenborg [later Helmer] gives her good hopes, is certain that all will turn out well. The maid opens the front door to the debt collector. Mrs. [Helmer] terrified; they exchange a few words; he is shown into the office. Mrs. [Helmer] and her friend; the circumstances of the debt collector are touched upon. [Helmer] enters in his overcoat; has sent the collector out the other way. Conversation about the friend's affairs; hesitation on his part. He and the friend go out; his wife follows them into the hall; the Nurse enters with the children. Mother and children play. The collector enters. Mrs. [Helmer] sends the children out to the left. Great scene between her and him. He goes. [Helmer] enters; has met him on the stairs; displeased; wants to know what he came back for? Her support? No intrigues. His wife cautiously tries to pump him. Strict legal answers. Exit to his room. She (repeating her words when the collector went out): But that's impossible. Why, I did it from love!

Second Act

The last day of the year. Midday. Nora and the old Nurse. Nora, impelled by uneasiness, is putting on her things to go out. Anxious random questions of one kind and another give a hint that thoughts of death are in her mind. Tries to banish these thoughts, to turn it off, hopes that some-

A Doll's House: Notes and Scenario

thing or other may intervene. But what? The Nurse goes off to the left. [Helmer] enters from his room. Short dialogue between him and Nora. The Nurse re-enters, looking for Nora; the youngest child is crying. Annoyance and questioning on [Helmer's] part; exit the Nurse; [Helmer] is going in to the children. Doctor [R]ank enters. Scene between him and [Helmer]. Nora soon re-enters; she has turned back; anxiety has driven her home again. Scene between her, the Doctor and [Helmer]. [Helmer] goes into his room. Scene between Nora and the Doctor. The Doctor goes out. Nora alone. Mrs. Linde enters. Scene between her and Nora. Krogstad enters. Short scene between him, Mrs. Linde and Nora. Mrs. Linde goes in to the children. Scene between Krogstad and Nora. She entreats and implores him for the sake of her little children; in vain. Krogstad goes out. The letter is seen to fall from outside into the letter box. Mrs. Linde re-enters after a short pause. Scene between her and Nora. Half confession. Mrs. Linde goes out. Nora alone. [Helmer] enters. Scene between him and Nora. He wants to empty the letter box. Entreaties, jests, half playful persuasion. He promises to let business wait till after New Year's Day; but at 12 o'clock midnight . . . ! Exit. Nora alone. Nora (looking at the clock): It is five o'clock. Five; seven hours till midnight. Twenty-four hours till the next midnight. Twenty-four and seven — thirty-one. Thirty-one hours to live.

Third Act

A muffled sound of dance music is heard from the floor above. A lighted lamp on the table. Mrs. Linde sits in an armchair and absently turns the pages of a book, tries to read, but seems unable to fix her attention; once or twice she looks at her watch. Nora comes down from the dance; uneasiness has driven her; surprise at finding Mrs. Linde, who pretends that she wanted to see Nora in her costume. Helmer [sic], displeased at her going away, comes to fetch her back. The Doctor also enters, but to say good-bye. Meanwhile Mrs. Linde has gone into the side room on the right. Scene between the Doctor, Helmer and Nora. He is going to bed, he says, never to get up again; they are not to come and see him; there is ugliness about a death bed. He goes out. Helmer goes upstairs again with Nora, after the latter has exchanged a few words of farewell with Mrs. Linde. Mrs. Linde alone. Then Krogstad. Scene and explanation between them. Both go out. Nora and the children. Then she alone. Then Helmer. He takes the letters out of the letter box. Short scene; goodnight; he goes into his room. Nora in despair prepares for the final step; is already at the door when Helmer enters with the open letter in his hand. Great scene. A ring. Letter to Nora from Krogstad. Final scene. Divorce. Nora leaves the house.

Translated by Eva Le Gallienne

A Doll's House

A PLAY IN THREE ACTS

CHARACTERS

TORVALD HELMER, *a lawyer*
NORA, *his wife*
DOCTOR RANK
MRS. KRISTINE LINDE
NILS KROGSTAD, *an attorney*

HELMER'S THREE SMALL CHILDREN
ANNE-MARIE,* *nurse at the Helmers'*
HELENE, *maid at the Helmers'*
A PORTER

The action takes place in the Helmer residence.

ACT ONE

Scene: A comfortable room furnished with taste, but not expensively. In the back wall a door on the right leads to the hall; another door on the left leads to HELMER's *study. Between the two doors a piano. In the left wall, center, a door; farther downstage a window. Near the window a round table with an armchair and a small sofa. In the right wall upstage a door, and further downstage a porcelain stove round which are grouped a couple of armchairs and a rocking chair. Between the stove and the door stands a small table. Engravings on the walls. A whatnot with china objects and various bric-a-brac. A small bookcase with books in fancy bindings. The floor is carpeted; a fire burns in the stove. A winter day.*

NORA. Be sure and hide the Christmas tree carefully, Helene, the children mustn't see it till this evening, when it's all decorated. (*To the* PORTER, *taking out her purse.*) How much?
PORTER. Fifty, Ma'am.
NORA. Here you are. No — keep the change. (*The* PORTER *thanks her and goes.* NORA *closes the door. She laughs gaily to herself as she takes off her*

---
* For stage purposes, often ANNA-MARIA.

A Doll's House

outdoor things. Takes a bag of macaroons out of her pocket and eats a couple, then she goes cautiously to the door of her husband's study and listens) Yes — he's home. *(She goes over to the table right, humming to herself again.)*

HELMER *(from his study).* Is that my little lark twittering out there?

NORA *(busily undoing the packages).* Yes, it is.

HELMER. Is that my little squirrel bustling about?

NORA. Yes.

HELMER. When did my squirrel get home?

NORA. Just this minute. *(She puts the bag of macaroons back in her pocket and wipes her mouth.)* Oh, Torvald, do come in here! You must see what I have bought.

HELMER. Now, don't disturb me! *(A moment afterwards he opens the door and looks in — pen in hand.)* Did you say "bought"? That — all *that*? Has my little spendthrift been flinging money about again?

NORA. But, Torvald, surely this year we ought to let ourselves go a bit! After all, it's the first Christmas we haven't had to be careful.

HELMER. Yes, but that doesn't mean we can afford to *squander* money.

NORA. Oh, Torvald, we can squander a bit, can't we? Just a little tiny bit? You're going to get a big salary and you'll be making lots and lots of money.

HELMER. After the first of the year, yes. But remember there'll be three whole months before my salary falls due.

NORA. We can always borrow in the meantime.

HELMER. Nora! *(Goes to her and pulls her ear playfully.)* There goes my little featherbrain! Let's suppose I borrowed a thousand crowns today, you'd probably squander it all during Christmas week; and then let's suppose that on New Year's Eve a tile blew off the roof and knocked my brains out —

NORA *(puts her hand over his mouth).* Don't say such frightful things!

HELMER. But let's suppose it happened — then what?

NORA. If anything as terrible as *that* happened, I shouldn't care whether I owed money or not.

HELMER. But what about the people I'd borrowed from?

NORA. Who cares about them? After all they're just strangers.

HELMER. Oh, Nora, Nora! What a little woman you are! But seriously, Nora, you know my feelings about such things. I'll have no borrowing — I'll have no debts! There can be no freedom — no, nor beauty either — in a home based upon loans and credit. We've held out bravely up to now, and we shall continue to do so for the short time that remains.

NORA *(goes toward the stove).* Just as you like, Torvald.

HELMER *(following her).* Come, come; the little lark mustn't droop her wings. Don't tell me my little squirrel is sulking! *(He opens his purse.)* Nora! Guess what I have here!

NORA *(turns quickly).* Money!

HELMER. There you are! *(He hands her some notes.)* Don't you suppose I know that money is needed at Christmas time?

NORA (*counts the notes*). Ten, twenty, thirty, forty. Oh thank you, thank you, Torvald — this'll last me a long time!

HELMER. Better see that it does!

NORA. Oh, it will — I know. But do come here. I want to show you everything I've bought, and all so cheap too! Here are some new clothes for Ivar, and a little sword — and this horse and trumpet are for Bob, and here's a doll for Emmy — and a doll's bed. They're not worth much, but she's sure to tear them to pieces in a minute anyway. This is some dress material and handkerchiefs for the maids. Old Anne-Marie really should have had something better.

HELMER. And what's in that other parcel?

NORA (*with a shriek*). No, Torvald! You can't see that until this evening!

HELMER. I can't, eh? But what about you — you little squanderer? Have you thought of anything for yourself?

NORA. Oh, there's nothing I want, Torvald.

HELMER. Of course there is! — now tell me something sensible you'd really like to have.

NORA. But there's nothing — really! Except of course —

HELMER. Well?

NORA (*she fingers the buttons on his coat; without looking at him*). Well — If you really want to give me something — you might — you might —

HELMER. Well, well, out with it!

NORA (*rapidly*). You might give me some money, Torvald — just anything you feel you could spare; and then one of these days I'll buy myself something with it.

HELMER. But Nora —

NORA. Oh, please do, dear Torvald — I beg you to! I'll wrap it up in beautiful gold paper and hang it on the Christmas tree. Wouldn't that be fun?

HELMER. What's the name of the bird that eats up money?

NORA. The Spendthrift bird — I know! But do let's do as I say, Torvald! — it will give me a chance to choose something I really need. Don't you think that's a sensible idea? Don't you?

HELMER (*smiling*). Sensible enough — providing you really *do* buy something for yourself with it. But I expect you'll fritter it away on a lot of unnecessary household expenses, and before I know it you'll be coming to me for more.

NORA. But, Torvald —

HELMER. You can't deny it, Nora dear. (*Puts his arm round her waist.*) The Spendthrift is a sweet little bird — but it costs a man an awful lot of money to support one!

NORA. How can you say such nasty things — I save all I can!

HELMER. Yes, I dare say — but that doesn't amount to much!

NORA (*hums softly and smiles happily*). You don't know, Torvald, what expenses we larks and squirrels have!

A *Doll's House* 11

HELMER. You're a strange little creature; exactly like your father. You'll go to any lengths to get a sum of money — but as soon as you have it, it just slips through your fingers. You don't know yourself what's become of it. Well, I suppose one must just take you as you are. It's in your blood. Oh, yes! such things are hereditary, Nora.

NORA. I only wish I had inherited a lot of Father's qualities.

HELMER. And I wouldn't wish you any different than you are, my own sweet little lark. But Nora, it's just occurred to me — isn't there something a little — what shall I call it — a little guilty about you this morning?

NORA. About me?

HELMER. Yes. Look me straight in the eye.

NORA (*looking at him*). Well?

HELMER (*wags a threatening finger at her*). Has my little sweet-tooth been breaking rules today?

NORA. No! What makes you think that?

HELMER. Are you sure the sweet-tooth didn't drop in at the confectioner's?

NORA. No, I assure you, Torvald —

HELMER. She didn't nibble a little candy?

NORA. No, really not.

HELMER. Not even a macaroon or two?

NORA. No, Torvald, I assure you — really —

HELMER. There, there! Of course I'm only joking.

NORA (*going to the table right*). It would never occur to me to go against your wishes.

HELMER. Of course I know that — and anyhow — you've given me your word — (*Goes to her.*) Well, my darling, I won't pry into your little Christmas secrets. They'll be unveiled tonight under the Christmas tree.

NORA. Did you remember to ask Dr. Rank?

HELMER. No, it really isn't necessary. He'll take it for granted he's to dine with us. However, I'll ask him, when he stops by this morning. I've ordered some specially good wine. I am so looking forward to this evening, Nora, dear!

NORA. So am I — And the children will have such fun!

HELMER. Ah! How nice it is to feel secure; to look forward to a good position with an ample income. It's a wonderful prospect — isn't it, Nora?

NORA. Its's simply marvelous!

HELMER. Do you remember last Christmas? For three whole weeks — you locked yourself up every evening until past midnight — making paper flowers for the Christmas tree — and a lot of other wonderful things you wanted to surprise us with. I was never so bored in my life!

NORA. I wasn't a bit bored.

HELMER (*smiling*). But it all came to rather a sad end, didn't it, Nora?

NORA. Oh, do you have to tease me about that again! How could I help the cat coming in and tearing it all to pieces?

HELMER. Of course you couldn't help it, you poor darling! You meant to give us a good time — that's the main thing. But it's nice to know those lean times are over.

NORA. It's wonderful!

HELMER. Now I don't have to sit here alone, boring myself to death; and you don't have to strain your dear little eyes, and prick your sweet little fingers —

NORA (*claps her hands*). No, I don't — do I, Torvald! Oh! How lovely it all is. (*Takes his arm.*) I want to tell you how I thought we'd arrange things after Christmas. (*The doorbell rings.*) Oh, there's the bell. (*Tidies up the room a bit.*) It must be a visitor — how tiresome!

HELMER. I don't care to see any visitors, Nora — remember that.

HELENE (*in the doorway*). There's a lady to see you, Ma'am.

NORA. Well, show her in.

HELENE (*to* HELMER). And the Doctor's here too, Sir.

HELMER. Did he go straight to my study?

HELENE. Yes, he did, Sir.

> HELMER *goes into his study.* HELENE *ushers in* MRS. LINDE *who is dressed in traveling clothes, and closes the door behind her.*

MRS. LINDE (*in subdued and hesitant tone*). How do you do, Nora?

NORA (*doubtfully*). How do you do?

MRS. LINDE. You don't recognize me, do you?

NORA. No, I don't think — and yet — I seem to — (*With a sudden outburst.*) Kristine! Is it really you?

MRS. LINDE. Yes; it's really I!

NORA. Kristine! And to think of my not knowing you! But how could I when — (*More softly.*) You've changed so, Kristine!

MRS. LINDE. Yes, I suppose I have. After all — it's nine or ten years —

NORA. It is *that* long since we met? Yes, so it is. Oh, these last eight years have been such happy ones! Fancy your being in town! And imagine taking that long trip in midwinter! How brave you are!

MRS. LINDE. I arrived by the morning boat.

NORA. You've come for the Christmas holidays, I suppose — what fun! Oh, what a good time we'll have! Do take off your things. You're not cold, are you? (*Helping her.*) There; now we'll sit here by the stove. No, you take the arm-chair; I'll sit here in the rocker. (*Seizes her hands.*) Now you look more like yourself again. It was just at first — you're a bit paler, Kristine — and perhaps a little thinner.

MRS. LINDE. And much, much older, Nora.

NORA. Well, perhaps a *little* older — a tiny, tiny bit — not much, though. (*She suddenly checks herself; seriously.*) Oh, but, Kristine! What a thoughtless wretch I am, chattering away like that — Dear, darling Kristine, do forgive me!

MRS. LINDE. What for, Nora, dear?

NORA (*softly*). You lost your husband, didn't you, Kristine! You're a widow.

MRS. LINDE. Yes; my husband died three years ago.

NORA. Yes, I remember; I saw it in the paper. Oh, I *did* mean to write to you, Kristine! But I kept on putting it off, and all sorts of things kept coming in the way.

MRS. LINDE. I understand, dear Nora.

NORA. No, it was beastly of me, Kristine! Oh, you poor darling! What you must have gone through! — And he died without leaving you anything, didn't he?

MRS. LINDE. Yes.

NORA. And you have no children?

MRS. LINDE. No.

NORA. Nothing then?

MRS. LINDE. Nothing — Not even grief, not even regret.

NORA (*looking at her incredulously*). But how is that possible, Kristine?

MRS. LINDE (*smiling sadly and stroking her hair*). It sometimes happens, Nora.

NORA. Imagine being so utterly alone! It must be dreadful for you, Kristine! I have three of the loveliest children! I can't show them to you just now, they're out with their nurse. But I want you to tell me all about yourself —

MRS. LINDE. No, no; I'd rather hear about you, Nora —

NORA. No, I want you to begin. I'm not going to be selfish today. I'm going to think only of you. Oh! but one thing I *must* tell you. You haven't heard about the wonderful thing that's just happened to us, have you?

MRS. LINDE. No. What is it?

NORA. My husband's been elected president of the Joint Stock Bank!

MRS. LINDE. Oh, Nora — How splendid!

NORA. Yes; isn't it? You see, a lawyer's position is so uncertain, especially if he refuses to handle any cases that are in the least bit — shady; Torvald is very particular about such things — and I agree with him, of course! You can imagine how glad we are. He's to start at the Bank right after the New Year; he'll make a big salary and all sorts of percentages. We'll be able to live quite differently from then on — we'll have everything we want. Oh, Kristine! I'm so happy and excited! Won't it be wonderful to have lots and lots of money, and nothing to worry about!

MRS. LINDE. It certainly would be wonderful to have enough for one's needs.

NORA. Oh, not just for one's *needs*, Kristine! But heaps and heaps of money!

MRS. LINDE (*with a smile*). Nora, Nora, I see you haven't grown up yet! I remember at school you were a frightful spendthrift.

NORA (*quietly; smiling*). Yes; that's what Torvald always says. (*Holding up her forefinger.*) But I haven't had much chance to be a spendthrift. We have had to work hard — both of us.

MRS. LINDE. You too?

NORA. Oh yes! I did all sorts of little jobs: needlework, embroidery, crochet —that sort of thing. (*Casually.*) And other things as well. I suppose you know that Torvald left the Government service right after we were married. There wasn't much chance of promotion in his department, and of course he had to earn more money when he had me to support. But that first year he overworked himself terribly. He had to undertake all sorts of odd jobs, worked from morning till night. He couldn't stand it; his health gave way and he became deathly ill. The doctors said he absolutely *must* spend some time in the South.

MRS. LINDE. Yes, I heard you spent a whole year in Italy.

NORA. Yes, we did. It wasn't easy to arrange, I can tell you. It was just after Ivar's birth. But of course we had to go. It was a wonderful trip, and it saved Torvald's life. But it cost a fearful lot of money, Kristine.

MRS. LINDE. Yes, it must have.

NORA. Twelve hundred dollars! Four thousand eight hundred crowns! That's an awful lot of money, you know.

MRS. LINDE. You were lucky to have it.

NORA. Well, you see, we got it from Father.

MRS. LINDE. Oh, I see. Wasn't it just about that time that your father died?

NORA. Yes, it was, Kristine. Just think! I wasn't able to go to him — I couldn't be there to nurse him! I was expecting Ivar at the time and then I had my poor sick Torvald to look after. Dear, darling Papa! I never saw him again, Kristine. It's the hardest thing I have had to go through since my marriage.

MRS. LINDE. I know you were awfully fond of him. And after that you went to Italy?

NORA. Yes; then we had the money, you see; and the doctors said we must lose no time; so we started a month later.

MRS. LINDE. And your husband came back completely cured?

NORA. Strong as an ox!

MRS. LINDE. But — what about the doctor then?

NORA. How do you mean?

MRS. LINDE. Didn't the maid say something about a doctor, just as I arrived?

NORA. Oh, yes; Dr. Rank. He's our best friend — it's not a professional call; he stops in to see us every day. No, Torvald hasn't had a moment's illness since; and the children are strong and well, and so am I. (*Jumps up and claps her hands.*) Oh Kristine, Kristine! How lovely it is to be alive and happy! But how disgraceful of me! Here I am talking about nothing but myself! (*Seats herself upon a footstool close to* KRISTINE *and lays her arms on her lap.*) Please don't be cross with me — Is it really true, Kristine, that you didn't love your husband? Why did you marry him, then?

MRS. LINDE. Well, you see — Mother was still alive; she was bedridden; completely helpless; and I had my two younger brothers to take care of. I didn't think it would be right to refuse him.

NORA. No, I suppose not. I suppose he had money then?

A Doll's House

MRS. LINDE. Yes, I believe he was quite well off. But his business was precarious, Nora. When he died it all went to pieces, and there was nothing left.

NORA. And then —?

MRS. LINDE. Then I had to struggle along as best I could. I had a small shop for a while, and then I started a little school. These last three years have been one long battle — but it is over now, Nora. My dear mother is at rest — She doesn't need me any more. And my brothers are old enough to work, and can look after themselves.

NORA. You must have such a free feeling!

MRS. LINDE. No — only one of complete emptiness. I haven't a soul to live for! (*Stands up restlessly.*) I suppose that's why I felt I had to get away. I should think here it would be easier to find something to do — something to occupy one's thoughts. I might be lucky enough to get a steady job here — some office work, perhaps —

NORA. But that's so terribly tiring, Kristine; and you look so tired already. What you need is a rest. Couldn't you go to some nice watering-place?

MRS. LINDE (*going to the window*). I have no father to give me the money, Nora.

NORA (*rising*). Oh, please don't be cross with me!

MRS. LINDE (*goes to her*). My dear Nora, you mustn't be cross with me! In my sort of position it's hard not to become bitter. One has no one to work for, and yet one can't give up the struggle. One must go on living, and it makes one selfish. I'm ashamed to admit it — but, just now, when you told me the good news about your husband's new position — I was glad — not so much for your sake as for mine.

NORA. How do you mean? Oh of course — I see! You think Torvald might perhaps help you.

MRS. LINDE. That's what I thought, yes.

NORA. And so he shall, Kristine. Just you leave it to me. I'll get him in a really good mood — and then bring it up quite casually. Oh, it would be such fun to help you!

MRS. LINDE. How good of you, Nora dear, to bother on my account! It's especially good of you — after all, you've never had to go through any hardship.

NORA. I? Not go through any —?

MRS. LINDE (*smiling*). Well — Good Heavens — a little needlework, and so forth — You're just a child, Nora.

NORA (*tosses her head and paces the room*). You needn't be so patronizing!

MRS. LINDE. No?

NORA. You're just like all the rest. You all think I'm incapable of being serious —

MRS. LINDE. Oh, come now —

NORA. You seem to think I've had no troubles — that I've been through nothing in my life!

MRS. LINDE. But you've just told me all your troubles, Nora dear.

NORA. I've only told you trifles! (*Softly.*) I haven't mentioned the important thing.

MRS. LINDE. Important thing? What do you mean?

NORA. I know you look down on me, Kristine; but you really shouldn't. You take pride in having worked so hard and so long for your mother.

MRS. LINDE. I don't look down on anyone, Nora; I can't help feeling proud and happy too, to have been able to make Mother's last days a little easier —

NORA. And you're proud of what you did for your brothers, too.

MRS. LINDE. I think I have a right to be.

NORA. Yes, so do I. But I want you to know, Kristine — that I, too, have something to be proud of.

MRS. LINDE. I don't doubt that. But what are you referring to?

NORA. Hush! We must talk quietly. It would be dreadful if Torvald overheard us! He must never know about it! No one must know about it, except you.

MRS. LINDE. And what is it, Nora?

NORA. Come over here. (*Draws her down beside her on sofa.*) Yes, I have something to be proud and happy about too. I saved Torvald's life, you see.

MRS. LINDE. Saved his life? But how?

NORA. I told you about our trip to Italy. Torvald would never have recovered if it hadn't been for that.

MRS. LINDE. Yes, I know — and your father gave you the necessary money.

NORA (*smiling*). That's what everyone thinks — Torvald too; but —

MRS. LINDE. Well —?

NORA. Papa never gave us a penny. I raised the money myself.

MRS. LINDE. All that money! You?

NORA. Twelve hundred dollars. Four thousand eight hundred crowns. What do you think of that?

MRS. LINDE. But, Nora, how on earth did you do it? Did you win it in the lottery?

NORA (*contemptuously*). The lottery! Of course not! Any fool could have done that!

MRS. LINDE. Where did you get it then?

NORA (*hums and smiles mysteriously*). H'm; tra-la-la-la.

MRS. LINDE. You certainly couldn't have borrowed it.

NORA. Why not?

MRS. LINDE. A wife can't borrow without her husband's consent.

NORA (*tossing her head*). Oh I don't know! If a wife has a good head on her shoulders — and has a little sense of business —

MRS. LINDE. I don't in the least understand, Nora —

NORA. Well, you needn't. I never said I borrowed the money. I may have got it some other way. (*Throws herself back on the sofa.*) Perhaps I got it from some admirer. After all when one is as attractive as I am —!

A Doll's House

MRS. LINDE. What a mad little creature you are!

NORA. I'm sure you're dying of curiosity, Kristine —

MRS. LINDE. Nora, are you sure you haven't been a little rash?

NORA (*sitting upright again*). Is it rash to save one's husband's life?

MRS. LINDE. But mightn't it be rash to do such a thing behind his back?

NORA. But I couldn't tell him — don't you understand that! He wasn't even supposed to know how ill he was. The doctors didn't tell him — they came to me privately, told me his life was in danger and that he could only be saved by living in the South for a while. At first I tried persuasion; I cried, I begged, I cajoled — I said how much I longed to take a trip abroad like other young wives; I reminded him of my condition and told him he ought to humor me — and finally, I came right out and suggested that we borrow the money. But then, Kristine, he was almost angry; he said I was being frivolous and that it was his duty as my husband not to indulge my whims and fancies — I think that's what he called them. Then I made up my mind he must be saved in spite of himself — and I thought of a way.

MRS. LINDE. But didn't he ever find out from your father that the money was not from him?

NORA. No; never. You see, Papa died just about that time. I was going to tell him all about it and beg him not to give me away. But he was so very ill — and then, it was no longer necessary — unfortunately.

MRS. LINDE. And you have never confided all this to your husband?

NORA. Good heavens, no! That's out of the question! He's much too strict in matters of that sort. And besides — Torvald could never bear to think of owing anything to me! It would hurt his self-respect — wound his pride. It would ruin everything between us. Our whole marriage would be wrecked by it!

MRS. LINDE. Don't you think you'll ever tell him?

NORA (*thoughtfully; half-smiling*). Perhaps some day — a long time from now when I'm no longer so pretty and attractive. No! Don't laugh! Some day when Torvald is no longer as much in love with me as he is now; when it no longer amuses him to see me dance and dress-up and act for him — then it might be useful to have something in reserve. (*Breaking off.*) Oh, what nonsense! That time will never come! Well — what do you think of my great secret, Kristine? Haven't I something to be proud of too? It's caused me endless worry, though. It hasn't been easy to fulfill my obligations. You know, in business there are things called installments, and quarterly interest — and they're dreadfully hard to meet on time. I've had to save a little here and there, wherever I could. I couldn't save much out of the housekeeping, for of course Torvald had to live well. And I couldn't let the children go about badly dressed; any money I got for them, I spent on them, the darlings!

MRS. LINDE. Poor Nora! I suppose it had to come out of your own allowance.

NORA. Yes, of course. But after all, the whole thing was my doing. Whenever Torvald gave me money to buy some new clothes, or other things I needed, I never spent more than half of it; I always picked out the simplest cheapest dresses. It's a blessing that almost anything looks well on me — so Torvald never knew the difference. But it's been hard sometimes, Kristine. It's so nice to have pretty clothes — isn't it?

MRS. LINDE. I suppose it is.

NORA. And I made money in other ways too. Last winter I was lucky enough to get a lot of copying to do. I shut myself up in my room every evening and wrote far into the night. Sometimes I was absolutely exhausted — but it was fun all the same — working like that and earning money. It made me feel almost like a man!

MRS. LINDE. How much have you managed to pay off?

NORA. Well, I really don't know exactly. It's hard to keep track of things like that. All I know is — I've paid every penny I coud scrape together. There were times when I didn't know which way to turn! (*Smiles.*) Then I used to sit here and pretend that some rich old gentleman had fallen madly in love with me —

MRS. LINDE. What are you talking about? *What* old gentleman?

NORA. I'm just joking! And then he was to die and when they opened his will, there in large letters were to be the words: "I leave all my fortune to that charming Nora Helmer to be handed over to her immediately."

MRS. LINDE. But who *is* this old gentleman?

NORA. Good heavens, can't you understand? There never *was* any such old gentleman; I just used to make him up, when I was at the end of my rope and didn't know where to turn for money. But it doesn't matter now — the tiresome old fellow can stay where he is as far as I am concerned. I no longer need him nor his money; for now my troubles are over. (*Springing up.*) Oh, isn't it wonderful to think of, Kristine. No more troubles! No more worry! I'll be able to play and romp about with the children; I'll be able to make a charming lovely home for Torvald — have everything just as he likes it. And soon spring will be here, with its great blue sky. Perhaps we might take a little trip — I might see the ocean again. Oh, it's so marvelous to be alive and to be happy!

The hall doorbell rings.

MRS. LINDE (*rising*). There's the bell. Perhaps I had better go.

NORA. No, no; do stay! It's probably just someone for Torvald.

HELENE (*in the doorway*). Excuse me, Ma'am; there's a gentleman asking for Mr. Helmer — but the doctor's in there — and I didn't know if I should disturb him —

NORA. Who is it?

KROGSTAD (*in the doorway*). It is I, Mrs. Helmer.

MRS. LINDE *starts and turns away to the window.*

NORA (*goes a step toward him, anxiously; in a low voice*). You? What is it? Why do you want to see my husband?

A Doll's House

KROGSTAD. It's to do with Bank business — more or less. I have a small position in the Joint Stock Bank, and I hear your husband is to be the new president.

NORA. Then it's just —?

KROGSTAD. Just routine business, Mrs. Helmer; nothing else.

NORA. Then, please be good enough to go into his study.

KROGSTAD *goes. She bows indifferently while she closes the door into the hall. Then she goes to the stove and tends the fire.*

MRS. LINDE. Who was that man, Nora?

NORA. A Mr. Krogstad — he's a lawyer.

MRS. LINDE. I was right, then.

NORA. Do you know him?

MRS. LINDE. I used to know him — many years ago. He worked in a law office in our town.

NORA. Yes, so he did.

MRS. LINDE. How he has changed!

NORA. He was unhappily married, they say.

MRS. LINDE. Is he a widower now?

NORA. Yes — with lots of children. There! That's better! (*She closes the door of the stove and moves the rocking chair a little to one side.*)

MRS. LINDE. I'm told he's mixed up in a lot of rather questionable business.

NORA. He may be; I really don't know. But don't let's talk about business — it's so tiresome.

DR. RANK *comes out of* HELMER'S *room.*

RANK (*still in the doorway*). No, no, I won't disturb you. I'll go in and see your wife for a moment. (*Sees* MRS. LINDE.) Oh, I beg your pardon. I seem to be in the way here, too.

NORA. Of course not! (*Introduces them.*) Dr. Rank — Mrs. Linde.

RANK. Well, well, I've often heard that name mentioned in this house; didn't I pass you on the stairs when I came in?

MRS. LINDE. Yes; I'm afraid I climb them very slowly. They wear me out!

RANK. A little on the delicate side — eh?

MRS. LINDE. No; just a bit overtired.

RANK. I see. So I suppose you've come to town for a good rest — on a round of dissipation!

MRS. LINDE. I have come to look for work.

RANK. Is that the best remedy for tiredness?

MRS. LINDE. One has to live, Doctor.

RANK. Yes, I'm told that's necessary.

NORA. Oh, come now, Dr. Rank! You're not above wanting to live yourself!

RANK. That's true enough. No matter how wretched I may be, I still want to hang on as long as possible. All my patients have that feeling too. Even the *morally* sick seem to share it. There's a wreck of a man in there with Helmer now —

MRS. LINDE (*softly*). Ah!

NORA. Whom do you mean?

RANK. A fellow named Krogstad, he's a lawyer — you wouldn't know anything about him. He's thoroughly depraved — rotten to the core — Yet even he declared, as though it were a matter of paramount importance, that he must live.

NORA. Really? What did he want with Torvald?

RANK. I've no idea; I gathered it was some Bank business.

NORA. I didn't know that Krog — that this man Krogstad had anything to do with the Bank?

RANK. He seems to have some sort of position there. (*To* MRS. LINDE.) I don't know if this is true in your part of the country — but there are men who make it a practice of prying about in other people's business, searching for individuals of doubtful character — and having discovered their secret, place them in positions of trust, where they can keep an eye on them, and make use of them at will. Honest men — men of strong moral fiber — they leave out in the cold.

MRS. LINDE. Perhaps the weaklings need more help.

RANK (*shrugs his shoulders*). That point-of-view is fast turning society into a clinic.

NORA, *deep in her own thoughts, breaks into half-stifled laughter and claps her hands.*

RANK. Why should that make you laugh? I wonder if you've any idea what "society" is?

NORA. Why should I care about your tiresome old "society"? I was laughing at something quite different — something frightfully amusing. Tell me, Dr. Rank — will all the employees at the Bank be dependent on Torvald now?

RANK. Is *that* what strikes you as so amusing?

NORA (*smiles and hums*). Never you mind! Never you mind! (*Walks about the room*) What fun to think that we — that Torvald — has such power over so many people. (*Takes the bag from her pocket.*) Dr. Rank, how about a macaroon?

RANK. Well, well! — Macaroons, eh? I thought they were forbidden here.

NORA. These are some Kristine brought —

MRS. LINDE. What! I —

NORA. Now, you needn't be so frightened. How could you possibly know that Torvald had forbidden them? He's afraid they'll spoil my teeth. Oh, well — just for once! Don't you agree, Dr. Rank? There you are! (*Puts a macaroon into his mouth.*) You must have one too, Kristine. And I'll have just one — just a tiny one, or at most two. (*Walks about again.*) Oh dear, I am so happy! There's just one thing in all the world that would give me the greatest pleasure.

RANK. What's that?

NORA. It's something I long to say in front of Torvald.

RANK. What's to prevent you?

NORA. Oh, I don't dare; it isn't nice.

MRS. LINDE. Not nice?

RANK. It might be unwise, then; but you can certainly say it to us. What is it you so long to say in front of Torvald?

NORA. I'd so love to say "Damn! — damn! — damn it all!"

RANK. Have you gone crazy?

MRS. LINDE. Good gracious, Nora —

RANK. Go ahead and say it — here he comes!

NORA. (*hides the macaroons*). Hush — sh — sh.

HELMER *comes out of his room; he carries his hat and overcoat.*

NORA (*going to him*). Well, Torvald, dear, did you get rid of him?

HELMER. He has just gone.

NORA. Let me introduce you — this is Kristine, who has just arrived in town —

HELMER. Kristine? I'm sorry — but I really don't —

NORA. Mrs. Linde, Torvald, dear — Kristine Linde.

HELMER. Oh yes! I suppose you're one of my wife's school friends?

MRS. LINDE. Yes; we knew each other as children.

NORA. Imagine, Torvald! She came all that long way just to talk to you.

HELMER. How do you mean?

MRS. LINDE. Well, it wasn't exactly —

NORA. Kristine is tremendously good at office-work, and her great dream is to get a position with a really clever man — so she can improve still more, you see —

HELMER. Very sensible, Mrs. Linde.

NORA. And when she heard that you had become president of the Bank — it was in the paper, you know — she started off at once; you *will* try and do something for Kristine, won't you, Torvald? For my sake?

HELMER. It's by no means impossible. You're a widow, I presume?

MRS. LINDE. Yes.

HELMER. And you've already had business experience?

MRS. LINDE. A good deal.

HELMER. Then, I think it's quite likely I may be able to find a place for you.

NORA (*clapping her hands*). There, you see! You see!

HELMER. You have come at a good moment, Mrs. Linde.

MRS. LINDE. How can I ever thank you —?

HELMER (*smiling*). Don't mention it. (*Puts on his overcoat.*) But just now, I'm afraid you must excuse me —

RANK. I'll go with you. (*Fetches his fur coat from the hall and warms it at the stove.*)

NORA. Don't be long, Torvald, dear.

HELMER. I shan't be more than an hour.

NORA. Are you going too, Kristine?

MRS. LINDE (*putting on her outdoor things*). Yes; I must go and find a place to live.

HELMER. We can all go out together.

NORA (*helping her*). How tiresome that we're so cramped for room, Kristine; otherwise —

MRS. LINDE. Oh, you mustn't think of that! Goodbye, dear Nora, and thanks for everything.

NORA. Goodbye for the present. Of course you'll come back this evening. And you too, Dr. Rank — eh? If you're well enough? But of course you'll be well enough! Wrap up warmly now! (*They go out talking, into the hall; children's voices are heard on the stairs*) Here they come! Here they come! (*She runs to the outer door and opens it. The nurse,* ANNE-MARIE, *enters the hall with the children*) Come in, come in — you darlings! Just look at them, Kristine. Aren't they sweet?

RANK. No chattering in this awful draught!

HELMER. Come along, Mrs. Linde; you have to be a mother to put up with this!

> DR. RANK, HELMER, *and* MRS. LINDE *go down the stairs;* ANNE-MARIE *enters the room with the children;* NORA *comes in too, shutting the door behind her.*

NORA. How fresh and bright you look! And what red cheeks! Like apples and roses. (*The children chatter to her during what follows.*) Did you have a good time? Splendid! You gave Emmy and Bob a ride on your sled? Both at once? You *are* a clever boy, Ivar! Let me hold her for a bit, Anne-Marie. My darling little doll-baby. (*Takes the smallest from the nurse and dances with her.*) All right, Bobbie! Mama will dance with you too. You threw snowballs, did you? I should have been in on that! Never mind, Anne; I'll undress them myself — oh, do let me — it's such fun. Go on into the nursery, you look half-frozen. There's some hot coffee in there on the stove. (*The nurse goes into the room on the left.* NORA *takes off the children's things and throws them down anywhere, while the children all talk together.*) Not really! You were chased by a big dog? But he didn't bite you? No; dogs don't bite tiny little doll-babies! Don't touch the packages, Ivar. What's in them? Wouldn't you like to know! No. No! Careful! It might bite! Come on, let's play. What will we play? Hide-and-seek? Let's play hide-and-seek. Bob, you hide first! Do you want me to? All right! I'll hide first then.

> *She and the children play, laughing and shouting, all over the room and in the adjacent room to the left. Finally* NORA *hides under the table; the children come rushing in, look for her, but cannot find her, hear her half-suppressed laughter, rush to the table, lift up the cover and see her. Loud shouts of delight. She creeps out, as though to frighten them. More shouts. Meanwhile there has been a knock at the door leading into the hall. No one has heard it. Now the door is half-opened and* KROGSTAD *appears. He waits a little — the game continues.*

KROGSTAD. I beg your pardon, Mrs. Helmer —

NORA (*with a stifled scream, turns round and half jumps up*). Oh! What do you want?

KROGSTAD. Excuse me; the outer door was ajar — someone must have forgotten to close it —

NORA (*standing up*). My husband is not at home, Mr. Krogstad.

KROGSTAD. I know that.

NORA. Then, what do you want here?

KROGSTAD. I want a few words with you.

NORA. With —? (*To the children, softly.*) Go in to Anne-Marie. What? No — the strange man won't do Mama any harm; when he's gone we'll go on playing. (*She leads the children into the right hand room, and shuts the door behind them; uneasy, in suspense.*) You want to speak to me?

KROGSTAD. Yes, I do.

NORA. Today? But it's not the first of the month yet —

KROGSTAD. No, it is Christmas Eve. It's up to you whether your Christmas is a merry one.

NORA. What is it you want? Today I can't possibly —

KROGSTAD. That doesn't concern me for the moment. This is about something else. You have a few minutes, haven't you?

NORA. I suppose so; although —

KROGSTAD. Good. I was sitting in the restaurant opposite, and I saw your husband go down the street —

NORA. Well?

KROGSTAD. — with a lady.

NORA. What of it?

KROGSTAD. May I ask if that lady was a Mrs. Linde?

NORA. Yes.

KROGSTAD. She's just come to town, hasn't she?

NORA. Yes. Today.

KROGSTAD. Is she a good friend of yours?

NORA. Yes, she is. But I can't imagine —

KROGSTAD. I used to know her too.

NORA. Yes, I know you did.

KROGSTAD. Then you know all about it. I thought as much. Now, tell me: is Mrs. Linde to have a place in the Bank?

NORA. How dare you question me like this, Mr. Krogstad — you, one of my husband's employees! But since you ask — you might as well know. Yes, Mrs. Linde is to have a position at the Bank, and it is I who recommended her. Does that satisfy you, Mr. Krogstad?

KROGSTAD. I was right, then.

NORA (*walks up and down*). After all, one has a little influence, now and then. Even if one is only a woman it doesn't always follow that — people in subordinate positions, Mr. Krogstad, ought really to be careful how they offend anyone who — h'm —

KROGSTAD. — has influence?

NORA. Precisely.

KROGSTAD (*taking another tone*). Then perhaps you'll be so kind, Mrs. Helmer, as to use your influence on *my* behalf?

NORA. What? How do you mean?

KROGSTAD. Perhaps you'll be good enough to see that I *retain* my subordinate position?

NORA. But, I don't understand. Who wants to take it from you?

KROGSTAD. Oh, don't try and play the innocent! I can well understand that it would be unpleasant for your friend to associate with me; and I understand too, whom I have to thank for my dismissal.

NORA. But I assure you —

KROGSTAD. Never mind all that — there is still time. But I advise you to use your influence to prevent this.

NORA. But, Mr. Krogstad, I *have* no influence — absolutely none!

KROGSTAD. Indeed! I thought you just told me yourself —

NORA. You misunderstood me — *really* you did! You must know my husband would never be influenced by me!

KROGSTAD. Your husband and I were at the University together — I know him well. I don't suppose he's any more inflexible than other married men.

NORA. Don't you dare talk disrespectfully about my husband, or I'll show you the door!

KROGSTAD. The little lady's plucky.

NORA. I'm no longer afraid of you. I'll soon be free of all this — after the first of the year.

KROGSTAD (*in a more controlled manner*). Listen to me, Mrs. Helmer. This is a matter of life and death to me. I warn you I shall fight with all my might to keep my position in the Bank.

NORA. So it seems.

KROGSTAD. It's not just the salary; that is the least important part of it — It's something else — Well, I might as well be frank with you. I suppose you know, like everyone else, that once — a long time ago — I got into quite a bit of trouble.

NORA. I have heard something about it, I believe.

KROGSTAD. The matter never came to court; but from that time on, all doors were closed to me. I then went into the business with which you are familiar. I had to do something; and I don't think I've been among the worst. But now I must get away from all that. My sons are growing up, you see; for their sake I'm determined to recapture my good name. This position in the Bank was to be the first step; and now your husband wants to kick me back into the mud again.

NORA. But I tell you, Mr. Krogstad, it's not in my power to help you.

KROGSTAD. Only because you don't really want to; but I can compel you to do it, if I choose.

NORA. You wouldn't tell my husband that I owe you money?

KROGSTAD. And suppose I were to?

NORA. But that would be an outrageous thing to do! (*With tears in her voice.*) My secret — that I've guarded with such pride — such joy! I couldn't bear to have him find it out in such an ugly, hateful way — to have him find it out from you! I couldn't bear it! It would be too horribly unpleasant!

KROGSTAD. Only unpleasant, Mrs. Helmer?

NORA (*vehemently*). But just you do it! You'll be the one to suffer; for then my husband will *really* know the kind of man you are — there'll be no chance of keeping your job then!

KROGSTAD. Didn't you hear my question? I asked if it were only unpleasantness you feared?

NORA. If my husband got to know about it, he'd naturally pay you off at once, and then we'd have nothing more to do with you.

KROGSTAD (*takes a step towards her*). Listen, Mrs. Helmer: Either you have a very bad memory, or you know nothing about business. I think I'd better make the position clear to you.

NORA. What do you mean?

KROGSTAD. When your husband fell ill, you came to me to borrow twelve hundred dollars.

NORA. I didn't know what else to do.

KROGSTAD. I promised to find you the money —

NORA. And you did find it.

KROGSTAD. I promised to find you the money, on certain conditions. At that time you were so taken up with your husband's illness and so anxious to procure the money for your journey, that you probably did not give much thought to details. Perhaps I'd better remind you of them. I promised to find you the amount in exchange for a note, which I drew up.

NORA. Yes, and I signed it.

KROGSTAD. Very good. But then I added a clause, stating that your father would stand sponsor for the debt. This clause your father was to have signed.

NORA. Was to —? He did sign it.

KROGSTAD. I left the date blank, so that your father himself should date his signature. You recall that?

NORA. Yes, I believe —

KROGSTAD. Then I gave you the paper, and you were to mail it to your father. Isn't that so?

NORA. Yes.

KROGSTAD. And you must have mailed it at once; for five or six days later you brought me back the document with your father's signature; and then I handed you the money.

NORA. Well? Haven't I made my payments punctually?

KROGSTAD. Fairly — yes. But to return to the point: That was a sad time for you, wasn't it, Mrs. Helmer?

NORA. It was indeed!

KROGSTAD. Your father was very ill, I believe?

NORA. Yes — he was dying.

KROGSTAD. And he did die soon after, didn't he?

NORA. Yes.

KROGSTAD. Now tell me, Mrs. Helmer: Do you happen to recollect the date of your father's death: the day of the month, I mean?

NORA. Father died on the 29th of September.

KROGSTAD. Quite correct. I have made inquiries. Now here is a strange thing, Mrs. Helmer — (*produces a paper*) something rather hard to explain.

NORA. What do you mean? What strange thing?

KROGSTAD. The strange thing about it is, that your father seems to have signed this paper three days after his death!

NORA. I don't understand —

KROGSTAD. Your father died on the 29th of September. But look at this: his signature is dated October 2nd! Isn't that rather strange, Mrs. Helmer? (NORA *is silent.*) Can you explain that to me? (NORA *continues silent.*) It is curious, too, that the words "October 2nd" and the year are not in your father's handwriting, but in a handwriting I seem to know. This could easily be explained, however; your father might have forgotten to date his signature, and someone might have added the date at random, before the fact of your father's death was known. There is nothing wrong in that. It all depends on the signature itself. It is of course genuine, Mrs. Helmer? It was your father himself who wrote his name here?

NORA (*after a short silence, throws her head back and looks defiantly at him*). No, it wasn't. I wrote father's name.

KROGSTAD. I suppose you realize, Mrs. Helmer, what a dangerous confession that is?

NORA. Why should it be dangerous? You will get your money soon enough!

KROGSTAD. I'd like to ask you a question: Why didn't you send the paper to your father?

NORA. It was impossible. Father was too ill. If I had asked him for his signature, he'd have wanted to know what the money was for. In his condition I simply could not tell him that my husband's life was in danger. That's why it was impossible.

KROGSTAD. Then wouldn't it have been wiser to give up the journey?

NORA. How could I? That journey was to save my husband's life. I simply couldn't give it up.

KROGSTAD. And it never occurred to you that you weren't being honest with me?

NORA. I really couldn't concern myself with that. You meant nothing to me — In fact I couldn't help disliking you for making it all so difficult — with your cold, business-like clauses and conditions — when you knew my husband's life was at stake.

KROGSTAD. You evidently haven't the faintest idea, Mrs. Helmer, what you

A Doll's House

have been guilty of. Yet let me tell you that it was nothing more and nothing worse that made me an outcast from society.

NORA. You don't expect me to believe that you ever did a brave thing to save your wife's life?

KROGSTAD. The law takes no account of motives.

NORA. It must be a very bad law, then!

KROGSTAD. Bad or not, if I produce this document in court, you will be condemned according to the law.

NORA. I don't believe that for a minute. Do you mean to tell me that a daughter has no right to spare her dying father worry and anxiety? Or that a wife has no right to save her husband's life? I may not know much about it — but I'm sure there must be something or other in the law that permits such things. You as a lawyer should be aware of that. You don't seem to know very much about the law, Mr. Krogstad.

KROGSTAD. Possibly not. But business — the kind of business we are concerned with — I *do* know something about. Don't you agree? Very well, then; do as you please. But I warn you: if I am made to suffer a second time, you shall keep me company. (*Bows and goes out through the hall.*)

NORA. (*stands a while thinking, then tosses her head*). What nonsense! He's just trying to frighten me. I'm not such a fool as all that! (*Begins folding the children's clothes. Pauses.*) And yet —? No, it's impossible! After all — I only did it for love's sake.

CHILDREN (*at the door, left*). Mama, the strange man has gone now.

NORA. Yes, yes, I know. But don't tell anyone about the strange man. Do you hear? Not even Papa!

CHILDREN. No, Mama; now will you play with us again?

NORA. No, not just now.

CHILDREN. But Mama! You promised!

NORA. But I can't just now. Run back to the nursery; I have so much to do. Run along now! Run along, my darlings! (*She pushes them gently into the inner room, and closes the door behind them. Sits on the sofa, embroiders a few stitches, but soon pauses.*) No! (*Throws down the work, rises, goes to the hall door and calls out.*) Helene, bring the tree in to me, will you? (*Goes to table, right, and opens the drawer; again pauses.*) No, it's utterly impossible!

HELENE (*carries in the Christmas tree*). Where shall I put it, Ma'am?

NORA. Right there; in the middle of the room.

HELENE. Is there anything else you need?

NORA. No, thanks; I have everything.

HELENE, *having put down the tree, goes out.*

NORA (*busy dressing the tree*). We'll put a candle here — and some flowers here — that dreadful man! But it's just nonsense! There's nothing to worry about. The tree will be lovely. I'll do everything to please you, Torvald; I'll sing for you, I'll dance for you —

Enter HELMER *by the hall door, with a bundle of documents.*

NORA. Oh! You're back already?

HELMER. Yes. Has somebody been here?

NORA. No. Nobody.

HELMER. That's odd. I just saw Krogstad leave the house.

NORA. Really? Well — as a matter of fact — Krogstad was here for a moment.

HELMER. Nora — I can tell by your manner — he came here to ask you to put in a good word for him, didn't he?

NORA. Yes, Torvald.

HELMER. And you weren't supposed to tell me he'd been here — You were to do it as if of your own accord — isn't that it?

NORA. Yes, Torvald; but —

HELMER. Nora, Nora! How could you consent to such a thing! To have dealings with a man like that — make him promises! And then to lie about it too!

NORA. Lie!

HELMER. Didn't you tell me that nobody had been here? (*Threatens with his finger.*) My little bird must never do that again! A song-bird must sing clear and true! No false notes! (*Puts arm around her.*) Isn't that the way it should be? Of course it is! (*Lets her go.*) And now we'll say no more about it. (*Sits down before the fire.*) It's so cozy and peaceful here! (*Glances through the documents.*)

NORA (*busy with the tree, after a short silence*). Torvald!

HELMER. Yes.

NORA. I'm so looking forward to the Stenborgs' fancy dress party, day after tomorrow.

HELMER. And I can't wait to see what surprise you have in store for me.

NORA. Oh, it's so awful, Torvald!

HELMER. *What* is?

NORA. I can't think of anything amusing. Everything seems so silly, so pointless.

HELMER. Has my little Nora come to *that* conclusion?

NORA (*behind his chair, with her arms on the back*). Are you very busy, Torvald?

HELMER. Well —

NORA. What are all those papers?

HELMER. Just Bank business.

NORA. Already!

HELMER. The board of directors has given me full authority to do some reorganizing — to make a few necessary changes in the staff. I'll have to work on it during Christmas week. I want it all settled by the New Year.

NORA. I see. So that was why that poor Krogstad —

HELMER. H'm.

NORA (*still leaning over the chair-back and slowly stroking his hair*). If you weren't so very busy, I'd ask you to do me a great, great favor, Torvald.

HELMER. Well, let's hear it! Out with it!

NORA. You have such perfect taste, Torvald; and I do so want to look well at the fancy dress ball. Couldn't you take me in hand, and decide what I'm to be, and arrange my costume for me?

HELMER. Well, well! So we're not so self-sufficient after all! We need a helping hand, do we?

NORA. Oh, please, Torvald! I know I shall *never* manage without your help!

HELMER. I'll think about it; we'll hit on something.

NORA. Oh, how sweet of you! (*Goes to the tree again; pause.*) Those red flowers show up beautifully! Tell me, Torvald; did that Krogstad do something very wrong?

HELMER. He committed forgery. Have you any idea of what that means?

NORA. Perhaps he did it out of necessity?

HELMER. Or perhaps he was just fool-hardy, like so many others. I am not so harsh as to condemn a man irrevocably for one mistake.

NORA. No, of course not!

HELMER. A man has a chance to rehabilitate himself, if he honestly admits his guilt and takes his punishment.

NORA. Punishment —

HELMER. But that wasn't Krogstad's way. He resorted to tricks and evasions; became thoroughly demoralized.

NORA. You really think it would —?

HELMER. When a man has that sort of thing on his conscience his life becomes a tissue of lies and deception. He's forced to wear a mask — even with those nearest to him — his own wife and children even. And the children — that's the worst part of it, Nora.

NORA. Why?

HELMER. Because the whole atmosphere of the home would be contaminated. The very air the children breathed would be filled with evil.

NORA (*closer behind him*). Are you sure of that?

HELMER. As a lawyer, I know it from experience. Almost all cases of early delinquency can be traced to dishonest mothers.

NORA. Why — only mothers?

HELMER. It usually stems from the mother's side; but of course it can come from the father too. We lawyers know a lot about such things. And this Krogstad has been deliberately poisoning his own children for years, by surrounding them with lies and hypocrisy — that is why I call him demoralized. (*Holds out both hands to her.*) So my sweet little Nora must promise not to plead his cause. Shake hands on it. Well? What's the matter? Give me your hand. There! That's all settled. I assure you it would have been impossible for me to work with him. It literally gives me a feeling of physical discomfort to come in contact with such people.

NORA *draws her hand away, and moves to the other side of the Christmas tree.*

NORA. It's so warm here. And I have such a lot to do.

HELMER (*rises and gathers up his papers*). I must try and look through some of these papers before dinner. I'll give some thought to your costume too. Perhaps I may even find something to hang in gilt paper on the Christmas tree! (*Lays his hand on her head.*) My own precious little song-bird! (*He goes into his study and closes the door after him.*)

NORA (*softly, after a pause*). It can't be —! It's impossible. Of course it's impossible!

ANNE-MARIE (*at the door, left*). The babies keep begging to come in and see Mama.

NORA. No, no! Don't let them come to me! Keep them with you, Anne-Marie.

ANNE-MARIE. Very well, Ma'am. (*Shuts the door.*)

NORA (*pale with terror*). Harm my children! — Corrupt my home! (*Short pause. She throws back her head.*) It's not true! I know it's not! It could never, never be true!

CURTAIN

ACT TWO

Scene: The same room. In the corner, beside the piano, stands the Christmas tree, stripped and with the candles burnt out. NORA's *outdoor things lie on the sofa.* NORA, *alone, is walking about restlessly. At last she stops by the sofa, and picks up her cloak.*

NORA (*puts the cloak down again*). Did someone come in? (*Goes to the hall and listens.*) No; no one; of course no one will come today, Christmas Day; nor tomorrow either. But perhaps — (*Opens the door and looks out.*) No, there's nothing in the mailbox; it's quite empty. (*Comes forward.*) Oh nonsense! He only meant to frighten me. There won't be any trouble. It's all impossible! Why, I — I have three little children!

ANNE-MARIE *enters from the left, with a large cardboard box.*

ANNE-MARIE. Well — I found the box with the fancy dress clothes at last, Miss Nora.

NORA. Thanks; put it on the table.

ANNE-MARIE (*does so*). I'm afraid they're rather shabby.

NORA. If I had my way I'd tear them into a thousand pieces!

ANNE-MARIE. Good gracious! They can be repaired — just have a little patience.

NORA. I'll go and get Mrs. Linde to help me.

A Doll's House

ANNE-MARIE. I wouldn't go out again in this awful weather! You might catch cold, Miss Nora, and get sick.

NORA. Worse things might happen — How are the children?

ANNE-MARIE. The poor little things are playing with their Christmas presents; but —

NORA. Have they asked for me?

ANNE-MARIE. They're so used to having Mama with them.

NORA. I know; but, you see, Anne-Marie, I won't be able to be with them as much as I used to.

ANNE-MARIE. Well, little children soon get used to anything.

NORA. You really think so? Would they forget me if I went away for good?

ANNE-MARIE. Good gracious! — for good!

NORA. Tell me something, Anne-Marie — I've so often wondered about it — how could you bear to part with your child — give it up to strangers?

ANNE-MARIE. Well, you see, I had to — when I came to nurse my little Nora.

NORA. Yes — but how could you *bear* to do it?

ANNE-MARIE. I couldn't afford to say "no" to such a good position. A poor girl who's been in trouble must take what comes. Of course *he* never offered to help me — the wicked sinner!

NORA. Then I suppose your daughter has forgotten all about you.

ANNE-MARIE. No — indeed she hasn't! She even wrote to me — once when she was confirmed and again when she was married.

NORA (*embracing her*). Dear old Anne-Marie — you were a good mother to me when I was little.

ANNE-MARIE. But then my poor little Nora *had* no mother of her own!

NORA. And if ever my little ones were left without — you'd look after them, wouldn't you? — Oh, that's just nonsense! (*Opens the box.*) Go back to them. Now I must — Just you wait and see how lovely I'll look tomorrow!

ANNE-MARIE. My Miss Nora will be the prettiest person there! (*She goes into the room on the left.*)

NORA (*takes the costume out of the box, but soon throws it down again*). I wish I dared go out — I'm afraid someone might come. I'm afraid something might happen while I'm gone. That's just silly! No one will come. I must try not to think — This muff needs cleaning. What pretty gloves — they're lovely! I must put it out of my head! One, two, three, four, five, six — (*With a scream.*) Ah! They're here!

Goes toward the door, then stands irresolute. MRS. LINDE *enters from the hall, where she has taken off her things.*

NORA. Oh, it's you, Kristine! There's no one else out there, is there? I'm so glad you have come!

MRS. LINDE. I got a message you'd been asking for me.

NORA. Yes, I just happened to be passing by. There's something I want you to help me with. Sit down here on the sofa. Now, listen: There's to be a fancy dress ball at the Stenborgs' tomorrow evening — they live just overhead — and Torvald wants me to go as a Neapolitan peasant girl, and dance the tarantella; I learned it while we were in Capri.

MRS. LINDE. So you're going to give a real performance, are you?

NORA. Torvald wants me to. Look, here's the costume; Torvald had it made for me down there. But it's all torn, Kristine, and I don't know whether —

MRS. LINDE. Oh, we'll soon fix that. It's only the trimming that has come loose here and there. Have you a needle and thread? Oh, yes. Here's everything I need.

NORA. It's awfully good of you!

MRS. LINDE (*sewing*). So you're going to be all dressed up, Nora — what fun! You know — I think I'll run in for a moment — just to see you in your costume — I haven't really thanked you for last night. I had such a happy time!

NORA (*rises and walks across the room*). Somehow it didn't seem as nice to me as usual. I wish you'd come to town a little earlier, Kristine. Yes — Torvald has a way of making things so gay and cozy.

MRS. LINDE. Well — so have you. That's your father coming out in you! But tell me — is Doctor Rank always so depressed?

NORA. No; last night it was worse than usual. He's terribly ill, you see — tuberculosis of the spine, or something. His father was a frightful man, who kept mistresses and all that sort of thing — that's why his son has been an invalid from birth —

MRS. LINDE (*lets her sewing fall into her lap*). Why, Nora! what do you know about such things?

NORA (*moving about the room*). After all — I've had three children; and those women who look after one at childbirth know almost as much as doctors; and they love to gossip.

MRS. LINDE (*goes on sewing; a short pause*). Does Doctor Rank come here every day?

NORA. Every single day. He's Torvald's best friend, you know — always has been; and he's *my* friend too. He's almost like one of the family.

MRS. LINDE. Do you think he's quite sincere, Nora? I mean — isn't he inclined to flatter people?

NORA. Quite the contrary. What gave you that impression?

MRS. LINDE. When you introduced us yesterday he said he had often heard my name mentioned here; but I noticed afterwards that your husband hadn't the faintest notion who I was. How could Doctor Rank —?

NORA. He was quite right, Kristine. You see Torvald loves me so tremendously that he won't share me with anyone; he wants me all to himself, as he says. At first he used to get terribly jealous if I even mentioned any of my old friends back home; so naturally I gave up doing it. But I often talk to Doctor Rank about such things — he likes to hear about them.

A Doll's House

MRS. LINDE. Listen to me, Nora! In many ways you are still a child. I'm somewhat older than you, and besides, I've had much more experience. I think you ought to put a stop to all this with Dr. Rank.

NORA. Put a stop to what?

MRS. LINDE. To the whole business. You said something yesterday about a rich admirer who was to give you money —

NORA. One who never existed, unfortunately. Go on.

MRS. LINDE. Has Doctor Rank money?

NORA. Why yes, he has.

MRS. LINDE. And he has no one dependent on him?

NORA. No, no one. But —

MRS. LINDE. And he comes here every single day?

NORA. Yes — I've just told you so.

MRS. LINDE. It's surprising that a sensitive man like that should be so importunate.

NORA. I don't understand you —

MRS. LINDE. Don't try to deceive me, Nora. Don't you suppose I can guess who lent you the twelve hundred dollars?

NORA. You must be out of your mind! How could you ever think such a thing? Why, he's a friend of ours; he comes to see us every day! The situation would have been impossible!

MRS. LINDE. So it wasn't he, then?

NORA. No, I assure you. Such a thing never even occurred to me. Anyway, he didn't have any money at that time; he came into it later.

MRS. LINDE. Perhaps that was just as well, Nora, dear.

NORA. No — it would never have entered my head to ask Dr. Rank — Still — I'm sure that if I did ask him —

MRS. LINDE. But you won't, of course.

NORA. No, of course not. Anyway — I don't see why it should be necessary. But I'm sure that if I talked to Doctor Rank —

MRS. LINDE. Behind your husband's back?

NORA. I want to get that thing cleared up; after all, that's behind his back too. I must get clear of it.

MRS. LINDE. That's just what I said yesterday; but —

NORA (*walking up and down*). It's so much easier for a man to manage things like that —

MRS. LINDE. One's own husband, yes.

NORA. Nonsense. (*Stands still.*) Surely if you pay back everything you owe — the paper is returned to you?

MRS. LINDE. Naturally.

NORA. Then you can tear it into a thousand pieces, and burn it up — the nasty, filthy thing!

MRS. LINDE (*looks at her fixedly, lays down her work, and rises slowly*). Nora, you are hiding something from me.

NORA. You can see it in my face, can't you?

MRS. LINDE. Something's happened to you since yesterday morning, Nora, what is it?

NORA (*going towards her*). Kristine —! (*Listens*) Hush! Here comes Torvald! Go into the nursery for a little while. Torvald hates anything to do with sewing. Get Anne-Marie to help you.

MRS. LINDE (*gathers the things together*). Very well; but I shan't leave until you have told me all about it. (*She goes out to the left, as* HELMER *enters from the hall.*)

NORA (*runs to meet him*). Oh, I've missed you so, Torvald, dear!

HELMER. Was that the dressmaker —?

NORA. No, it was Kristine. She's helping me fix my costume. It's going to look so nice.

HELMER. Wasn't that a good idea of mine?

NORA. Splendid! But don't you think it was good of me to let you have your way?

HELMER. Good of you! To let your own husband have his way! There, there, you crazy little thing; I'm only teasing. Now I won't disturb you. You'll have to try the dress on, I suppose.

NORA. Yes — and I expect you've work to do.

HELMER. I have. (*Shows her a bundle of papers.*) Look. I've just come from the Bank — (*Goes towards his room.*)

NORA. Torvald.

HELMER (*stopping*). Yes?

NORA. If your little squirrel were to beg you — with all her heart —

HELMER. Well?

NORA. Would you do something for her?

HELMER. That depends on what it is.

NORA. Be a darling and say "Yes," Torvald! Your squirrel would skip about and play all sorts of pretty tricks —

HELMER. Well — out with it!

NORA. Your little lark would twitter all day long —

HELMER. She does that anyway!

NORA. I'll pretend to be an elf and dance for you in the moonlight, Torvald.

HELMER. Nora — you're surely not getting back to what we talked about this morning?

NORA (*coming nearer*). Oh, Torvald, dear, I do most humbly beg you —!

HELMER. You have the temerity to bring that up again?

NORA. You must give in to me about this, Torvald! You *must* let Krogstad keep his place!

HELMER. I'm giving his place to Mrs. Linde.

NORA. That's awfully sweet of you. But instead of Krogstad — couldn't you dismiss some other clerk?

HELMER. This is the most incredible obstinacy! Because you were thoughtless enough to promise to put in a good word for him, am I supposed to —?

NORA. That's not the reason, Torvald. It's for your own sake. Didn't you tell me yourself he writes for the most horrible newspapers? He can do you no end of harm. Oh! I'm so afraid of him —

HELMER. I think I understand; you have some unpleasant memories — that's why you're frightened.

NORA. What do you mean?

HELMER. Aren't you thinking of your father?

NORA. Oh, yes — of course! You remember how those awful people slandered poor father in the newspapers? If you hadn't been sent to investigate the matter, and been so kind and helpful — he might have been dismissed.

HELMER. My dear Nora, there is a distinct difference between your father and me. Your father's conduct was not entirely unimpeachable. But mine is; and I trust it will remain so.

NORA. You never know what evil-minded people can think up. We could be so happy now, Torvald, in our lovely, peaceful home — you and I and the children! Oh! I implore you, Torvald —!

HELMER. The more you plead his cause the less likely I am to keep him on. It's already known at the Bank that I intend to dismiss Krogstad. If I were to change my mind, people might say I'd done it at the insistence of my wife —

NORA. Well — what of that?

HELMER. Oh, nothing, of course! As long as the obstinate little woman gets her way! I'd simply be the laughing-stock of the whole staff; they'd think I was weak and easily influenced — I should soon be made to feel the consequences. Besides — there is one factor that makes it quite impossible for Krogstad to work at the Bank as long as I'm head there.

NORA. What could that be?

HELMER. His past record I might be able to overlook —

NORA. Yes, you might, mightn't you, Torvald —?

HELMER. And I'm told he's an excellent worker. But unfortunately we were friendly during our college days. It was one of those impetuous friendships that subsequently often prove embarrassing. He's tactless enough to call me by my first name — regardless of the circumstances — and feels quite justified in taking a familiar tone with me. At any moment he comes out with "Torvald" this, and "Torvald" that! It's acutely irritating. It would make my position at the Bank intolerable.

NORA. You're surely not serious about this, Torvald?

HELMER. Why not?

NORA. But — it's all so petty.

HELMER. Petty! So you think I'm petty!

NORA. Of course not, Torvald — just the opposite; that's why —

HELMER. Never mind; you call my motives petty; so I must be petty too! Petty! Very well! — We'll put an end to this now — once and for all. (HELMER *goes to the door into the hall and calls* HELENE.)

NORA. What do you want?

HELMER (*searching among his papers*). I want this thing settled. (HELENE *enters.*) Take this letter, will you? Get a messenger and have him deliver it at once! It's urgent. Here's some money.

HELENE. Very good, Sir. (*Goes with the letter.*)

HELMER (*putting his papers together*). There, little Miss Obstinacy.

NORA (*breathless*). Torvald — what was in that letter?

HELMER. Krogstad's dismissal.

NORA. Call her back, Torvald! There's still time. Call her back! For my sake, for your own sake, for the sake of the children, don't send that letter! Torvald, do you hear? You don't realize what may come of this!

HELMER. It's too late.

NORA. Too late, yes.

HELMER. Nora, dear; I forgive your fears — though it's not exactly flattering to me to think I could ever be afraid of any spiteful nonsense Krogstad might choose to write about me! But I forgive you all the same — it shows how much you love me. (*Takes her in his arms.*) And that's the way it should be, Nora darling. No matter what happens, you'll see — I have strength and courage for us both. My shoulders are broad — I'll bear the burden.

NORA (*terror-struck*). How do you mean?

HELMER. The whole burden, my darling. Don't you worry any more.

NORA (*with decision*). No! You mustn't — I won't let you!

HELMER. Then we'll share it, Nora, as man and wife. That is as it should be. (*Petting her.*) Are you happy now? There! Don't look at me like a frightened little dove! You're just imagining things, you know — Now don't you think you ought to play the tarantella through — and practice your tambourine? I'll go into my study and close both doors, then you won't disturb me. You can make all the noise you like! (*Turns round in doorway.*) And when Rank comes, just tell him where I am. (*He nods to her, and goes with his papers to his room, closing the door.*)

NORA (*bewildered with terror, stands as though rooted to the ground, and whispers*). He'd do it too! He'd do it — in spite of anything! But he mustn't — never, never! Anything but that! There must be some way out! What shall I do? (*The hall bell rings.*) Dr. Rank —! Anything but that — anything, *any*thing but that!

> NORA *draws her hands over her face, pulls herself together, goes to the door and opens it.* RANK *stands outside hanging up his fur coat. During the following scene, darkness begins to fall.*

NORA. How are you, Doctor Rank? I recognized your ring. You'd better not go in to Torvald just now; I think he's busy.

RANK. How about you? (*Enters and closes the door.*)

NORA. You know I always have an hour to spare for you.

RANK. Many thanks. I'll make use of that privilege as long as possible.

NORA. What do you mean — as long as possible?

RANK. Does that frighten you?

NORA. No — but it's such a queer expression. Has anything happened?

RANK. I've been expecting it for a long time; but I never thought it would come quite so soon.

NORA. What is it you have found out? Doctor Rank, please tell me!

RANK (*sitting down by the stove*). I haven't much time left. There's nothing to do about it.

NORA (*with a sigh of relief*). Oh! Then — it's about you —?

RANK. Of course. What did you think? It's no use lying to one's self. I am the most miserable of all my patients, Mrs. Helmer. These past few days I've been taking stock of my position — and I find myself completely bankrupt. Within a month, I shall be rotting in the church-yard.

NORA. What a ghastly way to talk!

RANK. The whole business is pretty ghastly, you see. And the worst of it is, there are so many ghastly things to be gone through before it's over. I've just one last examination to make, then I shall know approximately when the final dissolution will begin. There's something I want to say to you: Helmer's sensitive nature is repelled by anything ugly. I couldn't bear to have him near me when —

NORA. But Doctor Rank —

RANK. No, I couldn't bear it! I won't have him there — I shall bar my door against him — As soon as I am absolutely certain of the worst, I'll send you my visiting-card marked with a black cross; that will mean that the final horror has begun.

NORA. Doctor Rank — you're absolutely impossible today! And I did so want you to be in a good humor.

RANK. With death staring me in the face? And why should I have to expiate another's sins! What justice is there in that? Well — I suppose in almost every family there are some such debts that have to be paid.

NORA (*stopping her ears*). Don't talk such nonsense! Come along! Cheer up!

RANK. One might as well laugh. It's really very funny when you come to think of it — that my poor innocent spine should be made to suffer for my father's exploits!

NORA (*at table, left*). He was much addicted to asparagus-tips and paté de foie gras, wasn't he?

RANK. Yes; and truffles.

NORA. Oh, of course — truffles, yes. And I suppose oysters too?

RANK. Oh, yes! Masses of oysters, certainly!

NORA. And all the wine and champagne that went with them! It does seem a shame that all these pleasant things should be so damaging to the spine, doesn't it?

RANK. Especially when it's a poor miserable spine that never had any of the fun!

NORA. Yes, that's the biggest shame of all!

RANK (*gives her a searching look*). H'm —

NORA (*a moment later*). Why did you smile?

RANK. No; you were the one that laughed.

NORA. No; you were the one that smiled, Doctor Rank!

RANK (*gets up*). You're more of a rogue than I thought you were.

NORA. I'm full of mischief today.

RANK. So it seems.

NORA. (*with her hands on his shoulders*). Dear, dear Doctor Rank, don't go and die and leave Torvald and me.

RANK. Oh, you won't miss me long! Those who go away — are soon forgotten.

NORA (*looks at him anxiously*). You really believe that?

RANK. People develop new interests, and soon —

NORA. What do you mean — new interests?

RANK. That'll happen to you and Helmer when I am gone. You seem to have made a good start already. What was that Mrs. Linde doing here last evening?

NORA. You're surely not jealous of poor old Kristine!

RANK. Yes, I am. She will be my successor in this house. When I'm gone she'll probably —

NORA. Sh — hh! She's in there.

RANK. She's here again today? You see!

NORA. She's just helping me with my costume. Good heavens, you *are* in an unreasonable mood! (*Sits on sofa.*) Now do try to be good, Doctor Rank. Tomorrow you'll see how beautifully I'll dance; and then you can pretend I'm doing it all to please you — and Torvald too, of course — that's understood.

RANK (*after a short silence*). You know — sitting here talking to you so informally — I simply can't imagine what would have become of me, if I had never had this house to come to.

NORA (*smiling*). You really *do* feel at home with us, don't you?

RANK (*in a low voice — looking straight before him*). And to be obliged to leave it all —

NORA. Nonsense! You're not going to leave anything.

RANK (*in the same tone*). And not to be able to leave behind one even the smallest proof of gratitude; at most a fleeting regret — an empty place to be filled by the first person who comes along.

NORA. And supposing I were to ask you for —? No —

RANK. For what?

NORA. For a great proof of your friendship.

RANK. Yes? — Yes?

NORA. No, I mean — if I were to ask you to do me a really tremendous favor —

RANK. You'd really, for once, give me that great happiness?

A Doll's House

NORA. Oh, but you don't know what it is.

RANK. Then tell me.

NORA. I don't think I can, Doctor Rank. It's much too much to ask — it's not just a favor — I need your help and advice as well —

RANK. So much the better. I've no conception of what you mean. But tell me about it. You trust me, don't you?

NORA. More than anyone. I know you are my best and truest friend — that's why I can tell you. Well then, Doctor Rank, there is something you must help me prevent. You know how deeply, how intensely Torvald loves me; he wouldn't hesitate for a moment to give up his life for my sake.

RANK (*bending towards her*). Nora — do you think he is the only one who —?

NORA (*with a slight start*). Who — what?

RANK. Who would gladly give his life for you?

NORA (*sadly*). I see.

RANK. I was determined that you should know this before I — went away. There'll never be a better chance to tell you. Well, Nora, now you know, and you must know too that you can trust me as you can no one else.

NORA (*standing up; simply and calmly*). Let me get by —

RANK (*makes way for her, but remains sitting*). Nora —

NORA (*in the doorway*). Bring in the lamp, Helene. (*Crosses to the stove.*) Oh, dear Doctor Rank, that was really horrid of you.

RANK (*rising*). To love you just as deeply as — as someone else does; is that horrid?

NORA. No — but the fact of your telling me. There was no need to do that.

RANK. What do you mean? Did you know —?

HELENE *enters with the lamp; sets it on the table and goes out again.*

RANK. Nora — Mrs. Helmer — tell me, did you know?

NORA. Oh, how do I know what I knew or didn't know. I really can't say — How could you be so clumsy, Doctor Rank? It was all so nice.

RANK. Well, at any rate, you know now that I stand ready to serve you body and soul. So — tell me.

NORA (*looking at him*). After this?

RANK. I beg you to tell me what it is.

NORA. I can't tell you anything now.

RANK. But you must! Don't punish me like that! Let me be of use to you; I'll do anything for you — anything within human power.

NORA. You can do nothing for me now. Anyway — I don't really need help. I was just imagining things, you see. Really! That's all it was! (*Sits in the rocking chair, looks at him and smiles.*) Well — you're a nice one, Doctor Rank! Aren't you a bit ashamed, now that the lamp's been lit?

RANK. No; really not. But I suppose I'd better go now — for good?

NORA. You'll do no such thing! You must come here just as you always have. Torvald could never get on without you!

RANK. But how about *you*?

NORA. You know I always love to have you here.

RANK. Yes — I suppose that's what misled me. I can't quite make you out. I've often felt you liked being with me almost as much as being with Helmer.

NORA. Well — you see — There are the people one loves best — and yet there are others one would almost rather *be* with.

RANK. Yes — there's something in that.

NORA. When I was still at home, it was of course Papa whom I loved best. And yet whenever I could, I used to slip down to the servants' quarters. I loved being with them. To begin with, they never lectured me a bit, and it was such fun to hear them talk.

RANK. I see; and now you have me instead!

NORA (*jumps up and hurries toward him*). Oh, dear, darling Doctor Rank. I didn't mean it like that! It's just that now, Torvald comes first — the way Papa did. *You* understand —!

HELENE *enters from the hall.*

HELENE. I beg your pardon, Ma'am — (*Whispers to* NORA, *and gives her a card.*)

NORA (*glancing at card*). Ah! (*Puts it in her pocket.*)

RANK. Anything wrong?

NORA. No, nothing! It's just — it's my new costume —

RANK. Isn't that your costume — there?

NORA. Oh, that one, yes. But this is a different one. It's one I've ordered — Torvald mustn't know —

RANK. So *that's* the great secret!

NORA. Yes, of course it is! Go in and see him, will you? He's in his study. Be sure and keep him there as long as —

RANK. Don't worry; he shan't escape me. (*Goes into* HELMER'S *room.*)

NORA (*to* HELENE). He's waiting in the kitchen?

HELENE. Yes, he came up the back stairs —

NORA. Why didn't you tell him I was busy?

HELENE. I did, but he insisted.

NORA. He won't go away?

HELENE. Not until he has spoken to you, Ma'am.

NORA. Very well, then; show him in; but quietly, Helene — and don't say a word to anyone; it's about a surprise for my husband.

HELENE. I understand, Ma'am. (*She goes out.*)

NORA. It's coming! It's going to happen after all! No, no! It can't happen. It *can't*!

She goes to HELMER'S *door and locks it.* HELENE *opens the hall door for* KROGSTAD, *and shuts it after him. He wears a traveling-coat, boots, and a fur cap.*

NORA. (*goes towards him*). Talk quietly; my husband is at home.

KROGSTAD. What's that to me?

NORA. What is it you want?

KROGSTAD. I want to make sure of something.

NORA. Well — what is it? Quickly!

KROGSTAD. I suppose you know I've been dismissed.

NORA. I couldn't prevent it, Mr. Krogstad. I did everything in my power, but it was useless.

KROGSTAD. So that's all your husband cares about you! He must realize what I can put you through, and yet, in spite of that, he dares to —

NORA. You don't imagine my husband knows about it?

KROGSTAD. No — I didn't really suppose he did. I can't imagine my friend Torvald Helmer showing that much courage.

NORA. I insist that you show respect when speaking of my husband, Mr. Krogstad!

KROGSTAD. With all due respect, I assure you! But am I right in thinking — since you are so anxious to keep the matter secret — that you have a clearer idea today than you had yesterday, of what you really did?

NORA. Clearer than *you* could ever give me!

KROGSTAD. Of course! I who know so little about the law —!

NORA. What do you want of me?

KROGSTAD. I just wanted to see how you were getting on, Mrs. Helmer. I've been thinking about you all day. You see — even a mere money-lender, a cheap journalist — in short, someone like me — is not entirely without feeling.

NORA. Then prove it; think of my little children.

KROGSTAD. Did you or your husband think of mine? But that's not the point. I only wanted to tell you not to take this matter too seriously. I shan't take any action — for the present, at least.

NORA. You won't, will you? I was sure you wouldn't!

KROGSTAD. It can all be settled quite amicably. It needn't be made public. It needn't go beyond us three.

NORA. But, my husband must never know.

KROGSTAD. How can you prevent it? Can you pay off the balance?

NORA. No, not immediately.

KROGSTAD. Have you any way of raising the money within the next few days?

NORA. None — that I will make use of.

KROGSTAD. And if you had, it would have made no difference. Even if you were to offer me the entire sum in cash — I still wouldn't give you back your note.

NORA. What are you going to do with it?

KROGSTAD. I shall simply keep it — I shall guard it carefully. No one, outside the three of us, shall know a thing about it. So, if you have any thought of doing something desperate —

NORA. I shall.

KROGSTAD. — of running away from home, for instance —
NORA. I shall!
KROGSTAD. — or perhaps even something worse —
NORA. How could you guess that?
KROGSTAD. — then put all such thoughts out of your head.
NORA. How did you know I had thought of *that*?
KROGSTAD. Most of us think of *that*, at first. I thought of it, too; but I didn't have the courage —
NORA (*tonelessly*). I haven't either.
KROGSTAD (*relieved*). No; you haven't the courage for it either, have you?
NORA. No! I haven't, I haven't!
KROGSTAD. Besides, it would be a very foolish thing to do. You'll just have to get through one domestic storm — and then it'll all be over. I have a letter for your husband, here in my pocket —
NORA. Telling him all about it?
KROGSTAD. Sparing you as much as possible.
NORA (*quickly*). He must never read that letter. Tear it up, Mr. Krogstad! I will manage to get the money somehow —
KROGSTAD. Excuse me, Mrs. Helmer, but I thought I just told you —
NORA. Oh, I'm not talking about the money I owe you. Just tell me how much money you want from my husband — I will get it somehow!
KROGSTAD. I want no money from your husband.
NORA. What *do* you want then?
KROGSTAD. Just this: I want a new start; I want to make something of myself; and your husband shall help me do it. For the past eighteen months my conduct has been irreproachable. It's been a hard struggle — I've lived in abject poverty; still, I was content to work my way up gradually, step by step. But now I've been kicked out, and now I shall not be satisfied to be merely reinstated — taken back on sufferance. I'm determined to make something of myself, I tell you. I intend to continue working in the Bank — but I expect to be promoted. Your husband shall create a new position for me —
NORA. He'll never do it!
KROGSTAD. Oh, yes he will; I know him — he'll do it without a murmur; he wouldn't dare do otherwise. And then — you'll see! Within a year I'll be his right hand man. It'll be Nils Krogstad, not Torvald Helmer, who'll run the Joint Stock Bank.
NORA. That will never happen.
KROGSTAD. No? Would you, perhaps —?
NORA. Yes! I have the courage for it now.
KROGSTAD. You don't frighten me! A dainty, pampered little lady such as you —
NORA. You'll see, you'll see!
KROGSTAD. Yes, I dare say! How would you like to lie there under the ice —

in that freezing, pitch-black water? And in the spring your body would be found floating on the surface — hideous, hairless, unrecognizable —

NORA. You can't frighten me!

KROGSTAD. You can't frighten me either. People don't do that sort of thing, Mrs. Helmer. And, anyway, what would be the use? I'd still have your husband in my power.

NORA. You mean — afterwards? Even if I were no longer —?

KROGSTAD. Remember — I'd still have your reputation in my hands! (NORA *stands speechless and looks at him.*) Well, I've given you fair warning. I wouldn't do anything foolish, if I were you. As soon as Helmer receives my letter, I shall expect to hear from him. And just remember this: I've been forced back into my former way of life — and your husband is responsible. I shall never forgive him for it. Good-bye, Mrs. Helmer.

Goes out through the hall. NORA *hurries to the door, opens it a little, and listens.*

NORA. He's gone. He didn't leave the letter. Of course he didn't — that would be impossible! (*Opens the door further and further.*) What's he doing? He's stopped outside the door. He's not going down the stairs. Has he changed his mind? Is he —? (*A letter falls into the box.* KROGSTAD's *footsteps are heard gradually receding down the stairs.* NORA *utters a suppressed shriek, and rushes forward towards the sofa table; pause.*) It's in the letter-box! (*Slips shrinkingly up to the hall door.*) It's there! — Torvald, Torvald — now we are lost!

MRS. LINDE *enters from the left with the costume.*

MRS. LINDE. There, I think it's all right now. If you'll just try it on —?

NORA (*hoarsely and softly*). Come here, Kristine.

MRS. LINDE (*throws down the dress on the sofa*). What's the matter with you? You look upset.

NORA. Come here. Do you see that letter? Do you see it — in the letter-box?

MRS. LINDE. Yes, yes, I see it.

NORA. It's from Krogstad —

MRS. LINDE. Nora — you don't mean Krogstad lent you the money!

NORA. Yes; and now Torvald will know everything.

MRS. LINDE. It'll be much the best thing for you both, Nora.

NORA. But you don't know everything. I committed forgery —

MRS. LINDE. Good heavens!

NORA. Now, listen to me, Kristine; I want you to be my witness —

MRS. LINDE. How do you mean "witness"? What am I to —?

NORA. If I should go out of my mind — that might easily happen —

MRS. LINDE. Nora!

NORA. Or if something should happen to me — something that would prevent my being here —!

MRS. LINDE. Nora, Nora, you're quite beside yourself!

NORA. In case anyone else should insist on taking all the blame upon himself — the whole blame — you understand —

MRS. LINDE. Yes, but what makes you think —?

NORA. Then you must bear witness to the fact that that isn't true. I'm in my right mind now; I know exactly what I'm saying; and I tell you nobody else knew anything about it; I did the whole thing on my own. Just remember that.

MRS. LINDE. Very well — I will. But I don't understand at all.

NORA. No — of course — you couldn't. It's the wonderful thing — It's about to happen, don't you see?

MRS. LINDE. What "wonderful thing"?

NORA. The wonderful — wonderful thing! But it must never be allowed to happen — never. It would be too terrible.

MRS. LINDE. I'll go and talk to Krogstad at once.

NORA. No, don't go to him! He might do you some harm.

MRS. LINDE. There was a time — he would have done anything in the world for me.

NORA. He?

MRS. LINDE. Where does he live?

NORA. How do I know —? Yes — (*Feels in her pocket.*) Here's his card. But the letter, the letter —!

HELMER (*from his study; knocking on the door*). Nora!

NORA (*shrieks in terror*). Oh! What is it? What do you want?

HELMER. Don't be frightened! We're not coming in; anyway, you've locked the door. Are you trying on?

NORA. Yes, yes, I'm trying on. I'm going to look so pretty, Torvald.

MRS. LINDE (*who has read the card*). He lives just round the corner.

NORA. But it won't do any good. It's too late now. The letter is in the box.

MRS. LINDE. I suppose your husband has the key?

NORA. Of course.

MRS. LINDE. Krogstad must ask for his letter back, unread. He must make up some excuse —

NORA. But this is the time that Torvald usually —

MRS. LINDE. Prevent him. Keep him occupied. I'll come back as quickly as I can. (*She goes out hastily by the hall door.*)

NORA. (*opens* HELMER's *door and peeps in*). Torvald!

HELMER (*in the study*). Well? May one venture to come back into one's own living-room? Come along, Rank — now we shall see — (*in the doorway*) Why — what's this?

NORA. What, Torvald, dear?

HELMER. Rank led me to expect some wonderful disguise.

RANK (*in the doorway*). That's what I understood. I must have been mistaken.

NORA. Not till tomorrow evening! Then I shall appear in all my splendor!

HELMER. But you look quite tired, Nora, dear. I'm afraid you've been practicing too hard.

NORA. Oh, I haven't practiced at all yet.

HELMER. You ought to, though —

NORA. Yes — I really should, Torvald! But I can't seem to manage without your help. I'm afraid I've forgotten all about it.

HELMER. Well — we'll see what we can do. It'll soon come back to you.

NORA. You will help me, won't you, Torvald? Promise! I feel so nervous — all those people! You must concentrate on me this evening — forget all about business. *Please*, Torvald, dear — promise me you will!

HELMER. I promise. This evening I'll be your slave — you sweet, helpless little thing —! Just one moment, though — I want to see — (*Going to hall door.*)

NORA. What do you want out there?

HELMER. I just want to see if there are any letters.

NORA. Oh, don't, Torvald! Don't bother about that now!

HELMER. Why not?

NORA. *Please* don't, Torvald! There aren't any.

HELMER. Just let me take a look — (*Starts to go.*)

NORA, *at the piano, plays the first bars of the tarantella.*

HELMER (*stops in the doorway*). Aha!

NORA. I shan't be able to dance tomorrow if I don't rehearse with you!

HELMER (*going to her*). Are you really so nervous, Nora, dear?

NORA. Yes, I'm terrified! Let's rehearse right away. We've plenty of time before dinner. Sit down and play for me, Torvald, dear; direct me — guide me; you know how you do!

HELMER. With pleasure, my darling, if you wish me to. (*Sits at piano.*)

NORA *snatches the tambourine out of the box, and hurriedly drapes herself in a long parti-colored shawl; then, with a bound, stands in the middle of the floor and cries out.*

NORA. Now play for me! Now I'll dance!

HELMER *plays and* NORA *dances.* RANK *stands at the piano behind* HELMER *and looks on.*

HELMER (*playing*). Too fast! Too fast!

NORA. I can't help it!

HELMER. Don't be so violent, Nora!

NORA. That's the way it *should* be!

HELMER (*stops*). No, no; this won't do at all!

NORA (*laughs and swings her tambourine*). You see? What did I tell you?

RANK. I'll play for her.

HELMER (*rising*). Yes, do — then I'll be able to direct her.

RANK *sits down at the piano and plays;* NORA *dances more and more wildly;* HELMER *stands by the stove and addresses frequent corrections to her; she seems not to hear. Her hair breaks loose, and falls over her shoulders. She does not notice it, but goes on dancing.* MRS. LINDE *enters and stands spellbound in the doorway.*

MRS. LINDE. Ah — !

NORA (*dancing*). We're having such fun, Kristine!

HELMER. Why, Nora, dear, you're dancing as if your life were at stake!

NORA. It is! It is!

HELMER. Rank, stop! This is absolute madness. Stop, I say!

RANK *stops playing, and* NORA *comes to a sudden standstill.*

HELMER (*going toward her*). I never would have believed it. You've forgotten everything I ever taught you.

NORA (*throws the tambourine away*). I told you I had!

HELMER. This needs an immense amount of work.

NORA. That's what I said; you see how important it is! You must work with me up to the very last minute. Will you promise me, Torvald?

HELMER. I most certainly will!

NORA. This evening and all day tomorrow you must think of nothing but me. You mustn't open a single letter — mustn't even *look* at the mail-box.

HELMER. Nora! I believe you're still worried about that wretched man —

NORA. Yes — yes, I am!

HELMER. Nora — Look at me — there's a letter from him in the box, isn't there?

NORA. Maybe — I don't know; I believe there is. But you're not to read anything of that sort now; nothing must come between us until the party's over.

RANK (*softly, to* HELMER). Don't go against her.

HELMER (*putting his arm around her*). Very well! The child shall have her way. But tomorrow night, when your dance is over —

NORA. Then you'll be free.

HELENE *appears in the doorway, right.*

HELENE. Dinner is served, Ma'am.

NORA. We'll have champagne, Helene.

HELENE. Very good, Ma'am. (*Goes out.*)

HELMER. Quite a feast, I see!

NORA. Yes — a real feast! We'll stay up till dawn drinking champagne! (*Calling out.*) Oh, and we'll have macaroons, Helene — lots of them! Why not — for once?

HELMER (*seizing her hand*). Come, come! Not so violent! Be my own little lark again.

NORA. I will, Torvald. But now — both of you go in — while Kristine helps me with my hair.

RANK (*softly, as they go*). Is anything special the matter? I mean — anything — ?

HELMER. No, no; nothing at all. It's just this childish fear I was telling you about. (*They go out to the right.*)

NORA. Well?

MRS. LINDE. He's gone out of town.

NORA. I saw it in your face.

MRS. LINDE. He'll be back tomorrow evening. I left a note for him.

NORA. You shouldn't have bothered. You couldn't prevent it anyway. After all, there's a kind of joy in waiting for the wonderful thing to happen.

MRS. LINDE. I don't understand. What *is* this thing you're waiting for?

NORA. I can't explain. Go in and join them. I'll be there in a moment.

MRS. LINDE *goes into the dining room.* NORA *stands for a moment as though pulling herself together; then looks at her watch.*

NORA. Five o'clock. Seven hours till midnight. Twenty-four hours till the next midnight and then the tarantella will be over. Twenty-four and seven? I've thirty-one hours left to live.

HELMER *appears at the door, right.*

HELMER. Well! What has become of the little lark?

NORA (*runs to him with open arms*). Here she is!

CURTAIN

ACT THREE

Scene: *The same room. The table, with the chairs around it, has been moved to stage-center. A lighted lamp on the table. The hall door is open. Dance music is heard from the floor above.* MRS. LINDE *sits by the table absent-mindedly turning the pages of a book. She tries to read, but seems unable to keep her mind on it. Now and then she listens intently and glances towards the hall door.*

MRS. LINDE (*looks at her watch*). Where can he be? The time is nearly up. I hope he hasn't — (*Listens again.*) Here he is now. (*She goes into the hall and cautiously opens the outer door; cautious footsteps are heard on the stairs; she whispers.*) Come in; there is no one here.

KROGSTAD (*in the doorway*). I found a note from you at home. What does it mean?

MRS. LINDE. I simply *must* speak to you.

KROGSTAD. Indeed? But why here? Why in this house?

MRS. LINDE. I couldn't see you at my place. My room has no separate entrance. Come in; we're quite alone. The servants are asleep, and the Helmers are upstairs at a party.

KROGSTAD (*coming into the room*). Well, well! So the Helmers are dancing tonight, are they?

MRS. LINDE. Why shouldn't they?

KROGSTAD. Well — why not!

MRS. LINDE. Let's have a talk, Krogstad.

KROGSTAD. Have we two anything to talk about?

MRS. LINDE. Yes. A great deal.

KROGSTAD. I shouldn't have thought so.

MRS. LINDE. But then, you see — you have never really understood me.

KROGSTAD. There wasn't much to understand, was there? A woman is heartless enough to break off with a man, when a better match is offered; it's quite an ordinary occurrence.

MRS. LINDE. You really think me heartless? Did you think it was so easy for me?

KROGSTAD. Wasn't it?

MRS. LINDE. You really believed that, Krogstad?

KROGSTAD. If not, why should you have written to me as you did?

MRS. LINDE. What else could I do? Since I was forced to break with you, I felt it was only right to try and kill your love for me.

KROGSTAD (*clenching his hands together*). So what was it! And you did this for money!

MRS. LINDE. Don't forget I had my mother and two little brothers to think of. We couldn't wait for you, Krogstad; things were so unsettled for you then.

KROGSTAD. That may be; but, even so, you had no right to throw me over — not even for their sake.

MRS. LINDE. Who knows? I've often wondered whether I did right or not.

KROGSTAD (*more softly*). When I had lost you, I felt the ground crumble beneath my feet. Look at me. I'm like a shipwrecked man clinging to a raft.

MRS. LINDE. Help may be nearer than you think.

KROGSTAD. Help was here! Then you came and stood in the way.

MRS. LINDE. I knew nothing about it, Krogstad. I didn't know until today that I was to replace *you* at the Bank.

KROGSTAD. Very well — I believe you. But now that you do know, will you withdraw?

MRS. LINDE. No; I'd do you no good by doing that.

KROGSTAD. "Good" or not — I'd withdraw all the same.

MRS. LINDE. I have learnt to be prudent, Krogstad — I've had to. The bitter necessities of life have taught me that.

KROGSTAD. And life has taught me not to believe in phrases.

MRS. LINDE. Then life has taught you a very wise lesson. But what about deeds? Surely you must still believe in them?

KROGSTAD. How do you mean?

MRS. LINDE. You just said you were like a shipwrecked man, clinging to a raft.

KROGSTAD. I have good reason to say so.

MRS. LINDE. Well — I'm like a shipwrecked *woman* clinging to a raft. I have no one to mourn for, no one to care for.

KROGSTAD. You made your choice.

MRS. LINDE. I *had* no choice, I tell you!

KROGSTAD. What then?

MRS. LINDE. Since we're both of us shipwrecked, couldn't we join forces, Krogstad?

KROGSTAD. You don't mean — ?

MRS. LINDE. Two people on a raft have a better chance than one.

KROGSTAD. Kristine!

MRS. LINDE. Why do you suppose I came here to the city?

KROGSTAD. You mean — you thought of me?

MRS. LINDE. I can't live without work; all my life I've worked, as far back as I can remember; it's always been my one great joy. Now I'm quite alone in the world; my life is empty — aimless. There's not much joy in working for one's self. You could help me, Nils; you could give me something and someone to work for.

KROGSTAD. I can't believe all this. It's an hysterical impulse — a woman's exaggerated craving for self-sacrifice.

MRS. LINDE. When have you ever found me hysterical?

KROGSTAD. You'd really be willing to do this? Tell me honestly — do you quite realize what my past has been?

MRS. LINDE. Yes.

KROGSTAD. And you know what people think of me?

MRS. LINDE. Didn't you just say you'd have been a different person if you'd been with me?

KROGSTAD. I'm sure of it.

MRS. LINDE. Mightn't that still be true?

KROGSTAD. You really mean this, Kristine, don't you? I can see it in your face. Are you sure you have the courage — ?

MRS. LINDE. I need someone to care for, and your children need a mother. We two need each other, Nils. I have faith in your fundamental goodness. I'm not afraid.

KROGSTAD (*seizing her hands*). Thank you — thank you, Kristine. I'll make others believe in me too — I won't fail you! But — I'd almost forgotten —

MRS. LINDE (*listening*). Hush! The tarantella! You must go!

KROGSTAD. Why? What is it?

MRS. LINDE. Listen! She's begun her dance; as soon as she's finished dancing, they'll be down.

KROGSTAD. Yes — I'd better go. There'd have been no need for all that — but, of course, you don't know what I've done about the Helmers.

MRS. LINDE. Yes, I do, Nils.

KROGSTAD. And yet you have the courage to — ?

MRS. LINDE. I know you were desperate — I understand.

KROGSTAD. I'd give anything to undo it!

MRS. LINDE. You can. Your letter's still in the mail-box.

KROGSTAD. Are you sure?

MRS. LINDE. Quite, but —

KROGSTAD (*giving her a searching look*). Could that be it? You're doing all this to save your friend? You might as well be honest with me! Is that it?

MRS. LINDE. I sold myself once for the sake of others, Nils; I'm not likely to do it again.

KROGSTAD. I'll ask for my letter back unopened.

MRS. LINDE. No, no.

KROGSTAD. Yes, of course. I'll wait till Helmer comes; I'll tell him to give me back the letter — I'll say it refers to my dismissal — and ask him not to read it —

MRS. LINDE. No, Nils; don't ask for it back.

KROGSTAD. But wasn't that actually your reason for getting me to come here?

MRS. LINDE. Yes, in my first moment of fear. But that was twenty-four hours ago, and since then I've seen incredible things happening here. Helmer must know the truth; this wretched business must no longer be kept secret; it's time those two came to a thorough understanding; there's been enough deceit and subterfuge.

KROGSTAD. Very well, if you like to risk it. But there's one thing I can do, and at once —

MRS. LINDE (*listening*). You must go now. Make haste! The dance is over; we're not safe here another moment.

KROGSTAD. I'll wait for you downstairs.

MRS. LINDE. Yes, do; then you can see me home.

KROGSTAD. Kristine! I've never been so happy! (KROGSTAD *goes out by the outer door. The door between the room and the hall remains open.*)

MRS. LINDE (*arranging the room and getting her outdoor things together*). How different things will be! Someone to work for, to live for; a home to make happy! How wonderful it will be to try! — I wish they'd come — (*Listens.*) Here they are! I'll get my coat — (*Takes bonnet and cloak.* HELMER's *and* NORA's *voices are heard outside, a key is turned in the lock, and* HELMER *drags* NORA *almost by force into the hall. She wears the Italian costume with a large black shawl over it. He is in evening dress and wears a black domino, open.*)

NORA (*struggling with him in the doorway*). No, no! I don't want to come home; I want to go upstairs again; I don't want to leave so early!

HELMER. Come — Nora dearest!

NORA. I beg you, Torvald! Please, *please* — just one hour more!

HELMER. Not one single minute more, Nora darling; don't you remember our agreement? Come along in, now; you'll catch cold. (*He leads her gently into the room in spite of her resistance.*)

MRS. LINDE. Good evening.

NORA. Kristine!

HELMER. Why, Mrs. Linde! What are you doing here so late?

MRS. LINDE. Do forgive me. I did so want to see Nora in her costume.

NORA. Have you been waiting for me all this time?

MRS. LINDE. Yes; I came too late to catch you before you went upstairs, and I didn't want to go away without seeing you.

HELMER (*taking* NORA's *shawl off*). And you *shall* see her, Mrs. Linde! She's worth looking at I can tell you! Isn't she lovely?

MRS. LINDE. Oh, Nora. How perfectly —!

HELMER. Absolutely exquisite, isn't she? That's what everybody said. But she's obstinate as a mule, is my sweet little thing! I don't know what to do with her! Will you believe it, Mrs. Linde, I had to drag her away by force?

NORA. You'll see — you'll be sorry, Torvald, you didn't let me stay, if only for another half-hour.

HELMER. Do you hear that, Mrs. Linde? Now, listen to this: She danced her tarantella to wild applause, and she deserved it, too, I must say — though, perhaps, from an artistic point of view, her interpretation was a bit too realistic. But never mind — the point is, she made a great success, a phenomenal success. Now — should I have allowed her to stay on and spoil the whole effect? Certainly not! I took my sweet little Capri girl — my capricious little Capri girl, I might say — in my arms; a rapid whirl round the room, a low curtsey to all sides, and — as they say in novels — the lovely apparition vanished! An exit should always be effective, Mrs. Linde; but I can't get Nora to see that. Phew! It's warm here. (*Throws his domino on a chair and opens the door to his room.*) Why — there's no light on in here! Oh no, of course — Excuse me — (*Goes in and lights candles.*)

NORA. (*whispers breathlessly*). Well?

MRS. LINDE (*softly*). I've spoken to him.

NORA. And —?

MRS. LINDE. Nora — you must tell your husband everything —

NORA (*tonelessly*). I knew it!

MRS. LINDE. You have nothing to fear from Krogstad; but you must speak out.

NORA. I shan't.

MRS. LINDE. Then the letter will.

NORA. Thank you, Kristine. Now I know what I must do. Hush —!

HELMER (*coming back*). Well, have you finished admiring her, Mrs. Linde?

MRS. LINDE. Yes, and now I must say good-night.

HELMER. Oh — must you be going already? Does this knitting belong to you?

MRS. LINDE (*takes it*). Oh, thank you; I almost forgot it.

HELMER. So you knit, do you?

MRS. LINDE. Yes.

HELMER. Why don't you do embroidery instead?

MRS. LINDE. Why?

HELMER. Because it's so much prettier. Now watch! You hold the embroidery in the left hand — so — and then, in the right hand, you hold the needle, and guide it — so — in a long graceful curve — isn't that right?

MRS. LINDE. Yes, I suppose so —

HELMER. Whereas, knitting can never be anything but ugly. Now, watch! Arms close to your sides, needles going up and down — there's something Chinese about it! — That really was splendid champagne they gave us.

MRS. LINDE. Well, good-night, Nora; don't be obstinate any more.

HELMER. Well said, Mrs. Linde!

MRS. LINDE. Good-night, Mr. Helmer.

HELMER (*accompanying her to the door*). Good-night, good-night; I hope you get home safely. I'd be only too glad to — but you've such a short way to go. Good-night, good-night. (*She goes;* HELMER *shuts the door after her and comes forward again.*) Well — thank God we've got rid of her; she's a dreadful bore, that woman.

NORA. You must be tired, Torvald.

HELMER. I? Not in the least.

NORA. But, aren't you sleepy?

HELMER. Not a bit. On the contrary, I feel exceedingly lively. But what about you? You seem to be very tired and sleepy.

NORA. Yes, I am very tired. But I'll soon sleep now.

HELMER. You see! I was right not to let you stay there any longer.

NORA. Everything you do is always right, Torvald.

HELMER (*kissing her forehead*). There's my sweet, sensible little lark! By the way, did you notice how gay Rank was this evening?

NORA. Was he? I didn't get a chance to speak to him.

HELMER. I didn't either, really; but it's a long time since I've seen him in such a jolly mood. (*Gazes at* NORA *for a while, then comes nearer her.*) It's so lovely to be home again — to be here alone with you. You glorious, fascinating creature!

NORA. Don't look at me like that, Torvald.

HELMER. Why shouldn't I look at my own dearest treasure? — at all this loveliness that is mine, wholly and utterly mine — mine alone!

NORA (*goes to the other side of the table*). You mustn't talk to me like that tonight.

HELMER (*following*). You're still under the spell of the tarantella — and it makes you even more desirable. Listen! The other guests are leaving now. (*More softly.*) Soon the whole house will be still, Nora.

NORA. I hope so.

HELMER. Yes, you do, don't you, my beloved? Do you know something — when I'm out with you among a lot of people — do you know why it is I hardly speak to you, why I keep away from you, and only occasionally steal a quick glance at you; do you know why that is? It's because I pretend that we love each other in secret, that we're secretly engaged, and that no one suspects there is anything between us.

NORA. Yes, yes; I know your thoughts are always round me.

HELMER. Then, when it's time to leave, and I put your shawl round your smooth, soft, young shoulders — round that beautiful neck of yours — I pretend that you are my young bride, that we've just come from the wedding, and that I'm taking you home for the first time — that for the first time I shall be alone with you — quite alone with you, in all your tremulous beauty. All evening I have been filled with longing for you. As I watched you swaying and whirling in the tarantella — my pulses began to throb until I thought I should go mad; that's why I carried you off — made you leave so early —

NORA. Please go, Torvald! Please leave me. I don't want you like this.

HELMER. What do you mean? You're teasing me, aren't you, little Nora? Not want me —! Aren't I your husband —?

A knock at the outer door.

NORA (*starts*). Listen —!

HELMER (*going toward the hall*). Who is it?

RANK (*outside*). It is I; may I come in a moment?

HELMER (*in a low tone, annoyed*). Why does he have to bother us now! (*Aloud.*) Just a second! (*Opens door.*) Well! How nice of you to look in.

RANK. I heard your voice, and I thought I'd like to stop in a minute. (*Looks round.*) These dear old rooms! You must be so cozy and happy here, you two!

HELMER. I was just saying how gay and happy you seemed to be, upstairs.

RANK. Why not? Why shouldn't I be? One should get all one can out of life; all one can, for as long as one can. That wine was excellent —

HELMER. Especially the champagne.

RANK. You noticed that, did you? It's incredible how much I managed to get down.

NORA. Torvald drank plenty of it too.

RANK. Oh?

NORA. It always puts him in such a jolly mood.

RANK. Well, why shouldn't one have a jolly evening after a well-spent day?

HELMER. Well-spent! I'm afraid mine wasn't much to boast of!

RANK (*slapping him on the shoulder*). But mine was, you see?

NORA. Did you by any chance make a scientific investigation, Doctor Rank?

RANK. Precisely.

HELMER. Listen to little Nora, talking about scientific investigations!

NORA. Am I to congratulate you on the result?

RANK. By all means.

NORA. It was good then?

RANK. The best possible, both for the doctor and the patient — certainty.

NORA (*quickly and searchingly*). Certainty?

RANK. Absolute certainty. Wasn't I right to spend a jolly evening after that?

NORA. You were quite right, Doctor Rank.

HELMER. I quite agree! Provided you don't have to pay for it, tomorrow.

RANK. You don't get anything for nothing in this life.

NORA. You like masquerade parties, don't you, Dr. Rank?

RANK. Very much — when there are plenty of amusing disguises —

NORA. What shall we two be at our next masquerade?

HELMER. Listen to her! Thinking of the next party already!

RANK. We two? I'll tell you. You must go as a precious talisman.

HELMER. How on earth would you dress that!

RANK. That's easy. She'd only have to be herself.

HELMER. Charmingly put. But what about you? Have you decided what you'd be?

RANK. Oh, definitely.

HELMER. Well?

RANK. At the next masquerade party I shall be invisible.

HELMER. That's a funny notion!

RANK. There's a large black cloak — you've heard of the invisible cloak, haven't you? You've only to put it around you and no one can see you any more.

HELMER (*with a suppressed smile*). Quite true!

RANK. But I almost forgot what I came for. Give me a cigar, will you, Helmer? One of the dark Havanas.

HELMER. Of course — with pleasure. (*Hands cigar case.*)

RANK (*takes one and cuts the end off*). Thanks.

NORA (*striking a wax match*). Let me give you a light.

RANK. I thank you. (*She holds the match. He lights his cigar at it.*) And now, I'll say good-bye!

HELMER. Good-bye, good-bye, my dear fellow.

NORA. Sleep well, Doctor Rank.

RANK. Thanks for the wish.

NORA. Wish me the same.

RANK. You? Very well, since you ask me — Sleep well. And thanks for the light. (*He nods to them both and goes out.*)

HELMER (*in an undertone*). He's had a lot to drink.

NORA (*absently*). I dare say. (HELMER *takes his bunch of keys from his pocket and goes into the hall.*) Torvald! What do you want out there?

HELMER. I'd better empty the mail-box; it's so full there won't be room for the papers in the morning.

NORA. Are you going to work tonight?

HELMER. No — you know I'm not. — Why, what's this? Someone has been at the lock.

NORA. The lock —?

HELMER. Yes — that's funny! I shouldn't have thought that the maids would — Here's a broken hair-pin. Why — it's one of yours, Nora.

NORA (*quickly*). It must have been the children —

A Doll's House

HELMER. You'll have to stop them doing that — There! I got it open at last. (*Takes contents out and calls out towards the kitchen.*) Helene? — Oh, Helene; put out the lamp in the hall, will you? (*He returns with letters in his hand, and shuts the door to the hall.*) Just look how they've stacked up. (*Looks through them.*) Why, what's this?

NORA (*at the window*). The letter! Oh, Torvald! No!

HELMER. Two visiting cards — from Rank.

NORA. From Doctor Rank?

HELMER (*looking at them*). Doctor Rank, physician. They were right on top. He must have stuck them in just now, as he left.

NORA. Is there anything on them?

HELMER. There's a black cross over his name. Look! What a gruesome thought. Just as if he were announcing his own death.

NORA. And so he is.

HELMER. What do you mean? What do you know about it? Did he tell you anything?

NORA. Yes. These cards mean that he has said good-bye to us for good. Now he'll lock himself up to die.

HELMER. Oh, my poor friend! I always knew he hadn't long to live, but I never dreamed it would be quite so soon —! And to hide away like a wounded animal —

NORA. When the time comes, it's best to go in silence. Don't you think so, Torvald?

HELMER (*walking up and down*). He'd become so a part of us. I can't imagine his having gone for good. With his suffering and loneliness he was like a dark, cloudy background to our lives — it made the sunshine of our happiness seem even brighter — Well, I suppose it's for the best — for him at any rate. (*Stands still.*) And perhaps for us too, Nora. Now we are more than ever dependent on each other. (*Takes her in his arms.*) Oh, my beloved wife! I can't seem to hold you close enough. Do you know something, Nora. I often wish you were in some great danger — so I could risk body and soul — my whole life — everything, everything, for your sake.

NORA (*tears herself from him and says firmly*). Now you must read your letters, Torvald.

HELMER. No, no; not tonight. I want to be with you, my beloved wife.

NORA. With the thought of your dying friend —?

HELMER. Of course — You are right. It's been a shock to both of us. A hideous shadow has come between us — thoughts of death and decay. We must try and throw them off. Until then — we'll stay apart.

NORA (*her arms round his neck*). Torvald! Good-night! Good-night!

HELMER (*kissing her forehead*). Good-night, my little song-bird; sleep well! Now I'll go and read my letters. (*He goes with the letters in his hand into his room and shuts the door.*)

NORA (*with wild eyes, gropes about her, seizes* HELMER's *domino, throws it round her, and whispers quickly, hoarsely, and brokenly*). I'll never see him again. Never, never, never. (*Throws her shawl over her head.*) I'll never see the children again. I'll never see them either — Oh the thought of that black, icy water! That fathomless —! If it were only over! He has it now; he's reading it. Oh, not yet — please! Not yet! Torvald, good-bye —! Good-bye to you and the children!

>*She is rushing out by the hall; at the same moment* HELMER *flings his door open, and stands there with an open letter in his hand.*

HELMER. Nora!

NORA (*shrieks*). Ah —!

HELMER. What does this mean? Do you know what is in this letter?

NORA. Yes, yes, I know. Let me go! Let me out!

HELMER (*holds her back*). Where are you going?

NORA (*tries to break away from him*). Don't try to save me, Torvald!

HELMER (*falling back*). So it's true! It's true what he writes? It's too horrible! It's impossible — it can't be true.

NORA. It *is* true. I've loved you more than all the world.

HELMER. Oh, come now! Let's have no silly nonsense!

NORA (*a step nearer him*). Torvald —!

HELMER. Do you realize what you've done?

NORA. Let me go — I won't have you suffer for it! I won't have you take the blame!

HELMER. Will you stop this play-acting! (*Locks the outer door.*) You'll stay here and give an account of yourself. Do you understand what you have done? Answer me! Do you understand it?

NORA (*looks at him fixedly, and says with a stiffening expression*). I think I'm beginning to understand for the first time.

HELMER (*walking up and down*). God! What an awakening! After eight years to discover that you who have been my pride and joy — are no better than a hypocrite, a liar — worse than that — a criminal! It's too horrible to think of! (NORA *says nothing, and continues to look fixedly at him.*) I might have known what to expect. I should have foreseen it. You've inherited all your father's lack of principle — be silent! — all of your father's lack of principle, I say! — no religion, no moral code, no sense of duty. This is my punishment for shielding him! I did it for your sake; and this is my reward!

NORA. I see.

HELMER. You've destroyed my happiness. You've ruined my whole future. It's ghastly to think of! I'm completely in the power of this scoundrel; he can force me to do whatever he likes, demand whatever he chooses; order me about at will; and I shan't dare open my mouth! My entire career is to be wrecked and all because of a lawless, unprincipled woman!

NORA. If I were no longer alive, then you'd be free.

HELMER. Oh yes! You're full of histrionics! Your father was just the same. Even if you "weren't alive," as you put it, what good would that do me? None

A Doll's House

whatever! He could publish the story all the same; I might even be suspected of collusion. People might say I was behind it all — that I had prompted you to do it. And to think I have you to thank for all this — you whom I've done nothing but pamper and spoil since the day of our marriage. Now do you realize what you've done to me?

NORA (*with cold calmness*). Yes.

HELMER. It's all so incredible, I can't grasp it. But we must try and come to some agreement. Take off that shawl. Take it off, I say! Of course, we must find some way to appease him — the matter must be hushed up at any cost. As far as we two are concerned, there must be no change in our way of life — in the eyes of the world, I mean. You'll naturally continue to live here. But you won't be allowed to bring up the children — I'd never dare trust them to you — God! to have to say this to the woman I've loved so tenderly — There can be no further thought of happiness between us. We must save what we can from the ruins — we can save appearances, at least — (*A ring;* HELMER *starts.*) What can that be? At this hour! You don't suppose he —! Could he —? Hide yourself, Nora; say you are ill.

NORA *stands motionless.* HELMER *goes to the door and opens it.*

HELENE (*half dressed, in the hall*). It's a letter for Mrs. Helmer.

HELMER. Give it to me. (*Seizes the letter and shuts the door.*) It's from him. I shan't give it to you. I'll read it myself.

NORA. Very well.

HELMER (*by the lamp*). I don't dare open it; this may be the end — for both of us. Still — I must know. (*Hastily tears the letter open; reads a few lines, looks at an enclosure; with a cry of joy.*) Nora! (NORA *looks inquiringly at him.*) Nora! — I can't believe it — I must read it again. But it's true — it's really true! Nora, I am saved! I'm saved!

NORA. What about me?

HELMER. You too, of course; we are both of us saved, both of us. Look! — he's sent you back your note — he says he's sorry for what he did and apologizes for it — that due to a happy turn of events he — Oh, what does it matter what he says! We are saved, Nora! No one can harm you now. Oh, Nora, Nora —; but let's get rid of this hateful thing. I'll just see — (*Glances at the I.O.U.*) No, no — I won't even look at it; I'll pretend it was all a horrible dream. (*Tears the I.O.U. and both letters in pieces. Throws them into the fire and watches them burn.*) There! Now it's all over — He said in his letter you've known about this since Christmas Eve — you must have had three dreadful days, Nora!

NORA. Yes. It's been very hard.

HELMER. How you must have suffered! And you saw no way out but — No! We'll forget the whole ghastly business. We'll just thank God and repeat again and again: It's over; all over! Don't you understand, Nora? You don't seem to grasp it: It's over. What's the matter with you? Why do you look so grim? My poor darling little Nora, I understand; but you mustn't worry — because I've forgiven you, Nora; I swear I have; I've forgiven everything. You did what you did because you loved me — I see that now.

NORA. Yes — that's true.

HELMER. You loved me as a wife should love her husband. You didn't realize what you were doing — you weren't able to judge how wrong it was. Don't think this makes you any less dear to me. Just you lean on me; let me guide you and advise you; I'm not a man for nothing! There's something very endearing about a woman's helplessness. And try and forget those harsh things I said just now. I was frantic; my whole world seemed to be tumbling about my ears. Believe me, I've forgiven you, Nora — I swear it — I've forgiven everything.

NORA. Thank you for your forgiveness, Torvald. (*Goes out, to the right.*)

HELMER. No! Don't go. (*Looking through the doorway.*) Why do you have to go in there?

NORA (*inside*). I want to get out of these fancy-dress clothes.

HELMER (*in the doorway*). Yes, do, my darling. Try to calm down now, and get back to normal, my poor frightened little song-bird. Don't you worry — you'll be safe under my wings — they'll protect you. (*Walking up and down near the door.*) How lovely our home is, Nora! You'll be sheltered here; I'll cherish you as if you were a little dove I'd rescued from the claws of some dreadful hawk. You'll see — your poor fluttering little heart will soon grow calm again. Tomorrow all this will appear in quite a different light — things will be just as they were. I won't have to keep on saying I've forgiven you — you'll be able to sense it. You don't really think I could ever drive you away, do you? That I could even so much as reproach you for anything? You'd understand if you could see into my heart. When a man forgives his wife whole-heartedly — as I have you — it fills him with such tenderness, such peace. She seems to belong to him in a double sense; it's as though he'd brought her to life again; she's become more than his wife — she's become his child as well. That's how it will be with us, Nora — my own bewildered, helpless little darling. From now on you mustn't worry about anything; just open your heart to me; just let me be both will and conscience to you. (NORA *enters in everyday dress.*) What's all this? I thought you were going to bed. You've changed your dress?

NORA. Yes, Torvald; I've changed my dress.

HELMER. But what for? At this hour?

NORA. I shan't sleep tonight.

HELMER. But, Nora dear —

NORA (*looking at her watch*). It's not so very late — Sit down, Torvald; we have a lot to talk about. (*She sits at one side of the table.*)

HELMER. Nora — what does this mean? Why that stern expression?

NORA. Sit down. It'll take some time. I have a lot to say to you.

HELMER *sits at the other side of the table.*

HELMER. You frighten me, Nora. I don't understand you.

NORA. No, that's just it. You don't understand me; and I have never understood you either — until tonight. No, don't interrupt me. Just listen to what I have to say. This is to be a final settlement, Torvald.

HELMER. How do you mean?

NORA (*after a short silence*). Doesn't anything special strike you as we sit here like this?

HELMER. I don't think so — why?

NORA. It doesn't occur to you, does it, that though we've been married for eight years, this is the first time that we two — man and wife — have sat down for a serious talk?

HELMER. What do you mean by serious?

NORA. During eight whole years, no — more than that — ever since the first day we met — we have never exchanged so much as one serious word about serious things.

HELMER. Why should I perpetually burden you with all my cares and problems? How could you possibly help me to solve them?

NORA. I'm not talking about cares and problems. I'm simply saying we've never once sat down seriously and tried to get to the bottom of anything.

HELMER. But, Nora, darling — why should you be concerned with serious thoughts?

NORA. That's the whole point! You've never understood me — A great injustice has been done me, Torvald; first by Father, and then by you.

HELMER. What a thing to say! No two people on earth could ever have loved you more than we have!

NORA (*shaking her head*). You never loved me. You just thought it was fun to be in love with me.

HELMER. This is fantastic!

NORA. Perhaps. But it's true all the same. While I was still at home I used to hear Father airing his opinions and they became my opinions; or if I didn't happen to agree, I kept it to myself — he would have been displeased otherwise. He used to call me his doll-baby, and played with me as I played with my dolls. Then I came to live in your house —

HELMER. What an expression to use about our marriage!

NORA (*undisturbed*). I mean — from Father's hands I passed into yours. You arranged everything according to your tastes, and I acquired the same tastes, or I pretended to — I'm not sure which — a little of both, perhaps. Looking back on it all, it seems to me I've lived here like a beggar, from hand to mouth. I've lived by performing tricks for you, Torvald. But that's the way you wanted it. You and Father have done me a great wrong. You've prevented me from becoming a real person.

HELMER. Nora, how can you be so ungrateful and unreasonable! Haven't you been happy here?

NORA. No, never. I thought I was; but I wasn't really.

HELMER. Not — not happy!

NORA. No; only merry. You've always been so kind to me. But our home has never been anything but a play-room. I've been your doll-wife, just as at home I was Papa's doll-child. And the children in turn, have been my dolls. I thought it fun when you played games with me, just as they thought it fun when I played games with them. And that's been our marriage, Torvald.

HELMER. There may be a grain of truth in what you say, even though it is distorted and exaggerated. From now on things will be different. Play-time is over now; tomorrow lessons begin!

NORA. Whose lessons? Mine, or the children's?

HELMER. Both, if you wish it, Nora, dear.

NORA. Torvald, I'm afraid you're not the man to teach me to be a real wife to you.

HELMER. How can you say that?

NORA. And I'm certainly not fit to teach the children.

HELMER. Nora!

NORA. Didn't you just say, a moment ago, you didn't dare trust them to me?

HELMER. That was in the excitement of the moment! You mustn't take it so seriously!

NORA. But you were quite right, Torvald. That job is beyond me; there's another job I must do first: I must try and educate myself. You could never help me to do that; I must do it quite alone. So, you see — that's why I'm going to leave you.

HELMER (*jumping up*). What did you say —?

NORA. I shall never get to know myself — I shall never learn to face reality — unless I stand alone. So I can't stay with you any longer.

HELMER. Nora! Nora!

NORA. I am going at once. I'm sure Kristine will let me stay with her tonight —

HELMER. But, Nora — this is madness! I shan't allow you to do this. I shall forbid it!

NORA. You no longer have the power to forbid me anything. I'll only take a few things with me — those that belong to me. I shall never again accept anything from you.

HELMER. Have you lost your senses?

NORA. Tomorrow I'll go home — to what *was* my home, I mean. It might be easier for me there, to find something to do.

HELMER. You talk like an ignorant child, Nora —!

NORA. Yes. That's just why I must educate myself.

HELMER. To leave your home — to leave your husband, and your children! What do you suppose people would say to that?

NORA. It makes no difference. This is something I *must* do.

HELMER. It's inconceivable! Don't you realize you'd be betraying your most sacred duty?

NORA. What do you consider that to be?

A Doll's House

HELMER. Your duty towards your husband and your children — I surely don't have to tell you that!

NORA. I've another duty just as sacred.

HELMER. Nonsense! What duty do you mean?

NORA. My duty towards myself.

HELMER. Remember — before all else you are a wife and mother.

NORA. I don't believe that anymore. I believe that before all else I am a human being, just as you are — or at least that I should try and become one. I know that most people would agree with you, Torvald — and that's what they say in books. But I can no longer be satisfied with what most people say — or what they write in books. I must think things out for myself — get clear about them.

HELMER. Surely your position in your home is clear enough? Have you no sense of religion? Isn't that an infallible guide to you?

NORA. But don't you see, Torvald — I don't really know what religion is.

HELMER. Nora! How *can* you!

NORA. All I know about it is what Pastor Hansen told me when I was confirmed. He taught me what he thought religion was — said it was *this* and *that*. As soon as I get away by myself, I shall have to look into that matter too, try and decide whether what he taught me was right — or whether it's right for *me*, at least.

HELMER. A nice way for a young woman to talk! It's unheard of! If religion means nothing to you, I'll appeal to your conscience; you must have some sense of ethics, I suppose? Answer me! Or have you none?

NORA. It's hard for me to answer you, Torvald. I don't think I know — all these things bewilder me. But I *do* know that I think quite differently from you about them. I've discovered that the law, for instance, is quite different from what I had imagined; but I find it hard to believe it can be right. It seems it's criminal for a woman to try and spare her old, sick, father, or save her husband's life! I can't agree with that.

HELMER. You talk like a child. You have no understanding of the society we live in.

NORA. No, I haven't. But I'm going to try and learn. I want to find out which of us is right — society or I.

HELMER. You are ill, Nora; you have a touch of fever; you're quite beside yourself.

NORA. I've never felt so sure — so clear-headed — as I do tonight.

HELMER. "Sure and clear-headed" enough to leave your husband and your children?

NORA. Yes.

HELMER. Then there is only one explanation possible.

NORA. What?

HELMER. You don't love me any more.

NORA. No; that is just it.

HELMER. Nora! — What are you saying!

NORA. It makes me so unhappy, Torvald; for you've always been so kind to me. But I can't help it. I don't love you any more.

HELMER (*mastering himself with difficulty*). You feel "sure and clear-headed" about this too?

NORA. Yes, utterly sure. That's why I can't stay here any longer.

HELMER. And can you tell me how I lost your love?

NORA. Yes, I can tell you. It was tonight — when the wonderful thing didn't happen; I knew then you weren't the man I always thought you were.

HELMER. I don't understand.

NORA. For eight years I've been waiting patiently; I knew, of course, that such things don't happen every day. Then, when this trouble came to me — I thought to myself: Now! Now the wonderful thing will happen! All the time Krogstad's letter was out there in the box, it never occurred to me for a single moment that you'd think of submitting to his conditions. I was absolutely convinced that you'd defy him — that you'd tell him to publish the thing to all the world; and that then —

HELMER. You mean you thought I'd let my wife be publicly dishonored and disgraced?

NORA. No. What I thought you'd do, was to take the blame upon yourself.

HELMER. Nora —!

NORA. I know! You think I never would have accepted such a sacrifice. Of course I wouldn't! But my word would have meant nothing against yours. That was the wonderful thing I hoped for, Torvald, hoped for with such terror. And it was to prevent that, that I chose to kill myself.

HELMER. I'd gladly work for you day and night, Nora — go through suffering and want, if need be — but one doesn't sacrifice one's honor for love's sake.

NORA. Millions of women have done so.

HELMER. You think and talk like a silly child.

NORA. Perhaps. But you neither think nor talk like the man I want to share my life with. When you'd recovered from your fright — and you never thought of me, only of yourself — when you had nothing more to fear — you behaved as though none of this had happened. I was your little lark again, your little doll — whom you would have to guard more carefully than ever, because she was so weak and frail. (*Stands up.*) At that moment it suddenly dawned on me that I had been living here for eight years with a stranger and that I'd borne him three children. I can't bear to think about it! I could tear myself to pieces!

HELMER (*sadly*). I see, Nora — I understand; there's suddenly a great void between us — Is there no way to bridge it?

NORA. Feeling as I do now, Torvald — I could never be a wife to you.

HELMER. But, if I were to change? Don't you think I'm capable of that?

NORA. Perhaps — when you no longer have your doll to play with.

A Doll's House

HELMER. It's inconceivable! I *can't* part with you, Nora. I can't endure the thought.

NORA (*going into room on the right*). All the more reason it should happen. (*She comes back with outdoor things and a small traveling-bag, which she places on a chair.*)

HELMER. But not at once, Nora — not now! At least wait till tomorrow.

NORA (*putting on cloak*). I can't spend the night in a strange man's house.

HELMER. Couldn't we go on living here together? As brother and sister, if you like — as friends.

NORA (*fastening her hat*). You know very well that wouldn't last, Torvald. (*Puts on the shawl.*) Good-bye. I won't go in and see the children. I know they're in better hands than mine. Being what I am — how can I be of any use to them?

HELMER. But surely, some day, Nora —?

NORA. How can I tell? How do I know what sort of person I'll become?

HELMER. You are my wife, Nora, now and always!

NORA. Listen to me, Torvald — I've always heard that when a wife deliberately leaves her husband as I am leaving you, he is legally freed from all responsibility towards her. At any rate, I release you now from all responsibility. You mustn't feel yourself bound, any more than I shall. There must be complete freedom on both sides. Here is your ring. Now give me mine.

HELMER. That too?

NORA. That too.

HELMER. Here it is.

NORA. So — it's all over now. Here are the keys. The servants know how to run the house — better than I do. I'll ask Kristine to come by tomorrow, after I've left town; there are a few things I brought with me from home; she'll pack them up and send them on to me.

HELMER. You really mean it's over, Nora? *Really* over? You'll never think of me again?

NORA. I expect I shall often think of you; of you — and the children, and this house.

HELMER. May I write to you?

NORA. No — never. You mustn't! Please!

HELMER. At least, let me send you —

NORA. Nothing!

HELMER. But, you'll let me help you, Nora —

NORA. No, I say! I can't accept anything from strangers.

HELMER. Must I always be a stranger to you, Nora?

NORA (*taking her traveling-bag*). Yes. Unless it were to happen — the most wonderful thing of all —

HELMER. What?

NORA. Unless we both could change so that — Oh, Torvald! I no longer *believe* in miracles, you see!

HELMER. Tell me! Let *me* believe! Unless we both could change so that —?

NORA. — So that our life together might truly be a marriage. Good-bye. (*She goes out by the hall door.*)

HELMER (*sinks into a chair by the door with his face in his hands*). Nora! Nora! (*He looks around the room and rises.*) She is gone! How empty it all seems! (*A hope springs up in him.*) The most wonderful thing of all —?

From below is heard the reverberation of a heavy door closing.

CURTAIN

NATURALISM

August Strindberg

MISS JULIE

[1888]

August Strindberg [1849-1912]

With good reason we think of August Strindberg as morbid, anguished, and unbalanced. His psychological life, as we know it from his autobiographical volumes and his plays, was turbulent. Three attempts at suicide before he was forty, a year's stay in a sanitarium, irrational obsessions, and repeated failures in marriage all illustrate his unhappy and disturbed life. Denied a mother's love and attention as a child and reared in an uncongenial household, Strindberg continually pursued love and happiness in marriage, only to have three marriages disintegrate shortly after they were celebrated. Apparently he could not live without women — but certainly he could not live with them. To know something of Strindberg's intimate life is to be able to understand the darkness of his naturalistic plays.

Strindberg has been called the dramatist of the division in the modern soul. As the sensitive, though often obsessive, prober of the deepest conflicts of unusual people, he has been praised as an original by twentieth-century playwrights as no other modern dramatist has. Sean O'Casey has called Strindberg "the greatest of them all," and Eugene O'Neill has unqualifiedly said that "Strindberg was the precursor of all modernity in our present theater." His modernity lies in his having developed in notable ways both the naturalistic and the expressionist drama. (For a discussion of the latter, see the introduction to *A Dream Play*.)

Literary naturalism is distinguished by two distinct but related and interdependent characteristics: the first is the presentation of certain philosophical presuppositions (such as Strindberg outlines in the first part of his foreword to *Miss Julie*), and the second is the dramatic method — which bodies forth the world view. The two are not separate, and are ultimately not separable; it would be difficult to conceive of a naturalistic play which was not naturalistic in both content and form. The literary naturalist tends to view life as a struggle, and sees some deterministic force at work in the lives of his characters. The force may be broadly environmental, or more particularly psychological; it is both in *Miss Julie*. But whatever the force, it is likely to be ultimately determinative of the action. In his effort to get at the truth the naturalist is likely to make some pretensions to objectivity of presentation; he often attempts to withhold any judgments, though this aim is frequently not realized. Further, in a naturalistic play a good deal of emphasis may be placed on a literal fidelity to the actual details of the life portrayed. The naturalist often chooses his subject from low life or some other fringe of society in order that he may find life at its most "real," where the veneer of convention and affectation is thinnest.

In his foreword to *Miss Julie*, which has emerged as one of the most important documents in modern dramatic literature, Strindberg states explicitly that "there is no such thing as absolute evil," and that he as a naturalist "has abolished guilt with God." He

Strindberg and Naturalism

enjoys the struggles of life, and he is centrally interested in revealing the many motives (determining forces) which precipitate each action. Further, he devotes several pages to discussing the shortcomings of the contemporary stage, advocating among other innovations the rejection of such artificial stage conventions as act divisions, painted properties, and playing toward the audience (as well as to it), in favor of a true fourth wall convention.

In *The Father* (1887) and *Miss Julie* Strindberg has introduced to the modern drama an emphasis on the neurotic (or even the psychotic) in his characters. (See also Ibsen's *Hedda Gabler*, 1890.) This short full-length play is a duel to the death between Jean and Julie, who are here representatives of the two sexes. Strindberg's own view of women was that they were predatory creatures, usually stronger and more ruthless than the susceptible male. In this play, however, the male (for any special reasons?) finally dominates. The unbalanced protagonist irrationally succumbs to the powers of the valet.

Among other questions which might be asked about *Miss Julie* are these: What is the special effect of the lack of an intermission? What is the function of Julie's dream? How is her past involved? Does Julie, as Strindberg says she does, arouse pity? These questions and their answers suggest some qualities characteristic of literary naturalism.

AUTHOR'S FOREWORD TO
MISS JULIE*

Theatre has long seemed to me — in common with much other art — a *Biblia Pauperum*, a Bible in pictures for those who cannot read what is written or printed; and I see the playwright as a lay preacher peddling the ideas of his time in popular form, popular enough for the middleclasses, mainstay of theatre audiences, to grasp the gist of the matter without troubling their brains too much. For this reason theatre has always been an elementary school for the young, the semi-educated and for women who still have a primitive capacity for deceiving themselves and letting themselves be deceived — who, that is to say, are susceptible to illusion and to suggestion from the author. I have therefore thought it not unlikely that in these days, when that rudimentary and immature thought-process operating through fantasy appears to be developing into reflection, research and analysis, that theatre, like religion, might be discarded as an outworn form for whose appreciation we lack the necessary conditions. This opinion is confirmed by the major crisis still prevailing in the theatres of Europe, and still more by the fact that in those countries of culture, producing the greatest thinkers of the age, namely England and Germany, drama — like other fine arts — is dead.

Some countries, it is true, have attempted to create a new drama by using the old forms with up-to-date contents, but not only has there been insufficient time for these new ideas to be popularized, so that the audience can grasp them, but also people have been so wrought up by the taking of sides that pure, disinterested appreciation has become impossible. One's deepest impressions are upset when an applauding or a hissing majority dominates as forcefully and openly as it can in the theatre. Moreover, as no new form has been devised for these new contents, the new wine has burst the old bottles.

In this play I have not tried to do anything new, for this cannot be done, but only to modernize the form to meet the demands which may, I think, be made on this art today. To this end I chose — or surrendered myself to — a theme which claims to be outside the controversial issues of today, since questions of social climbing or falling, of higher or lower, better or worse, of man and woman, are, have been and will be of lasting interest. When I took

* Translated by Elizabeth Sprigge.

this theme from a true story told me some years ago, which made a deep impression, I saw it as a subject for tragedy, for as yet it is tragic to see one favoured by fortune go under, and still more to see a family heritage die out, although a time may come when we have grown so developed and enlightened that we shall view with indifference life's spectacle, now seeming so brutal, cynical and heartless. Then we shall have dispensed with those inferior, unreliable instruments of thought called feelings, which become harmful and superfluous as reasoning develops.

The fact that my heroine rouses pity is solely due to weakness; we cannot resist fear of the same fate overtaking us. The hyper-sensitive spectator may, it is true, go beyond this kind of pity, while the man with belief in the future may actually demand some suggestion for remedying the evil — in other words some kind of policy. But, to begin with, there is no such thing as absolute evil; the downfall of one family is the good fortune of another, which thereby gets a chance to rise, and, fortune being only comparative, the alternation of rising and falling is one of life's principal charms. Also, to the man of policy, who wants to remedy the painful fact that the bird of prey devours the dove, and lice the bird of prey, I should like to put the question: why should it be remedied? Life is not so mathematically idiotic as only to permit the big to eat the small; it happens just as often that the bee kills the lion or at least drives it mad.

That my tragedy depresses many people is their own fault. When we have grown strong as the pioneers of the French revolution, we shall be happy and relieved to see the national parks cleared of ancient rotting trees which have stood too long in the way of others equally entitled to a period of growth — as relieved as we are when an incurable invalid dies.

My tragedy "The Father" was recently criticised for being too sad — as if one wants cheerful tragedies! Everybody is clamouring for this supposed "joy of life," and theatre managers demand farces, as if the joy of life consisted in being ridiculous and portraying all human beings as suffering from St. Vitus's dance or total idiocy. I myself find the joy of life in its strong and cruel struggles, and my pleasure in learning, in adding to my knowledge. For this reason I have chosen for this play an unusual situation, but an instructive one — an exception, that is to say, but a great exception, one proving the rule, which will no doubt annoy all lovers of the commonplace. What will offend simple minds is that my plot is not simple, nor its point of view single. In real life an action — this, by the way, is a somewhat new discovery — is generally caused by a whole series of motives, more or less fundamental, but as a rule the spectator chooses just one of these — the one which his mind can most easily grasp or that does most credit to his intelligence. A suicide is committed. Business troubles, says the man of affairs. Unrequited love, say the women. Sickness, says the invalid. Despair, says the down-and-out. But it is possible that the motive lay in all or none of these directions, or that the dead man concealed his actual motive by revealing quite another, likely to reflect more to his glory.

I see Miss Julie's tragic fate to be the result of many circumstances: the mother's character, the father's mistaken upbringing of the girl, her own nature, and the influence of her fiancé on a weak, degenerate mind. Also, more directly, the festive mood of Midsummer Eve, her father's absence, her monthly indisposition, her pre-occupation with animals, the excitement of dancing, the magic of dusk, the strongly aphrodisiac influence of flowers, and finally the chance that drives the couple into a room alone — to which must be added the urgency of the excited man.

My treatment of the theme, moreover, is neither exclusively physiological nor psychological. I have not put the blame wholly on the inheritance from her mother, nor on her physical condition at the time, nor on immorality. I have not even preached a moral sermon; in the absence of a priest I leave this to the cook.

I congratulate myself on this multiplicity of motives as being up-to-date, and if others have done the same thing before me, then I congratulate myself on not being alone in my "paradoxes," as all innovations are called.

In regard to the drawing of the characters, I have made my people somewhat "characterless" for the following reasons. In the course of time the word *character* has assumed manifold meanings. It must have originally signified the dominating trait of the soul-complex, and this was confused with temperament. Later it became the middle-class term for the automaton, one whose nature had become fixed or who had adapted himself to a particular role in life. In fact a person who had ceased to grow was called a character, while one continuing to develop — the skilful navigator of life's river, sailing not with sheets set fast, but veering before the wind to luff again — was called characterless, in a derogatory sense, of course, because he was so hard to catch, classify and keep track of. This middle-class conception of the immobility of the soul was transferred to the stage where the middle-class has always ruled. A character came to signify a man fixed and finished: one who invariably appeared either drunk or jocular or melancholy, and characterization required nothing more than a physical defect such as a club-foot, a wooden leg, a red nose; or the fellow might be made to repeat some such phrase as: "That's capital!" or "Barkis is willin'!" This simple way of regarding human beings still survives in the great Molière. Harpagon is nothing but a miser, although Harpagon might have been not only a miser, but also a first-rate financier, an excellent father and a good citizen. Worse still, his "failing" is a distinct advantage to his son-in-law and his daughter, who are his heirs, and who therefore cannot criticise him, even if they have to wait a while to get to bed. I do not believe, therefore, in simple stage characters; and the summary judgments of authors — this man is stupid, that one brutal, this jealous, that stingy, and so forth — should be challenged by the Naturalists who know the richness of the soul-complex and realise that vice has a reverse side very much like virtue.

Because they are modern characters, living in a period of transition more feverishly hysterical than its predecessor at least, I have drawn my figures vacillating, disintegrated, a blend of old and new. Nor does it seem to me unlikely that, through newspapers and conversations, modern ideas may have filtered down to the level of the domestic servant.

My souls (characters) are conglomerations of past and present stages of civilization, bits from books and newspapers, scraps of humanity, rags and tatters of fine clothing, patched together as is the human soul. And I have added a little evolutionary history by making the weaker steal and repeat the words of the stronger, and by making the characters borrow ideas or "suggestions" from one another.

Miss Julie is a modern character, not that the half-woman, the man-hater, has not existed always, but because now that she has been discovered she has stepped to the front and begun to make a noise. The half-woman is a type who thrusts herself forward, selling herself nowadays for power, decorations, distinctions, diplomas, as formerly for money. The type implies degeneration; it is not a good type and it does not endure; but it can unfortunately transmit its misery, and degenerate men seem instinctively to choose their mates from among such women, and so they breed, producing offspring of indeterminate sex to whom life is torture. But fortunately they perish, either because they cannot come to terms with reality, or because their repressed instincts break out uncontrollably, or again because their hopes of catching up with men are shattered. The type is tragic, revealing a desperate fight against nature, tragic too in its Romantic inheritance now dissipated by Naturalism, which wants nothing but happiness — and for happiness strong and sound species are required.

But Miss Julie is also a relic of the old warrior nobility now giving way to the new mobility of nerve and brain. She is a victim of the discord which a mother's "crime" has produced in a family, a victim too of the day's complaisance, of circumstances, of her own defective constitution, all of which are equivalent to the Fate or Universal Law of former days. The Naturalist has abolished guilt with God, but the consequences of the action — punishment, imprisonment or the fear of it — he cannot abolish, for the simple reason that they remain whether he is acquitted or not. An injured fellow-being is not so complacent as outsiders, who have not been injured, can afford to be. Even if the father had felt impelled to take no vengeance, the daughter would have taken vengeance on herself, as she does here, from that innate or acquired sense of honour which the upper-classes inherit — whether from Barbarism or Aryan forebears, or from the chivalry of the Middle Ages, who knows? It is a very beautiful thing, but it has become a danger nowadays to the preservation of the race. It is the nobleman's *hara-kiri*, the Japanese law of inner conscience which compels him to cut his own stomach open at the insult of another, and which survives in modified form in the duel, a privilege of the nobility. And so the valet Jean lives on, but Miss Julie cannot live without honour. This is the thrall's advantage over the nobleman, that he lacks this fatal preoccupation with honour. And in all of us Aryans there is something of the nobleman, or the Don Quixote, which makes us sympathize with the man who commits suicide because he has done something ignoble and lost his honour. And we are noblemen enough to suffer at the sight of fallen greatness littering the earth like a corpse — yes, even if the fallen rise again and make restitution by honourable deeds. Jean, the valet, is a race-builder, a man of marked characteristics. He was a labourer's son who has educated himself towards becoming a gentleman. He has learnt easily, through his well-developed senses (smell, taste, vision) — and he also has a sense of beauty. He has already bettered himself, and is thick-skinned enough to have no scruples about using other people's services. He is already foreign to his associates, despising them as part of the life he has turned his back on, yet also fearing and fleeing from them because they know his secrets, pry into his plans, watch his rise with envy, and look forward with pleasure to his fall. Hence his dual, indeterminate character, vacillating between love of the heights and hatred of those who have already achieved them. He is, he says himself, an aristocrat; he has learned the secrets of good society. He is polished, but vulgar within; he already wears his tails with taste, but there is no guarantee of his personal cleanliness.

He has some respect for his young lady, but he is frightened of Kristin, who knows his dangerous secrets, and he is sufficiently callous not to allow the night's events to wreck his plans for the future. Having both the slave's brutality and the master's lack of squeamishness, he can see blood without fainting and take disaster by the horns. Consequently he emerges from the battle unscathed, and probably ends his days as a hotel-keeper. And even if *he* does not become a Roumanian Count, his son will doubtless go to the university and perhaps become a county attorney.

The light which Jean sheds on a lower-class conception of life, life seen from below, is on the whole illuminating — when he speaks the truth, which is not often, for he says what is favourable to himself rather than what is true. When Miss Julie suggests that the lower-classes must be oppressed by the attitude of their superiors, Jean naturally agrees, as his object is to gain her sympathy; but when he perceives the advantage of separating himself from the common herd, he at once takes back his words.

It is not because Jean is now rising that he has the upper hand of Miss Julie, but because he is a man. Sexually he is the aristocrat because of his virility, his keener senses and his capacity for taking the initiative. His inferiority is mainly due to the social environment in which he lives, and he can probably shed it with his valet's livery.

The slave mentality expresses itself in the worship of the Count (the boots), and his religious superstition; but he worships the Count chiefly because he holds that higher position for which Jean himself is striving. And this worship remains even when he has won the daughter of the house and seen how empty is that lovely shell.

I do not believe that a love relationship in the "higher" sense could exist between two individuals of such different quality, but I have made Miss Julie imagine that she is in love, so as to lessen her sense of guilt, and I let Jean suppose that if his social position were altered he would truly love her. I think love is like the hyacinth which has to strike roots in darkness *before* it can produce a vigorous flower. In this case it shoots up quickly, blossoms and goes to seed all at the same time, which is why the plant dies so soon.

As for Kristin, she is a female slave, full of servility and sluggishness acquired in front of the kitchen fire, and stuffed full of morality and religion, which are her cloak and scape-goat. She goes to church as a quick and easy way of unloading her household thefts on to Jesus and taking on a fresh cargo of guiltlessness. For the rest she is a minor character, and I have therefore sketched her in the same manner as the Pastor and the Doctor in "The Father," where I wanted ordinary human beings, as are most country pastors and provincial doctors. If these minor characters seem abstract to some people this is due to the fact that ordinary people are to a certain extent abstract in pursuit of their work; that is to say, they are without individuality, showing, while working, only one side of themselves. And as long as the spectator does not feel a need to see them from other sides, there is nothing wrong with my abstract presentation.

In regard to the dialogue, I have departed somewhat from tradition by not making my characters catechists who ask stupid questions in order to elicit a smart reply. I have avoided the symmetrical, mathematical construction of French dialogue, and let people's minds work irregularly, as they do in real life where, during a conversation, no topic is drained to the dregs, and one mind finds in another a chance cog to engage in. So too the dialogue wanders, gathering in the opening scenes material which is later picked up, worked over, repeated, expounded and developed like the theme in a musical composition.

The plot speaks for itself, and as it really only concerns two people, I have concentrated on these, introducing only one minor character, the cook, and keeping the unhappy spirit of the father above and behind the action. I have done this because it seems to me that the psychological process is what interests people most today. Our inquisitive souls are no longer satisfied with seeing a thing happen; we must also know how it happens. We want to see the wires themselves, to watch the machinery, to examine the box with the false bottom, to take hold of the magic ring in order to find the join, and look at the cards to see how they are marked.

In this connection I have had in view the documentary novels of the brothers de Goncourt, which appeal to me more than any other modern literature.

As far as the technical side of the work is concerned I have made the experiment of abolishing the division into acts. This is because I have come to the conclusion that our capacity for illusion is disturbed by the intervals, during which the audience has time to reflect and escape from the suggestive influence of the author-hypnotist. My play will probably take an hour and a half, and as one can listen to a lecture, a sermon or a parliamentary debate for as long as that or longer, I do not think a theatrical performance will be fatiguing in the same length of time. As early as 1872, in one of my first dramatic attempts, "The Outlaw," I tried this concentrated form, although with scant success. The play was written in five acts, and only when finished did I become aware of the restless, disjointed effect that it produced. The script was burnt and from the ashes rose a single well-knit act — fifty pages of print, playable in one hour. The form of the present play is, therefore, not new, but it appears to be my own, and changing tastes may make it timely. My hope is one day to have an audience educated enough to sit through a whole evening's entertainment in one act, but one would have to try this out to see. Meanwhile, in order to provide respite for the audience and the players, without allowing the audience to escape from the illusion, I have introduced three art forms: monologue, mime and ballet. These are all part of drama, having their origins in classic tragedy, monody having become monologue and the chorus, ballet.

Monologue is now condemned by our realists as unnatural, but if one provides motives for it one makes it natural, and then can use it to advantage. It is, surely, natural for a public speaker to walk up and down the room practicing his speech, natural for an actor to read his part aloud, for a servant girl to talk to her cat, a mother to prattle to her child, an old maid to chatter to her parrot, and a sleeper to talk in his sleep. And in order that the actor may have a chance, for once, of working independently, free from the author's direction, it is better that the monologue should not be written, but only indicated. For since it is of small importance what is said in one's sleep or to the parrot or to the cat — none of it influences the action — a talented actor, identifying himself with the atmosphere and the situation, may improvise better than the author, who cannot calculate ahead how much may be said or how long taken without waking the audience from the illusion.

Some Italian theatres have, as we know, returned to improvisation, thereby producing actors who are creative, although within the bounds set by the author. This may well be a step forward, or even the beginning of a new artform worthy to be called *productive*.

In places where monologue would be unnatural I have used mime, leaving here an even wider scope for the actor's imagination, and more chance for him to win independent laurels. But so as not to try the audience beyond endurance, I have introduced music — fully justified by the Midsummer Eve dance — to exercise its powers of persuasion during the dumb show. But I beg the musical director to consider carefully his choice of compositions, so that conflicting moods are not induced by selections from the current operetta or dance show, or by folk-tunes of too local a character.

The ballet I have introduced cannot be replaced by the usual kind of "crowd-scene," for such scenes are too badly played — a lot of grinning idiots seizing the opportunity to show off and thus destroying the illusion. And as peasants cannot improvise their taunts, but use ready-made phrases with a double meaning, I have not composed their lampoon, but taken a little-known song and dance which I myself noted down in the Stockholm district. The words are not quite to the point, but this too is intentional, for the cunning, i.e. weakness, of the slave prevents him from direct attack. Nor can there be clowning in a serious action, or coarse joking in a situation which nails the lid on a family coffin.

As regards the scenery, I have borrowed from impressionist painting its asymmetry and its economy; thus, I think, strengthening the illusion. For the fact that one does not see the whole room and all the furniture leaves scope for conjecture — that is to say imagination is roused and complements what is seen. I have succeeded too in getting rid of those tiresome exits through doors, since scenery doors are made of canvas, and rock at the slightest touch. They cannot even express the wrath of an irate head of the family who, after a bad dinner, goes out slamming the door behind him, "so that the whole house shakes." On the stage it rocks. I have also kept to a single set, both in order to let the characters develop in their métier and to break away from over-decoration. When one has only one set, one may expect it to be realistic; but as a matter of fact nothing is harder than to get a stage room that looks something like a room, however easily the scene painter can produce flaming volcanoes and water-falls. Presumably the walls must be of canvas; but it seems about time to dispense with painted shelves and cooking utensils. We are asked to accept so many stage conventions that we might at least be spared the pain of painted pots and pans.

I have set the back wall and the table diagonally so that the actors may play full-face and in half-profile when they are sitting opposite one another at the table. In the opera *Aïda* I saw a diagonal background, which led the eye to unfamiliar perspectives and did not look like mere reaction against boring straight lines.

Another much needed innovation is the abolition of foot-lights. This lighting from below is said to have the purpose of making the actors' faces fatter. But why, I ask, should all actors have fat faces? Does not this underlighting flatten out all the subtlety of the lower part of the face, specially the jaw, falsify the shape of the nose and throw shadows up over the eyes? Even if this were not so, one thing is certain: that the lights hurt the performers' eyes, so that the full play of their expression is lost. The foot-lights strike part of the retina usually protected — except in sailors who have to watch sunlight on water — and therefore one seldom sees anything other than a crude rolling of the eyes, either sideways or up towards the gallery, showing their whites.

Perhaps this too causes that tiresome blinking of the eyelashes, especially by actresses. And when anyone on the stage wants to speak with his eyes, the only thing he can do is to look straight at the audience, with whom he or she then gets into direct communication, outside the framework of the set — a habit called, rightly or wrongly, "greeting one's friends."

Would not sufficiently strong side-lighting, with some kind of reflectors, add to the actor's powers of expression by allowing him to use the face's greatest asset: — the play of the eyes?

I have few illusions about getting the actors to play *to* the audience instead of *with* it, although this is what I want. That I shall see an actor's back throughout a critical scene is beyond my dreams, but I do wish crucial scenes could be played, not in front of the prompter's box, like duets expecting applause, but in the place required by the action. So, no revolutions, but just some small modifications, for to make the stage into a real room with the fourth wall missing would be too upsetting altogether.

I dare not hope that the actresses will listen to what I have to say about make-up, for they would rather be beautiful than life-like, but the actor might consider whether it is to his advantage to create an abstract character with grease-paint, and cover his face with it like a mask. Take the case of a man who draws a choleric charcoal line between his eyes and then, in this fixed state of wrath, has to smile at some repartee. What a frightful grimace the result is! And equally, how is that false forehead, smooth as a billiard ball, to wrinkle when the old man loses his temper?

In a modern psychological drama, where the subtlest reactions of a character need to be mirrored in the face rather than expressed by sound and gesture, it would be worth while experimenting with powerful side-lighting on a small stage and a cast without make-up, or at least with the minimum.

If, in addition, we could abolish the visible orchestra, with its distracting lamps and its faces turned toward the audience; if we could have the stalls raised so that the spectators' eyes were higher than the players' knees; if we could get rid of the boxes (the centre of my target), with their tittering diners and supper-parties, and have total darkness in the auditorium during the performance; and if, first and foremost, we could have a *small* stage and a *small* house, then perhaps a new dramatic art might arise, and theatre once more become a place of entertainment for educated people. While waiting for such a theatre it is as well for us to go on writing so as to stock that repertory of the future.

I have made an attempt. If it has failed, there is time enough to try again.

Translated by Elizabeth Sprigge

Miss Julie

A TRAGEDY IN ONE ACT

CHARACTERS

MISS JULIE, *aged 25*
JEAN, *the valet, aged 30*
KRISTIN, *the cook, aged 35*

Scene: The large kitchen of a Swedish manor house in a country district in the eighties.

Midsummer eve.

The kitchen has three doors, two small ones into Jean's and Kristin's bedrooms, and a large, glass-fronted double one, opening on to a courtyard. This is the only way to the rest of the house.

Through these glass doors can be seen part of a fountain with a cupid, lilac bushes in flower and the tops of some Lombardy poplars. On one wall are shelves edged with scalloped paper on which are kitchen utensils of copper, iron and tin.

To the left is the corner of a large tiled range and part of its chimney-hood, to the right the end of the servants' dinner table with chairs beside it.

The stove is decorated with birch boughs, the floor strewn with twigs of juniper. On the end of the table is a large Japanese spice jar full of lilac.

There are also an ice-box, a scullery table and a sink. Above the double door hangs a big old-fashioned bell; near it is a speaking-tube.

A fiddle can be heard from the dance in the barn near-by.

KRISTIN *is standing at the stove, frying something in a pan. She wears a light-coloured cotton dress and a big apron.*

JEAN *enters, wearing livery and carrying a pair of large riding-boots with spurs, which he puts in a conspicuous place.*

All rights whatsoever in this play are strictly reserved and applications for performances, etc. should be made to Willis Kingsley Wing, 24 East 38th Street, New York 16, New York.

Miss Julie

JEAN. Miss Julie's crazy again to-night, absolutely crazy.

KRISTIN. Oh, so you're back, are you?

JEAN. When I'd taken the Count to the station, I came back and dropped in at the Barn for a dance. And who did I see there but our young lady leading off with the gamekeeper. But the moment she sets eyes on me, up she rushes and invites me to waltz with her. And how she waltzed — I've never seen anything like it! She's crazy.

KRISTIN. Always has been, but never so bad as this last fortnight since the engagement was broken off.

JEAN. Yes, that was a pretty business, to be sure. He's a decent enough chap, too, even if he isn't rich. Oh, but they're choosy! (*Sits down at the end of the table.*) In any case, it's a bit odd that our young — er — lady would rather stay at home with the yokels than go with her father to visit her relations.

KRISTIN. Perhaps she feels a bit awkward, after that bust-up with her fiancé.

JEAN. Maybe. That chap had some guts, though. Do you know the sort of thing that was going on, Kristin? I saw it with my own eyes, though I didn't let on I had.

KRISTIN. You saw them ...?

JEAN. Didn't I just! Came across the pair of them one evening in the stable-yard. Miss Julie was doing what she called "training" him. Know what that was? Making him jump over her riding-whip — the way you teach a dog. He did it twice and got a cut each time for his pains, but when it came to the third go, he snatched the whip out of her hands and broke it into smithereens. And then he cleared off.

KRISTIN. What goings on! I never did!

JEAN. Well, that's how it was with that little affair ... Now, what have you got for me, Kristin? Something tasty?

KRISTIN (*serving from the pan to his plate*). Well, it's just a little bit of kidney I cut off their joint.

JEAN (*smelling it*). Fine! That's my special delice. (*Feels the plate.*) But you might have warmed the plate.

KRISTIN. When you choose to be finicky you're worse than the Count himself. (*Pulls his hair affectionately.*)

JEAN (*crossly*). Stop pulling my hair. You know how sensitive I am.

KRISTIN. There, there! It's only love, you know.

    JEAN *eats.* KRISTIN *brings a bottle of beer.*

JEAN. Beer on Midsummer Eve? No thanks! I've got something better than that. (*From a drawer in the table brings out a bottle of red wine with a yellow seal.*) Yellow seal, see! Now get me a glass. You use a glass with a stem of course when you're drinking it straight.

KRISTIN (*giving him a wine-glass*). Lord help the woman who gets you for a husband, you old fusser! (*She puts the beer in the ice-box and sets a small saucepan on the stove.*)

JEAN. Nonsense! You'll be glad enough to get a fellow as smart as me.

And I don't think it's done you any harm people calling me your fiancé. (*Tastes the wine.*) Good. Very good indeed. But not quite warmed enough. (*Warms the glass in his hand.*) We bought this in Dijon. Four francs the litre without the bottle, and duty on top of that. What are you cooking now? It stinks.

KRISTIN. Some bloody muck Miss Julie wants for Diana.

JEAN. You should be more refined in your speech, Kristin. But why should you spend a holiday cooking for that bitch? Is she sick or what?

KRISTIN. Yes, she's sick. She sneaked out with the pug at the lodge and got in the usual mess. And that, you know, Miss Julie won't have.

JEAN. Miss Julie's too high-and-mighty in some respects, and not enough in others, just like her mother before her. The Countess was more at home in the kitchen and cowsheds than anywhere else, but would she ever go driving with only one horse? She went round with her cuffs filthy, but she had to have the coronet on the cuff-links. Our young lady — to come back to her — hasn't any proper respect for herself or her position. I mean she isn't refined. In the Barn just now she dragged the gamekeeper away from Anna and made him dance with her — no waiting to be asked. We wouldn't do a thing like that. But that's what happens when the gentry try to behave like the common people — they become common ... Still she's a fine girl. Smashing! What shoulders! And what — er — etcetera!

KRISTIN. Oh come off it! I know what Clara says, and she dresses her.

JEAN. Clara? Pooh, you're all jealous! But I've been out riding with her ... and as for her dancing!

KRISTIN. Listen, Jean. You will dance with me, won't you, as soon as I'm through?

JEAN. Of course I will.

KRISTIN. Promise?

JEAN. Promise? When I say I'll do a thing I do it. Well, thanks for the supper. It was a real treat. (*Corks the bottle.*)

    JULIE *appears in the doorway, speaking to someone outside.*

JULIE. I'll be back in a moment. Don't wait.

    JEAN *slips the bottle into the drawer and rises respectfully.* JULIE *enters and joins* KRISTIN *at the stove.*

Well, have you made it? (KRISTIN *signs that* JEAN *is near them.*)

JEAN (*gallantly*). Have you ladies got some secret?

JULIE (*flipping his face with her handkerchief*). You're very inquisitive.

JEAN. What a delicious smell! Violets.

JULIE (*coquettishly*). Impertinence! Are you an expert of scent too? I must say you know how to dance. Now don't look. Go away. (*The music of a schottische begins.*)

JEAN (*with impudent politeness*). Is it some witches' brew you're cooking on Midsummer Eve? Something to tell your stars by, so you can see your future?

JULIE (*sharply*). If you could see that you'd have good eyes. (*To* KRISTIN.)

Miss Julie

Put it in a bottle and cork it tight. Come and dance this schottische with me, Jean.

JEAN (*hesitating*). I don't want to be rude, but I've promised to dance this one with Kristin.

JULIE. Well, she can have another, can't you, Kristin? You'll lend me Jean, won't you?

KRISTIN (*bottling*). It's nothing to do with me. When you're so condescending, Miss, it's not his place to say no. Go on, Jean, and thank Miss Julie for the honour.

JEAN. Frankly speaking, Miss, and no offence meant, I wonder if it's wise for you to dance twice running with the same partner, specially as those people are so ready to jump to conclusions.

JULIE (*flaring up*). What did you say? What sort of conclusions? What do you mean?

JEAN (*meekly*). As you choose not to understand, Miss Julie, I'll have to speak more plainly. It looks bad to show a preference for one of your retainers when they're all hoping for the same unusual favour.

JULIE. Show a preference! The very idea! I'm surprised at you. I'm doing the people an honour by attending their ball when I'm mistress of the house, but if I'm really going to dance, I mean to have a partner who can lead and doesn't make me look ridiculous.

JEAN. If those are your orders, Miss, I'm at your service.

JULIE (*gently*). Don't take it as an order. To-night we're all just people enjoying a party. There's no question of class. So now give me your arm. Don't worry, Kristin. I shan't steal your sweetheart.

JEAN gives JULIE his arm and leads her out.

Left alone, KRISTIN plays her scene in an unhurried, natural way, humming to the tune of the schottische, played on a distant violin. She clears JEAN's place, washes up and puts things away, then takes off her apron, brings out a small mirror from a drawer, props it against the jar of lilac, lights a candle, warms a small pair of tongs and curls her fringe. She goes to the door and listens, then turning back to the table finds MISS JULIE's forgotten handkerchief. She smells it, then meditatively smooths it out and folds it.

Enter JEAN.

JEAN. She really *is* crazy. What a way to dance! With people standing grinning at her too from behind the doors. What's got into her, Kristin?

KRISTIN. Oh, it's just her time coming on. She's always queer then. Are you going to dance with me now?

JEAN. Then you're not wild with me for cutting that one?

KRISTIN. You know I'm not — for a little thing like that. Besides I know my place.

JEAN (*putting his arm around her waist*). You're a sensible girl, Kristin, and you'll make a very good wife...

Enter JULIE, unpleasantly surprised.

JULIE (*with forced gaiety*). You're a fine beau — running away from your partner.

JEAN. Not away, Miss Julie, but as you see back to the one I deserted.

JULIE (*changing her tone*). You really can dance, you know. But why are you wearing your livery on a holiday? Take it off at once.

JEAN. Then I must ask you to go away for a moment, Miss. My black coat's here. (*Indicates it hanging on the door to his room.*)

JULIE. Are you so shy of me — just over changing a coat? Go into your room then — or stay here and I'll turn my back.

JEAN. Excuse me then, Miss. (*He goes to his room and is partly visible as he changes his coat.*)

JULIE. Tell me, Kristin, is Jean your fiancé? You seem very intimate.

KRISTIN. My fiancé? Yes, if you like. We call it that.

JULIE. Call it?

KRISTIN. Well, you've had a fiancé yourself, Miss, and ...

JULIE. But we really were engaged.

KRISTIN. All the same it didn't come to anything.

JEAN *returns in his black coat.*

JULIE. Très gentil, Monsieur Jean. Très gentil.

JEAN. Vous voulez plaisanter, Madame.

JULIE. Et vous voulez parler français. Where did you learn it?

JEAN. In Switzerland, when I was sommelier at one of the biggest hotels in Lucerne.

JULIE. You look quite the gentleman in that get-up. Charming. (*Sits at the table.*)

JEAN. Oh, you're just flattering me!

JULIE (*annoyed*). Flattering you?

JEAN. I'm too modest to believe you would pay real compliments to a man like me, so I must take it you are exaggerating — that this is what's known as flattery.

JULIE. Where on earth did you learn to make speeches like that? Perhaps you've been to the theatre a lot.

JEAN. That's right. And travelled a lot too.

JULIE. But you come from this neighbourhood, don't you?

JEAN. Yes, my father was a labourer on the next estate — the District Attorney's place. I often used to see you, Miss Julie, when you were little, though you never noticed me.

JULIE. Did you really?

JEAN. Yes. One time specially I remember ... but I can't tell you about that.

JULIE. Oh do! Why not? This is just the time.

JEAN. No, I really can't now. Another time perhaps.

JULIE. Another time means never. What harm in now?

JEAN. No harm, but I'd rather not. (*Points to* KRISTIN, *now fast asleep.*) Look at her.

Miss Julie

JULIE. She'll make a charming wife, won't she? I wonder if she snores.
JEAN. No, she doesn't, but she talks in her sleep.
JULIE (*cynically*). How do you know she talks in her sleep?
JEAN (*brazenly*). I've heard her. (*Pause. They look at one another.*)
JULIE. Why don't you sit down?
JEAN. I can't take such a liberty in your presence.
JULIE. Supposing I order you to.
JEAN. I'll obey.
JULIE. Then sit down. No, wait a minute. Will you get me a drink first?
JEAN. I don't know what's in the ice-box. Only beer, I expect.
JULIE. There's no only about it. My taste is so simple I prefer it to wine.
   JEAN *takes a bottle from the ice-box, fetches a glass and plate and serves the beer.*
JEAN. At your service.
JULIE. Thank you. Won't you have some yourself?
JEAN. I'm not really a beer-drinker, but if it's an order . . .
JULIE. Order? I should have thought it was ordinary manners to keep your partner company.
JEAN. That's a good way of putting it. (*He opens another bottle and fetches a glass.*)
JULIE. Now drink my health. (*He hesitates.*) I believe the man really is shy.
   JEAN *kneels and raises his glass with mock ceremony.*
JEAN. To the health of my lady!
JULIE. Bravo! Now kiss my shoe and everything will be perfect. (*He hesitates, then boldly takes hold of her foot and lightly kisses it.*) Splendid. You ought to have been an actor.
JEAN (*rising*). We can't go on like this, Miss Julie. Someone might come in and see us.
JULIE. Why would that matter?
JEAN. For the simple reason that they'd talk. And if you knew the way their tongues were wagging out there just now, you . . .
JULIE. What were they saying? Tell me. Sit down.
JEAN (*sitting*). No offence meant, Miss, but . . . well, their language wasn't nice, and they were hinting . . . oh, you know quite well what. You're not a child, and if a lady's seen drinking alone at night with a man — and a servant at that — then . . .
JULIE. Then what? Besides, we're not alone. Kristin's here.
JEAN. Yes, asleep.
JULIE. I'll wake her up. (*Rises.*) Kristin, are you asleep? (KRISTIN *mumbles in her sleep.*) Kristin! Goodness, how she sleeps!
KRISTIN (*in her sleep*). The Count's boots are cleaned — put the coffee on — yes, yes, at once . . . (*Mumbles incoherently.*)
JULIE (*tweaking her nose*). Wake up, can't you!
JEAN (*sharply*). Let her sleep.

JULIE. What?

JEAN. When you've been standing at the stove all day you're likely to be tired at night. And sleep should be respected.

JULIE (*changing her tone*). What a nice idea. It does you credit. Thank you for it. (*Holds out her hand to him.*) Now come out and pick some lilac for me.

During the following KRISTIN *goes sleepily in to her bedroom.*

JEAN. Out with you, Miss Julie?

JULIE. Yes.

JEAN. It wouldn't do. It really wouldn't.

JULIE. I don't know what you mean. You can't possibly imagine that ...

JEAN. I don't, but others do.

JULIE. What? That I'm in love with the valet?

JEAN. I'm not a conceited man, but such a thing's been known to happen, and to these rustics nothing's sacred.

JULIE. You, I take it, are an aristocrat.

JEAN. Yes, I am.

JULIE. And I am coming down in the world.

JEAN. Don't come down, Miss Julie. Take my advice. No one will believe you came down of your own accord. They'll all say you fell.

JULIE. I have a higher opinion of our people than you. Come and put it to the test. Come on. (*Gazes into his eyes.*)

JEAN. You're very strange, you know.

JULIE. Perhaps I am, but so are you. For that matter everything is strange. Life, human beings, everything, just scum drifting about on the water until it sinks — down and down. That reminds me of a dream I sometimes have, in which I'm on top of a pillar and can't see any way of getting down. When I look down I'm dizzy; I have to get down but I haven't the courage to jump. I can't stay there and I long to fall, but I don't fall. There's no respite. There can't be any peace at all for me until I'm down, right down on the ground. And if I did get to the ground I'd want to be under the ground ... Have you ever felt like that?

JEAN. No. In my dream I'm lying under a great tree in a dark wood. I want to get up, up to the top of it, and look out over the bright landscape where the sun is shining and rob that high nest of its golden eggs. And I climb and climb, but the trunk is so thick and smooth and it's so far to the first branch. But I know if I can once reach that first branch I'll go to the top just as if I'm on a ladder. I haven't reached it yet, but I shall get there, even if only in my dreams.

JULIE. Here I am chattering about dreams with you. Come on. Only into the park. (*She takes his arm and they go towards the door.*)

JEAN. We must sleep on nine midsummer flowers tonight; then our dreams will come true, Miss Julie. (*They turn at the door. He has a hand to his eye.*)

JULIE. Have you got something in your eye? Let me see.

Miss Julie   85

JEAN. Oh, it's nothing. Just a speck of dust. It'll be gone in a minute.

JULIE. My sleeve must have rubbed against you. Sit down and let me see to it. (*Takes him by the arm and makes him sit down, bends his head back and tries to get the speck out with the corner of her handkerchief.*) Keep still now, quite still. (*Slaps his hand.*) Do as I tell you. Why, I believe you're trembling, big, strong man though you are! (*Feels his biceps.*) What muscles!

JEAN (*warning*). Miss Julie!

JULIE. Yes, Monsieur Jean?

JEAN. Attention. Je ne suis qu'un homme.

JULIE. Will you stay still! There now. It's out. Kiss my hand and say thank you.

JEAN (*rising*). Miss Julie, listen. Kristin's gone to bed now. Will you listen?

JULIE. Kiss my hand first.

JEAN. Very well, but you'll have only yourself to blame.

JULIE. For what?

JEAN. For what! Are you still a child at twenty-five? Don't you know it's dangerous to play with fire?

JULIE. Not for me. I'm insured.

JEAN (*bluntly*). No, you're not. And even if you are, there's still stuff here to kindle a flame.

JULIE. Meaning yourself?

JEAN. Yes. Not because I'm me, but because I'm a man and young and . . .

JULIE. And good-looking? What incredible conceit! A Don Juan perhaps? Or a Joseph? Good Lord, I do believe you are a Joseph!

JEAN. Do you?

JULIE. I'm rather afraid so.

JEAN *goes boldly up and tries to put his arms round her and kiss her. She boxes his ears.*

How dare you!

JEAN. Was that in earnest or a joke?

JULIE. In earnest.

JEAN. Then what went before was in earnest too. You take your games too seriously and that's dangerous. Anyhow I'm tired of playing now and beg leave to return to my work. The Count will want his boots first thing and it's past midnight now.

JULIE. Put those boots down.

JEAN. No. This is my work, which it's my duty to do. But I never undertook to be your playfellow and I never will be. I consider myself too good for that.

JULIE. You're proud.

JEAN. In some ways — not all.

JULIE. Have you ever been in love?

JEAN. We don't put it that way, but I've been gone on quite a few girls. And once I went sick because I couldn't have the one I wanted. Sick, I mean, like those princes in the Arabian Nights who couldn't eat or drink for love.

JULIE. Who was she? (*No answer.*) Who was she?

JEAN. You can't force me to tell you that.

JULIE. If I ask as an equal, ask as a — friend? Who was she?

JEAN. You.

JULIE (*sitting*). How absurd!

JEAN. Yes, ludicrous if you like. That's the story I wouldn't tell you before, see, but now I will . . . Do you know what the world looks like from below? No, you don't. No more than the hawks and falcons do whose backs one hardly ever sees because they're always soaring up aloft. I lived in a labourer's hovel with seven other children and a pig, out in the grey fields where there isn't a single tree. But from the window I could see the wall round the Count's park with apple-trees above it. That was the Garden of Eden, guarded by many terrible angels with flaming swords. All the same I and the other boys managed to get to the tree of life. Does all this make you despise me?

JULIE. Goodness, all boys steal apples!

JEAN. You say that now, but all the same you do despise me. However, one time I went into the Garden of Eden with my mother to weed the onion beds. Close to the kitchen garden there was a Turkish pavilion hung all over with jasmine and honeysuckle. I hadn't any idea what it was used for, but I'd never seen such a beautiful building. People used to go in and then come out again, and one day the door was left open. I crept up and saw the walls covered with pictures of kings and emperors, and the windows had red curtains with fringes — you know now what the place was, don't you? I . . . (*Breaks off a piece of lilac and holds it for* JULIE *to smell. As he talks, she takes it from him.*) I had never been inside the manor, never seen anything but the church, and this was more beautiful. No matter where my thoughts went, they always came back — to that place. The longing went on growing in me to enjoy it fully, just once. Enfin, I sneaked in, gazed and admired. Then I heard someone coming. There was only one way out for the gentry, but for me there was another and I had no choice but to take it. (JULIE *drops the lilac on the table.*) Then I took to my heels, plunged through the raspberry canes, dashed across the strawberry beds and found myself on the rose terrace. There I saw a pink dress and a pair of white stockings — it was you. I crawled into a weed pile and lay there right under it among prickly thistles and damp rank earth. I watched you walking among the roses and said to myself: "If it's true that a thief can get to heaven and be with the angels, it's pretty strange that a labourer's child here on God's earth mayn't come in the park and play with the Count's daughter."

JULIE (*sentimentally*). Do you think all poor children feel the way you did?

JEAN (*taken aback, then rallying*). *All* poor children? . . . Yes, of course they do. Of course.

JULIE. It must be terrible to be poor.

JEAN (*with exaggerated distress*). Oh yes, Miss Julie, yes. A dog may lie on the Countess's sofa, a horse may have his nose stroked by a young lady, but a servant ... (*change of tone*) well, yes, now and then you meet one with guts enough to rise in the world, but how often? Anyhow, do you know what I did? Jumped in the millstream with my clothes on, was pulled out and got a hiding. But the next Sunday, when Father and all the rest went to Granny's, I managed to get left behind. Then I washed with soap and hot water, put my best clothes on and went to church so as to see you. I did see you and went home determined to die. But I wanted to die beautifully and peacefully, without any pain. Then I remembered it was dangerous to sleep under an elder bush. We had a big one in full bloom, so I stripped it and climbed into the oats-bin with the flowers. Have you ever noticed how smooth oats are? Soft to touch as human skin ... Well, I closed the lid and shut my eyes, fell asleep, and when they woke me I was very ill. But I didn't die, as you see. What I meant by all that I don't know. There was no hope of winning you — you were simply a symbol of the hopelessness of ever getting out of the class I was born in.

JULIE. You put things very well, you know. Did you go to school?

JEAN. For a while. But I've read a lot of novels and been to the theatre. Besides, I've heard educated folk talking — that's what's taught me most.

JULIE. Do you stand round listening to what we're saying?

JEAN. Yes, of course. And I've heard quite a bit too! On the carriage box or rowing the boat. Once I heard you, Miss Julie, and one of your young lady friends ...

JULIE. Oh! Whatever did you hear?

JEAN. Well, it wouldn't be nice to repeat it. And I must say I was pretty startled. I couldn't think where you had learnt such words. Perhaps, at bottom, there isn't as much difference between people as one's led to believe.

JULIE. How dare you! We don't behave as you do when we're engaged.

JEAN (*looking hard at her*). Are you sure? It's no use making out so innocent to me.

JULIE. The man I gave my love to was a rotter.

JEAN. That's what you always say — afterwards.

JULIE. Always?

JEAN. I think it must be always. I've heard the expression several times in similar circumstances.

JULIE. What circumstances?

JEAN. Like those in question. The last time ...

JULIE (*rising*). Stop. I don't want to hear any more.

JEAN. Nor did *she* — curiously enough. May I go to bed now please?

JULIE (*gently*). Go to bed on Midsummer Eve?

JEAN. Yes. Dancing with that crowd doesn't really amuse me.

JULIE. Get the key of the boathouse and row me out on the lake. I want to see the sun rise.

JEAN. Would that be wise?

JULIE. You sound as though you're frightened for your reputation.

JEAN. Why not? I don't want to be made a fool of, nor to be sent packing without a character when I'm trying to better myself. Besides, I have Kristin to consider.

JULIE. So now it's Kristin.

JEAN. Yes, but it's you I'm thinking about too. Take my advice and go to bed.

JULIE. Am I to take orders from you?

JEAN. Just this once, for your own sake. Please. It's very late and sleepiness goes to one's head and makes one rash. Go to bed. What's more, if my ears don't deceive me, I hear people coming this way. They'll be looking for me, and if they find us here, you're done for.

The CHORUS *approaches, singing. During the following dialogue the song is heard in snatches, and in full when the peasants enter.*

> *Out of the wood two women came,*
> *Tridiri-ralla, tridiri-ra.*
> *The feet of one were bare and cold,*
> *Tridiri-ralla-la.*
>
> *The other talked of bags of gold,*
> *Tridiri-ralla, tridiri-ra.*
> *But neither had a sou to her name,*
> *Tridiri-ralla-la.*
>
> *The bridal wreath I give to you,*
> *Tridiri-ralla, tridiri-ra.*
> *But to another I'll be true,*
> *Tridiri-ralla-la.*

JULIE. I know our people and I love them, just as they do me. Let them come. You'll see.

JEAN. No, Miss Julie, they don't love you. They take your food, then spit at it. You must believe me. Listen to them, just listen to what they're singing . . . No, don't listen.

JULIE (*listening*). What are they singing?

JEAN. They're mocking — you and me.

JULIE. Oh no! How horrible! What cowards!

JEAN. A pack like that's always cowardly. But against such odds there's nothing we can do but run away.

JULIE. Run away? Where to? We can't get out and we can't go into Kristin's room.

JEAN. Into mine then. Necessity knows no rules. And you can trust me. I really am your true and devoted friend.

JULIE. But supposing . . . supposing they were to look for you in there?
JEAN. I'll bolt the door, and if they try to break in I'll shoot. Come on. (*Pleading.*) Please come.
JULIE (*tensely*). Do you promise . . . ?
JEAN. I swear!

JULIE *goes quickly into his room and he excitedly follows her.*

Led by the fiddler, the peasants enter in festive attire with flowers in their hats. They put a barrel of beer and a keg of spirits, garlanded with leaves, on the table, fetch glasses and begin to carouse. The scene becomes a ballet. They form a ring and dance and sing and mime: "Out of the wood two women came." *Finally they go out, still singing.*

JULIE *comes in alone. She looks at the havoc in the kitchen, wrings her hands, then takes out her powder puff and powders her face.*

JEAN *enters in high spirits.*

JEAN. Now you see! And you heard, didn't you? Do you still think it's possible for us to stay here?
JULIE. No, I don't. But what can we do?
JEAN. Run away. Far away. Take a journey.
JULIE. Journey? But where to?
JEAN. Switzerland. The Italian lakes. Ever been there?
JULIE. No. Is it nice?
JEAN. Ah! Eternal summer, oranges, evergreens . . . ah!
JULIE. But what would we do there?
JEAN. I'll start a hotel. First-class accommodation and first-class customers.
JULIE. Hotel?
JEAN. There's life for you. New faces all the time, new languages — no time for nerves or worries, no need to look for something to do — work rolling up of its own accord. Bells ringing night and day, trains whistling, buses coming and going, and all the time gold pieces rolling on to the counter. There's life for you!
JULIE. For *you*. And I?
JEAN. Mistress of the house, ornament of the firm. With your looks, and your style . . . oh, it's bound to be a success! Terrific! You'll sit like a queen in the office and set your slaves in motion by pressing an electric button. The guests will file past your throne and nervously lay their treasure on your table. You've no idea the way people tremble when they get their bills. I'll salt the bills and you'll sugar them with your sweetest smiles. Ah, let's get away from here! (*Produces a time-table.*) At once, by the next train. We shall be at Malmö at six-thirty, Hamburg eight-forty next morning, Frankfurt-Basle the following day, and Como by the St. Gothard pass in — let's see — three days. Three days!
JULIE. That's all very well. But Jean, you must give me courage. Tell me you love me. Come and take me in your arms.
JEAN (*reluctantly*). I'd like to, but I daren't. Not again in this house. I

love you — that goes without saying. You can't doubt that, Miss Julie, can you?

JULIE (*shyly, very feminine*). Miss? Call me Julie. There aren't any barriers between us now. Call me Julie.

JEAN (*uneasily*). I can't. As long as we're in this house, there *are* barriers between us. There's the past and there's the Count. I've never been so servile to anyone as I am to him. I've only got to see his gloves on a chair to feel small. I've only got to hear his bell and I shy like a horse. Even now, when I look at his boots, standing there so proud and stiff, I feel my back beginning to bend. (*Kicks the boots.*) It's those old, narrow-minded notions drummed into us as children . . . but they can soon be forgotten. You've only got to get to another country, a republic, and people will bend themselves double before my porter's livery. Yes, double they'll bend themselves, but I shan't. I wasn't born to bend. I've got guts, I've got character, and once I reach that first branch, you'll watch me climb. Today I'm valet, next year I'll be proprietor, in ten years I'll have made a fortune, and then I'll go to Roumania, get myself decorated and I may, I only say *may*, mind you, end up as a Count.

JULIE (*sadly*). That would be very nice.

JEAN. You see in Roumania one can buy a title, and then you'll be a Countess after all. My Countess.

JULIE. What do I care about all that? I'm putting those things behind me. Tell me you love me, because if you don't . . . if you don't, what am I?

JEAN. I'll tell you a thousand times over — later. But not here. No sentimentality now or everything will be lost. We must consider this thing calmly like reasonable people. (*Takes a cigar, cuts and lights it.*) You sit down there and I'll sit here and we'll talk as if nothing has happened.

JULIE. My God, have you no feelings at all?

JEAN. Nobody has more. But I know how to control them.

JULIE. A short time ago you were kissing my shoe. And now . . .

JEAN (*harshly*). Yes, that was then. Now we have something else to think about.

JULIE. Don't speak to me so brutally.

JEAN. I'm not. Just sensibly. One folly's been committed, don't let's have more. The Count will be back at any moment and we've got to settle our future before that. Now, what do you think of my plans? Do you approve?

JULIE. It seems a very good idea — but just one thing. Such a big undertaking would need a lot of capital. Have you got any?

JEAN (*chewing his cigar*). I certainly have. I've got my professional skill, my wide experience and my knowledge of foreign languages. That's capital worth having, it seems to me.

JULIE. But it won't buy even one railway ticket.

JEAN. Quite true. That's why I need a backer to advance some ready cash.

JULIE. How could you get that at a moment's notice?

JEAN. You must get it, if you want to be my partner.

JULIE. I can't. I haven't any money of my own. (*Pause.*)
JEAN. Then the whole thing's off.
JULIE. And...?
JEAN. We go on as we are.
JULIE. Do you think I'm going to stay under this roof as your mistress? With everyone pointing at me. Do you think I can face my father after this? No. Take me away from here, away from this shame, this humiliation. Oh my God, what have I done? My God, my God! (*Weeps.*)
JEAN. So that's the tune now, is it? What have you done? Same as many before you.
JULIE (*hysterically*). And now you despise me. I'm falling, I'm falling.
JEAN. Fall as far as me and I'll lift you up again.
JULIE. Why was I so terribly attracted to you? The weak to the strong, the falling to the rising? Or was it love? Is that love? Do you know what love is?
JEAN. Do I? You bet I do. Do you think I never had a girl before?
JULIE. The things you say, the things you think!
JEAN. That's what life's taught me, and that's what I am. It's no good getting hysterical or giving yourself airs. We're both in the same boat now. Here, my dear girl, let me give you a glass of something special. (*Opens the drawer, takes out the bottle of wine and fills two used glasses.*)
JULIE. Where did you get that wine?
JEAN. From the cellar.
JULIE. My father's burgundy.
JEAN. Why not, for his son-in-law?
JULIE. And I drink beer.
JEAN. That only shows your taste's not so good as mine.
JULIE. Thief!
JEAN. Are you going to tell on me?
JULIE. Oh God! The accomplice of a petty thief! Was I blind drunk? Have I dreamt this whole night? Midsummer Eve, the night for innocent merrymaking.
JEAN. Innocent, eh?
JULIE. Is anyone on earth as wretched as I am now?
JEAN. Why should *you* be? After such a conquest. What about Kristin in there? Don't you think she has any feelings?
JULIE. I did think so, but I don't any longer. No. A menial is a menial...
JEAN. And a whore is a whore.
JULIE (*falling to her knees, her hands clasped*). O God in heaven, put an end to my miserable life! Lift me out of this filth in which I'm sinking. Save me! Save me!
JEAN. I must admit I'm sorry for you. When I was in the onion bed and saw you up there among the roses, I... yes, I'll tell you now... I had the same dirty thoughts as all boys.
JULIE. You, who wanted to die because of me?

JEAN. In the oats-bin? That was just talk.

JULIE. Lies, you mean.

JEAN (*getting sleepy*). More or less. I think I read a story in some paper about a chimney-sweep who shut himself up in a chest full of lilac because he'd been summonsed for not supporting some brat . . .

JULIE. So this is what you're like.

JEAN. I had to think up something. It's always the fancy stuff that catches the women.

JULIE. Beast!

JEAN. Merde!

JULIE. Now you have seen the falcon's back.

JEAN. Not exactly its *back*.

JULIE. I was to be the first branch.

JEAN. But the branch was rotten.

JULIE. I was to be a hotel sign.

JEAN. And I the hotel.

JULIE. Sit at your counter, attract your clients and cook their accounts.

JEAN. I'd have done that myself.

JULIE. That any human being can be so steeped in filth!

JEAN. Clean it up then.

JULIE. Menial! Lackey! Stand up when I speak to you.

JEAN. Menial's whore, lackey's harlot, shut your mouth and get out of here! Are you the one to lecture me for being coarse? Nobody of my kind would ever be as coarse as you were tonight. Do you think any servant girl would throw herself at a man that way? Have you ever seen a girl of my class asking for it like that? I haven't. Only animals and prostitutes.

JULIE (*broken*). Go on. Hit me, trample on me — it's all I deserve. I'm rotten. But help me! If there's any way out at all, help me.

JEAN (*more gently*). I'm not denying myself a share in the honour of seducing you, but do you think anybody in my place would have dared look in your direction if you yourself hadn't asked for it? I'm still amazed . . .

JULIE. And proud.

JEAN. Why not? Though I must admit the victory was too easy to make me lose my head.

JULIE. Go on hitting me.

JEAN (*rising*). No. On the contrary I apologise for what I've said. I don't hit a person who's down — least of all a woman. I can't deny there's a certain satisfaction in finding that what dazzled one below was just moonshine, that that falcon's back is grey after all, that there's powder on the lovely cheek, that polished nails can have black tips, that the handkerchief is dirty although it smells of scent. On the other hand it hurts to find that what I was struggling to reach wasn't high and isn't real. It hurts to see you fallen so low you're far lower than your own cook. Hurts like when you see the last flowers of summer lashed to pieces by rain and turned to mud.

JULIE. You're talking as if you're already my superior.

JEAN. I am. I might make you a Countess, but you could never make me a Count, you know.

JULIE. But I am the child of a Count, and you could never be that.

JEAN. True, but I might be the father of Counts if . . .

JULIE. You're a thief. I'm not.

JEAN. There are worse things than being a thief — much lower. Besides, when I'm in a place I regard myself as a member of the family to some extent, as one of the children. You don't call it stealing when children pinch a berry from overladen bushes. (*His passion is roused again.*) Miss Julie, you're a glorious woman, far too good for a man like me. You were carried away by some kind of madness, and now you're trying to cover up your mistake by persuading yourself you're in love with me. You're not, although you may find me physically attractive, which means your love's no better than mine. But I wouldn't be satisfied with being nothing but an animal for you, and I could never make you love me.

JULIE. Are you sure?

JEAN. You think there's a chance? Of my loving you, yes, of course. You're beautiful, refined — (*takes her hand*) — educated, and you can be nice when you want to be. The fire you kindle in a man isn't likely to go out. (*Puts his arm round her.*) You're like mulled wine, full of spices, and your kisses . . . (*He tries to pull her to him, but she breaks away.*)

JULIE. Let go of me! You won't win me that way.

JEAN. Not that way, how then? Not by kisses and fine speeches, not by planning the future and saving you from shame? How then?

JULIE. How? How? I don't know. There isn't any way. I loathe you — loathe you as I loathe rats, but I can't escape from you.

JEAN. Escape with me.

JULIE (*pulling herself together*). Escape? Yes, we must escape. But I'm so tired. Give me a glass of wine. (*He pours it out. She looks at her watch.*) First we must talk. We still have a little time. (*Empties the glass and holds it out for more.*)

JEAN. Don't drink like that. You'll get tipsy.

JULIE. What's that matter?

JEAN. What's it matter? It's vulgar to get drunk. Well, what have you got to say?

JULIE. We've got to run away, but we must talk first — or rather, I must, for so far you've done all the talking. You've told me about your life, now I want to tell you about mine, so that we really know each other before we begin this journey together.

JEAN. Wait. Excuse my saying so, but don't you think you may be sorry afterwards if you give away your secrets to me?

JULIE. Aren't you my friend?

JEAN. On the whole. But don't rely on me.

JULIE. You can't mean that. But anyway everyone knows my secrets. Listen. My mother wasn't well-born; she came of quite humble people, and was brought up with all those new ideas of sex-equality and women's rights and so on. She thought marriage was quite wrong. So when my father proposed to her, she said she would never become his *wife* . . . but in the end she did. I came into the world, as far as I can make out, against my mother's will, and I was left to run wild, but I had to do all the things a boy does — to prove women are as good as men. I had to wear boys' clothes; I was taught to handle horses — and I wasn't allowed in the dairy. She made me groom and harness and go out hunting; I even had to try to plough. All the men on the estate were given the women's jobs, and the women the men's, until the whole place went to rack and ruin and we were the laughing-stock of the neighbourhood. At last my father seems to have come to his senses and rebelled. He changed everything and ran the place his own way. My mother got ill — I don't know what was the matter with her, but she used to have strange attacks and hide herself in the attic or the garden. Sometimes she stayed out all night. Then came the great fire which you have heard people talking about. The house and the stables and the barns — the whole place burnt to the ground. In very suspicious circumstances. Because the accident happened the very day the insurance had to be renewed, and my father had sent the new premium, but through some carelessness of the messenger it arrived too late. (*Refills her glass and drinks.*)

JEAN. Don't drink any more.

JULIE. Oh, what does it matter? We were destitute and had to sleep in the carriages. My father didn't know how to get money to rebuild, and then my mother suggested he should borrow from an old friend of hers, a local brick manufacturer. My father got the loan and, to his surprise, without having to pay interest. So the place was rebuilt. (*Drinks.*) Do you know who set fire to it?

JEAN. Your lady mother.

JULIE. Do you know who the brick manufacturer was?

JEAN. Your mother's lover?

JULIE. Do you know whose the money was?

JEAN. Wait . . . no, I don't know that.

JULIE. It was my mother's.

JEAN. In other words the Count's, unless there was a settlement.

JULIE. There wasn't any settlement. My mother had a little money of her own which she didn't want my father to control, so she invested it with her — friend.

JEAN. Who grabbed it.

JULIE. Exactly. He appropriated it. My father came to know all this. He couldn't bring an action, couldn't pay his wife's lover, nor prove it was his wife's money. That was my mother's revenge because he made himself master in his own house. He nearly shot himself then — at least there's a rumour he tried and didn't bring it off. So he went on living, and my mother had to pay dearly for what she'd done. Imagine what those five years were like for me. My natural sympathies were with my father, yet I took my mother's side, because I didn't know the facts. I'd learnt from her to hate and distrust men — you know how she loathed the whole male sex. And I swore to her I'd never become the slave of any man.

JEAN. And so you got engaged to that attorney.

JULIE. So that he should be my slave.

JEAN. But he wouldn't be.

JULIE. Oh yes, he wanted to be, but he didn't have the chance. I got bored with him.

JEAN. Is that what I saw — in the stable-yard?

JULIE. What did you see?

JEAN. What I saw was him breaking off the engagement.

JULIE. That's a lie. It was I who broke it off. Did he say it was him? The cad.

JEAN. He's not a cad. Do you hate men, Miss Julie?

JULIE. Yes . . . most of the time. But when that weakness comes, oh . . . the shame!

JEAN. Then do you hate me?

JULIE. Beyond words. I'd gladly have you killed like an animal.

JEAN. Quick as you'd shoot a mad dog, eh?

JULIE. Yes.

JEAN. But there's nothing here to shoot with — and there isn't a dog. So what do we do now?

JULIE. Go abroad.

JEAN. To make each other miserable for the rest of our lives?

JULIE. No, to enjoy ourselves for a day or two, for a week, for as long as enjoyment lasts, and then — to die . . .

JEAN. Die? How silly! I think it would be far better to start a hotel.

JULIE (*without listening*) . . . die on the shores of Lake Como, where the sun always shines and at Christmas time there are green trees and glowing oranges.

JEAN. Lake Como's a rainy hole and I didn't see any oranges outside the shops. But it's a good place for tourists. Plenty of villas to be rented by — er — honeymoon couples. Profitable business that. Know why? Because they all sign a lease for six months and all leave after three weeks.

JULIE (*naïvely*). After three weeks? Why?

JEAN. They quarrel, of course. But the rent has to be paid just the same. And then it's let again. So it goes on and on, for there's plenty of love although it doesn't last long.

JULIE. You don't want to die with me?

JEAN. I don't want to die at all. For one thing I like living and for another I consider suicide's a sin against the Creator who gave us life.

JULIE. You believe in God — *you?*

JEAN. Yes, of course. And I go to church every Sunday. Look here, I'm tired of all this. I'm going to bed.

JULIE. Indeed! And do you think I'm going to leave things like this? Don't you know what you owe the woman you've ruined?

JEAN (*taking out his purse and throwing a silver coin on the table*). There you are. I don't want to be in anybody's debt.

JULIE (*pretending not to notice the insult*). Don't you know what the law is?

JEAN. There's no law unfortunately that punishes a woman for seducing a man.

JULIE. But can you see anything for it but to go abroad, get married and then divorce?

JEAN. What if I refuse this mésalliance?

JULIE. Mésalliance?

JEAN. Yes, for me. I'm better bred than you, see! Nobody in my family committed arson.

JULIE. How do you know?

JEAN. Well, you can't prove otherwise, because we haven't any family records outside the Registrar's office. But I've seen your family tree in that book on the drawing-room table. Do you know who the founder of your family was? A miller who let his wife sleep with the King one night during the Danish war. I haven't any ancestors like that. I haven't any ancestors at all, but I might become one.

JULIE. This is what I get for confiding in someone so low, for sacrificing my family honour . . .

JEAN. Dishonour! Well, I told you so. One shouldn't drink, because then one talks. And one shouldn't talk.

JULIE. Oh, how ashamed I am, how bitterly ashamed! If at least you loved me!

JEAN. Look here — for the last time — what do you want? Am I to burst into tears? Am I to jump over your riding whip? Shall I kiss you and carry you off to Lake Como for three weeks, after which . . . What am I to do? What do you want? This is getting unbearable, but that's what comes of playing around with women. Miss Julie, I can see how miserable you are; I know you're going through hell, but I don't understand you. We don't have scenes like this; we don't go in for hating each ther. We make love for fun in our spare time, but we haven't all day and all night for it like you. I think you must be ill. I'm sure you're ill.

JULIE. Then you must be kind to me. You sound almost human now.

JEAN. Well, be human yourself. You spit at me, then won't let me wipe it off — on you.

JULIE. Help me, help me! Tell me what to do, where to go.

JEAN. Jesus, as if I knew!

JULIE. I've been mad, raving mad, but there must be a way out.

JEAN. Stay here and keep quiet. Nobody knows anything.
JULIE. I can't. People do know. Kristin knows.
JEAN. They don't know and they wouldn't believe such a thing.
JULIE (*hesitating*). But — it might happen again.
JEAN. That's true.
JULIE. And there might be — consequences.
JEAN (*in panic*). Consequences! Fool that I am I never thought of that. Yes, there's nothing for it but to go. At once. I can't come with you. That would be a complete giveaway. You must go alone — abroad — anywhere.
JULIE. Alone? Where to? I can't.
JEAN. You must. And before the Count gets back. If you stay, we know what will happen. Once you've sinned you feel you might as well go on, as the harm's done. Then you get more reckless and in the end you're found out. No. You must go abroad. Then write to the Count and tell him everything, except that it was me. He'll never guess that — and I don't think he'll want to.
JULIE. I'll go if you come with me.
JEAN. Are you crazy, woman? "Miss Julie elopes with valet." Next day it would be in the headlines, and the Count would never live it down.
JULIE. I can't go. I can't stay. I'm so tired, so completely worn out. Give me orders. Set me going. I can't think any more, can't act . . .
JEAN. You see what weaklings you are. Why do you give yourselves airs and turn up your noses as if you're the lords of creation? Very well, I'll give you orders. Go upstairs and dress. Get money for the journey and come down here again.
JULIE (*softly*). Come up with me.
JEAN. To your room? Now you've gone crazy again. (*Hesitates a moment.*) No! Go along at once. (*Takes her hand and pulls her to the door.*)
JULIE (*as she goes*). Speak kindly to me, Jean.
JEAN. Orders always sound unkind. Now you know. Now you know.
> Left alone, JEAN *sighs with relief, sits down at the table, takes out a notebook and pencil and adds up figures, now and then aloud. Dawn begins to break.* KRISTIN *enters dressed for church, carrying his white dickey and tie.*

KRISTIN. Lord Jesus, look at the state the place is in! What have you been up to? (*Turns out the lamp.*)
JEAN. Oh, Miss Julie invited the crowd in. Did you sleep through it? Didn't you hear anything?
KRISTIN. I slept like a log.
JEAN. And dressed for church already.
KRISTIN. Yes, you promised to come to Communion with me today.
JEAN. Why, so I did. And you've got my bib and tucker, I see. Come on then. (*Sits.* KRISTIN *begins to put his things on. Pause. Sleepily.*) What's the lesson today?
KRISTIN. It's about the beheading of John the Baptist, I think.

JEAN. That's sure to be horribly long. Hi, you're choking me! Oh Lord, I'm so sleepy, so sleepy!

KRISTIN. Yes, what have you been doing up all night? You look absolutely green.

JEAN. Just sitting here talking with Miss Julie.

KRISTIN. She doesn't know what's proper, that one. (*Pause.*)

JEAN. I say, Kristin.

KRISTIN. What?

JEAN. It's queer really, isn't it, when you come to think of it? Her.

KRISTIN. What's queer?

JEAN. The whole thing. (*Pause.*)

KRISTIN (*looking at the half-filled glasses on the table*). Have you been drinking together too?

JEAN. Yes.

KRISTIN. More shame you. Look me straight in the face.

JEAN. Yes.

KRISTIN. Is it possible? Is it possible?

JEAN (*after a moment*). Yes, it is.

KRISTIN. Oh! This I would never have believed. How low!

JEAN. You're not jealous of her, surely?

KRISTIN. No, I'm not. If it had been Clara or Sophie I'd have scratched your eyes out. But not of her. I don't know why; that's how it is though. But it's disgusting.

JEAN. You're angry with her then.

KRISTIN. No. With you. It was wicked of you, very very wicked. Poor girl. And, mark my words, I won't stay here any longer now — in a place where one can't respect one's employers.

JEAN. Why should one respect them?

KRISTIN. You should know since you're so smart. But you don't want to stay in the service of people who aren't respectable, do you? I wouldn't demean myself.

JEAN. But it's rather a comfort to find out they're no better than us.

KRISTIN. I don't think so. If they're no better there's nothing for us to live up to. Oh and think of the Count! Think of him. He's been through so much already. No, I won't stay in the place any longer. A fellow like you too! If it had been that attorney now or somebody of her own class . . .

JEAN. Why, what's wrong with . . .

KRISTIN. Oh, you're all right in your own way, but when all's said and done there is a difference between one class and another. No, this is something I'll never be able to stomach. That our young lady who was so proud and so down on men you'd never believe she'd let one come near her should go and give herself to one like you. She who wanted to have poor Diana shot for running after the lodge-keeper's pug. No, I must say. . . ! Well, I won't stay here any longer. On the twenty-fourth of October I quit.

Miss Julie

JEAN. And then?

KRISTIN. Well, since you mention it, it's about time you began to look around, if we're ever going to get married.

JEAN. But what am I to look for? I shan't get a place like this when I'm married.

KRISTIN. I know you won't. But you might get a job as porter or caretaker in some public institution. Government rations are small but sure, and there's a pension for the widow and children.

JEAN. That's all very fine, but it's not in my line to start thinking at once about dying for my wife and children. I must say I had rather bigger ideas.

KRISTIN. You and your ideas! You've got obligations too, and you'd better start thinking about them.

JEAN. Don't *you* start pestering me about obligations. I've had enough of that. (*Listens to a sound upstairs.*) Anyway we've plenty of time to work things out. Go and get ready now and we'll be off to church.

KRISTIN. Who's that walking about upstairs?

JEAN. Don't know — unless it's Clara.

KRISTIN (*going*). You don't think the Count could have come back without our hearing him?

JEAN (*scared*). The Count? No, he can't have. He'd have rung for me.

KRISTIN. God help us! I've never known such goings on. (*Exit.*)

The sun has now risen and is shining on the treetops. The light gradually changes until it slants in through the windows. JEAN *goes to the door and beckons.* JULIE *enters in travelling clothes, carrying a small bird-cage covered with a cloth which she puts on a chair.*

JULIE. I'm ready.

JEAN. Hush! Kristin's up.

JULIE (*in a very nervous state*). Does she suspect anything?

JEAN. Not a thing. But, my God, what a sight you are!

JULIE. Sight? What do you mean?

JEAN. You're white as a corpse and — pardon me — your face is dirty.

JULIE. Let me wash then. (*Goes to the sink and washes her face and hands.*) There. Give me a towel. Oh! The sun is rising!

JEAN. And that breaks the spell.

JULIE. Yes. The spell of Midsummer Eve . . . But listen, Jean. Come with me. I've got the money.

JEAN (*sceptically*). Enough?

JULIE. Enough to start with. Come with me. I can't travel alone today. It's Midsummer Day, remember. I'd be packed into a suffocating train among crowds of people who'd all stare at me. And it would stop at every station while I yearned for wings. No, I can't do that, I simply can't. There will be memories too; memories of Midsummer Days when I was little. The leafy church — birch and lilac — the gaily spread dinner table, relatives, friends — evening in the park — dancing and music and flowers and fun. Oh, however far you run away — there'll always be memories in the baggage car — and remorse and guilt.

JEAN. I will come with you, but quickly now then, before it's too late. At once.

JULIE. Put on your things. (*Picks up the cage.*)

JEAN. No luggage mind. That would give us away.

JULIE. No, only what we can take with us in the carriage.

JEAN (*fetching his hat*). What on earth have you got there? What is it?

JULIE. Only my greenfinch. I don't want to leave it behind.

JEAN. Well, I'll be damned! We're to take a bird-cage along, are we? You're crazy. Put that cage down.

JULIE. It's the only thing I'm taking from my home. The only living creature who cares for me since Diana went off like that. Don't be cruel. Let me take it.

JEAN. Put that cage down, I tell you — and don't talk so loud. Kristin will hear.

JULIE. No, I won't leave it in strange hands. I'd rather you killed it.

JEAN. Give the little beast here then and I'll wring its neck.

JULIE. But don't hurt it, don't . . . no, I can't.

JEAN. Give it here. I *can*.

JULIE (*taking the bird out of the cage and kissing it*). Dear little Serena, must you die and leave your mistress?

JEAN. Please don't make a scene. It's *your* life and future we're worrying about. Come on, quick now!

He snatches the bird from her, puts it on a board and picks up a chopper. JULIE *turns away.*

You should have learnt how to kill chickens instead of target-shooting. Then you wouldn't faint at a drop of blood.

JULIE (*screaming*). Kill me too! Kill me! You who can butcher an innocent creature without a quiver. Oh, how I hate you, how I loathe you! There is blood between us now. I curse the hour I first saw you. I curse the hour I was conceived in my mother's womb.

JEAN. What's the use of cursing. Let's go.

JULIE (*going to the chopping-block as if drawn against her will*). No, I won't go yet. I can't . . . I must look. Listen! There's a carriage. (*Listens without taking her eyes off the board and chopper.*) You don't think I can bear the sight of blood. You think I'm so weak. Oh, how I should like to see your blood and your brains on a chopping-block! I'd like to see the whole of your sex swimming like that in a sea of blood. I think I could drink out of your skull, bathe my feet in your broken breast and eat your heart roasted whole. You think I'm weak. You think I love you, that my womb yearned for your seed and I want to carry your offspring under my heart and nourish it with my blood. You think I want to bear your child and take your name. By the way, what is your name? I've never heard your surname. I don't sup-

Miss Julie

pose you've got one. I should be "Mrs. Hovel" or "Madam Dunghill." You dog wearing my collar, you lackey with my crest on your buttons! I share you with my cook; I'm my own servant's rival! Oh! Oh! Oh! . . . You think I'm a coward and will run away. No, now I'm going to stay — and let the storm break. My father will come back . . . find his desk broken open . . . his money gone. Then he'll ring that bell — twice for the valet — and then he'll send for the police . . . and I shall tell everything. Everything. Oh how wonderful to make an end of it all — a real end! He has a stroke and dies and that's the end of all of us. Just peace and quietness . . . eternal rest. The coat of arms broken on the coffin and the Count's line extinct . . . But the valet's line goes on in an orphanage, wins laurels in the gutter and ends in jail.

JEAN. There speaks the noble blood! Bravo, Miss Julie. But now, don't let the cat out of the bag.

KRISTIN *enters dressed for church, carrying a prayer-book.* JULIE *rushes to her and flings herself into her arms for protection.*

JULIE. Help me, Kristin! Protect me from this man!

KRISTIN (*unmoved and cold*). What goings-on for a feast day morning! (*Sees the board.*) And what a filthy mess. What's it all about? Why are you screaming and carrying on so?

JULIE. Kristin, you're a woman and my friend. Beware of that scoundrel!

JEAN (*embarrassed*). While you ladies are talking things over, I'll go and shave. (*Slips into his room.*)

JULIE. You must understand. You must listen to me.

KRISTIN. I certainly don't understand such loose ways. Where are you off to in those travelling clothes? And he had his hat on, didn't he, eh?

JULIE. Listen, Kristin. Listen, I'll tell you everything.

KRISTIN. I don't want to know anything.

JULIE. You must listen.

KRISTIN. What to? Your nonsense with Jean? I don't care a rap about that; it's nothing to do with me. But if you're thinking of getting him to run off with you, we'll soon put a stop to that.

JULIE (*very nervously*). Please try to be calm, Kristin, and listen. I can't stay here, nor can Jean — so we must go abroad.

KRISTIN. Hm, hm!

JULIE (*brightening*). But you see, I've had an idea. Supposing we all three go — abroad — to Switzerland and start a hotel together . . . I've got some money, you see . . . and Jean and I could run the whole thing — and I thought you would take charge of the kitchen. Wouldn't that be splendid? Say yes, do. If you come with us everything will be fine. Oh do say yes! (*Puts her arms round* KRISTIN.)

KRISTIN (*coolly thinking*). Hm, hm.

JULIE (*presto tempo*). You've never travelled, Kristin. You should go abroad and see the world. You've no idea how nice it is travelling by train — new faces all the time and new countries. On our way through Hamburg we'll go to the zoo — you'll love that — and we'll go to the theatre and the opera too . . . and when we get to Munich there'll be the museums, dear, and pictures by Rubens and Raphael — the great painters, you know . . . You've heard of Munich, haven't you? Where King Ludwig lived — you know, the king who went mad. . . . We'll see his castles — some of his castles are still just like in fairy-tales . . . and from there it's not far to Switzerland — and the Alps. Think of the Alps, Kristin dear, covered with snow in the middle of summer . . . and there are oranges there and trees that are green the whole year round . . .

>JEAN *is seen in the door of his room, sharpening his razor on a strop which he holds with his teeth and his left hand. He listens to the talk with satisfaction and now and then nods approval.* JULIE *continues, tempo prestissimo.*

And then we'll get a hotel . . . and I'll sit at the desk, while Jean receives the guests and goes out marketing and writes letters . . . There's life for you! Trains whistling, buses driving up, bells ringing upstairs and downstairs . . . and I shall make out the bills — and I shall cook them too . . . you've no idea how nervous travellers are when it comes to paying their bills. And you — you'll sit like a queen in the kitchen . . . of course there won't be any standing at the stove for you. You'll always have to be nicely dressed and ready to be seen, and with your looks — no, I'm not flattering you — one fine day you'll catch yourself a husband . . . some rich Englishman, I shouldn't wonder — they're the ones who are easy — (*slowing down*) — to catch . . . and then we'll get rich and build ourselves a villa on Lake Como . . . of course it rains there a little now and then — but — (*dully*) — the sun must shine there too sometimes — even though it seems gloomy — and if not — then we can come home again — come back — (*pause*) — here — or somewhere else . . .

>KRISTIN. Look here, Miss Julie, do you believe all that yourself?

>JULIE (*exhausted*). Do I believe it?

>KRISTIN. Yes.

>JULIE (*wearily*). I don't know. I don't believe anything any more. (*Sinks down on the bench; her head in her arms on the table.*) Nothing. Nothing at all.

>KRISTIN (*turning to* JEAN). So you meant to beat it, did you?

>JEAN (*disconcerted, putting the razor on the table*). Beat it? What are you talking about? You've heard Miss Julie's plan, and though she's tired now with being up all night, it's a perfectly sound plan.

>KRISTIN. Oh, is it? If you thought I'd work for that . . .

>JEAN (*interrupting*). Kindly use decent language in front of your mistress. Do you hear?

>KRISTIN. Mistress?

>JEAN. Yes.

>KRISTIN. Well, well, just listen to that!

Miss Julie

JEAN. Yes, it would be a good thing if you did listen and talked less. Miss Julie is your mistress and what's made you lose your respect for her now ought to make you feel the same about yourself.

KRISTIN. I've always had enough self-respect ——

JEAN. To despise other people.

KRISTIN. — not to go below my own station. Has the Count's cook ever gone with the groom or the swineherd? Tell me that.

JEAN. No, you were lucky enough to have a high-class chap for your beau.

KRISTIN. High-class all right — selling the oats out of the Count's stable.

JEAN. You're a fine one to talk — taking a commission on the groceries and bribes from the butcher.

KRISTIN. What the devil...?

JEAN. And now you can't feel any respect for your employers. You, you!

KRISTIN. Are you coming to church with me? I should think you need a good sermon after your fine deeds.

JEAN. No, I'm not going to church today. You can go alone and confess your own sins.

KRISTIN. Yes, I'll do that and bring back enough forgiveness to cover yours too. The Saviour suffered and died on the cross for all our sins, and if we go to Him with faith and a penitent heart, He takes all our sins upon Himself.

JEAN. Even grocery thefts?

JULIE. Do you believe that, Kristin?

KRISTIN. That is my living faith, as sure as I stand here. The faith I learnt as a child and have kept ever since, Miss Julie. "But where sin abounded, grace did much more abound."

JULIE. Oh, if I had your faith! Oh, if...

KRISTIN. But you see you can't have it without God's special grace, and it's not given to all to have that.

JULIE. Who is it given to then?

KRISTIN. That's the great secret of the workings of grace, Miss Julie. God is no respecter of persons, and with Him the last shall be first...

JULIE. Then I suppose He does respect the last.

KRISTIN (*continuing*) ... and it is easier for a camel to go through the eye of a needle than for a rich man to enter into the kingdom of God. That's how it is, Miss Julie. Now I'm going — alone, and on my way I shall tell the groom not to let any of the horses out, in case anyone should want to leave before the Count gets back. Goodbye. (*Exit.*)

JEAN. What a devil! And all on account of a greenfinch.

JULIE (*wearily*). Never mind the greenfinch. Do you see any way out of this, any end to it?

JEAN (*pondering*). No.

JULIE. If you were in my place, what would you do?

JEAN. In your place? Wait a bit. If I was a woman — a lady of rank who had — fallen. I don't know. Yes, I do know now.

JULIE (*picking up the razor and making a gesture*). This?

JEAN. Yes. But I wouldn't do it, you know. There's a difference between us.

JULIE. Because you're a man and I'm a woman? What is the difference?

JEAN. The usual difference — between man and woman.

JULIE (*holding the razor*). I'd like to. But I can't. My father couldn't either, that time he wanted to.

JEAN. No, he didn't want to. He had to be revenged first.

JULIE. And now my mother is revenged again, through me.

JEAN. Didn't you ever love your father, Miss Julie?

JULIE. Deeply, but I must have hated him too — unconsciously. And he let me be brought up to despise my own sex, to be half woman, half man. Whose fault is what's happened? My father's, my mother's or my own? My own? I haven't anything that's my own. I haven't one single thought that I didn't get from my father, one emotion that didn't come from my mother, and as for this last idea — about all people being equal — I got that from him, my fiancé — that's why I call him a cad. How can it be my fault? Push the responsibility on to Jesus, like Kristin does? No, I'm too proud and — thanks to my father's teaching — too intelligent. As for all that about a rich person not being able to get into heaven, it's just a lie, but Kristin, who has money in the savings-bank, will certainly not get in. Whose fault is it? What does it matter whose fault it is? In any case I must take the blame and bear the consequences.

JEAN. Yes, but . . . (*There are two sharp rings on the bell.* JULIE *jumps to her feet.* JEAN *changes into his livery.*) The Count is back. Supposing Kristin . . . (*Goes to the speaking-tube, presses it and listens.*)

JULIE. Has he been to his desk yet?

JEAN. This is Jean, sir. (*Listens.*) Yes, sir. (*Listens.*) Yes, sir, very good, sir. (*Listens.*) At once, sir? (*Listens.*) Very good, sir. In half an hour.

JULIE (*in panic*). What did he say? My God, what did he say?

JEAN. He ordered his boots and his coffee in half an hour.

JULIE. Then there's half an hour . . . I'm so tired! I can't do anything. Can't be sorry, can't run away, can't stay, can't live — can't die. Help me. Order me, and I'll obey like a dog. Do me this last service — save my honour, save his name. You know what I ought to do, but haven't the strength to do. Use your strength and order me to do it.

JEAN. I don't know why — I can't now — I don't understand . . . It's just as if this coat made me — I can't give you orders — and now that the Count has spoken to me — I can't quite explain, but . . . well, that devil of a lackey is bending my back again. I believe if the Count came down now and ordered me to cut my throat, I'd do it on the spot.

JULIE. Then pretend you're him and I'm you. You did some fine acting before, when you knelt to me and played the aristocrat. Or . . . Have you ever seen a hypnotist at the theatre? (*He nods.*) He says to the person "Take the broom," and he takes it. He says "Sweep," and he sweeps . . .

JEAN. But the person has to be asleep.

JULIE (*as if in a trance*). I am asleep already . . . the whole room has turned to smoke — and you look like a stove — a stove like a man in black with a tall hat — your eyes are glowing like coals when the fire is low — and your face is a white patch like ashes. (*The sunlight has now reached the floor and lights up* JEAN.) How nice and warm it is! (*She holds out her hands as though warming them at a fire.*) And so light — and so peaceful.

JEAN (*putting the razor in her hand*). Here is the broom. Go now while it's light — out to the barn — and . . . (*Whispers in her ear.*)

JULIE (*waking*). Thank you. I am going now — to rest. But just tell me that even the first can receive the gift of grace.

JEAN. The first? No, I can't tell you that. But wait . . . Miss Julie, I've got it! You aren't one of the first any longer. You're one of the last.

JULIE. That's true. I'm one of the very last. I *am* the last. Oh! . . . But now I can't go. Tell me again to go.

JEAN. No, I can't now either. I can't.

JULIE. And the first shall be last.

JEAN. Don't think, don't think. You're taking my strength away too and making me a coward. What's that? I thought I saw the bell move . . . To be so frightened of a bell! Yes, but it's not just a bell. There's somebody behind it — a hand moving it — and something else moving the hand — and if you stop your ears — if you stop your ears — yes, then it rings louder than ever. Rings and rings until you answer — and then it's too late. Then the police come and . . . and . . . (*The bell rings twice loudly.* JEAN *flinches, then straightens himself up.*) It's horrible. But there's no other way to end it . . . Go!

JULIE *walks firmly out through the door.*

CURTAIN

SYMBOLISM

Maurice Maeterlinck

PELLÉAS AND MÉLISANDE

[1892]

Maurice Maeterlinck [1862–1949]

Maurice Maeterlinck, winner of the Nobel Prize for literature in 1911, was celebrated in the 1890's as the creator of a new kind of drama, a so-called interior drama. As the decade wore on into the twentieth century, Maeterlinck produced some plays of great popularity, notably *The Blue Bird* (1908); however, he did not equal his early work. Today Maeterlinck is remembered for his one-act plays, among them *The Blind* (1890), *The Intruder* (1890), and *Interior* (1894), and for *Pelléas and Mélisande*. With even this small body of work plus his critical essays, Maeterlinck's contribution to the history of the modern drama is quite important.

As Edmund Wilson says in *Axel's Castle*, "The peculiar subtlety and difficulty of Symbolism is indicated by the name itself." As we know, symbolism of one sort or another has been pervasive in literature. For example, Hebrew poetry used symbols; so did Dante, and so did Shelley. But a peculiar way of choosing and using symbols has led to the designation of certain writers as Symbolists. Among the Symbolist school, as it may be called, is the tendency to choose symbols arbitrarily and to use them in a personal, perhaps a unique, way. What then is a symbol, and how does the Symbolist use it?

Arthur Symons begins his *The Symbolist Movement in Literature* with an epigraph from Carlyle's chapter on symbols in *Sartor Resartus*, and Maeterlinck opens his first essay, on silence, in *The Treasure of the Humble* with a long quotation from the same chapter. There Carlyle says, "In the Symbol proper, what we can call a Symbol, there is ever, more or less distinctly and directly, some embodiment and revelation of the Infinite; the Infinite is made to blend itself with the Finite, to stand visible, and as it were, attainable there." And a few paragraphs later he writes, "It

Maeterlinck and Symbolism

is in and through *Symbols* that man, consciously or unconsciously, lives, works, and has his being: those ages, moreover, are accounted the noblest which can the best recognize symbolical worth, and prize it the highest." With these words Maeterlinck and most other Symbolists could easily agree. Symbolism, coming, Edmund Wilson says, as "the second flood of the same tide" as Romanticism, is yet distinct from it. To a much greater degree than was true of Romanticism, Symbolism is "an attempt to spiritualize literature." Yeats has said that "wisdom first speaks in images," but these images are susceptible of various interpretations and consequently the attempt to hint at states of soul-experience may be only partially successful. Impressions, moods, feelings, evocations, suggestions — in short, the mysterious and the transcendental identify Symbolist literature.

The Symbolists thought of their writing as literature of the soul as opposed to literature of the rational intellect and of the senses (though their writing can be highly sensuous); as a result, we often find a tone of religiosity in Symbolism. To the Symbolists, intuitions and vague feelings, since they may be the stirrings of the soul, are more likely to be true than objective facts; the more uncertain and inexpressible, the more true, it would seem. Since the written word of everyday use is inadequate to express the refinements of feeling of which the soul is capable, symbols (or correspondences in which things seen or apprehended stand for the unseen, but still real) are needed. The highly subjective nature of their symbols led the Symbolists to indefiniteness and lack of precise statement: the Symbolists may mean what they say — but they do not, directly at least, say what they mean.

Pelléas and Mélisande is a shadowy, twilight drama in which atmosphere carries much of the meaning and in which silences are suggestive. In his essay "Silence," Maeterlinck presents the rationale for his drama of pauses. He writes, "It is idle to think that, by means of words, any real communication can ever pass from one man to another." And later he says that it is the "quality" of the "silences that alone [reveal] the quality" of a love between two people. He approves, in a literal way, the old saying "Silence is golden"; it represents the most important moments in human experience.

Maeterlinck espouses a drama of stasis and of silence, one from which the reader or viewer must infer the meaning. While silences may be highly significant in real life, the dramatization of silences presents very great problems. At times the playwright (often with the important collaboration of the director and the stage designer) is thus confined to creating atmosphere — a fragile and uncertain state at best. *Pelléas and Mélisande* (performed behind a gauze curtain in its first production in English in 1898) illustrates many of the characteristics of Symbolism. As a result of the dramatic theory which it exemplifies, it intentionally (sometimes unintentionally?) raises questions. Who are the three old men? What does the dove suggest? What of the golden ball? What of the King's weak eyesight? What are the effects of the numerous ellipses in the text, and of the number of scenes? And what is the total effect on a reader or a viewer of all these and other unanswered questions? Can we agree with Eric Bentley when he says of the Symbolists, "The aim was to find the essence of life; the result was . . . leaving life behind"?

THE TRAGICAL IN DAILY LIFE*

by Maurice Maeterlinck

There is a tragic element in the life of every day that is far more real, far more penetrating, far more akin to the true self that is in us than the tragedy that lies in great adventure. But, readily as we all may feel this, to prove it is by no means easy, inasmuch as this essential tragic element comprises more than that which is merely material or merely psychological. It goes beyond the determined struggle of man against man, and desire against desire: it goes beyond the eternal conflict of duty and passion. Its province is rather to reveal to us how truly wonderful is the mere act of living, and to throw light upon the existence of the soul, self-contained in the midst of ever-restless immensities; to hush the discourse of reason and sentiment, so that above the tumult may be heard the solemn, uninterrupted whisperings of man and his destiny. It is its province to point out to us the uncertain, dolorous footsteps of the being, as he approaches, or wanders from, his truth, his beauty, or his God. And further, to show us, and make us understand, the countless other things therewith connected, of which tragic poets have but vouchsafed us passing glimpses. And here do we come to an essential point, for could not these things, of which we have had only passing glimpses, be placed in front of the others, and shown to us first of all? The mysterious chant of the Infinite, the ominous silence of the soul and of God, the murmur of Eternity on the horizon, the destiny or fatality that we are conscious of within us, though by what tokens none can tell — do not all these underlie King Lear, Macbeth, Hamlet? And would it not be possible, by some interchanging of the roles, to bring them nearer to us, and send the actors farther off? Is it beyond the mark to say that the true tragic element, normal, deep-rooted, and universal, that the true tragic element of life only begins at the moment when so-called adventures, sorrows, and dangers have disappeared? Is the arm of happiness not longer than that of sorrow, and do not certain of its attributes draw nearer to the soul? Must we indeed roar like the Atrides, before the Eternal God will reveal Himself in our life? and is He never by our side at times when the air is calm, and the lamp burns on, unflickering? When we think of it, is it not the tranquillity that is terrible, the tranquillity watched by the stars? and is it in tumult or in silence that the spirit of life quickens within us? Is it not

* From *The Treasure of the Humble*, trans. Alfred Sutro (New York: Dodd, Mead, 1900), pp. 97–119.

when we are told, at the end of the story, "They were happy," that the great disquiet should intrude itself? What is taking place while they are happy? Are there not elements of deeper gravity and stability in happiness, in a single moment of repose, than in the whirlwind of passion? Is it not then that we at last behold the march of time — ay, and of many another on-stealing besides, more secret still — is it not then that the hours rush forward? Are not deeper chords set vibrating by all these things than by the dagger-stroke of conventional drama? Is it not at the very moment when a man believes himself secure from bodily death that the strange and silent tragedy of the being and the immensities does indeed raise its curtain on the stage? Is it while I flee before a naked sword that my existence touches its most interesting point? Is life always at its sublimest in a kiss? Are there not other moments, when one hears purer voices that do not fade away so soon? Does the soul only flower on nights of storm? Hitherto, doubtless, this belief has prevailed. It is only the life of violence, the life of bygone days, that is perceived by nearly all our tragic writers; and truly may one say that anachronism dominates the stage, and that dramatic art dates back as many years as the art of sculpture. Far different is it with the other arts — with painting and music, for instance — for these have learned to select and reproduce those obscurer phases of daily life that are not the less deep-rooted and amazing. They know that all that life has lost, as regards mere superficial ornament, has been more than counterbalanced by the depth, the intimate meaning and the spiritual gravity it has acquired. The true artist no longer chooses Marius triumphing over the Cimbrians, or the assassination of the Duke of Guise, as fit subjects for his art; for he is well aware that the psychology of victory or murder is but elementary and exceptional, and that the solemn voice of men and things, the voice that issues forth so timidly and hesitatingly, cannot be heard amidst the idle uproar of acts of violence. And therefore will he place on his canvas a house lost in the heart of the country, an open door at the end of a passage, a face or hands at rest, and by these simple images will he add to our consciousness of life, which is a possession that it is no longer possible to lose.

But to the tragic author, as to the mediocre painter who still lingers over historical pictures, it is only the violence of the anecdote that appeals, and in his representation thereof does the entire interest of his work consist. And he imagines, forsooth, that we shall delight in witnessing the very same acts that brought joy to the hearts of the barbarians, with whom murder, outrage and treachery were matters of daily occurrence. Whereas it is far away from bloodshed, battle-cry and sword-thrust that the lives of most of us flow on, and men's tears are silent today, and invisible, and almost spiritual. . . .*

Indeed, when I go to a theatre, I feel as though I were spending a few hours with my ancestors, who conceived life as something that was primitive, arid, and brutal; but this conception of theirs scarcely even lingers in my

---

* The ellipses throughout this essay are Maeterlinck's.

The Tragical in Daily Life

memory, and surely it is not one that I can share. I am shown a deceived husband killing his wife, a woman poisoning her lover, a son avenging his father, a father slaughtering his children, children putting their father to death, murdered kings, ravished virgins, imprisoned citizens — in a word, all the sublimity of tradition, but alas, how superficial and material! Blood, surface tears, and death! What can I learn from creatures who have but one fixed idea, and who have no time to live, for there is a rival, or a mistress, whom it behooves them to put to death?

I had hoped to be shown some act of life, traced back to its sources and to its mystery by connecting links, that my daily occupations afford me neither power nor occasion to study. I had gone there hoping that the beauty, the grandeur, and the earnestness of my humble day-by-day existence would, for one instant, be revealed to me, that I would be shown the I know not what presence, power, or God that is ever with me in my room. I was yearning for one of the strange moments of a higher life that flit unperceived through my dreariest hours; whereas, almost invariably, all that I beheld was but a man who would tell me, at wearisome length, why he was jealous, why he poisoned, or why he killed.

I admire Othello, but he does not appear to me to live the august daily life of a Hamlet, who has the time to live, inasmuch as he does not act. Othello is admirably jealous. But is it not perhaps an ancient error to imagine that it is at the moments when this passion, or others of equal violence, possesses us, that we live our truest lives? I have grown to believe that an old man, seated in his armchair, waiting patiently, with his lamp beside him; giving unconscious ear to all the eternal laws that reign about his house, interpreting, without comprehending, the silence of doors and windows and the quivering voice of the light, submitting with bent head to the presence of his soul and his destiny — an old man, who conceives not that all the powers of this world, like so many heedful servants, are mingling and keeping vigil in his room, who suspects not that the very sun itself is supporting in space the little table against which he leans, or that every star in heaven and every fiber of the soul are directly concerned in the movement of an eyelid that closes, or a thought that springs to birth — I have grown to believe that he, motionless as he is, does yet live in reality a deeper, more human, and more universal life than the lover who strangles his mistress, the captain who conquers in battle, or "the husband who avenges his honor."

I shall be told, perhaps, that a motionless life would be invisible, that therefore animation must be conferred upon it, and movement, and that such varied movement as would be acceptable is to be found only in the few passions of which use has hitherto been made. I do not know whether it be true that a static theatre is impossible. Indeed, to me it seems to exist already. Most of the tragedies of Aeschylus are tragedies without movement. In both the *Prometheus* and the *Suppliants,* events are lacking; and the entire tragedy of the *Choephori* — surely the most terrible drama of antiquity — does but cling, nightmarelike, around the tomb of Agamemnon, till murder darts forth, as a lightning flash, from the accumulation of prayers, ever falling back upon themselves. Consider, from this point of view, a few more of the finest tragedies of the ancients: *The Eumenides, Antigone, Electra, Oedipus at Colonus.* "They have admired," said Racine in his preface to *Berenice*, "they have admired the *Ajax* of Sophocles, wherein there is nothing but Ajax killing himself with regret for the fury into which he fell after the arms of Achilles were denied him. They have admired *Philoctetes*, whose entire subject is but the coming of Ulysses with intent to seize the arrows of Hercules. Even the *Oedipus*, though full of recognitions, contains less subject matter than the simplest tragedy of our days."

What have we here but life that is almost motionless? In most cases, indeed, you will find that psychological action — infinitely loftier in itself than mere material action, and truly, one might think, well-nigh indispensable — that psychological action even has been suppressed, or at least vastly diminished, in a truly marvelous fashion, with the result that the interest centers solely and entirely in the individual, face to face with the universe. Here we are no longer with the barbarians, nor is man now fretting himself in the midst of elementary passions, as though, forsooth, these were the only things worthy of note: he is at rest, and we have time to observe him. It is no longer a violent, exceptional moment of life that passes before our eyes — it is life itself. Thousands and thousands of laws there are, mightier and more venerable than those of passion; but, in common with all that is endowed with resistless force, these laws are silent, and discreet, and slow-moving; and hence it is only in the twilight that they can be seen and heard, in the meditation that comes to us at the tranquil moments of life.

When Ulysses and Neoptolemus come to Philoctetes and demand of him the arms of Hercules, their action is in itself as simple and ordinary as that of a man of our day who goes into a house to visit an invalid, of a traveler who knocks at the door of an inn, or of a mother who, by the fireside, awaits the return of her child. Sophocles indicates the character of his heroes by means of the lightest and quickest of touches. But it may safely be said that the chief interest of the tragedy does not lie in the struggle we witness between cunning and loyalty, between love of country, rancor, and headstrong pride. There is more beyond: for it is man's loftier existence that is laid bare to us. The poet adds to ordinary life something, I know not what, which is the poet's secret: and there comes to us a sudden revelation of life in its stupendous grandeur, in its submissiveness to the unknown powers, in its endless affinities, in its awe-inspiring misery. Let but the chemist pour a few mysterious drops into a vessel that seems to contain the purest water, and at once masses of crystals will rise to the surface, thus revealing to us all that lay in abeyance there where nothing was visible before to our incomplete eyes. And even thus is it in *Philoctetes*; the primitive psychology of the three leading characters would seem to be merely the sides of the vessel containing the clear water; and this itself is our ordinary life, into which the poet is about to let fall the revelation-bearing drops of his genius. . . .

Indeed, it is not in the actions but in the words that are found the beauty and greatness of tragedies that are truly beautiful and great; and this not solely in the words that accompany and explain the action, for there must perforce be another dialogue besides the one which is superficially necessary. And indeed the only words that count in the play are those that at first seemed useless, for it is therein that the essence lies. Side by side with the necessary dialogue will you almost always find another dialogue that seems superfluous; but examine it carefully, and it will be borne home to you that this is the only one that the soul can listen to profoundly, for here alone is it the soul that is being addressed. You will see, too, that it is the quality and the scope of this unnecessary dialogue that determine the quality and the immeasurable range of the work. Certain it is that, in the ordinary drama, the indispensable dialogue by no means corresponds to reality; and it is just those words that are spoken by the side of the rigid, apparent truth, that constitute the mysterious beauty of the most beautiful tragedies, inasmuch as these are words that conform to a deeper truth, and one that lies incomparably nearer to the invisible soul by which the poem is upheld. One may even affirm that a poem draws the nearer to beauty and loftier truth in the measure that it eliminates words that merely explain the action, and substitutes for them others that reveal, not the so-called "soul-state," but I know not what intangible and unceasing striving of the soul toward its own beauty and truth. And so much the nearer, also, does it draw to the true life. To every man does it happen, in his workaday existence, that some situation of deep seriousness has to be unraveled by means of words. Reflect for an instant. At moments such as those — nay, at the most commonplace of times — is it the thing you say or the reply you receive that has the most value? Are not other forces, other words one cannot hear, brought into being, and do not these determine the event? What I say often counts for so little; but my presence, the attitude of my soul, my future and my past, that which will take birth in me and that which is dead, a secret thought, the stars that approve, my destiny, the thousands of mysteries which surround me and float about yourself — all this it is that speaks to you at that tragic moment, all this it is that brings to me your answer. There is all this beneath every one of my words, and each one of yours; it is this, above all, that we see, it is this above all, that we hear, ourselves notwithstanding. If you have come, you, the "outraged husband," the "deceived lover," the "forsaken wife," intending to kill me, your arm will not be stayed by my most moving entreaty; but it may be that there will come toward you, at that moment, one of these unexpected forces; and my soul, knowing of their vigil near to me, may whisper a secret word whereby, haply, you shall be disarmed. These are the spheres wherein adventures come to issue, this is the dialogue whose echo should be heard. And it is this echo that one does hear — extremely attenuated and variable, it is true — in some of the great works mentioned above. But might we not try to draw nearer to the spheres where it is "in reality" that everything comes to pass?

It would seem as though the endeavor were being made. Some time ago, when dealing with *The Master Builder*, which is the one of Ibsen's dramas wherein this dialogue of the "second degree" attains the deepest tragedy, I endeavored, unskillfully enough, to fix its secrets. For indeed they are kindred handmarks traced on the same wall by the same sightless being, groping for the same light. "What is it," I asked, "what is it that, in *The Master Builder*, the poet has added to life, thereby making it appear so strange, so profound, and so disquieting beneath its trivial surface?" The discovery is not easy, and the old master hides from us more than one secret. It would even seem as though what he has wished to say were but little by the side of what he has been compelled to say. He has freed certain powers of the soul that have never yet been free, and it may well be that these have held him in thrall. "Look you, Hilda," exclaims Solness, "look you! There is sorcery in you, too, as there is in me. It is this sorcery that imposes action on the powers of the beyond. And we *have* to yield to it. Whether we want to or not, we *must*."

There is sorcery in them, as in us all. Hilda and Solness are, I believe, the first characters in drama who feel, for an instant, that they are living in the atmosphere of the soul; and the discovery of this essential life that exists in them, beyond the life of every day, comes fraught with terror. Hilda and Solness are two souls to whom a flash has revealed their situation in the true life. Diverse ways there are by which knowledge of our fellows may come to us. Two or three men, perhaps, are seen by me almost daily. For a long time it is merely by their gestures that I distinguish them, by their habits, be these of mind or body, by the manner in which they feel, act, or think. But, in the course of every friendship of some duration, there comes to us a mysterious moment when we seem to perceive the exact relationship of our friend to the unknown that surrounds him, when we discover the attitude destiny has assumed toward him. And it is from this moment that he truly belongs to us. We have seen, once and for all, the treatment held in store for him by events. We know that however such a one may seclude himself in the recesses of his dwelling, in dread lest his slightest movement stir up that which lies in the great reservoirs of the future, his forethought will avail him nothing, and the innumerable events that destiny holds in reserve will discover him wherever he hides, and will knock one after another at his door. And even so do we know that this other will sally forth in vain in pursuit of adventure. He will ever return emptyhanded. No sooner are our eyes thus opened than unerring knowledge would seem to spring to life, self-created, within our soul; and we know with absolute conviction that the event that seems to be impending over the head of a certain man will nevertheless most assuredly not reach him.

From this moment a special part of the soul reigns over the friendship of even the most unintelligent, the obscurest of men. Life has become, as it were, transposed. And when it happens that we meet one of the men who are thus known to us, though we do but speak of the snow that is falling or the women that pass by, something there is in each of us which nods to the other, which examines and asks its questions without our knowledge, which interests itself in contingencies and hints at events that it is impossible for us to understand. . . .

Thus do I conceive it to be with Hilda and Solness; it is thus surely that they regard each other. Their conversation resembles nothing that we have ever heard, inasmuch as the poet has endeavored to blend in one expression both the inner and the outer dialogue. A new, indescribable power dominates this somnambulistic drama. All that is said therein at once hides and reveals the sources of an unknown life. And if we are bewildered at times, let us not forget that our soul appears to our feeble eyes to be but the maddest of forces, and that there are in man many regions more fertile, more profound, and more interesting than those of his reason or his intelligence. . . .

Translated by Richard Hovey

Pelléas and Mélisande

PERSONS

ARKËL, *King of Allemonde*
GENEVIÈVE, *mother of Pelléas and Golaud*
PELLÉAS, } *grandsons of Arkël*
GOLAUD, }
MÉLISANDE

LITTLE YNIOLD, *son of Golaud (by a former marriage)*
A PHYSICIAN
THE PORTER
Servants, Beggars, etc.

ACT FIRST

SCENE I. — *The gate of the castle.*

MAIDSERVANTS (*within*). Open the gate! Open the gate!
PORTER (*within*). Who is there? Why do you come and wake me up? Go out by the little gates; there are enough of them!
A MAIDSERVANT (*within*). We have come to wash the threshold, the gate, and the steps; open, then! open!
ANOTHER MAIDSERVANT (*within*). There are going to be great happenings!
THIRD MAIDSERVANT (*within*). There are going to be great fêtes! Open quickly! . . .
THE MAIDSERVANTS. Open! open!
PORTER. Wait! wait! I do not know whether I shall be able to open it; . . . it is never opened. . . . Wait till it is light. . . .
FIRST MAIDSERVANT. It is light enough without; I see the sunlight through the chinks. . . .
PORTER. Here are the great keys. . . . Oh! oh! how the bolts and the locks grate! . . . Help me! help me! . . .
MAIDSERVANTS. We are pulling; we are pulling. . . .
SECOND MAIDSERVANT. It will not open. . . .
FIRST MAIDSERVANT. Ah, ah! It is opening! it is opening slowly!
PORTER. How it shrieks! how it shrieks! It will wake up everybody. . . .
SECOND MAIDSERVANT (*appearing on the threshold*). Oh, how light it is already out of doors!

FIRST MAIDSERVANT. The sun is rising on the sea!
PORTER. It is open. . . . It is wide open! . . .
All the maidservants appear on the threshold and pass over it.
FIRST MAIDSERVANT. I am going to wash the sill first. . . .
SECOND MAIDSERVANT. We shall never be able to clean all this.
OTHER MAIDSERVANTS. Fetch the water! fetch the water!
PORTER. Yes, yes; pour on water; pour on water; pour on all the water of the Flood! You will never come to the end of it. . . .

Scene II. — *A forest.*

MÉLISANDE *discovered at the brink of a spring.*
Enter GOLAUD.

GOLAUD. I shall never be able to get out of this forest again. — God knows where that beast has led me. And yet I thought I had wounded him to death; and here are traces of blood. But now I have lost sight of him; I believe I am lost myself — my dogs can no longer find me — I shall retrace my steps. . . . — I hear weeping . . . Oh! oh! what is there yonder by the water's edge? . . . A little girl weeping by the water's edge? (*He coughs.*) — She does not hear me. I cannot see her face. (*He approaches and touches* MÉLISANDE *on the shoulder.*) Why weepest thou? (MÉLISANDE *trembles, starts up, and would flee.*) — Do not be afraid. You have nothing to fear. Why are you weeping here all alone?
MÉLISANDE. Do not touch me! do not touch me!
GOLAUD. Do not be afraid. . . . I will not do you any . . . Oh, you are beautiful!
MÉLISANDE. Do not touch me! do not touch me! or I throw myself in the water! . . .
GOLAUD. I will not touch you. . . . See, I will stay here, against the tree. Do not be afraid. Has any one hurt you?
MÉLISANDE. Oh! yes! yes! yes! . . . (*She sobs profoundly.*)
GOLAUD. Who has hurt you?
MÉLISANDE. Every one! every one!
GOLAUD. What hurt have they done you?
MÉLISANDE. I will not tell! I cannot tell! . . .
GOLAUD. Come; do not weep so. Whence come you?
MÉLISANDE. I have fled! . . . fled . . . fled. . . .
GOLAUD. Yes; but whence have you fled?
MÉLISANDE. I am lost! . . . lost! . . . Oh! oh! lost here. . . . I am not of this place. . . . I was not born here. . . .
GOLAUD. Whence are you? Where were you born?
MÉLISANDE. Oh! oh! far away from here! . . . far away . . . far away. . . .
GOLAUD. What is it shining so at the bottom of the water?

MÉLISANDE. Where? — Ah! it is the crown he gave me. It fell as I was weeping. . . .

GOLAUD. A crown? — Who was it gave you a crown? — I will try to get it. . . .

MÉLISANDE. No, no; I will have no more of it! I will have no more of it! . . . I had rather die . . . die at once. . . .

GOLAUD. I could easily pull it out. The water is not very deep.

MÉLISANDE. I will have no more of it! If you take it out, I throw myself in its place!

GOLAUD. No, no! I will leave it there. It could be reached without difficulty, nevertheless. It seems very beautiful. — Is it long since you fled?

MÉLISANDE. Yes, yes! . . . Who are you?

GOLAUD. I am Prince Golaud — grandson of Arkël, the old King of Allemonde. . . .

MÉLISANDE. Oh, you have gray hairs already. . . .

GOLAUD. Yes; some, here, by the temples.

MÉLISANDE. And in your beard, too. . . . Why do you look at me so?

GOLAUD. I am looking at your eyes. — Do you never shut your eyes?

MÉLISANDE. Oh, yes; I shut them at night.

GOLAUD. Why do you look so astonished?

MÉLISANDE. You are a giant?

GOLAUD. I am a man like the rest. . . .

MÉLISANDE. Why have you come here?

GOLAUD. I do not know, myself. I was hunting in the forest. I was chasing a wild boar. I mistook the road. — You look very young. How old are you?

MÉLISANDE. I am beginning to be cold. . . .

GOLAUD. Will you come with me?

MÉLISANDE. No, no; I will stay here. . . .

GOLAUD. You cannot stay here all alone. You cannot stay here all night long. . . . What is your name?

MÉLISANDE. Mélisande.

GOLAUD. You cannot stay here, Mélisande. Come with me. . . .

MÉLISANDE. I will stay here. . . .

GOLAUD. You will be afraid, all alone. We do not know what there may be here . . . all night long . . . all alone . . . it is impossible. Mélisande, come, give me your hand. . . .

MÉLISANDE. Oh, do not touch me! . . .

GOLAUD. Do not scream. . . . I will not touch you again. But come with me. The night will be very dark and very cold. Come with me. . . .

MÉLISANDE. Where are you going? . . .

GOLAUD. I do not know. . . . I am lost too. . . .

(*Exeunt.*)

Scene III. — *A hall in the castle.*

ARKËL *and* GENEVIÈVE *discovered.*

GENEVIÈVE. Here is what he writes to his brother, Pelléas: "I found her all in tears one evening, beside a spring in the forest where I had lost myself. I do not know her age, nor who she is, nor whence she comes, and I dare not question her, for she must have had a sore fright; and when you ask her what has happened to her, she falls at once a-weeping like a child, and sobs so heavily you are afraid. Just as I found her by the spring, a crown of gold had slipped from her hair and fallen to the bottom of the water. She was clad, besides, like a princess, though her garments had been torn by the briers. It is now six months since I married her and I know no more about it than on the day of our meeting. Meanwhile, dear Pelléas, thou whom I love more than a brother, although we were not born of the same father; meanwhile make ready for my return. . . . I know my mother will willingly forgive me. But I am afraid of the King, our venerable grandsire, I am afraid of Arkël, in spite of all his kindness, for I have undone by this strange marriage all his plans of state, and I fear the beauty of Mélisande will not excuse my folly to eyes so wise as his. If he consents nevertheless to receive her as he would receive his own daughter, the third night following this letter, light a lamp at the top of the tower that overlooks the sea. I shall perceive it from the bridge of our ship; otherwise I shall go far away again and come back no more. . . ." What say you of it?

ARKËL. Nothing. He has done what he probably must have done. I am very old, and nevertheless I have not yet seen clearly for one moment into myself; how would you that I judge what others have done? I am not far from the tomb and do not succeed in judging myself. . . . One always mistakes when one does not close his eyes. That may seem strange to us; but that is all. He is past the age to marry and he weds, like a child, a little girl he finds by a spring. . . . That may seem strange to us, because we never see but the reverse of destinies . . . the reverse even of our own. . . . He has always followed my counsels hitherto; I had thought to make him happy in sending him to ask the hand of Princess Ursula. . . . He could not remain alone; since the death of his wife he has been sad to be alone; and that marriage would have put an end to long wars and old hatreds. . . . He would not have it so. Let it be as he would have it; I have never put myself athwart a destiny; and he knows better than I his future. There happen perhaps no useless events. . . .

GENEVIÈVE. He has always been so prudent, so grave, and so firm. . . . If it were Pelléas, I should understand. . . . But he . . . at his age. . . . Who is it he is going to introduce here? — An unknown found along the roads. . . . Since his wife's death, he has no longer lived for aught but his son, the little Yniold, and if he were about to marry again, it was because you had wished it. . . . And now . . . a little girl in the forest. . . . He has forgotten everything. . . . What shall we do? . . .

Enter PELLÉAS.

ARKËL. Who is coming in there?

GENEVIÈVE. It is Pelléas. He has been weeping.

ARKËL. Is it thou, Pelléas? — Come a little nearer, that I may see thee in the light. . . .

PELLÉAS. Grandfather, I received another letter at the same time as my brother's; a letter from my friend Marcellus. . . . He is about to die and calls for me. He would see me before dying. . . .

ARKËL. Thou wouldst leave before thy brother's return? — Perhaps thy friend is less ill than he thinks. . . .

PELLÉAS. His letter is so sad you can see death between the lines. . . . He says he knows the very day when death must come. . . . He tells me I can arrive before it if I will, but that there is no more time to lose. The journey is very long, and if I wait Golaud's return, it will be perhaps too late.

ARKËL. Thou must wait a little while, nevertheless. . . . We do not know what this return has in store for us. And besides, is not thy father here, above us, more sick perhaps than thy friend? . . . Couldst thou choose between the father and the friend? . . . (*Exit.*)

GENEVIÈVE. Have a care to keep the lamp lit from this evening, Pelléas. . . .
(*Exeunt severally.*)

SCENE IV. — *Before the castle.*

Enter GENEVIÈVE *and* MÉLISANDE.

MÉLISANDE. It is gloomy in the gardens. And what forests, what forests all about the palaces! . . .

GENEVIÈVE. Yes; that astonished me too when I came hither; it astonishes everybody. There are places where you never see the sun. But one gets used to it so quickly. . . . It is long ago, it is long ago. . . . It is nearly forty years that I have lived here. . . . Look toward the other side, you will have the light of the sea.

MÉLISANDE. I hear a noise below us. . . .

GENEVIÈVE. Yes; it is some one coming up toward us. . . . Ah! it is Pelléas. . . . He seems still tired from having waited so long for you. . . .

MÉLISANDE. He has not seen us.

GENEVIÈVE. I think he has seen us but does not know what he should do. . . . Pelléas, Pelléas, is it thou? . . .

Enter PELLÉAS.

PELLÉAS. Yes! . . . I was coming toward the sea. . . .

GENEVIÈVE. So were we; we were seeking the light. It is a little lighter here than elsewhere; and yet the sea is gloomy.

PELLÉAS. We shall have a storm tonight. There has been one every night for some time, and yet it is so calm now. . . . One might embark unwittingly and come back no more.

MÉLISANDE. Something is leaving the port.

PELLÉAS. It must be a big ship. . . . The lights are very high, we shall see it in a moment, when it enters the band of light. . . .

GENEVIÈVE. I do not know whether we shall be able to see it . . . there is still a fog on the sea. . . .

PELLÉAS. The fog seems to be rising slowly.

MÉLISANDE. Yes; I see a little light down there, which I had not seen. . . .

PELLÉAS. It is a lighthouse; there are others we cannot see yet.

MÉLISANDE. The ship is in the light. . . . It is already very far away. . . .

PELLÉAS. It is a foreign ship. It looks larger than ours. . . .

MÉLISANDE. It is the ship that brought me here! . . .

PELLÉAS. It flies away under full sail. . . .

MÉLISANDE. It is the ship that brought me here. It has great sails. . . . I recognized it by its sails.

PELLÉAS. There will be a rough sea tonight.

MÉLISANDE. Why does it go away tonight? . . . You can hardly see it any longer. . . . Perhaps it will be wrecked. . . .

PELLÉAS. The night falls very quickly. . . .

A silence.

GENEVIÈVE. No one speaks any more? . . . You have nothing more to say to each other? . . . It is time to go in. Pelléas, show Mélisande the way. I must go see little Yniold a moment. (*Exit.*)

PELLÉAS. Nothing can be seen any longer on the sea. . . .

MÉLISANDE. I see more lights.

PELLÉAS. It is the other lighthouses. . . . Do you hear the sea? . . . It is the wind rising. . . . Let us go down this way. Will you give me your hand?

MÉLISANDE. See, see, my hands are full. . . .

PELLÉAS. I will hold you by the arm, the road is steep and it is very gloomy there. . . . I am going away perhaps tomorrow. . . .

MÉLISANDE. Oh! . . . why do you go away? (*Exeunt.*)

ACT SECOND

SCENE I. — *A fountain in the park.*

Enter PELLÉAS *and* MÉLISANDE.

PELLÉAS. You do not know where I have brought you? — I often come to sit here, toward noon, when it is too hot in the gardens. It is stifling today, even in the shade of the trees.

MÉLISANDE. Oh, how clear the water is! . . .

PELLÉAS. It is as cool as winter. It is an old abandoned spring. It seems to have been a miraculous spring — it opened the eyes of the blind — they still call it "Blind Man's Spring."

MÉLISANDE. It no longer opens the eyes of the blind?

PELLÉAS. Since the King has been nearly blind himself, no one comes any more. . . .

MÉLISANDE. How alone one is here! . . . There is no sound.

PELLÉAS. There is always a wonderful silence here. . . . One could hear the water sleep. . . . Will you sit down on the edge of the marble basin? There is one linden where the sun never comes. . . .

MÉLISANDE. I am going to lie down on the marble. — I should like to see the bottom of the water. . . .

PELLÉAS. No one has ever seen it. — It is as deep, perhaps, as the sea. — It is not known whence it comes. — Perhaps it comes from the bottom of the earth. . . .

MÉLISANDE. If there were anything shining at the bottom, perhaps one could see it. . . .

PELLÉAS. Do not lean over so. . . .

MÉLISANDE. I would like to touch the water. . . .

PELLÉAS. Have a care of slipping. . . . I will hold your hand. . . .

MÉLISANDE. No, no, I would plunge both hands in it. . . . You would say my hands were sick today. . . .

PELLÉAS. Oh! oh! take care! take care! Mélisande! . . . Mélisande! . . . — Oh! your hair! . . .

MÉLISANDE (*starting upright*). I cannot, . . . I cannot reach it. . . .

PELLÉAS. Your hair dipped in the water. . . .

MÉLISANDE. Yes, it is longer than my arms. . . . It is longer than I. . . .

    A *silence.*

PELLÉAS. It was at the brink of a spring, too, that he found you?

MÉLISANDE. Yes. . . .

PELLÉAS. What did he say to you?

MÉLISANDE. Nothing; — I no longer remember. . . .

PELLÉAS. Was he quite near you?

MÉLISANDE. Yes; he would have kissed me.

PELLÉAS. And you would not?

MÉLISANDE. No.

PELLÉAS. Why would you not?

MÉLISANDE. Oh! oh! I saw something pass at the bottom of the water. . . .

PELLÉAS. Take care! take care! — You will fall! What are you playing with?

MÉLISANDE. With the ring he gave me. . . .

PELLÉAS. Take care; you will lose it. . . .

MÉLISANDE. No, no; I am sure of my hands. . . .

PELLÉAS. Do not play so, over so deep a water. . . .

MÉLISANDE. My hands do not tremble.

PELLÉAS. How it shines in the sunlight! — Do not throw it so high in the air. . . .
MÉLISANDE. Oh! . . .
PELLÉAS. It has fallen?
MÉLISANDE. It has fallen into the water!
PELLÉAS. Where is it? where is it? . . .
MÉLISANDE. I do not see it sink. . . .
PELLÉAS. I think I see it shine. . . .
MÉLISANDE. My ring?
PELLÉAS. Yes, yes; down yonder. . . .
MÉLISANDE. Oh! oh! It is so far away from us! . . . no, no, that is not it . . . that is not it . . . It is lost . . . lost. . . . There is nothing any more but a great circle on the water. . . . What shall we do? What shall we do now? . . .
PELLÉAS. You need not be so troubled for a ring. It is nothing. . . . We shall find it again, perhaps. Or else we will find another.
MÉLISANDE. No, no; we shall never find it again; we shall never find any others either. . . . And yet I thought I had it in my hands. . . . I had already shut my hands, and it is fallen in spite of all. . . . I threw it too high, toward the sun. . . .
PELLÉAS. Come, come, we will come back another day; . . . come, it is time. They will come to meet us. It was striking noon at the moment the ring fell.
MÉLISANDE. What shall we say to Golaud if he ask where it is?
PELLÉAS. The truth, the truth, the truth. . . . (*Exeunt.*)

SCENE II. — *An apartment in the castle.*

GOLAUD *discovered, stretched upon his bed;* MÉLISANDE, *by his bedside.*
GOLAUD. Ah! ah! all goes well; it will amount to nothing. But I cannot understand how it came to pass. I was hunting quietly in the forest. All at once my horse ran away, without cause. Did he see anything unusual? . . . I had just heard the twelve strokes of noon. At the twelfth stroke he suddenly took fright and ran like a blind madman against a tree. I heard no more. I do not yet know what happened. I fell, and he must have fallen on me. I thought I had the whole forest on my breast; I thought my heart was crushed. But my heart is sound. It is nothing, apparently. . . .
MÉLISANDE. Would you like a little water?
GOLAUD. Thanks, thanks; I am not thirsty.
MÉLISANDE. Would you like another pillow? . . . There is a little spot of blood on this.
GOLAUD. No, no; it is not worth while. I bled at the mouth just now. I shall bleed again perhaps. . . .
MÉLISANDE. Are you quite sure? . . . You are not suffering too much?
GOLAUD. No, no; I have seen a good many more like this. I was made of

iron and blood. . . . These are not the little bones of a child; do not alarm yourself. . . .

MÉLISANDE. Close your eyes and try to sleep. I shall stay here all night. . . .

GOLAUD. No, no; I do not wish you to tire yourself so. I do not need anything; I shall sleep like a child. . . . What is the matter, Mélisande? Why do you weep all at once?

MÉLISANDE (*bursting into tears*). I am . . . I am ill too. . . .

GOLAUD. Thou art ill? . . . What ails thee, then; what ails thee, Mélisande? . . .

MÉLISANDE. I do not know. . . . I am ill here. . . . I had rather tell you today; my lord, my lord, I am not happy here. . . .

GOLAUD. Why, what has happened, Mélisande? What is it? . . . And I suspecting nothing. . . . What has happened? . . . Some one has done thee harm? . . . Some one has given thee offense?

MÉLISANDE. No, no; no one has done me the least harm. . . . It is not that. . . . It is not that. . . . But I can live here no longer. I do not know why. . . . I would go away, go away! . . . I shall die if I am left here.

GOLAUD. But something has happened? You must be hiding something from me? . . . Tell me the whole truth, Mélisande. . . . Is it the King? . . . Is it my mother? . . . Is it Pelléas? . . .

MÉLISANDE. No, no; it is not Pelléas. It is not anybody. . . . You could not understand me. . . .

GOLAUD. Why should I not understand? . . . If you tell me nothing, what will you have me do? . . . Tell me everything and I shall understand everything.

MÉLISANDE. I do not know myself what it is. . . . I do not know just what it is. . . . If I could tell you, I would tell you. . . . It is something stronger than I. . . .

GOLAUD. Come; be reasonable, Mélisande. — What would you have me do? — You are no longer a child. — Is it I whom you would leave?

MÉLISANDE. Oh! no, no; it is not that. . . . I would go away with you. . . . It is here that I can live no longer. . . . I feel that I shall not live a long while. . . .

GOLAUD. But there must be a reason, nevertheless. You will be thought mad. It will be thought child's dreams. — Come, is it Pelléas, perhaps? — I think he does not often speak to you.

MÉLISANDE. Yes, yes; he speaks to me sometimes. I think he does not like me; I have seen it in his eyes. . . . But he speaks to me when he meets me. . . .

GOLAUD. You must not take it ill of him. He has always been so. He is a little strange. And just now he is sad; he thinks of his friend Marcellus, who is at the point of death, and whom he cannot go to see. . . . He will change, he will change, you will see; he is young. . . .

MÉLISANDE. But it is not that . . . it is not that. . . .

GOLAUD. What is it, then? — Can you not get used to the life one leads here? Is it too gloomy here? — It is true the castle is very old and very somber. . . . It is very cold, and very deep. And all those who dwell in it are already old. And the country may seem gloomy too, with all its forests, all its old forests without light. But that may all be enlivened if we will. And then, joy, joy: one does not have it every day; we must take things as they come. But tell me something; no matter what; I will do everything you could wish. . . .

MÉLISANDE. Yes, yes; it is true. . . . You never see the sky here. I saw it for the first time this morning. . . .

GOLAUD. It is that, then, that makes you weep, my poor Mélisande? — It is only that, then? — You weep, not to see the sky? — Come, come, you are no longer at the age when one may weep for such things. . . . And then, is not the summer yonder? You will see the sky every day. — And then, next year. . . . Come, give me your hand; give me both your little hands. (*He takes her hands.*) Oh! oh! these little hands that I could crush like flowers. . . . — Hold! where is the ring I gave you?

MÉLISANDE. The ring?

GOLAUD. Yes; our wedding-ring, where is it?

MÉLISANDE. I think . . . I think it has fallen. . . .

GOLAUD. Fallen? — Where has it fallen? — You have not lost it?

MÉLISANDE. No, no; it fell . . . it must have fallen . . . but I know where it is. . . .

GOLAUD. Where is it?

MÉLISANDE. You know . . . you know well . . . the grotto by the sea-shore? . . .

GOLAUD. Yes.

MÉLISANDE. Well then, it is there. . . . It must be it is there. . . . Yes, yes; I remember. . . . I went there this morning to pick up shells for little Yniold. . . . There were some very fine ones. . . . It slipped from my finger. . . . then the sea came in; and I had to go out before I had found it.

GOLAUD. Are you sure it is there?

MÉLISANDE. Yes, yes; quite sure. . . . I felt it slip . . . then, all at once, the noise of the waves. . . .

GOLAUD. You must go look for it at once.

MÉLISANDE. I must go look for it at once?

GOLAUD. Yes.

MÉLISANDE. Now? — at once? — in the dark?

GOLAUD. Now, at once, in the dark. You must go look for it at once. I had rather have lost all I have than have lost that ring. You do not know what it is. You do not know whence it came. The sea will be very high tonight. The sea will come to take it before you. . . . Make haste. You must go look for it at once. . . .

MÉLISANDE. I dare not. . . . I dare not go alone. . . .

GOLAUD. Go, go with no matter whom. But you must go at once, do you understand? — Make haste; ask Pelléas to go with you.

MÉLISANDE. Pelléas? — With Pelléas? — But Pelléas would not. . . .

GOLAUD. Pelléas will do all you ask of him. I know Pelléas better than you do. Go, go; hurry! I shall not sleep until I have the ring.

MÉLISANDE. Oh! oh! I am not happy! . . . I am not happy! . . .

(*Exit, weeping.*)

SCENE III. — *Before a grotto.*

Enter PELLÉAS *and* MÉLISANDE.

PELLÉAS (*speaking with great agitation*). Yes; it is here; we are there. It is so dark you cannot tell the entrance of the grotto from the rest of the night. . . . There are no stars on this side. Let us wait till the moon has torn through that great cloud; it will light up the whole grotto, and then we can enter without danger. There are dangerous places, and the path is very narrow between two lakes whose bottom has not yet been found. I did not think to bring a torch or a lantern, but I think the light of the sky will be enough for us. — You have never gone into this grotto?

MÉLISANDE. No. . . .

PELLÉAS. Let us go in; let us go in. . . . You must be able to describe the place where you lost the ring, if he questions you. . . . It is very big and very beautiful. There are stalactites that look like plants and men. It is full of blue darks. It has not yet been explored to the end. There are great treasures hidden there, it seems. You will see the remains of ancient shipwrecks there. But you must not go far in it without a guide. There have been some who never have come back. I myself dare not go forward too far. We will stop the moment we no longer see the light of the sea or the sky. When you strike a little light there, you would say the vault was covered with stars like the sky. It is bits of crystal or salt, they say, that shine so in the rock. — Look, look, I think the sky is going to clear. . . . Give me your hand; do not tremble, do not tremble so. There is no danger; we will stop the moment we no longer see the light of the sea. . . . Is it the noise of the grotto that frightens you? It is the noise of the night or the noise of silence. . . . Do you hear the sea behind us? — It does not seem happy tonight. . . . Ah! look, the light! . . .

The moon lights up abundantly the entrance and part of the darkness of the grotto; and at a certain depth are seen three old beggars with white hair, seated side by side, leaning upon each other and asleep against a boulder.

MÉLISANDE. Ah!

PELLÉAS. What is it?

MÉLISANDE. There are . . . there are . . . (*She points out the three beggars.*)

PELLÉAS. Yes, yes; I have seen them too. . . .

MÉLISANDE. Let us go! . . . Let us go! . . .

PELLÉAS. Yes . . . it is three old poor men fallen asleep. . . . There is a famine in the country. . . . Why have they come to sleep here? . . .

MÉLISANDE. Let us go! . . . Come, come. . . . Let us go! . . .

PELLÉAS. Take care; do not speak so loud. . . . Let us not wake them. . . . They are still sleeping heavily. . . . Come.

MÉLISANDE. Leave me, leave me; I prefer to walk alone. . . .

PELLÉAS. We will come back another day. (*Exeunt.*)

SCENE IV. — *An apartment in the castle.*

ARKËL *and* PELLÉAS *discovered.*

ARKËL. You see that everything retains you here just now and forbids you this useless journey. We have concealed your father's condition from you until now; but it is perhaps hopeless; and that alone should suffice to stop you on the threshold. But there are so many other reasons. . . . And it is not in the day when our enemies awake, and when the people are dying of hunger and murmur about us, that you have the right to desert us. And why this journey? Marcellus is dead; and life has graver duties than the visit to a tomb. You are weary, you say, of your inactive life; but activity and duty are not found on the highways. They must be waited for upon the threshold, and let in as they go by; and they go by every day. You have never seen them? I hardly see them any more myself; but I will teach you to see them, and I will point them out to you the day when you would make them a sign. Nevertheless, listen to me; if you believe it is from the depths of your life this journey is exacted, I do not forbid your undertaking it, for you must know better than I the events you must offer to your being or your fate. I shall ask you only to wait until we know what must take place ere long. . . .

PELLÉAS. How long must I wait?

ARKËL. A few weeks; perhaps a few days.

PELLÉAS. I will wait. . . .

ACT THIRD

SCENE I. — *An apartment in the castle.*

PELLÉAS *and* MÉLISANDE *discovered.* MÉLISANDE *plies her distaff at the back of the room.*

PELLÉAS. Yniold does not come back; where has he gone?

MÉLISANDE. He had heard something in the corridor; he has gone to see what it is.

PELLÉAS. Mélisande. . . .

MÉLISANDE. What is it?

PELLÉAS. Can you still see to work there? . . .

MÉLISANDE. I work as well in the dark. . . .

PELLÉAS. I think everybody is already asleep in the castle. Golaud does not come back from the chase. It is late, nevertheless. . . . He no longer suffers from his fall? . . .

MÉLISANDE. He said he no longer suffered from it.

PELLÉAS. He must be more prudent; his body is no longer as supple as at twenty years. . . . I see the stars through the window and the light of the moon on the trees. It is late; he will not come back now. (*Knocking at the door.*) Who is there? . . . Come in! . . .

Little YNIOLD *opens the door and enters the room.*

It was you knocking so? . . . That is not the way to knock at doors. It is as if a misfortune had arrived; look, you have frightened little mother.

LITTLE YNIOLD. I only knocked a tiny little bit.

PELLÉAS. It is late; little father will not come back tonight; it is time for you to go to bed.

LITTLE YNIOLD. I shall not go to bed before you do.

PELLÉAS. What? . . . What is that you are saying?

LITTLE YNIOLD. I say . . . not before you . . . not before you. . . .

Bursts into sobs and takes refuge by MÉLISANDE.

MÉLISANDE. What is it, Yniold? . . . What it is? . . . why do you weep all at once?

YNIOLD (*sobbing*). Because . . . oh! oh! because . . .

MÉLISANDE. Because what? . . . Because what? . . . Tell me. . . .

YNIOLD. Little mother . . . little mother . . . you are going away. . . .

MÉLISANDE. But what has taken hold of you, Yniold? . . . I have never dreamed of going away. . . .

YNIOLD. Yes, you have; yes, you have; little father has gone away. . . . Little father does not come back, and you are going to go away too. . . . I have seen it . . . I have seen it. . . .

MÉLISANDE. But there has never been any idea of that, Yniold. . . . Why, what makes you think that I would go away? . . .

YNIOLD. I have seen it . . . I have seen it. . . . You have said things to uncle that I could not hear . . .

PELLÉAS. He is sleepy. . . . He has been dreaming. . . . Come here, Yniold; asleep already? . . . Come and look out at the window; the swans are fighting with the dogs.

YNIOLD (*at the window*). Oh! oh! they are chasing the dogs! . . . They are chasing them! . . . Oh! oh! the water! . . . the wings . . . the wings . . . they are afraid.

PELLÉAS (*coming back by* MÉLISANDE). He is sleepy; he is struggling against sleep; his eyes were closing. . . .

MÉLISANDE (*singing softly as she spins*). Saint Daniel and Saint Michaël. . . . Saint Michaël and Saint Raphaël. . . .

YNIOLD (*at the window*). Oh! oh! little mother! . . .

MÉLISANDE (*rising abruptly*). What is it, Yniold? . . . What is it? . . .

YNIOLD. I saw something at the window . . .

PELLÉAS *and* MÉLISANDE *run to the window*

PELLÉAS. What is there at the window? . . . What have you seen? . . .

YNIOLD. Oh! oh! I saw something! . . .
PELLÉAS. But there is nothing. I see nothing. . . .
MÉLISANDE. Nor I. . . .
PELLÉAS. Where did you see something? Which way? . . .
YNIOLD. Down there, down there! . . . It is no longer there. . . .
PELLÉAS. He does not know what he is saying. He must have seen the light of the moon on the forest. There are often strange reflections, . . . or else something must have passed on the highway . . . or in his sleep. For see, see, I believe he is quite asleep. . . .
YNIOLD (*at the window*). Little father is there! little father is there!
PELLÉAS (*going to the window*). He is right; Golaud is coming into the courtyard. . . .
YNIOLD. Little father! . . . little father! . . . I am going to meet him! . . .
(*Exit, running. — A silence.*)
   Enter GOLAUD *and* LITTLE YNIOLD *with a lamp.*
GOLAUD. You are still waiting in the dark?
YNIOLD. I have brought a light, little mother, a big light! . . . (*He lifts the lamp and looks at* MÉLISANDE.) You have been weeping, little mother? . . . You have been weeping? . . . (*He lifts the lamp toward* PELLÉAS *and looks in turn at him.*) You too, you too, you have been weeping? . . . Little father, look, little father; they have both been weeping. . . .
GOLAUD. Do not hold the light under their eyes so. . . .

SCENE II. — *One of the towers of the castle.*

A *watchman's round passes under a window in the tower.*
MÉLISANDE (*at the window, combing her unbound hair*).
      My long locks fall foaming
         To the threshold of the tower, —
      My locks await your coming
         All along the tower,
         And all the long, long hour,
         And all the long, long hour.

Saint Daniel and Saint Michaël,
Saint Michaël and Saint Raphaël.

      I was born on a Sunday,
         A Sunday at high noon. . . .

   Enter PELLÉAS *by the watchman's round.*
PELLÉAS. Holà! Holà! ho! . . .
MÉLISANDE. Who is there?
PELLÉAS. I, I, and I! . . . What art thou doing there at the window, singing like a bird that is not native here?
MÉLISANDE. I am doing my hair for the night. . . .

PELLÉAS. Is it that I see upon the wall? . . . I thought you had some light. . . .

MÉLISANDE. I have opened the window; it is too hot in the tower. . . . It is beautiful tonight. . . .

PELLÉAS. There are innumerable stars; I have never seen so many as tonight; . . . but the moon is still upon the sea. . . . Do not stay in the shadow, Mélisande; lean forward a little till I see your unbound hair. . . .

MÉLISANDE. I am frightful so. (*She leans out at the window.*)

PELLÉAS. Oh! oh! Mélisande! . . . oh, thou art beautiful! . . . thou art beautiful so! . . . Lean out! lean out! . . . Let me come nearer thee . . .

MÉLISANDE. I cannot come nearer thee. . . . I am leaning out as far as I can. . . .

PELLÉAS. I cannot come up higher; . . . give me at least thy hand tonight . . . before I go away. . . . I leave tomorrow. . . .

MÉLISANDE. No, no, no! . . .

PELLÉAS. Yes, yes, yes; I leave, I shall leave tomorrow. . . . Give me thy hand, thy hand, thy little hand upon my lips. . . .

MÉLISANDE. I give thee not my hand if thou wilt leave. . . .

PELLÉAS. Give, give, give! . . .

MÉLISANDE. Thou wilt not leave? . . .

PELLÉAS. I will wait; I will wait. . . .

MÉLISANDE. I see a rose in the shadows. . . .

PELLÉAS. Where? . . . I see only the boughs of the willow hanging over the wall. . . .

MÉLISANDE. Further down, further down, in the garden; further down, in the somber green. . . .

PELLÉAS. It is not a rose. . . . I will go see by and by, but give me thy hand first; first thy hand. . . .

MÉLISANDE. There, there; . . . I cannot lean our further. . . .

PELLÉAS. I cannot reach thy hand with my lips. . . .

MÉLISANDE. I cannot lean out further. . . . I am on the point of falling. . . . Oh! oh! my hair is falling down the tower! . . .

Her tresses fall suddenly over her head as she is leaning out so, and stream over PELLÉAS.

PELLÉAS. Oh! oh! what is it? . . . Thy hair, thy hair is falling down to me! . . . All thy locks, Mélisande, all thy locks have fallen down the tower! . . . I hold them in my hands; I hold them in my mouth. . . . I hold them in my arms; I put them about my neck. . . . I will not open my hands again tonight. . . .

MÉLISANDE. Let me go! let me go! . . . Thou wilt make me fall! . . .

PELLÉAS. No, no, no; . . . I have never seen such hair as thine, Mélisande! . . . See, see, see; it comes from so high and yet it floods me to the heart! . . . And yet it floods me to the knees! . . . And it is sweet, sweet as if it fell from heaven! . . . I see the sky no longer through thy locks. Thou seest, thou

Pelléas and Mélisande

seest? . . . I can no longer hold them with both hands; there are some on the boughs of the willow. . . . They are alive like birds in my hands, . . . and they love me, they love me more than thou! . . .

MÉLISANDE Let me go; let me go! . . . Some one might come. . . .

PELLÉAS. No, no, no; I shall not set thee free tonight. . . . Thou art my prisoner tonight; all night, all night! . . .

MÉLISANDE. Pelléas! Pelléas! . . .

PELLÉAS. I tie them, I tie them to the willow boughs. . . . thou shalt not go away now. . . . Look, look, I am kissing thy hair. . . . I suffer no more in the midst of thy hair. . . . Hearest thou my kisses along thy hair? . . . They mount along thy hair. . . . Each hair must bring thee some. . . . Thou seest, thou seest, I can open my hands. . . . My hands are free, and thou canst not leave me now. . . .

MÉLISANDE. Oh! oh! thou hurtest me. . . . (*Doves come out of the tower and fly about them in the night.*) — What is that, Pelléas? — What is it flying about me?

PELLÉAS. It is the doves coming out of the tower. . . . I have frightened them; they are flying away. . . .

MÉLISANDE. It is my doves, Pelléas. — Let us go away, let me go; they will not come back again. . . .

PELLÉAS. Why will they not come back again?

MÉLISANDE. They will be lost in the dark. . . . Let me go; let me lift my head. . . . I hear a noise of footsteps. . . . Let me go! — It is Golaud! . . . I believe it is Golaud! . . . He has heard us. . . .

PELLÉAS. Wait! Wait! . . . Thy hair is about the boughs. . . . It is caught there in the darkness. . . . Wait, wait! . . . It is dark. . . .

Enter GOLAUD, *by the watchman's round.*

GOLAUD. What do you here?

PELLÉAS. What do I here? . . . I . . .

GOLAUD. You are children. . . . Mélisande, do not lean out so at the window; you will fall. . . . Do you not know it is late? — It is nearly midnight. — Do not play so in the darkness. — You are children. . . . (*Laughing nervously.*) What children! . . . What children! . . .   (*Exit, with* PELLÉAS.)

SCENE III. — *The vaults of the castle.*

Enter GOLAUD *and* PELLÉAS.

GOLAUD. Take care; this way, this way. — You have never penetrated into these vaults?

PELLÉAS. Yes; once, of old; but it was long ago. . . .

GOLAUD. They are prodigious great; it is a succession of enormous crypts that end God knows where. The whole castle is builded on these crypts. Do you smell the deathly odor that reigns here? — That is what I wished to show you. In my opinion, it comes from the little underground lake I am going to have you see. Take care; walk before me, in the light of my lantern. I will warn you when we are there. (*They continue to walk in silence.*) Hey! hey! Pelléas! stop! stop! — (*He seizes him by the arm.*) For God's sake! . . . Do you not see? — One step more, and you had been in the gulf! . . .

PELLÉAS. But I did not see it! . . . The lantern no longer lighted me. . . .

GOLAUD. I made a misstep, . . . but if I had not held you by the arm . . . Well, this is the stagnant water that I spoke of to you. . . . Do you perceive the smell of death that rises? — Let us go to the end of this overhanging rock, and do you lean over a little. It will strike you in the face.

PELLÉAS. I smell it already; . . . you would say a smell of the tomb.

GOLAUD. Further, further. . . . It is this that on certain days has poisoned the castle. The King will not believe it comes from here. — The crypt should be walled up in which this standing water is found. It is time, besides, to examine these vaults a little. Have you noticed those lizards on the walls and pillars of the vaults? — There is a labor hidden here you would not suspect; and the whole castle will be swallowed up one of these nights, if it is not looked out for. But what will you have? nobody likes to come down this far. . . . There are strange lizards in many of the walls. . . . Oh! here . . . do you perceive the smell of death that rises?

PELLÉAS. Yes; there is a smell of death rising about us. . . .

GOLAUD. Lean over; have no fear. . . . I will hold you . . . give me . . . no, no, not your hand . . . it might slip . . . your arm, your arm! . . . Do you see the gulf? (*Moved.*) — Pelléas? Pelléas? . . .

PELLÉAS. Yes; I think I see the bottom of the gulf. . . . Is it the light that trembles so? . . . You . . . (*He straightens up, turns, and looks at* GOLAUD.)

GOLAUD (*with a trembling voice*). Yes; it is the lantern. . . . See, I shook it to lighten the walls. . . .

PELLÉAS. I stifle here; . . . let us go out. . . .

GOLAUD. Yes; let us go out. . . .

(*Exeunt in silence.*)

SCENE IV. — *A terrace at the exit of the vaults.*

Enter GOLAUD *and* PELLÉAS.

PELLÉAS. Ah! I breathe at last! . . . I thought, one moment, I was going to be ill in those enormous crypts; I was on the point of falling. . . . There is a damp air there, heavy as a leaden dew, and darkness thick as a poisoned paste. . . . And now, all the air of all the sea! . . . There is a fresh wind, see; fresh as a leaf that has just opened, over the little green waves. . . . Hold! the flowers have just been watered at the foot of the terrace, and the smell of the verdure and the wet roses comes up to us. . . . It must be nearly noon; they are already in the shadow of the tower. . . . It is noon; I hear the bells ringing, and the children are going down to the beach to bathe. . . . I did not know that we had stayed so long in the caverns. . . .

GOLAUD. We went down toward eleven o'clock. . . .
PELLÉAS. Earlier; it must have been earlier; I heard it strike half-past ten.
GOLAUD. Half-past ten or a quarter to eleven.
PELLÉAS. They have opened all the windows of the castle. It will be unusually hot this afternoon. . . . Look, there is mother with Mélisande at a window of the tower. . . .
GOLAUD. Yes; they have taken refuge on the shady side. — Speaking of Mélisande, I heard what passed and what was said last night. I am quite aware all that is but child's play; but it need not be repeated. Mélisande is very young and very impressionable; and she must be treated the more circumspectly that she is perhaps with child at this moment. . . . She is very delicate, hardly woman; and the least emotion might bring on a mishap. It is not the first time I have noticed there might be something between you. . . . You are older than she; it will suffice to have told you. . . . Avoid her as much as possible; without affectation moreover; without affectation. . . . — What is it I see yonder on the highway toward the forest? . . .
PELLÉAS. Some herds they are leading to the city. . . .
GOLAUD. They cry like lost children; you would say they smelt the butcher already. — It will be time for dinner. — What a fine day! What a capital day for the harvest! . . .

(*Exeunt.*)

SCENE V. — *Before the castle.*

Enter GOLAUD *and* LITTLE YNIOLD.

GOLAUD. Come, we are going to sit down here, Yniold; sit on my knee; we shall see from here what passes in the forest. I do not see you any more at all now. You abandon me too; you are always at little mother's. . . . Why, we are sitting just under little mother's windows. — Perhaps she is saying her evening prayer at this moment. . . . But tell me, Yniold, she is often with your uncle Pelléas, isn't she?
YNIOLD. Yes, yes; always, little father; when you are not there, little father. . . .
GOLAUD. Ah! — look; some one is going by with a lantern in the garden. — But I have been told they did not like each other. . . . It seems they often quarrel; . . . no? Is it true?
YNIOLD. Yes, yes; it is true.
GOLAUD. Yes? — Ah! ah! — But what do they quarrel about?
YNIOLD. About the door.
GOLAUD. What? about the door? — What are you talking about? — No, come, explain yourself; why do they quarrel about the door?
YNIOLD. About its being open.
GOLAUD. Who wants it to stay open? — Come, why do they quarrel?
YNIOLD. I don't know, little father; about the light.
GOLAUD. I am not talking to you about the light; we will talk of that by

and by. I am talking to you about the door. Answer what I ask you; you must learn to talk; it is time. . . . Do not put your hand in your mouth so; . . . come. . . .

YNIOLD. Little father! little father! . . . I won't do it any more. . . . (*He cries.*)

GOLAUD. Come; what are you crying for now? What has happened?

YNIOLD. Oh! oh! little father, you hurt me. . . .

GOLAUD. I hurt you? — Where did I hurt you? I did not mean to. . . .

YNIOLD. Here, here; on my little arm. . . .

GOLAUD. I did not mean to; come, don't cry any more, and I will give you something tomorrow.

YNIOLD. What, little father?

GOLAUD. A quiver and some arrows; but tell me what you know about the door.

YNIOLD. Big arrows?

GOLAUD. Yes, yes; very big arrows. — But why don't they want the door to be open? — Come, answer me sometime! — no, no; do not open your mouth to cry. I am not angry. We are going to have a quiet talk, like Pelléas and little mother when they are together. What do they talk about when they are together?

YNIOLD. Pelléas and little mother?

GOLAUD. Yes; what do they talk about?

YNIOLD. About me; always about me.

GOLAUD. And what do they say about you?

YNIOLD. They say I am going to be very big.

GOLAUD. Oh, plague of my life! . . . I am here like a blind man searching for his treasure at the bottom of the ocean! . . . I am here like a new-born child lost in the forest, and you . . . Come, come, Yniold, I was wandering; we are going to talk seriously. Do Pelléas and little mother never speak of me when I am not there? . . .

YNIOLD. Yes, yes, little father; they are always speaking of you.

GOLAUD. Ah! . . . And what do they say of me?

YNIOLD. They say I shall grow as big as you are.

GOLAUD. You are always by them?

YNIOLD. Yes, yes, always, always, little father.

GOLAUD. They never tell you to go play somewhere else?

YNIOLD. No, little father; they are afraid when I am not there.

GOLAUD. They are afraid? . . . What makes you think they are afraid?

YNIOLD. Little mother aways says, "Don't go away; don't go away!" . . . They are unhappy, but they laugh. . . .

GOLAUD. But that does not prove they are afraid.

YNIOLD. Yes, yes, little father; she is afraid. . . .

GOLAUD. Why do you say she is afraid?

YNIOLD. They always weep in the dark.

GOLAUD. Ah! ah! . . .

YNIOLD. That makes one weep too.
GOLAUD. Yes, yes! . . .
YNIOLD. She is pale, little father.
GOLAUD. Ah! ah . . . patience, my God, patience! . . .
YNIOLD. What, little father?
GOLAUD. Nothing, nothing, my child. — I saw a wolf go by in the forest. — Then they get on well together? — I am glad to learn they are on good terms. — They kiss each other sometimes? — No? . . .
YNIOLD. Kiss each other, little father? — No, no, — ah! yes, little father, yes, yes; once . . . once when it rained. . . .
GOLAUD. They kissed? — But how, how did they kiss?
YNIOLD. So, little father, so! . . . (*He gives him a kiss on the mouth, laughing.*) Ah! ah! your beard, little father! . . . It pricks! it pricks! it pricks! It is getting all gray, little father, and your hair, too; all gray, all gray, all gray. . . . (*The window under which they are sitting is lighted up at this moment, and the light falls upon them.*) Ah, ah! little mother has lit her lamp. It is light, little father; it is light. . . .
GOLAUD. Yes; it is beginning to be light. . . .
YNIOLD. Let us go there too, little father; let us go there too. . . .
GOLAUD. Where do you want to go?
YNIOLD. Where it is light, little father.
GOLAUD. No, no, my child; let us stay in the dark a little longer. . . . One cannot tell, one cannot tell yet. . . . Do you see those poor people down there trying to kindle a little fire in the forest? — It has rained. And over there, do you see the old gardener trying to lift that tree the wind has blown down across the road? — He cannot; the tree is too big; the tree is too heavy, and it will lie where it fell. All that cannot be helped. . . . I think Pelléas is mad. . . .
YNIOLD. No, little father, he is not mad; he is very good.
GOLAUD. Do you want to see little mother?
YNIOLD. Yes, yes; I want to see her!
GOLAUD. Don't make any noise; I am going to hoist you up to the window. It is too high for me, for all I am so big. . . . (*He lifts the child.*) Do not make the least noise; little mother would be terribly afraid. . . . Do you see her? — Is she in the room?
YNIOLD. Yes. . . . Oh, how light it is!
GOLAUD. She is alone?
YNIOLD. Yes; . . . no, no; Uncle Pelléas is there, too.
GOLAUD. He — . . . !
YNIOLD. Ah! ah! little father! you have hurt me! . . .
GOLAUD. It is nothing; be still; I will not do it any more; look, look, Yniold! . . . I stumbled; speak lower. What are they doing? —
YNIOLD. They are not doing anything, little father; they are waiting for something.
GOLAUD. Are they near each other?

YNIOLD. No, little father.

GOLAUD. And ... and the bed? are they near the bed?

YNIOLD. The bed, little father? — I can't see the bed.

GOLAUD. Lower, lower; they will hear you. Are they speaking?

YNIOLD. No, little father; they do not speak.

GOLAUD. But what are they doing? — They must be doing something....

YNIOLD. They are looking at the light.

GOLAUD. Both?

YNIOLD. Yes, little father.

GOLAUD. They do not say anything?

YNIOLD. No, little father; they do not close their eyes.

GOLAUD. They do not come near each other?

YNIOLD. No, little father; they do not stir.

GOLAUD. They are sitting down?

YNIOLD. No, little father; they are standing upright against the wall.

GOLAUD. They make no gestures? — They do not look at each other? — They make no signs? ...

YNIOLD. No, little father. — Oh! oh! little father; they never close their eyes.... I am terribly afraid....

GOLAUD. Be still. They do not stir yet?

YNIOLD. No, little father. — I am afraid, little father; let me come down! ...

GOLAUD. Why, what are you afraid of? — Look! look! ...

YNIOLD. I dare not look any more, little father! ... Let me come down! ...

GOLAUD. Look! look! ...

YNIOLD. Oh! oh! I am going to cry, little father! — Let me come down; let me come down! ...

GOLAUD. Come; we will go see what has happened.

(*Exeunt.*)

ACT FOURTH

SCENE I. — *A corridor in the castle.*

Enter PELLÉAS *and* MÉLISANDE, *meeting.*

PELLÉAS. Where goest thou? I must speak to thee tonight. Shall I see thee?

MÉLISANDE. Yes.

PELLÉAS. I have just left my father's room. He is getting better. The physician has told us he is saved.... And yet this morning I had a presentiment this day would end ill. I have had a rumor of misfortune in my ears for some time.... Then, all at once there was a great change; today it is no longer anything but a question of time. All the windows in his room have been thrown open. He speaks; he seems happy. He does not speak yet like an ordinary man, but already his ideas no longer all come from the other world. . . . He recognized me. He took my hand and said with that strange air he has had since he fell sick: "Is it thou, Pelléas? Why, why, I had not noticed it before, but thou hast the grave and friendly look of those who will not live long. . . . You must travel; you must travel. . . ." It is strange; I shall obey him. . . . My mother listened to him and wept for joy. — Hast thou not been aware of it? — The whole house seems already to revive: you hear breathing; you hear speaking; you hear walking. . . . Listen; I hear some one speaking behind that door. Quick, quick! answer quickly! where shall I see thee?

MÉLISANDE. Where wouldst thou?

PELLÉAS. In the park; near "Blind Man's Spring." — Wilt thou? — Wilt thou come?

MÉLISANDE. Yes.

PELLÉAS. It will be the last night; — I am going to travel, as my father said. Thou wilt not see me more. . . .

MÉLISANDE. Do not say that, Pelléas. . . . I shall see thee always; I shall look upon thee always. . . .

PELLÉAS. Thou wilt look in vain. . . . I shall be so far away thou couldst no longer see me. . . . I shall try to go very far away. . . . I am full of joy, and you would say I had all the weight of heaven and earth on my body today. . . .

MÉLISANDE. What has happened, Pelléas? — I no longer understand what you say. . . .

PELLÉAS. Go, go; let us separate. I hear some one speaking behind that door. . . . It is the strangers who came to the castle this morning. . . . They are going out. . . . Let us go; it is the strangers. . . .

(*Exeunt severally.*)

SCENE II. — *An apartment in the castle.*

ARKËL and MÉLISANDE discovered.

ARKËL. Now that Pelléas's father is saved, and sickness, the old handmaid of Death, has left the castle, a little joy and a little sunlight will at last come into the house again. . . . It was time! — For, since thy coming, we have only lived here whispering about a closed room. . . . And truly I have pitied thee, Mélisande. . . . Thou camest here all joyous, like a child seeking a gala-day, and at the moment thou enteredst in the vestibule I saw thy face change, and probably thy soul, as the face changes in spite of us when we enter at noon into a grotto too gloomy and too cold. . . . And since — since, on account of all that, I have often no longer understood thee. . . . I observed thee, thou wert there, listless perhaps, but with the strange, astray look of one awaiting ever a great trouble, in the sunlight, in a beautiful garden. . . . I cannot explain. . . . But I was sad to see thee so; for thou art too young and too beautiful to live already day and night under the breath of death. . . . But now all that will change. At my age, — and there perhaps is the surest fruit of my life, — at my age I have gained I know not what faith in the fidelity of events, and I have always seen that every young and beautiful being creates about itself young, beautiful, and happy events. . . . And it is thou who wilt now open the door for the new era I have glimpses of. . . . Come here; why dost thou stay there without answering and without lifting thine eyes? — I have kissed thee but once only hitherto, — the day of thy coming; and yet old men need sometimes to touch with their lips a woman's forehead or a child's cheek, to believe still in the freshness of life and avert awhile the menaces. . . . Art thou afraid of my old lips? How I have pitied thee these months! . . .

MÉLISANDE. Grandfather, I have not been unhappy. . . .

ARKËL. Perhaps you were of those who are unhappy without knowing it, . . . and they are the most unhappy. . . . Let me look at thee, so, quite near, a moment; . . . we have such need of beauty beside Death. . . .

Enter GOLAUD.

GOLAUD. Pelléas leaves tonight.

ARKËL. Thou hast blood on thy forehead. What hast thou done?

GOLAUD. Nothing, nothing. . . . I have passed through a hedge of thorns.

MÉLISANDE. Bend down your head a little, my lord. . . . I will wipe your forehead. . . .

GOLAUD (*repulsing her*). I will not that you touch me, do you understand? Go, go! — I am not speaking to you. — Where is my sword? — I came to seek my sword. . . .

MÉLISANDE. Here; on the praying-stool.

GOLAUD. Bring it. (*To* ARKËL.) — They have just found another peasant dead of hunger, along by the sea. You would say they all meant to die under our eyes. — (*To* MÉLISANDE.) Well, my sword? — Why do you tremble so? — I am not going to kill you. I would simply examine the blade. I do not employ the sword for these uses. Why do you examine me like a beggar? — I do not come to ask alms of you. You hope to see something in my eyes without my seeing anything in yours? — Do you think I may know something? — (*To* ARKËL.) — Do you see those great eyes? — It is as if they were proud of their richness. . . .

ARKËL. I see there only a great innocence. . . .

GOLAUD. A great innocence! . . . They are greater than innocence! . . . They are purer than the eyes of a lamb. . . . They would give God lessons in innocence! A great innocence! Listen: I am so near them I feel the freshness of their lashes when they wink; and yet I am less far away from the great secrets of the other world than from the smallest secret of those eyes! . . . A great innocence! . . . More than innocence! You would say the angels of heaven celebrated there an eternal baptism! . . . I know those eyes! I have seen them at their work! Close them! close them! or I shall close them for a long while! . . . — Do not put your right hand to your throat so; I am saying a very simple thing. . . . I have no under-thought. . . . If I had an under-thought, why should I not say it? Ah! ah! — do not attempt to flee! — Here! — Give me that hand! — Ah! your hands are too hot. . . . Go away! Your flesh disgusts me! . . . Here! — There is no more question of fleeing now! — (*He seizes her by the hair.*) — You shall follow me on your knees! — On your knees! — On your knees before me! — Ah! ah! your long hair serves some purpose at last! . . . Right, . . . left! — Left, . . . right! — Absalom! Absalom. — Forward! back! To the ground! to the ground! . . . You see, you see; I laugh already like an old man. . . .

ARKËL (*running up*). Golaud! . . .

GOLAUD (*affecting a sudden calm*). You will do as you may please, look you. — I attach no importance to that. — I am too old; and, besides, I am not a spy. I shall await chance; and then . . . Oh! then! . . . simply because it is the custom; simply because it is the custom. . . .   (*Exit.*)

ARKËL. What ails him? — He is drunk?

MÉLISANDE (*in tears*). No, no; he does not love me any more. . . . I am not happy! . . . I am not happy! . . .

ARKËL. If I were God, I would have pity on men's hearts. . . .

SCENE III. — *A terrace of the castle.*

LITTLE YNIOLD *discovered, trying to lift a boulder.*

LITTLE YNIOLD. Oh, this stone is heavy! . . . It is heavier than I am. . . . It is heavier than everybody. . . . It is heavier than everything that ever happened. . . . I can see my golden ball between the rock and this naughty stone, and I cannot reach it. . . . My little arm is not long enough . . . and this stone won't be lifted. . . . I can't lift it . . . and nobody could lift it. . . . It is heavier than the whole house; . . . you would think it had roots in the earth. . . . (*The bleatings of a flock heard far away.*) — Oh! oh! I hear the sheep crying. . . . (*He goes to look, at the edge of the terrace.*) Why! there is no more sun. . . . They are coming . . . the little sheep . . . they are coming. There is a lot of them! . . . There is a lot of them! . . . They are afraid of the dark. . . . They crowd together! they crowd together! . . . They can hardly walk any more. . . . They are crying! they are crying! and they go quick! . . . They go quick! . . . They are already at the great crossroads. Ah! ah! They don't know where they ought to go any more. . . . They don't cry any more. . . . They wait. . . . Some of them want to go to the right. . . . They all want to go to the right . . . They cannot! . . . The shepherd is throwing earth at them. . . . Ah! ah! They are going to pass by here. . . . They obey! They obey! They are going to pass under the terrace. . . . They are going to pass under the rocks. . . . I am going to see them near by. . . . Oh! oh! what a lot of them! . . . What a lot of them! . . . The whole road is full of them. . . .

They all keep still now. . . . Shepherd! shepherd! why don't they speak any more?

THE SHEPHERD (*who is out of sight*). Because it is no longer the road to the stable. . . .

YNIOLD. Where are they going? — Shepherd! shepherd! — where are they going? — He doesn't hear me any more. They are too far away already. . . . They go quick. . . . They are not making a noise any more. . . . It is no longer the road to the stable. . . . Where are they going to sleep tonight? — Oh! oh! — It is too dark. . . . I am going to tell something to somebody. . . .

(Exit.)

SCENE IV. — A *fountain in the park.*

Enter PELLÉAS.

PELLÉAS. It is the last evening . . . the last evening. It must all end. I have played like a child about a thing I did not guess. . . . I have played a-dream about the snares of fate. . . . Who has awakened me all at once? I shall flee, crying out for joy and woe like a blind man fleeing from his burning house. . . . I am going to tell her I shall flee. . . . My father is out of danger; and I have no more reason to lie to myself. . . . It is late; she does not come. . . . I should do better to go away without seeing her again. . . . I must look well at her this time. . . . There are some things that I no longer recall. . . . It seems at times as if I had not seen her for a hundred years. . . . And I have not yet looked upon her look. . . . There remains nought to me if I go away thus. And all those memories . . . it is as if I were to take away a little water in a muslin bag. . . . I must see her one last time, to the bottom of her heart. . . . I must tell her all that I have never told her.

Enter MÉLISANDE.

MÉLISANDE. Pelléas!

PELLÉAS. Mélisande! — Is it thou, Mélisande?

MÉLISANDE. Yes.

PELLÉAS. Come hither; do not stay at the edge of the moonlight. — Come hither. We have so many things to tell each other. . . . Come hither in the shadow of the linden.

MÉLISANDE. Let me stay in the light. . . .

PELLÉAS. We might be seen from the windows of the tower. Come hither; here, we have nothing to fear. — Take care; we might be seen. . . .

MÉLISANDE. I wish to be seen. . . .

PELLÉAS. Why, what doth ail thee? — Thou wert able to come out without being seen?

MÉLISANDE. Yes; your brother slept. . . .

PELLÉAS. It is late. — In an hour they will close the gates. We must be careful. Why art thou come so late?

MÉLISANDE. Your brother had a bad dream. And then my gown was caught on the nails of the gate. See, it is torn. I lost all this time, and ran. . . .

Pelléas and Mélisande

PELLÉAS. My poor Mélisande! . . . I should almost be afraid to touch thee. . . . Thou art still out of breath, like a hunted bird. . . . It is for me, for me, thou doest all that? . . . I hear thy heart beat as if it were mine. . . . Come hither . . . nearer, nearer me. . . .

MÉLISANDE. Why do you laugh?

PELLÉAS. I do not laugh; — or else I laugh for joy, unwittingly. . . . It were a weeping matter, rather. . . .

MÉLISANDE. We have come here before. . . . I recollect. . . .

PELLÉAS. Yes . . . yes. . . . Long months ago. — I knew not then. . . . Knowest thou why I asked thee to come here tonight?

MÉLISANDE. No.

PELLÉAS. It is perhaps the last time I shall see thee. . . . I must go away forever. . . .

MÉLISANDE. Why sayest thou always thou wilt go away? . . .

PELLÉAS. I must tell thee what thou knowest already? — Thou knowest not what I am going to tell thee?

MÉLISANDE. Why, no; why, no; I know nothing — . . .

PELLÉAS. Thou knowest not why I must go afar. . . . Thou knowest not it is because . . . (*He kisses her abruptly.*) I love thee. . . .

MÉLISANDE (*in a low voice*). I love thee too. . . .

PELLÉAS. Oh! oh! What saidst thou, Mélisande? . . . I hardly heard it! . . . Thou sayest that in a voice coming from the end of the world! . . . I hardly heard thee. . . . Thou lovest me? — Thou lovest me too? . . . Since when lovest thou me? . . .

MÉLISANDE. Since always. . . . Since I saw thee. . . .

PELLÉAS. Oh, how thou sayest that! . . . Thy voice seems to have blown across the sea in spring! . . . I have never heard it until now; . . . one would say it had rained on my heart! . . . Thou sayest that so frankly! . . . Like an angel questioned! . . . I cannot believe it, Mélisande! . . . Why shouldst thou love me? — Nay, why dost thou love me? — Is what thou sayest true? — Thou dost not mock me? — Thou dost not lie a little, to make me smile? . . .

MÉLISANDE. No; I never lie; I lie but to thy brother. . . .

PELLÉAS. Oh, how thou sayest that! . . . Thy voice! thy voice! . . . It is cooler and more frank than the water is! . . . It is like pure water on my lips! . . . It is like pure water on my hands. . . . Give me, give me thy hands! . . . Oh, how small thy hands are! . . . I did not know thou wert so beautiful! . . . I have never seen anything so beautiful before thee. . . . I was full of unrest; I sought throughout the house. . . . I sought throughout the country. . . . And I found not beauty. . . . And now I have found thee! . . . I have found thee! . . . I do not think there could be on the earth a fairer woman! . . . Where art thou? — I no longer hear thee breathe. . . .

MÉLISANDE. Because I look on thee. . . .

PELLÉAS. Why dost thou look so gravely on me? — We are already in the shadow. — It is too dark under this tree. Come into the light. We cannot see how happy we are. Come, come; so little time remains to us. . . .

MÉLISANDE. No, no; let us stay here. . . . I am nearer thee in the dark. . . .

PELLÉSA. Where are thine eyes? — Thou art not going to fly me? — Thou dost not think of me just now.

MÉLISANDE. Oh, yes; oh, yes; I only think of thee. . . .

PELLÉAS. Thou wert looking elsewhere. . . .

MÉLISANDE. I saw thee elsewhere. . . .

PELLÉAS. Thy soul is far away. . . . What ails thee, then — Meseems thou art not happy. . . .

MÉLISANDE. Yes, yes; I am happy, but I am sad. . . .

PELLÉAS. One is sad often when one loves. . . .

MÉLISANDE. I weep always when I think of thee. . . .

PELLÉAS. I too. . . . I too, Mélisande. . . . I am quite near thee; I weep for joy, and yet . . . (*He kisses her again.*) — Thou art strange when I kiss thee so. . . . Thou art so beautiful that one would think thou wert about to die. . . .

MÉLISANDE. Thou too. . . .

PELLÉAS. There, there. . . . We do not what we will. . . . I did not love thee the first time I saw thee. . . .

MÉLISANDE. Nor I . . . nor I. . . . I was afraid. . . .

PELLÉAS. I could not admit thine eyes. . . . I would have gone away at once . . . and then . . .

MÉLISANDE. And I — I would not have come. . . . I do not yet know why — I was afraid to come. . . .

PELLÉAS. There are so many things one never knows. We are ever waiting; and then. . . . What is that noise? — They are closing the gates! . . .

MÉLISANDE. Yes, they have closed the gates. . . .

PELLÉAS. We cannot go back now? — Hearest thou the bolts? — Listen! listen! . . . the great chains! . . . the great chains! . . . It is too late; it is too late! . . .

MÉLISANDE. All the better! all the better! all the better! . . .

PELLÉAS. Thou — . . . ? Behold, behold! . . . It is no longer we who will it so! . . . All's lost, all's saved! all is saved tonight! — Come, come. . . . My heart beats like a madman — up to my very throat. . . . (*They embrace.*) Listen! listen! my heart is almost strangling me. . . . Come! come! . . . Ah, how beautiful it is in the shadows! . . .

MÉLISANDE. There is some one behind us! . . .

PELLÉAS. I see no one. . . .

MÉLISANDE. I heard a noise. . . .

PELLÉAS. I hear only thy heart in the dark. . . .

MÉLISANDE. I heard the crackling of dead leaves. . . .

PELLÉAS. Because the wind is silent all at once. . . . It fell as we were kissing. . . .

MÉLISANDE. How long our shadows are tonight! . . .

PELLÉAS. They embrace to the very end of the garden. Oh, how they kiss far away from us! . . . Look! look! . . .

MÉLISANDE (*in a stifled voice*). A-a-h! — He is behind a tree!
PELLÉAS. Who?
MÉLISANDE. Golaud!
PELLÉAS. Golaud! — where? — I see nothing. . . .
MÉLISANDE. There . . . at the end of our shadows. . . .
PELLÉAS. Yes, yes; I saw him. . . . Let us not turn abruptly. . . .
MÉLISANDE. He has his sword. . . .
PELLÉAS. I have not mine. . . .
MÉLISANDE. He saw us kiss. . . .
PELLÉAS. He does not know we have seen him. . . . Do not stir; do not turn your head. . . . He would rush headlong on us. . . . He will remain there while he thinks we do not know. He watches us. . . . He is still motionless. . . . Go, go at once this way. . . . I will wait for him. . . . I will stop him. . . .
MÉLISANDE. No, no, no! . . .
PELLÉAS. Go! go! he has seen all! . . . He will kill us! . . .
MÉLISANDE. All the better! all the better! all the better! . . .
PELLÉAS. He comes! he comes! . . . Thy mouth! . . . Thy mouth! . . .
MÉLISANDE. Yes! . . . yes! yes! . . .

They kiss desperately.

PELLÉAS. Oh! oh! All the stars are falling! . . .
MÉLISANDE. Upon me too! upon me too! . . .
PELLÉAS. Again! Again! . . . Give! give! . . .
MÉLISANDE. All! all! all! . . .

GOLAUD *rushes upon them, sword in hand, and strikes* PELLÉAS, *who falls at the brink of the fountain.* MÉLISANDE *flees terrified.*

MÉLISANDE (*fleeing*). Oh! oh! I have no courage! . . . I have no courage! . . .

GOLAUD *pursues her through the wood in silence.*

ACT FIFTH

SCENE I. — A *lower hall in the castle.*

The women servants discovered, gathered together, while without children are playing before one of the ventilators of the hall.

AN OLD SERVANT. You will see, you will see, my daughters; it will be tonight. — Some one will come to tell us by and by. . . .
ANOTHER SERVANT. They will not come to tell us. . . . They don't know what they are doing any longer. . . .
THIRD SERVANT. Let us wait here. . . .
FOURTH SERVANT. We shall know well enough when we must go up. . . .
FIFTH SERVANT. When the time is come, we shall go up of ourselves. . . .
SIXTH SERVANT. There is no longer a sound heard in the house. . . .

SEVENTH SERVANT. We ought to make the children keep still, who are playing before the ventilator.

EIGHTH SERVANT. They will be still of themselves by and by.

NINTH SERVANT. The time has not yet come. . . .

Enter an old Servant.

THE OLD SERVANT. No one can go in the room any longer. I have listened more than an hour. . . . You could hear the flies walk on the doors. . . . I heard nothing. . . .

FIRST SERVANT. Has she been left alone in the room?

THE OLD SERVANT. No, no; I think the room is full of people.

FIRST SERVANT. They will come, they will come, by and by. . . .

THE OLD SERVANT. Lord! Lord! It is not happiness that has come into the house. . . . One may not speak, but if I could say what I know. . . .

SECOND SERVANT. It was you who found them before the gate?

THE OLD SERVANT. Why, yes! why, yes! it was I who found them. The porter says it was he who saw them first; but it was I who waked him. He was sleeping on his face and would not get up. — And now he comes saying, "It was I who saw them first." Is that just? — See, I burned myself lighting a lamp to go down cellar. — Now what was I going to do down cellar? — I can't remember any more what I was going to do down cellar. — At any rate I got up very early; it was not yet very light; I said to myself, I will go across the courtyard, and then I will open the gate. Good; I go down the stairs on tiptoe, and I open the gate as if it were an ordinary gate. . . . My God! my God! What do I see? Divine a little what I see! . . .

FIRST SERVANT. They were before the gate?

THE OLD SERVANT. They were both stretched out before the gate! . . . Exactly like poor folk that are too hungry. . . . They were huddled together like little children who are afraid. . . . The little princess was nearly dead, and the great Golaud had still his sword in his side. . . . There was blood on the sill. . . .

SECOND SERVANT. We ought to make the children keep still. . . . They are screaming with all their might before the ventilator. . . .

THIRD SERVANT. You can't hear yourself speak. . . .

FOURTH SERVANT. There is nothing to be done: I have tried already; they won't keep still. . . .

FIRST SERVANT. It seems he is nearly cured?

THE OLD SERVANT. Who?

FIRST SERVANT. The great Golaud.

THIRD SERVANT. Yes, yes; they have taken him to his wife's room. I met them just now, in the corridor. They were holding him up as if he were drunk. He cannot yet walk alone.

THE OLD SERVANT. He could not kill himself; he is too big. But she is hardly wounded, and it is she who is going to die. . . . Can you understand that?

FIRST SERVANT. You have seen the wound?

THE OLD SERVANT. As I see you, my daughter. — I saw everything, you understand. . . . I saw it before all the others. . . . A tiny little wound under her little left breast — a little wound that wouldn't kill a pigeon. Is it natural?

FIRST SERVANT. Yes, yes; there is something underneath. . . .

SECOND SERVANT. Yes; but she was delivered of her babe three days ago. . . .

THE OLD SERVANT. Exactly! . . . She was delivered on her death-bed; is that a little sign? — And what a child! Have you seen it? — A wee little girl a beggar would not bring into the world. . . . A little wax figure that came much too soon; . . . a little wax figure that must live in lambs' wool. . . . Yes, yes; it is not happiness that has come into the house. . . .

FIRST SERVANT. Yes, yes; it is the hand of God that has been stirring. . . .

SECOND SERVANT. Yes, yes; all that did not happen without reason. . . .

THIRD SERVANT. It is as good lord Pelléas . . . where is he? — No one knows. . . .

THE OLD SERVANT. Yes, yes; everybody knows. . . . But nobody dare speak of it. . . . One does not speak of this; . . . one does not speak of that; . . . one speaks no more of anything; . . . one no longer speaks truth. . . . But *I* know he was found at the bottom of Blind Man's Spring; . . . but no one, no one could see him. . . . Well, well, we shall only know all that at the last day. . . .

FIRST SERVANT. I dare not sleep here any longer. . . .

THE OLD SERVANT. Yes, yes; once ill-fortune is in the house, one keeps silence in vain. . . .

THIRD SERVANT. Yes; it finds you all the same. . . .

THE OLD SERVANT. Yes, yes; but we do not go where we would. . . .

FOURTH SERVANT. Yes, yes; we do not do what we would. . . .

FIRST SERVANT. They are afraid of us now. . . .

SECOND SERVANT. They all keep silence. . . .

THIRD SERVANT. They cast down their eyes in the corridors.

FOURTH SERVANT. They do not speak any more except in a low voice.

FIFTH SERVANT. You would think they had all done it together.

SIXTH SERVANT. One doesn't know what they have done. . . .

SEVENTH SERVANT. What is to be done when the masters are afraid? . . .

(*A silence.*)

FIRST SERVANT. I no longer hear the children screaming.

SECOND SERVANT. They are sitting down before the ventilator.

THIRD SERVANT. They are huddled against each other.

THE OLD SERVANT. I no longer hear anything in the house. . . .

FIRST SERVANT. You no longer even hear the children breathe. . . .

THE OLD SERVANT. Come, come; it is time to go up. . . .

(*Exeunt, in silence.*)

SCENE II. — *An apartment in the castle.*

ARKËL, GOLAUD, *and the* PHYSICIAN *discovered in one corner of the room.* MÉLISANDE *is stretched upon her bed.*

THE PHYSICIAN. It cannot be of that little wound she is dying; a bird would not have died of it. . . . It is not you, then, who have killed her, good my lord; do not be so disconsolate. . . . She could not have lived. . . . She was born without reason . . . to die; and she dies without reason. . . . And then, it is not sure we shall not save her. . . .

ARKËL. No, no; it seems to me we keep too silent, in spite of ourselves, in her room. . . . It is not a good sign. . . . Look how she sleeps . . . slowly, slowly; . . . it is as if her soul was cold forever. . . .

GOLAUD. I have killed her without cause! I have killed her without cause! . . . Is it not enough to make the stones weep? . . . They had kissed like little children. . . . They had simply kissed. . . . They were brother and sister. . . . And I, and I at once! . . . I did it in spite of myself, look you. . . . I did it in spite of myself. . . .

THE PHYSICIAN. Stop; I think she is waking. . . .

MÉLISANDE. Open the window . . . open the window. . . .

ARKËL. Shall I open this one, Mélisande?

MÉLISANDE. No, no; the great window . . . the great window. . . . It is to see. . . .

ARKËL. Is not the sea air too cold tonight?

THE PHYSICIAN. Do it; do it. . . .

MÉLISANDE. Thanks. . . . Is it sunset?

ARKËL. Yes; it is sunset on the sea; it is late. — How are you, Mélisande?

MÉLISANDE. Well, well. — Why do you ask that? I have never been better. — And yet it seems to me I know something. . . .

ARKËL. What sayest thou? — I do not understand thee. . . .

MÉLISANDE. Neither do I understand all I say, you see. . . . I do not know what I am saying. . . . I do not know what I know. I no longer say what I would. . . .

ARKËL. Why, yes! why, yes! . . . I am quite happy to hear thee speak so; thou hast raved a little these last days, and one no longer understood thee. . . . But now all that is far away. . . .

MÉLISANDE. I do not know. . . . — Are you all alone in the room, grandfather?

ARKËL. No, there is the physician, besides, who cured thee. . . .

MÉLISANDE. Ah! . . .

ARKËL. And then there is still some one else. . . .

MÉLISANDE. Who is it?

ARKËL. It is . . . thou must not be frightened. . . . He does not wish thee the least harm, be sure. . . . If thou'rt afraid, he will go away. . . . He is very unhappy. . . .

MÉLISANDE. Who is it?

ARKËL. It is thy . . . thy husband. . . . It is Golaud. . . .

MÉLISANDE. Golaud is here? Why does he not come by me?

GOLAUD (*dragging himself toward the bed*). Mélisande . . . Mélisande. . . .

MÉLISANDE. Is it you, Golaud? I should hardly recognize you any more. ... It is the evening sunlight in my eyes. ... Why look you on the walls? You have grown thin and old. ... Is it a long while since we saw each other?

GOLAUD (*to* ARKËL *and the* PHYSICIAN). Will you withdraw a moment, if you please? ... I will leave the door wide open. ... One moment only. ... I would say something to her; else I could not die. ... Will you? — Go clear to the end of the corridor; you can come back at once, at once. ... Do not refuse me this. ... I am a wretch. ... (*Exit* ARKËL *and the* PHYSICIAN.) — Mélisande, hast thou pity on me, as I have pity on thee? ... Mélisande? ... Dost thou forgive me, Mélisande? ...

MÉLISANDE. Yes, yes, I do forgive thee. ... What must I forgive? ...

GOLAUD. I have wrought thee so much ill, Mélisande. ... I cannot tell thee the ill I have wrought thee. ... But I see it, I see it so clearly today ... since the first day. ... And all I did not know till now leaps in my eyes tonight. ... And it is all my fault, all that has happened, all that will happen. ... If I could tell it, thou wouldst see as I do! ... I see all! I see all! ... But I loved thee so! ... I loved thee so! ... But now there is some one dying. ... It is I who am dying. ... And I would know ... I would ask thee. ... Thou'lt bear me no ill-will ... I would ... The truth must be told to a dying man. ... He must know the truth, or else he could not sleep. ... Swearest thou to tell me the truth?

MÉLISANDE. Yes.

GOLAUD. Didst thou love Pelléas?

MÉLISANDE. Why, yes; I loved him. — Where is he?

GOLAUD. Thou dost not understand me? — Thou wilt not understand me? — It seems to me ... it seems to me ... Well, then, here: I ask thee if thou lovedst him with a forbidden love? ... Wert thou ... were you guilty? Say, say, yes, yes, yes! ...

MÉLISANDE. No, no; we were not guilty. — Why do you ask that?

GOLAUD. Mélisande! ... tell me the truth, for the love of God!

MÉLISANDE. Why have I not told the truth?

GOLAUD. Do not lie so any more, at the moment of death!

MÉLISANDE. Who is dying? — Is it I?

GOLAUD. Thou, thou! and I, I too, after thee! ... And we must have the truth. ... We must have the truth at last, dost thou understand? ... Tell me all! Tell me all! I forgive thee all! ...

MÉLISANDE. Why am I going to die? — I did not know it. ...

GOLAUD. Thou knowest it now! ... It is time! It is time! ... Quick! quick! ... The truth! the truth! ...

MÉLISANDE. The truth ... the truth ...

GOLAUD. Where art thou? — Mélisande! — Where art thou? — It is not natural! Mélisande! Where art thou? — Where goest thou? (*Perceiving* ARKËL *and the* PHYSICIAN *at the door of the room.*) — Yes, yes; you may come in. ... I know nothing; it is useless. ... It is too late; she is already too far away from us. . . . I shall never know! . . . I shall die here like a blind man! . . .

ARKËL. What have you done? You will kill her. . . .
GOLAUD. I have already killed her. . . .
ARKËL. Mélisande. . . .
MÉLISANDE. Is it you, grandfather?
ARKËL. Yes, my daughter. . . . What would you have me do?
MÉLISANDE. Is it true that the winter is beginning? . . .
ARKËL. Why dost thou ask?
MÉLISANDE. Because it is cold, and there are no more leaves. . . .
ARKËL. Thou art cold? — Wilt thou have the windows closed?
MÉLISANDE. No, no, . . . not till the sun be at the bottom of the sea. — It sinks slowly; then it is the winter beginning?
ARKËL. Yes. — Thou dost not like the winter?
MÉLISANDE. Oh! no. I am afraid of the cold. — I am so afraid of the great cold. . . .
ARKËL. Dost thou feel better?
MÉLISANDE. Yes, yes; I have no longer all those qualms. . . .
ARKËL. Wouldst thou see thy child?
MÉLISANDE. What child?
ARKËL. Thy child. — Thou art a mother. . . . Thou hast brought a little daughter into the world. . . .
MÉLISANDE. Where is she?
ARKËL. Here. . . .
MÉLISANDE. It is strange. . . . I cannot lift my arms to take her. . . .
ARKËL. Because you are still very weak. . . . I will hold her myself; look. . . .
MÉLISANDE. She does not laugh. . . . She is little. . . . She is going to weep too. . . . I pity her. . . .

The room has been invaded, little by little, by the women servants of the castle, who range themselves in silence along the walls and wait.

GOLAUD (*rising abruptly*). What is the matter? — What are all these women coming here for? . . .
THE PHYSICIAN. It is the servants. . . .
ARKËL. Who was it called them?
THE PHYSICIAN. It was not I. . . .
GOLAUD. Why do you come here? — No one has asked for you. . . . What come you here to do? — But what is it, then? — Answer me! . . .

The servants make no answer.

ARKËL. Do not speak too loud. . . . She is going to sleep; she has closed her eyes. . . .
GOLAUD. It is not . . . ?
THE PHYSICIAN. No, no; see, she breathes. . . .
ARKËL. Her eyes are full of tears. — It is her soul weeping now. . . . Why does she stretch her arms out so? — What would she?

THE PHYSICIAN. It is toward the child, without doubt. . . . It is the struggle of motherhood against . . .

GOLAUD. At this moment? — At this moment? — You must say. Say! Say! . . .

THE PHYSICIAN. Perhaps.

GOLAUD. At once? . . . Oh! oh! I must tell her. . . . — Mélisande! Mélisande! . . . Leave me alone! leave me alone with her! . . .

ARKËL. No, no; do not come near. . . . Trouble her not. . . . Speak no more to her. . . . You know not what the soul is. . . .

GOLAUD. It is not my fault! . . . It is not my fault!

ARKËL. Hush! . . . Hush! . . . We must speak softly now. — She must not be disturbed. . . . The human soul is very silent. . . . The human soul likes to depart alone. . . . It suffers so timorously. . . . But the sadness, Golaud . . . the sadness of all we see! . . . Oh! oh! oh! . . .

At this moment, all the servants fall suddenly on their knees at the back of the chamber.

ARKËL (*turning*). What is the matter?

THE PHYSICIAN (*approaching the bed and feeling the body*). They are right. . . .

A long silence.

ARKËL. I saw nothing. — Are you sure? . . .

THE PHYSICIAN. Yes, yes.

ARKËL. I heard nothing. . . . So quick, so quick! . . . All at once! . . . She goes without a word. . . .

GOLAUD (*sobbing*). Oh! oh! oh!

ARKËL. Do not stay here, Golaud. . . . She must have silence now. . . . Come, come. . . . It is terrible, but it is not your fault. . . . 'Twas a little being, so quiet, so fearful, and so silent. . . . 'Twas a poor little mysterious being, like everybody. . . . She lies there as if she were the big sister of her child. . . . Come, come. . . . My God! My God! . . . I shall never understand it at all. . . . Let us not stay here. — Come; the child must not stay here in this room . . . She must live now in her place. . . . It is the poor little one's turn. . . .

They go out in silence.

CURTAIN

EXPRESSIONISM

August Strindberg

A DREAM PLAY

[1902]

August Strindberg [1849-1912]

About the time that Strindberg divorced his first wife, Siri von Essen, in 1891, he began intensive experimentation and investigation in such arcane subjects as mesmerism and alchemy. Not until 1897 did he return to literary writing, and after that date his plays are very different from those of his earlier period. His writing then took a mystical, and sometimes misty, turn. Beginning with the impressive trilogy *To Damascus* (1898-1901), Strindberg developed a new style of drama. The symbolist-expressionist trilogy was followed by *Easter* (1901), *A Dream Play* (1902), and *The Ghost Sonata* (1907), among many others. In all of these plays Strindberg dramatizes feelings and states of mind, with an infusion of religious emotion. As he himself was struggling toward some resolution of life's problems, he dramatized the struggle. Perhaps in some ways he reached his goal, having experienced his Damascus: he died in 1912, holding the Bible to his breast and saying, "All is atoned for."

Like so many other literary terms, expressionism is variously defined; some have labeled "expressionist" almost any nonrepresentational convention. However, if the word is to be useful, it must delimit in some meaningful way the particular dramatic phenomenon which it designates. Key ideas connected with expressionism are subjectivity, distortion, and vehemence. The term applies to a style of play writing, of stage design, and of production — even of acting, which is not always psychologically realistic, but may be declamatory in an "unnatural" way. The German playwright

Strindberg and Expressionism

Kasimir Edschmidt has said, "The expressionist believes in a reality which he himself creates against all other reality." This statement suggests the often subjective attitude of the playwright and the appropriately subjective means which he may use to communicate whatever he wishes to dramatize. The objective world is deformed in order to suggest an ultimate, inner reality. As a result, expressionist plays often have a nightmare quality about them, which in turn creates an intense, sometimes aggressive effect. The subjectivity may be in the mind of either the playwright or the protagonist. If the former, the entire play is shaped by the omniscient author who says in effect, "This is the world as I see it"; if the latter, we view experience through the (usually distorted) vision of the main character. The distorted world is dramatized through the use, often self-conscious and obtrusive, of lighting, sound effects, scenery, and stage properties. The physical theater is important to the expressionist.

It happens that the best expressionist plays have been primarily social or strongly philosophical; the psychological problems of strongly individuated characters have not been dramatized much by the expressionists. Although Strindberg introduced the new style around the turn of the century, it did not flourish in Europe until the time of World War I, and not in America until the early 1920's. Its success and impact were spectacular, but pure expressionism was a roman candle which glowed brilliantly for a short time and then died. What has remained, though, is an extremely

Strindberg and Expressionism

influential afterglow. (Expressionist techniques have been used with notable success, for example, by Tennessee Williams in *A Streetcar Named Desire* and by Arthur Miller in *Death of a Salesman*.) Expressionism, following realism, is the second radical phase of the modern drama, rejecting the objective, everyday world for some more intense and more "real" subjective world.

Joseph Wood Krutch in his excellent short book, *"Modernism" in the Modern Drama*, says that *A Dream Play* "is generally and probably properly credited with being the precursor of the whole nonrepresentational modern drama." Building upon the knowledge of the dream life and of the unconscious which Freud and others revealed, and upon Strindberg's dramatic example, many modern dramatists have followed to some degree the path set by *A Dream Play*. As Strindberg says in his prefatory note, such things as memories and fancies in nonlogical juxtaposition are woven together to form the fabric of the drama. If one finds it difficult to understand the rationale or the logic of the play, he must remember that the consciousness of the dreamer with its vagaries is the shaping force.

Strindberg often felt that his whole life was a dream, and in *A Dream Play* the characters are fragments of his dream. Certain of them especially reflect the mind of the dreamer: the Daughter of Indra, the Officer, the Lawyer, the Quarantine Master, and the Poet can be identified with the dreamer. They all see the hypocrisy

Strindberg and Expressionism

and the evil of the world; they can agree with the lament which recurs again and again in the words of Indra's Daughter, "Human beings are to be pitied."* The theme of the play is thus simply stated. The characters who dramatize the theme are abstractions without real personality; they are merely spokesmen for attitudes and ideas, they are the workings of the dreamer's unconscious and not real people. As a result, the boundaries between the real and the unreal, between the objective and the subjective worlds are abolished.

In order to fuse the two worlds, the objective and the symbolic-subjective, Strindberg has created his own mode (which is indebted here to Maeterlinck). From the moment that the curtain rises on the play proper, revealing the Growing Castle, we are aware of a nonrealistic and symbolic use of the set: "Under the walls of the castle [with its flower-bud summit] lie heaps of straw and stable-muck." The weird lights which accompany the speech of the Officer, the make-up on the Lawyer's face, the subdued music, and the final opening of the chrysanthemum bud all produce effects dependent upon exploiting the resources of the physical theater. Expressionism is, above all, of the theater.

---

* As Miss Sprigge says in the introduction to her translation of the play, "Strindberg never once alters the Daughter's phrase." However, in order to suggest more fully in translation the subtleties of the original Swedish, she has seen fit to alter the line from place to place.

AUTHOR'S NOTE TO

A DREAM PLAY*

In this dream play, as in his former dream play *To Damascus*, the Author has sought to reproduce the disconnected but apparently logical form of a dream. Anything can happen; everything is possible and probable. Time and space do not exist; on a slight groundwork of reality, imagination spins and weaves new patterns made up of memories, experiences, unfettered fancies, absurdities and improvisations.

The characters are split, double and multiply; they evaporate, crystallise, scatter and converge. But a single consciousness holds sway over them all — that of the dreamer. For him there are no secrets, no incongruities, no scruples and no law. He neither condemns nor acquits, but only relates, and since on the whole, there is more pain than pleasure in the dream, a tone of melancholy, and of compassion for all living things, runs through the swaying narrative. Sleep, the liberator, often appears as a torturer, but when the pain is at its worst, the sufferer awakes — and is thus reconciled with reality. For however agonising real life may be, at this moment, compared with the tormenting dream, it is a joy.

* Translated by Elizabeth Sprigge.

Translated by Elizabeth Sprigge

A Dream Play

DRAMATIS PERSONÆ*

(*The voice of*) FATHER INDRA
INDRA'S DAUGHTER
THE GLAZIER
THE OFFICER
THE FATHER
THE MOTHER
LINA
THE DOORKEEPER
THE BILLSTICKER
THE PROMPTER
THE POLICEMAN
THE LAWYER
THE DEAN OF PHILOSOPHY
THE DEAN OF THEOLOGY
THE DEAN OF MEDICINE
THE DEAN OF LAW
THE CHANCELLOR
KRISTIN
THE QUARANTINE MASTER
THE ELDERLY FOP
SINGERS AND DANCERS (*Members of the Opera Company*)
    CLERKS, GRADUATES, MAIDS, SCHOOLBOYS,
    CHILDREN, CREW, RIGHTEOUS PEOPLE.

THE COQUETTE
THE FRIEND
THE POET
HE
SHE (*doubles with Victoria's voice*)
THE PENSIONER
UGLY EDITH
EDITH'S MOTHER
THE NAVAL OFFICER
ALICE
THE SCHOOLMASTER
NILS
THE HUSBAND
THE WIFE
THE BLIND MAN
1ST COAL HEAVER
2ND COAL HEAVER
THE GENTLEMAN
THE LADY

* There is no list of characters in the original. E.S.

PROLOGUE

An impression of clouds, crumbling cliffs, ruins of castles and fortresses. The constellations Leo, Virgo and Libra are seen, with the planet Jupiter

---

All rights whatsoever in this play are strictly reserved and applications for performances, etc. should be made to Willis Kingsley Wing, 24 East 38th Street, New York 16, New York.

shining brightly among them. On the highest cloud-peak stands THE DAUGHTER OF INDRA. INDRA'S VOICE is heard from above.

INDRA'S VOICE. Where art thou, Daughter?
DAUGHTER. Here, Father, here!
INDRA'S VOICE. Thou hast strayed, my child.
Take heed, thou sinkest.
How cam'st thou here?
DAUGHTER. Borne on a cloud, I followed the lightning's
blazing trail from the ethereal heights.
But the cloud sank, and still is falling.
Tell me, great Father Indra, to what region
am I come? The air's so dense, so hard to breathe.
INDRA'S VOICE. Leaving the second world thou camest to the third.
From Cucra, Star of the Morning,
Far art thou come and enterest
Earth's atmosphere. Mark there
The Sun's Seventh House that's called the Scales.
The Morning Star is at the autumn weighing,
When day and night are equal.
DAUGHTER. Thou speak'st of Earth. Is that the dark
and heavy world the moon lights up?
INDRA'S VOICE. It is the darkest and the heaviest
of all the spheres that swing in space.
DAUGHTER. Does not the sun shine there?
INDRA'S VOICE. It shines, but not unceasingly.
DAUGHTER. Now the clouds part, and I can see ...
INDRA'S VOICE. What see'st thou, child?
DAUGHTER. I see ... that Earth is fair ... It has green woods,
blue waters, white mountains, yellow fields.
INDRA'S VOICE. Yes, it is fair, as all that Brahma shaped,
yet in the dawn of time
was fairer still. Then came a change,
a shifting of the orbit, maybe of more.
Revolt followed by crime which had to be suppressed.
DAUGHTER. Now I hear sounds arising ...
What kind of creatures dwell down there?
INDRA'S VOICE. Go down and see. The Creator's children I would not decry,
but it's their language that thou hearest.
DAUGHTER. It sounds as if ... it has no cheerful ring.
INDRA'S VOICE. So I believe. Their mother-tongue
is called Complaint. Truly a discontented,
thankless race is this of Earth.

A Dream Play

DAUGHTER. *Ah, say not so! Now I hear shouts of joy,*
and blare and boom. I see the lightning flash.
Now bells are pealing and the fires are lit.
A thousand thousand voices rise,
singing their praise and thanks to heaven.
Pause.
Thy judgment is too hard on them, my Father.

INDRA. *Descend and see, and hear, then come again*
and tell me if their lamentations
and complaint are justified.

DAUGHTER. *So be it. I descend. Come with me, Father!*

INDRA. *No. I cannot breathe their air.*

DAUGHTER. *Now the cloud sinks. It's growing dense. I suffocate!*
This is not air, but smoke and water that I breathe,
so heavy that it drags me down and down.
And now I clearly feel its reeling!
This third is surely not the highest world.

INDRA. *Neither the highest, truly, nor the lowest.*
It is called Dust, and whirls with all the rest,
And so at times its people, struck with dizziness,
live on the borderline of folly and insanity . . .
Courage, my child, for this is but a test!

DAUGHTER, *on her knees as the cloud descends.*
I am sinking!

[*The curtain rises on* The Growing Castle.]
The background shows a forest of giant hollyhocks in bloom: white, pink, crimson, sulphur-yellow and violet. Above this rises the gilded roof of a castle with a flower-bud crowning its summit. Under the walls of the castle lie heaps of straw and stable-muck. On each side of the stage are stylised representations of interiors, architecture and landscape which remain unchanged throughout the play. The GLAZIER *and the* DAUGHTER *enter together.*

DAUGHTER. The castle keeps on growing up out of the earth. Do you see how it has grown since last year?

GLAZIER (*to himself*). I've never seen that castle before — and I've never heard of a castle growing . . . but . . . (*to the* DAUGHTER *with conviction.*) Yes, it's grown six feet, but that's because they've manured it. And if you look carefully, you'll see it's put out a wing on the sunny side.

DAUGHTER. Ought it not to blossom soon? We are already halfway through the summer.

GLAZIER. Don't you see the flower up there?

DAUGHTER (*joyfully*). Yes, I see it. Father, tell me something. Why do flowers grow out of dirt?

GLAZIER. They don't like the dirt, so they shoot up as fast as they can into the light — to blossom and to die.

DAUGHTER. Do you know who lives in the castle?

GLAZIER. I used to know, but I've forgotten.

DAUGHTER. I believe there is a prisoner inside, waiting for me to set him free.

GLAZIER. What will you get if you do?

DAUGHTER. One does not bargain about what one has to do. Let us go into the castle.

GLAZIER. Very well, we will.

They go towards the background which slowly vanishes to the sides, disclosing a simple bare room with a table and a few chairs. A screen cuts the stage in two [the other half unlighted]. A YOUNG OFFICER *in an unconventional modern uniform sits rocking his chair and striking the table with his sword. [The* DAUGHTER *and the* GLAZIER *enter.] She goes up to the* OFFICER *and gently takes the sword from his hands.*

DAUGHTER. No, no, you mustn't do that.

OFFICER. Please, Agnes, let me keep my sword.

DAUGHTER. But you are cutting the table to pieces. (*To the* GLAZIER.) Father, you go down to the harness room and put in that window pane, and we will meet later.

Exit GLAZIER.

DAUGHTER. You are a prisoner in your own room. I have come to set you free.

OFFICER. I have been waiting for this, but I wasn't sure you would want to.

DAUGHTER. The castle is strong — it has seven walls — but it shall be done. Do you want to be set free — or not?

OFFICER. To tell the truth, I don't know. Either way I'll suffer. Every joy has to be paid for twice over with sorrow. It's wretched here, but I'd have to endure three times the agony for the joys of freedom . . . Agnes, I'll bear it, if only I may see you.

DAUGHTER. What do you see in me?

OFFICER. The beautiful, which is the harmony of the universe. There are lines in your form which I have only found in the movement of the stars, in the melody of strings, in the vibrations of light. You are a child of heaven.

DAUGHTER. So are you.

OFFICER. Then why do I have to groom horses, clean stables and have the muck removed?

DAUGHTER. So that you may long to get away.

OFFICER. I do. But it's so hard to pull oneself out of it all.

DAUGHTER. It is one's duty to seek freedom in the light.

A Dream Play

OFFICER. Duty? Life has not done its duty by me.

DAUGHTER. You feel wronged by life?

OFFICER. Yes. It has been unjust. . . .

Voices are now heard from behind the dividing screen, which is drawn aside [as the lights go up on the other set: a homely living-room]. The OFFICER *and the* DAUGHTER *stand watching, gestures and expression held. The* MOTHER, *an invalid, sits at a table. In front of her is a lighted candle, which from time to time she trims with snuffers. On the table are piles of new underclothing, which she is marking with a quill pen. Beyond is a brown cupboard. The* FATHER *brings her a silk shawl.*

FATHER (*gently*). I have brought you this.

MOTHER. What use is a silk shawl to me, my dear, when I am going to die so soon?

FATHER. You believe what the doctor says?

MOTHER. What he says too, but most of all I believe the voice that speaks within me.

FATHER (*sorrowfully*). Then it really is grave . . . And you are thinking of your children, first and last.

MOTHER. They were my life, my justification, my happiness, and my sorrow.

FATHER. Kristina, forgive me . . . for everything.

MOTHER. For what? Ah, my dear, forgive *me!* We have both hurt each other. Why, we don't know. We could not do otherwise . . . However, here is the children's new linen. See that they change twice a week — on Wednesdays and Sundays, and that Louisa washes them — all over . . . Are you going out?

FATHER. I have to go to the school at eleven.

MOTHER. Before you go ask Alfred to come.

FATHER (*pointing to the* OFFICER). But, dear heart, he is here.

MOTHER. My sight must be going too . . . Yes, it's getting so dark. (*Snuffs candle.*) Alfred, come!

The FATHER *goes out through the middle of the wall, nodding goodbye. The* OFFICER *moves forward to the* MOTHER.

MOTHER. Who is that girl?

OFFICER (*whispering*). That's Agnes.

MOTHER. Oh, is it Agnes? Do you know what they are saying? That she is the daughter of the God Indra, who begged to come down to Earth so as to know what it is really like for human beings. But don't say anything.

OFFICER. She *is* a child of the Gods.

MOTHER (*raising her voice*). Alfred, my son, I shall soon be leaving you and your brothers and sisters. I want to say one thing — for you to remember all your life.

OFFICER (*sadly*). What is it, Mother?

MOTHER. Only one thing: never quarrel with God.

OFFICER. What do you mean, Mother?

MOTHER. You must not go on feeling you have been wronged by life.

OFFICER. But I've been treated so unjustly.

MOTHER. You're still harping on the time you were unjustly punished for taking that money which was afterwards found.

OFFICER. Yes. That piece of injustice gave a twist to the whole of my life.

MOTHER. I see. Well now, you just go over to that cupboard . . .

OFFICER (*ashamed*). So you know about that. The . . .

MOTHER. "The Swiss Family Robinson" which . . .

OFFICER. Don't say any more . . .

MOTHER. Which your brother was punished for . . . when it was *you* who had torn it to pieces and hidden it.

OFFICER. Think of that cupboard still being there after twenty years. We have moved so many times — and my mother died ten years ago.

MOTHER. Yes. What of it? You are always questioning everything, and so spoiling the best of life for yourself . . . Ah, here's Lina!

Enter LINA.

LINA. Thank you very much all the same, Ma'am, but I can't go to the christening.

MOTHER. Why not, child?

LINA. I've got nothing to wear.

MOTHER. You can borrow this shawl of mine.

LINA. Oh no, Ma'am, you're very kind, but that would never do.

MOTHER. I can't see why not. I shan't be going to any more parties.

OFFICER. What will Father say? After all, it's a present from him.

MOTHER. What small minds!

FATHER (*putting his head in*). Are you going to lend my present to the maid?

MOTHER. Don't talk like that! Remember I was in service once myself. Why should you hurt an innocent girl?

FATHER. Why should you hurt me, your husband?

MOTHER. Ah, this life! If you do something good, someone else is sure to think it bad; if you are kind to one person, you're sure to harm another. Ah, this life!

She snuffs the candle so that it goes out. The room grows dark and the screen is drawn forward again.

DAUGHTER. Human beings are to be pitied.

OFFICER. Do you think so?

DAUGHTER. Yes, life is hard. But love conquers everything. Come and see.

They withdraw and the background disappears. The OFFICER *vanishes and the* DAUGHTER *comes forward alone.*

The new scene shows an old derelict wall. In the middle of the wall a gate opens on an alley leading to a green plot where a giant blue monks-

A Dream Play

hood is growing. To the left of the gate is the door-window of the Stage Doorkeeper's lodge. The Stage Doorkeeper is sitting with a grey shawl over her head and shoulders, crocheting a star-patterned coverlet. On the right is an announcement-board which the BILLSTICKER *is washing. Near him is a fishnet with a green handle and a green fish box. Further right the cupboard [from the previous set] has become a door with an air-hole shaped like a four-leafed clover. To the left is a small lime tree with a coal-black stem and a few pale green leaves. The* DAUGHTER *goes up to the* DOORKEEPER.

DAUGHTER. Isn't the star coverlet finished yet?

DOORKEEPER. No, my dear. Twenty-six years is nothing for such a piece of work.

DAUGHTER. And your sweetheart never came back?

DOORKEEPER. No, but it wasn't his fault. He *had* to take himself off, poor fellow. That was thirty years ago.

DAUGHTER (*to* BILLSTICKER). She was in the ballet, wasn't she? Here — at the Opera.

BILLSTICKER. She was the prima ballerina, but when *he* went away, it seems he took her dancing with him . . . so she never got any more parts.

DAUGHTER. All complain — with their eyes, and with their voices too.

BILLSTICKER. I haven't much to complain of — not now I've got my net and a green fish box.

DAUGHTER. Does that make you happy?

BILLSTICKER. Yes, very happy. That was my dream when I was little, and now it's come true. I'm all of fifty now, you know.

DAUGHTER. Fifty years for a fishnet and a box!

BILLSTICKER. A *green* box, a *green* one . . .

DAUGHTER (*to* DOORKEEPER). Let me have that shawl now, and I'll sit here and watch the children of men. But you must stand behind and tell me about them.

The DAUGHTER *puts on the shawl and sits down by the gate.*

DOORKEEPER. This is the last day of the Opera season. They hear now if they've been engaged for the next.

DAUGHTER. And those who have not?

DOORKEEPER. Lord Jesus, what a scene! I always pull my shawl over my head.

DAUGHTER. Poor things!

DOORKEEPER. Look, here's one coming. She's not been engaged. See how she's crying!

The SINGER *rushes in from the right and goes through the gate with her handkerchief to her eyes. She pauses a moment in the alley beyond and leans her head against the wall, then goes quickly out.*

DAUGHTER. Human beings are to be pitied.

DOORKEEPER. But here comes one who seems happy enough.

The OFFICER *comes down the alley, wearing a frock-coat and top hat. He carries a bouquet of roses and looks radiantly happy.*

DOORKEEPER. He's going to marry Miss Victoria.

OFFICER (*downstage, looks up and sings*). Victoria!

DOORKEEPER. The young lady will be down in a minute.

WOMAN'S VOICE (*from above, sings*). I am here!

OFFICER (*pacing*). Well, I am waiting.

DAUGHTER. Don't you know me?

OFFICER. No, I know only one woman — Victoria! Seven years I have come here to wait for her — at noon when the sun reaches the chimneys, and in the evening as darkness falls. Look at the paving. See? Worn by the steps of the faithful lover? Hurrah! She is mine. (*Sings.*) Victoria! (*No answer.*) Well, she's dressing now. (*To the* BILLSTICKER.) Ah, a fishnet I see! Everyone here at the Opera is crazy about fishnets — or rather about fish. Dumb fish — because they cannot sing . . . What does a thing like that cost?

BILLSTICKER. It's rather dear.

OFFICER (*sings*). Victoria! . . . (*Shakes the lime tree.*) Look, it's budding again! For the eighth time. (*Sings.*) Victoria! . . . Now she's doing her hair . . . (*To* DAUGHTER.) Madam, kindly allow me to go up and fetch my bride.

DOORKEEPER. Nobody's to go on the stage.

OFFICER. Seven years I've walked up and down here. Seven times three hundred and sixty-five I make two thousand five hundred and fifty-five. (*Stops and pokes the door with the clover-shaped hole.*) Then this door I've seen two thousand five hundred and fifty-five times and I still don't know where it leads to. And this clover leaf to let in the light. Who does it let the light in for? Is anyone inside? Does anybody live there?

DOORKEEPER. I don't know. I've never seen it open.

OFFICER. It looks like a larder door I saw when I was four years old, when I went out one Sunday afternoon with the maid — to see another family and other maids. But I only got as far as the kitchen, where I sat between the water barrel and the salt tub. I've seen so many kitchens in my time, and the larders are always in the passage, with round holes and a clover leaf in the door. But the Opera can't have a larder as it hasn't got a kitchen. (*Sings.*) Victoria! (*To* DAUGHTER.) Excuse me, madam, she can't leave by any other way, can she?

DOORKEEPER. No, there is no other way.

OFFICER. Good. Then I'm bound to meet her.

Members of the Opera Company swarm out of the building, scrutinised by the OFFICER. *They go out by the gate.*

She's sure to come. (*To* DAUGHTER.) Madam, that blue monkshood out there — I saw it when I was a child. Is it the same one? I remember it in a rectory garden when I was seven — with two doves, blue doves, under the hood. Then a bee came and went into the hood, and I thought: "Now I've got you," so I grabbed the flower, but the bee stung through it, and I burst into tears. However, the rector's wife came and put moist earth on it — and

A Dream Play

then we had wild strawberries and milk for supper . . . I believe it's growing dark already. Where are you off to, Billsticker?

BILLSTICKER. Home to my supper.

Exit with fishnet and box.

OFFICER (*rubbing his eyes*). Supper? At this time of day? . . . (*To* DAUGHTER.) Excuse me, may I just step inside a moment and telephone to the Growing Castle?

DAUGHTER. What do you want to say to them?

OFFICER. I want to tell the glazier to put in the double windows. It will be winter soon and I'm so dreadfully cold.

The OFFICER *goes into the* DOORKEEPER's *Lodge.*

DAUGHTER. Who is Miss Victoria?

DOORKEEPER. She is his love.

DAUGHTER. A true answer. What she is to us or others doesn't matter to him. Only what she is to *him*, that's what she *is*.

It grows dark suddenly.

DOORKEEPER (*lighting the lantern*). Dusk falls quickly today.

DAUGHTER. To the gods a year is as a minute.

DOORKEEPER. While to human beings a minute may be as long as a year.

The OFFICER *comes out again. He looks shabbier, and the roses are withered.*

OFFICER. Hasn't she come yet?

DOORKEEPER. No.

OFFICER. She's sure to come. She'll come. (*Paces up and down.*) But all the same . . . perhaps it would be wiser to cancel that luncheon . . . as it's now evening. Yes, that's what I'll do. (*Goes in and telephones.*)

DOORKEEPER (*to* DAUGHTER). May I have my shawl now?

DAUGHTER. No, my friend. You rest and I'll take your place, because I want to know about human beings and life — to find out if it really is as hard as they say.

DOORKEEPER. But you don't get any sleep on this job. Never any sleep, night or day.

DAUGHTER. No sleep at night?

DOORKEEPER. Well, if you can get any with the bell wire on your arm, because the night watchmen go up on the stage and are changed every three hours . . .

DAUGHTER. That must be torture.

DOORKEEPER. So you think, but we others are glad enough to get such a job. If you knew how much I'm envied.

DAUGHTER. Envied? Does one envy the tortured?

DOORKEEPER. Yes. But I'll tell you what's worse than nightwatching and drudgery and draughts and cold and damp. That's having to listen, as I do, to all their tales of woe. They all come to me. Why? Perhaps they read in my wrinkles the runes of suffering, and that makes them talk. In that shawl, my dear, thirty years of torment's hidden — my own and others.

DAUGHTER. That's why it is so heavy and stings like nettles.

DOORKEEPER. Wear it if you like. When it gets too heavy, call me and I'll come and relieve you of it.

DAUGHTER. Goodbye. What you can bear, surely I can.

DOORKEEPER. We shall see. But be kind to my young friends and put up with their complaining.

The DOORKEEPER disappears down the alley. The stage is blacked out. When light returns, the lime tree is bare, the blue monkshood withered, and the green plot at the end of the alley has turned brown.

The OFFICER enters. His hair is grey and he has a grey beard. His clothes are ragged; his collar soiled and limp. He still carries the bouquet of roses, but the petals have dropped.

OFFICER (*wandering round*). By all the signs, summer is over and autumn at hand. I can tell that by the lime tree — and the monkshood. (*Pacing.*) But autumn is *my* spring, for then the theatre opens again. And then she is bound to come. (*To* DAUGHTER.) Dear lady, may I sit on this chair for a while?

DAUGHTER. Do, my friend. I can stand.

OFFICER (*sitting*). If only I could sleep a little it would be better.

He falls asleep for a moment, then starts up and begins walking again. He stops by the clover-leaf door and pokes it.

OFFICER. This door — it gives me no peace. What is there behind it? Something must be. (*Soft ballet music is heard from above.*) Ah, the rehearsals have begun! (*The lights come and go like a lighthouse beam.*) What's this? (*Speaking in time with the flashes.*) Light and darkness; light and darkness.

DAUGHTER (*with the same timing*). Day and night; day and night. A merciful providence wants to shorten your waiting. And so the days fly, chasing the nights.

The light is now constant. The BILLSTICKER enters with his net and his implements.

OFFICER. Here's the Billsticker with his net. How was the fishing?

BILLSTICKER. Not too bad. The summer was hot and a bit long ... the net was all right, but not quite what I had in mind.

OFFICER. "Not quite what I had in mind." Excellently put. Nothing ever is as one imagined it — because one's mind goes further than the act, goes beyond the object. (*He walks up and down striking the bouquet against the walls until the last leaves fall.*)

BILLSTICKER. Hasn't she come down yet?

OFFICER. No, not yet, but she'll come soon. Do you know what's behind that door, Billsticker?

BILLSTICKER. No, I've never seen it open.

OFFICER. I'm going to telephone to a locksmith to come and open it. (*Goes into the Lodge. The BILLSTICKER pastes up a poster and moves away.*)

A Dream Play

DAUGHTER. What was wrong with the fishnet?

BILLSTICKER. Wrong? Well, there wasn't anything wrong exactly. But it wasn't what I'd had in mind, and so I didn't enjoy it *quite* as much . . .

DAUGHTER. How did you imagine the net?

BILLSTICKER. How? I can't quite tell you . . .

DAUGHTER. Let me tell you. In your imagination it was different — green but not *that* green.

BILLSTICKER. You understand, Madam. You understand everything. That's why they all come to you with their troubles. Now if you'd only listen to me, just this once . . .

DAUGHTER. But I will, gladly. Come in here and pour out your heart. (*She goes into the Lodge. The* BILLSTICKER *stays outside and talks to her through the window.*)

The stage is blacked out again, then gradually the lights go up. The lime tree is in leaf; the monkshood in bloom; the sun shines on the greenery at the end of the alley. The BILLSTICKER *is still at the window and the* DAUGHTER *can be seen inside.*

The OFFICER *enters from the Lodge. He is old and white-haired; his clothes and shoes are in rags. He carries the stems of the bouquet. He totters backwards and forwards slowly like a very old man, and reads the poster. A* BALLET GIRL [*comes out of the Theatre*].

OFFICER. Has Miss Victoria gone?

BALLET GIRL. No, she hasn't.

OFFICER. Then I'll wait. Will she come soon?

BALLET GIRL (*gravely*). Yes, she's sure to.

OFFICER. Don't go — then you'll be able to see what's behind that door. I've sent for the locksmith.

BALLET GIRL. That will be really interesting to see this door opened. The door and the Growing Castle. Do you know the Growing Castle?

OFFICER. Do I? Wasn't I imprisoned there?

BALLET GIRL. Really, was that you? But why did they have so many horses there?

OFFICER. It was a stable castle, you see.

BALLET GIRL (*distressed*). How silly of me not to have thought of that.

[*Moves towards the Lodge. A* CHORUS GIRL *comes out of the Theatre.*]

OFFICER. Has Miss Victoria gone?

CHORUS GIRL (*gravely*). No, she hasn't gone. She never goes.

OFFICER. That's because she loves me. No, you mustn't go before the locksmith comes. He's going to open this door.

CHORUS GIRL. Oh, is the door going to be opened? Really? What fun! I just want to ask the Doorkeeper something.

[*She joins the* BILLSTICKER *at the window. The* PROMPTER *comes out of the Theatre.*]

OFFICER. Has Miss Victoria gone?

PROMPTER. Not so far as I know.

OFFICER. There you are! Didn't I say she was waiting for me? No, don't go. The door's going to be opened.

PROMPTER. Which door?

OFFICER. Is there more than one door?

PROMPTER. Oh, I see — the one with the clover-leaf! Of course I'll stay. I just want to have a few words with the Doorkeeper.

[*He joins the group at the window. They all speak in turn to the* DAUGHTER.] *The* GLAZIER *comes through the gate.*

OFFICER. Are you the locksmith?

GLAZIER. No, the locksmith had company. But a glazier's just as good.

OFFICER. Yes, indeed . . . indeed. But . . . er . . . have you brought your diamond with you?

GLAZIER. Of course. A glazier without a diamond — what good would that be?

OFFICER. None. Let's get to work then. (*He claps his hands. All group themselves in a circle round the door.* MALE CHORUS *in costumes of Die Meistersinger, and* GIRL DANCERS *from Aïda come out of the theatre and join them.*) Locksmith — or Glazier — do your duty! (*The* GLAZIER *goes towards the door holding out his diamond.*) A moment such as this does not recur often in a lifetime. Therefore, my good friends, I beg you to reflect seriously upon . . .

[*During the last words the* POLICEMAN *has entered by the gate.*]

POLICEMAN. In the name of the law I forbid the opening of this door.

OFFICER. Oh God, what a fuss there is whenever one wants to do anything new and great! Well — we shall take proceedings . . . To the lawyer then, and we will see if the law holds good. To the lawyer!

Without any lowering of the curtain the scene changes to the LAWYER'S *office. The gate has now become the gate in an office railing stretching across the stage. The* DOORKEEPER'S *Lodge is a recess for the* LAWYER'S *desk, the lime tree, leafless, a coat-and-hat stand. The announcement-board is covered with proclamations and Court decrees and the clover-door is a document cupboard.*

The LAWYER *in frock coat and white tie is sitting on the left inside the railing of the gate, at this high desk covered with papers. His appearance bears witness to unspeakable suffering. His face is chalk-white, furrowed and purple-shadowed. He is hideous; his face mirrors all the crime and vice with which, through his profession, he has been involved.*

Of his two clerks one has only one arm; the other a single eye.

The people, who had gathered to witness the opening of the door, are now clients waiting to see the LAWYER, *and look as if they have always been there.*

The DAUGHTER, *wearing the shawl, and the* OFFICER *are in front. The* OFFICER *looks curiously at the cupboard door and from time to time pokes it. The* LAWYER *goes up to the* DAUGHTER.

A Dream Play

LAWYER. If you let me have that shawl, my dear, I'll hang it here until the stove is lighted and then I'll burn it with all its griefs and miseries.

DAUGHTER. Not yet, my friend. I must let it get quite full first, and I want above all to gather *your* sufferings up in it, the crimes you have absorbed from others, the vices, swindles, slanders, libel . . .

LAWYER. My child, your shawl would not be big enough. Look at these walls! Isn't the wall-paper stained as if by every kind of sin? Look at these documents in which I write records of evil! Look at me! . . . Nobody who comes here ever smiles. Nothing but vile looks, bared teeth, clenched fists, and all of them squirt their malice, their envy, their suspicions over me. Look, my hands are black and can never be clean! See how cracked they are and bleeding! I can never wear my clothes for more than a few days because they stink of other people's crimes. Sometimes I have the place fumigated with sulphur, but that doesn't help. I sleep in the next room and dream of nothing but crime. I have a murder case in Court now — that's bad enough — but do you know what's worst of all? Separating husbands and wives. Then earth and heaven seem to cry aloud, to cry treason against primal power, the source of good, against love! And then, do you know, after reams of paper have been filled with mutual accusations, if some kindly person takes one or other of the couple aside and asks them in a friendly sort of way the simple question — "What have your really got against your husband — or your wife?" — then he, or she, stands speechless. They don't know. Oh, once it was something to do with a salad, another time about some word. Usually it's about nothing at all. But the suffering, the agony! All this I have to bear. Look at me! Do you think, marked as I am by crime, I can ever win a woman's love? Or that anyone wants to be the friend of a man who has to enforce payment of all the debts of the town? It's misery to be human.

DAUGHTER. Human life is pitiable!

LAWYER. It is indeed. And what people live on is a mystery to me. They marry with an income of two thousand crowns when they need four. They borrow, to be sure, they all borrow, and so scrape along somehow by the skin of their teeth until they die. Then the estate is always insolvent. Who has to pay up in the end? Tell me that.

DAUGHTER. He who feeds the birds.

LAWYER. Well, if He who feeds the birds would come down to earth and see the plight of the unfortunate children of men, perhaps He would have some compassion . . .

DAUGHTER. Human life is pitiful.

LAWYER. Yes, that's the truth. (*To the* OFFICER.) What do you want?

OFFICER. I only want to ask if Miss Victoria has gone.

LAWYER. No, she hasn't. You can rest assured of that. Why do you keep poking my cupboard?

OFFICER. I thought the door was so very like . . .

LAWYER. Oh, no, no, no!

Church bells ring.

OFFICER. Is there a funeral in the town?

LAWYER. No, it's Graduation — the conferring of Doctors' degrees. I myself am about to receive the degree of Doctor of Laws. Perhaps you would like to graduate and receive a laurel wreath?

OFFICER. Why not? It would be a little distraction.

LAWYER. Then perhaps we should proceed at once to the solemn rites. But you must go and change.

Exit OFFICER.

The stage is blacked out and changes to the interior of the Church.

The barrier now serves as the chancel rail. The announcement-board shows the numbers of the hymns. The lime-tree hatstand has become a candelabra, the Lawyer's desk is the Chancellor's lectern, and the Cloverdoor leads to the vestry. The Chorus from Die Meistersinger are ushers with wands. The dancers carry the laurel wreaths.

The rest of the people are the congregation.

The new background shows only a gigantic organ, with a mirror over the keyboard.

Music is heard. At the sides stand the four Deans of the Faculties — Philosophy, Theology, Medicine and Law. For a moment there is no movement, then:

The USHERS *come forward from the right.**

The DANCERS *follow, holding laurel wreaths in their outstretched hands.*

Three GRADUATES *come in from the left, are crowned in turn by the* DANCERS *and go out to the right.*

The LAWYER *advances to receive his wreath.*

The DANCERS *turn away, refusing to crown him, and go out.*

The LAWYER, *greatly agitated, leans against a pillar.*

Everyone disappears. The LAWYER *is alone.*

The DAUGHTER *enters with a white shawl over her head and shoulders.*

DAUGHTER. Look, I have washed the shawl. But what are you doing here? Didn't you get your laurels?

LAWYER. No. I was discredited.

DAUGHTER. Why? Because you have defended the poor, said a good word for the sinner, eased the burden of the guilty, obtained reprieve for the condemned? Woe to mankind! Men are not angels, but pitiable creatures.

LAWYER. Do not judge men harshly. It is my business to plead for them.

DAUGHTER (*leaning against the organ*). Why do they strike their friends in the face?

---

* This scene follows exactly the normal ceremony in a Swedish university when Doctors' degrees are conferred. As each Graduate has the wreath put on his head, a gun outside is fired. The Chancellor and the Faculties bow. Then the new doctor bows to them.

One of the Graduates should be the Officer and another the Schoolmaster of the later scene.

A Dream Play

LAWYER. They know no better.

DAUGHTER. Let us enlighten them — you and I together. Will you?

LAWYER. There can be no enlightenment for them. Oh that the gods in heaven might hear our woe!

DAUGHTER. It shall reach the throne. (*Sits at the organ.*) Do you know what I see in this mirror? The world as it should be. For as it is it's wrong way up.

LAWYER. How did it come to be wrong way up?

DAUGHTER. When the copy was made.

LAWYER. Ah! You yourself have said it — the copy! I always felt this must be a poor copy, and when I began to remember its origin nothing satisfied me. Then they said I was cynical and had a jaundiced eye, and so forth.

DAUGHTER. It is a mad world. Consider these four Faculties. Organized society subsidizes all four: Theology, the doctrine of Divinity, continually attacked and ridiculed by Philosophy claiming wisdom for itself; and Medicine always giving the lie to Philosophy and discounting Theology as one of the sciences, calling it superstition. And there they sit together on the Council, whose function is to teach young men respect for the University. Yes, it's a madhouse. And woe to him who first recovers his senses!

LAWYER. The first to discover it are the theologians. For their preliminary studies they take Philosophy, which teaches them that Theology is nonsense, and then they learn from Theology that Philosophy is nonsense. Madness.

DAUGHTER. Then there's Law, serving all but its servants.

LAWYER. Justice, to the just unjust. Right so often wrong.

DAUGHTER. Thus you have made it, O Children of Men! Child, come! You shall have a wreath from me . . . one more fitting. (*She puts a crown of thorns on his head.*)* Now I will play to you. (*She sits at the organ and plays a Kyrie, but instead of the organ, voices are heard singing. The last note of each phrase is sustained.*)

CHILDREN'S VOICES. Lord! Lord!

WOMEN'S VOICES. Be merciful!

MEN'S VOICES (*tenor*). Deliver us for Thy mercy's sake.

MEN'S VOICES (*bass*). Save Thy children, O Lord, and be not wrathful against us.

ALL. Be merciful! Hear us! Have compassion for mortals. Are we so far from Thee? Out of the depths we call. Grace, Lord! Let not the burden be too heavy for Thy children. Hear us! Hear us!

The stage darkens as the DAUGHTER *rises and approaches the* LAWYER.

By means of lighting the organ is changed to the wall of a grotto. The sea seeps in between basalt pillars with a harmony of waves and wind.

LAWYER. Where are we?

---

* In Molander's production, as the Daughter put the crown of thorns on the Lawyer's head he knelt, facing the audience, his arms outstretched in the form of a crucifix.

DAUGHTER. What do you hear?

LAWYER. I hear drops falling.

DAUGHTER. Those are the tears of mankind weeping. What more do you hear?

LAWYER. A sighing ... a moaning ... a wailing.

DAUGHTER. The lamentation of mortals has reached so far, no further. But why this endless lamentation? Is there no joy in life?

LAWYER. Yes. The sweetest which is also the bitterest — love! Marriage and a home. The highest and the lowest.

DAUGHTER. Let me put it to the test.

LAWYER. With me?

DAUGHTER. With you. You know the rocks, the stumbling stones. Let us avoid them.

LAWYER. I am poor.

DAUGHTER. Does that matter if we love one another? And a little beauty costs nothing.

LAWYER. My antipathies may be your sympathies.

DAUGHTER. They can be balanced.

LAWYER. Supposing we tire?

DAUGHTER. Children will come, bringing ever new interests.

LAWYER. You? You will take me, poor, ugly, despised, discredited?

DAUGHTER. Yes. Let us join our destinies.

LAWYER. So be it.

The scene changes to a very simple room adjoining the LAWYER's *office. On the right is a large curtained double bed, close to it a window with double panes; on the left a stove and kitchen utensils.*

At the back an open door leads to the office, where a number of poor people can be seen awaiting admission. KRISTIN, *the maid, is pasting strips of paper along the edges of the inner window. The* DAUGHTER, *pale and worn, is at the stove.*

KRISTIN. I paste, I paste.

DAUGHTER. You are shutting out the air. I am suffocating.

KRISTIN. Now there's only one small crack left.

DAUGHTER. Air, air! I cannot breathe.

KRISTIN. I paste, I paste.

LAWYER (*from the office*). That's right, Kristin. Warmth is precious.

KRISTIN *pastes the last crack.*

DAUGHTER. Oh, it's as if you are glueing up my mouth!

LAWYER (*coming to the doorway with a document in his hand*). Is the child asleep?

DAUGHTER. Yes, at last.

LAWYER (*mildly*). That screaming frightens away my clients.

DAUGHTER (*gently*). What can be done about it?

A Dream Play

LAWYER. Nothing.

DAUGHTER. We must take a bigger flat.

LAWYER. We have no money.

DAUGHTER. May I open the window, please? This bad air is choking me.

LAWYER. Then the warmth would escape, and we should freeze.

DAUGHTER. It's horrible! Can't we at least scrub the place?

LAWYER. You can't scrub — neither can I, and Kristin must go on pasting. She must paste up the whole house, every crack in floor and walls and ceiling.

[*Exit* KRISTIN, *delighted.*]

DAUGHTER. I was prepared for poverty, not dirt.

LAWYER. Poverty is always rather dirty.

DAUGHTER. This is worse than I dreamt.

LAWYER. We haven't had the worst. There's still food in the pot.

DAUGHTER. But what food!

LAWYER. Cabbage is cheap, nourishing and good.

DAUGHTER. For those who like cabbage. To me it's repulsive.

LAWYER. Why didn't you say so?

DAUGHTER. Because I loved you. I wanted to sacrifice my taste.

LAWYER. Now I must sacrifice my taste for cabbage. Sacrifices must be mutual.

DAUGHTER. Then what shall we eat? Fish? But you hate fish.

LAWYER. And it's dear.

DAUGHTER. This is harder than I believed.

LAWYER (*gently*). You see how hard it is. And the child which should be our bond and blessing is our undoing.

DAUGHTER. Dearest! I am dying in this air, in this room with its backyard view, with babies screaming through endless sleepless hours, and those people out there wailing and quarrelling and accusing . . . Here I can only die.

LAWYER. Poor little flower, without light, without air.

DAUGHTER. And you say there are others worse off.

LAWYER. I am one of the envied of the neighbourhood.

DAUGHTER. None of it would matter, if only I could have some beauty in our home.

LAWYER. I know what you're thinking of — a plant, a heliotrope to be exact; but that costs as much as six quarts of milk or half a bushel of potatoes.

DAUGHTER. I would gladly go without food to have my flower.

LAWYER. There is one kind of beauty that costs nothing. Not to have it in his home is sheer torture for a man with any sense of beauty.

DAUGHTER. What is that?

LAWYER. If I tell you, you will lose your temper.

DAUGHTER. We agreed never to lose our tempers.

LAWYER. We agreed. Yes. All will be well, Agnes, if we can avoid those sharp hard tones. You know them — no, not yet.

DAUGHTER. We shall never hear those.

LAWYER. Never, if it depends on me.

DAUGHTER. Now tell me.

LAWYER. Well, when I come into a house, first I look to see how the curtains are hung. (*Goes to the window and adjusts the curtain.*) If they hang like a bit of string or rag, I soon leave. Then I glance at the chairs. If they are in their places, I stay. (*Puts a chair straight against the wall.*) Next I look at the candlesticks. If the candles are crooked, then the whole house is askew. (*Straightens a candle on the bureau.*) That you see, my dear, is the beauty which costs nothing.

DAUGHTER (*bowing her head*). Not that sharp tone, Axel!

LAWYER. It wasn't sharp.

DAUGHTER. Yes it was.

LAWYER. The devil take it!

DAUGHTER. What kind of language is that?

LAWYER. Forgive me, Agnes. But I have suffered as much from your untidiness as you do from the dirt. And I haven't dared straighten things myself, because you would have been offended and thought I was reproaching you. Oh, shall we stop this?

DAUGHTER. It is terribly hard to be married, harder than anything. I think one has to be an angel.

LAWYER. I think one has.

DAUGHTER. I am beginning to hate you after all this.

LAWYER. Alas for us then! But let us prevent hatred. I promise never to mention untidiness again, although it is torture to me.

DAUGHTER. And I will eat cabbage, although that is torment to me.

LAWYER. And so — life together is a torment. One's pleasure is the other's pain.

DAUGHTER. Human beings are pitiful.

LAWYER. You see that now?

DAUGHTER. Yes. But in God's name let us avoid the rocks, now that we know them so well.

LAWYER. Let us do that. We are tolerant, enlightened people. Of course we can make allowances and forgive.

DAUGHTER. Of course we can smile at trifles.

LAWYER. We, only we can do it. Do you know, I read in the paper this morning . . . By the way, where is the paper?

DAUGHTER (*embarrassed*). Which paper?

LAWYER (*harshly*). Do I take more than one newspaper?

DAUGHTER. Smile — and don't speak harshly! I lit the fire with your newspaper.

LAWYER (*violently*). The devil you did!

DAUGHTER. Please smile. I burnt it because it mocked what to me is holy.

LAWYER. What to me is unholy! Huh! (*Striking his hands together, beside himself.*) I'll smile, I'll smile till my back teeth show. I'll be tolerant and swallow my opinions and say yes to everything and cant and cringe. So you've

A Dream Play

burnt my paper, have you? (*Pulls the bed curtains.*) Very well. Now I'm going to tidy up until you lose your temper ... Agnes, this is quite impossible!

DAUGHTER. Indeed it is.

LAWYER. Yet we must stay together. Not for our vows' sake, but for the child's.

DAUGHTER. That's true — for the child's sake. Yes, yes, we must go on.

LAWYER. And now I must attend to my clients. Listen to them muttering. They can't wait to tear one another to pieces, to get each other fined and imprisoned. Benighted souls!

Enter KRISTIN *with pasting materials.*

DAUGHTER. Wretched, wretched beings! And all this pasting! (*She bows her head in dumb despair.*)

KRISTIN. I paste, I paste!

The LAWYER *standing by the door, nervously fingers the handle.*

DAUGHTER. Oh how that handle squeaks! It is as if you were twisting my heart-strings.

LAWYER. I twist, I twist!

DAUGHTER. Don't!

LAWYER. I twist ...

DAUGHTER. No!

LAWYER. I ...

The OFFICER [*now middle-aged*] *takes hold of the handle from inside the office.*

OFFICER. May I?

LAWYER (*letting go of the handle*). Certainly. As you have got your degree.

OFFICER (*entering*). The whole of life is now mine. All paths are open to me. I have set foot on Parnassus, the laurels are won. Immortality, fame, all are mine!

LAWYER. What are you going to live on?

OFFICER. Live on?

LAWYER. You'll need a roof surely, and clothes and food?

OFFICER. Those are always to be had, as long as there's someone who cares for you.

LAWYER. Fancy that now, fancy that! Paste, Kristin, paste! Until they cannot breathe. (*Goes out backwards, nodding.*)

KRISTIN. I paste, I paste! Until they cannot breathe.

OFFICER. Will you come now?

DAUGHTER. Oh quickly! But where to?

OFFICER. To Fairhaven, where it is summer and the sun is shining. Youth is there, children and flowers, singing and dancing, feasting and merrymaking.

[*Exit* KRISTIN.]

DAUGHTER. I would like to go there.

OFFICER. Come!

LAWYER (*entering*). Now I shall return to my first hell. This one was the second — and worst. The sweetest hell is the worst. Look, she's left hairpins all over the floor again! (*Picks one up.*)

OFFICER. So he has discovered the hairpins too.

LAWYER. Too? Look at this one. There are two prongs but one pin. Two and yet one. If I straighten it out, it becomes one single piece. If I bend it, it is two, without ceasing to be one. In other words the two are one. But if I break it — like this — (*breaks it in half*) — then the two are two. (*He throws away the pieces.*)

OFFICER. So much he has seen. But before one can break it, the prongs must diverge. If they converge, it holds.

LAWYER. And if they are parallel, they never meet. Then it neither holds nor breaks.

OFFICER. The hairpin is the most perfect of all created things. A straight line which is yet two parallel lines.

LAWYER. A lock that closes when open.

OFFICER. Closes open — a plait of hair loosed while bound.

LAWYER. Like this door. When I close it, I open the way out, for you, Agnes.

Goes out, closing the door.

DAUGHTER. And now?

The scene changes. The bed with its hangings is transformed into a tent, the stove remaining. The new background shows a beautiful wooded shore, with beflagged landing stages and white boats, some with sails set. Among the trees are little Italianesque villas, pavilions, kiosks and marble statues.

In the middle distance is a strait.

The foreground presents a sharp contrast with the background. Burnt hillsides, black and white tree stumps as after a forest fire, red heather, red pigsties and outhouses. On the right is an open-air establishment for remedial exercises, where people are being treated on machines resembling instruments of torture.

On the left is part of the Quarantine Station; open sheds with furnaces, boilers and pipes.

[*The* DAUGHTER *and the* OFFICER *are standing as at the end of the previous scene.*]

The QUARANTINE MASTER, *dressed as a blackamoor, comes along the shore.*

OFFICER (*going up and shaking hands with the* QUARANTINE MASTER). What? You here, old Gasbags?*

Q. MASTER. Yes, I'm here.

OFFICER. Is this place Fairhaven?

---

* Original "Ordström," meaning "Stream of Words."

A Dream Play

Q. MASTER. No, that's over there. (*Points across the strait.*) This is Foulstrand.

OFFICER. Then we've come wrong.

Q. MASTER. We! Aren't you going to introduce me?

OFFICER. It wouldn't do. (*Low.*) That is the Daughter of Indra.

Q. MASTER. Of Indra? I thought it must be Varuna himself. Well, aren't you surprised to find me black in the face?

OFFICER. My dear fellow, I am over fifty, at which age one ceases to be surprised. I assumed at once that you were going to a fancy dress ball this afternoon.

Q. MASTER. Quite correct. I hope you'll come with me.

OFFICER. Certainly, for there doesn't seem to be any attraction in this place. What kind of people live here?

Q. MASTER. The sick live here, and the healthy over there.

OFFICER. But surely only the poor here?

Q. MASTER. No, my boy, here you have the rich. (*Indicates the gymnasium.*) Look at that man on the rack. He's eaten too much paté-de-foie-gras with truffles, and drunk so much Burgundy that his feet are knotted.

OFFICER. Knotted?

Q. MASTER. He's got knotted feet, and that one lying on the guillotine has drunk so much brandy that his backbone's got to be mangled.

OFFICER. That's not very pleasant either.

Q. MASTER. What's more here on this side live all those who have some misery to hide. Look at this one coming now, for instance.

> *An elderly fop is wheeled on to the stage in a bath chair, accompanied by a gaunt and hideous coquette of sixty, dressed in the latest fashion and attended by the "Friend," a man of forty.*

OFFICER. It's the Major! Our schoolfellow.

Q. MASTER. Don Juan! You see, he's still in love with the spectre at his side. He doesn't see that she has grown old, that she is ugly, faithless, cruel.

OFFICER. There's true love for you. I never would have thought that flighty fellow had it in him to love so deeply and ardently.

Q. MASTER. That's a nice way of looking at it.

OFFICER. I've been in love myself — with Victoria. As a matter of fact I still pace up and down the alley, waiting for her.

Q. MASTER. So you're the fellow who waits in the alley?

OFFICER. I am he.

Q. MASTER. Well, have you got that door open yet?

OFFICER. No, we're still fighting the case. The Billsticker is out with his fishnet, you see, which delays the taking of evidence. Meanwhile, the Glazier has put in windowpanes at the castle, which has grown half a story. It has been an unusually good year this year — warm and damp.

Q. MASTER (*pointing to the sheds*). But you've certainly had nothing like the heat of my place there.

OFFICER. What's the temperature of your furnaces then?

Q. MASTER. When we're disinfecting cholera suspects, we keep them at sixty degrees.

OFFICER. But is there cholera about again?

Q. MASTER. Didn't you know?

OFFICER. Of course I know. But I so often forget what I know.

Q. MASTER. And I so often wish I could forget — especially myself. That's why I go in for masquerades, fancy dress, theatricals.

OFFICER. Why. What's the matter with you?

Q. MASTER. If I talk, they say I'm bragging. If I hold my tongue they call me a hypocrite.

OFFICER. Is that why you blacked your face?

Q. MASTER. Yes. A shade blacker than I am.

OFFICER. Who's this coming?

Q. MASTER. Oh, he's a poet! He's going to have his mud bath.

The POET *enters, looking at the sky and carrying a pail of mud.*

OFFICER. But, good heavens, he ought to bathe in light and air!

Q. MASTER. No, he lives so much in the higher spheres that he gets homesick for the mud. It hardens his skin to wallow in the mire, just as it does with pigs. After his bath he doesn't feel the gadflies stinging.

OFFICER. What a strange world of contradictions!

POET (*ecstatically*). Out of clay the god Ptah fashioned man on a potter's wheel, a lathe (*mockingly*), or some other damned thing . . . (*Ecstatically.*) Out of clay the sculptor fashions his more or less immortal masterpieces (*mockingly*), which are usually only rubbish. (*Ecstatically.*) Out of clay are formed those objects, so domestically essential bearing the generic name of pots and pans. (*Mockingly.*) Not that it matters in the least to me what they're called. (*Ecstatically.*) Such is clay! When clay is fluid, it is called mud. *C'est mon affaire!* (*Calls.*) Lina!

Enter LINA *with a bucket.*

POET. Lina, show yourself to Miss Agnes. She knew you ten years ago when you were a young, happy, and, let me add, pretty girl. (*To* DAUGHTER.) Look at her now! Five children, drudgery, squalling, hunger, blows. See how beauty has perished, how joy has vanished in the fulfilment of duties which should give that inner contentment which shows in the harmonious lines of a face, in the tranquil shining of the eyes . . .

Q. MASTER (*putting a hand to the* POET'S *lips*). Shut up! Shut up!

POET. That's what they all say. But if you are silent, they tell you to talk. How inconsistent people are!

Distant dance music is heard.

DAUGHTER (*going up to* LINA). Tell me your troubles.

LINA. No, I daren't. I'd catch it all the worse if I did.

DAUGHTER. Who is so cruel?

LINA. I daren't talk about it. I'll be beaten.

POET. May be, but I shall talk about it even if the Blackamoor knocks my teeth out. I shall talk about all the injustice there is here. Agnes, Daughter of the Gods, do you hear that music up on the hill? Well, that's a dance for Lina's sister, who has come home from town — where she went astray, you understand. Now they are killing the fatted calf, while Lina, who stayed at home, has to carry the swill pail and feed the pigs.

DAUGHTER. There is rejoicing in that home because the wanderer has forsaken the path of evil, not only because she has come home. Remember that.

POET. Then give a ball and a supper every evening for this blameless servant who has never gone astray. Do that for her — they never do. On the contrary, when Lina is free, she has to go to prayer meetings where she's reprimanded for not being perfect. Is that justice?

DAUGHTER. Your questions are difficult to answer, because there are so many unknown factors.

POET. The Caliph, Harun the Just, was of the same opinion. Sitting quietly on his exalted throne he could never see how those below were faring. Presently complaints reached his lofty ear, so one fine day he stepped down in disguise and walked unobserved among the crowd to watch the workings of justice.

DAUGHTER. You do not think I am Harun the Just, do you?

OFFICER. Let's change the subject. Here are newcomers.

A white boat, shaped like a dragon, glides into the Strait. It has a light blue silken sail on a gilded yard, and a golden mast with a rose-red pennon. At the helm, with their arms round each other's waists, sit HE *and* SHE.

There you see perfect happiness, utter bliss, the ecstasy of young love.

The light grows stronger. HE *stands up in the boat and sings.*

HE.   Hail fairest bay!
                   Where I passed youth's spring tide,
                   where I dreamed its first roses,
                   I come now again,
                   no longer alone.
                   Forests and havens,
                   heaven and sea,
                   greet her!
                   My love, my bride,
                   my sun, my life!

The flags on Fairhaven dip in salute. White handkerchiefs wave from villas and shores. The music of harps and violins sound over the strait.

POET. See how light streams from them! And sound rings across the water! Eros!

OFFICER. It is Victoria.

Q. MASTER. Well, if it is . . .

OFFICER. It is his Victoria. I have my own, and mine no one will ever see. Now hoist the quarantine flag while I haul in the catch.

> *The* QUARANTINE MASTER *waves a yellow flag. The* OFFICER *pulls on a line which causes the boat to turn in towards Foulstrand.*

Hold hard there!

> HE *and* SHE *become aware of the dreadful landscape and show their horror.*

Q. MASTER. Yes, yes, it's hard lines, but everyone has to land here, everyone coming from infectious areas.

POET. Think of being able to speak like that — to behave like that when you see two human beings joined in love. Do not touch them! Do not lay hands on love — that is high treason. Alas, alas! All that is most lovely will now be dragged down, down into the mud.

> HE *and* SHE *come ashore, shamed and sad.*

HE. What is it? What have we done?*

Q. MASTER. You don't have to do anything in order to meet with life's little discomforts.

SHE. How brief are joy and happiness!

HE. How long must we stay here?

Q. MASTER. Forty days and forty nights.

SHE. We would rather throw ourselves into the sea.

HE. Live here — among burnt hills and pigsties?

POET. Love can overcome everything, even sulphur fumes and carbolic acid.†

> *The* QUARANTINE MASTER *goes into a shed. Blue sulphurous vapour pours out.*

Q. MASTER (*coming out*). I'm burning the sulphur. Will you kindly step inside.

SHE. Oh, my blue dress will lose its colour!

Q. MASTER. And turn white. Your red roses will turn white too.

HE. So will your cheeks, in forty days.

SHE (*to the* OFFICER). That will please you.

OFFICER. No, it won't. True, your happiness was the source of my misery, but . . . that's no matter. (HE *and* SHE *go into the shed. To* DAUGHTER.) I've got my degree now, and a job as tutor over there. (*Indicates Fairhaven.*) Heigho! And in the fall I'll get a post in a school, teaching the boys the same lessons I learnt myself, all through my childhood, all through my youth. Teach them the same lessons I learnt all through my manhood and finally all through my old age. The same lessons! What is twice two? How many times does two go into four without remainder? Until I get a pension and have

---

* Literally "woe to us."

† The Poet does not speak again and is not mentioned until the end of the later quayside scene, so perhaps here he goes out.

nothing to do but wait for meals and the newspapers, until in the end I'm carried out to the crematorium and burnt to ashes. (*To* QUARANTINE MASTER *as he comes out of the shed.*) Have you no pensioners here? To be a pensioner is the worst fate after twice two is four, going to school again when one's taken one's degree, asking the same questions until one dies . . .

An elderly man walks past with his hands behind his back.

Look, there goes a pensioner waiting for his life to ebb. A Captain, probably, who failed to become a Major, or a Clerk to the Court who was never promoted. Many are called, but few are chosen. He's just walking about, waiting for breakfast.

PENSIONER. No, for the paper, the morning paper!

OFFICER. And he is only fifty-four. He may go on for another twenty-five years, waiting for meals and the newspaper. Isn't that dreadful?

PENSIONER. What is not dreadful? Tell me that. Tell me that.

OFFICER. Yes. Let him tell who can.

Exit PENSIONER.

Now I shall teach boys twice two is four. How many times does two go into four without remainder? (*He clutches his head in despair.*)

Enter HE *and* SHE *from the shed. Her dress and roses are white, her face pale. His clothes are also bleached.*

And Victoria whom I loved, for whom I desired the greatest happiness on earth, she has her happiness now, the greatest happiness she can know, while I suffer, suffer, suffer!

SHE. Do you think I can be happy, seeing your suffering? How can you believe that? Perhaps it comforts you to know that I shall be a prisoner here for forty days and forty nights. Tell me, does it comfort you?

OFFICER. Yes and no. I cannot have pleasure while you have pain. Oh!

HE. And do you think my happiness can be built on your agony?

OFFICER. We are all to be pitied — all of us.

All lift their hands to heaven. A discordant cry of anguish breaks from their lips.

ALL. Oh!

DAUGHTER. O God, hear them! Life is evil! Mankind is to be pitied.

ALL (*as before*). Oh!

The stage is blacked out and the scene changes.

The whole landscape is in winter dress with snow on the ground and on the leafless trees. Foulstrand is in the background, in shadow.

The strait is still in the middle distance. On the near side is a landing stage with white boats and flags flying from flagstaffs. In the strait a white warship, a brig with gunports, is anchored.

The foreground presents Fairhaven, in full light.

On the right is a corner of the Assembly Rooms with open windows through which are seen couples dancing.

On a box outside stand three MAIDS, *their arms round each other's waists, watching the dancing.*

On the steps is a bench on which UGLY EDITH *is sitting, bareheaded and sorrowful, with long dishevelled hair, before an open piano.*

On the left is a yellow wooden house outside which two children in summer dresses are playing ball.

The DAUGHTER *and* OFFICER *enter.*

DAUGHTER. Here is peace and happiness. Holiday time. Work over, every day a festival, everyone in holiday attire. Music and dancing even in the morning. (*To the* MAIDS.) Why don't you go in and dance, my dears?

SERVANTS. Us?

OFFICER. But they are servants.

DAUGHTER. True. But why is Edith sitting there instead of dancing?

EDITH *buries her face in her hands.*

OFFICER. Don't ask her! She has been sitting there for three hours without being invited to dance. (*He goes into the yellow house.*)

DAUGHTER. What cruel pleasure!

The MOTHER, *in a décolleté dress, comes out of the Assembly Rooms and goes up to* EDITH.

MOTHER. Why don't you go in as I told you?

EDITH. Because . . . because I can't be my own partner. I know I'm ugly and no one wants to dance with me, but I can avoid being reminded of it. (*She begins to play Bach's Toccata con Fuga, No. 10.*)

The waltz at the ball is heard too, first faintly, then growing louder as if in competition with the Toccata. Gradually EDITH *overcomes it and reduces it to silence. Dance couples appear in the doorway, and everyone stands reverently listening. A* NAVAL OFFICER *seizes* ALICE, *one of the guests, by the waist.*

N. OFFICER. Come, quick! (*He leads her down to the landing stage.* EDITH *breaks off, rises and watches them in despair. She remains standing as if turned to stone.*)

The front wall of the yellow house vanishes. Boys are sitting on forms, among them the OFFICER *looking uncomfortable and worried. In front of them stands the* SCHOOLMASTER, *wearing spectacles and holding chalk and a cane.*

SCHOOLMASTER (*to the* OFFICER). Now, my boy, can you tell me what twice two is?

The OFFICER *remains seated, painfully searching his memory without finding an answer.*

You must stand up when you are asked a question.

OFFICER (*rising anxiously*). Twice two . . . let me see . . . That makes two twos.

S. MASTER. Aha! So you have not prepared your lesson.

A Dream Play

OFFICER (*embarrassed*). Yes, I have, but . . . I know what it is, but I can't say it.

S. MASTER. You're quibbling. You know the answer, do you? But you can't say it. Perhaps I can assist you. (*Pulls the* OFFICER's *hair.*)

OFFICER. Oh, this is dreadful, really dreadful!

S. MASTER. Yes, it is dreadful that such a big boy should have no ambition.

OFFICER (*agonised*). A *big* boy. Yes, I certainly am big, much bigger than these others. I am grown up, I have left school . . . (*As if waking.*) I have even graduated. Why am I sitting here then? Haven't I got my degree?

S. MASTER. Certainly. But you have got to stay here and mature. Do you see? You must mature. Isn't that so?

OFFICER (*clasping his head*). Yes, that's so, one must mature . . . Twice two — is two, and this I will demonstrate by analogy, the highest form of proof. Listen! Once one is one, therefore twice two is two. For that which applies to the one must also apply to the other.

S. MASTER. The proof is perfectly in accord with the laws of logic, but the answer is wrong.

OFFICER. What is in accord with the laws of logic cannot be wrong. Let us put it to the test. One into one goes once, therefore two into two goes twice.

S. MASTER. Quite correct according to analogy. But what then is once three?

OFFICER. It is three.

S. MASTER. Consequently twice three is also three.

OFFICER (*pondering*). No, that can't be right . . . It can't be, for if so . . . (*Sits down in despair.*) No, I am not mature yet . . .

S. MASTER. No, you are not mature by a long way.

OFFICER. Then how long shall I have to stay here?

S. MASTER. How long? Here? You believe that time and space exist? Assuming time does exist, you ought to be able to say what time is. What is time?

OFFICER. Time . . . (*Considers.*) I can't say, although I know what it is. Ergo, I may know what twice two is without being able to say it. Can you yourself say what time is?

S. MASTER. Certainly I can.

ALL THE BOYS. Tell us then!

S. MASTER. Time? . . . Let me see. (*Stands motionless with his finger to his nose.*) While we speak, time flies. Consequently time is something which flies while I am speaking.

BOY (*rising*). You're speaking now, sir, and while you're speaking, I fly. Consequently I am time. (*Flies.*)

S. MASTER. That is quite correct according to the laws of logic.

OFFICER. Then the laws of logic are absurd, for Nils, though he did fly, can't be time.

S. MASTER. That is also quite correct according to the laws of logic, although it is absurd.

OFFICER. Then logic is absurd.

S. MASTER. It really looks like it. But if logic is absurd, then the whole world is absurd . . . and I'll be damned if I stay here and teach you absurdities! If anyone will stand us a drink, we'll go and bathe.

OFFICER. That's a *posterus prius*, a world back to front, for it's customary to bathe first and have one's drink afterwards. You old fossil!

S. MASTER. Don't be so conceited, Doctor.

OFFICER. Captain, if you please. I am an officer, and I don't understand why I should sit here among a lot of schoolboys and be insulted.

S. MASTER (*wagging his finger*). We must mature!

Enter QUARANTINE MASTER.

Q. MASTER. The quarantine period has begun.

OFFICER. So there you are. Fancy this fellow making me sit here on a form, when I've taken my degree.

Q. MASTER. Well, why don't you go away?

OFFICER. Go away? That's easier said than done.

S. MASTER. So I should think. Try!

OFFICER (*to* QUARANTINE MASTER). Save me! Save me from his eyes!

Q. MASTER. Come on then! Come and help us dance. We must dance before the plague breaks out. We must.

OFFICER. Will the ship sail then?

Q. MASTER. The ship will sail first. A lot of tears will be shed of course.

OFFICER. Always tears; when she comes in and when she sails. Let's go.

They go out. The SCHOOLMASTER *continues to give his lesson in mime. The* MAIDS, *who were standing at the window of the ballroom, walk sadly down to the quay.* EDITH, *until then motionless beside the piano, follows them.*

DAUGHTER (*to* OFFICER). Isn't there one happy person in this paradise?

OFFICER. Yes, here comes a newly wed couple. Listen to them.

The NEWLY WED COUPLE *enter.*

HUSBAND (*to* WIFE). My happiness is so complete that I wish to die.

WIFE. But why to die?

HUSBAND. In the midst of happiness grows a seed of unhappiness. Happiness consumes itself like a flame. It cannot burn for ever, it must go out, and the presentiment of its end destroys it at its very peak.

WIFE. Let us die together, now at once.

HUSBAND. Die! Yes, let us die. For I fear happiness, the deceiver.

They go towards the sea and disappear.

DAUGHTER (*to the* OFFICER). Life is evil. Human beings are to be pitied!

OFFICER. Look who's coming now. This is the most envied mortal in the place. (*The* BLIND MAN *is led in.*) He is the owner of these hundreds of Italian villas. He owns all these bays and creeks and shores and woods, the fish in the water, the birds in the air and the game in the woods. These

A Dream Play

thousands of people are his tenants, and the sun rises over his sea and sets over his lands.

DAUGHTER. And does he complain too?

OFFICER. Yes, with good cause, as he cannot see.

Q. MASTER. He is blind.

DAUGHTER. The most envied of all!

OFFICER. Now he's going to see the ship sail with his son aboard.

BLIND MAN. I do not see, but I hear. I hear the fluke of the anchor tearing the clay bed, just as when the hook is dragged out of a fish and the heart comes up too through the gullet. My son, my only child, is going to journey to strange lands across the great sea. Only my thoughts can go with him . . . Now I hear the chain clanking . . . and there's something flapping and lashing like washing on a clothes line . . . Wet handkerchiefs perhaps . . . And I hear a sound of sighing . . . or sobbing . . . like people crying . . . Maybe the plash of small waves against the hull, or maybe the girls on the quay, the abandoned, the inconsolable. I once asked a child why the sea was salt, and the child, whose father was on a long voyage, replied at once: "The sea is salt because sailors cry so much." "But why do sailors cry so much?" "Well," he said, "because they keep going away . . . And so they're always drying their handkerchiefs up on the masts." "And why do people cry when they're sad?" I asked. "Oh," said he, "that's because the eye window must be washed sometimes, so we can see better."

The brig has set sail and glided away. The girls on the quay alternately wave their handkerchiefs and dry their eyes. Now on the topmast is hoisted the signal "YES," a red ball on a white ground. ALICE *waves a triumphant reply.*

DAUGHTER (*to* OFFICER). What does that flag mean?

OFFICER. It means "yes." It is the lieutenant's "yes" in red, red as heart's blood, written on the blue cloth of the sky.

DAUGHTER. Then what is "no" like?

OFFICER. Blue as tainted blood in blue veins. Look how elated Alice is.

DAUGHTER. And how Edith is weeping.

BLIND MAN. Meeting and parting, parting and meeting. That's life. I met his mother, then she went away. My son was left; now he has gone.

DAUGHTER. But he will come back.

BLIND MAN. Who is speaking to me? I have heard that voice before. In my dreams, in boyhood when summer holidays began, in early married life when my child was born. Whenever life smiled, I heard that voice, like the whisper of the South wind, like the sounds of a heavenly harp, like the angels' greeting, as I imagine it, on Christmas Eve.

The LAWYER *enters, goes up to the* BLIND MAN *and whispers.*
Really?

LAWYER. Yes, it's a fact. (*Goes across to the* DAUGHTER.) You have seen most things now, but you have not yet experienced the worst thing of all.

DAUGHTER. What can that be?

LAWYER. Repetitions, reiterations. Going back. Doing one's lessons again ... Come!

DAUGHTER. Where to?

LAWYER. To your duties.

DAUGHTER. What are they?

LAWYER. Everything you abominate. Everything you least want to do, and yet must. They are to abstain and renounce, to go without, to leave behind. They are everything that is disagreeable, repulsive, painful.

DAUGHTER. Are there no pleasant duties?

LAWYER. They become pleasant when they are done.

DAUGHTER. When they no longer exist. So duty is altogether unpleasant. What then can one enjoy?

LAWYER. What one enjoys is sin.

DAUGHTER. Sin?

LAWYER. Which is punished. Yes. If I enjoy myself one day, one evening, the next day I have a bad conscience and go through the torments of hell.

DAUGHTER. How strange!

LAWYER. I wake in the morning with a headache, and then the repetition begins, but it is a distorted repetition, so that everything which was charming and witty and beautiful the night before appears in memory ugly, stupid, repulsive. Pleasure stinks, and enjoyment falls to pieces. What people call success is always a step towards the next failure. The successes in my life have been my downfall. Men have an instinctive dread of another's good fortune. They feel it's unjust that fate should favour any one man, so try to restore the balance by rolling boulders across his path. To have talent is to be in danger of one's life — one may so easily starve to death. However, you must go back to your duties, or I shall take proceedings against you, and we shall go through all three Courts, first, second, third.

DAUGHTER. Go back? To the stove and the cabbage and the baby clothes?

LAWYER. Yes. And it's washing day — the big wash when all the handkerchiefs have to be done.

DAUGHTER. Oh, must I do that again?

LAWYER. The whole of life is only repetition. Look at the schoolmaster there. Yesterday he took his doctor's degree, was crowned with laurels, scaled Parnassus, was embraced by the monarch. Today he is back at school, asking what twice two is ... and that's what he will go on doing until he dies. But come now, back to your home.

DAUGHTER. I would rather die.

LAWYER. Die? One can't do that. To begin with taking one's own life is so dishonourable that even one's corpse is dishonoured. And to add to that one is damned, for it is a mortal sin.

DAUGHTER. It is not easy to be human.

ALL. Hear, hear!

DAUGHTER. I will not go back with you to humiliation and dirt. I shall

A Dream Play

return to the place from which I came. But first the door must be opened, so that I may know the secret. I wish the door to be opened.

Enter the POET.

LAWYER. Then you must retrace your steps, go back the way you came, and put up with all the horrors of a lawsuit; the repetitions, the redraftings, the reiterations.

DAUGHTER. So be it. But first I shall seek solitude in the wilderness to find myself. We shall meet again. (*To the* POET.) Come with me.

A distant cry of lamentation rises.

VOICES. Oh! oh! oh!

DAUGHTER. What was that?

LAWYER. The doomed at Foulstrand.

DAUGHTER. Why do they wail so today?

LAWYER. Because here the sun is shining, here is music and dance and youth. This makes them suffer more.

DAUGHTER. We must set them free.

LAWYER. Try! Once a deliverer came, but he was hanged upon a cross.

DAUGHTER. By whom?

LAWYER. By all the righteous.

DAUGHTER. Who are they?

LAWYER. Don't you know the righteous? Well, you will.

DAUGHTER. Was it they who refused you your degree?

LAWYER. Yes.

DAUGHTER. Then I do know them.

The scene changes to a Mediterranean resort. In the background are villas, a Casino with a terrace, and a blue strip of sea. In the foreground is a white wall over which hang branches of orange trees in fruit. Below this to one side a huge heap of coal and two wheel barrows.

The DAUGHTER *and the* LAWYER *come on to the terrace.*

DAUGHTER. This is paradise.

1ST. COAL HEAVER. This is hell.

2ND. C. H. A hundred and twenty in the shade.

1ST. C. H. Shall we get into the sea?

2ND. C. H. Then the police'd come: "You mustn't bathe here!"

1ST. C. H. Can't we have a bit of fruit off that tree?

2ND. C. H. No. The police would come.

1ST. C. H. One can't work in this heat. I'm going to chuck it.

2ND. C. H. Then the police will come and take you up. (*Pause.*) Besides, you'll have nothing to eat.

1ST. C. H. Nothing to eat! We, who do the most work, get the least food. And the rich, who do nothing, get it all. Might one not, without taking liberties with the truth, call this unjust? What has the Daughter of the Gods up there to say about it?

DAUGHTER. I have no answer. But, tell me, what have you done to get so black and have so hard a lot?

1ST. C. H. What have we done? Got ourselves born of poor and pretty bad parents. Been sentenced a couple of times maybe.

DAUGHTER. Sentenced?

1ST. C. H. Yes. The ones that don't get caught sit up there in the Casino eating eight course dinners with wine.

DAUGHTER (*to* LAWYER). Can this be true?

LAWYER. More or less, yes.

DAUGHTER. Do you mean that everyone at some time or other deserves imprisonment?

LAWYER. Yes.

DAUGHTER. Even you?

LAWYER. Yes.

DAUGHTER. Is it true those poor men aren't allowed to bathe in that sea?

LAWYER. No, not even with their clothes on. Only those who try to drown themselves avoid paying. And they are more than likely to get beaten up at the police station.

DAUGHTER. Can't they go and bathe outside the town — in the country?

LAWYER. There is no country. It's all fenced in.

DAUGHTER. I mean where it is open and free.

LAWYER. Nothing is free. Everything is owned.

DAUGHTER. Even the sea, the vast, wide . . . ?

LAWYER. Everything. You can't go out in a boat, nor can you land, without it all being booked and paid for. It's marvellous.

DAUGHTER. This is not paradise.

LAWYER. I promise you that.

DAUGHTER. Why don't people do anything to improve conditions?

LAWYER. They certainly do. But all reformers end in prison or the madhouse.

DAUGHTER. Who puts them in prison?

LAWYER. All the righteous, all the respectable.

DAUGHTER. Who puts them in the madhouse?

LAWYER. Their own despair when they see the hopelessness of the struggle.

DAUGHTER. Has it occurred to anyone that there may be unknown reasons for this state of things?

LAWYER. Yes, the well-off always think that is so.

DAUGHTER. That there is nothing wrong with things as they are?

1ST. C. H. And yet we are the foundation of society. If there's no coal, the kitchen stove goes out and the fire on the hearth too. The machines in the factory stop working; the lights in streets and shops and homes all go out. Darkness and cold descend on you. That's why we sweat like hell carrying filthy coal. What do you give us in return?

LAWYER (*to* DAUGHTER). Help them. (*Pause.*) I know things can't be exactly the same for everybody, but why should there be such inequality?

A Dream Play

The GENTLEMAN *and the* LADY *cross the terrace.*

LADY. Are you coming to play cards?

GENTLEMAN. No, I must go for a little walk to get an appetite for dinner. *Exeunt.*

1ST. C. H. To *get* an appetite!

2ND. C. H. To *get* . . .!

Children enter. When they catch sight of the black workers they scream with terror [and run off].

1ST. C. H. They scream when they see us. They scream!

2ND. C. H. Curse it! We'd better get out the scaffolds soon and execute this rotten body.

1ST. C. H. Curse it, I say too!

LAWYER (*to* DAUGHTER). It's all wrong. It's not the people who are so bad, but . . .

DAUGHTER. But?

LAWYER. The system.

DAUGHTER (*hiding her face in her hands*). This is not paradise.

1ST. C. H. No. This is hell, pure hell.

The scene changes to [the earlier set of] Fingal's Cave. Long green billows roll gently into the cave. A red bellbuoy rocks upon the waves, but gives no sound until later. Music of the winds. Music of the waves.

The DAUGHTER *is with the* POET.

POET. Where have you brought me?

DAUGHTER. Far from the murmur and wailing of the children of men. To this grotto at the ends of the oceans to which we give the name *Indra's Ear*, for here, it is said, the King of Heaven listens to the lamentations of mortals.

POET. Why here?

DAUGHTER. Do you not see that this cave is shaped like a shell? Yes, you see it. Do you not know that your ear is shaped like a shell? You know, but you have given it no thought. (*She picks up a shell.*) As a child, did you never hold a shell to your ear and listen to the whisper of your heart's blood, to the humming of thoughts in your brain, to the parting of a thousand little worn-out tissues in the fabric of your body? All this you can hear in a small shell. Think then what may be heard in this great one.

POET (*listening*). I hear nothing but the sighing of the wind.

DAUGHTER. Then I will be its interpreter. Listen to the lamentation of the winds. (*She speaks to soft music.*)

> Born under heaven's clouds,
> chased were we by Indra's fires
> down to the crust of earth.
> The mould of acres soiled our feet,
> we had to bear
> the dust of roads and city smoke,
> the kitchen's reek and fumes of wine.

> *Out to these spacious seas we blew,*
> *to air our lungs,*
> *to shake our wings*
> *and bathe our feet.*
> *Indra, Lord of Heaven,*
> *hear us!*
> *Listen to our sighing!*
> *Earth is not clean,*
> *life is not just,*
> *men are not evil*
> *nor are they good.*
> *They live as best they may*
> *from one day to another,*
> *Sons of dust in dust they walk,*
> *born of the dust,*
> *dust they become.*
> *Feet they have to trudge,*
> *no wings.*
> *Dust-soiled they grow.*
> *Is the fault theirs*
> *or Thine?*

POET. So I heard once . . .

DAUGHTER. Hush! The winds are still singing. (*Continues to soft music.*)
> *We, the winds, the sons of air,*
> *bear man's lamentation.*
> *Thou hast heard us*
> *on autumn eves in the chimney stack,*
> *in the stove-pipe's vent,*
> *in the window cracks,*
> *as the rain wept on the tiles.*
> *Or on winter nights,*
> *mid the pine-wood's snows,*
> *or on the stormy ocean,*
> *hast heard the moaning and the whine,*
> *of rope and sail.*
> *That is us, the winds,*
> *the sons of air,*
> *who from human breasts*
> *we pierced ourselves,*
> *these sounds of suffering learnt.*
> *In sickroom, on the battlefield,*
> *and most where the newborn lie,*
> *screaming, complaining,*
> *of the pain of being alive.*

A Dream Play

> *It is we, we, the winds*
> *who whine and whistle,*
> *woe! woe! woe!*

POET. It seems to me that once before...

DAUGHTER. Hush! The waves are singing. (*Speaks to soft music.*)
> *It is we, we the waves,*
> *that rock the winds*
> *to rest.*
> *Green cradling waves,*
> *wet are we and salt.*
> *Like flames of fire,*
> *wet flames we are.*
> *Quenching, burning,*
> *cleansing, bathing,*
> *generating, multiplying.*
> *We, we the waves,*
> *that rock the winds*
> *to rest.*

False waves and faithless. Everything on earth that is not burned is drowned by those waves. Look there! (*She points to the wreckage.*) Look what the sea has stolen and destroyed! All that remains of those sunken ships is their figureheads ... and the names — Justice, Friendship, Golden Peace, and Hope. That's all that's left of hope, treacherous hope. Spars, rowlocks, bailers. And see! The lifebuoy which saved itself, letting those in need perish.

POET (*searching the wreckage*). Here is the name of the ship Justice. This is the ship which sailed from Fairhaven with the Blind Man's son on board. So she sank. And Alice's sweetheart was in her too, Edith's hopeless love.

DAUGHTER. The blind man? Fairhaven? Surely that I dreamt. Alice's sweetheart, ugly Edith, Foulstrand and the quarantine, the sulphur and carbolic, graduation in the church, the lawyer's office, the alley and Victoria. The Growing Castle and the Officer ... These things I dreamt.

POET. Of these things I once made poetry.

DAUGHTER. You know then what poetry is?

POET. I know what dreams are. What is poetry?

DAUGHTER. Not reality, but more than reality. Not dreams, but waking dreams.

POET. Yet the children of men believe that poets merely play — invent and fabricate.

DAUGHTER. It is just as well, my friend, or else the world would be laid waste from lack of endeavour. All men would lie upon their backs, gazing at the heavens; no hand would be lifted to plough or spade, or plane or axe.

POET. Do you speak thus, Daughter of Indra? You, who are half of heaven?

DAUGHTER. You are right to reproach me. I have lived too long down here, and like you have bathed in mud. My thoughts can no longer fly. Clay is on their wings and soil about their feet. And I myself — (*she raises her arms*) — I am sinking, sinking! Help me, Father, God of Heaven! (*Silence.*) No longer can I hear His answer. The ether no longer carries the sound of His lips to the shell of my ear . . . the silver thread has snapped. Alas, I am earthbound!

POET. Do you mean then soon — to go?

DAUGHTER. As soon as I have burnt this earthly matter, for the waters of the ocean cannot cleanse me. Why do you ask?

POET. I have a prayer — a petition.

DAUGHTER. A petition?

POET. A petition from mankind to the ruler of the universe, drawn up by a dreamer.

DAUGHTER. Who is to present it?

POET. Indra's Daughter.

DAUGHTER. Can you speak the words?

POET. I can.

DAUGHTER. Speak them then.

POET. It is better that you should.

DAUGHTER. Where shall I read them?

POET. In my thoughts — or here. (*He gives her a scroll.*)

DAUGHTER. So be it. I will speak them. (*She takes the scroll but does not read.*)

> *"Why with anguish are you born?*
> *Why do you hurt your mother so,*
> *Child of man, when bringing her*
> *the joy of motherhood,*
> *joy beyond all other joys?*
> *Why wake to life,*
> *why greet the light*
> *with a cry of fury and of pain,*
> *Child of man, when to be glad*
> *should be the gift of life?*
> *Why are we born like animals?*
> *We who stem from God and man,*
> *whose souls are longing to be clothed*
> *in other than this blood and filth.*
> *Must God's own image cut its teeth?"*

(*Speaking her own thoughts.*)
>   Silence! No more! The work may not condemn the master.
>   Life's riddle still remains unsolved.

(*Continuing the* POET's *bitter words.*)
> *"And then the journey's course begins,*
> *over thistles, thorns and stones.*
> *If it should touch a beaten track,*

A Dream Play

> comes at once the cry: 'Keep off!'
> Pluck a flower, straight you'll find
> the bloom you picked to be another's.
> If cornfields lie across your path
> and you must pursue your way,
> trampling on another's crops,
> others then will trample yours
> that your loss may equal theirs.
> Every pleasure you enjoy
> brings to all your fellows sorrow,
> yet your sorrow gives no gladness.
> So sorrow, sorrow upon sorrow
> on your way — until you're dead
> and then, alas, give others bread."

(*Her own thought.*)
> Is it thus, O son of dust,
> You seek to win the ear of God?

POET. How may son of dust find words,
so pure, so light, so luminous,
that they can rise up from the earth?
Child of the Gods translate for me,
this lamentation into speech
fit for Immortal ears.

DAUGHTER. I will.

POET (*pointing*). What is floating there — a buoy?

DAUGHTER. Yes.

POET. It is like a lung with a windpipe.

DAUGHTER. It is the watchman of the sea. When danger is abroad it sings.

POET. It seems to me that the sea is rising, and the waves beginning to ...

DAUGHTER. You are not mistaken.

POET. Alas, what do I see? A ship — on the rocks.

DAUGHTER. What ship can it be?

POET. I believe it is the ghost-ship.

DAUGHTER. What is that?

POET. The Flying Dutchman.

DAUGHTER. He? Why is he punished so cruelly, and why does he not come ashore?

POET. Because he had seven unfaithful wives.

DAUGHTER. Shall he be punished for that?

POET. Yes. All righteous men condemned him.

DAUGHTER. Incomprehensible world! How can he be freed from this curse?

POET. Freed? One would beware of freeing him.

DAUGHTER. Why?

POET. Because . . . No, that is not the Dutchman. It is an ordinary ship in distress. Then why does the buoy not sound? Look how the sea is rising! The waves are towering, and soon we shall be imprisoned in this cave. Now the ship's bell is ringing. Soon there will be another figurehead in here. Cry out buoy! Watchman, do your duty!

The buoy sounds a four-part chord in fifths and sixths, like foghorns. The crew is waving to us . . . but we ourselves perish.

DAUGHTER. Do you not want to be set free?

POET. Yes, yes I do! But not now . . . and not by water!

THE CREW (*singing four-part*). Christ Kyrie!

POET. They are calling and the sea is calling. But no one hears.

CREW (*singing as before*). Christ Kyrie!

DAUGHTER. Who is it coming there?

POET. Walking upon the water! Only One walks upon the water. It is not Peter, the rock, for he sank like a stone.

A white light appears over the sea.

CREW (*as before*). Christ Kyrie!

DAUGHTER. Is it He?

POET. It is He, the crucified.

DAUGHTER. Why, tell me why He was crucified.

POET. Because He wished to set men free.

DAUGHTER. Who — I have forgotten — who crucified Him?

The cave grows darker.

POET. All righteous men.

DAUGHTER. This incomprehensible world!

POET. The sea is rising. Darkness is falling on us. The storm is growing wilder.

The CREW *shriek.*

The crew are screaming with horror because they have seen their Saviour . . . and now . . . they are throwing themselves overboard in terror of the Redeemer.

The CREW *shriek again.*

Now they are screaming because they are going to die. They were born screaming and they die screaming.

The mounting waves threaten to drown them in the cave. The light begins to change.

DAUGHTER. If I were sure it was a ship . . .

POET. Indeed, I do not think it is a ship. It's a two storied house, with trees round it . . . and a telephone tower — a tower reaching to the skies. It's the modern Tower of Babel, sending up its wires to communicate with those above.

DAUGHTER. Child, man's thought needs no wires for its flight. The prayers of the devout penetrate all worlds. That is surely no Tower of Babel. If you wish to storm the heavens, storm them with your prayers.

POET. No, it's not a house ... not a telephone tower. Do you see?
DAUGHTER. What do you see?

During the following speech, the scene changes to the alley of the Opera House.
POET. I see a snow-covered heath ... a parade ground. The winter sun is shining behind a church on the hill, so that the tower casts its long shadow on the snow. Now a troop of soldiers comes marching over the heath. They march on the tower and up the spire ... Now they are on the cross, and I seem to know that the first to tread on the weathercock must die ... They are drawing near it. It's the Corporal at their head who ... Ah! A cloud is sailing over the heath, across the sun ... Now everything has gone. The moisture of the cloud has put out the fire of the sun. The sunlight created a shadowy image of the tower, but the shadow of the cloud smothered the image of the tower.

[*It is springtime. The tree and the monkshood are in bud. The* STAGE DOORKEEPER *sits in her old place. The* DAUGHTER *enters, followed by the* POET.]

DAUGHTER (*to* DOORKEEPER). Has the Chancellor arrived yet?
DOORKEEPER. No.
DAUGHTER. Nor the Deans?
DOORKEEPER. No.
DAUGHTER. You must send for them at once. The door is going to be opened.
DOORKEEPER. Is it so urgent?
DAUGHTER. Yes. It's thought that the answer to the riddle of the universe is locked up in there. So send for the Chancellor and the Deans of the four Faculties. (*The* DOORKEEPER *blows a whistle.*) And don't forget the Glazier and his diamond, or nothing can be done.

The personnel of the Opera pour from the building as in the earlier scene. The OFFICER [*young again*], *in morning coat and top hat, comes through the gate, carrying a bouquet of roses and looking radiantly happy.*
OFFICER (*singing*). Victoria!
DOORKEEPER. The young lady will be down in a minute.
OFFICER. Good. The carriage is waiting, the table is laid, the champagne is on the ice ... Let me embrace you, Madam. (*Embraces the* DOORKEEPER.) Victoria!
WOMAN'S VOICE (*from above, singing*). I am here.
OFFICER (*pacing*). Well, I am waiting.
POET. I seem to have lived through all this before.
DAUGHTER. I too.
POET. Perhaps I dreamt it.
DAUGHTER. Or made a poem of it.
POET. Or made a poem.

DAUGHTER. You know then what poetry is.

POET. I know what dreaming is.

DAUGHTER. I feel that once before, somewhere else, we said these words.

POET. Then soon you will know what reality is.

DAUGHTER. Or dreaming.

POET. Or poetry.

Enter the CHANCELLOR *and the* DEANS OF THEOLOGY, PHILOSOPHY, MEDICINE *and* LAW, [*followed by the* GLAZIER *and a group of* RIGHTEOUS PEOPLE].

CHANCELLOR. It's all a question of the door, you understand. What does the Dean of Theology think about it?

DEAN OF THEOLOGY. I don't think — I believe. Credo.

DEAN OF PHILOSOPHY. I think.

DEAN OF MEDICINE. I know.

DEAN OF LAW. I doubt — until I have heard the evidence and witnesses.

CHANCELLOR. Now they will quarrel again. Well then, first what does Theology believe?

THEOLOGY. I believe that this door ought not to be opened, as it conceals dangerous truths.

PHILOSOPHY. The truth is never dangerous.

MEDICINE. What is truth?

LAW. Whatever can be proved by two witnesses.

THEOLOGY. Anything can be proved by two false witnesses — if you're a pettifogger.

PHILOSOPHY. Truth is wisdom, and wisdom and knowledge are philosophy itself. Philosophy is the science of sciences, the knowledge of knowledge. All other sciences are its servants.

MEDICINE. The only science is natural science. Philosophy is not science. It is mere empty speculation.

THEOLOGY. Bravo!

PHILOSOPHY (*to* DEAN OF THEOLOGY). You say bravo. And what, may I ask, are you? The arch enemy of knowledge, the antithesis of science. You are ignorance and darkness.

MEDICINE. Bravo!

THEOLOGY (*to* DEAN OF MEDICINE). And you say bravo — you who can't see further than the end of your own nose in a magnifying glass. You who believe in nothing but your deceptive senses — in your eyes, for instance, which may be long-sighted, short-sighted, blind, purblind, squinting, one-eyed, colour-blind, red-blind, green-blind . . .

MEDICINE. Blockhead!

THEOLOGY. Ass!

They fight.

CHANCELLOR. Enough! Birds of a feather shouldn't peck each other's eyes out.

PHILOSOPHY. Had I to choose between these two, Theology and Medicine, I should choose — neither.

LAW. And if I had to sit in judgment over you three, I should condemn — every one of you . . . You can't agree upon a single point, and never have been able to. Let's get back to the matter in hand. What's your opinion, Chancellor, of this door and the opening of it?

CHANCELLOR. Opinion? I don't have opinions. I am merely appointed by the Government to see you don't break each other's arms and legs in the Senate in the course of educating the young. Opinions? No, I take good care not to have any. I had a few once, but they were soon exploded. Opinions always are exploded — by opponents, of course. Perhaps we had better have the door opened now, even at the risk of it concealing dangerous truths.

LAW. What is truth? What is the truth?

THEOLOGY. I am the Truth and the Life . . .

PHILOSOPHY. I am the knowledge of knowledge.

MEDICINE. I am exact knowledge . . .

LAW. I doubt.

They fight.

DAUGHTER. Shame on you, teachers of youth!

LAW. Chancellor, as delegate of the Government and head of the teaching staff, denounce this woman. She has cried "shame on you" which is contumely, and she has ironically referred to you as "teachers of youth," which is slander.

DAUGHTER. Poor youth!

LAW. She pities youth, and that's tantamount to accusing us. Chancellor, denounce her!

DAUGHTER. Yes, I accuse you — all of you — of sowing the seeds of doubt and dissension in the minds of the young.

LAW. Listen to her! She herself is raising doubts in the young as to our authority, yet she is accusing us of raising doubts. I appeal to all righteous men. Is this not a criminal offence?

ALL THE RIGHTEOUS. Yes, it is criminal.

LAW. The righteous have condemned you. Go in peace with your gains. Otherwise . . .

DAUGHTER. My gains? Otherwise what?

LAW. Otherwise you will be stoned.

POET. Or crucified.

DAUGHTER (*to the* POET). I am going. Come with me and learn the answer to the riddle.

POET. Which riddle?

DAUGHTER. What does he mean by my "gains"?

POET. Probably nothing at all. That's what we call idle chatter. He was just chattering.

DAUGHTER. But that hurt me more than anything else.

POET. That's why he said it. Human beings are like that.

The GLAZIER *opens the door and looks inside.*

ALL THE RIGHTEOUS. Hurrah! The door is open.

The DEANS *look inside.*

CHANCELLOR. What was concealed behind that door?

GLAZIER. I can't see anything.

CHANCELLOR. He can't see anything. Well, I'm not surprised. Deans! What was concealed behind that door?

THEOLOGY. Nothing. That is the solution of the riddle of the universe. Out of nothing in the beginning God created heaven and earth.

PHILOSOPHY. Out of nothing comes nothing.

MEDICINE. Bosh! That is nothing.

LAW. I doubt everything. And there's some swindle here. I appeal to all righteous men.

DAUGHTER (*to* POET). Who are these righteous?

POET. Let him tell you who can. All the righteous are often just one person. Today they are me and mine, tomorrow you and yours. One is nominated for the post, or rather, one nominates oneself.

ALL THE RIGHTEOUS. We have been swindled.

CHANCELLOR. Who has swindled you?

ALL THE RIGHTEOUS. The Daughter!

CHANCELLOR. Will the Daughter kindly inform us what her idea was in having the door opened.

DAUGHTER. No, my friends. If I told you, you would not believe it.

MEDICINE. But there's nothing there.

DAUGHTER. What you say is correct. But you have not understood it.

MEDICINE. What she says is bosh.

ALL. Bosh!

DAUGHTER (*to* POET). They are to be pitied.

POET. Do you mean that seriously?

DAUGHTER. Very seriously.

POET. Do you think the righteous are to be pitied too?

DAUGHTER. They most of all perhaps.

POET. And the four Faculties?

DAUGHTER. They too, and not least. Four heads and four minds with a single body. Who created such a monster?

ALL. She does not answer.

CHANCELLOR. Then stone her!

DAUGHTER. This is the answer.

CHANCELLOR. Listen! She is answering.

ALL. Stone her! She is answering.

Enter LAWYER.

DAUGHTER. If she answers, or if she does not answer, stone her! (*To* POET.) Come, you Seer, and I will answer the riddle, but far from here, out in the wilderness, where none can hear us, none can see us. For . . .

A Dream Play

The LAWYER *interrupts by taking hold of her arm.*

LAWYER. Have you forgotten your duties?

DAUGHTER. God knows I have not. But I have higher duties.

LAWYER. But your child?

DAUGHTER. My child? Yes?

LAWYER. Your child is calling you.

DAUGHTER. My child! Alas, I am earthbound! And this anguish in my breast, this agony, what is it?

LAWYER. Don't you know?

DAUGHTER. No.

LAWYER. It is the pangs of conscience.

DAUGHTER. The pangs of conscience?

LAWYER. Yes. They come after every neglected duty, after every pleasure, however innocent — if there is such a thing as an innocent pleasure, which is doubtful. And they also come every time one causes pain to one's neighbour.

DAUGHTER. Is there no remedy?

LAWYER. Yes, but only one. To do one's duty instantly.

DAUGHTER. You look like a devil when you say the word "duty." But when one has, as I, two duties?

LAWYER. Fulfil first one and then the other.

DAUGHTER. The higher first. Therefore, you look after my child, and I will do my duty.

LAWYER. Your child is unhappy without you. Can you let another suffer on your account?

DAUGHTER. There is conflict in my soul. It is pulled this way and that until it is torn in two.

LAWYER. These, you see, are life's little trials.

DAUGHTER. Oh, how they tear one!

POET. You would have nothing to do with me, if you knew what misery I have caused through following my vocation — yes, my vocation, which is the highest duty of all.

DAUGHTER. What do you mean?

POET. I had a father, whose hopes were centred in me, his only son. I was to have carried on his business, but I ran away from the Commercial College. Worry brought my father to his grave. My mother wanted me to be religious. I couldn't be religious. She disowned me. I had a friend who helped me when I was desperate, but that friend turned out to be a tyrant to the very people whose cause I upheld. So to save my soul I had to strike down my friend and benefactor. Since that time I have had no peace. I am considered base, contemptible, the scum of the earth. Nor do I get any comfort from my conscience when it tells me I did right, for the next moment it assures me I did wrong. That is the way of life.

DAUGHTER. Come with me, out into the wilderness.

LAWYER. Your child!

DAUGHTER (*indicating all present*). These are my children. Each one of them is good, but as soon as they are together they fight and turn into devils. Farewell!

[*Blackout. When the lights go up the scene has changed to*] Outside the Castle.

The set is the same as the earlier one, except that now the ground is covered with blue monkshood, aconite and other flowers. The chrysanthemum bud at the top of the tower is on the point of bursting. The Castle windows are lit with candles. [*In the foreground is a fire.*]

DAUGHTER. The hour is at hand when with the aid of fire I shall ascend again into the ether. This is what you call death and approach with so much fear.

POET. Fear of the unknown.

DAUGHTER. Which yet you know.

POET. Who knows it?

DAUGHTER. Mankind. Why do you not believe your prophets?

POET. Prophets have never been believed. Why is that? If they truly speak with the voice of God, why then do men not believe? His power to convince should be irresistible.

DAUGHTER. Have you always doubted?

POET. No, I have had faith many times, but after a while it drifted away, like a dream when one awakens.

DAUGHTER. To be mortal is not easy.

POET. You understand this now?

DAUGHTER. Yes.

POET. Tell me, did not Indra once send his son down to earth to hear man's complaint?

DAUGHTER. He did. And how was he received?

POET. How did he fulfil his mission? — to answer with a question.

DAUGHTER. To answer with another — was not the state of mankind bettered by his visit to the earth? Answer truly.

POET. Bettered? Yes, a little, a very little. Now, instead of further questions, will you tell me the answer to the riddle?

DAUGHTER. What purpose would that serve? You would not believe me.

POET. I shall believe you, for I know who you are.

DAUGHTER. Then I will tell you. In the dawn of time, before your sun gave light, Brahma, the divine primal force, let himself be seduced by Maya, the World Mother, that he might propagate. This mingling of the divine element with the earthly was the Fall from heaven. This world, its life and its inhabitants are therefore only a mirage, a reflection, a dream image.

POET. My dream!

DAUGHTER. A true dream. But, in order to be freed from the earthly element, the descendants of Brahma sought renunciation and suffering. And so you have suffering as the deliverer. But this yearning for suffering comes into

A Dream Play

conflict with the longing for joy, for love. Now you understand what love is; supreme joy in the greatest suffering, the sweetest is the most bitter. Do you understand now what woman is? Woman, through whom sin and death entered into life.

POET. I understand. And the outcome?

DAUGHTER. What you yourself know. Conflict between the pain of joy and the joy of pain, between the anguish of the penitent and the pleasure of the sensual.

POET. And the conflict?

DAUGHTER. The conflict of opposites generates power, as fire and water create the force of steam.

POET. But peace? Rest?

DAUGHTER. Hush! You must ask no more, nor may I answer. The altar is decked for the sacrifice, the flowers keep vigil, the candles are lighted, the white sheet hangs in the window, the threshold is strewn with pine.*

POET. How calmly you speak! As if suffering did not exist for you.

DAUGHTER. Not exist? I suffered all your sufferings a hundred fold because my sensibilities were finer.

POET. Tell me your sorrows.

DAUGHTER. Poet, could you tell your own with utter truth? Could your words ever once convey your thoughts?

POET. You are right. No. To myself I have always seemed a deaf mute, and while the crowd was acclaiming my song, to me it seemed a jangle. And so, you see, I was always ashamed when men paid me homage.

DAUGHTER. And yet you wish me to speak? Look into my eyes.

POET. I cannot endure your gaze.

DAUGHTER. How then will you endure my words, if I speak in my own language?

POET. Even so, before you go, tell me from what you suffered most down here.

DAUGHTER. From living. From feeling my vision dimmed by having eyes, my hearing dulled by having ears, and my thought, my airy, luminous thought, bound down in a labyrinth of fat. You have seen a brain. What twisting channels, what creeping ways!

POET. Yes, and that is why the minds of the righteous are twisted.

DAUGHTER. Cruel, always cruel, each one of you.

POET. How can we be otherwise?

DAUGHTER. Now first I shake the dust from my feet, the earth, the clay. (*She takes off her shoes and puts them in the fire.*)

> One after another the following characters come in, put their contributions on the fire, cross the stage and go out, while the POET and the DAUGHTER stand watching.

* Signs of mourning in Sweden.

DOORKEEPER. Perhaps I may burn my shawl too?

OFFICER. And I my roses, of which only the thorns are left.

BILLSTICKER. The posters can go, but my fishnet never.

GLAZIER. Farewell to the diamond that opened the door.

LAWYER. The report of the proceedings in the High Court touching the Pope's beard or the diminishing water supply in the sources of the Ganges.

QUARANTINE MASTER. A small contribution in the shape of the black mask which turned me into a blackamoor against my will.

VICTORIA [SHE]. My beauty — my sorrow.

EDITH. My ugliness — my sorrow.

BLINDMAN (*putting his hand in the fire*). I give my hand which is my sight.

DON JUAN *is pushed in in the bathchair [accompanied by the* COQUETTE *and the* FRIEND].

DON JUAN. Make haste, make haste! Life is short.

POET. I have read that when a life is nearing its end, everything and everyone pass by in a single stream. Is this the end?

DAUGHTER. For me, yes. Farewell!

POET. Say a parting word!

DAUGHTER. No, I cannot. Do you think your language can express our thoughts?

Enter the DEAN OF THEOLOGY, *raging*.

THEOLOGY. I am disowned by God; I am persecuted by men; I am abandoned by the Government, and scorned by my colleagues. How can I have faith when no one else has faith? How can I defend a God who does not defend His own people? It's all bosh!

He throws a book on the fire and goes out. The POET *snatches the book from the flames.*

POET. Do you know what this is? A Book of Martyrs, a calendar with a martyr for each day of the year.

DAUGHTER. A martyr?

POET. Yes, one who was tortured and put to death for his faith. Tell me why. Do you believe all who are tortured suffer, all who are put to death feel pain? Surely suffering is redemption and death deliverance.

KRISTIN *enters with her paste and strips of paper.*

KRISTIN. I paste, I paste, till there is nothing left to paste.

POET. If heaven itself cracked open, you would try to paste it up. Go away!

KRISTIN. Are there no inner windows in the Castle?

POET. No, none there.

KRISTIN. I'll go then, I'll go.

Exit.

As the DAUGHTER *speaks her last lines the flames rise until the Castle is on fire.*

DAUGHTER. *The parting time has come; the end draws near.*
    Farewell, you child of man, dreamer,
    poet, who knows best the way to live.

A Dream Play

> *Above the earth on wings you hover,*
> *plunging at times to graze the dust,*
> *but not to be submerged.*
> *Now I am going, now the hour has come*
> *to leave both friend and place,*
> *how sharp the loss of all I loved,*
> *how deep regret for all destroyed!*
> *Ah, now I know the whole of living's pain!*
> *This then it is to be a human being —*
> *ever to miss the thing one never prized*
> *and feel remorse for what one never did,*
> *to yearn to go, yet long to stay.*
> *And so the human heart is split in two,*
> *emotions by wild horses torn —*
> *conflict, discord and uncertainty.*
> *Farewell! Tell all on earth I shall remember them.*
> *Where I am going, and in your name*
> *carry their lamentations to the throne.*
> *Farewell!*

She goes into the Castle. Music is heard. The background is lighted up by the burning Castle, and now shows a wall of human faces, questioning, mourning, despairing. While the Castle is burning, the flower-bud on the roof bursts into a giant chrysanthemum.

THE DRAMA OF

DISCUSSION

George Bernard Shaw

MAN AND SUPERMAN
A COMEDY AND A PHILOSOPHY

[1903]

George Bernard Shaw [1856–1950]

O rare Bernard Shaw! Archibald Henderson in his "official" biography of Shaw has somewhat immoderately called him "man of the century," and there is no reason to think that Shaw would flinch at the phrase. A supreme egotist, Shaw was also a supreme writer of dramatic prose, and many of his plays seem destined to become permanent items in the modern repertory. A failure as a novelist, Shaw was in turn art critic, music critic, and drama critic, as well as dramatist and dedicated Fabian Socialist. He said at one time that he would rather be remembered for helping to found the Labour Party than for his plays; at another he said that his "vocation is that of a prophet"; and, again, "I suspect and hope that most of my readers are unconscious of my literary virtuosity and keen on my ideas." All of which is to emphasize the identity of Shaw the playwright and Shaw the economist, political thinker, reformer, pamphleteer, and lecturer.

Shaw (the most quotable of modern playwrights) wrote in the "Author's Apology" to *Mrs. Warren's Profession:*

> I am convinced that fine art is the subtlest, the most seductive, the most effective means of propagandism in the world, excepting only the example of personal conduct; . . . [my determination is] to accept problem as the normal material of the drama. . . . It will be seen that only in the problem play is there any real drama, because drama is no mere setting up of the camera to nature: it is the presentation in parable of the conflict between Man's will and his environment: in a word, of problem.

When Shaw delivered his lecture on Ibsen to the Fabian Society in 1890 (the year before Ibsen's *Ghosts* first appeared in London), he put a good deal of himself into it. And the expanded form which appeared in 1891 as *The Quintessence of Ibsenism* emphasizes what Shaw saw and admired in Ibsen. The so-called Ibsenite plays dealt with problems and with man in his relation to society and institutions. Furthermore, they vigorously attacked falsehoods and lies (often disguised as "ideals"). Thus Shaw can say that the destroyer of so-called ideals "is in fact sweeping the world clear of lies." He had no doubt about the way society should be treated; he writes in *The Quintessence:*

> The plain working truth is that it is not only good for people to be shocked occasionally, but absolutely necessary to the progress of society that they should be shocked pretty often.

The drama of discussion could do this. With Ibsen, and pre-eminently with Shaw, the theater became a forum where ideas were paraded in dramatic form and a place where speeches might even be made (for example, see Tanner's long speeches in *Man and Superman*, and King Magnus's eleven-minute tour de force in *The Apple Cart*). With the triumph of Shaw, intelligent, intelligible discussion became a staple of the modern drama — though admittedly few playwrights were as articulate as Shaw.

Man and Superman, which Archibald Henderson terms "the most brilliant comedy ever written," is particularly important in the career of Shaw and in the history of the modern drama, of which it is one of the glories. It established Shaw as a favorite of the intellectuals when it was produced at the Royal Court Theatre in 1905, and it showed that drama consisting largely of talk could sustain itself, and even achieve popularity. Though the scene of

Shaw and Drama of Discussion

the action does move, and though there is some plot intrigue, the play is essentially a series of discussions over proper morality and the roles of the artist-philosopher and the female of the species. Sandwiched into the play proper (the third act is seldom included in a production of the play) is a philosophical discourse in dialogue form in which Don Juan speaks the following key lines:

> I tell you that as long as I can conceive something better than myself I cannot be easy unless I am striving to bring it into existence or clearing the way for it. That is the law of my life. That is the working within me of Life's incessant aspiration to higher organization, wider, deeper, intenser self-consciousness, and clearer self-understanding.

The Life Force, Creative Evolution, Evolutionary Appetite — this is the main subject of Shaw's play. "The philosopher is Nature's pilot," Juan says, and unquestionably Shaw would agree. But, as Shaw asks in his lengthy preface, does he get all of this into the main part of *Man and Superman*? Does he dramatize (that is, act out) the ideas he is so eager to communicate? In this "most serious play of the most serious man alive," as G. K. Chesterton wrote, who is the protagonist? And who is the villain? Can we agree with Chesterton when he says that in *Man and Superman* "Shaw follows the banner of life; but austerely, not joyously. For him Nature has authority, but hardly charm"? And can we accept Shaw's assertion that the play is popular because it is "the only play on the subject of sex ever written"?

EPISTLE DEDICATORY TO
MAN AND SUPERMAN

TO ARTHUR BINGHAM WALKLEY

My dear Walkley

You once asked me why I did not write a Don Juan play. The levity with which you assumed this frightful responsibility has probably by this time enabled you to forget it; but the day of reckoning has arrived: here is your play! I say *your* play, because *qui facit per alium facit per se*. Its profits, like its labor, belong to me: its morals, its manners, its philosophy, its influence on the young, are for you to justify. You were of mature age when you made the suggestion; and you knew your man. It is hardly fifteen years since, as twin pioneers of the New Journalism of that time, we two, cradled in the same new sheets, began an epoch in the criticism of the theatre and the opera house by making it a pretext for a propaganda of our own views of life. So you cannot plead ignorance of the character of the force you set in motion. You meant me to *épater le bourgeois*; and if he protests, I hereby refer him to you as the accountable party.

I warn you that if you attempt to repudiate your responsibility, I shall suspect you of finding the play too decorous for your taste. The fifteen years have made me older and graver. In you I can detect no such becoming change. Your levities and audacities are like the loves and comforts prayed for by Desdemona: they increase, even as your days do grow. No mere pioneering journal dares meddle with them now: the stately *Times* itself is alone sufficiently above suspicion to act as your chaperone; and even the *Times* must sometimes thank its stars that new plays are not produced every day, since after each such event its gravity is compromised, its platitude turned to epigram, its portentousness to wit, its propriety to elegance, and even its decorum into naughtiness by criticisms which the traditions of the paper do not allow you to sign at the end, but which you take care to sign with the most extravagant flourishes between the lines. I am not sure that this is not a portent of Revolution. In eighteenth-century France the end was at hand when men bought the *Encyclopedia* and found Diderot there. When I buy the *Times* and find you there, my prophetic ear catches a rattle of twentieth-century tumbrils.

However, that is not my present anxiety. The question is, will you not be disappointed with a Don Juan play in which not one of that hero's *mille e tre* adventures is brought upon the stage? To propitiate you, let me explain myself. You will retort that I never do anything else: it is your favorite jibe at me that what I call drama is nothing but explanation. But you must not expect me to adopt your inexplicable, fantastic, petulant, fastidious ways: you must take me as I am, a reasonable, patient, consistent, apologetic, laborious person, with the temperament of a schoolmaster and the pursuits of a vestryman. No doubt that literary knack of mine which happens to amuse the British public distracts attention from my character; but the character is there none the less, solid as bricks. I have a conscience; and conscience is always anxiously explanatory. You, on the contrary, feel that a man who discusses his conscience is much like a woman who discusses her modesty. The only moral force you condescend to parade is the force of your wit: the only demand you make in public is the demand of your artistic temperament for symmetry, elegance, style, grace, refinement, and the cleanliness which comes next to godliness if not before it. But my conscience is the genuine pulpit article: it annoys me to see people comfortable when they ought to be uncomfortable; and I insist on making them think in order to bring them to conviction of sin. If you don't like my preaching you must lump it. I really cannot help it.

In the preface to my *Plays for Puritans* I explained the predicament of our contemporary English drama, forced to deal almost exclusively with cases of sexual attraction, and yet forbidden to exhibit the incidents of that attraction or even to discuss its nature. Your suggestion that I should write a Don Juan play was virtually a challenge to me to treat this subject myself dramatically. The challenge was difficult enough to be worth accepting, because, when you come to think of it, though we have plenty of dramas with heroes and heroines who are in love and must accordingly marry or perish at the end of the play, or about people whose relations with one another have been complicated by the marriage laws, not to mention the looser sort of plays which trade on the tradition that illicit love affairs are at once vicious and delightful, we have no modern English plays in which the natural attraction of the sexes for one another is made the mainspring of the action. That is why we insist on beauty in our performers, differing herein from the countries our friend William Archer holds up as examples of seriousness to our childish theatres. There the Juliets and Isoldes, the Romeos and Tristans, might be our mothers and fathers. Not so the English actress. The heroine she impersonates is not allowed to discuss the elemental relations of men and women: all her romantic twaddle about novelet-made love, all her purely legal dilemmas as to whether she was married or "betrayed," quite miss our hearts and worry our minds. To console ourselves we must just look at her. We do so; and her beauty feeds our starving emotions. Sometimes we grumble ungallantly at the lady because she does not act as well as she looks. But in a drama which, with all its preoccupation with sex, is really void of sexual interest, good looks are more desired than histrionic skill.

Let me press this point on you, since you are too clever to raise the fool's cry of paradox whenever I take hold of a stick by the right instead of the wrong end. Why are our occasional attempts to deal with the sex problem on the stage so repulsive and dreary that even those who are most determined that sex questions shall be held open and their discussion kept free, cannot pretend to relish these joyless attempts at social sanitation? Is it not because at bottom they are utterly sexless? What is the usual formula for such plays? A woman has, on some past occasion, been brought into conflict with the law which regulates the relations of the sexes. A man, by falling in love with her, or marrying her, is brought into conflict with the social convention which discountenances the woman. Now the conflicts of individuals with law and convention can be dramatized like all other human conflicts; but they are purely judicial; and the fact that we are much more curious about the suppressed relations between the man and the woman than about the relations between both and our courts of law and private juries of matrons, produces that sensation of evasion, of dissatisfaction, of fundamental irrelevance, of shallowness, of useless disagreeableness, of total failure to edify and partial failure to interest, which is as familiar to you in the theatres as it was to me when I, too, frequented those uncomfortable buildings, and found our popular playwrights in the mind to (as they thought) emulate Ibsen.

I take it that when you asked me for a Don Juan play you did not want that sort of thing. Nobody does: the successes such plays sometimes obtain are due to the incidental conventional melodrama with which the experienced popular author instinctively saves himself from failure. But what did you want? Owing to your unfortunate habit — you now, I hope, feel its inconvenience — of not explaining yourself, I have had to discover this for myself. First, then, I have had to ask myself, what is a Don Juan? Vulgarly, a libertine. But your dislike of vulgarity is pushed to the length of a defect (universality of character is impossible without a share of vulgarity); and even if you could acquire the taste, you would find yourself overfed from ordinary sources without troubling me. So I took it that you demanded a Don Juan in the philosophic sense.

Philosophically, Don Juan is a man who, though gifted enough to be exceptionally capable of distinguishing between good and evil, follows his own instincts without regard to the common, statute, or canon law; and therefore, whilst gaining the ardent sympathy of our rebellious instincts (which are flattered by the brilliancies with which Don Juan associates them), finds himself in mortal conflict with existing institutions, and defends himself by fraud and force as unscrupulously as a farmer defends his crops by the same means against vermin. The prototypic Don Juan, invented early in the sixteenth century by a Spanish monk, was presented, according to the ideas of that time, as the enemy of God, the approach of whose vengeance is felt throughout the drama, growing in menace from minute to minute. No anxiety is caused on Don Juan's account by any minor antagonist: he easily eludes the police, temporal and spiritual; and when an indignant father seeks private redress with the sword, Don Juan kills him without an effort. Not until the slain father returns from heaven as the agent of God, in the form of his own statue, does he prevail against his slayer and cast him into hell. The moral is a monkish one: repent and reform now; for tomorrow it may be too late. This is really the only point on which Don Juan is sceptical; for he is a devout believer in an ultimate hell, and risks damnation only because, as he is young, it seems so far off that repentance can be postponed until he has amused himself to his heart's content.

But the lesson intended by an author is hardly ever the lesson the world chooses to learn from his book. What attracts and impresses us in *El Burlador de Sevilla* is not the immediate urgency of repentance, but the heroism of daring to be the enemy of God. From Prometheus to my own *Devil's Disciple*, such enemies have always been popular. Don Juan became such a pet that the world could not bear his damnation. It reconciled him sentimentally to God in a second version, and clamored for his canonization for a whole century, thus treating him as English journalism has treated that comic foe of the gods, Punch. Molière's Don Juan casts back to the original in point of impenitence; but in piety he falls off greatly. True, he also proposes to repent; but in what terms! "*Oui, ma foi! il faut s'amender. Encore vingt ou trente ans de cette vie-ci, et puis nous songerons à nous.*" After Molière comes the artist-enchanter, the master of masters, Mozart, who reveals the hero's spirit in magical harmonies, elfin tones, and elate darting rhythms as of summer lightning made audible. Here you have freedom in love and in morality mocking exquisitely at slavery to them, and interesting you, attracting you, tempting you, inexplicably forcing you to range the hero with his enemy the statue on a transcendant plane, leaving the prudish daughter and her priggish lover on a crockery shelf below to live piously ever after.

After these completed works Byron's fragment does not count for much philosophically. Our vagabond libertines are no more interesting from that point of view than the sailor who has a wife in every port; and Byron's hero is, after all, only a vagabond libertine. And he is dumb: he does not discuss himself with a Sganarelle-Leporello or with the fathers or brothers of his mistresses: he does not even, like Casanova, tell his own story. In fact he is not a true Don Juan at all; for he is no more an enemy of God than any romantic and adventurous young sower of wild oats. Had you and I been in his place at his age, who knows whether we might not have done as he did, unless indeed your fastidiousness had saved you from the Empress Catherine. Byron was as little of a philosopher as Peter the Great: both were instances of that rare and useful, but unedifying variation, an energetic genius born without the prejudices or superstitions of his contemporaries. The resultant unscrupulous freedom of thought made Byron a greater poet than Wordsworth just as it made Peter a greater king than George III; but as it was, after all, only a negative qualification, it did not prevent Peter from being an appalling blackguard and an arrant poltroon, nor did it enable Byron to become a religious force like Shelley. Let us, then, leave Byron's Don Juan out of account. Mozart's is the last of the true Don Juans; for by the time he was of age, his cousin Faust had, in the hands of Goethe, taken his place and carried both his warfare and his reconciliation with the gods far beyond mere lovemaking into politics, high art, schemes for reclaiming new continents from the ocean, and recognition of an eternal womanly principle in the universe. Goethe's *Faust* and Mozart's *Don Juan* were the last words of the eighteenth century on the subject; and by the time the polite critics of the nineteenth century, ignoring William Blake as superficially as the eighteenth had ignored Hogarth or the seventeenth Bunyan, had got past the Dickens-Macaulay Dumas-Guizot stage and the Stendhal-Meredith-Turgenieff stage, and were confronted with philosophic fiction by such pens as Ibsen's and Tolstoy's, Don Juan had changed his sex and become Doña Juana, breaking out of the Doll's House and asserting herself as an individual instead of a mere item in a moral pageant.

Now it is all very well for you at the beginning of the twentieth century to ask me for a Don Juan play; but you will see from the foregoing survey that Don Juan is a full century out of date for you and for me; and if there are millions of less literate people who are still in the eighteenth century, have they not Molière and Mozart, upon whose art no human hand can improve? You would laugh at me if at this time of day I dealt in duels and ghosts and "womanly" women. As to mere libertinism, you would be the first to remind me that the *Festin de Pierre* of Molière is not a play for amorists, and that one bar of the voluptuous sentimentality of Gounod or Bizet would appear as a licentious stain on the score of *Don Giovanni*. Even the more abstract parts of the Don Juan play are dilapidated past use: for instance, Don Juan's supernatural antagonist hurled those who refuse to repent into lakes of burning brimstone, there to be tormented by devils with horns and tails. Of that antagonist, and of that conception of repentance, how much is left that could be used in a play by me dedicated to you? On the other hand, those forces of middle class public opinion which hardly existed for a Spanish nobleman in the days of the first Don Juan, are now triumphant everywhere. Civilized society is one huge bourgeoisie: no nobleman dares now shock his greengrocer. The women, *"marchesane, principesse, cameriere, cittadine"* and all, are become equally dangerous: the sex is aggressive, powerful: when women are wronged they do not group themselves pathetically to sing *"Protegga il giusto cielo"*: they grasp formidable legal and social weapons, and retaliate. Political parties are wrecked and public careers undone by a single indiscretion. A man had better have all the statues in London to supper with him, ugly as they are, than be brought to the bar of the Nonconformist Conscience by Donna Elvira. Excommunication has become almost as serious a business as it was in the tenth century.

As a result, Man is no longer, like Don Juan, victor in the duel of sex.

Whether he has ever really been may be doubted: at all events the enormous superiority of Woman's natural position in this matter is telling with greater and greater force. As to pulling the Nonconformist Conscience by the beard as Don Juan plucked the beard of the Commandant's statue in the convent of San Francisco, that is out of the question nowadays: prudence and good manners alike forbid it to a hero with any mind. Besides, it is Don Juan's own beard that is in danger of plucking. Far from relapsing into hypocrisy, as Sganarelle feared, he has unexpectedly discovered a moral in his immorality. The growing recognition of his point of view is heaping responsibility on him. His former jests he has had to take as seriously as I have had to take some of the jests of Mr. W. S. Gilbert. His scepticism, once his least tolerated quality, has now triumphed so completely that he can no longer assert himself by witty negations, and must, to save himself from cipherdom, find an affirmative position. His thousand and three affairs of gallantry, after becoming, at most, two immature intrigues leading to sordid and prolonged complications and humiliations, have been discarded altogether as unworthy of his philosophic dignity and compromising to his newly acknowledged position as the founder of a school. Instead of pretending to read Ovid he does actually read Schopenhauer and Nietzsche, studies Westermark, and is concerned for the future of the race instead of for the freedom of his own instincts. Thus his profligacy and his dare-devil airs have gone the way of his sword and mandoline into the rag shop of anachronisms and superstitions. In fact, he is now more Hamlet than Don Juan; for though the lines put into the actor's mouth to indicate to the pit that Hamlet is a philosopher are for the most part mere harmonious platitude which, with a little debasement of the word-music, would be properer to Pecksniff, yet if you separate the real hero, inarticulate and unintelligible to himself except in flashes of inspiration, from the performer who has to talk at any cost through five acts; and if you also do what you must always do in Shakespear's tragedies: that is, dissect out the absurd sensational incidents and physical violences of the borrowed story from the genuine Shakespearian tissue, you will get a true Promethean foe of the gods, whose instinctive attitude towards women much resembles that to which Don Juan is now driven. From this point of view Hamlet was a developed Don Juan whom Shakespear palmed off as a reputable man just as he palmed poor Macbeth off as a murderer. Today the palming off is no longer necessary (at least on your plane and mine) because Don Juanism is no longer misunderstood as mere Casanovism. Don Juan himself is almost ascetic in his desire to avoid that misunderstanding; and so my attempt to bring him up to date by launching him as a modern Englishman into a modern English environment has produced a figure superficially quite unlike the hero of Mozart.

And yet I have not the heart to disappoint you wholly of another glimpse of the Mozartian *dissoluto punito* and his antagonist the statue. I feel sure you would like to know more of the statue — to draw him out when he is off

Man and Superman: Epistle Dedicatory

duty, so to speak. To gratify you, I have resorted to the trick of the strolling theatrical manager who advertises the pantomime of Sinbad the Sailor with a stock of second-hand picture posters designed for Ali Baba. He simply thrusts a few oil jars into the valley of diamonds, and so fulfils the promise held out by the hoardings to the public eye. I have adapted this simple device to our occasion by thrusting into my perfectly modern three-act play a totally extraneous act in which my hero, enchanted by the air of the Sierra, has a dream in which his Mozartian ancestor appears and philosophizes at great length in a Shavio-Socratic dialogue with the lady, the statue, and the devil.

But this pleasantry is not the essence of the play. Over this essence I have no control. You propound a certain social substance, sexual attraction to wit, for dramatic distillation; and I distil it for you. I do not adulterate the product with aphrodisiacs nor dilute it with romance and water; for I am merely executing your commission, not producing a popular play for the market. You must therefore (unless, like most wise men, you read the play first and the preface afterwards) prepare yourself to face a trumpery story of modern London life, a life in which, as you know, the ordinary man's main business is to get means to keep up the position and habits of a gentleman, and the ordinary woman's business is to get married. In 9,999 cases out of 10,000, you can count on their doing nothing, whether noble or base, that conflicts with these ends; and that assurance is what you rely on as their religion, their morality, their principles, their patriotism, their reputation, their honor and so forth.

On the whole, this is a sensible and satisfactory foundation for society. Money means nourishment and marriage means children; and that men should put nourishment first and women children first is, broadly speaking, the law of Nature and not the dictate of personal ambition. The secret of the prosaic man's success, such as it is, is the simplicity with which he pursues these ends: the secret of the artistic man's failure, such as that is, is the versatility with which he strays in all directions after secondary ideals. The artist is either a poet or a scallawag: as poet, he cannot see, as the prosaic man does, that chivalry is at bottom only romantic suicide: as scallawag, he cannot see that it does not pay to sponge and beg and lie and brag and neglect his person. Therefore do not misunderstand my plain statement of the fundamental constitution of London society as an Irishman's reproach to your nation. From the day I first set foot on this foreign soil I knew the value of the prosaic qualities of which Irishmen teach Englishmen to be ashamed as well as I knew the vanity of the poetic qualities of which Englishmen teach Irishmen to be proud. For the Irishman instinctively disparages the quality which makes the Englishman dangerous to him; and the Englishman instinctively flatters the fault that makes the Irishman harmless and amusing to him. What is wrong with the prosaic Englishman is what is wrong with the prosaic men of all countries: stupidity. The vitality which places nourishment and children first, heaven and hell a somewhat remote second, and the health of society as an organic whole nowhere, may muddle successfully through the comparatively tribal stages of gregariousness; but in nineteenth-century nations and twentieth-century empires the determination of every man to be rich at all costs, and of every woman to be married at all costs, must, without a highly scientific social organization, produce a ruinous development of poverty, celibacy, prostitution, infant mortality, adult degeneracy, and everything that wise men most dread. In short, there is no future for men, however brimming with crude vitality, who are neither intelligent nor politically educated enough to be socialists. So do not misunderstand me in the other direction either: if I appreciate the vital qualities of the Englishman as I appreciate the vital qualities of the bee, I do not guarantee the Englishman against being, like the bee (or the Canaanite) smoked out and unloaded of his honey by beings inferior to himself in simple acquisitiveness, combativeness, and fecundity, but superior to him in imagination and cunning.

The Don Juan play, however, is to deal with sexual attraction, and not with nutrition, and to deal with it in a society in which the serious business of sex is left by men to women, as the serious business of nutrition is left by women to men. That the men, to protect themselves against a too aggressive prosecution of the women's business, have set up a feeble romantic convention that the initiative in sex business must always come from the man, is true; but the pretence is so shallow that even in the theatre, that last sanctuary of unreality, it imposes only on the inexperienced. In Shakespear's plays the woman always takes the initiative. In his problem plays and his popular plays alike the love interest is the interest of seeing the woman hunt the man down. She may do it by blandishment, like Rosalind, or by stratagem, like Mariana; but in every case the relation between the woman and the man is the same: she is the pursuer and contriver, he the pursued and disposed of. When she is baffled, like Ophelia, she goes mad and commits suicide; and the man goes straight from her funeral to a fencing match. No doubt Nature, with very young creatures, may save the woman the trouble of scheming: Prospero knows that he has only to throw Ferdinand and Miranda together and they will mate like a pair of doves; and there is no need for Perdita to capture Florizel as the lady doctor in *All's Well That Ends Well* (an early Ibsenite heroine) captures Bertram. But the mature cases all illustrate the Shakespearian law. The one apparent exception, Petruchio, is not a real one: he is most carefully characterized as a purely commercial matrimonial adventurer. Once he is assured that Katharine has money, he undertakes to marry her before he has seen her. In real life we find not only Petruchios, but Mantalinis and Dobbins who pursue women with appeals to their pity or jealousy or vanity, or cling to them in a romantically infatuated way. Such effeminates do not count in the world scheme: even Bunsby dropping like a fascinated bird into the jaws of Mrs.

MacStinger is by comparison a true tragic object of pity and terror. I find in my own plays that Woman, projecting herself dramatically by my hands (a process over which I assure you I have no more real control than I have over my wife), behaves just as Woman did in the plays of Shakespear.

And so your Don Juan has come to birth as a stage projection of the tragi-comic love chase of the man by the woman; and my Don Juan is the quarry instead of the huntsman. Yet he is a true Don Juan, with a sense of reality that disables convention, defying to the last the fate which finally overtakes him. The woman's need of him to enable her to carry on Nature's most urgent work, does not prevail against him until his resistance gathers her energy to a climax at which she dares to throw away her customary exploitations of the conventional affectionate and dutiful poses, and claim him by natural right for a purpose that far transcends their mortal personal purposes.

Among the friends to whom I have read this play in manuscript are some of our own sex who are shocked at the "unscrupulousness," meaning the total disregard of masculine fastidiousness, with which the woman pursues her purpose. It does not occur to them that if women were as fastidious as men, morally or physically, there would be an end of the race. Is there anything meaner than to throw necessary work upon other people and then disparage it as unworthy and indelicate. We laugh at the haughty American nation because it makes the Negro clean its boots and then proves the moral and physical inferiority of the Negro by the fact that he is a shoeblack; but we ourselves throw the whole drudgery of creation on one sex, and then imply that no female of any womanliness or delicacy would initiate any effort in that direction. There are no limits to male hypocrisy in this matter. No doubt there are moments when man's sexual immunities are made acutely humiliating to him. When the terrible moment of birth arrives, its supreme importance and its superhuman effort and peril, in which the father has no part, dwarf him into the meanest insignificance: he slinks out of the way of the humblest petticoat, happy if he be poor enough to be pushed out of the house to outface his ignominy by drunken rejoicings. But when the crisis is over he takes his revenge, swaggering as the breadwinner, and speaking of Woman's "sphere" with condescension, even with chivalry, as if the kitchen and the nursery were less important than the office in the city. When his swagger is exhausted he drivels into erotic poetry or sentimental uxoriousness; and the Tennysonian King Arthur posing at Guinevere becomes Don Quixote grovelling before Dulcinea. You must admit that here Nature beats Comedy out of the field: the wildest hominist or feminist farce is insipid after the most commonplace "slice of life." The pretence that women do not take the initiative is part of the farce. Why, the whole world is strewn with snares, traps, gins and pitfalls for the capture of men by women. Give women the vote, and in five years there will be a crushing tax on bachelors. Men, on the other hand, attach penalties to marriage, depriving women of property, of the franchise, of the free use of their limbs, of that ancient symbol of immortality, the right to make oneself at home in the house of God by taking off the hat, of everything that he can force Woman to dispense with without compelling himself to dispense with her. All in vain. Woman must marry because the race must perish without her travail: if the risk of death and the certainty of pain, danger and unutterable discomforts cannot deter her, slavery and swaddled ankles will not. And yet we assume that the force that carries women through all these perils and hardships, stops abashed before the primnesses of our behavior for young ladies. It is assumed that the woman must wait, motionless, until she is wooed. Nay, she often does wait motionless. That is how the spider waits for the fly. But the spider spins her web. And if the fly, like my hero, shews a strength that promises to extricate him, how swiftly does she abandon her pretence of passiveness, and openly fling coil after coil about him until he is secured for ever!

If the really impressive books and other art-works of the world were produced by ordinary men, they would express more fear of women's pursuit than love of their illusory beauty. But ordinary men cannot produce really impressive art-works. Those who can are men of genius: that is, men selected by Nature to carry on the work of building up an intellectual consciousness of her own instinctive purpose. Accordingly, we observe in the man of genius all the unscrupulousness and all the "self-sacrifice" (the two things are the same) of Woman. He will risk the stake and the cross; starve, when necessary, in a garret all his life; study women and live on their work and care as Darwin studied worms and lived upon sheep; work his nerves into rags without payment, a sublime altruist in his disregard of himself, an atrocious egoist in his disregard of others. Here Woman meets a purpose as impersonal, as irresistible as her own; and the clash is sometimes tragic. When it is complicated by the genius being a woman, then the game is one for a king of critics: your George Sand becomes a mother to gain experience for the novelist and to develop her, and gobbles up men of genius, Chopins, Mussets and the like, as mere hors d'oeuvres.

I state the extreme case, of course; but what is true of the great man who incarnates the philosophic consciousness of Life and the woman who incarnates its fecundity, is true in some degree of all geniuses and all women. Hence it is that the world's books get written, its pictures painted, its statues modelled, its symphonies composed, by people who are free of the otherwise universal dominion of the tyranny of sex. Which leads us to the conclusion, astonishing to the vulgar, that art, instead of being before all things the expression of the normal sexual situation, is really the only department in which sex is a superseded and secondary power, with its consciousness so confused and its purpose so perverted, that its ideas are mere fantasy to common men. Whether the artist becomes poet or philosopher, moralist or founder of a religion, his sexual doctrine is nothing but a barren special pleading for pleasure, excitement, and knowledge when he is young, and for contemplative tranquillity when he is old and satiated. Romance and Asceticism, Amorism and Puritanism are equally unreal in the great Philistine world. The world shewn us in books, whether the books be confessed epics or professed gospels, or in codes, or in political rations, or in philosphic systems, is not the main world at all: it is only the self-consciousness of certain abnormal people who have the specific artistic talent and temperament. A serious matter this for you and me, because the man whose consciousness does not correspond to that of the majority is a madman; and the old habit of worshipping madmen is giving way to the new habit of locking them up. And since what we call education and culture is for the most part nothing but the substitution of reading for experience, of literature for life, of the obsolete fictitious for the contemporary real, education, as you no doubt observed at Oxford, destroys, by supplantation, every mind that is not strong enough to see through the imposture and to use the great Masters of Arts as what they really are and no more: that is, patentees of highly questionable methods of thinking, and manufacturers of highly questionable, and for the majority but half valid representations of life. The schoolboy who uses his Homer to throw at his fellow's head makes perhaps the safest and most rational use of him; and I observe with reassurance that you occasionally do the same, in your prime, with your Aristotle.

Fortunately for us, whose minds have been so overwhelmingly sophisticated by literature, what produces all these treatises and poems and scriptures of one sort or another is the struggle of Life to become divinely conscious of itself instead of blindly stumbling hither and thither in the line of least resistance. Hence there is a driving towards truth in all books on matters where the writer, though exceptionally gifted, is normally constituted, and has no private axe to grind. Copernicus had no motive for misleading his fellowmen as to the place of the sun in the solar system: he looked for it as honestly as a shepherd seeks his path in a mist. But Copernicus would not have written love stories scientifically. When it comes to sex relations, the man of genius does not share the common man's danger of capture, nor the woman of genius the common woman's overwhelming specialization. And that is why our scriptures and other art works, when they deal with love, turn from honest attempts at science in physics to romantic nonsense, erotic ecstasy, or the stern asceticism of satiety ("the road of excess leads to the palace of wisdom" said William Blake; for "you never know what is enough unless you know what is more than enough").

There is a political aspect of this sex question which is too big for my comedy, and too momentous to be passed over without culpable frivolity. It is impossible to demonstrate that the initiative in sex transactions remains with Woman, and has been confirmed to her, so far, more and more by the suppression of rapine and discouragement of importunity, without being driven to very serious reflections on the fact that this initiative is politically the most important of all the initiatives, because our political experiment of democracy, the last refuge of cheap misgovernment, will ruin us if our citizens are ill bred.

When we two were born, this country was still dominated by a selected class bred by political marriages. The commercial class had not then completed the first twenty-five years of its new share of political power; and it was itself selected by money qualification, and bred, if not by political marriage, at least by a pretty rigorous class marriage. Aristocracy and plutocracy still furnish the figureheads of politics; but they are now dependent on the votes of the promiscuously bred masses. And this, if you please, at the very moment when the political problem, having suddenly ceased to mean a very limited and occasional interference, mostly by way of jobbing public appointments, in the mismanagement of a tight but parochial little island, with occasional meaningless prosecution of dynastic wars, has become the industrial reorganization of Britain, the construction of a practically international Commonwealth, and the partition of the whole of Africa and perhaps the whole of Asia by the civilized Powers. Can you believe that the people whose conceptions of society and conduct, whose power of attention and scope of interest, are measured by the British theatre as you know it today, can either handle this colossal task themselves, or understand and support the sort of mind and character that is (at least comparatively) capable of handling it? For remember: what our voters are in the pit and gallery they are also in the polling booth. We are all now under what Burke called "the hoofs of the swinish multitude." Burke's language gave great offence because the implied exceptions to its universal application made it a class insult; and it certainly was not for the pot to call the kettle black. The aristocracy he defended, in spite of the political marriages by which it tried to secure breeding for itself, had its mind undertrained by silly schoolmasters and governesses, its character corrupted by gratuitous luxury, its self-respect adulterated to complete spuriousness by flattery and flunkeyism. It is no better today and never will be any better: our very peasants have something morally hardier in them that culminates occasionally in a Bunyan, a Burns, or a Carlyle. But observe, this aristocracy, which was overpowered from 1832 to 1885 by the middle class, has come back to power by the votes of "the swinish multitude." Tom Paine has triumphed over Edmund Burke; and the swine are now courted electors. How many of their own class have these electors sent to parliament? Hardly a dozen out of 670, and these only under the persuasion of conspicuous personal qualifications and popular eloquence. The multitude thus pronounces judgment on its own units: it admits itself unfit to govern, and will vote only for a man morphologically and generically transfigured by palatial residence and equipage, by transcendent tailoring, by the glamor of aristocratic kinship. Well, we two know these transfigured persons, these college passmen, these well groomed monocular Algys and Bobbies, these cricketers to whom age brings golf instead of wisdom, these plutocratic products of "the nail and sarspan business as he got his money by." Do you know whether to laugh or cry at the notion that they, poor devils! will drive a team of continents as they drive a four-in-hand; turn a jostling anarchy of casual trade and speculation into an ordered productivity; and federate our colonies into a world-Power of the first magnitude? Give these people the most perfect political constitution and the soundest political program that benevolent omniscience can devise for them, and they will interpret it into mere fashionable folly or canting charity as infallibly as a savage converts the philosophical theology of a Scotch missionary into crude African idolatry.

I do not know whether you have any illusions left on the subject of education, progress, and so forth. I have none. Any pamphleteer can shew the way to better things; but when there is no will there is no way. My nurse was fond of remarking that you cannot make a silk purse out of a sow's ear; and the more I see of the efforts of our churches and universities and literary sages to raise the mass above its own level, the more convinced I am that my nurse was right. Progress can do nothing but make the most of us all as we are, and that most would clearly not be enough even if those who are already raised out of the lowest abysses would allow the others a chance. The bubble of Heredity has been pricked: the certainty that acquirements are negligible as elements in practical heredity has demolished the hopes of the educationists as well as the terrors of the degeneracy mongers; and we know now that there is no hereditary "governing class" any more than a hereditary hooliganism. We must either breed political capacity or be ruined by Democracy, which was forced on us by the failure of the older alternatives. Yet if Despotism failed only for want of a capable benevolent despot, what chance has Democracy, which requires a whole population of capable voters: that is, of political critics who, if they cannot govern in person for lack of spare energy or specific talent for administration, can at least recognize and appreciate capacity and benevolence in others, and so govern through capably benevolent representatives? Where are such voters to be found today? Nowhere. Promiscuous breeding has produced a weakness of character that is too timid to face the full stringency of a thoroughly competitive struggle for existence and too lazy and petty to organize the commonwealth co-operatively. Being cowards, we defeat natural selection under cover of philanthropy: being sluggards, we neglect artificial selection under cover of delicacy and morality.

Yet we must get an electorate of capable critics or collapse as Rome and Egypt collapsed. At this moment the Roman decadent phase of *panem et circenses* is being inaugurated under our eyes. Our newspapers and melodramas are blustering about our imperial destiny; but our eyes and hearts turn eagerly to the American millionaire. As his hand goes down to his pocket, our fingers go up to the brims of our hats by instinct. Our ideal prosperity is not the prosperity of the industrial north, but the prosperity of the Isle of Wight, of Folkestone and Ramsgate, of Nice and Monte Carlo. That is the only prosperity you see on the stage, where the workers are all footmen, parlormaids, comic lodging-letters and fashionable professional men, whilst the heroes and heroines are miraculously provided with unlimited dividends, and eat gratuitously, like the knights in Don Quixote's books of chivalry. The city papers prate of the competition of Bombay with Manchester and the like. The real competition is the competition of Regent Street with the Rue de Rivoli, of Brighton and the south coast with the Riviera, for the spending money of the American Trusts. What is all this growing love of pageantry, this effusive loyalty, this officious rising and uncovering at a wave from a flag or a blast from a brass band? Imperialism? Not a bit of it. Obsequiousness, servility, cupidity roused by the prevailing smell of money. When Mr. Carnegie rattled his millions in his pockets all England became one rapacious cringe. Only, when Rhodes (who had probably been reading my *Socialism for Millionaires*) left word that no idler was to inherit his estate, the bent backs straightened mistrustfully for a moment. Could it be that the Diamond King was no gentleman after all? However, it was easy to ignore a rich man's solecism. The ungentlemanly clause was not mentioned again; and the backs soon bowed themselves back into their natural shape.

But I hear you asking me in alarm whether I have actually put all this tub thumping into a Don Juan comedy. I have not. I have only made my Don Juan a political pamphleteer, and given you his pamphlet in full by way of appendix. You will find it at the end of the book. I am sorry to say that it is a common practice with romancers to announce their hero as a man of extraordinary genius, and to leave his works entirely to the reader's imagination; so that at the end of the book you whisper to yourself ruefully that but for the author's solemn preliminary assurance you should hardly have given the gentleman credit for ordinary good sense. You cannot accuse me of this pitiable barrenness, this feeble evasion. I not only tell you that my hero wrote a revolutionists' handbook: I give you the handbook at full length for your edification if you care to read it. And in that handbook you will find the politics of the sex question as I conceive Don Juan's descendant to understand them. Not that I disclaim the fullest responsibility for his opinions and for those of all my characters, pleasant and unpleasant. They are all right from their several points of view; and their points of view are, for the dramatic moment, mine also. This may puzzle the people who believe that there is such a thing as an absolutely right point of view, usually their own. It may seem to them that nobody who doubts this can be in a state of grace. However that may be, it is certainly true that nobody who agrees with them can possibly be a dramatist, or indeed anything else that turns upon a knowledge of mankind. Hence it has been pointed out that Shakespear had no conscience. Neither have I, in that sense.

You may, however, remind me that this digression of mine into politics was preceded by a very convincing demonstration that the artist never catches the point of view of the common man on the question of sex, because he is not in the same predicament. I first prove that anything I write on the relation of the sexes is sure to be misleading; and then I proceed to write a Don Juan play. Well, if you insist on asking me why I behave in this absurd way, I can only reply that you asked me to, and that in any case my treatment of the subject may be valid for the artist, amusing to the amateur, and at least intelligible and therefore possibly suggestive to the Philistine. Every man who records his illusions is providing data for the genuinely scientific psychology which the world still waits for. I plank down my view of the existing relations of men to women in the most highly civilized society for what it is worth. It is a view like any other view and no more, neither true nor false, but, I hope, a way of looking at the subject which throws into the familiar order of cause and effect a sufficient body of fact and experience to be interesting to you, if not to the playgoing public of London. I have certainly shewn little consideration for that public in this enterprise; but I know that it has the friendliest disposition towards you and me as far as it has any consciousness of our existence, and quite understands that what I write for you must pass at a considerable height over its simple romantic head. It will take my books as read and my genius for granted, trusting me to put forth work of such quality as shall bear out its verdict. So we may disport ourselves on our own plane to the top of our bent; and if any gentleman points out that neither this epistle dedicatory nor the dream of Don Juan in the third act of the ensuing comedy is suitable for immediate production at a popular theatre we need not contradict him. Napoleon provided Talma with a pit of kings, with what effect on Talma's acting is not recorded. As for me, what I have always wanted is a pit of philosophers; and this is a play for such a pit.

I should make formal acknowledgment to the authors whom I have pillaged in the following pages if I could recollect them all. The theft of the brigand-poetaster from Sir Arthur Conan Doyle is deliberate; and the metamorphosis of Leporello into Enry Straker, motor engineer and New Man, is an intentional dramatic sketch of the contemporary embryo of Mr. H. G. Wells's anticipation of the efficient engineering class which will, he hopes, finally sweep the jabberers out of the way of civilization. Mr. Barrie has also, whilst I am correcting my proofs, delighted London with a servant who knows more than his masters. The conception of Mendoza Limited I trace back to a certain West Indian colonial secretary, who, at a period when he and I and Mr. Sidney Webb were sowing our political wild oats as a sort of Fabian Three Musketeers, without any prevision of the surprising respectability of the crop that followed, recommended Webb, the encyclopedic and inexhaustible, to form himself into a company for the benefit of the shareholders. Octavius I take over unaltered from Mozart; and I hereby authorize any actor who impersonates him, to sing "*Dalla sua pace*" (if he can) at any convenient moment during the representation. Ann was suggested to me by the fifteenth century Dutch morality called Everyman, which Mr. William Poel has lately resuscitated so triumphantly. I trust he will work that vein further, and recognize that Elizabethan Renascence fustian is no more bearable after medieval poesy than Scribe after Ibsen. As I sat watching Everyman at the Charterhouse, I said to myself Why not Everywoman? Ann was the result: every woman is not Ann; but Ann is Everywoman.

That the author of Everyman was no mere artist, but an artist-philosopher, and that the artist-philosophers are the only sort of artists I take quite seriously, will be no news to you. Even Plato and Boswell, as the dramatists who invented Socrates and Dr. Johnson, impress me more deeply than the romantic playwrights. Ever since, as a boy, I first breathed the air of the transcendental regions at a performance of Mozart's *Zauberflöte*, I have been proof against the garish splendors and alcoholic excitements of the ordinary stage combinations of Tappertitian romance with the police intelligence. Bunyan, Blake, Hogarth, and Turner (these four apart and above all the English classics), Goethe, Shelley, Schopenhauer, Wagner, Ibsen, Morris, Tolstoy, and Nietzsche are among the writers whose peculiar sense of the world I recognize as more or less akin to my own. Mark the word peculiar. I read Dickens and Shakespear without shame or stint; but their pregnant observations and demonstrations of life are not co-ordinated into any philosophy or religion: on the contrary Dickens's sentimental assumptions are violently contradicted by his observations; and Shakespear's pessimism is only his wounded humanity. Both have the specific genius of the fictionist and the common sympathies of human feeling and thought in pre-eminent degree. They are often saner and shrewder than the philosophers just as Sancho Panza was often saner and shrewder than Don Quixote. They clear away vast masses of oppressive gravity by their sense of the ridiculous, which is at bottom a combination of sound moral judgment with lighthearted good humor. But they are concerned with the diversities of the world instead of with its unities: they are so irreligious that they exploit popular religion for professional purposes without delicacy or scruple (for example, Sydney Carton and the ghost in Hamlet!): they are anarchical, and cannot balance their exposures of Angelo and Dogberry, Sir Leicester Dedlock and Mr. Tite Barnacle, with any portrait of a prophet or a worthy leader: they have no constructive ideas: they regard those who have them as dangerous fanatics: in all their fictions there is no leading thought or inspiration for which any man could conceivably risk the spoiling of his hat in a shower, much less his life. Both are alike forced to borrow motives for the more strenuous actions of their personages from the common stockpot of melodramatic plots; so that Hamlet has to be stimulated by the prejudices of a policeman and Macbeth by the cupidities of a bushranger. Dickens, without the excuse of having to manufacture motives for Hamlets and Macbeths, superfluously punts his crew down the stream of his monthly parts by mechanical devices which I leave you to describe, my own memory being quite baffled by the simplest question as to Monks in *Oliver Twist*, or the long lost parentage of Smike, or the relations between the Dorrit and Clennam families so inopportunely discovered by Monsieur Rigaud Blandois. The truth is, the world was to Shakespear a great "stage of fools" on which he was utterly bewildered. He could see no sort of sense in living at all; and Dickens saved himself from the despair of the dream in The Chimes by taking the world for granted and busying himself with its details. Neither of them could do anything with a serious positive character: they could place a human figure before you with perfect verisimilitude; but when the moment came for making it live and move, they found, unless it made them laugh, that they had a puppet on their hands, and had to invent some artificial external stimulus to make it work. This is what is the matter with Hamlet all through: he has no will except in his bursts of temper. Foolish Bardolaters make a virtue of this after their fashion: they declare that the play is the tragedy of irresolution; but all Shakespear's projections of the deepest humanity he knew have the same defect: their characters and manners are lifelike; but their actions are forced on them from without, and the external force is grotesquely inapppropriate except when it is quite conventional, as in the case of Henry V. Falstaff is more vivid than any of these reflective characters, because he is self-acting: his motives are his own appetites and instincts and humors. Richard III, too, is delightful as the whimsical comedian who stops a funeral to make love to the corpse's widow; but when, in the next act, he is replaced by a stage villain who smothers babies and offs with people's heads, we are revolted at the imposture and repudiate the changeling. Faulconbridge, Coriolanus, Leontes are admirable descriptions of instinctive temperaments: indeed the play of *Coriolanus* is the greatest of Shakespear's comedies; but description is not philosophy; and comedy neither compromises the author nor reveals him. He must be judged by those characters into which he puts what he knows of himself, his Hamlets and Macbeths and Lears and Prosperos. If these characters are agonizing in a void about factitious melodramatic murders and revenges and the like, whilst the comic characters walk with their feet on solid ground, vivid and amusing, you know that the author has much to shew and nothing to teach. The comparison between Falstaff and Prospero is like the comparison between Micawber and David Copperfield. At the end of the book you know Micawber, whereas you only know what has happened to David, and are not interested enough in him to wonder what his politics or religion might be if anything so stupendous as a religious or political idea, or a general idea of any sort, were to occur to him. He is tolerable as a child; but he never becomes a man, and might be left out of his own biography altogether but for his usefulness as a stage confidant, a Horatio or "Charles his friend" — what they call on the stage a feeder.

Now you cannot say this of the works of the artist-philosophers. You cannot say it, for instance, of *The Pilgrim's Progress*. Put your Shakespearian hero and coward, Henry V and Pistol or Parolles, beside Mr. Valiant and Mr. Fearing, and you have a sudden revelation of the abyss that lies between the fashionable author who could see nothing in the world but personal aims and the tragedy of their disappointment or the comedy of their incongruity, and the field preacher who achieved virtue and courage by identifying himself with the purpose of the world as he understood it. The contrast is enormous: Bunyan's coward stirs your blood more than Shakespear's hero, who actually leaves you cold and secretly hostile. You suddenly see that Shakespear, with all his flashes and divinations, never understood virtue and courage, never conceived how any man who was not a fool could, like Bunyan's hero, look back from the brink of the river of death over the strife and labor of his pilgrimage, and say "yet do I not repent me"; or, with the panache of a millionaire, bequeath "my sword to him that shall succeed me in my pilgrimage, and my courage and skill to him that can get it." This is the true joy in life, the being used for a purpose recognized by yourself as a mighty one; the being thoroughly worn out before you are thrown on the scrap heap; the being a force of Nature instead of a feverish selfish little clod of ailments and grievances complaining that the world will not devote itself to making you happy. And also the only real tragedy in life is the being used by personally minded men for purposes which you recognize to be base. All the rest is at worst mere misfortune or mortality: this alone is misery, slavery, hell on earth; and the revolt against it is the only force that offers a man's work to the poor artist, whom our personally minded rich people would so willingly employ as pander, buffoon, beauty monger, sentimentalizer and the like.

It may seem a long step from Bunyan to Nietzsche; but the difference between their conclusions is purely formal. Bunyan's perception that righteousness is filthy rags, his scorn for Mr. Legality in the village of Morality, his defiance of the Church as the supplanter of religion, his insistence on courage as the virtue of virtues, his estimate of the career of the conventionally respectable and sensible Worldly Wiseman as no better at bottom than the life and death of Mr. Badman: all this, expressed by Bunyan in the terms of a tinker's theology, is what Nietzsche has expressed in terms of post-Darwinian, post-Schopenhauerian philosophy; Wagner in terms of polytheistic mythology; and Ibsen in terms of mid-nineteenth century Parisian dramaturgy. Nothing is new in these matters except their novelties: for instance, it is a novelty to call Justification by Faith "Wille," and Justification by Works "Vorstellung." The sole use of the novelty is that you and I buy and read Schopenhauer's treatise on Will and Representation when we should not dream of buying a set of sermons on Faith versus Works. At bottom the controversy is the same, and the dramatic results are the same. Bunyan makes no attempt to present his pilgrims as more sensible or better conducted than Mr. Worldly Wiseman. Mr. W. W.'s worst enemies, Mr. Embezzler, Mr. Never-go-to-Church-on-Sunday, Mr. Bad Form, Mr. Murderer, Mr. Burglar, Mr. Co-respondent, Mr. Blackmailer, Mr. Cad, Mr. Drunkard, Mr. Labor Agitator and so forth, can read *The Pilgrim's Progress* without finding a word said against them; whereas the respectable people who snub them and put them in prison, such as Mr. W. W. himself and his young friend Civility; Formalist and Hypocrisy; Wildhead, Inconsiderate, and Pragmatick (who were clearly young university men of good family and high feeding); that brisk lad Ignorance, Talkative, By-Ends of Fairspeech and his mother-in-law Lady Feigning, and other reputable gentlemen and citizens, catch it very severely. Even Little

Faith, though he gets to heaven at last, is given to understand that it served him right to be mobbed by the brothers Faint Heart, Mistrust, and Guilt, all three recognized members of respectable society and veritable pillars of the law. The whole allegory is a consistent attack on morality and respectability, without a word that one can remember against vice and crime. Exactly what is complained of in Nietzsche and Ibsen, is it not? And also exactly what would be complained of in all the literature which is great enough and old enough to have attained canonical rank, officially or unofficially, were it not that books are admitted to the canon by a compact which confesses their greatness in consideration of abrogating their meaning; so that the reverend rector can agree with the prophet Micah as to his inspired style without being committed to any complicity in Micah's furiously Radical opinions. Why, even I, as I force myself, pen in hand, into recognition and civility, find all the force of my onslaught destroyed by a simple policy of nonresistance. In vain do I redouble the violence of the language in which I proclaim my heterodoxies. I rail at the theistic credulity of Voltaire, the amoristic superstition of Shelley, the revival of tribal soothsaying and idolatrous rites which Huxley called Science and mistook for an advance on the Pentateuch, no less than at the welter of ecclesiastical and professional humbug which saves the face of the stupid system of violence and robbery which we call Law and Industry. Even atheists reproach me with infidelity and anarchists with nihilism because I cannot endure their moral tirades. And yet, instead of exclaiming "Send this inconceivable Satanist to the stake," the respectable newspapers pith me by announcing "another book by this brilliant and thoughtful writer." And the ordinary citizen, knowing that an author who is well spoken of by a respectable newspaper must be all right, reads me, as he reads Micah, with undisturbed edification from his own point of view. It is narrated that in the eighteen-seventies an old lady, a very devout Methodist, moved from Colchester to a house in the neighborhood of the City Road, in London, where, mistaking the Hall of Science for a chapel, she sat at the feet of Charles Bradlaugh for many years, entranced by his eloquence, without questioning his orthodoxy or moulting a feather of her faith. I fear I shall be defrauded of my just martyrdom in the same way.

However, I am digressing, as a man with a grievance always does. And after all, the main thing in determining the artistic quality of a book is not the opinions it propagates, but the fact that the writer has opinions. The old lady from Colchester was right to sun her simple soul in the energetic radiance of Bradlaugh's genuine beliefs and disbeliefs rather than in the chill of such mere painting of light and heat as elocution and convention can achieve. My contempt for belles-lettres, and for amateurs who become the heroes of the fanciers of literary virtuosity, is not founded on any illusion of mind as to the permanence of those forms of thought (call them opinions) by which I strive to communicate my bent to my fellows. To younger men they are already outmoded; for though they have no more lost their logic than an eighteenth century pastel has lost its drawing or its color, yet, like the pastel, they grow indefinably shabby, and will grow shabbier until they cease to count at all, when my books will either perish, or, if the world is still poor enough to want them, will have to stand, with Bunyan's, by quite amorphous qualities of temper and energy. With this conviction I cannot be a bellettrist. No doubt I must recognize, as even the Ancient Mariner did, that I must tell my story entertainingly if I am to hold the wedding guest spellbound in spite of the siren sounds of the loud bassoon. But "for art's sake" alone I would not face the toil of writing a single sentence. I know that there are men who, having nothing to say and nothing to write, are nevertheless so in love with oratory and with literature that they keep desperately repeating as much as they can understand of what others have said or written aforetime. I know that the leisurely tricks which their want of conviction leaves them free to play with the diluted and misapprehended message supply them with a pleasant parlor game which they call style. I can pity their dotage and even sympathize with their fancy. But a true original style is never achieved for its own sake: a man may pay from a shilling to a guinea, according to his means, to see, hear, or read another man's act of genius; but he will not pay with his whole life and soul to become a mere virtuoso in literature, exhibiting an accomplishment which will not even make money for him, like fiddle playing. Effectiveness of assertion is the Alpha and Omega of style. He who has nothing to assert has no style and can have none: he who has something to assert will go as far in power of style as its momentousness and his conviction will carry him. Disprove his assertion after it is made, yet its style remains. Darwin has no more destroyed the style of Job nor of Handel than Martin Luther destroyed the style of Giotto. All the assertions get disproved sooner or later; and so we find the world full of a magnificent débris of artistic fossils, with the matter-of-fact credibility gone clean out of them, but the form still splendid. And that is why the old masters play the deuce with our mere susceptibles. Your Royal Academician thinks he can get the style of Giotto without Giotto's beliefs, and correct his perspective into the bargain. Your man of letters thinks he can get Bunyan's or Shakespear's style without Bunyan's conviction or Shakespear's apprehension, especially if he takes care not to split his infinitives. And so with your Doctors of Music, who, with their collections of discords duly prepared and resolved or retarded or anticipated in the manner of the great composers, think they can learn the art of Palestrina from Cherubini's treatise. All this academic art is far worse than the trade in sham antique furniture; for the man who sells me an oaken chest which he swears was made in the thirteenth century, though as a matter of fact he made it himself only yesterday, at least does not pretend that there are any modern ideas in it, whereas your academic copier of fossils offers them to you as the latest outpouring of the human spirit, and, worst of all, kidnaps young people as pupils and persuades them that his limitations are rules, his observances dexterities, his timidities good taste, and his emptinesses purities. And when he declares that art should not be didactic, all the people who have nothing to teach and all the people who dont want to learn agree with him emphatically.

I pride myself on not being one of these susceptibles. If you study the electric light with which I supply you in that Bumbledonian public capacity of mine over which you make merry from time to time, you will find that your house contains a great quantity of highly susceptible copper wire which gorges itself with electricity and gives you no light whatever. But here and there occurs a scrap of intensely insusceptible, intensely resistant material; and that stubborn scrap grapples with the current and will not let it through until it has made itself useful to you as those two vital qualities of literature, light and heat. Now if I am to be no mere copper wire amateur but a luminous author, I must also be a most intensely refractory person, liable to go out and to go wrong at inconvenient moments, and with incendiary possibilities. These are the faults of my qualities; and I assure you that I sometimes dislike myself so much that when some irritable reviewer chances at that moment to pitch into me with zest, I feel unspeakably relieved and obliged. But I never dream of reforming, knowing that I must take myself as I am and get what work I can out of myself. All this you will understand; for there is community of material between us: we are both critics of life as well as of art; and you have perhaps said to yourself when I have passed your windows "There, but for the grace of God, go I." An awful and chastening reflection, which shall be the closing cadence of this immoderately long letter from yours faithfully,

G. BERNARD SHAW

Woking, 1903.

Man and Superman

ACT ONE

ROEBUCK RAMSDEN *is in his study, opening the morning's letters. The study, handsomely and solidly furnished, proclaims the man of means. Not a speck of dust is visible: it is clear that there are at least two housemaids and a parlormaid downstairs, and a housekeeper upstairs who does not let them spare elbow-grease. Even the top of* ROEBUCK'S *head is polished: on a sunshiny day he could heliograph his orders to distant camps by merely nodding. In no other respect, however, does he suggest the military man. It is in active civil life that men get his broad air of importance, his dignified expectation of deference, his determinate mouth disarmed and refined since the hour of his success by the withdrawal of opposition and the concession of comfort and precedence and power. He is more than a highly respectable man: he is marked out as a president of highly respectable men, a chairman among directors, an alderman among councillors, a mayor among aldermen. Four tufts of iron-grey hair, which will soon be as white as isinglass, and are in other respects not at all unlike it, grow in two symmetrical pairs above his ears and at the angles of his spreading jaws. He wears a black frock coat, a white waistcoat (it is bright spring weather), and trousers, neither black nor perceptibly blue, of one of those indefinitely mixed hues which the modern clothier has produced to harmonize with the religions of respectable men. He has not been out of doors yet to-day; so he still wears his slippers, his boots being ready for him on the hearth-rug. Surmising that he has no valet, and seeing that he has no secretary with a shorthand notebook and a typewriter, one meditates on how little our great burgess domesticity has been disturbed by new fashions and methods, or by the enterprise of the railway and hotel companies which sell you a Saturday to Monday of life at Folkestone as a real gentleman for two guineas, first class fares both ways included.*

How old is ROEBUCK? *The question is important on the threshold of a drama of ideas; for under such circumstances everything depends on whether his adolescence belonged to the sixties or to the eighties. He was born, as a matter of fact, in 1839, and was a Unitarian and Free Trader from his boyhood, and an Evolutionist from the publication of the* Origin of Species. *Consequently he has always classed himself as an advanced thinker and fearlessly outspoken reformer.*

Sitting at his writing table, he has on his right the windows giving on Portland Place. Through these, as through a proscenium, the curious spectator may contemplate his profile as well as the blinds will permit. On his left is the inner wall, with a stately bookcase, and the door not quite in the middle, but somewhat further from him. Against the wall opposite him are two busts on pillars: one, to his left, of John Bright; the other, to his right, of Mr. Herbert Spencer. Between them hang an engraved portrait of Richard Cobden; enlarged photographs of Martineau, Huxley, and George Eliot; autotypes of allegories by Mr. G. F. Watts (for ROEBUCK *believes in the fine arts with all the earnestness of a man who does not understand them), and an impression of Dupont's engraving of Delaroche's Beaux Arts hemicycle, representing the great men of all ages. On the wall behind him, above the mantelshelf, is a family portrait of impenetrable obscurity.*

A chair stands near the writing table for the convenience of business visitors. Two other chairs are against the wall between the busts.

A PARLORMAID *enters with a visitor's card.* ROEBUCK *takes it, and nods, pleased. Evidently a welcome caller.*

RAMSDEN. Shew him in.

The PARLORMAID *goes out and returns with the visitor.*

THE MAID. Mr. Robinson.

MR. ROBINSON *is really an uncommonly nice looking young fellow. He must, one thinks, be the jeune premier; for it is not in reason to suppose that a second such attractive male figure should appear in one story. The slim, shapely frame, the elegant suit of new mourning, the small head and regular features, the pretty little moustache, the frank clear eyes, the wholesome bloom on the youthful complexion, the well brushed glossy hair, not curly, but of fine texture and good dark color, the arch of good nature in the eyebrows, the erect forehead and neatly pointed chin, all announce the man who will love and suffer later on. And that he will not do so without sympathy is guaranteed by an engaging sincerity and eager modest serviceableness which stamp him as a man of amiable nature. The moment he appears,* RAMSDEN's *face expands into fatherly liking and welcome, an expression which drops into one of decorous grief as the young man approaches him with sorrow in his face as well as in his black clothes.* RAMSDEN *seems to know the nature of the bereavement. As the visitor advances silently to the writing table, the old man rises and shakes his hand across it without a word: a long, affectionate shake which tells the story of a recent sorrow common to both.*

RAMSDEN (*concluding the handshake and cheering up*). Well, well, Octavius, it's the common lot. We must all face it some day. Sit down.

OCTAVIUS *takes the visitor's chair.* RAMSDEN *replaces himself in his own.*

OCTAVIUS. Yes: we must face it, Mr. Ramsden. But I owed him a great deal. He did everything for me that my father could have done if he had lived.

RAMSDEN. He had no son of his own, you see.

OCTAVIUS. But he had daughters; and yet he was as good to my sister as to me. And his death was so sudden! I always intended to thank him — to let him know that I had not taken all his care of me as a matter of course, as any boy takes his father's care. But I waited for an opportunity; and now he is dead — dropped without a moment's warning. He will never know what I felt. (*He takes out his handkerchief and cries unaffectedly.*)

RAMSDEN. How do we know that, Octavius? He may know it: we cannot tell. Come! dont grieve. (OCTAVIUS *masters himself and puts up his handkerchief.*) Thats right. Now let me tell you something to console you. The last time I saw him — it was in this very room — he said to me: "Tavy is a generous lad and the soul of honor; and when I see how little consideration other men get from their sons, I realize how much better than a son he's been to me." There! Doesnt that do you good?

OCTAVIUS. Mr. Ramsden: he used to say to me that he had met only one man in the world who was the soul of honor, and that was Roebuck Ramsden.

RAMSDEN. Oh, that was his partiality: we were very old friends, you know. But there was something else he used to say about you. I wonder whether I ought to tell you or not!

OCTAVIUS. You know best.

RAMSDEN. It was something about his daughter.

OCTAVIUS (*eagerly*). About Ann! Oh, do tell me that, Mr. Ramsden.

RAMSDEN. Well, he said he was glad, after all, you were not his son, because he thought that someday Annie and you — (OCTAVIUS *blushes vividly.*) Well, perhaps I shouldnt have told you. But he was in earnest.

OCTAVIUS. Oh, if only I thought I had a chance! You know, Mr. Ramsden, I dont care about money or about what people call position; and I cant bring myself to take an interest in the business of struggling for them. Well, Ann has a most exquisite nature; but she is so accustomed to be in the thick of that sort of thing that she thinks a man's character incomplete if he is not ambitious. She knows that if she married me she would have to reason herself out of being ashamed of me for not being a big success of some kind.

RAMSDEN (*getting up and planting himself with his back to the fireplace*). Nonsense, my boy, nonsense! Youre too modest. What does she know about the real value of men at her age? (*More seriously.*) Besides, she's a wonderfully dutiful girl. Her father's wish would be sacred to her. Do you know that since she grew up to years of discretion, I dont believe she has ever once given her own wish as a reason for doing anything or not doing it. It's always "Father wishes me to," or "Mother wouldnt like it." It's really almost a fault in her. I have often told her she must learn to think for herself.

OCTAVIUS (*shaking his head*). I couldnt ask her to marry me because her father wished it, Mr. Ramsden.

RAMSDEN. Well, perhaps not. No: of course not. I see that. No: you certainly couldnt. But when you win her on your own merits, it will be a great happiness to her to fulfil her father's desire as well as her own. Eh? Come! youll ask her, wont you?

OCTAVIUS (*with sad gaiety*). At all events I promise you I shall never ask anyone else.

RAMSDEN. Oh, you shant need to. She'll accept you, my boy — although (*here he suddenly becomes very serious indeed*) you have one great drawback.

OCTAVIUS (*anxiously*). What drawback is that, Mr. Ramsden? I should rather say which of my many drawbacks?

RAMSDEN. I'll tell you, Octavius. (*He takes from the table a book bound in red cloth*). I have in my hand a copy of the most infamous, the most scandalous, the most mischievous, the most blackguardly book that ever escaped burning at the hands of the common hangman. I have not read it: I would not soil my mind with such filth; but I have read what the papers say of it. The title is quite enough for me. (*He reads it.*) The Revolutionist's Handbook and Pocket Companion. By John Tanner, M.I.R.C., Member of the Idle Rich Class.

OCTAVIUS (*smiling*). But Jack —

RAMSDEN (*testily*). For goodness' sake, dont call him Jack under my roof. (*He throws the book violently down on the table. Then, somewhat relieved, he comes past the table to* OCTAVIUS, *and addresses him at close quarters with impressive gravity.*) Now, Octavius, I know that my dead friend was right when he said you were a generous lad. I know that this man was your schoolfellow, and that you feel bound to stand by him because there was a boyish friendship between you. But I ask you to consider the altered circumstances. You were treated as a son in my friend's house. You lived there; and your friends could not be turned from the door. This man Tanner was in and out there on your account almost from his childhood. He addresses Annie by her Christian name as freely as you do. Well, while her father was alive, that was her father's business, not mine. This man Tanner was only a boy to him: his opinions were something to be laughed at, like a man's hat on a child's head. But now Tanner is a grown man and Annie a grown woman. And her father is gone. We dont as yet know the exact terms of his will; but he often talked it over with me; and I have no more doubt than I have that youre sitting there that the will appoints me Annie's trustee and guardian. (*Forcibly.*) Now I tell you, once for all, I cant and I wont have Annie placed in such a position that she must, out of regard for you, suffer the intimacy of this fellow Tanner. It's not fair: it's not right: it's not kind. What are you going to do about it?

OCTAVIUS. But Ann herself has told Jack that whatever his opinions are, he will always be welcome because he knew her dear father.

RAMSDEN (*out of patience*). That girl's mad about her duty to her parents.

(*He starts off like a goaded ox in the direction of John Bright, in whose expression there is no sympathy for him. As he speaks he fumes down to Herbert Spencer, who receives him still more coldly.*) Excuse me, Octavius; but there are limits to social toleration. You know that I am not a bigoted or prejudiced man. You know that I am plain Roebuck Ramsden when other men who have done less have got handles to their names, because I have stood for equality and liberty of conscience while they were truckling to the Church and to the aristocracy. Whitefield and I lost chance after chance through our advanced opinions. But I draw the line at Anarchism and Free Love and that sort of thing. If I am to be Annie's guardian, she will have to learn that she has a duty to me: I wont have it: I will not have it. She must forbid John Tanner the house; and so must you.

The PARLORMAID *returns.*

OCTAVIUS. But —

RAMSDEN (*calling his attention to the servant*). Ssh! Well?

THE MAID. Mr. Tanner wishes to see you, sir.

RAMSDEN. Mr. Tanner!

OCTAVIUS. Jack!

RAMSDEN. How dare Mr. Tanner call on me! Say I cannot see him.

OCTAVIUS (*hurt*). I am sorry you are turning my friend from your door like that.

THE MAID (*calmly*). He's not at the door, sir. He's upstairs in the drawing-room with Miss Ramsden. He came with Mrs. Whitefield and Miss Ann and Miss Robinson, sir. (RAMSDEN's *feelings are beyond words.*)

OCTAVIUS (*grinning*). Thats very like Jack, Mr. Ramsden. You must see him, even if it's only to turn him out.

RAMSDEN (*hammering out his words with suppressed fury*). Go upstairs and ask Mr. Tanner to be good enough to step down here. (*The* PARLORMAID *goes out; and* RAMSDEN *returns to the fireplace, as to a fortified position.*) I must say that of all the confounded pieces of impertinence — well, if these are Anarchist manners, I hope you like them. And Annie with him! Annie! A — (*He chokes.*)

OCTAVIUS. Yes: thats what surprises me. He's so desperately afraid of Ann. There must be something the matter.

MR. JOHN TANNER *suddenly opens the door and enters. He is too young to be described simply as a big man with a beard. But it is already plain that middle life will find him in that category. He has still some of the slimness of youth; but youthfulness is not the effect he aims at: his frock coat would befit a prime minister; and a certain high chested carriage of the shoulders, a lofty pose of the head; and the Olympian majesty with which a mane, or rather a huge wisp, of hazel colored hair is thrown back from an imposing brow, suggest Jupiter rather than Apollo. He is prodigiously fluent of speech, restless, excitable [mark the snorting nostril and the restless blue eye, just the thirty-second of an inch too wide open], possibly a little mad. He is carefully dressed, not from the vanity that cannot resist finery, but from a sense of the importance of everything he does which leads him to make as much of paying a call as other men do of getting married or laying a foundation stone. A sensitive, susceptible, exaggerative, earnest man: a megalomaniac, who would be lost without a sense of humor.*

Just at present the sense of humor is in abeyance. To say that he is excited is nothing: all his moods are phases of excitement. He is now in the panic-stricken phase; and he walks straight up to RAMSDEN *as if with the fixed intention of shooting him on his own hearthrug. But what he pulls from his breast pocket is not a pistol, but a foolscap document which he thrusts under the indignant nose of* RAMSDEN *as he exclaims —*

TANNER. Ramsden: do you know what that is?

RAMSDEN (*loftily*). No, sir.

TANNER. It's a copy of Whitefield's will. Ann got it this morning.

RAMSDEN. When you say Ann, you mean, I presume, Miss Whitefield.

TANNER. I mean our Ann, your Ann, Tavy's Ann, and now, Heaven help me, my Ann!

OCTAVIUS (*rising, very pale*). What do you mean?

TANNER. Mean! (*He holds up the will.*) Do you know who is appointed Ann's guardian by this will?

RAMSDEN (*coolly*). I believe I am.

TANNER. You! You and I, man. I! I!! I!!! Both of us! (*He flings the will down on the writing table.*)

RAMSDEN. You! Impossible.

TANNER. It's only too hideously true. (*He throws himself into* OCTAVIUS's *chair.*) Ramsden: get me out of it somehow. You dont know Ann as well as I do. She'll commit every crime a respectable woman can; and she'll justify every one of them by saying that it was the wish of her guardians. She'll put everything on us; and we shall have no more control over her than a couple of mice over a cat.

OCTAVIUS. Jack: I wish you wouldnt talk like that about Ann.

TANNER. This chap's in love with her: thats another complication. Well, she'll either jilt him and say I didnt approve of him, or marry him and say you ordered her to. I tell you, this is the most staggering blow that has ever fallen on a man of my age and temperament.

RAMSDEN. Let me see that will, sir. (*He goes to the writing table and picks it up.*) I cannot believe that my old friend Whitefield would have shewn such a want of confidence in me as to associate me with — (*His countenance falls as he reads.*)

TANNER. It's all my own doing: thats the horrible irony of it. He told me one day that you were to be Ann's guardian; and like a fool I began arguing with him about the folly of leaving a young woman under the control of an old man with obsolete ideas.

RAMSDEN (*stupended*). My ideas obsolete ! ! ! ! ! ! !

TANNER. Totally. I had just finished an essay called Down with Government by the Greyhaired; and I was full of arguments and illustrations. I said the proper thing was to combine the experience of an old hand with the vitality of a young one. Hang me if he didnt take me at my word and alter his will — it's dated only a fortnight after that conversation — appointing me as joint guardian with you!

RAMSDEN (*pale and determined*). I shall refuse to act.

TANNER. Whats the good of that? Ive been refusing all the way from Richmond; but Ann keeps on saying that of course she's only an orphan; and that she cant expect the people who were glad to come to the house in her father's time to trouble much about her now. Thats the latest game. An orphan! It's like hearing an ironclad talk about being at the mercy of the winds and waves.

OCTAVIUS. This is not fair, Jack. She is an orphan. And you ought to stand by her.

TANNER. Stand by her! What danger is she in? She has the law on her side; she has popular sentiment on her side; she has plenty of money and no conscience. All she wants with me is to load up all her moral responsibilities on me, and do as she likes at the expense of my character. I cant control her; and she can compromise me as much as she likes. I might as well be her husband.

RAMSDEN. You can refuse to accept the guardianship. I shall certainly refuse to hold it jointly with you.

TANNER. Yes; and what will she say to that? what does she say to it? Just that her father's wishes are sacred to her, and that she shall always look up to me as her guardian whether I care to face the responsibility or not. Refuse! You might as well refuse to accept the embraces of a boa constrictor when once it gets round your neck.

OCTAVIUS. This sort of talk is not kind to me, Jack.

TANNER (*rising and going to* OCTAVIUS *to console him, but still lamenting*). If he wanted a young guardian, why didnt he appoint Tavy?

RAMSDEN. Ah! why indeed?

OCTAVIUS. I will tell you. He sounded me about it; but I refused the trust because I loved her. I had no right to let myself be forced on her as a guardian by her father. He spoke to her about it; and she said I was right. You know I love her, Mr. Ramsden; and Jack knows it too. If Jack loved a woman, I would not compare her to a boa constrictor in his presence, however much I might dislike her. (*He sits down between the busts and turns his face to the wall.*)

RAMSDEN. I do not believe that Whitefield was in his right senses when he made that will. You have admitted that he made it under your influence.

TANNER. You ought to be pretty well obliged to me for my influence. He leaves you two thousand five hundred for your trouble. He leaves Tavy a dowry for his sister and five thousand for himself.

OCTAVIUS (*his tears flowing afresh*). Oh, I cant take it. He was too good to us.

TANNER. You wont get it, my boy, if Ramsden upsets the will.

RAMSDEN. Ha! I see. You have got me in a cleft stick.

TANNER. He leaves me nothing but the charge of Ann's morals, on the ground that I have already more money than is good for me. That shews that he had his wits about him, doesnt it?

RAMSDEN (*grimly*). I admit that.

OCTAVIUS (*rising and coming from his refuge by the wall*). Mr. Ramsden: I think you are prejudiced against Jack. He is a man of honor, and incapable of abusing —

TANNER. Dont, Tavy: youll make me ill. I am not a man of honor: I am a man struck down by a dead hand. Tavy: you must marry her after all and take her off my hands. And I had set my heart on saving you from her!

OCTAVIUS. Oh, Jack, you talk of saving me from my highest happiness.

TANNER. Yes, a lifetime of happiness. If it were only the first half hour's happiness, Tavy, I would buy it for you with my last penny. But a lifetime of happiness! No man alive could bear it: it would be hell on earth.

RAMSDEN (*violently*). Stuff, sir. Talk sense; or else go and waste someone else's time: I have something better to do than listen to your fooleries. (*He positively kicks his way to his table and resumes his seat.*)

TANNER. You hear him, Tavy! Not an idea in his head later than eighteen sixty. We cant leave Ann with no other guardian to turn to.

RAMSDEN. I am proud of your contempt for my character and opinions, sir. Your own are set forth in that book, I believe.

TANNER (*eagerly going to the table*). What! Youve got my book! What do you think of it?

RAMSDEN. Do you suppose I would read such a book, sir?

TANNER. Then why did you buy it?

RAMSDEN. I did not buy it, sir. It has been sent me by some foolish lady who seems to admire your views. I was about to dispose of it when Octavius interrupted me. I shall do so now, with your permission. (*He throws the book into the waste paper basket with such vehemence that* TANNER *recoils under the impression that it is being thrown at his head.*)

TANNER. You have no more manners than I have myself. However, that saves ceremony between us. (*He sits down again.*) What do you intend to do about this will?

OCTAVIUS. May I make a suggestion?

RAMSDEN. Certainly, Octavius.

OCTAVIUS. Arnt we forgetting that Ann herself may have some wishes in this matter?

RAMSDEN. I quite intend that Annie's wishes shall be consulted in every reasonable way. But she is only a woman, and a young and inexperienced woman at that.

TANNER. Ramsden: I begin to pity you.

RAMSDEN (*hotly*). I dont want to know how you feel towards me, Mr. Tanner.

TANNER. Ann will do just exactly what she likes. And whats more, she'll force us to advise her to do it; and she'll put the blame on us if it turns out badly. So, as Tavy is longing to see her —

OCTAVIUS (*shyly*). I am not, Jack.

TANNER. You lie, Tavy: you are. So lets have her down from the drawing-room and ask her what she intends us to do. Off with you, Tavy, and fetch her. (TAVY *turns to go.*) And dont be long; for the strained relations between myself and Ramsden will make the interval rather painful. (RAMSDEN *compresses his lips, but says nothing.*)

OCTAVIUS. Never mind him, Mr. Ramsden. He's not serious. (*He goes out.*)

RAMSDEN (*very deliberately*). Mr. Tanner: you are the most impudent person I have ever met.

TANNER (*seriously*). I know it, Ramsden. Yet even I cannot wholly conquer shame. We live in an atmosphere of shame. We are ashamed of everything that is real about us; ashamed of ourselves, of our relatives, of our incomes, of our accents, of our opinions, of our experience, just as we are ashamed of our naked skins. Good Lord, my dear Ramsden, we are ashamed to walk, ashamed to ride in an omnibus, ashamed to hire a hansom instead of keeping a carriage, ashamed of keeping one horse instead of two and a groom-gardener instead of a coachman and footman. The more things a man is ashamed of, the more respectable he is. Why, youre ashamed to buy my book, ashamed to read it: the only thing youre not ashamed of is to judge me for it without having read it; and even that only means that youre ashamed to have heterodox opinions. Look at the effect I produce because my fairy godmother withheld from me this gift of shame. I have every possible virtue that a man can have except —

RAMSDEN. I am glad you think so well of yourself.

TANNER. All you mean by that is that you think I ought to be ashamed of talking about my virtues. You dont mean that I havnt got them: you know perfectly well that I am as sober and honest a citizen as yourself, as truthful personally, and much more truthful politically and morally.

RAMSDEN (*touched on his most sensitive point*). I deny that. I will not allow you or any man to treat me as if I were a mere member of the British public. I detest its prejudices; I scorn its narrowness; I demand the right to think for myself. You pose as an advanced man. Let me tell you that I was an advanced man before you were born.

TANNER. I knew it was a long time ago.

RAMSDEN. I am as advanced as ever I was. I defy you to prove that I have ever hauled down the flag. I am more advanced than ever I was. I grow more advanced every day.

TANNER. More advanced in years, Polonius.

RAMSDEN. Polonius! So you are Hamlet, I suppose.

TANNER. No: I am only the most impudent person youve ever met. Thats your notion of a thoroughly bad character. When you want to give me a piece of your mind, you ask yourself, as a just and upright man, what is the worst you can fairly say of me. Thief, liar, forger, adulterer, perjurer, glutton, drunkard? Not one of these names fits me. You have to fall back on my deficiency in shame. Well, I admit it. I even congratulate myself; for if I were ashamed of my real self, I should cut as stupid a figure as any of the rest of you. Cultivate a little impudence, Ramsden; and you will become quite a remarkable man.

RAMSDEN. I have no —

TANNER. You have no desire for that sort of notoriety. Bless you, I knew that answer would come as well as I know that a box of matches will come out of an automatic machine when I put a penny in the slot: you would be ashamed to say anything else.

The crushing retort for which RAMSDEN *has been visibly collecting his forces is lost for ever; for at this point* OCTAVIUS *returns with* MISS ANN WHITEFIELD *and her mother; and* RAMSDEN *springs up and hurries to the door to receive them. Whether* ANN *is good-looking or not depends upon your taste; also and perhaps chiefly on your age and sex. To* OCTAVIUS *she is an enchantingly beautiful woman, in whose presence the world becomes transfigured, and the puny limits of individual consciousness are suddenly made infinite by a mystic memory of the whole life of the race to its beginnings in the east, or even back to the paradise from which it fell. She is to him the reality of romance, the inner good sense of nonsense, the unveiling of his eyes, the freeing of his soul, the abolition of time, place and circumstance, the etherealization of his blood into rapturous rivers of the very water of life itself, the revelation of all the mysteries and the sanctification of all the dogmas. To her mother she is, to put it as moderately as possible, nothing whatever of the kind. Not that* OCTAVIUS's *admiration is in any way ridiculous or discreditable.* ANN *is a well formed creature, as far as that goes; and she is perfectly ladylike, graceful, and comely, with ensnaring eyes and hair. Besides, instead of making herself an eyesore, like her mother, she has devised a mourning costume of black and violet silk which does honor to her late father and reveals the family tradition of brave unconventionality by which* RAMSDEN *sets such store.*

But all this is beside the point as an explanation of ANN's *charm. Turn up her nose, give a cast to her eye, replace her black and violet confection by the apron and feathers of a flower girl, strike all the aitches out of her speech, and* ANN *would still make men dream. Vitality is as common as humanity; but, like humanity, it sometimes rises to genius; and* ANN *is one of the vital geniuses. Not at all, if you please, an oversexed person: that is a vital defect, not a true excess. She is a perfectly respectable, perfectly self-controlled woman, and looks it; though her pose is fashionably frank and impulsive. She inspires confidence as a person who will do nothing she does not mean to do; also some fear, perhaps, as a woman who will probably do everything she means to do without taking more account of other people than may be necessary and what she calls right. In short, what the weaker of her own sex sometimes call a cat.*

Nothing can be more decorous than her entry and her reception by RAMSDEN, *whom she kisses. The late Mr. Whitefield would be gratified almost to impatience by the long faces of the men [except* TANNER, *who is fidgety], the silent handgrasps, the sympathetic placing of chairs, the sniffing of the widow, and the liquid eye of the daughter, whose heart, apparently, will not let her control her tongue to speech.* RAMSDEN *and* OCTAVIUS *take the two chairs from the wall, and place them for the two ladies; but* ANN *comes to* TANNER *and takes his chair, which he offers with a brusque gesture, subsequently relieving his irritation by sitting down on the corner of the writing table with studied indecorum.* OCTAVIUS *gives* MRS. WHITEFIELD *a chair next* ANN, *and himself takes the vacant one which* RAMSDEN *has placed under the nose of the effigy of Mr. Herbert Spencer.*

MRS. WHITEFIELD, *by the way, is a little woman, whose faded flaxen hair looks like straw on an egg. She has an expression of muddled shrewdness, a squeak of protest in her voice, and an odd air of continually elbowing away some larger person who is crushing her into a corner. One guesses her as one of those women who are conscious of being treated as silly and negligible, and who, without having strength enough to assert themselves effectually, at any rate never submit to their fate. There is a touch of chivalry in* OCTAVIUS'S *scrupulous attention to her, even whilst his whole soul is absorbed by* ANN.

RAMSDEN *goes solemnly back to his magisterial seat at the writing table, ignoring* TANNER, *and opens the proceedings.*

RAMSDEN. I am sorry, Annie, to force business on you at a sad time like the present. But your poor dear father's will has raised a very serious question. You have read it, I believe?

ANN *assents with a nod and a catch of her breath, too much affected to speak.*

I must say I am surprised to find Mr. Tanner named as joint guardian and trustee with myself of you and Rhoda. (*A pause. They all look portentous; but they have nothing to say.* RAMSDEN, *a little ruffled by the lack of any response, continues.*) I dont know that I can consent to act under such conditions. Mr. Tanner has, I understand, some objection also; but I do not profess to understand its nature: he will no doubt speak for himself. But we are agreed that we can decide nothing until we know your views. I am afraid I shall have to ask you to choose between my sole guardianship and that of Mr. Tanner; for I fear it is impossible for us to undertake a joint arrangement.

ANN (*in a low musical voice*). Mamma —

MRS. WHITEFIELD (*hastily*). Now, Ann, I do beg you not to put it on me. I have no opinion on the subject, and if I had, it would probably not be attended to. I am quite content with whatever you three think best.

TANNER *turns his head and looks fixedly at* RAMSDEN, *who angrily refuses to receive this mute communication.*

ANN (*resuming in the same gentle voice, ignoring her mother's bad taste*). Mamma knows that she is not strong enough to bear the whole responsibility for me and Rhoda without some help and advice. Rhoda must have a guardian; and though I am older, I do not think any young unmarried woman should be left quite to her own guidance. I hope you agree with me, Granny?

TANNER (*starting*). Granny! Do you intend to call your guardians Granny?

ANN. Dont be foolish, Jack. Mr. Ramsden has always been Grandpapa Roebuck to me: I am Granny's Annie; and he is Annie's Granny. I christened him so when I first learned to speak.

RAMSDEN (*sarcastically*). I hope you are satisfied, Mr. Tanner. Go on, Annie: I quite agree with you.

ANN. Well, if I am to have a guardian, can I set aside anybody whom my dear father appointed for me?

RAMSDEN (*biting his lip*). You approve of your father's choice, then?

ANN. It is not for me to approve or disapprove. I accept it. My father loved me and knew best what was good for me.

RAMSDEN. Of course I understand your feeling, Annie. It is what I should have expected of you; and it does you credit. But it does not settle the question so completely as you think. Let me put a case to you. Suppose you were to discover that I had been guilty of some disgraceful action — that I was not the man your poor dear father took me for! Would you still consider it right that I should be Rhoda's guardian?

ANN. I cant imagine you doing anything disgraceful, Granny.

TANNER (*to* RAMSDEN). You havnt done anything of the sort, have you?

RAMSDEN (*indignantly*). No sir.

MRS. WHITEFIELD (*placidly*). Well, then, why suppose it?

ANN. You see, Granny, Mamma would not like me to suppose it.

RAMSDEN (*much perplexed*). You are both so full of natural and affectionate feeling in these family matters that it is very hard to put the situation fairly before you.

TANNER. Besides, my friend, you are not putting the situation fairly before them.

RAMSDEN (*sulkily*). Put it yourself, then.

TANNER. I will. Ann: Ramsden thinks I am not fit to be your guardian; and I quite agree with him. He considers that if your father had read my book, he wouldnt have appointed me. That book is the disgraceful action he has been talking about. He thinks it's your duty for Rhoda's sake to ask him to act alone and to make me withdraw. Say the word; and I will.

ANN. But I havnt read your book, Jack.

TANNER (*diving at the waste-paper basket and fishing the book out for her*). Then read it at once and decide.

RAMSDEN (*vehemently*). If I am to be your guardian, I positively forbid you to read that book, Annie. (*He smites the table with his fist and rises.*)

ANN. Of course not if you dont wish it. (*She puts the book on the table.*)

TANNER. If one guardian is to forbid you to read the other guardian's book, how are we to settle it? Suppose I order you to read it! What about your duty to me?

ANN (*gently*). I am sure you would never purposely force me into a painful dilemma, Jack.

RAMSDEN (*irritably*). Yes, yes, Annie: this is all very well, and, as I said, quite natural and becoming. But you must make a choice one way or the other. We are as much in a dilemma as you.

ANN. I feel that I am too young, too inexperienced, to decide. My father's wishes are sacred to me.

MRS. WHITEFIELD. If you two men wont carry them out I must say it is rather hard that you should put the responsibility on Ann. It seems to me that people are always putting things on other people in this world.

RAMSDEN. I am sorry you take it in that way.

ANN (*touchingly*). Do you refuse to accept me as your ward, Granny?

RAMSDEN. No: I never said that. I greatly object to act with Mr. Tanner: thats all.

MRS. WHITEFIELD. Why? What's the matter with poor Jack?

TANNER. My views are too advanced for him.

RAMSDEN (*indignantly*). They are not. I deny it.

ANN. Of course not. What nonsense! Nobody is more advanced than Granny. I am sure it is Jack himself who has made all the difficulty. Come, Jack! be kind to me in my sorrow. You dont refuse to accept me as your ward, do you?

TANNER (*gloomily*). No. I let myself in for it; so I suppose I must face it. (*He turns away to the bookcase, and stands there, moodily studying the titles of the volumes.*)

ANN (*rising and expanding with subdued but gushing delight*). Then we are all agreed; and my dear father's will is to be carried out. You dont know what a joy that is to me and to my mother! (*She goes to* RAMSDEN *and presses both his hands, saying*) And I shall have my dear Granny to help and advise me. (*She casts a glance at* TANNER *over her shoulder.*) And Jack the Giant Killer. (*She goes past her mother to* OCTAVIUS.) And Jack's inseparable friend Ricky-ticky-tavy. (*He blushes and looks inexpressibly foolish.*)

MRS. WHITEFIELD (*rising and shaking her widow's weeds straight*). Now that you are Ann's guardian, Mr. Ramsden, I wish you would speak to her about her habit of giving people nicknames. They cant be expected to like it. (*She moves towards the door.*)

ANN. How can you say such a thing, Mamma! (*Glowing with affectionate remorse.*) Oh, I wonder can you be right! Have I been inconsiderate? (*She turns to* OCTAVIUS, *who is sitting astride his chair with his elbows on the back of it. Putting her hand on his forehead she turns his face up suddenly.*) Do you want to be treated like a grown up man? Must I call you Mr. Robinson in future?

OCTAVIUS (*earnestly*). Oh please call me Ricky-ticky-tavy. "Mr. Robinson" would hurt me cruelly. (*She laughs and pats his cheek with her finger; then comes back to* RAMSDEN.)

ANN. You know I'm beginning to think that Granny is rather a piece of impertinence. But I never dreamt of its hurting you.

RAMSDEN (*breezily, as he pats her affectionately on the back*). My dear Annie, nonsense. I insist on Granny. I wont answer to any other name than Annie's Granny.

ANN (*gratefully*). You all spoil me, except Jack.

TANNER (*over his shoulder, from the bookcase*). I think you ought to call me Mr. Tanner.

ANN (*gently*). No you dont, Jack. Thats like the things you say on purpose to shock people: those who know you pay no attention to them. But, if you like, I'll call you after your famous ancestor Don Juan.

RAMSDEN. Don Juan!

ANN (*innocently*). Oh, is there any harm in it? I didnt know. Then I certainly wont call you that. May I call you Jack until I can think of something else?

TANNER. Oh, for Heaven's sake dont try to invent anything worse. I capitulate. I consent to Jack. I embrace Jack. Here endeth my first and last attempt to assert my authority.

ANN. You see, Mamma, they all really like to have pet names.

MRS. WHITEFIELD. Well, I think you might at least drop them until we are out of mourning.

ANN (*reproachfully, stricken to the soul*). Oh, how could you remind me, mother? (*She hastily leaves the room to conceal her emotion.*)

MRS. WHITEFIELD. Of course. My fault as usual! (*She follows* ANN.)

TANNER (*coming from the bookcase*). Ramsden: we're beaten — smashed — nonentitized, like her mother.

RAMSDEN. Stuff, sir. (*He follows* MRS. WHITEFIELD *out of the room.*)

TANNER (*left alone with* OCTAVIUS, *stares whimsically at him*). Tavy: do you want to count for something in the world?

OCTAVIUS. I want to count for something as a poet: I want to write a great play.

TANNER. With Ann as the heroine?

OCTAVIUS. Yes: I confess it.

TANNER. Take care, Tavy. The play with Ann as the heroine is all right; but if youre not very careful, by Heaven she'll marry you.

OCTAVIUS (*sighing*). No such luck, Jack!

TANNER. Why, man, your head is in the lioness's mouth: you are half swallowed already — in three bites — Bite One, Ricky; Bite Two, Ticky; Bite Three, Tavy; and down you go.

OCTAVIUS. She is the same to everybody, Jack: you know her ways.

TANNER. Yes: she breaks everybody's back with the stroke of her paw; but the question is, which of us will she eat? My own opinion is that she means to eat you.

OCTAVIUS (*rising, pettishly*). It's horrible to talk like that about her when she is upstairs crying for her father. But I do so want her to eat me that I can bear your brutalities because they give me hope.

TANNER. Tavy; thats the devilish side of a woman's fascination: she makes you will your own destruction.

OCTAVIUS. But it's not destruction: it's fulfilment.

TANNER. Yes, of her purpose; and that purpose is neither her happiness nor yours, but Nature's. Vitality in a woman is a blind fury of creation. She sacrifices herself to it: do you think she will hesitate to sacrifice you?

OCTAVIUS. Why, it is just because she is self-sacrificing that she will not sacrifice those she loves.

TANNER. That is the profoundest of mistakes, Tavy. It is the self-sacrificing women that sacrifice others most recklessly. Because they are unselfish, they are kind in little things. Because they have a purpose which is not their own purpose, but that of the whole universe, a man is nothing to them but an instrument of that purpose.

OCTAVIUS. Dont be ungenerous, Jack. They take the tenderest care of us.

TANNER. Yes, as a soldier takes care of his rifle or a musician of his violin. But do they allow us any purpose or freedom of our own? Will they lend us to one another? Can the strongest man escape from them when once he is appropriated? They tremble when we are in danger, and weep when we die; but the tears are not for us, but for a father wasted, a son's breeding thrown away. They accuse us of treating them as a mere means to our pleasure; but how can so feeble and transient a folly as a man's selfish pleasure enslave a woman as the whole purpose of Nature embodied in a woman can enslave a man?

OCTAVIUS. What matter, if the slavery makes us happy?

TANNER. No matter at all if you have no purpose of your own, and are, like most men, a mere breadwinner. But you, Tavy, are an artist: that is, you have a purpose as absorbing and as unscrupulous as a woman's purpose.

OCTAVIUS. Not unscrupulous.

TANNER. Quite unscrupulous. The true artist will let his wife starve, his children go barefoot, his mother drudge for his living at seventy, sooner than work at anything but his art. To women he is half vivisector, half vampire. He gets into intimate relations with them to study them, to strip the mask of convention from them, to surprise their inmost secrets, knowing that they have the power to rouse his deepest creative energies, to rescue him from his cold reason, to make him see visions and dream dreams, to inspire him, as he calls it. He persuades women that they may do this for their own purpose whilst he really means them to do it for his. He steals the mother's milk and blackens it to make printer's ink to scoff at her and glorify ideal women with. He pretends to spare her the pangs of child-bearing so that he may have for himself the tenderness and fostering that belong of right to her children. Since marriage began, the great artist has been known as a bad husband. But he is worse: he is a child-robber, a blood-sucker, a hypocrite and a cheat. Perish the race and wither a thousand women if only the sacrifice of them enable him to act Hamlet better, to paint a finer picture, to write a deeper poem, a greater play, a profounder philosophy! For mark you, Tavy, the artist's work is to shew us ourselves as we really are. Our minds are nothing but this knowledge of ourselves; and he who adds a jot to such knowledge creates new mind as surely as any woman creates new men. In the rage of that creation he is as ruthless as the woman, as dangerous to her as she to him, and as horribly fascinating. Of all human struggles there is none so treacherous and remorseless as the struggle between the artist man and the mother woman. Which shall use up the other? that is the issue between them. And it is all the deadlier because, in your romanticist cant, they love one another.

OCTAVIUS. Even if it were so — and I dont admit it for a moment — it is out of the deadliest struggles that we get the noblest characters.

TANNER. Remember that the next time you meet a grizzly bear or a Bengal tiger, Tavy.

OCTAVIUS. I meant where there is love, Jack.

TANNER. Oh, the tiger will love you. There is no love sincerer than the love of food. I think Ann loves you that way: she patted your cheek as if it were a nicely underdone chop.

OCTAVIUS. You know, Jack, I should have to run away from you if I did not make it a fixed rule not to mind anything you say. You come out with perfectly revolting things sometimes.

RAMSDEN *returns, followed by* ANN. *They come in quickly, with their former leisurely air of decorous grief changed to one of genuine concern, and, on* RAMSDEN'S *part, of worry. He comes between the two men, intending to address* OCTAVIUS, *but pulls himself up abruptly as he sees* TANNER.

RAMSDEN. I hardly expected to find you still here, Mr. Tanner.

TANNER. Am I in the way? Good morning, fellow guardian. (*He goes towards the door.*)

ANN. Stop, Jack. Granny: he must know, sooner or later.

RAMSDEN. Octavius: I have a very serious piece of news for you. It is of the most private and delicate nature — of the most painful nature too, I am sorry to say. Do you wish Mr. Tanner to be present whilst I explain?

OCTAVIUS (*turning pale*). I have no secrets from Jack.

RAMSDEN. Before you decide that finally, let me say that the news concerns your sister, and that it is terrible news.

OCTAVIUS. Violet! What has happened? Is she — dead?

RAMSDEN. I am not sure that it is not even worse than that.

OCTAVIUS. Is she badly hurt? Has there been an accident?

RAMSDEN. No: nothing of that sort.

TANNER. Ann: will you have the common humanity to tell us what the matter is?

ANN (*half whispering*). I cant. Violet has done something dreadful. We shall have to get her away somewhere. (*She flutters to the writing table and sits in* RAMSDEN's *chair, leaving the three men to fight it out between them.*)

OCTAVIUS (*enlightened*). Is that what you meant, Mr. Ramsden?

RAMSDEN. Yes. (OCTAVIUS *sinks upon a chair, crushed.*) I am afraid there is no doubt that Violet did not really go to Eastbourne three weeks ago when we thought she was with the Parry Whitefields. And she called on a strange doctor yesterday with a wedding ring on her finger. Mrs. Parry Whitefield met her there by chance; and so the whole thing came out.

OCTAVIUS (*rising with his fists clenched*). Who is the scoundrel?

ANN. She wont tell us.

OCTAVIUS (*collapsing into the chair again*). What a frightful thing!

TANNER (*with angry sarcasm*). Dreadful. Appalling. Worse than death, as Ramsden says. (*He comes to* OCTAVIUS.) What would you not give, Tavy, to turn it into a railway accident, with all her bones broken, or something equally respectable and deserving of sympathy?

OCTAVIUS. Dont be brutal, Jack.

TANNER. Brutal! Good Heavens, man, what are you crying for? Here is a woman whom we all supposed to be making bad water color sketches, practising Grieg and Brahms, gadding about to concerts and parties, wasting her life and her money. We suddenly learn that she has turned from these sillinesses to the fulfilment of her highest purpose and greatest function — to increase, multiply and replenish the earth. And instead of admiring her courage and rejoicing in her instinct; instead of crowning the completed womanhood and raising the triumphal strain of "Unto us a child is born: unto us a son is given," here you are — you who have been as merry as grigs in your mourning for the dead — all pulling long faces and looking as ashamed and disgraced as if the girl had committed the vilest of crimes.

RAMSDEN (*roaring with rage*). I will not have these abominations uttered in my house. (*He smites the writing table with his fist.*)

TANNER. Look here: if you insult me again I'll take you at your word and leave your house. Ann: where is Violet now?

ANN. Why? Are you going to her?

TANNER. Of course I am going to her. She wants help; she wants money; she wants respect and congratulation; she wants every chance for her child. She does not seem likely to get it from you: she shall from me. Where is she?

ANN. Dont be so headstrong, Jack. She's upstairs.

TANNER. What! Under Ramsden's sacred roof! Go and do your miserable duty, Ramsden. Hunt her out into the street. Cleanse your threshold from her contamination. Vindicate the purity of your English home. I'll go for a cab.

ANN (*alarmed*). Oh, Granny, you mustnt do that.

OCTAVIUS (*broken-heartedly, rising*). I'll take her away, Mr. Ramsden. She had no right to come to your house.

RAMSDEN (*indignantly*). But I am only too anxious to help her. (*Turning on* TANNER.) How dare you, sir, impute such monstrous intentions to me? I protest against it. I am ready to put down my last penny to save her from being driven to run to you for protection.

TANNER (*subsiding*). It's all right, then. He's not going to act up to his principles. It's agreed that we all stand by Violet.

OCTAVIUS. But who is the man? He can make reparation by marrying her; and he shall, or he shall answer for it to me.

RAMSDEN. He shall, Octavius. There you speak like a man.

TANNER. Then you dont think him a scoundrel, after all?

OCTAVIUS. Not a scoundrel! He is a heartless scoundrel.

RAMSDEN. A damned scoundrel. I beg your pardon, Annie; but I can say no less.

TANNER. So we are to marry your sister to a damned scoundrel by way of reforming her character! On my soul, I think you are all mad.

ANN. Dont be absurd, Jack. Of course you are quite right, Tavy; but we dont know who he is: Violet wont tell us.

TANNER. What on earth does it matter who he is? He's done his part; and Violet must do the rest.

RAMSDEN (*beside himself*). Stuff! lunacy! There is a rascal in our midst, a libertine, a villain worse than a murderer; and we are not to learn who he is! In our ignorance we are to shake him by the hand; to introduce him into our homes; to trust our daughters with him; to — to —

ANN (*coaxingly*). There, Granny, dont talk so loud. It's most shocking: we must all admit that; but if Violet wont tell us, what can we do? Nothing. Simply nothing.

RAMSDEN. Hmph! I'm not so sure of that. If any man has paid Violet any special attention, we can easily find that out. If there is any man of notoriously loose principles among us —

TANNER. Ahem!

RAMSDEN (*raising his voice*). Yes, sir, I repeat, if there is any man of notoriously loose principles among us —

TANNER. Or any man notoriously lacking in self-control.

RAMSDEN (*aghast*). Do you dare to suggest that *I* am capable of such an act?

TANNER. My dear Ramsden, this is an act of which every man is capable.

That is what comes of getting at cross purposes with Nature. The suspicion you have just flung at me clings to us all. It's a sort of mud that sticks to the judge's ermine or the cardinal's robe as fast as to the rags of the tramp. Come, Tavy: don't look so bewildered: it might have been me: it might have been Ramsden; just as it might have been anybody. If it had, what could we do but lie and protest — as Ramsden is going to protest.

RAMSDEN (*choking*). I — I — I —

TANNER. Guilt itself could not stammer more confusedly. And yet you know perfectly well he's innocent, Tavy.

RAMSDEN (*exhausted*). I am glad you admit that, sir. I admit, myself, that there is an element of truth in what you say, grossly as you may distort it to gratify your malicious humor. I hope, Octavius, no suspicion of me is possible in your mind.

OCTAVIUS. Of you! No, not for a moment.

TANNER (*drily*). I think he suspects me just a little.

OCTAVIUS. Jack: you couldnt — you wouldnt —

TANNER. Why not?

OCTAVIUS (*appalled*). Why not!

TANNER. Oh, well, I'll tell you why not. First, you would feel bound to quarrel with me. Second, Violet doesnt like me. Third, if I had the honor of being the father of Violet's child, I should boast of it instead of denying it. So be easy: our friendship is not in danger.

OCTAVIUS. I should have put away the suspicion with horror if only you would think and feel naturally about it. I beg your pardon.

TANNER. My pardon! nonsense! And now lets sit down and have a family council. (*He sits down. The rest follow his example, more or less under protest.*) Violet is going to do the State a service; consequently she must be packed abroad like a criminal until it's over. Whats happening upstairs?

ANN. Violet is in the housekeeper's room — by herself, of course.

TANNER. Why not in the drawingroom?

ANN. Dont be absurd, Jack. Miss Ramsden is in the drawingroom with my mother, considering what to do.

TANNER. Oh! the housekeeper's room is the penitentiary, I suppose; and the prisoner is waiting to be brought before her judges. The old cats!

ANN. Oh, Jack!

RAMSDEN. You are at present a guest beneath the roof of one of the old cats, sir. My sister is the mistress of this house.

TANNER. She would put me in the housekeeper's room, too, if she dared, Ramsden. However, I withdraw cats. Cats would have more sense. Ann: as your guardian, I order you to go to Violet at once and be particularly kind to her.

ANN. I have seen her, Jack. And I am sorry to say I am afraid she is going to be rather obstinate about going abroad. I think Tavy ought to speak to her about it.

OCTAVIUS. How can I speak to her about such a thing? (*He breaks down.*)

ANN. Dont break down, Ricky. Try to bear it for all our sakes.

RAMSDEN. Life is not all plays and poems, Octavius. Come! face it like a man.

TANNER (*chafing again*). Poor dear brother! Poor dear friends of the family! Poor dear Tabbies and Grimalkins! Poor dear everybody except the woman who is going to risk her life to create another life! Tavy: dont you be a selfish ass. Away with you and talk to Violet; and bring her down here if she cares to come. (*Octavius rises*). Tell her we'll stand by her.

RAMSDEN (*rising*). No, sir —

TANNER (*rising also and interrupting him*). Oh, we understand: it's against your conscience; but still youll do it.

OCTAVIUS. I assure you all, on my word, I never meant to be selfish. It's so hard to know what to do when one wishes earnestly to do right.

TANNER. My dear Tavy, your pious English habit of regarding the world as a moral gymnasium built expressly to strengthen your character in, occasionally leads you to think about your own confounded principles when you should be thinking about other people's necessities. The need of the present hour is a happy mother and a healthy baby. Bend your energies on that; and you will see your way clearly enough.

OCTAVIUS, *much perplexed, goes out.*

RAMSDEN (*facing* TANNER *impressively*). And Morality, sir? What is to become of that?

TANNER. Meaning a weeping Magdalen and an innocent child branded with her shame. Not in our circle, thank you. Morality can go to its father the devil.

RAMSDEN. I thought so, sir. Morality sent to the devil to please our libertines, male and female. That is to be the future of England, is it?

TANNER. Oh, England will survive your disapproval. Meanwhile, I understand that you agree with me as to the practical course we are to take?

RAMSDEN. Not in your spirit, sir. Not for your reasons.

TANNER. You can explain that if anybody calls you to account, here or hereafter. (*He turns away, and plants himself in front of Mr. Herbert Spencer, at whom he stares gloomily.*)

ANN (*rising and coming to* RAMSDEN). Granny: hadnt you better go up to the drawingroom and tell them what we intend to do?

RAMSDEN (*looking pointedly at* TANNER). I hardly like to leave you alone with this gentleman. Will you not come with me?

ANN. Miss Ramsden would not like to speak about it before me, Granny. I ought not to be present.

RAMSDEN. You are right: I should have thought of that. You are a good girl, Annie.

He pats her on the shoulder. She looks up at him with beaming eyes; and he goes out, much moved. Having disposed of him, she looks at

TANNER. *His back being turned to her, she gives a moment's attention to her personal appearance, then softly goes to him and speaks almost into his ear.*

ANN. Jack (*he turns with a start*): are you glad that you are my guardian? You dont mind being made responsible for me, I hope.

TANNER. The latest addition to your collection of scapegoats, eh?

ANN. Oh, that stupid old joke of yours about me! Do please drop it. Why do you say things that you know must pain me? I do my best to please you, Jack: I suppose I may tell you so now that you are my guardian. You will make me so unhappy if you refuse to be friends with me.

TANNER (*studying her as gloomily as he studied the bust*). You need not go begging for my regard. How unreal our moral judgments are! You seem to me to have absolutely no conscience — only hypocrisy; and you cant see the difference — yet there is a sort of fascination about you. I always attend to you, somehow. I should miss you if I lost you.

ANN (*tranquilly slipping her arm into his and walking about with him*). But isnt that only natural, Jack? We have known each other since we were children. Do you remember —

TANNER (*abruptly breaking loose*). Stop! I remember everything.

ANN. Oh, I daresay we were often very silly; but —

TANNER. I wont have it, Ann. I am no more that schoolboy now than I am the dotard of ninety I shall grow into if I live long enough. It is over: let me forget it.

ANN. Wasnt it a happy time? (*She attempts to take his arm again.*)

TANNER. Sit down and behave yourself. (*He makes her sit down in the chair next the writing table.*) No doubt it was a happy time for you. You were a good girl and never compromised yourself. And yet the wickedest child that ever was slapped could hardly have had a better time. I can understand the success with which you bullied the other girls: your virtue imposed on them. But tell me this: did you ever know a good boy?

ANN. Of course. All boys are foolish sometimes; but Tavy was always a good boy.

TANNER (*struck by this*). Yes: youre right. For some reason you never tempted Tavy.

ANN. Tempted! Jack!

TANNER. Yes, my dear Lady Mephistopheles, tempted. You were insatiably curious as to what a boy might be capable of, and diabolically clever at getting through his guard and surprising his inmost secrets.

ANN. What nonsense! All because you used to tell me long stories of the wicked things you had done — silly boy's tricks! And you call such things inmost secrets! Boys' secrets are just like men's; and you know what they are!

TANNER (*obstinately*). No I dont. What are they, pray?

ANN. Why, the things they tell everybody, of course.

TANNER. Now I swear I told you things I told no one else. You lured me into a compact by which we were to have no secrets from one another. We were to tell one another everything. I didnt notice that you never told me anything.

ANN. You didnt want to talk about me, Jack. You wanted to talk about yourself.

TANNER. Ah, true, horribly true. But what a devil of a child you must have been to know that weakness and to play on it for the satisfaction of your own curiosity! I wanted to brag to you, to make myself interesting. And I found myself doing all sorts of mischievous things simply to have something to tell you about. I fought with boys I didnt hate; I lied about things I might just as well have told the truth about; I stole things I didnt want; I kissed little girls I didnt care for. It was all bravado: passionless and therefore unreal.

ANN. I never told of you, Jack.

TANNER. No; but if you had wanted to stop me you would have told of me. You wanted me to go on.

ANN (*flashing out*). Oh, thats not true: it's not true, Jack. I never wanted you to do those dull, disappointing, brutal, stupid, vulgar things. I always hoped that it would be something really heroic at last. (*Recovering herself.*) Excuse me, Jack; but the things you did were never a bit like the things I wanted you to do. They often gave me great uneasiness; but I could not tell on you and get you into trouble. And you were only a boy. I knew you would grow out of them. Perhaps I was wrong.

TANNER (*sardonically*). Do not give way to remorse, Ann. At least nineteen twentieths of the exploits I confessed to you were pure lies. I soon noticed that you didnt like the true stories.

ANN. Of course I knew that some of the things couldnt have happened. But —

TANNER. You are going to remind me that some of the most disgraceful ones did.

ANN (*fondly, to his great terror*). I dont want to remind you of anything. But I knew the people they happened to, and heard about them.

TANNER. Yes; but even the true stories were touched up for telling. A sensitive boy's humiliations may be very good fun for ordinary thickskinned grown-ups; but to the boy himself they are so acute, so ignominious, that he cannot confess them — cannot but deny them passionately. However, perhaps it was as well for me that I romanced a bit; for, on the one occasion when I told you the truth, you threatened to tell of me.

ANN. Oh, never. Never once.

TANNER. Yes, you did. Do you remember a dark-eyed girl named Rachel Rosetree? (ANN's *brows contract for an instant involuntarily.*) I got up a love affair with her; and we met one night in the garden and walked about very uncomfortably with our arms round one another, and kissed at parting, and were most conscientiously romantic. If that love affair had gone on, it would have bored me to death; but it didnt go on; for the next thing that happened was that Rachel cut me because she found out that I had told you. How did she find it out? From you. You went to her and held the guilty secret over her head, leading her a life of abject terror and humiliation by threatening to tell on her.

ANN. And a very good thing for her, too. It was my duty to stop her misconduct; and she is thankful to me for it now.

TANNER. Is she?

ANN. She ought to be, at all events.

TANNER. It was not your duty to stop my misconduct, I suppose.

ANN. I did stop it by stopping her.

TANNER. Are you sure of that? You stopped my telling you about my adventures; but how do you know that you stopped the adventures?

ANN. Do you mean to say that you went on in the same way with other girls?

TANNER. No. I had enough of that sort of romantic tomfoolery with Rachel.

ANN (*unconvinced*). Then why did you break off our confidences and become quite strange to me?

TANNER (*enigmatically*). It happened just then that I got something that I wanted to keep all to myself instead of sharing it with you.

ANN. I am sure I shouldnt have asked for any of it if you had grudged it.

TANNER. It wasnt a box of sweets, Ann. It was something youd never have let me call my own.

ANN (*incredulously*). What?

TANNER. My soul.

ANN. Oh, do be sensible, Jack. You know youre talking nonsense.

TANNER. The most solemn earnest, Ann. You didnt notice at that time that you were getting a soul too. But you were. It was not for nothing that you suddenly found you had a moral duty to chastise and reform Rachel. Up to that time you had traded pretty extensively in being a good child; but you had never set up a sense of duty to others. Well, I set one up too. Up to that time I had played the boy buccaneer with no more conscience than a fox in a poultry farm. But now I began to have scruples, to feel obligations to find that veracity and honor were no longer goody-goody expressions in the mouths of grown-up people, but compelling principles in myself.

ANN (*quietly*). Yes, I suppose youre right. You were beginning to be a man, and I to be a woman.

TANNER. Are you sure it was not that we were beginning to be something more? What does the beginning of manhood and womanhood mean in most people's mouths? You know: it means the beginning of love. But love began long before that for me. Love played its part in the earliest dreams and follies and romances I can remember — may I say the earliest follies and romances we can remember? — though we did not understand it at the time. No: the change that came to me was the birth in me of moral passion; and I declare that according to my experience moral passion is the only real passion.

ANN. All passions ought to be moral, Jack.

TANNER. Ought! Do you think that anything is strong enough to impose oughts on a passion except a stronger passion still?

ANN. Our moral sense controls passion, Jack. Dont be stupid.

TANNER. Our moral sense! And is that not a passion? Is the devil to have all the passions as well as all the good tunes? If it were not a passion — if it were not the mightiest of the passions, all the other passions would sweep it away like a leaf before a hurricane. It is the birth of that passion that turns a child into a man.

ANN. There are other passions, Jack. Very strong ones.

TANNER. All the other passions were in me before; but they were idle and aimless — mere childish greedinesses and cruelties, curiosities and fancies, habits and superstitions, grotesque and ridiculous to the mature intelligence. When they suddenly began to shine like newly lit flames it was by no light of their own, but by the radiance of the dawning moral passion. That passion dignified them, gave them conscience and meaning, found them a mob of appetites and organized them into an army of purposes and principles. My soul was born of that passion.

ANN. I noticed that you got more sense. You were a dreadfully destructive boy before that.

TANNER. Destructive! Stuff! I was only mischievous.

ANN. Oh Jack, you were very destructive. You ruined all the young fir trees by chopping off their leaders with a wooden sword. You broke all the cucumber frames with your catapult. You set fire to the common: the police arrested Tavy for it because he ran away when he couldnt stop you. You —

TANNER. Pooh! pooh! pooh! these were battles, bombardments, stratagems to save our scalps from the red Indians. You have no imagination, Ann. I am ten times more destructive now than I was then. The moral passion has taken my destructiveness in hand and directed it to moral ends. I have become a reformer, and, like all reformers, an iconoclast. I no longer break cucumber frames and burn gorse bushes: I shatter creeds and demolish idols.

ANN (*bored*). I am afraid I am too feminine to see any sense in destruction. Destruction can only destroy.

TANNER. Yes. That is why it is so useful. Construction cumbers the ground with institutions made by busybodies. Destruction clears it and gives us breathing space and liberty.

ANN. It's no use, Jack. No woman will agree with you there.

TANNER. Thats because you confuse construction and destruction with creation and murder. Theyre quite different: I adore creation and abhor murder. Yes: I adore it in tree and flower, in bird and beast, even in you. (*A flush of interest and delight suddenly chases the growing perplexity and boredom from her face.*) It was the creative instinct that led you to attach me to you by bonds that have left their mark on me to this day. Yes, Ann: the old childish compact between us was an unconscious love compact —

ANN. Jack!

TANNER. Oh, dont be alarmed —

ANN. I am not alarmed.

TANNER (*whimsically*). Then you ought to be: where are your principles?

ANN. Jack: are you serious or are you not?

TANNER. Do you mean about the moral passion?

ANN. No, no; the other one. (*Confused.*) Oh! you are so silly: one never knows how to take you.

TANNER. You must take me quite seriously. I am your guardian; and it is my duty to improve your mind.

ANN. The love compact is over, then, is it? I suppose you grew tired of me?

TANNER. No; but the moral passion made our childish relations impossible. A jealous sense of my new individuality arose in me —

ANN. You hated to be treated as a boy any longer. Poor Jack!

TANNER. Yes, because to be treated as a boy was to be taken on the old footing. I had become a new person; and those who knew the old person laughed at me. The only man who behaved sensibly was my tailor: he took my measure anew every time he saw me, whilst all the rest went on with their old measurements and expected them to fit me.

ANN. You became frightfully self-conscious.

TANNER. When you go to heaven, Ann, you will be frightfully conscious of your wings for the first year or so. When you meet your relatives there, and they persist in treating you as if you were still a mortal, you will not be able to bear them. You will try to get into a circle which has never known you except as an angel.

ANN. So it was only your vanity that made you run away from us after all?

TANNER. Yes, only my vanity, as you call it.

ANN. You need not have kept away from me on that account.

TANNER. From you above all others. You fought harder than anybody against my emancipation.

ANN (*earnestly*). Oh, how wrong you are! I would have done anything for you.

TANNER. Anything except let me get loose from you. Even then you had acquired by instinct that damnable woman's trick of heaping obligations on a man, of placing yourself so entirely and helplessly at his mercy that at last he dare not take a step without running to you for leave. I know a poor wretch whose one desire in life is to run away from his wife. She prevents him by threatening to throw herself in front of the engine of the train he leaves her in. That is what all women do. If we try to go where you do not want us to go there is no law to prevent us; but when we take the first step your breasts are under our foot as it descends: your bodies are under our wheels as we start. No woman shall ever enslave me in that way.

ANN. But, Jack, you cannot get through life without considering other people a little.

TANNER. Ay; but what other people? It is this consideration of other people — or rather this cowardly fear of them which we call consideration — that makes us the sentimental slaves we are. To consider you, as you call it, is to substitute your will for my own. How if it be a baser will than mine? Are women taught better than men or worse? Are mobs of voters taught better than statesmen or worse? Worse, of course, in both cases. And then what sort of world are you going to get, with its public men considering its voting mobs, and its private men considering their wives? What does Church and State mean nowadays? The Woman and the Ratepayer.

ANN (*placidly*). I am so glad you understand politics, Jack: it will be most useful to you if you go into parliament. (*He collapses like a pricked bladder.*) But I am sorry you thought my influence a bad one.

TANNER. I dont say it was a bad one. But bad or good, I didnt choose to be cut to your measure. And I wont be cut to it.

ANN. Nobody wants you to, Jack. I assure you — really on my word — I dont mind your queer opinions one little bit. You know we have all been brought up to have advanced opinions. Why do you persist in thinking me so narrow minded?

TANNER. Thats the danger of it. I know you dont mind, because youve found out that it doesnt matter. The boa constrictor doesnt mind the opinions of a stag one little bit when once she has got her coils round it.

ANN (*rising in sudden enlightenment*). O-o-o-o-oh! now I understand why you warned Tavy that I am a boa constrictor. Granny told me. (*She laughs and throws her boa round his neck.*) Doesnt it feel nice and soft, Jack?

TANNER (*in the toils*). You scandalous woman, will you throw away even your hypocrisy?

ANN. I am never hypocritical with you, Jack. Are you angry? (*She withdraws the boa and throws it on a chair.*) Perhaps I shouldnt have done that.

TANNER (*contemptuously*). Pooh, prudery! Why should you not, if it amuses you?

ANN (*shyly*). Well, because — because I suppose what you really mean by the boa constrictor was this. (*She puts her arm round his neck.*)

TANNER (*staring at her*). Magnificent audacity! (*She laughs and pats his cheeks.*) Now just to think that if I mentioned this episode not a soul would believe me except the people who would cut me for telling, whilst if you accused me of it nobody would believe my denial!

ANN (*taking her arms away with perfect dignity*). You are incorrigible, Jack. But you should not jest about our affection for one another. Nobody could possibly misunderstand it. You do not misunderstand it, I hope.

TANNER. My blood interprets for me, Ann. Poor Ricky Ticky Tavy!

ANN (*looking quickly at him as if this were a new light*). Surely you are not so absurd as to be jealous of Tavy.

TANNER. Jealous! Why should I be? But I dont wonder at your grip of him. I feel the coils tightening round my very self, though you are only playing with me.

ANN. Do you think I have designs on Tavy?

TANNER. I know you have.

ANN (*earnestly*). Take care, Jack. You may make Tavy very unhappy if you mislead him about me.

TANNER. Never fear: he will not escape you.

ANN. I wonder are you really a clever man!

TANNER. Why this sudden misgiving on the subject?

ANN. You seem to understand all the things I dont understand; but you are a perfect baby in the things I do understand.

TANNER. I understand how Tavy feels for you, Ann; you may depend on that, at all events.

ANN. And you think you understand how I feel for Tavy, dont you?

TANNER. I know only too well what is going to happen to poor Tavy.

ANN. I should laugh at you, Jack, if it were not for poor papa's death. Mind! Tavy will be very unhappy.

TANNER. Yes; but he wont know it, poor devil. He is a thousand times too good for you. Thats why he is going to make the mistake of his life about you.

ANN. I think men make more mistakes by being too clever than by being too good. (*She sits down, with a trace of contempt for the whole male sex in the elegant carriage of her shoulders.*)

TANNER. Oh, I know you dont care very much about Tavy. But there is always one who kisses and one who only allows the kiss. Tavy will kiss; and you will only turn the cheek. And you will throw him over if anybody better turns up.

ANN (*offended*). You have no right to say such things, Jack. They are not true, and not delicate. If you and Tavy choose to be stupid about me, that is not my fault.

TANNER (*remorsefully*). Forgive my brutalities, Ann. They are levelled at this wicked world, not at you. (*She looks up at him, pleased and forgiving. He becomes cautious at once.*) All the same, I wish Ramsden would come back. I never feel safe with you: there is a devilish charm — or no: not a charm, a subtle interest. (*She laughs.*) — Just so: you know it; and you triumph in it. Openly and shamelessly triumph in it!

ANN. What a shocking flirt you are, Jack!

TANNER. A flirt! ! I ! ! !

ANN. Yes, a flirt. You are always abusing and offending people; but you never really mean to let go your hold of them.

TANNER. I will ring the bell. This conversation has already gone further than I intended.

> RAMSDEN *and* OCTAVIUS *come back with* MISS RAMSDEN, *a hardheaded old maiden lady in a plain brown silk gown, with enough rings, chains and brooches to shew that her plainness of dress is a matter of principle, not of poverty. She comes into the room very determinedly: the two men,*

perplexed and downcast, following her. ANN *rises and goes eagerly to meet her.* TANNER *retreats to the wall between the busts and pretends to study the pictures.* RAMSDEN *goes to his table as usual; and* OCTAVIUS *clings to the neighborhood of* TANNER.

MISS RAMSDEN (*almost pushing* ANN *aside as she comes to* MRS. WHITEFIELD's *chair and plants herself there resolutely*). I wash my hands of the whole affair.

OCTAVIUS (*very wretched*). I know you wish me to take Violet away, Miss Ramsden. I will. (*He turns irresolutely to the door.*)

RAMSDEN. No, no —

MISS RAMSDEN. What is the use of saying no, Roebuck? Octavius knows that I would not turn any truly contrite and repentant woman from your doors. But when a woman is not only wicked, but intends to go on being wicked, she and I part company.

ANN. Oh, Miss Ramsden, what do you mean? What has Violet said?

RAMSDEN. Violet is certainly very obstinate. She wont leave London. I dont understand her.

MISS RAMSDEN. I do. It's as plain as the nose on your face, Roebuck, that she wont go because she doesnt want to be separated from this man, whoever he is.

ANN. Oh, surely, surely! Octavius: did you speak to her?

OCTAVIUS. She wont tell us anything. She wont make any arrangement until she has consulted somebody. It cant be anybody else than the scoundrel who has betrayed her.

TANNER (*to* OCTAVIUS). Well, let her consult him. He will be glad enough to have her sent abroad. Where is the difficulty?

MISS RAMSDEN (*taking the answer out of* OCTAVIUS's *mouth*). The difficulty, Mr. Jack, is that when I offered to help her I didnt offer to become her accomplice in her wickedness. She either pledges her word never to see that man again, or else she finds some new friends; and the sooner the better.

The PARLORMAID *appears at the door.* ANN *hastily resumes her seat, and looks as unconcerned as possible.* OCTAVIUS *instinctively imitates her.*

THE MAID. The cab is at the door, ma'am.

MISS RAMSDEN. What cab?

THE MAID. For Miss Robinson.

MISS RAMSDEN. Oh! (*Recovering herself.*) All right. (*The* MAID *withdraws.*) She has sent for a cab.

TANNER. I wanted to send for that cab half an hour ago.

MISS RAMSDEN. I am glad she understands the position she has placed herself in.

RAMSDEN. I dont like her going away in this fashion, Susan. We had better not do anything harsh.

OCTAVIUS. No: thank you again and again; but Miss Ramsden is quite right. Violet cannot expect to stay.

ANN. Hadnt you better go with her, Tavy?

OCTAVIUS. She wont have me.

MISS RAMSDEN. Of course she wont. She's going straight to that man.

TANNER. As a natural result of her virtuous reception here.

RAMSDEN (*much troubled*). There, Susan! You hear! and theres some truth in it. I wish you could reconcile it with your principles to be a little patient with this poor girl. She's very young; and theres a time for everything.

MISS RAMSDEN. Oh, she will get all the sympathy she wants from the men. I'm surprised at you, Roebuck.

TANNER. So am I, Ramsden, most favorably.

VIOLET *appears at the door. She is as impenitent and self-possessed a young lady as one would desire to see among the best behaved of her sex. Her small head and tiny resolute mouth and chin; her haughty crispness of speech and trimness of carriage; the ruthless elegance of her equipment, which includes a very smart hat with a dead bird in it, mark a personality which is as formidable as it is exquisitely pretty. She is not a siren, like* ANN: *admiration comes to her without any compulsion or even interest on her part; besides, there is some fun in* ANN, *but in this woman none, perhaps no mercy either: if anything restrains her, it is intelligence and pride, not compassion. Her voice might be the voice of a schoolmistress addressing a class of girls who had disgraced themselves, as she proceeds with complete composure and some disgust to say what she has come to say.*

VIOLET. I have only looked in to tell Miss Ramsden that she will find her birthday present to me, the filigree bracelet, in the housekeeper's room.

TANNER. Do come in, Violet, and talk to us sensibly.

VIOLET. Thank you: I have had quite enough of the family conversation this morning. So has your mother, Ann: she has gone home crying. But at all events, I have found out what some of my pretended friends are worth. Good bye.

TANNER. No, no: one moment. I have something to say which I beg you to hear. (*She looks at him without the slightest curiosity, but waits, apparently as much to finish getting her glove on as to hear what he has to say.*) I am altogether on your side in this matter. I congratulate you, with the sincerest respect, on having the courage to do what you have done. You are entirely in the right; and the family is entirely in the wrong.

Sensation. ANN *and* MISS RAMSDEN *rise and turn towards the two.* VIOLET, *more surprised than any of the others, forgets her glove, and comes forward into the middle of the room, both puzzled and displeased.* OCTAVIUS *alone does not move ar raise his head: he is overwhelmed with shame.*

ANN (*pleading to* TANNER *to be sensible*). Jack!

MISS RAMSDEN (*outraged*). Well, I must say!

VIOLET (*sharply to* TANNER). Who told you?

TANNER. Why, Ramsden and Tavy of course. Why should they not?

VIOLET. But they dont know.

TANNER. Dont know what?

VIOLET. They dont know that I am in the right, I mean.

TANNER. Oh, they know it in their hearts, though they think themselves bound to blame you by their silly superstitions about morality and propriety and so forth. But I know, and the whole world really knows, though it dare not say so, that you were right to follow your instinct; that vitality and bravery are the greatest qualities a woman can have, and motherhood her solemn initiation into womanhood; and that the fact of your not being legally married matters not one scrap either to your own worth or to our real regard for you.

VIOLET (*flushing with indignation*). Oh! You think me a wicked woman, like the rest. You think I have not only been vile, but that I share your abominable opinions. Miss Ramsden: I have borne your hard words because I knew you would be sorry for them when you found out the truth. But I wont bear such a horrible insult as to be complimented by Jack on being one of the wretches of whom he approves. I have kept my marriage a secret for my husband's sake. But now I claim my right as a married woman not to be insulted.

OCTAVIUS (*raising his head with inexpressible relief*). You are married!

VIOLET. Yes; and I think you might have guessed it. What business had you all to take it for granted that I had no right to wear my wedding ring? Not one of you even asked me: I cannot forget that.

TANNER (*in ruins*). I am utterly crushed. I meant well. I apologize — abjectly apologize.

VIOLET. I hope you will be more careful in future about the things you say. Of course one does not take them seriously; but they are very disagreeable, and rather in bad taste, I think.

TANNER (*bowing to the storm*). I have no defence: I shall know better in future than to take any woman's part. We have all disgraced ourselves in your eyes, I am afraid, except Ann. She befriended you. For Ann's sake, forgive us.

VIOLET. Yes: Ann has been very kind; but then Ann knew.

TANNER (*with a desperate gesture*). Oh!!! Unfathomable deceit! Double crossed!

MISS RAMSDEN (*stiffly*). And who, pray, is the gentleman who does not acknowledge his wife?

VIOLET (*promptly*). That is my business, Miss Ramsden, and not yours. I have my reasons for keeping my marriage a secret for the present.

RAMSDEN. All I can say is that we are extremely sorry, Violet. I am shocked to think of how we have treated you.

OCTAVIUS (*awkwardly*). I beg your pardon, Violet. I can say no more.

MISS RAMSDEN (*still loth to surrender*). Of course what you say puts a very different complexion on the matter. All the same, I owe it to myself —

VIOLET (*cutting her short*). You owe me an apology, Miss Ramsden: thats what you owe both to yourself and to me. If you were a married woman you would not like sitting in the housekeeper's room and being treated like a naughty child by young girls and old ladies without any serious duties and responsibilities.

TANNER. Dont hit us when we're down, Violet. We seem to have made fools of ourselves; but really it was you who made fools of us.

VIOLET. It was no business of yours, Jack, in any case.

TANNER. No business of mine! Why, Ramsden as good as accused me of being the unknown gentleman.

RAMSDEN *makes a frantic demonstration; but* VIOLET's *cool keen anger extinguishes it.*

VIOLET. You! Oh, how infamous! how abominable! how disgracefully you have all been talking about me! If my husband knew it he would never let me speak to any of you again. (*To* RAMSDEN.) I think you might have spared me that, at least.

RAMSDEN. But I assure you I never — at least it is a monstrous perversion of something I said that —

MISS RAMSDEN. You neednt apologize, Roebuck. She brought it all on herself. It is for her to apologize for having deceived us.

VIOLET. I can make allowances for you, Miss Ramsden: you cannot understand how I feel on this subject, though I should have expected rather better taste from people of greater experience. However, I quite feel that you have placed yourselves in a very painful position; and the most truly considerate thing for me to do is to go at once. Good morning.

She goes, leaving them staring.

MISS RAMSDEN. Well, I must say!

RAMSDEN (*plaintively*). I dont think she is quite fair to us.

TANNER. You must cower before the wedding ring like the rest of us, Ramsden. The cup of our ignominy is full.

ACT TWO

On the carriage drive in the park of a country house near Richmond a motor car has broken down. It stands in front of a clump of trees round which the drive sweeps to the house, which is partly visible through them: indeed TANNER, *standing in the drive with the car on his right hand, could get an unobstructed view of the west corner of the house on his left were he not far too much interested in a pair of supine legs in dungaree overalls which protrude from beneath the machine. He is watching them intently with bent back and hands supported on his* knees. His leathern overcoat and peaked cap proclaim him one of the dismounted passengers.

THE LEGS. Aha! I got him.

TANNER. All right now?

THE LEGS. Aw rawt nah.

TANNER *stoops and takes the legs by the ankles, drawing their owner forth like a wheelbarrow, walking on his hands, with a hammer in his mouth. He is a young man in a neat suit of blue serge, clean shaven, dark eyed, square fingered, with short well brushed black hair and rather irregular sceptically turned eyebrows. When he is manipulating the car his movements are swift and sudden, yet attentive and deliberate. With* TANNER *and* TANNER'S *friends his manner is not in the least deferential, but cool and reticent, keeping them quite effectually at a distance whilst giving them no excuse for complaining of him. Nevertheless he has a vigilant eye on them always, and that, too, rather cynically, like a man who knows the world well from its seamy side. He speaks slowly and with a touch of sarcasm; and as he does not at all affect the gentleman in his speech, it may be inferred that his smart appearance is a mark of respect to himself and his own class, not to that which employs him.*

He now gets into the car to stow away his tools and divest himself of his overalls. TANNER *takes off his leathern overcoat and pitches it into the car with a sigh of relief, glad to be rid of it. The* CHAUFFEUR, *noting this, tosses his head contemptuously, and surveys his employer sardonically.*

THE CHAUFFEUR. Had enough of it, eh?

TANNER. I may as well walk to the house and stretch my legs and calm my nerves a little. (*Looking at his watch.*) I suppose you know that we have come from Hyde Park Corner to Richmond in twenty-one minutes.

THE CHAUFFEUR. I'd ha done it under fifteen if I'd had a clear road all the way.

TANNER. Why do you do it? Is it for love of sport or for the fun of terrifying your unfortunate employer?

THE CHAUFFEUR. What are you afraid of?

TANNER. The police, and breaking my neck.

THE CHAUFFEUR. Well, if you like easy going, you can take a bus, you know. It's cheaper. You pay me to save your time and give you the value of what you paid for the car. (*He sits down calmly.*)

TANNER. I am the slave of that car and of you too. I dream of the accursed thing at night.

THE CHAUFFEUR. Youll get over that all right. If youre going up to the house, may I ask how long youre goin to stay? Because if you mean to put in the whole morning in there, talkin to the ladies, I'll put the car in the garage and make myself agreeable with a view to lunching here. If not, I'll keep the car on the go about here til you come.

TANNER. Better wait here. We shant be long. Theres a young American gentleman, a Mr. Malone, who is driving Mr. Robinson down in his new American steam car.

THE CHAUFFEUR (*springing up and coming hastily out of the car to* TANNER). American steam car! Wot! racin us dahn from London!

TANNER. Perhaps theyre here already.

THE CHAUFFEUR. If I'd known it! (*With deep reproach.*) Why didnt you tell me, Mr. Tanner?

TANNER. Because Ive been told that this car is capable of 84 miles an hour; and I already know what you are capable of when there is a rival car on the road. No, Henry: there are things it is not good for you to know; and this was one of them. However, cheer up: we are going to have a day after your own heart. The American is to take Mr. Robinson and his sister and Miss Whitefield. We are to take Miss Rhoda.

THE CHAUFFEUR (*consoled, and musing on another matter*). Thats Miss Whitefield's sister, isnt it?

TANNER. Yes.

THE CHAUFFEUR. And Miss Whitefield herself is goin in the other car? Not with you?

TANNER. Why the devil should she come with me? Mr. Robinson will be in the other car. (*The* CHAUFFEUR *looks at* TANNER *with cool incredulity, and turns to the car, whistling a popular air softly to himself.* TANNER, *a little annoyed, is about to pursue the subject when he hears the footsteps of* OCTAVIUS *on the gravel.* OCTAVIUS *is coming from the house, dressed for motoring, but without his overcoat.*) Weve lost the race, thank Heaven: heres Mr. Robinson. Well, Tavy, is the steam car a success?

OCTAVIUS. I think so. We came from Hyde Park Corner here in seventeen minutes. (*The* CHAUFFEUR, *furious, kicks the car with a groan of vexation.*) How long were you?

TANNER. Oh, about three quarters of an hour or so.

THE CHAUFFEUR (*remonstrating*). Now, now, Mr. Tanner, come now! We could ha done it easy under fifteen.

TANNER. By the way, let me introduce you. Mr. Octavius Robinson: Mr. Enry Straker.

STRAKER. Pleased to meet you, sir. Mr. Tanner is gittin at you with is Enry Straker, you know. You call it Henery. But I dont mind, bless you.

TANNER. You think it's simply bad taste in me to chaff him, Tavy. But you're wrong. This man takes more trouble to drop his aitches than ever his father did to pick them up. It's a mark of caste to him. I have never met anybody more swollen with the pride of class than Enry is.

STRAKER. Easy, easy! A little moderation, Mr. Tanner.

TANNER. A little moderation, Tavy, you observe. You would tell me to draw it mild. But this chap has been educated. Whats more, he knows that we havnt. What was that Board School of yours, Straker?

STRAKER. Sherbrooke Road.

Man and Superman 265

TANNER. Sherbrooke Road! Would any of us say Rugby! Harrow! Eton! in that tone of intellectual snobbery? Sherbrooke Road is a place where boys learn something: Eton is a boy farm where we are sent because we are nuisances at home, and because in after life, whenever a Duke is mentioned, we can claim him as an old schoolfellow.

STRAKER. You dont know nothing about it, Mr. Tanner. It's not the Board School that does it: it's the Polytechnic.

TANNER. His university, Octavius. Not Oxford, Cambridge, Durham, Dublin or Glasgow. Not even those Nonconformist holes in Wales. No, Tavy. Regent Street, Chelsea, the Borough — I don't know half their confounded names: these are his universities, not mere shops for selling class limitations like ours. You despise Oxford, Enry, dont you?

STRAKER. No, I dont. Very nice sort of place, Oxford, I should think, for people that like that sort of place. They teach you to be a gentleman there. In the Polytechnic they teach you to be an engineer or such like. See?

TANNER. Sarcasm, Tavy, sarcasm! Oh, if you could only see into Enry's soul, the depth of his contempt for a gentleman, the arrogance of his pride in being an engineer, would appal you. He positively likes the car to break down because it brings out my gentlemanly helplessness and his workmanlike skill and resource.

STRAKER. Never you mind him, Mr. Robinson. He likes to talk. We know him, dont we?

OCTAVIUS (*earnestly*). But theres a great truth at the bottom of what he says. I believe most intensely in the dignity of labor.

STRAKER (*unimpressed*). That's because you never done any, Mr. Robinson. My business is to do away with labor. Youll get more out of me and a machine than you will out of twenty laborers, and not so much to drink either.

TANNER. For Heaven's sake, Tavy, dont start him on political economy. He knows all about it; and we dont. Youre only a poetic Socialist, Tavy: he's a scientific one.

STRAKER (*unperturbed*). Yes. Well, this conversation is very improvin; but Ive got to look after the car; and you two want to talk about your ladies. I know. (*He pretends to busy himself about the car, but presently saunters off to indulge in a cigaret.*)

TANNER. Thats a very momentous social phenomenon.

OCTAVIUS. What is?

TANNER. Straker is. Here have we literary and cultured persons been for years setting up a cry of the New Woman whenever some unusually old fashioned female came along; and never noticing the advent of the New Man. Straker's the New Man.

OCTAVIUS. I see nothing new about him, except your way of chaffing him. But I dont want to talk about him just now. I want to speak to you about Ann.

TANNER. Straker knew even that. He learnt it at the Polytechnic, probably. Well, what about Ann? Have you proposed to her?

OCTAVIUS (*self-reproachfully*). I was brute enough to do so last night.

TANNER. Brute enough! What do you mean?

OCTAVIUS (*dithyrambically*). Jack: we men are all coarse: we never understand how exquisite a woman's sensibilities are. How could I have done such a thing!

TANNER. Done what, you maudlin idiot?

OCTAVIUS. Yes, I am an idiot. Jack: if you had heard her voice! if you had seen her tears! I have lain awake all night thinking of them. If she had reproached me, I could have borne it better.

TANNER. Tears! thats dangerous. What did she say?

OCTAVIUS. She asked me how she could think of anything now but her dear father. She stifled a sob — (*He breaks down.*)

TANNER (*patting him on the back*). Bear it like a man, Tavy, even if you feel it like an ass. It's the old game: she's not tired of playing with you yet.

OCTAVIUS (*impatiently*). Oh, dont be a fool, Jack. Do you suppose this eternal shallow cynicism of yours has any real bearing on a nature like hers?

TANNER. Hm! Did she say anything else?

OCTAVIUS. Yes; and that is why I expose myself and her to your ridicule by telling you what passed.

TANNER (*remorsefully*). No, dear Tavy, not ridicule, on my honor! However, no matter. Go on.

OCTAVIUS. Her sense of duty is so devout, so perfect, so —

TANNER. Yes: I know. Go on.

OCTAVIUS. You see, under this new arrangement, you and Ramsden are her guardians; and she considers that all her duty to her father is now transferred to you. She said she thought I ought to have spoken to you both in the first instance. Of course she is right; but somehow it seems rather absurd that I am to come to you and formally ask to be received as a suitor for your ward's hand.

TANNER. I am glad that love has not totally extinguished your sense of humor, Tavy.

OCTAVIUS. That answer wont satisfy her.

TANNER. My official answer is, obviously, Bless you, my children: may you be happy!

OCTAVIUS. I wish you would stop playing the fool about this. If it is not serious to you, it is to me, and to her.

TANNER. You know very well that she is as free to choose as you are.

OCTAVIUS. She does not think so.

TANNER. Oh, doesnt she! just! However, say what you want me to do?

OCTAVIUS. I want you to tell her sincerely and earnestly what you think about me. I want you to tell her that you can trust her to me — that is, if you feel you can.

TANNER. I have no doubt that I can trust her to you. What worries me is the idea of trusting you to her. Have you read Maeterlinck's book about the bee?

OCTAVIUS (*keeping his temper with difficulty*). I am not discussing literature at present.

TANNER. Be just a little patient with me. I am not discussing literature: the book about the bee is natural history. It's an awful lesson to mankind. You think that you are Ann's suitor; that you are the pursuer and she the pursued; that it is your part to woo, to persuade, to prevail, to overcome. Fool: it is you who are the pursued, the marked down quarry, the destined prey. You need not sit looking longingly at the bait through the wires of the trap: the door is open, and will remain so until it shuts behind you for ever.

OCTAVIUS. I wish I could believe that, vilely as you put it.

TANNER. Why, man, what other work has she in life but to get a husband? It is a woman's business to get married as soon as possible, and a man's to keep unmarried as long as he can. You have your poems and your tragedies to work at: Ann has nothing.

OCTAVIUS. I cannot write without inspiration. And nobody can give me that except Ann.

TANNER. Well, hadnt you better get it from her at a safe distance? Petrarch didn't see half as much of Laura, nor Dante of Beatrice, as you see of Ann now; and yet they wrote first-rate poetry — at least so I'm told. They never exposed their idolatry to the test of domestic familiarity; and it lasted them to their graves. Marry Ann; and at the end of a week youll find no more inspiration in her than in a plate of muffins.

OCTAVIUS. You think I shall tire of her!

TANNER. Not at all: you dont get tired of muffins. But you dont find inspiration in them; and you wont in her when she ceases to be a poet's dream and becomes a solid eleven stone wife. Youll be forced to dream about somebody else; and then there will be a row.

OCTAVIUS. This sort of talk is no use, Jack. You dont understand. You have never been in love.

TANNER. I! I have never been out of it. Why, I am in love even with Ann. But I am neither the slave of love nor its dupe. Go to the bee, thou poet: consider her ways and be wise. By Heaven, Tavy, if women could do without our work, and we ate their children's bread instead of making it, they would kill us as the spider kills her mate or as the bees kill the drone. And they would be right if we were good for nothing but love.

OCTAVIUS. Ah, if we were only good enough for Love! There is nothing like Love: there is nothing else but Love: without it the world would be a dream of sordid horror.

TANNER. And this — this is the man who asks me to give him the hand of my ward! Tavy: I believe we were changed in our cradles, and that you are the real descendant of Don Juan.

OCTAVIUS. I beg you not to say anything like that to Ann.

TANNER. Dont be afraid. She has marked you for her own; and nothing will stop her now. You are doomed. (STRAKER *comes back with a newspaper.*) Here comes the New Man, demoralizing himself with a halfpenny paper as usual.

STRAKER. Now would you believe it, Mr. Robinson, when we're out motoring we take in two papers, the Times for him, the Leader or the Echo for me. And do you think I ever see my paper? Not much. He grabs the Leader and leaves me to stodge myself with his Times.

OCTAVIUS. Are there no winners in the Times?

TANNER. Enry dont old with bettin, Tavy. Motor records are his weakness. Whats the latest?

STRAKER. Paris to Biskra at forty mile an hour average, not countin the Mediterranean.

TANNER. How many killed?

STRAKER. Two silly sheep. What does it matter? Sheep dont cost such a lot; they were glad to ave the price without the trouble o sellin em to the butcher. All the same, d'y'see, therell be a clamor agin it presently; and then the French Government'll stop it; an our chance'll be gone, see? Thats what makes me fairly mad: Mr. Tanner wont do a good run while he can.

TANNER. Tavy: do you remember my uncle James?

OCTAVIUS. Yes. Why?

TANNER. Uncle James had a first rate cook: he couldnt digest anything except what she cooked. Well, the poor man was shy and hated society. But his cook was proud of her skill, and wanted to serve up dinners to princes and ambassadors. To prevent her from leaving him, that poor old man had to give a big dinner twice a month, and suffer agonies of awkwardness. Now here am I; and here is this chap Enry Straker, the New Man. I loathe travelling; but I rather like Enry. He cares for nothing but tearing along in a leather coat and goggles, with two inches of dust all over him, at sixty miles an hour and the risk of his life and mine. Except, of course, when he is lying on his back in the mud under the machine trying to find out where it has given way. Well, if I dont give him a thousand mile run at least once a fortnight I shall lose him. He will give me the sack and go to some American millionaire; and I shall have to put up with a nice respectful groom-gardener-amateur, who will touch his hat and know his place. I am Enry's slave, just as Uncle James was his cook's slave.

STRAKER (*exasperated*). Garn! I wish I had a car that would go as fast as you can talk, Mr. Tanner. What I say is that you lose money by a motor car unless you keep it workin. Might as well ave a pram and a nussmaid to wheel you in it as that car and me if you dont git the last inch out of us both.

TANNER (*soothingly*). All right, Henry, all right. We'll go out for half an hour presently.

STRAKER (*in disgust*). Arf an ahr! (*He returns to his machine; seats himself in it; and turns up a fresh page of his paper in search of more news.*)

OCTAVIUS. Oh, that reminds me. I have a note for you from Rhoda. (*He gives* TANNER *a note.*)

TANNER (*opening it*). I rather think Rhoda is heading for a row with Ann. As a rule there is only one person an English girl hates more than she hates her eldest sister; and thats her mother. But Rhoda positively prefers her mother to Ann. She — (*indignantly.*) Oh, I say!

OCTAVIUS. Whats the matter?

TANNER. Rhoda was to have come with me for a ride in the motor car. She says Ann has forbidden her to go out with me.

> STRAKER *suddenly begins whistling his favorite air with remarkable deliberation. Surprised by this burst of larklike melody, and jarred by a sardonic note in its cheerfulness, they turn and look inquiringly at him. But he is busy with his paper; and nothing comes of their movement.*

OCTAVIUS (*recovering himself*). Does she give any reason?

TANNER. Reason! An insult is not a reason. Ann forbids her to be alone with me on any occasion. Says I am not a fit person for a young girl to be with. What do you think of your paragon now?

OCTAVIUS. You must remember that she has a very heavy responsibility now that her father is dead. Mrs. Whitefield is too weak to control Rhoda.

TANNER (*staring at him*). In short, you agree with Ann.

OCTAVIUS. No; but I think I understand her. You must admit that your views are hardly suited for the formation of a young girl's mind and character.

TANNER. I admit nothing of the sort. I admit that the formation of a young lady's mind and character usually consists in telling her lies; but I object to the particular lie that I am in the habit of abusing the confidence of girls.

OCTAVIUS. Ann doesnt say that, Jack.

TANNER. What else does she mean?

STRAKER (*catching sight of* ANN *coming from the house*). Miss Whitefield, gentlemen. (*He dismounts and strolls away down the avenue with the air of a man who knows he is no longer wanted.*)

ANN (*coming between* OCTAVIUS *and* TANNER). Good morning, Jack. I have come to tell you that poor Rhoda has got one of her headaches and cannot go out with you to-day in the car. It is a cruel disappointment to her, poor child!

TANNER. What do you say now, Tavy.

OCTAVIUS. Surely you cannot misunderstand, Jack. Ann is shewing you the kindest consideration, even at the cost of deceiving you.

ANN. What do you mean?

TANNER. Would you like to cure Rhoda's headache, Ann?

ANN. Of course.

TANNER. Then tell her what you said just now; and add that you arrived about two minutes after I had received her letter and read it.

ANN. Rhoda has written to you!

TANNER. With full particulars.

OCTAVIUS. Never mind him, Ann. You were right — quite right. Ann was only doing her duty, Jack; and you know it. Doing it in the kindest way, too.

ANN (*going to* OCTAVIUS). How kind you are, Tavy! How helpful! How well you understand!

OCTAVIUS *beams.*

TANNER. Ay: tighten the coils. You love her, Tavy, dont you?

OCTAVIUS. She knows I do.

ANN. Hush. For shame, Tavy!

TANNER. Oh, I give you leave. I am your guardian; and I commit you to Tavy's care for the next hour. I am off for a turn in the car.

ANN. No, Jack. I must speak to you about Rhoda. Ricky: will you go back to the house and entertain your American friend. He's rather on Mamma's hands so early in the morning. She wants to finish her housekeeping.

OCTAVIUS. I fly, dearest Ann. (*He kisses her hand.*)

ANN (*tenderly*). Ricky Ticky Tavy!

He looks at her with an eloquent blush, and runs off.

TANNER (*bluntly*). Now look here, Ann. This time youve landed yourself; and if Tavy were not in love with you past all salvation he'd have found out what an incorrigible liar you are.

ANN. You misunderstand, Jack. I didnt dare tell Tavy the truth.

TANNER. No: your daring is generally in the opposite direction. What the devil do you mean by telling Rhoda that I am too vicious to associate with her? How can I ever have any human or decent relations with her again, now that you have poisoned her mind in that abominable way?

ANN. I know you are incapable of behaving badly —

TANNER. Then why did you lie to her?

ANN. I had to.

TANNER. Had to!

ANN. Mother made me.

TANNER (*his eye flashing*). Ha! I might have known it. The mother! Always the mother!

ANN. It was that dreadful book of yours. You know how timid mother is. All timid women are conventional: we must be conventional, Jack, or we are so cruelly, so vilely misunderstood. Even you, who are a man, cannot say what you think without being misunderstood and vilified — yes: I admit it: I have had to vilify you. Do you want to have poor Rhoda misunderstood and vilified in the same way? Would it be right for mother to let her expose herself to such treatment before she is old enough to judge for herself?

TANNER. In short, the way to avoid misunderstanding is for everybody to lie and slander and insinuate and pretend as hard as they can. That is what obeying your mother comes to.

ANN. I love my mother, Jack.

TANNER (*working himself up into a sociological rage*). Is that any reason why you are not to call your soul your own? Oh, I protest against this vile abjection of youth to age! Look at fashionable society as you know it. What does it pretend to be? An exquisite dance of nymphs. What is it? A horrible procession of wretched girls, each in the claws of a cynical, cunning, avaricious, disillusioned, ignorantly experienced, foul-minded old woman whom she calls mother, and whose duty it is to corrupt her mind and sell her to the highest bidder. Why do these unhappy slaves marry anybody, however old and vile, sooner than not marry at all? Because marriage is their only means of escape from these decrepit fiends who hide their selfish ambitions, their jealous hatreds of the young rivals who have supplanted them, under the mask of maternal duty and family affection. Such things are abominable: the voice of nature proclaims for the daughter a father's care and for the son a mother's. The law for father and son and mother and daughter is not the law of love: it is the law of revolution, of emancipation, of final supersession of the old and worn-out by the young and capable. I tell you, the first duty of manhood and womanhood is a Declaration of Independence: the man who pleads his father's authority is no man: the woman who pleads her mother's authority is unfit to bear citizens to a free people.

ANN (*watching him with quiet curiosity*). I suppose you will go in seriously for politics some day, Jack.

TANNER (*heavily let down*). Eh? What? Wh —? (*Collecting his scattered wits.*) What has that got to do with what I have been saying?

ANN. You talk so well.

TANNER. Talk! Talk! It means nothing to you but talk. Well, go back to your mother, and help her to poison Rhoda's imagination as she has poisoned yours. It is the tame elephants who enjoy capturing the wild ones.

ANN. I am getting on. Yesterday I was a boa constrictor: to-day I am an elephant.

TANNER. Yes. So pack your trunk and begone: I have no more to say to you.

ANN. You are so utterly unreasonable and impracticable. What can I do?

TANNER. Do! Break your chains. Go your way according to your own conscience and not according to your mother's. Get your mind clean and vigorous; and learn to enjoy a fast ride in a motor car instead of seeing nothing in it but an excuse for a detestable intrigue. Come with me to Marseilles and across to Algiers and to Biskra, at sixty miles an hour. Come right down to the Cape if you like. That will be a Declaration of Independence with a vengeance. You can write a book about it afterwards. That will finish your mother and make a woman of you.

ANN (*thoughtfully*). I dont think there would be any harm in that, Jack. You are my guardian: you stand in my father's place, by his own wish. Nobody could say a word against our travelling together. It would be delightful: thank you a thousand times, Jack. I'll come.

TANNER (*aghast*). Youll come!!!

ANN. Of course.

TANNER. But — (*He stops, utterly appalled; then resumes feebly.*) No: look here, Ann: if theres no harm in it theres no point in doing it.

ANN. How absurd you are! You dont want to compromise me, do you?

TANNER. Yes: thats the whole sense of my proposal.

ANN. You are talking the greatest nonsense; and you know it. You would never do anything to hurt me.

TANNER. Well, if you dont want to be compromised, dont come.

ANN (*with simple earnestness*). Yes, I will come, Jack, since you wish it. You are my guardian; and I think we ought to see more of one another and come to know one another better. (*Gratefully.*) It's very thoughtful and very kind of you, Jack, to offer me this lovely holiday, especially after what I said about Rhoda. You really are good — much better than you think. When do we start?

TANNER. But ——

The conversation is interrupted by the arrival of MRS. WHITEFIELD *from the house. She is accompanied by the American gentleman, and followed by* RAMSDEN *and* OCTAVIUS.

HECTOR MALONE *is an Eastern American; but he is not at all ashamed of his nationality. This makes English people of fashion think well of him, as of a young fellow who is manly enough to confess to an obvious disadvantage without any attempt to conceal or extenuate it. They feel that he ought not to be made to suffer for what is clearly not his fault, and make a point of being specially kind to him. His chivalrous manners to women, and his elevated moral sentiments, being both gratuitous and unusual, strike them as being a little unfortunate; and though they find his vein of easy humor rather amusing when it has ceased to puzzle them (as it does at first), they have had to make him understand that he really must not tell anecdotes unless they are strictly personal and scandalous, and also that oratory is an accomplishment which belongs to a cruder stage of civilization than that in which his migration has landed him. On these points* HECTOR *is not quite convinced: he still thinks that the British are apt to make merits of their stupidities, and to represent their various incapacities as points of good breeding. English life seems to him to suffer from a lack of edifying rhetoric (which he calls moral tone); English behavior to shew a want of respect for womanhood; English pronunciation to fail very vulgarly in tackling such words as world, girl, bird, etc.; English society to be plain spoken to an extent which stretches occasionally to intolerable coarseness; and English intercourse to need enlivening by games and stories and other pastimes; so he does not feel called upon to acquire these defects after taking great pains to cultivate himself in a first rate manner before venturing across the Atlantic. To this culture he finds English people either totally indifferent, as they very commonly are to all culture, or else politely evasive, the truth being that* HECTOR's *culture is nothing but a state of saturation with our literary exports of thirty years ago, reimported by him to be unpacked at a moment's notice and hurled at the head of English literature, science and art, at every conversational opportunity. The dismay set up by these sallies encourages him in his belief that he is helping to educate England. When he finds people chattering harmlessly about Anatole France and Nietzsche, he devastates them with Matthew Arnold, the Autocrat of the Breakfast Table, and even Macaulay; and as he is devoutly religious at bottom, he first leads the unwary, by humorous irreverence, to leave popular theology out of account in discussing moral questions with him, and then scatters them in confusion by demanding whether the carrying out of his ideals of conduct was not the manifest object of God Almighty in creating honest men and pure women. The engaging freshness of his personality and the dumbfounding staleness of his culture make it extremely difficult to decide whether he is worth knowing; for whilst his company is undeniably pleasant and enlivening, there is intellectually nothing new to be got out of him, especially as he despises politics, and is careful not to talk commercial shop, in which department he is probably much in advance of his English capitalist friends. He gets on best with romantic Christians of the amoristic sect: hence the friendship which has sprung up between him and* OCTAVIUS.

In appearance HECTOR *is a neatly built young man of twenty-four, with a short, smartly trimmed black beard, clear, well shaped eyes, and an ingratiating vivacity of expression. He is, from the fashionable point of view, faultlessly dressed. As he comes along the drive from the house with* MRS. WHITEFIELD *he is sedulously making himself agreeable and entertaining, and thereby placing on her slender wit a burden it is unable to bear. An Englishman would let her alone, accepting boredom and indifference as their common lot; and the poor lady wants to be either let alone or let prattle about the things that interest her.*

RAMSDEN *strolls over to inspect the motor car.* OCTAVIUS *joins* HECTOR.

ANN (*pouncing on her mother joyously*). Oh, mamma, what do you think! Jack is going to take me to Nice in his motor car. Isnt it lovely? I am the happiest person in London.

TANNER (*desperately*). Mrs. Whitefield objects. I am sure she objects. Doesnt she, Ramsden?

RAMSDEN. I should think it very likely indeed.

ANN. You dont object, do you, mother?

MRS. WHITEFIELD. I object! Why should I? I think it will do you good, Ann. (*Trotting over to* TANNER.) I meant to ask you to take Rhoda out for a run occasionally: she is too much in the house; but it will do when you come back.

TANNER. Abyss beneath abyss of perfidy!

ANN (*hastily, to distract attention from this outburst*). Oh, I forgot: you have not met Mr. Malone. Mr. Tanner, my guardian: Mr. Hector Malone.

HECTOR. Please to meet you, Mr. Tanner. I should like to suggest an extension of the travelling party to Nice, if I may.

ANN. Oh, we're all coming. Thats understood, isn't it?

HECTOR. I also am the mawdest possessor of a motor car. If Miss Rawbnsn will allow me the privilege of taking her, my car is at her service.

OCTAVIUS. Violet!

General constraint.

ANN (*subduedly*). Come, mother: we must leave them to talk over the arrangements. I must see to my travelling kit.

MRS. WHITEFIELD looks bewildered; but ANN draws her discreetly away; and they disappear round the corner towards the house.

HECTOR. I think I may go so far as to say that I can depend on Miss Rawbnsn's consent.

Continued embarrassment.

OCTAVIUS. I'm afraid we must leave Violet behind. There are circumstances which make it impossible for her to come on such an expedition.

HECTOR (*amused and not at all convinced*). Too American, eh? Must the young lady have a chaperone?

OCTAVIUS. It's not that, Malone — at least not altogether.

HECTOR. Indeed! May I ask what other objection applies?

TANNER (*impatiently*). Oh, tell him, tell him. We shall never be able to keep the secret unless everybody knows what it is. Mr. Malone: if you go to Nice with Violet, you go with another man's wife. She is married.

HECTOR (*thunderstruck*). You dont tell me so!

TANNER. We do. In confidence.

RAMSDEN (*with an air of importance, lest MALONE should suspect a misalliance*). Her marriage has not yet been made known: she desires that it shall not be mentioned for the present.

HECTOR. I shall respect the lady's wishes. Would it be indiscreet to ask who her husband is, in case I should have an opportunity of cawnsulting him about this trip?

TANNER. We dont know who he is.

HECTOR (*retiring into his shell in a very marked manner*). In that case, I have no more to say.

They become more embarrassed than ever.

OCTAVIUS. You must think this very strange.

HECTOR. A little singular. Pardn mee for saying so.

RAMSDEN (*half apologetic, half huffy*). The young lady was married secretly; and her husband has forbidden her, it seems, to declare his name. It is only right to tell you, since you are interested in Miss — er — in Violet.

OCTAVIUS (*sympathetically*). I hope this is not a disappointment to you.

HECTOR (*softened, coming out of his shell again*). Well: it is a blow. I can hardly understand how a man can leave his wife in such a position. Surely it's not custoMary. It's not manly. It's not considerate.

OCTAVIUS. We feel that, as you may imagine, pretty deeply.

RAMSDEN (*testily*). It is some young fool who has not enough experience to know what mystifications of this kind lead to.

HECTOR (*with strong symptoms of moral repugnance*). I hope so. A man need be very young and pretty foolish too to be excused for such conduct. You take a very lenient view, Mr. Ramsden. Too lenient to my mind. Surely marriage should ennoble a man.

TANNER (*sardonically*). Ha!

HECTOR. Am I to gather from that cacchination that you dont agree with me, Mr. Tanner?

TANNER (*drily*). Get married and try. You may find it delightful for a while: you certainly wont find it ennobling. The greatest common measure of a man and a woman is not necessarily greater than the man's single measure.

HECTOR. Well, we think in America that a woman's morl number is higher than a man's, and that the purer nature of a woman lifts a man right out of himself, and makes him better than he was.

OCTAVIUS (*with conviction*). So it does.

TANNER. No wonder American women prefer to live in Europe! It's more comfortable than standing all their lives on an altar to be worshipped. Anyhow, Violet's husband has not been ennobled. So whats to be done?

HECTOR (*shaking his head*). I cant dismiss that man's cawnduct as lightly as you do, Mr. Tanner. However, I'll say no more. Whoever he is, he's Miss Rawbnsn's husband; and I should be glad for her sake to think better of him.

OCTAVIUS (*touched; for he divines a secret sorrow*). I'm very sorry, Malone. Very sorry.

HECTOR (*gratefully*). Youre a good fellow, Rawbnsn. Thank you.

TANNER. Talk about something else. Violet's coming from the house.

HECTOR. I should esteem it a very great favor, gentlemen, if you would take the opportunity to let me have a few words with the lady alone. I shall have to cry off this trip; and it's rather a dullicate —

RAMSDEN (*glad to escape*). Say no more. Come, Tanner. Come, Tavy. (*He strolls away into the park with* OCTAVIUS *and* TANNER, *past the motor car.*)

   VIOLET *comes down the avenue to* HECTOR.

VIOLET. Are they looking?

HECTOR. No.

   She kisses him.

VIOLET. Have you been telling lies for my sake?

HECTOR. Lying! Lying hardly describes it. I overdo it. I get carried away in an ecstasy of mendacity. Violet: I wish youd let me own up.

VIOLET (*instantly becoming serious and resolute*). No, no, Hector: you promised me not to.

HECTOR. I'll keep my prawmis until you release me from it. But I feel mean, lying to those men, and denying my wife. Just dastardly.

VIOLET. I wish your father were not so unreasonable.

HECTOR. He's not unreasonable. He's right from his point of view. He has a prejudice against the English middle class.

VIOLET. It's too ridiculous. You know how I dislike saying such things to you, Hector; but if I were to — oh, well, no matter.

HECTOR. I know. If you were to marry the son of an English manufacturer of awffice furniture, your friends would consider it a misalliance. And here's my silly old dad, who is the biggest awffice furniture man in the world, would shew me the door for marrying the most perfect lady in England merely because she has no handle to her name. Of course it's just absurd. But I tell you, Violet, I dont like deceiving him. I feel as if I was stealing his money. Why wont you let me own up?

VIOLET. We cant afford it. You can be as romantic as you please about love, Hector; but you mustnt be romantic about money.

HECTOR (*divided between his uxoriousness and his habitual elevation of moral sentiment*). Thats very English. (*Appealing to her impulsively.*) Violet: dad's bound to find us out someday.

VIOLET. Oh yes, later on of course. But dont lets go over this every time we meet, dear. You promised —

HECTOR. All right, all right, I —

VIOLET (*not to be silenced*). It is I and not you who suffer by this concealment; and as to facing a struggle and poverty and all that sort of thing I simply will not do it. It's too silly.

HECTOR. You shall not. I'll sort of borrow the money from my dad until I get on my own feet; and then I can own up and pay up at the same time.

VIOLET (*alarmed and indignant*). Do you mean to work? Do you want to spoil our marriage?

HECTOR. Well, I dont mean to let marriage spoil my character. Your friend Mr. Tanner has got the laugh on me a bit already about that; and —

VIOLET. The beast! I hate Jack Tanner.

HECTOR (*magnanimously*). Oh, hee's all right: he only needs the love of a good woman to ennoble him. Besides, he's proposed a motoring trip to Nice; and I'm going to take you.

VIOLET. How jolly!

HECTOR. Yes; but how are we going to manage? You see, theyve warned me off going with you, so to speak. Theyve told me in cawnfidence that youre married. Thats just the most overwhelming cawnfidence Ive ever been honored with.

TANNER *returns with* STRAKER, *who goes to his car.*

TANNER. Your car is a great success, Mr. Malone. Your engineer is showing it off to Mr. Ramsden.

HECTOR (*eagerly — forgetting himself*). Lets come, Vi.

VIOLET (*coldly, warning him with her eyes*). I beg your pardon, Mr. Malone, I did not quite catch —

HECTOR (*recollecting himself*). I ask to be allowed the pleasure of shewing you my little American steam car, Miss Rawbnsn.

VIOLET. I shall be very pleased. (*They go off together down the avenue.*)

TANNER. About this trip, Straker.

STRAKER (*preoccupied with the car*). Yes?

TANNER. Miss Whitefield is supposed to be coming with me.

STRAKER. So I gather.

TANNER. Mr. Robinson is to be one of the party.

STRAKER. Yes.

TANNER. Well, if you can manage so as to be a good deal occupied with me, and leave Mr. Robinson a good deal occupied with Miss Whitefield, he will be deeply grateful to you.

STRAKER (*looking round at him*). Evidently.

TANNER. "Evidently"! Your grandfather would have simply winked.

STRAKER. My grandfather would have touched his at.

TANNER. And I should have given your good nice respectful grandfather a sovereign.

STRAKER. Five shillins, more likely. (*He leaves the car and approaches* TANNER.) What about the lady's views?

TANNER. She is just as willing to be left to Mr. Robinson as Mr. Robinson is to be left to her. (STRAKER *looks at his principal with cool scepticism; then turns to the car whistling his favorite air.*) Stop that aggravating noise. What do you mean by it? (STRAKER *calmly resumes the melody and finishes it.* TANNER *politely hears it out before he again addresses* STRAKER, *this time with elaborate seriousness.*) Enry: I have ever been a warm advocate of the spread of music among the masses; but I object to your obliging the company whenever Miss Whitefield's name is mentioned. You did it this morning, too.

STRAKER (*obstinately*). It's not a bit o use. Mr. Robinson may as well give it up first as last.

TANNER. Why?

STRAKER. Garn! You know why. Course it's not my business; but you neednt start kiddin me about it.

TANNER. I am not kidding. I dont know why.

STRAKER (*cheerfully sulky*). Oh, very well. All right. It aint my business.

TANNER (*impressively*). I trust, Enry, that, as between employer and engineer, I shall always know how to keep my proper distance, and not intrude my private affairs on you. Even our business arrangements are subject to the approval of your Trade Union. But dont abuse your advantages. Let me remind you that Voltaire said that what was too silly to be said could be sung.

STRAKER. It wasnt Voltaire: it was Bow Mar Shay.

TANNER. I stand corrected: Beaumarchais of course. Now you seem to think that what is too delicate to be said can be whistled. Unfortunately your whistling, though melodious, is unintelligible. Come! theres nobody listening: neither my genteel relatives nor the secretary of your confounded Union. As man to man, Enry, why do you think that my friend has no chance with Miss Whitefield?

STRAKER. Cause she's arter summun else.

TANNER. Bosh; who else?

STRAKER. You.

TANNER. Me!!!

STRAKER. Mean to tell me you didnt know? Oh, come, Mr. Tanner!

TANNER (*in fierce earnest*). Are you playing the fool, or do you mean it?

STRAKER (*with a flash of temper*). I'm not playin no fool. (*More coolly.*) Why, it's as plain as the nose on your face. If you aint spotted that, you dont know much about these sort of things. (*Serene again.*) Ex-cuse me, you know, Mr. Tanner; but you asked me as man to man; and I told you as man to man.

TANNER (*wildly appealing to the heavens*). Then I — I am the bee, the spider, the marked down victim, the destined prey.

STRAKER. I dunno about the bee and the spider. But the marked down victim, thats what you are and no mistake; and a jolly good job for you, too, I should say.

TANNER (*momentously*). Henry Straker: the golden moment of your life has arrived.

STRAKER. What d'y' mean?

TANNER. That record to Biskra.

STRAKER (*eagerly*). Yes?

TANNER. Break it.

STRAKER (*rising to the height of his destiny*). D'y'mean it?

TANNER. I do.

STRAKER. When?

TANNER. Now. Is that machine ready to start?

STRAKER (*quailing*). But you cant —

TANNER (*cutting him short by getting into the car*). Off we go. First to the bank for money; then to my rooms for my kit; then to your rooms for your kit; then break the record from London to Dover or Folkestone; then across the channel and away like mad to Marseilles, Gibraltar, Genoa, any port from which we can sail to a Mahometan country where men are protected from women.

STRAKER. Garn! youre kiddin.

TANNER (*resolutely*). Stay behind then. If you wont come I'll do it alone. (*He starts the motor.*)

STRAKER (*running after him*). Here! Mister! arf a mo! steady on! (*He scrambles in as the car plunges forward.*)

ACT THREE

Evening in the Sierra Nevada. Rolling slopes of brown, with olive trees instead of apple trees in the cultivated patches, and occasional prickly pears instead of gorse and bracken in the wilds. Higher up, tall stone peaks and precipices, all handsome and distinguished. No wild nature here: rather a most aristocratic mountain landscape made by a fastidious artist-creator. No vulgar profusion of vegetation: even a touch of aridity in the frequent patches of stones: Spanish magnificence and Spanish economy everywhere.

Not very far north of a spot at which the high road over one of the passes crosses a tunnel on the railway from Malaga to Granada, is one of the mountain amphitheatres of the Sierra. Looking at it from the wide end of the horse-shoe, one sees, a little to the right, in the face of the cliff, a romantic cave which is really an abandoned quarry, and towards the left a little hill, commanding a view of the road, which skirts the amphitheatre on the left, maintaining its higher level on embankments and an occasional stone arch. On the hill, watching the road, is a man who is either a Spaniard or a Scotchman. Probably a Spaniard, since he wears the dress of a Spanish goatherd and seems at home in the Sierra Nevada, but very like a Scotchman for all that. In the hollow, on the slope leading to the quarry-cave, are about a dozen men who, as they recline at their ease round a heap of smouldering white ashes of dead leaf and brushwood, have an air of being conscious of themselves as picturesque scoundrels honoring the Sierra by using it as an effective pictorial background. As a matter of artistic fact they are not picturesque; and the mountains tolerate them as lions tolerate lice. An English policeman or Poor Law Guardian would recognize them as a selected band of tramps and ablebodied paupers.

This description of them is not wholly contemptuous. Whoever has intelligently observed the tramp, or visited the ablebodied ward of a workhouse, will admit that our social failures are not all drunkards and weaklings. Some of them are men who do not fit the class they were born into. Precisely the same qualities that make the educated gentleman an artist may make an uneducated manual laborer an ablebodied pauper. There are men who fall helplessly into the workhouse because they are good for nothing; but there are also men who are there because they are strongminded enough to disregard the social convention (obviously not a disinterested one on the part of the ratepayer) which bids a man live by heavy and badly paid drudgery when he has the alternative of walking into the workhouse, announcing himself as a destitute person, and legally compelling the Guardians to feed, clothe and house him better than he could feed, clothe and house himself without great exertion. When a man who is born a poet refuses a stool in a stockbroker's office, and starves in a garret, sponging on a poor landlady or on his friends and relatives sooner than work against his grain; or when a lady, because she is a lady, will face any extremity of parasitic dependence rather than take a situation as cook or parlormaid, we make large allowances for them. To such allowances the ablebodied pauper, and his nomadic variant the tramp, are equally entitled.

Further, the imaginative man, if his life is to be tolerable to him, must have leisure to tell himself stories, and a position which lends itself to imaginative decoration. The ranks of unskilled labor offer no such positions. We misuse our laborers horribly; and when a man refuses to be misused, we have no right to say that he is refusing honest work. Let us be frank in this matter before we go on with our play; so that we may enjoy it without hyprocrisy. If we were reasoning, farsighted people, four fifths of us would go straight to the Guardians for relief, and knock the whole social system to pieces with most beneficial reconstructive results. The reason we do not do this is because we work like bees or ants, by instinct or habit, not reasoning about the matter at all. Therefore when a man comes along who can and does reason, and who, applying the Kantian test to his conduct, can truly say to us, If everybody did as I do, the world would be compelled to reform itself industrially, and abolish slavery and squalor, which exist only because everybody does as you do, let us honor that man and seriously consider the advisability of following his example. Such a man is the ablebodied, ableminded pauper. Were he a gentleman doing his best to get a pension or a sinecure instead of sweeping a crossing, nobody would blame him for deciding that so long as the alternative lies between living mainly at the expense of the community and allowing the community to live mainly at his, it would be folly to accept what is to him personally the greater of the two evils.

We may therefore contemplate the tramps of the Sierra without prejudice, admitting cheerfully that our objects — briefly, to be gentlemen of fortune — are much the same as theirs, and the difference in our position and methods merely accidental. One or two of them, perhaps, it would be wiser to kill without malice in a friendly and frank manner; for there are bipeds, just as there are quadrupeds, who are too dangerous to be left unchained and unmuzzled; and these cannot fairly expect to have other men's lives wasted in the work of watching them. But as society has not the courage to kill them, and, when it catches them, simply wreaks on them some superstitious expiatory rites of torture and degradation, and then lets them loose with heightened qualifications for mischief, it is just as well that they are at large in the Sierra, and in the hands of a chief who looks as if he might possibly, on provocation, order them to be shot.

This chief, seated in the centre of the group on a squared block of stone from the quarry, is a tall strong man, with a striking cockatoo nose, glossy black hair, pointed beard, upturned moustache, and a Mephistophelean affectation which is fairly imposing, perhaps because the scenery admits of a larger swagger than Piccadilly, perhaps because of a certain sentimentality in the man which gives him that touch of grace which alone can excuse deliberate picturesqueness. His eyes and mouth are by no means rascally; he has a fine voice and a ready wit; and whether he is really the strongest man in the party or not, he looks it. He is certainly the best fed, the best dressed, and the best trained. The fact that he speaks English is not unexpected, in spite of the Spanish landscape; for with the exception of one man who might be guessed as a bullfighter ruined by drink, and one unmistakable Frenchman, they are all cockney or American; therefore, in a land of cloaks and sombreros, they mostly wear seedy overcoats, woollen mufflers, hard hemispherical hats, and dirty brown gloves. Only a very few dress after their leader, whose broad sombrero with a cock's feather in the band, and voluminous cloak descending to his high boots, are as un-English as possible. None of them are armed; and the ungloved ones keep their hands in their pockets because it is their national belief that it must be dangerously cold in the open air with the night coming on. (It is as warm an evening as any reasonable man could desire).

Except the bullfighting inebriate there is only one person in the company who looks more than, say, thirty-three. He is a small man with reddish whiskers, weak eyes, and the anxious look of a small tradesman in difficulties. He wears the only tall hat visible: it shines in the sunset with the sticky glow of some sixpenny patent hat reviver, often applied and constantly tending to produce a worse state of the original surface than the ruin it was applied to remedy. He has a collar and cuffs of celluloid; and his brown Chesterfield overcoat, with velvet collar, is still presentable. He is pre-eminently the respectable man of the party, and is certainly over forty, possibly over fifty. He is the corner man on the leader's right, opposite three men in scarlet ties on his left. One of these three is the Frenchman. Of the remaining two, who are both English, one is argumentative, solemn, and obstinate; the other rowdy and mischievous.

The CHIEF, *with a magnificent fling of the end of his cloak across his left shoulder, rises to address them. The applause which greets him shews that he is a favorite orator.*

THE CHIEF. Friends and fellow brigands. I have a proposal to make to this meeting. We have now spent three evenings in discussing the question Have Anarchists or Social-Democrats the most personal courage? We have gone into the principles of Anarchism and Social-Democracy at great length. The cause of Anarchy has been ably represented by our one Anarchist, who doesnt know what Anarchism means (*Laughter*) —

THE ANARCHIST (*rising*). A point of order, Mendoza —

MENDOZA (*forcibly*). No, by thunder: your last point of order took half an hour. Besides, Anarchists dont believe in order.

THE ANARCHIST (*mild, polite but persistent: he is, in fact, the respectable looking elderly man in the celluloid collar and cuffs*). That is a vulgar error. I can prove —

MENDOZA. Order, order.

THE OTHERS (*shouting*). Order, order. Sit down. Chair! Shut up.

The ANARCHIST *is suppressed.*

MENDOZA. On the other hand we have three Social-Democrats among us. They are not on speaking terms; and they have put before us three distinct and incompatible views of Social-Democracy.

THE THREE MEN IN SCARLET TIES. 1. Mr. Chairman, I protest. A personal explanation. 2. It's a lie. I never said so. Be fair, Mendoza. 3. Je demande la parole. C'est absolument faux. C'est faux! faux!! faux!!! Assas-s-s-s-sin!!!!!!

MENDOZA. Order, order.

THE OTHERS. Order, order, order! Chair!

The SOCIAL-DEMOCRATS *are suppressed.*

MENDOZA. Now, we tolerate all opinions here. But after all, comrades, the vast majority of us are neither Anarchists nor Socialists, but gentlemen and Christians.

THE MAJORITY (*shouting assent*). Hear, hear! So we are. Right.

THE ROWDY SOCIAL-DEMOCRAT (*smarting under suppression*). You aint no Christian. Youre a Sheeny, you are.

MENDOZA (*with crushing magnanimity*). My friend: I am an exception to all rules. It is true that I have the honor to be a Jew; and when the Zionists need a leader to reassemble our race on its historic soil of Palestine, Mendoza will not be the last to volunteer. (*Sympathetic applause — hear, hear, &c.*) But I am not a slave to any superstition. I have swallowed all the formulas, even that of Socialism; though, in a sense, once a Socialist, always a Socialist.

THE SOCIAL-DEMOCRATS. Hear, hear!

MENDOZA. But I am well aware that the ordinary man — even the ordinary brigand, who can scarcely be called an ordinary man [Hear, hear!] — is not a philosopher. Common sense is good enough for him; and in our business affairs common sense is good enough for me. Well, what is our business here in the Sierra Nevada, chosen by the Moors as the fairest spot in Spain? Is it to discuss abstruse questions of political economy? No: it is to hold up motor cars and secure a more equitable distribution of wealth.

THE SULKY SOCIAL-DEMOCRAT. All made by labor, mind you.

MENDOZA (*urbanely*). Undoubtedly. All made by labor, and on its way to be squandered by wealthy vagabonds in the dens of vice that disfigure the sunny shores of the Mediterranean. We intercept that wealth. We restore it to circulation among the class that produced it and that chiefly needs it — the working class. We do this at the risk of our lives and liberties, by the exercise of the virtues of courage, endurance, foresight, and abstinence —

especially abstinence. I myself have eaten nothing but prickly pears and broiled rabbit for three days.

THE SULKY SOCIAL-DEMOCRAT (*stubbornly*). No more aint we.

MENDOZA (*indignantly*). Have I taken more than my share?

THE SULKY SOCIAL-DEMOCRAT (*unmoved*). Why should you?

THE ANARCHIST. Why should he not? To each according to his needs: from each according to his means.

THE FRENCHMAN (*shaking his fist at the* ANARCHIST). Fumiste!

MENDOZA (*diplomatically*). I agree with both of you.

THE GENUINELY ENGLISH BRIGANDS. Hear, hear! Bravo, Mendoza!

MENDOZA. What I say is, let us treat one another as gentlemen, and strive to excel in personal courage only when we take the field.

THE ROWDY SOCIAL-DEMOCRAT (*derisively*). Shikespear.

A whistle comes from the GOATHERD *on the hill. He springs up and points excitedly forward along the road to the north.*

THE GOATHERD. Automobile! Automobile! (*He rushes down the hill and joins the rest, who all scramble to their feet.*)

MENDOZA (*in ringing tones*). To arms! Who has the gun?

THE SULKY SOCIAL-DEMOCRAT (*handing a rifle to* MENDOZA). Here.

MENDOZA. Have the nails been strewn in the road?

THE ROWDY SOCIAL-DEMOCRAT. Two ahnces of em.

MENDOZA. Good! (*To the Frenchman.*) With me, Duval. If the nails fail, puncture their tires with a bullet. (*He gives the rifle to* DUVAL, *who follows him up the hill.* MENDOZA *produces an opera glass. The others hurry across to the road and disappear to the north.*)

MENDOZA (*on the hill, using his glass*). Two only, a capitalist and his chauffeur. They look English.

DUVAL. Angliche! Aoh yess. Cochons! (*Handling the rifle.*) Faut tirer, n'est-ce-pas?

MENDOZA. No: the nails have gone home. Their tire is down: they stop.

DUVAL (*shouting to the others*). Fondez sur eux, nom de Dieu!

MENDOZA (*rebuking his excitement*). Du calme, Duval: keep your hair on. They take it quietly. Let us descend and receive them.

MENDOZA *descends, passing behind the fire and coming forward, whilst* TANNER *and* STRAKER, *in their motoring goggles, leather coats, and caps, are led in from the road by the brigands.*

TANNER. Is this the gentleman you describe as your boss? Does he speak English?

THE ROWDY SOCIAL-DEMOCRAT. Course e daz. Y' downt suppowz we Hinglishmen luts ahrselves be bossed by a bloomin Spenniard, do you?

MENDOZA (*with dignity*). Allow me to introduce myself: Mendoza, President of the League of the Sierra! (*Posing loftily.*) I am a brigand: I live by robbing the rich.

TANNER (*promptly*). I am a gentleman: I live by robbing the poor. Shake hands.

THE ENGLISH SOCIAL-DEMOCRATS. Hear, hear!
> *General laughter and good humor.* TANNER *and* MENDOZA *shake hands. The* BRIGANDS *drop into their former places.*

STRAKER. Ere! where do I come in?

TANNER (*introducing*). My friend and chauffeur.

THE SULKY SOCIAL-DEMOCRAT (*suspiciously*). Well, which is he? friend or show-foor? It makes all the difference, you know.

MENDOZA (*explaining*). We should expect ransom for a friend. A professional chauffeur is free of the mountains. He even takes a trifling percentage of his principal's ransom if he will honor us by accepting it.

STRAKER. I see. Just to encourage me to come this way again. Well, I'll think about it.

DUVAL (*impulsively rushing across to* STRAKER). Mon frère! (*He embraces him rapturously and kisses him on both cheeks.*)

STRAKER (*disgusted*). Ere, git aht: dont be silly. Who are you, pray?

DUVAL. Duval: Social-Democrat.

STRAKER. Oh, youre a Social-Democrat, are you?

THE ANARCHIST. He means that he has sold out to the parliamentary humbugs and the bourgeoisie. Compromise! that is his faith.

DUVAL (*furiously*). I understand what he say. He say Bourgeois. He say Compromise. Jamais de la vie! Misérable menteur —

STRAKER. See here, Captain Mendoza, ah mach o this sort o thing do you put up with here? Are we avin a pleasure trip in the mountains, or are we at a Socialist meetin?

THE MAJORITY. Hear, hear! Shut up. Chuck it. Sit down, &c. &c. (*The* SOCIAL-DEMOCRATS *and the* ANARCHIST *are hustled into the background.* STRAKER, *after superintending this proceeding with satisfaction, places himself on* MENDOZA'S *left,* TANNER *being on his right.*)

MENDOZA. Can we offer you anything? Broiled rabbit and prickly pears —

TANNER. Thank you: we have dined.

MENDOZA (*to his followers*). Gentlemen: business is over for the day. Go as you please until morning.

> *The* BRIGANDS *disperse into groups lazily. Some go into the cave. Others sit down or lie down to sleep in the open. A few produce a pack of cards and move off towards the road; for it is now starlight; and they know that motor cars have lamps which can be turned to account for lighting a card party.*

STRAKER (*calling after them*). Dont none of you go fooling with that car, d'ye hear?

MENDOZA. No fear, Monsieur le Chauffeur. The first one we captured cured us of that.

STRAKER (*interested*). What did it do?

MENDOZA. It carried three brave comrades of ours, who did not know how to stop it, into Granada, and capsized them opposite the police station. Since

Man and Superman

then we never touch one without sending for the chauffeur. Shall we chat at our ease?

TANNER. By all means.

TANNER, MENDOZA, and STRAKER sit down on the turf by the fire. MENDOZA delicately waives his presidential dignity, of which the right to sit on the squared stone block is the appanage, by sitting on the ground like his guests, and using the stone only as a support for his back.

MENDOZA. It is the custom in Spain always to put off business until to-morrow. In fact, you have arrived out of office hours. However, if you would prefer to settle the question of ransom at once, I am at your service.

TANNER. To-morrow will do for me. I am rich enough to pay anything in reason.

MENDOZA *(respectfully, much struck by this admission)*. You are a remarkable man, sir. Our guests usually describe themselves as miserably poor.

TANNER. Pooh! Miserably poor people dont own motor cars.

MENDOZA. Precisely what we say to them.

TANNER. Treat us well: we shall not prove ungrateful.

STRAKER. No prickly pears and broiled rabbits, you know. Dont tell me you cant do us a bit better than that if you like.

MENDOZA. Wine, kids, milk, cheese and bread can be procured for ready money.

STRAKER *(graciously)*. Now youre talkin.

TANNER. Are you all Socialists here, may I ask?

MENDOZA *(repudiating this humiliating misconception)*. Oh no, no, no: nothing of the kind, I assure you. We naturally have modern views as to the justice of the existing distribution of wealth: otherwise we should lose our self-respect. But nothing that you could take exception to, except two or three faddists.

TANNER. I had no intention of suggesting anything discreditable. In fact, I am a bit of a Socialist myself.

STRAKER *(drily)*. Most rich men are, I notice.

MENDOZA. Quite so. It has reached us, I admit. It is in the air of the century.

STRAKER. Socialism must be lookin up a bit if your chaps are taking to it.

MENDOZA. That is true, sir. A movement which is confined to philosophers and honest men can never exercise any real political influence: there are too few of them. Until a movement shews itself capable of spreading among brigands, it can never hope for a political majority.

TANNER. But are your brigands any less honest than ordinary citizens?

MENDOZA. Sir: I will be frank with you. Brigandage is abnormal. Abnormal professions attract two classes: those who are not good enough for ordinary bourgeois life and those who are too good for it. We are dregs and scum, sir: the dregs very filthy, the scum very superior.

STRAKER. Take care! some o the dregs'll hear you.

MENDOZA. It does not matter: each brigand thinks himself scum, and likes to hear the others called dregs.

TANNER. Come! you are a wit. (MENDOZA *inclines his head, flattered.*) May one ask you a blunt question?

MENDOZA. As blunt as you please.

TANNER. How does it pay a man of your talent to shepherd such a flock as this on broiled rabbit and prickly pears? I have seen men less gifted, and I'll swear less honest, supping at the Savoy on foie gras and champagne.

MENDOZA. Pooh! they have all had their turn at the broiled rabbit, just as I shall have my turn at the Savoy. Indeed, I have had a turn there already — as waiter.

TANNER. A waiter! You astonish me!

MENDOZA (*reflectively*). Yes: I, Mendoza of the Sierra, was a waiter. Hence, perhaps, my cosmopolitanism. (*With sudden intensity.*) Shall I tell you the story of my life?

STRAKER (*apprehensively*). If it aint too long, old chap —

TANNER (*interrupting him*). Tsh-sh: you are a Philistine, Henry: you have no romance in you. (*To* MENDOZA.) You interest me extremely, President. Never mind Henry: he can go to sleep.

MENDOZA. The woman I loved —

STRAKER. Oh, this is a love story, is it? Right you are. Go on: I was only afraid you were going to talk about yourself.

MENDOZA. Myself! I have thrown myself away for her sake: that is why I am here. No matter: I count the world well lost for her. She had, I pledge you my word, the most magnificent head of hair I ever saw. She had humor; she had intellect; she could cook to perfection; and her highly strung temperament made her uncertain, incalculable, variable, capricious, cruel, in a word, enchanting.

STRAKER. A six shillin novel sort o woman, all but the cookin. Er name was Lady Gladys Plantagenet, wasnt it?

MENDOZA. No, sir: she was not an earl's daughter. Photography, reproduced by the half-tone process, has made me familiar with the appearance of the daughters of the English peerage; and I can honestly say that I would have sold the lot, faces, dowries, clothes, titles, and all, for a smile from this woman. Yet she was a woman of the people, a worker: otherwise — let me reciprocate your bluntness — I should have scorned her.

TANNER. Very properly. And did she respond to your love?

MENDOZA. Should I be here if she did? She objected to marry a Jew.

TANNER. On religious grounds?

MENDOZA. No: she was a freethinker. She said that every Jew considers in his heart that English people are dirty in their habits.

TANNER (*surprised*). Dirty!

MENDOZA. It shewed her extraordinary knowledge of the world; for it is undoubtedly true. Our elaborate sanitary code makes us unduly contemptuous of the Gentile.

TANNER. Did you ever hear that, Henry?

STRAKER. Ive heard my sister say so. She was cook in a Jewish family once.

MENDOZA. I could not deny it; neither could I eradicate the impression it made on her mind. I could have got round any other objection; but no woman can stand a suspicion of indelicacy as to her person. My entreaties were in vain: she always retorted that she wasnt good enough for me, and recommended me to marry an accursed barmaid named Rebecca Lazarus, whom I loathed. I talked of suicide: she offered me a packet of beetle poison to do it with. I hinted at murder: she went into hysterics; and as I am a living man I went to America so that she might sleep without dreaming that I was stealing upstairs to cut her throat. In America I went out west and fell in with a man who was wanted by the police for holding up trains. It was he who had the idea of holding up motors cars in the South of Europe: a welcome idea to a desperate and disappointed man. He gave me some valuable introductions to capitalists of the right sort. I formed a syndicate; and the present enterprise is the result. I became leader, as the Jew always becomes leader, by his brains and imagination. But with all my pride of race I would give everything I possess to be an Englishman. I am like a boy: I cut her name on the trees and her initials on the sod. When I am alone I lie down and tear my wretched hair and cry Louisa —

STRAKER (*startled*). Louisa!

MENDOZA. It is her name — Louisa — Louisa Straker —

TANNER. Straker!

STRAKER (*scrambling up on his knees most indignantly*). Look here: Louisa Straker is my sister, see? Wot do you mean by gassin about her like this? Wotshe got to do with you?

MENDOZA. A dramatic coincidence! You are Enry, her favorite brother!

STRAKER. Oo are you callin Enry? What call have you to take a liberty with my name or with hers? For two pins I'd punch your fat edd, so I would.

MENDOZA (*with grandiose calm*). If I let you do it, will you promise to brag of it afterwards to her? She will be reminded of her Mendoza: that is all I desire.

TANNER. This is genuine devotion, Henry. You should respect it.

STRAKER (*fiercely*). Funk, more likely.

MENDOZA (*springing to his feet*). Funk! Young man: I come of a famous family of fighters; and as your sister well knows, you would have as much chance against me as a perambulator against your motor car.

STRAKER (*secretly daunted, but rising from his knees with an air of reckless pugnacity*). I aint afraid of you. With your Louisa! Louisa! Miss Straker is good enough for you, I should think.

MENDOZA. I wish you could persuade her to think so.

STRAKER (*exasperated*). Here —

TANNER (*rising quickly and interposing*). Oh come, Henry: even if you could fight the President you cant fight the whole League of the Sierra. Sit down again and be friendly. A cat may look at a king; and even a President of brigands may look at your sister. All this family pride is really very old fashioned.

STRAKER (*subdued, but grumbling*). Let him look at her. But wot does he mean by makin out that she ever looked at im? (*Reluctantly resuming his couch on the turf.*) Ear him talk, one ud think she was keepin company with him. (*He turns his back on them and composes himself to sleep.*)

MENDOZA (*to* TANNER, *becoming more confidential as he finds himself virtually alone with a sympathetic listener in the still starlight of the mountains; for all the rest are asleep by this time*). It was just so with her, sir. Her intellect reached forward into the twentieth century: her social prejudices and family affections reached back into the dark ages. Ah, sir, how the words of Shakespear seem to fit every crisis in our emotions!

> I loved Louisa: 40,000 brothers
> Could not with all their quantity of love
> Make up my sum.

And so on. I forget the rest. Call it madness if you will — infatuation. I am an able man, a strong man: in ten years I should have owned a first-class hotel. I met her; and — you see! — I am a brigand, an outcast. Even Shakespear cannot do justice to what I feel for Louisa. Let me read you some lines that I have written about her myself. However slight their literary merit may be, they express what I feel better than any casual words can. (*He produces a packet of hotel bills scrawled with manuscript, and kneels at the fire to decipher them, poking it with a stick to make it glow.*)

TANNER (*slapping him rudely on the shoulder*). Put them in the fire, President.

MENDOZA (*startled*). Eh?

TANNER. You are sacrificing your career to a monomania.

MENDOZA. I know it.

TANNER. No you dont. No man would commit such a crime against himself if he really knew what he was doing. How can you look round at these august hills, look up at this divine sky, taste this finely tempered air, and then talk like a literary hack on a second floor in Bloomsbury?

MENDOZA (*shaking his head*). The Sierra is no better than Bloomsbury when once the novelty has worn off. Besides, these mountains make you dream of women — of women with magnificent hair.

TANNER. Of Louisa, in short. They will not make me dream of women, my friend: I am heartwhole.

MENDOZA. Do not boast until morning, sir. This is a strange country for dreams.

TANNER. Well, we shall see. Goodnight. (*He lies down and composes himself to sleep.*)

MENDOZA, *with a sigh, follows his example; and for a few moments there is peace in the Sierra. Then* MENDOZA *sits up suddenly and says pleadingly to* TANNER —

MENDOZA. Just allow me to read a few lines before you go to sleep. I should really like your opinion of them.

TANNER (*drowsily*). Go on. I am listening.

MENDOZA. I saw thee first in Whitsun week
        Louisa, Louisa —

TANNER (*rousing himself*). My dear President, Louisa is a very pretty name; but it really doesnt rhyme well to Whitsun week.

MENDOZA. Of course not. Louisa is not the rhyme, but the refrain.

TANNER (*subsiding*). Ah, the refrain. I beg your pardon. Go on.

MENDOZA. Perhaps you do not care for that one: I think you will like this better. (*He recites, in rich soft tones, and in slow time.*)
        Louisa, I love thee.
        I love thee, Louisa.
        Louisa, Louisa, Louisa, I love thee.
        One name and one phrase make my music, Louisa.
        Louisa, Louisa, Louisa, I love thee.

        Mendoza thy lover,
        Thy lover, Mendoza,
        Mendoza adoringly lives for Louisa.
        There's nothing but that in the world for Mendoza.
        Louisa, Louisa, Mendoza adores thee.

(*Affected.*) There is no merit in producing beautiful lines upon such a name. Louisa is an exquisite name, is it not?

TANNER (*all but asleep, responds with a faint groan*).

MENDOZA. O wert thou, Louisa,
        The wife of Mendoza,
        Mendoza's Louisa, Louisa Mendoza,
        How blest were the life of Louisa's Mendoza!
        How painless his longing of love for Louisa!

That is real poetry — from the heart — from the heart of hearts. Dont you think it will move her?

No answer.

(*Resignedly.*) Asleep, as usual. Doggerel to all the world: heavenly music to me! Idiot that I am to wear my heart on my sleeve! (*He composes himself to sleep, murmuring*) Louisa, I love thee; I love thee, Louisa; Louisa, Louisa, Louisa, I —

    STRAKER *snores; rolls over on his side; and relapses into sleep. Stillness settles on the Sierra; and the darkness deepens. The fire has again buried itself in white ash and ceased to glow. The peaks shew unfathomably dark against the starry firmament; but now the stars dim and vanish; and the sky seems to steal away out of the universe. Instead of the Sierra there is nothing; omnipresent nothing. No sky, no peaks, no light, no sound, no time nor space, utter void. Then somewhere the beginning of a pallor, and with it a faint throbbing buzz as of a ghostly violoncello palpitating on the same note endlessly. A couple of ghostly violins presently take advantage of this bass*

and therewith the pallor reveals a man in the void, an incorporeal but visible man, seated, absurdly enough, on nothing. For a moment he raises his head as the music passes him by. Then, with a heavy sigh, he droops in utter dejection; and the violins, discouraged, retrace their melody in despair and at last give it up, extinguished by wailings from uncanny wind instruments, thus: —

It is all very odd. One recognizes the Mozartian strain; and on this hint, and by the aid of certain sparkles of violet light in the pallor, the man's costume explains itself as that of a Spanish nobleman of the XV–XVI century. DON JUAN, of course; but where? why? how? Besides, in the brief lifting of his face, now hidden by his hat brim, there was a curious suggestion of TANNER. A more critical, fastidious, handsome face, paler and colder, without TANNER's impetuous credulity and enthusiasm, and without a touch of his modern plutocratic vulgarity, but still a resemblance, even an identity. The name too: Don Juan Tenorio, John Tanner. Where on earth — or elsewhere — have we got to from the XX century and the Sierra?

Another pallor in the void, this time not violet, but a disagreeable smoky yellow. With it, the whisper of a ghostly clarionet turning this tune into infinite sadness:

The yellowish pallor moves: there is an old crone wandering in the void, bent and toothless; draped, as well as one can guess, in the coarse brown *frock of some religious order. She wanders and wanders in her slow hopeless way, much as a wasp flies in its rapid busy way, until she blunders against the thing she seeks: companionship. With a sob of relief the poor old creature clutches at the presence of the man and addresses him in her dry unlovely voice, which can still express pride and resolution as well as suffering.*

THE OLD WOMAN. Excuse me; but I am so lonely; and this place is so awful.

DON JUAN. A new comer?

THE OLD WOMAN. Yes: I suppose I died this morning. I confessed; I had extreme unction; I was in bed with my family about me and my eyes fixed on the cross. Then it grew dark; and when the light came back it was this light by which I walk seeing nothing. I have wandered for hours in horrible loneliness.

DON JUAN (*sighing*). Ah! you have not yet lost the sense of time. One soon does, in eternity.

THE OLD WOMAN. Where are we?

DON JUAN. In hell.

THE OLD WOMAN (*proudly*). Hell! I in hell! How dare you?

DON JUAN (*unimpressed*). Why not, Señora?

THE OLD WOMAN. You do not know to whom you are speaking. I am a lady, and a faithful daughter of the Church.

DON JUAN. I do not doubt it.

THE OLD WOMAN. But how then can I be in hell? Purgatory, perhaps: I have not been perfect: who has? But hell! oh, you are lying.

DON JUAN. Hell, Señora, I assure you; hell at its best: that is, its most solitary — though perhaps you would prefer company.

THE OLD WOMAN. But I have sincerely repented; I have confessed —

DON JUAN. How much?

THE OLD WOMAN. More sins than I really committed. I loved confession.

DON JUAN. Ah, that is perhaps as bad as confessing too little. At all events, Señora, whether by oversight or intention, you are certainly damned, like myself; and there is nothing for it now but to make the best of it.

THE OLD WOMAN (*indignantly*). Oh! and I might have been so much wickeder! All my good deeds wasted! It is unjust.

DON JUAN. No: you were fully and clearly warned. For your bad deeds, vicarious atonement, mercy without justice. For your good deeds, justice without mercy. We have many good people here.

THE OLD WOMAN. Were you a good man?

DON JUAN. I was a murderer.

THE OLD WOMAN. A murderer! Oh, how dare they send me to herd with murderers! I was not as bad as that: I was a good woman. There is some mistake: where can I have it set right?

DON JUAN. I do not know whether mistakes can be corrected here. Probably they will not admit a mistake even if they have made one.

THE OLD WOMAN. But whom can I ask?

DON JUAN. I should ask the Devil, Señora: he understands the ways of this place, which is more than I ever could.

THE OLD WOMAN. The Devil! *I* speak to the Devil!

DON JUAN. In hell, Señora, the Devil is the leader of the best society.

THE OLD WOMAN. I tell you, wretch, I know I am not in hell.

DON JUAN. How do you know?

THE OLD WOMAN. Because I feel no pain.

DON JUAN. Oh, then there is no mistake: you are intentionally damned.

THE OLD WOMAN. Why do you say that?

DON JUAN. Because hell, Señora, is a place for the wicked. The wicked are quite comfortable in it: it was made for them. You tell me you feel no pain. I conclude you are one of those for whom Hell exists.

THE OLD WOMAN. Do you feel no pain?

DON JUAN. I am not one of the wicked, Señora; therefore it bores me, bores me beyond description, beyond belief.

THE OLD WOMAN. Not one of the wicked! You said you were a murderer.

DON JUAN. Only a duel. I ran my sword through an old man who was trying to run his through me.

THE OLD WOMAN. If you were a gentleman, that was not a murder.

DON JUAN. The old man called it murder, because he was, he said, defending his daughter's honor. By this he meant that because I foolishly fell in love with her and told her so, she screamed; and he tried to assassinate me after calling me insulting names.

THE OLD WOMAN. You were like all men. Libertines and murderers all, all, all!

DON JUAN. And yet we meet here, dear lady.

THE OLD WOMAN. Listen to me. My father was slain by just such a wretch as you, in just such a duel, for just such a cause. I screamed: it was my duty. My father drew on my assailant: his honor demanded it. He fell: that was the reward of honor. I am here: in hell, you tell me: that is the reward of duty. Is there justice in heaven?

DON JUAN. No; but there is justice in hell: heaven is far above such idle human personalities. You will be welcome in hell, Señora. Hell is the home of honor, duty, justice, and the rest of the seven deadly virtues. All the wickedness on earth is done in their name: where else but in hell should they have their reward? Have I not told you that the truly damned are those who are happy in hell?

THE OLD WOMAN. And are you happy here?

DON JUAN (*springing to his feet*). No; and that is the enigma on which I ponder in darkness. Why am I here? I, who repudiated all duty, trampled honor underfoot, and laughed at justice!

THE OLD WOMAN. Oh, what do I care why you are here? Why am *I* here? I, who sacrificed all my inclinations to womanly virtue and propriety!

DON JUAN. Patience, lady: you will be perfectly happy and at home here. As saith the poet, "Hell is a city much like Seville."

THE OLD WOMAN. Happy! here! where I am nothing! where I am nobody!

DON JUAN. Not at all: you are a lady; and wherever ladies are is hell. Do not be surprised or terrified: you will find everything here that a lady can desire, including devils who will serve you from sheer love of servitude, and magnify your importance for the sake of dignifying their service — the best of servants.

THE OLD WOMAN. My servants will be devils!

DON JUAN. Have you ever had servants who were not devils?

THE OLD WOMAN. Never: they were devils, perfect devils, all of them. But that is only a manner of speaking. I thought you meant that my servants here would be real devils.

DON JUAN. No more real devils than you will be a real lady. Nothing is real here. That is the horror of damnation.

THE OLD WOMAN. Oh, this is all madness. This is worse than fire and the worm.

DON JUAN. For you, perhaps, there are consolations. For instance: how old were you when you changed from time to eternity?

THE OLD WOMAN. Do not ask me how old I was — as if I were a thing of the past. I am 77.

DON JUAN. A ripe age, Señora. But in hell old age is not tolerated. It is too real. Here we worship Love and Beauty. Our souls being entirely damned, we cultivate our hearts. As a lady of 77, you would not have a single acquaintance in hell.

THE OLD WOMAN. How can I help my age, man?

DON JUAN. You forget that you have left your age behind you in the realm of time. You are no more 77 than you are 7 or 17 or 27.

THE OLD WOMAN. Nonsense!

DON JUAN. Consider, Señora: was not this true even when you lived on earth? When you were 70, were you really older underneath your wrinkles and your grey hairs than when you were 30?

THE OLD WOMAN. No, younger: at 30 I was a fool. But of what use is it to feel younger and look older?

DON JUAN. You see, Señora, the look was only an illusion. Your wrinkles lied, just as the plump smooth skin of many a stupid girl of 17, with heavy spirits and decrepit ideas, lies about her age. Well, here we have no bodies: we see each other as bodies only because we learnt to think about one another under that aspect when we were alive; and we still think in that way, knowing no other. But we can appear to one another at what age we choose. You have but to will any of your old looks back, and back they will come.

THE OLD WOMAN. It cannot be true.

DON JUAN. Try.

THE OLD WOMAN. Seventeen!

DON JUAN. Stop. Before you decide, I had better tell you that these things are a matter of fashion. Occasionally we have a rage for 17; but it does not last long. Just at present the fashionable age is 40 — or say 37; but there are signs of a change. If you were at all good-looking at 27, I should suggest your trying that, and setting a new fashion.

THE OLD WOMAN. I do not believe a word you are saying. However, 27 be it. (*Whisk! the old woman becomes a young one, and so handsome that in the radiance into which her dull yellow halo has suddenly lightened one might almost mistake her for* ANN WHITEFIELD.)

DON JUAN. Doña Ana de Ulloa!

ANA. What? You know me!

DON JUAN. And you forget me!

ANA. I cannot see your face. (*He raises his hat.*) Don Juan Tenorio! Monster! You who slew my father! even here you pursue me.

DON JUAN. I protest I do not pursue you. Allow me to withdraw. (*Going.*)

ANA (*seizing his arm*). You shall not leave me alone in this dreadful place.

DON JUAN. Provided my staying be not interpreted as pursuit.

ANA (*releasing him*). You may well wonder how I can endure your presence. My dear, dear father!

DON JUAN. Would you like to see him?

ANA. My father here! ! !

DON JUAN. No: he is in heaven.

ANA. I knew it. My noble father! He is looking down on us now. What must he feel to see his daughter in this place, and in conversation with his murderer!

DON JUAN. By the way, if we should meet him —

ANA. How can we meet him? He is in heaven.

DON JUAN. He condescends to look in upon us here from time to time. Heaven bores him. So let me warn you that if you meet him he will be mortally offended if you speak of me as his murderer! He maintains that he was a much better swordsman than I, and that if his foot had not slipped he would have killed me. No doubt he is right: I was not a good fencer. I never dispute the point; so we are excellent friends.

ANA. It is no dishonor to a soldier to be proud of his skill in arms.

DON JUAN. You would rather not meet him, probably.

ANA. How dare you say that?

DON JUAN. Oh, that is the usual feeling here. You may remember that on earth — though of course we never confessed it — the death of anyone we knew, even those we liked best, was always mingled with a certain satisfaction at being finally done with them.

ANA. Monster! Never, never.

DON JUAN (*placidly*). I see you recognize the feeling. Yes: a funeral was always a festivity in black, especially the funeral of a relative. At all events, family ties are rarely kept up here. Your father is quite accustomed to this: he will not expect any devotion from you.

ANA. Wretch: I wore mourning for him all my life.

DON JUAN. Yes: it became you. But a life of mourning is one thing: an eternity of it quite another. Besides, here you are as dead as he. Can anything be more ridiculous than one dead person mourning for another? Do not look shocked, my dear Ana; and do not be alarmed: there is plenty of humbug in hell (indeed there is hardly anything else); but the humbug of death and age and change is dropped because here we are all dead and all eternal. You will pick up our ways soon.

ANA. And will all the men call me their dear Ana?

DON JUAN. No. That was a slip of the tongue. I beg your pardon.

ANA (*almost tenderly*). Juan: did you really love me when you behaved so disgracefully to me?

DON JUAN (*impatiently*). Oh, I beg you not to begin talking about love. Here they talk of nothing else but love — its beauty, its holiness, its spirituality, its devil knows what! — excuse me; but it does so bore me. They dont know what theyre talking about. I do. They think they have achieved the perfection of love because they have no bodies. Sheer imaginative debauchery! Faugh!

ANA. Has even death failed to refine your soul, Juan? Has the terrible judgment of which my father's statue was the minister taught you no reverence?

DON JUAN. How is that very flattering statue, by the way? Does it still come to supper with naughty people and cast them into this bottomless pit?

ANA. It has been a great expense to me. The boys in the monastery school would not let it alone: the mischievous ones broke it; and the studious ones wrote their names on it. Three new noses in two years, and fingers without end. I had to leave it to its fate at last; and now I fear it is shockingly mutilated. My poor father!

DON JUAN. Hush! Listen! (*Two great chords rolling on syncopated waves of sound break forth: D minor and its dominant: a sound of dreadful joy to all musicians.*) Ha! Mozart's statue music. It is your father. You had better disappear until I prepare him (*She vanishes.*)

> *From the void comes a living* STATUE *of white marble, designed to represent a majestic old man. But he waives his majesty with infinite grace; walks with a feather-like step; and makes every wrinkle in his war worn visage brim over with holiday joyousness. To his sculptor he owes a perfectly trained figure, which he carries erect and trim; and the ends of his moustache curl up, elastic as watchsprings, giving him an air which, but for its Spanish dignity, would be called jaunty. He is on the pleasantest terms with* DON JUAN. *His voice, save for a much more distinguished intonation, is so like the voice of* ROEBUCK RAMSDEN *that it calls attention to the fact that they are not unlike one another in spite of their very different fashions of shaving.*

DON JUAN. Ah, here you are, my friend. Why dont you learn to sing the splendid music Mozart has written for you?

THE STATUE. Unluckily he has written it for a bass voice. Mine is a counter tenor. Well: have you repented yet?

DON JUAN. I have too much consideration for you to repent, Don Gonzalo.

If I did, you would have no excuse for coming from Heaven to argue with me.

THE STATUE. True. Remain obdurate, my boy. I wish I had killed you, as I should have done but for an accident. Then I should have come here; and you would have had a statue and a reputation for piety to live up to. Any news?

DON JUAN. Yes: your daughter is dead.

THE STATUE (*puzzled*). My daughter? (*Recollecting.*) Oh! the one you were taken with. Let me see: what was her name?

DON JUAN. Ana.

THE STATUE. To be sure: Ana. A goodlooking girl, if I recollect aright. Have you warned Whatshisname — her husband?

DON JUAN. My friend Ottavio? No: I have not seen him since Ana arrived.

Ana comes indignantly to light.

ANA. What does this mean? Ottavio here and your friend! And you, father, have forgotten my name. You are indeed turned to stone.

THE STATUE. My dear: I am so much more admired in marble than I ever was in my own person that I have retained the shape the sculptor gave me. He was one of the first men of his day: you must acknowledge that.

ANA. Father! Vanity! personal vanity! from you!

THE STATUE. Ah, you outlived that weakness, my daughter: you must be nearly 80 by this time. I was cut off (by an accident) in my 64th year, and am considerably your junior in consequence. Besides, my child, in this place, what our libertine friend here would call the farce of parental wisdom is dropped. Regard me, I beg, as a fellow creature, not as a father.

ANA. You speak as this villain speaks.

THE STATUE. Juan is a sound thinker, Ana. A bad fencer, but a sound thinker.

ANA (*horror creeping upon her*). I begin to understand. These are devils, mocking me. I had better pray.

THE STATUE (*consoling her*). No, no, no, my child: do not pray. If you do, you will throw away the main advantage of this place. Written over the gate here are the words "Leave every hope behind, ye who enter." Only think what a relief that is! For what is hope? A form of moral responsibility. Here there is no hope, and consequently no duty, no work, nothing to be gained by praying, nothing to be lost by doing what you like. Hell, in short, is a place where you have nothing to do but amuse yourself. (DON JUAN *sighs deeply.*) You sigh, friend Juan; but if you dwelt in heaven, as I do, you would realize your advantages.

DON JUAN. You are in good spirits to-day, Commander. You are positively brilliant. What is the matter?

THE STATUE. I have come to a momentous decision, my boy. But first, where is our friend the Devil? I must consult him in the matter. And Ana would like to make his acquaintance, no doubt.

ANA. You are preparing some torment for me.

DON JUAN. All that is superstition, Ana. Reassure yourself. Remember: the devil is not so black as he is painted.

THE STATUE. Let us give him a call.

At the wave of the statue's hand the great chords roll out again; but this time Mozart's music gets grotesquely adulterated with Gounod's. A scarlet halo begins to glow; and into it the DEVIL *rises, very Mephistophelean, and not at all unlike* MENDOZA, *though not so interesting. He looks older; is getting prematurely bald; and, in spite of an effusion of goodnature and friendliness, is peevish and sensitive when his advances are not reciprocated. He does not inspire much confidence in his powers of hard work or endurance, and is, on the whole, a disagreeably self-indulgent looking person; but he is clever and plausible, though perceptibly less well bred than the two other men, and enormously less vital than the woman.*

THE DEVIL (*heartily*). Have I the pleasure of again receiving a visit from the illustrious Commander of Calatrava? (*Coldly.*) Don Juan, your servant. (*Politely.*) And a strange lady? My respects, Señora.

ANA. Are you —

THE DEVIL (*bowing*). Lucifer, at your service.

ANA. I shall go mad.

THE DEVIL (*gallantly*). Ah, Señora, do not be anxious. You come to us from earth, full of the prejudices and terrors of that priest-ridden place. You have heard me ill spoken of; and yet, believe me, I have hosts of friends there.

ANA. Yes: you reign in their hearts.

THE DEVIL (*shaking his head*). You flatter me, Señora; but you are mistaken. It is true that the world cannot get on without me; but it never gives me credit for that: in its heart it mistrusts and hates me. Its sympathies are all with misery, with poverty, with starvation of the body and of the heart. I call on it to sympathize with joy, with love, with happiness, with beauty —

DON JUAN (*nauseated*). Excuse me: I am going. You know I cannot stand this.

THE DEVIL (*angrily*). Yes: I know that you are no friend of mine.

THE STATUE. What harm is he doing you, Juan? It seems to me that he was talking excellent sense when you interrupted him.

THE DEVIL (*warmly shaking the* STATUE's *hand*). Thank you, my friend: thank you. You have always understood me: he has always disparaged and avoided me.

DON JUAN. I have treated you with perfect courtesy.

THE DEVIL. Courtesy! What is courtesy? I care nothing for mere courtesy. Give me warmth of heart, true sincerity, the bond of sympathy with love and joy —

DON JUAN. You are making me ill.

THE DEVIL. There! (*Appealing to the* STATUE.) You hear, sir! Oh, by what irony of fate was this cold selfish egotist sent to my kingdom, and you taken to the icy mansions of the sky!

THE STATUE. I cant complain. I was a hypocrite; and it served me right to be sent to heaven.

THE DEVIL. Why, sir, do you not join us, and leave a sphere for which your temperament is too sympathetic, your heart too warm, your capacity for enjoyment too generous?

THE STATUE. I have this day resolved to do so. In future, excellent Son of the Morning, I am yours. I have left Heaven for ever.

THE DEVIL (*again grasping his hand*). Ah, what an honor for me! What a triumph for our cause! Thank you, thank you. And now, my friend — I may call you so at last — could you not persuade him to take the place you have left vacant above?

THE STATUE (*shaking his head*). I cannot conscientiously recommend anybody with whom I am on friendly terms to deliberately make himself dull and uncomfortable.

THE DEVIL. Of course not; but are you sure he would be uncomfortable? Of course you know best: you brought him here originally; and we had the greatest hopes of him. His sentiments were in the best taste of our best people. You remember how he sang? (*He begins to sing in a nasal operatic baritone, tremulous from an eternity of misuse in the French manner.*)

Vivan le femmine!
Viva il buon vino!

THE STATUE (*taking up the tune an octave higher in his counter tenor*).

Sostegno e gloria
D'umanità.

THE DEVIL. Precisely. Well, he never sings for us now.

DON JUAN. Do you complain of that? Hell is full of musical amateurs: music is the brandy of the damned. May not one lost soul be permitted to abstain?

THE DEVIL. You dare blaspheme against the sublimest of the arts!

DON JUAN (*with cold disgust*). You talk like a hysterical woman fawning on a fiddler.

THE DEVIL. I am not angry. I merely pity you. You have no soul; and you are unconscious of all that you lose. Now you, Señor Commander, are a born musician. How well you sing! Mozart would be delighted if he were still here; but he moped and went to heaven. Curious how these clever men, whom you would have supposed born to be popular here, have turned out social failures, like Don Juan!

DON JUAN. I am really very sorry to be a social failure.

THE DEVIL. Not that we dont admire your intellect, you know. We do. But I look at the matter from your own point of view. You dont get on with us. The place doesnt suit you. The truth is, you have — I wont say no heart; for we know that beneath all your affected cynicism you have a warm one —

DON JUAN (*shrinking*). Dont, please dont.

THE DEVIL (*nettled*). Well, youve no capacity for enjoyment. Will that satisfy you?

DON JUAN. It is a somewhat less insufferable form of cant than the other. But if youll allow me, I'll take refuge, as usual, in solitude.

THE DEVIL. Why not take refuge in Heaven? Thats the proper place for you. (*To* ANA.) Come, Señora! could you not persuade him for his own good to try change of air?

ANA. But can he go to Heaven if he wants to?

THE DEVIL. Whats to prevent him?

ANA. Can anybody — can *I* go to Heaven if I want to?

THE DEVIL (*rather contemptuously*). Certainly, if your taste lies that way.

ANA. But why doesnt everybody go to Heaven, then?

THE STATUE (*chuckling*). I can tell you that, my dear. It's because heaven is the most angelically dull place in all creation: thats why.

THE DEVIL. His excellency the Commander puts it with military bluntness; but the strain of living in Heaven is intolerable. There is a notion that I was turned out of it; but as a matter of fact nothing could have induced me to stay there. I simply left it and organized this place.

THE STATUE. I dont wonder at it. Nobody could stand an eternity of heaven.

THE DEVIL. Oh, it suits some people. Let us be just, Commander: it is a question of temperament. I dont admire the heavenly temperament: I dont understand it: I dont know that I particularly want to understand it; but it takes all sorts to make a universe. There is no accounting for tastes: there are people who like it. I think Don Juan would like it.

DON JUAN. But — pardon my frankness — could you really go back there if you desired to; or are the grapes sour?

THE DEVIL. Back there! I often go back there. Have you never read the book of Job? Have you any canonical authority for assuming that there is any barrier between our circle and the other one?

ANA. But surely there is a great gulf fixed.

THE DEVIL. Dear lady: a parable must not be taken literally. The gulf is the difference between the angelic and the diabolic temperament. What more impassable gulf could you have? Think of what you have seen on earth. There is no physical gulf between the philosopher's class room and the bull ring; but the bull fighters do not come to the class room for all that. Have you ever been in the country where I have the largest following — England? There they have great racecourses, and also concert rooms where they play the classical compositions of his Excellency's friend Mozart. Those who go to the racecourses can stay away from them and go to the classical concerts instead if they like: there is no law against it; for Englishmen never will be slaves: they are free to do whatever the Government and public opinion allow them to do. And the classical concert is admitted to be a higher, more cultivated, poetic, intellectual, ennobling place than the racecourse. But do the lovers of racing desert their sport and flock to the concert room? Not they. They would suffer there all the weariness the Commander has suffered in heaven. There is the great gulf of the parable between the two places. A mere physical gulf they could bridge; or at least I could bridge it for them (the earth is full of Devil's Bridges); but the gulf of dislike is impassable and eternal. And that is the only gulf that separates my friends here from those who are invidiously called the blest.

ANA. I shall go to heaven at once.

THE STATUE. My child; one word of warning first. Let me complete my friend Lucifer's similitude of the classical concert. At every one of those concerts in England you will find rows of weary people who are there, not because they really like classical music, but because they think they ought to like it. Well, there is the same thing in heaven. A number of people sit there in glory, not because they are happy, but because they think they owe it to their position to be in heaven. They are almost all English.

THE DEVIL. Yes: the Southerners give it up and join me just as you have done. But the English really do not seem to know when they are thoroughly miserable. An Englishman thinks he is moral when he is only uncomfortable.

THE STATUE. In short, my daughter, if you go to Heaven without being naturally qualified for it, you will not enjoy yourself there.

ANA. And who dares say that I am not naturally qualified for it? The most distinguished princes of the Church have never questioned it. I owe it to myself to leave this place at once.

THE DEVIL (*offended*). As you please, Señora. I should have expected better taste from you.

ANA. Father: I shall expect you to come with me. You cannot stay here. What will people say?

THE STATUE. People! Why, the best people are here — princes of the church and all. So few go to Heaven, and so many come here, that the blest, once called a heavenly host, are a continually dwindling minority. The saints, the fathers, the elect of long ago are the cranks, the faddists, the outsiders of to-day.

THE DEVIL. It is true. From the beginning of my career I knew that I should win in the long run by sheer weight of public opinion, in spite of the long campaign of misrepresentation and calumny against me. At bottom the universe is a constitutional one; and with such a majority as mine I cannot be kept permanently out of office.

DON JUAN. I think, Ana, you had better stay here.

ANA (*jealously*). You do not want me to go with you.

DON JUAN. Surely you do not want to enter Heaven in the company of a reprobate like me.

ANA. All souls are equally precious. You repent, do you not?

DON JUAN. My dear Ana, you are silly. Do you suppose heaven is like earth, where people persuade themselves that what is done can be undone by repentance; that what is spoken can be unspoken by withdrawing it; that what is true can be annihilated by a general agreement to give it the lie? No: heaven is the home of the masters of reality: that is why I am going thither.

ANA. Thank you: I am going to heaven for happiness. I have had quite enough of reality on earth.

DON JUAN. Then you must stay here; for hell is the home of the unreal and of the seekers for happiness. It is the only refuge from heaven, which is, as I tell you, the home of the masters of reality, and from earth, which is the home of the slaves of reality. The earth is a nursery in which men and women play at being heroes and heroines, saints and sinners; but they are dragged down from their fool's paradise by their bodies: hunger and cold and thirst, age and decay and disease, death above all, make them slaves of reality: thrice a day meals must be eaten and digested: thrice a century a new generation must be engendered: ages of faith, of romance, and of science are all driven at last to have but one prayer "Make me a healthy animal." But here you escape this tyranny of the flesh; for here you are not an animal at all: you are a ghost, an appearance, an illusion, a convention, deathless, ageless: in a word, bodiless. There are no social questions here, no political questions, no religious questions, best of all, perhaps, no sanitary questions. Here you call your appearance beauty, your emotions love, your sentiments heroism, your aspirations virtue, just as you did on earth; but here there are no hard facts to contradict you, no ironic contrast of your needs with your pretensions, no human comedy, nothing but a perpetual romance, a universal melodrama. As our German friend put it in his poem, "the poetically nonsensical here is good sense; and the Eternal Feminine draws us ever upward and on" — without getting us a step farther. And yet you want to leave this paradise!

ANA. But if Hell be so beautiful as this, how glorious must heaven be!

The DEVIL, *the* STATUE, *and* DON JUAN *all begin to speak at once in violent protest; then stop, abashed.*

DON JUAN. I beg your pardon.

THE DEVIL. Not at all. I interrupted you.

THE STATUE. You were going to say something.

DON JUAN. After you, gentlemen.

THE DEVIL (*to* DON JUAN). You have been so eloquent on the advantages of my dominions that I leave you to do equal justice to the drawbacks of the alternative establishment.

DON JUAN. In Heaven, as I picture it, dear lady, you live and work instead of playing and pretending. You face things as they are; you escape nothing but glamor; and your steadfastness and your peril are your glory. If the play still goes on here and on earth, and all the world is a stage, Heaven is at least behind the scenes. But Heaven cannot be described by metaphor. Thither I shall go presently, because there I hope to escape at last from lies and from the tedious, vulgar pursuit of happiness, to spend my eons in contemplation —

THE STATUE. Ugh!

DON JUAN. Señor Commander: I do not blame your disgust: a picture gallery is a dull place for a blind man. But even as you enjoy the contemplation of such romantic mirages as beauty and pleasure; so would I enjoy the contemplation of that which interests me above all things: namely, Life: the force that ever strives to attain greater power of contemplating itself. What made this brain of mine, do you think? Not the need to move my limbs; for a rat with half my brains moves as well as I. Not merely the need to do, but the need to know what I do, lest in my blind efforts to live I should be slaying myself.

THE STATUE. You would have slain yourself in your blind efforts to fence but for my foot slipping, my friend.

DON JUAN. Audacious ribald: your laughter will finish in hideous boredom before morning.

THE STATUE. Ha ha! Do you remember how I frightened you when I said something like that to you from my pedestal in Seville? It sounds rather flat without my trombones.

DON JUAN. They tell me it generally sounds flat with them, Commander.

ANA. Oh, do not interrupt with these frivolities, father. Is there nothing in Heaven but contemplation, Juan?

DON JUAN. In the Heaven I seek, no other joy. But there is the work of helping Life in its struggle upward. Think of how it wastes and scatters itself, how it raises up obstacles to itself and destroys itself in its ignorance and blindness. It needs a brain, this irresistible force, lest in its ignorance it should resist itself. What a piece of work is man! says the poet. Yes: but what a blunderer! Here is the highest miracle of organization yet attained by life, the most intensely alive thing that exists, the most conscious of all the organisms; and yet, how wretched are his brains! Stupidity made sordid and cruel by the realities learnt from toil and poverty: Imagination resolved to starve sooner than face these realities, piling up illusions to hide them, and calling itself cleverness, genius! And each accusing the other of its own defect: Stupidity accusing Imagination of folly, and Imagination accusing Stupidity of ignorance: whereas, alas! Stupidity has all the knowledge, and Imagination all the intelligence.

THE DEVIL. And a pretty kettle of fish they make of it between them. Did I not say, when I was arranging that affair of Faust's, that all Man's reason has done for him is to make him beastlier than any beast. One splendid body is worth the brains of a hundred dyspeptic, flatulent philosophers.

DON JUAN. You forget that brainless magnificence of body has been tried. Things immeasurably greater than man in every respect but brain have existed and perished. The megatherium, the icthyosaurus have paced the earth with seven-league steps and hidden the day with cloud vast wings. Where are they now? Fossils in museums, and so few and imperfect at that, that a knuckle bone or a tooth of one of them is prized beyond the lives of a thousand soldiers. These things lived and wanted to live; but for lack of brains they did not know how to carry out their purpose, and so destroyed themselves.

THE DEVIL. And is Man any the less destroying himself for all this boasted brain of his? Have you walked up and down upon the earth lately? I have; and I have examined Man's wonderful inventions. And I tell you that in the arts of life man invents nothing; but in the arts of death he outdoes Nature herself, and produces by chemistry and machinery all the slaughter of plague, pestilence and famine. The peasant I tempt to-day eats and drinks what was eaten and drunk by the peasants of ten thousand years ago; and the house he lives in has not altered as much in a thousand centuries as the fashion of a lady's bonnet in a score of weeks. But when he goes out to slay, he carries a marvel of mechanism that lets loose at the touch of his finger all the hidden molecular energies, and leaves the javelin, the arrow, the blowpipe of his fathers far behind. In the arts of peace Man is a bungler. I have seen his cotton factories and the like, with machinery that a greedy dog could have invented if it had wanted money instead of food. I know his clumsy typewriters and bungling locomotives and tedious bicycles: they are toys compared to the Maxim gun, the submarine torpedo boat. There is nothing in Man's industrial machinery but his greed and sloth: his heart is in his weapons. This marvellous force of Life of which you boast is a force of Death: Man measures his strength by his destructiveness. What is his religion? An excuse for hating me. What is his law? An excuse for hanging you. What is his morality? Gentility! an excuse for consuming without producing. What is his art? An excuse for gloating over pictures of slaughter. What are his politics? Either the worship of a despot because a despot can kill, or parliamentary cockfighting. I spent an evening lately in a certain celebrated legislature, and heard the pot lecturing the kettle for its blackness, and ministers answering questions. When I left I chalked up on the door the old nursery saying "Ask no questions and you will be told no lies." I bought a sixpenny family magazine, and found it full of pictures of young men shooting and stabbing one another. I saw a man die: he was a London bricklayer's laborer with seven children. He left seventeen pounds club money; and his wife spent it all on his funeral and went into the workhouse with the children next day. She would not have spent sevenpence on her children's schooling: the law had to force her to let them be taught gratuitously; but on death she spent all she had. Their imagination glows, their energies rise up at the idea of death, these people: they love it; and the more horrible it is the more they enjoy it. Hell is a place far above their comprehension: they derive their notion of it from two of the greatest fools that ever lived, an Italian and an Englishman. The Italian described it as a place of mud, frost, filth, fire, and venomous serpents: all torture. This ass, when he was not lying about me, was maundering about some woman whom he saw once in the street. The Englishman described me as being expelled from Heaven by cannons and gunpowder; and to this day every Briton believes that the whole of his silly story is in the Bible. What else he says I do not know; for it is all in a long poem which neither I nor anyone else ever succeeded in wading through. It is the same in everything. The highest form of literature is the tragedy, a play in which everybody is murdered at the end. In the old chronicles you read of earthquakes and pestilences, and are told that these shewed the power and majesty of God and the littleness of Man. Nowadays the chronicles describe battles. In a battle two bodies of men shoot at one another with bullets and explosive shells until one body runs away, when the others chase the fugitives on horseback and cut them to pieces as they fly. And this, the chronicle concludes, shews the greatness and majesty of empires, and the littleness of the vanquished. Over such battles the people run about the streets yelling with delight, and egg their Governments on to spend hundreds of millions of money in the slaughter, whilst the strongest Ministers dare not spend an extra penny in the pound against the poverty and pestilence through which they themselves daily walk. I could give you a thousand instances; but they all come to the same thing: the power that governs the earth is not the power of Life but of Death; and the inner need that has nerved Life to the effort of organizing itself into the human being is not the need for higher life but for a more efficient engine of destruction. The plague, the famine, the earthquake, the tempest were too spasmodic in their action; the tiger and crocodile were too easily satiated and not cruel enough: something more constantly, more ruthlessly, more ingeniously destructive was needed; and that something was Man, the inventor of the rack, the stake, the gallows, the electric chair; of sword and gun and poison gas: above all, of justice, duty, patriotism and all the other isms by which even those who are clever enough to be humanely disposed are persuaded to become the most destructive of all the destroyers.

DON JUAN. Pshaw! all this is old. Your weak side, my diabolic friend, is that you have always been a gull: you take Man at his own valuation. Nothing would flatter him more than your opinion of him. He loves to think of himself as bold and bad. He is neither one nor the other: he is only a coward. Call him tyrant, murderer, pirate, bully; and he will adore you, and swagger about with the consciousness of having the blood of the old sea kings in his veins. Call him liar and thief; and he will only take an action against you for libel. But call him coward; and he will go mad with rage: he will face death to outface that stinging truth. Man gives every reason for his conduct save one, every excuse for his crimes save one, every plea for his safety save one; and that one is his cowardice. Yet all his civilization is founded on his cowardice, on his abject tameness, which he calls his respectability. There are limits to what a mule or an ass will stand; but Man will suffer himself to be degraded until his vileness becomes so loathsome to his oppressors that they themselves are forced to reform it.

THE DEVIL. Precisely. And these are the creatures in whom you discover what you call a Life Force!

DON JUAN. Yes; for now comes the most surprising part of the whole business.

THE STATUE. Whats that?

DON JUAN. Why, that you can make any of these cowards brave by simply putting an idea into his head.

THE STATUE. Stuff! As an old soldier I admit the cowardice: it's as universal as sea sickness, and matters just as little. But that about putting an idea into a man's head is stuff and nonsense. In a battle all you need to make you fight is a little hot blood and the knowledge that it's more dangerous to lose than to win.

DON JUAN. That is perhaps why battles are so useless. But men never really overcome fear until they imagine they are fighting to further a universal purpose — fighting for an idea, as they call it. Why was the Crusader braver than the pirate? Because he fought, not for himself, but for the Cross. What force was it that met him with a valor as reckless as his own? The force of men who fought, not for themselves, but for Islam. They took Spain from us, though we were fighting for our very hearths and homes; but when we, too, fought for that mighty idea, a Catholic Church, we swept them back to Africa.

THE DEVIL (*ironically*). What! you a Catholic, Señor Don Juan! A devotee! My congratulations.

THE STATUE (*seriously*). Come come! as a soldier, I can listen to nothing against the Church.

DON JUAN. Have no fear, Commander: this idea of a Catholic Church will survive Islam, will survive the Cross, will survive even that vulgar pageant of incompetent schoolboyish gladiators which you call the Army.

THE STATUE. Juan: you will force me to call you to account for this.

DON JUAN. Useless: I cannot fence. Every idea for which Man will die will be a Catholic idea. When the Spaniard learns at last that he is no better than the Saracen, and his prophet no better than Mahomet, he will arise, more Catholic than ever, and die on a barricade across the filthy slum he starves in, for universal liberty and equality.

THE STATUE. Bosh!

DON JUAN. What you call bosh is the only thing men dare die for. Later on, Liberty will not be Catholic enough: men will die for human perfection, to which they will sacrifice all their liberty gladly.

THE DEVIL. Ay: they will never be at a loss for an excuse for killing one another.

DON JUAN. What of that? It is not death that matters, but the fear of death. It is not killing and dying that degrades us, but base living, and accepting the wages and profits of degradation. Better ten dead men than one live slave or his master. Men shall yet rise up, father against son and brother against brother, and kill one another for the great Catholic idea of abolishing slavery.

THE DEVIL. Yes, when the Liberty and Equality of which you prate shall have made free white Christians cheaper in the labor market than black heathen slaves sold by auction at the block.

DON JUAN. Never fear! the white laborer shall have his turn too. But I am not now defending the illusory forms the great ideas take. I am giving you examples of the fact that this creature Man, who in his own selfish affairs is a coward to the backbone, will fight for an idea like a hero. He may be abject as a citizen; but he is dangerous as a fanatic. He can only be enslaved whilst he is spiritually weak enough to listen to reason. I tell you, gentlemen, if you can shew a man a piece of what he now calls God's work to do, and what he will later on call by many new names, you can make him entirely reckless of the consequences to himself personally.

ANA. Yes: he shirks all his responsibilities, and leaves his wife to grapple with them.

THE STATUE. Well said, daughter. Do not let him talk you out of your common sense.

THE DEVIL. Alas! Señor Commander, now that we have got on to the subject of Woman, he will talk more than ever. However, I confess it is for me the one supremely interesting subject.

DON JUAN. To a woman, Señora, man's duties and responsibilities begin and end with the task of getting bread for her children. To her, Man is only a means to the end of getting children and rearing them.

ANA. Is that your idea of a woman's mind? I call it cynical and disgusting materialism.

DON JUAN. Pardon me, Ana: I said nothing about a woman's whole mind. I spoke of her view of Man as a separate sex. It is no more cynical than her view of herself as above all things a Mother. Sexually, Woman is Nature's contrivance for perpetuating its highest achievement. Sexually, Man is Woman's contrivance for fulfilling Nature's behest in the most economical way. She knows by instinct that far back in the evolutionary process she invented him, differentiated him, created him in order to produce something better than the single-sexed process can produce. Whilst he fulfils the purpose for which she made him, he is welcome to his dreams, his follies, his ideals, his heroisms, provided that the keystone of them all is the worship of woman, of motherhood, of the family, of the hearth. But how rash and dangerous it was to invent a separate creature whose sole function was her own impregnation! For mark what has happened. First, Man has multiplied on her hands until there are as many men as women; so that she has been unable to employ for her purposes more than a fraction of the immense energy she has left at his disposal by saving him the exhausting labor of gestation. This superfluous energy has gone to his brain and to his muscle. He has become too strong to be controlled by her bodily, and too imaginative and mentally vigorous to be content with mere self-reproduction. He has created civilization without consulting her, taking her domestic labor for granted as the foundation of it.

Man and Superman

ANA. That is true, at all events.

THE DEVIL. Yes; and this civilization! what is it, after all?

DON JUAN. After all, an excellent peg to hang your cynical commonplaces on; but before all, it is an attempt on Man's part to make himself something more than the mere instrument of Woman's purpose. So far, the result of Life's continual effort not only to maintain itself, but to achieve higher and higher organization and completer self-consciousness, is only, at best, a doubtful campaign between its forces and those of Death and Degeneration. The battles in this campaign are mere blunders, mostly won, like actual military battles, in spite of the commanders.

THE STATUE. That is a dig at me. No matter: go on, go on.

DON JUAN. It is a dig at a much higher power than you, Commander. Still, you must have noticed in your profession that even a stupid general can win battles when the enemy's general is a little stupider.

THE STATUE (*very seriously*). Most true, Juan, most true. Some donkeys have amazing luck.

DON JUAN. Well, the Life Force is stupid; but it is not so stupid as the forces of Death and Degeneration. Besides, these are in its pay all the time. And so Life wins, after a fashion. What mere copiousness of fecundity can supply and mere greed preserve, we possess. The survival of whatever form of civilization can produce the best rifle and the best fed riflemen is assured.

THE DEVIL. Exactly! the survival, not of the most effective means of Life but of the most effective means of Death. You always come back to my point, in spite of your wrigglings and evasions and sophistries, not to mention the intolerable length of your speeches.

DON JUAN. Oh come! who began making long speeches? However, if I overtax your intellect, you can leave us and seek the society of love and beauty and the rest of your favorite boredoms.

THE DEVIL (*much offended*). This is not fair, Don Juan, and not civil. I am also on the intellectual plane. Nobody can appreciate it more than I do. I am arguing fairly with you, and, I think, utterly refuting you. Let us go on for another hour if you like.

DON JUAN. Good: let us.

THE STATUE. Not that I see any prospect of your coming to any point in particular, Juan. Still, since in this place, instead of merely killing time we have to kill eternity, go ahead by all means.

DON JUAN (*somewhat impatiently*). My point, you marble-headed old masterpiece, is only a step ahead of you. Are we agreed that Life is a force which has made innumerable experiments in organizing itself; that the mammoth and the man, the mouse and the megatherium, the flies and the fleas and the Fathers of the Church, are all more or less successful attempts to build up that raw force into higher and higher individuals, the ideal individual being omnipotent, omniscient, infallible, and withal completely, unilludedly self-conscious: in short, a god?

THE DEVIL. I agree, for the sake of argument.

THE STATUE. I agree, for the sake of avoiding argument.

ANA. I most emphatically disagree as regards the Fathers of the Church; and I must beg you not to drag them into the argument.

DON JUAN. I did so purely for the sake of alliteration, Ana; and I shall make no further allusion to them. And now, since we are, with that exception, agreed so far, will you not agree with me further that Life has not measured the success of its attempts at godhead by the beauty of bodily perfection of the result, since in both these respects the birds, as our friend Aristophanes long ago pointed out, are so extraordinarily superior, with their power of flight and their lovely plumage, and, may I add, the touching poetry of their loves and nestings, that it is inconceivable that Life, having once produced them, should, if love and beauty were her object, start off on another line and labor at the clumsy elephant and the hideous ape, whose grandchildren we are?

ANA. Aristophanes was a heathen; and you, Juan, I am afraid, are very little better.

THE DEVIL. You conclude, then, that Life was driving at clumsiness and ugliness?

DON JUAN. No, perverse devil that you are, a thousand times no. Life was driving at brains — at its darling object: an organ by which it can attain not only self-consciousness but self-understanding.

THE STATUE. This is metaphysics, Juan. Why the devil should — (*To the* DEVIL) I beg your pardon.

THE DEVIL. Pray dont mention it. I have always regarded the use of my name to secure additional emphasis as a high compliment to me. It is quite at your service, Commander.

THE STATUE. Thank you: thats very good of you. Even in heaven, I never quite got out of my old military habits of speech. What I was going to ask Juan was why Life should bother itself about getting a brain. Why should it want to understand itself? Why not be content to enjoy itself?

DON JUAN. Without a brain, Commander, you would enjoy yourself without knowing it, and so lose all the fun.

THE STATUE. True, most true. But I am quite content with brain enough to know that I'm enjoying myself. I dont want to understand why. In fact, I'd rather not. My experience is that one's pleasures dont bear thinking about.

DON JUAN. That is why intellect is so unpopular. But to Life, the force behind the Man, intellect is a necessity, because without it he blunders into death. Just as Life, after ages of struggle, evolved that wonderful bodily organ the eye, so that the living organism could see where it was going and what was coming to help or threaten it and thus avoid a thousand dangers that formerly slew it, so it is evolving today a mind's eye that shall see, not the physical world, but the purpose of Life, and thereby enable the individual to work for that purpose instead of thwarting and baffling it by setting up shortsighted personal aims as at present. Even as it is, only one sort of man has ever been happy, has ever been universally respected among all the conflicts of interests and illusions.

THE STATUE. You mean the military man.

DON JUAN. Commander: I do not mean the military man. When the military man approaches, the world locks up its spoons and packs off its womankind. No: I sing, not arms and the hero, but the philosophic man: he who seeks in contemplation to discover the inner will of the world, in invention to discover the means of fulfilling that will, and in action to do that will by the so-discovered means. Of all other sorts of men I declare myself tired. They are tedious failures. When I was on earth, professors of all sorts prowled round me feeling for an unhealthy spot in me on which they could fasten. The doctors of medicine bade me consider what I must do to save my body, and offered me quack cures for imaginary diseases. I replied that I was not a hypochondriac; so they called me Ignoramus and went their way. The doctors of divinity bade me consider what I must do to save my soul; but I was not a spiritual hypochondriac any more than a bodily one, and would not trouble myself about that either; so they called me Atheist and went their way. After them came the politician, who said there was only one purpose in Nature, and that was to get him into parliament. I told him I did not care whether he got into parliament or not; so he called me Mugwump and went his way. Then came the romantic man, the Artist, with his love songs and his paintings and his poems; and with him I had great delight for many years, and some profit; for I cultivated my senses for his sake; and his songs taught me to hear better, his paintings to see better, and his poems to feel more deeply. But he led me at last into the worship of Woman.

ANA. Juan!

DON JUAN. Yes: I came to believe that in her voice was all the music of the song, in her face all the beauty of the painting, and in her soul all the emotion of the poem.

ANA. And you were disappointed, I suppose. Well, was it her fault that you attributed all these perfections to her?

DON JUAN. Yes, partly. For with a wonderful instinctive cunning, she kept silent and allowed me to glorify her; to mistake my own visions, thoughts, and feelings for hers. Now my friend the romantic man was often too poor or too timid to aproach those women who were beautiful or refined enough to seem to realize his ideal; and so he went to his grave believing in his dream. But I was more favored by nature and circumstance. I was of noble birth and rich; and when my person did not please, my conversation flattered, though I generally found myself fortunate in both.

THE STATUE. Coxcomb!

DON JUAN. Yes; but even my coxcombry pleased. Well, I found that when I had touched a woman's imagination, she would allow me to persuade myself that she loved me; but when my suit was granted she never said "I am happy:

my love is satisfied": she always said, first, "At last, the barriers are down," and second, "When will you come again?"

ANA. That is exactly what men say.

DON JUAN. I protest I never said it. But all women say it. Well, these two speeches always alarmed me; for the first meant that the lady's impulse had been solely to throw down my fortifications and gain my citadel; and the second openly announced that henceforth she regarded me as her property, and counted my time as already wholly at her disposal.

THE DEVIL. That is where your want of heart came in.

THE STATUE (*shaking his head*). You shouldnt repeat what a woman says, Juan.

ANA (*severely*). It should be sacred to you.

THE STATUE. Still, they certainly do always say it. I never minded the barriers; but there was always a slight shock about the other, unless one was very hard hit indeed.

DON JUAN. Then the lady, who had been happy and idle enough before, became anxious, preoccupied with me, always intriguing, conspiring, pursuing, watching, waiting, bent wholly on making sure of her prey — I being the prey, you understand. Now this was not what I had bargained for. It may have been very proper and very natural; but it was not music, painting, poetry and joy incarnated in a beautiful woman. I ran away from it. I ran away from it very often: in fact I became famous for running away from it.

ANA. Infamous, you mean.

DON JUAN. I did not run away from you. Do you blame me for running away from the others?

ANA. Nonsense, man. You are talking to a woman of 77 now. If you had had the chance, you would have run away from me too — if I had let you. You would not have found it so easy with me as with some of the others. If men will not be faithful to their home and their duties, they must be made to be. I daresay you all want to marry lovely incarnations of music and painting and poetry. Well, you cant have them, because they dont exist. If flesh and blood is not good enough for you you must go without: thats all. Women have to put up with flesh-and-blood husbands — and little enough of that too, sometimes; and you will have to put up with flesh-and-blood wives. (*The* DEVIL *looks dubious. The* STATUE *makes a wry face.*) I see you dont like that, any of you; but it's true, for all that; so if you dont like it you can lump it.

DON JUAN. My dear lady, you have put my whole case against romance into a few sentences. That is just why I turned my back on the romantic man with the artist nature, as he called his infatuation. I thanked him for teaching me to use my eyes and ears; but I told him that his beauty worshipping and happiness hunting and woman idealizing was not worth a dump as a philosophy of life; so he called me Philistine and went his way.

ANA. It seems that Woman taught you something, too, with all her defects.

DON JUAN. She did more: she interpreted all the other teaching for me. Ah, my friends, when the barriers were down for the first time, what an astounding illumination! I had been prepared for infatuation, for intoxication, for all the illusions of love's young dream; and lo! never was my perception clearer, nor my criticism more ruthless. The most jealous rival of my mistress never saw every blemish in her more keenly than I. I was not duped: I took her without chloroform.

ANA. But you did take her.

DON JUAN. That was the revelation. Up to that moment I had never lost the sense of being my own master; never consciously taken a single step until my reason had examined and approved it. I had come to believe that I was a purely rational creature: a thinker! I said, with the foolish philosopher, "I think; therefore I am." It was Woman who taught me to say "I am; therefore I think." And also "I would think more; therefore I must be more."

THE STATUE. This is extremely abstract and metaphysical, Juan. If you would stick to the concrete, and put your discoveries in the form of entertaining anecdotes about your adventures with women, your conversation would be easier to follow.

DON JUAN. Bah! what need I add? Do you not understand that when I stood face to face with Woman, every fibre in my clear critical brain warned me to spare her and save myself. My morals said No. My conscience said No. My chivalry and pity for her said No. My prudent regard for myself said No. My ear, practised on a thousand songs and symphonies; my eye, exercised on a thousand paintings; tore her voice, her features, her color to shreds. I caught all those tell-tale resemblances to her father and mother by which I knew what she would be like in thirty years' time. I noted the gleam of gold from a dead tooth in the laughing mouth: I made curious observations of the strange odors of the chemistry of the nerves. The visions of my romantic reveries, in which I had trod the plains of heaven with a deathless, ageless creature of coral and ivory, deserted me in that supreme hour. I remembered them and desperately strove to recover their illusion; but they now seemed the emptiest of inventions: my judgment was not to be corrupted: my brain still said No on every issue. And whilst I was in the act of framing my excuse to the lady, Life seized me and threw me into her arms as a sailor throws a scrap of fish into the mouth of a seabird.

THE STATUE. You might as well have gone without thinking such a lot about it, Juan. You are like all the clever men: you have more brains than is good for you.

THE DEVIL. And were you not the happier for the experience, Señor Don Juan?

DON JUAN. The happier, no: the wiser, yes. That moment introduced me for the first time to myself, and, through myself, to the world. I saw then how useless it is to attempt to impose conditions on the irresistible force of Life; to preach prudence, careful selection, virtue, honor, chastity —

ANA. Don Juan: a word against chastity is an insult to me.

DON JUAN. I say nothing against your chastity, Señora, since it took the form of a husband and twelve children. What more could you have done had you been the most abandoned of women?

ANA. I could have had twelve husbands and no children: thats what I could have done, Juan. And let me tell you that that would have made all the difference to the earth which I replenished.

THE STATUE. Bravo Ana! Juan: you are floored, quelled, annihilated.

DON JUAN. No; for though that difference is the true essential difference — Doña Ana has, I admit, gone straight to the real point — yet it is not a difference of love or chastity, or even constancy; for twelve children by twelve different husbands would have replenished the earth perhaps more effectively. Suppose my friend Ottavio had died when you were thirty, you would never have remained a widow: you were too beautiful. Suppose the successor of Ottavio had died when you were forty, you would still have been irresistible; and a woman who marries twice marries three times if she becomes free to do so. Twelve lawful children borne by one highly respectable lady to three different fathers is not impossible nor condemned by public opinion. That such a lady may be more law abiding than the poor girl whom we used to spurn into the gutter for bearing one unlawful infant is no doubt true; but dare you say she is less self-indulgent?

ANA. She is less virtuous: that is enough for me.

DON JUAN. In that case, what is virtue but the Trade Unionism of the married? Let us face the facts, dear Ana. The Life Force respects marriage only because marriage is a contrivance of its own to secure the greatest number of children and the closest care of them. For honor, chastity and all the rest of your moral figments it cares not a rap. Marriage is the most licentious of human institutions —

ANA. Juan!

THE STATUE (*protesting*). Really! —

DON JUAN (*determinedly*). I say the most licentious of human institutions: that is the secret of its popularity. And a woman seeking a husband is the most unscrupulous of all the beasts of prey. The confusion of marriage with morality has done more to destroy the conscience of the human race than any other single error. Come, Ana! do not look shocked: you know better than any of us that marriage is a mantrap baited with simulated accomplishments and delusive idealizations. When your sainted mother, by dint of scoldings and punishments, forced you to learn how to play half a dozen pieces on the spinet — when she hated as much as you did — had she any other purpose than to delude your suitors into the belief that your husband would have in his home an angel who would fill it with melody, or at least play him to sleep after dinner? You married my friend Ottavio: well, did you ever open the spinet from the hour when the Church united him to you?

ANA. You are a fool, Juan. A young married woman has something else to do than sit at the spinet without any support for her back; so she gets out of the habit of playing.

DON JUAN. Not if she loves music. No: believe me, she only throws away the bait when the bird is in the net.

ANA (*bitterly*). And men, I suppose, never throw off the mask when their bird is in the net. The husband never becomes negligent, selfish, brutal — oh never!

DON JUAN. What do these recriminations prove, Ana? Only that the hero is as gross an imposture as the heroine.

ANA. It is all nonsense: most marriages are perfectly comfortable.

DON JUAN. "Perfectly" is a strong expression, Ana. What you mean is that sensible people make the best of one another. Send me to the galleys and chain me to the felon whose number happens to be next before mine; and I must accept the inevitable and make the best of the companionship. Many such companionships, they tell me, are touchingly affectionate; and most are at least tolerably friendly. But that does not make a chain a desirable ornament nor the galleys an abode of bliss. Those who talk most about the blessings of marriage and the constancy of its vows are the very people who declare that if the chain were broken and the prisoners left free to choose, the whole social fabric would fly asunder. You cannot have the argument both ways. If the prisoner is happy, why lock him in? If he is not, why pretend that he is?

ANA. At all events, let me take an old woman's privilege again, and tell you flatly that marriage peoples the world and debauchery does not.

DON JUAN. How if a time come when this shall cease to be true? Do you not know that where there is a will there is a way — that whatever Man really wishes to do he will finally discover a means of doing? Well, you have done your best, your virtuous ladies, and others of your way of thinking, to bend Man's mind wholly towards honorable love as the highest good, and to understand by honorable love romance and beauty and happiness in the possession of beautiful, refined, delicate, affectionate women. You have taught women to value their own youth, health, shapeliness, and refinement above all things. Well, what place have squalling babies and household cares in this exquisite paradise of the senses and emotions? Is it not the inevitable end of it all that the human will shall say to the human brain: Invent me a means by which I can have love, beauty, romance, emotion, passion without their wretched penalties, their expenses, their worries, their trials, their illnesses and agonies and risks of death, their retinue of servants and nurses and doctors and schoolmasters.

THE DEVIL. All this, Señor Don Juan, is realized here in my realm.

DON JUAN. Yes, at the cost of death. Man will not take it at that price: he demands the romantic delights of your hell whilst he is still on earth. Well, the means will be found: the brain will not fail when the will is in earnest. The day is coming when great nations will find their numbers dwindling from census to census; when the six roomed villa will rise in price above the family mansion; when the viciously reckless poor and the stupidly pious rich will delay the extinction of the race only by degrading it; whilst the boldly prudent, the thriftily selfish and ambitious, the imaginative and poetic, the lovers of money and solid comfort, the worshippers of success, of art, and of love, will all oppose to the Force of Life the device of sterility.

THE STATUE. That is all very eloquent, my young friend; but if you had lived to Ana's age, or even to mine, you would have learned that the people who get rid of the fear of poverty and children and all the other family troubles, and devote themselves to having a good time of it, only leave their minds free for the fear of old age and ugliness and impotence and death. The childless laborer is more tormented by his wife's idleness and her constant demands for amusement and distraction than he could be by twenty children; and his wife is more wretched than he. I have had my share of vanity; for as a young man I was admired by women; and as a statue I am praised by art critics. But I confess that had I found nothing to do in the world but wallow in these delights I should have cut my throat. When I married Ana's mother — or perhaps, to be strictly correct, I should rather say when I at last gave in and allowed Ana's mother to marry me — I knew that I was planting thorns in my pillow, and that marriage for me, a swaggering young officer thitherto unvanquished, meant defeat and capture.

ANA (*scandalized*). Father!

THE STATUE. I am sorry to shock you, my love; but since Juan has stripped every rag of decency from the discussion I may as well tell the frozen truth.

ANA. Hmf! I suppose I was one of the thorns.

THE STATUE. By no means: you were often a rose. You see, your mother had most of the trouble you gave.

DON JUAN. Then may I ask, Commander, why you have left Heaven to come here and wallow, as you express it, in sentimental beatitudes which you confess would once have driven you to cut your throat?

THE STATUE (*struck by this*). Egad, thats true.

THE DEVIL (*alarmed*). What! You are going back from your word! (*To* DON JUAN.) And all your philosophizing has been nothing but a mask for proselytizing! (*To the* STATUE.) Have you forgotten already the hideous dulness from which I am offering you a refuge here? (*To* DON JUAN.) And does your demonstration of the approaching sterilization and extinction of mankind lead to anything better than making the most of those pleasures of art and love which you yourself admit refined you, elevated you, developed you?

DON JUAN. I never demonstrated the extinction of mankind. Life cannot will its own extinction either in its blind amorphous state or in any of the forms into which it has organized itself. I had not finished when His Excellency interrupted me.

THE STATUE. I begin to doubt whether you ever will finish, my friend. You are extremely fond of hearing yourself talk.

DON JUAN. True; but since you have endured so much, you may as well endure to the end. Long before this sterilization which I described becomes more than a clearly foreseen possibility, the reaction will begin. The great central purpose of breeding the race, ay, breeding it to heights now deemed superhuman: that purpose which is now hidden in a mephitic cloud of love and romance and prudery and fastidiousness, will break through into clear sunlight as a purpose no longer to be confused with the gratification of personal fancies, the impossible realization of boys' and girls' dreams of bliss, or the need of older people for companionship or money. The plain-spoken marriage services of the vernacular Churches will no longer be abbreviated and half suppressed as indelicate. The sober decency, earnestness and authority of their declaration of the real purpose of marriage will be honored and accepted, whilst their romantic vowings and pledgings and until-death-do-us-partings and the like will be expunged as unbearable frivolities. Do my sex the justice to admit, Señora, that we have always recognized that the sex relation is not a personal or friendly relation at all.

ANA. Not a personal or friendly relation! What relation is more personal? more sacred? more holy?

DON JUAN. Sacred and holy, if you like, Ana, but not personally friendly. Your relation to God is sacred and holy: dare you call it personally friendly? In the sex relation the universal creative energy, of which the parties are both the helpless agents, over-rides and sweeps away all personal considerations and dispenses with all personal relations. The pair may be utter strangers to one another, speaking different languages, differing in race and color, in age and disposition, with no bond between them but a possibility of that fecundity for the sake of which the Life Force throws them into one another's arms at the exchange of a glance. Do we not recognize this by allowing marriages to be made by parents without consulting the woman? Have you not often expressed your disgust at the immorality of the English nation, in which women and men of noble birth become acquainted and court each other like peasants? And how much does even the peasant know of his bride or she of him before he engages himself? Why, you would not make a man your lawyer or your family doctor on so slight an acquaintance as you would fall in love with and marry him!

ANA. Yes, Juan: we know the libertine's philosophy. Always ignore the consequences to the woman.

DON JUAN. The consequences, yes: they justify her fierce grip of the man. But surely you do not call that attachment a sentimental one. As well call the policeman's attachment to his prisoner a love relation.

ANA. You see you have to confess that marriage is necessary, though, according to you, love is the slightest of all the relations.

DON JUAN. How do you know that it is not the greatest of all the relations? far too great to be a personal matter. Could your father have served his country if he had refused to kill any enemy of Spain unless he personally hated him? Can a woman serve her country if she refuses to marry any man she does not personally love? You know it is not so: the woman of noble birth marries as the man of noble birth fights, on political and family grounds, not on personal ones.

THE STATUE (*impressed*). A very clever point that, Juan: I must think it over. You are really full of ideas. How did you come to think of this one?

DON JUAN. I learnt it by experience. When I was on earth, and made those proposals to ladies which, though universally condemned, have made me so interesting a hero of legend, I was not infrequently met in some such way as this. The lady would say that she would countenance my advances, provided they were honorable. On inquiring what that proviso meant, I found that it meant that I proposed to get possession of her property if she had any, or to undertake her support for life if she had not; that I desired her continual companionship, counsel and conversation to the end of my days, and would bind myself under penalties to be always enraptured by them; and, above all, that I would turn my back on all other women for ever for her sake. I did not object to these conditions because they were exorbitant and inhuman: it was their extraordinary irrelevance that prostrated me. I invariably replied with perfect frankness that I had never dreamt of any of these things; that unless the lady's character and intellect were equal or superior to my own, her conversation must degrade and her counsel mislead me; that her constant companionship might, for all I knew, become intolerably tedious to me; that I could not answer for my feelings for a week in advance, much less to the end of my life; that to cut me off from all natural and unconstrained relations with the rest of my fellow creatures would narrow and warp me if I submitted to it, and, if not, would bring me under the curse of clandestinity; that, finally, my proposals to her were wholly unconnected with any of these matters, and were the outcome of a perfectly simple impulse of my manhood towards her womanhood.

ANA. You mean that it was an immoral impulse.

DON JUAN. Nature, my dear lady, is what you call immoral. I blush for it; but I cannot help it. Nature is a pander, Time a wrecker, and Death a murderer. I have always preferred to stand up to those facts and build institutions on their recognition. You prefer to propitiate the three devils by proclaiming their chastity, their thrift, and their loving kindness; and to base your institutions on these flatteries. Is it any wonder that the institutions do not work smoothly?

THE STATUE. What used the ladies to say, Juan?

DON JUAN. Oh come! Confidence for confidence. First tell me what you used to say to the ladies.

THE STATUE. I! Oh, I swore that I would be faithful to the death; that I should die if they refused me; that no woman could ever be to me what she was —

ANA. She! Who?

THE STATUE. Whoever it happened to be at the time, my dear. I had certain things I always said. One of them was that even when I was eighty, one white hair of the woman I loved would make me tremble more than the thickest gold tress from the most beautiful young head. Another was that I could not bear the thought of anyone else being the mother of my children.

DON JUAN (*revolted*). You old rascal!

THE STATUE (*stoutly*). Not a bit; for I really believed it with all my soul at the moment. I had a heart: not like you. And it was this sincerity that made me successful.

DON JUAN. Sincerity! To be fool enough to believe a ramping, stamping, thumping lie: that is what you call sincerity! To be so greedy for a woman that you deceive yourself in your eagerness to deceive her: sincerity, you call it!

THE STATUE. Oh, damn your sophistries! I was a man in love, not a lawyer. And the women loved me for it, bless them!

DON JUAN. They made you think so. What will you say when I tell you that though I played the lawyer so callously, they made me think so too? I also had my moments of infatuation in which I gushed nonsense and believed it. Sometimes the desire to give pleasure by saying beautiful things so rose in me on the flood of emotion that I said them recklessly. At other times I argued against myself with a devilish coldness that drew tears. But I found it just as hard to escape in the one case as in the others. When the lady's instinct was set on me, there was nothing for it but lifelong servitude or flight.

ANA. You dare boast, before me and my father, that every woman found you irresistible.

DON JUAN. Am I boasting? It seems to me that I cut the most pitiable of figures. Besides, I said "when the lady's instinct was set on me." It was not always so; and then, heavens! what transports of virtuous indignation! what overwhelming defiance to the dastardly seducer! what scenes of Imogen and Iachimo!

ANA. I made no scenes. I simply called my father.

DON JUAN. And he came, sword in hand, to vindicate outraged honor and morality by murdering me.

THE STATUE. Murdering! What do you mean? Did I kill you or did you kill me?

DON JUAN. Which of us was the better fencer?

THE STATUE. I was.

DON JUAN. Of course you were. And yet you, the hero of those scandalous adventures you have just been relating to us, you had the effrontery to pose as the avenger of outraged morality and condemn me to death! You would have slain me but for an accident.

THE STATUE. I was expected to, Juan. That is how things were arranged on earth. I was not a social reformer; and I always did what it was customary for a gentleman to do.

DON JUAN. That may account for your attacking me, but not for the revolting hypocrisy of your subsequent proceedings as a statue.

THE STATUE. That all came of my going to Heaven.

THE DEVIL. I still fail to see, Señor Don Juan, that these episodes in your earthly career and in that of the Señor Commander in any way discredit my view of life. Here, I repeat, you have all that you sought without anything that you shrank from.

DON JUAN. On the contrary, here I have everything that disappointed me without anything that I have not already tried and found wanting. I tell you that as long as I can conceive something better than myself I cannot be easy unless I am striving to bring it into existence or clearing the way for it. That is the law of my life. That is the working within me of Life's incessant aspiration to higher organization, wider, deeper, intenser self-consciousness, and clearer self-understanding. It was the supremacy of this purpose that reduced love for me to the mere pleasure of a moment, art for me to the mere schooling of my faculties, religion for me to a mere excuse for laziness, since it had set up a God who looked at the world and saw that it was good, against the instinct in me that looked through my eyes at the world and saw that it could be improved. I tell you that in the pursuit of my own pleasure, my own health, my own fortune, I have never known happiness. It was not love for Woman that delivered me into her hands: it was fatigue, exhaustion. When I was a child, and bruised my head against a stone, I ran to the nearest woman and cried away my pain against her apron. When I grew up, and bruised my soul against the brutalities and stupidities with which I had to strive, I did again just what I had done as a child. I have enjoyed, too, my rests, my recuperations, my breathing times, my very prostrations after strife; but rather would I be dragged through all the circles of the foolish Italian's Inferno than through the pleasures of Europe. That is what has made this place of eternal pleasures so deadly to me. It is the absence of this instinct in you that makes you that strange monster called a Devil. It is the success with which you have diverted the attention of men from their real purpose, which in one degree or another is the same as mine, to yours, that has earned you the name of The Tempter. It is the fact that they are doing your will, or rather drifting with your want of will, instead of doing their own, that makes them the uncomfortable, false, restless, artificial, petulant, wretched creatures they are.

THE DEVIL (*mortified*). Señor Don Juan: you are uncivil to my friends.

DON JUAN. Pooh! why should I be civil to them or to you? In this Palace of Lies a truth or two will not hurt you. Your friends are all the dullest dogs I know. They are not beautiful: they are only decorated. They are not clean: they are only shaved and starched. They are not dignified: they are only fashionably dressed. They are not educated: they are only college passmen. They are not religious: they are only pewrenters. They are not moral: they are only conventional. They are not virtuous: they are only cowardly. They are not even vicious: they are only "frail." They are not artistic: they are only lascivious. They are not prosperous: they are only rich. They are not loyal, they are only servile; not dutiful, only sheepish; not public spirited, only patriotic; not courageous, only quarrelsome; not determined, only obstinate; not masterful, only domineering; not self-controlled, only obtuse; not self-respecting, only vain; not kind, only sentimental; not social, only gregarious; not considerate, only polite; not intelligent, only opinionated; not progressive, only factious; not imaginative, only superstitious; not just, only vindictive; not generous, only propitiatory; not disciplined, only cowed; and not truthful at all — liars every one of them, to the very backbone of their souls.

THE STATUE. Your flow of words is simply amazing, Juan. How I wish I could have talked like that to my soldiers.

THE DEVIL. It is mere talk, though. It has all been said before; but what change has it ever made? What notice has the world ever taken of it?

DON JUAN. Yes, it is mere talk. But why is it mere talk? Because, my friend, beauty, purity, respectability, religion, morality, art, patriotism, bravery and the rest are nothing but words which I or anyone else can turn inside out like a glove. Were they realities, you would have to plead guilty to my indictment; but fortunately for your self-respect, my diabolical friend, they are not realities. As you say, they are mere words, useful for duping barbarians into adopting civilization, or the civilized poor into submitting to be robbed and enslaved. That is the family secret of the governing caste; and if we who are of that caste aimed at more Life for the world instead of at more power and luxury for our miserable selves, that secret would make us great. Now, since I, being a nobleman, am in the secret too, think how tedious to me must be your unending cant about all these moralistic figments, and how squalidly disastrous your sacrifice of your lives to them! If you even believed in your moral game enough to play it fairly, it would be interesting to watch; but you dont: you cheat at every trick; and if your opponent outcheats you, you upset the table and try to murder him.

THE DEVIL. On earth there may be some truth in this, because the people are uneducated and cannot appreciate my religion of love and beauty; but here —

DON JUAN. Oh yes: I know. Here there is nothing but love and beauty. Ugh! it is like sitting for all eternity at the first act of a fashionable play, before the complications begin. Never in my worst moments of superstitious terror on earth did I dream that Hell was so horrible. I live, like a hairdresser, in the continual contemplation of beauty, toying with silken tresses. I breathe an atmosphere of sweetness, like a confectioner's shopboy. Commander: are there any beautiful women in Heaven?

THE STATUE. None. Absolutely none. All dowdies. Not two pennorth of jewellery among a dozen of them. They might be men of fifty.

DON JUAN. I am impatient to get there. Is the word beauty ever mentioned; and are there any artistic people?

THE STATUE. I give you my word they wont admire a fine statue even when it walks past them.

DON JUAN. I go.

THE DEVIL. Don Juan: shall I be frank with you?

DON JUAN. Were you not so before?

THE DEVIL. As far as I went, yes. But I will now go further, and confess to you that men get tired of everything, of heaven no less than of hell; and that all history is nothing but a record of the oscillations of the world between these two extremes. An epoch is but a swing of the pendulum; and each generation thinks the world is progressing because it is always moving. But when you are as old as I am; when you have a thousand times wearied of heaven, like myself and the Commander, and a thousand times wearied of hell, as you are wearied now, you will no longer imagine that every swing from heaven to hell is an emancipation, every swing from hell to heaven an evolution. Where you now see reform, progress, fulfilment of upward tendency, continual ascent by Man on the stepping stones of his dead selves to higher things, you will see nothing but an infinite comedy of illusion. You will discover the profound truth of the saying of my friend Koheleth, that there is nothing new under the sun. Vanitas vanitatum —

DON JUAN (*out of all patience*). By Heaven, this is worse than your cant about love and beauty. Clever dolt that you are, is a man no better than a worm, or a dog than a wolf, because he gets tired of everything? Shall he give up eating because he destroys his appetite in the act of gratifying it? Is a field idle when it is fallow? Can the Commander expend his hellish energy here without accumulating heavenly energy for his next term of blessedness? Granted that the great Life Force has hit on the device of the clockmaker's pendulum, and uses the earth for its bob; that the history of each oscillation, which seems so novel to us the actors, is but the history of the last oscillation repeated; nay more, that in the unthinkable infinitude of time the sun throws off the earth and catches it again a thousand times as a circus rider throws up a ball, and that the total of all our epochs is but the moment between the toss and the catch, has the colossal mechanism no purpose?

THE DEVIL. None, my friend. You think, because you have a purpose, Nature must have one. You might as well expect it to have fingers and toes because you have them.

DON JUAN. But I should not have them if they served no purpose. And I, my friend, am as much a part of Nature as my own finger is a part of me. If my finger is the organ by which I grasp the sword and the mandoline, my brain is the organ by which Nature strives to understand itself. My dog's brain serves only my dog's purposes; but my brain labors at a knowledge which does nothing for me personally but make my body bitter to me and my decay and death a calamity. Were I not possessed with a purpose beyond my own I had better be a ploughman than a philosopher; for the ploughman lives as long as the philosopher, eats more, sleeps better, and rejoices in the wife of his bosom with less misgiving. This is because the philosopher is in the grip of the Life Force. This Life Force says to him "I have done a thousand wonderful things unconsciously by merely willing to live and following the line of least resistance: now I want to know myself and my destination,

Man and Superman

and choose my path; so I have made a special brain — a philosopher's brain — to grasp this knowledge for me as the husbandman's hand grasps the plough for me. And this" says the Life Force to the philosopher "must thou strive to do for me until thou diest, when I will make another brain and another philosopher to carry on the work."

THE DEVIL. What is the use of knowing?

DON JUAN. Why, to be able to choose the line of greatest advantage instead of yielding in the direction of the least resistance. Does a ship sail to its destination no better than a log drifts nowhither? The philosopher is Nature's pilot. And there you have our difference: to be in hell is to drift: to be in heaven is to steer.

THE DEVIL. On the rocks, most likely.

DON JUAN. Pooh! which ship goes oftenest on the rocks or to the bottom — the drifting ship or the ship with a pilot on board?

THE DEVIL. Well, well, go your way, Señor Don Juan. I prefer to be my own master and not the tool of any blundering universal force. I know that beauty is good to look at; that music is good to hear; that love is good to feel; and that they are all good to think about and talk about. I know that to be well exercised in these sensations, emotions, and studies is to be a refined and cultivated being. Whatever they may say of me in churches on earth, I know that it is universally admitted in good society that the Prince of Darkness is a gentleman; and that is enough for me. As to your Life Force, which you think irresistible, it is the most resistible thing in the world for a person of any character. But if you are naturally vulgar and credulous, as all reformers are, it will thrust you first into religion, where you will sprinkle water on babies to save their souls from me; then it will drive you from religion into science, where you will snatch the babies from the water sprinkling and inoculate them with disease to save them from catching it accidentally; then you will take to politics, where you will become the catspaw of corrupt functionaries and the henchman of ambitious humbugs; and the end will be despair and decrepitude, broken nerve and shattered hopes, vain regrets for that worst and silliest of wastes and sacrifices, the waste and sacrifice of the power of enjoyment: in a word, the punishment of the fool who pursues the better before he has secured the good.

DON JUAN. But at least I shall not be bored. The service of the Life Force has that advantage, at all events. So fare you well, Señor Satan.

THE DEVIL (*amiably*). Fare you well, Don Juan. I shall often think of our interesting chats about things in general. I wish you every happiness: Heaven, as I said before, suits some people. But if you should change your mind, do not forget that the gates are always open here to the repentant prodigal. If you feel at any time that warmth of heart, sincere unforced affection, innocent enjoyment, and warm, breathing, palpitating reality —

DON JUAN. Why not say flesh and blood at once, though we have left those two greasy commonplaces behind us?

THE DEVIL (*angrily*). You throw my friendly farewell back in my teeth, then, Don Juan?

DON JUAN. By no means. But though there is much to be learnt from a cynical devil, I really cannot stand a sentimental one. Señor Commander: you know the way to the frontier of hell and heaven. Be good enough to direct me.

THE STATUE. Oh, the frontier is only the difference between two ways of looking at things. Any road will take you across it if you really want to get there.

DON JUAN. Good. (*Saluting* DOÑA ANA.) Señora: your servant.

ANA. But I am going with you.

DON JUAN. I can find my own way to heaven, Ana; but I cannot find yours. (*He vanishes.*)

ANA. How annoying!

THE STATUE (*calling after him*). Bon voyage, Juan! (*He wafts a final blast of his great rolling chords after him as a parting salute. A faint echo of the first ghostly melody comes back in acknowledgment.*) Ah! there he goes. (*Puffing a long breath out through his lips*) Whew! How he does talk! Theyll never stand it in heaven.

THE DEVIL (*gloomily*). His going is a political defeat. I cannot keep these Life Worshippers: they all go. This is the greatest loss I have had since that Dutch painter went — a fellow who would paint a hag of 70 with as much enjoyment as a Venus of 20.

THE STATUE. I remember: he came to heaven. Rembrandt.

THE DEVIL. Ay, Rembrandt. There is something unnatural about these fellows. Do not listen to their gospel, Señor Commander: it is dangerous. Beware of the pursuit of the Superhuman: it leads to an indiscriminate contempt for the Human. To a man, horses and dogs and cats are mere species, outside the moral world. Well, to the Superman, men and women are a mere species too, also outside the moral world. This Don Juan was kind to women and courteous to men as your daughter here was kind to her pet cats and dogs; but such kindness is a denial of the exclusively human character of the soul.

THE STATUE. And who the deuce is the Superman?

THE DEVIL. Oh, the latest fashion among the Life Force fanatics. Did you not meet in Heaven, among the new arrivals, that German Polish madman — what was his name? Nietzsche?

THE STATUE. Never heard of him.

THE DEVIL. Well, he came here first, before he recovered his wits. I had some hopes of him; but he was a confirmed Life Force worshipper. It was he who raked up the Superman, who is as old as Prometheus; and the twentieth century will run after this newest of the old crazes when it gets tired of the world, the flesh, and your humble servant.

THE STATUE. Superman is a good cry; and a good cry is half the battle. I should like to see this Nietzsche.

THE DEVIL. Unfortunately he met Wagner here, and had a quarrel with him.

THE STATUE. Quite right, too. Mozart for me!

THE DEVIL. Oh, it was not about music. Wagner once drifted into Life Force worship, and invented a Superman called Siegfried. But he came to his senses afterwards. So when they met here, Nietzsche denounced him as a renegade; and Wagner wrote a pamphlet to prove that Nietzsche was a Jew; and it ended in Nietzsche's going to heaven in a huff. And a good riddance too. And now, my friend, let us hasten to my palace and celebrate your arrival with a grand musical service.

THE STATUE. With pleasure: youre most kind.

THE DEVIL. This way, Commander. We go down the old trap. (*He places himself on the grave trap.*)

THE STATUE. Good. (*Reflectively.*) All the same, the Superman is a fine conception. There is something statuesque about it. (*He places himself on the grave trap beside the* DEVIL. *It begins to descend slowly. Red glow from the abyss.*) Ah, this reminds me of old times.

THE DEVIL. And me also.

ANA. Stop! (*The trap stops.*)

THE DEVIL. You, Señora, cannot come this way. You will have an apotheosis. But you will be at the palace before us.

ANA. That is not what I stopped you for. Tell me: where can I find the Superman?

THE DEVIL. He is not yet created, Señora.

THE STATUE. And never will be, probably. Let us proceed: the red fire will make me sneeze. (*They descend.*)

ANA. Not yet created! Then my work is not yet done. (*Crossing herself devoutly.*) I believe in the Life to Come. (*Crying to the universe.*) A father — a father for the Superman!

> She vanishes into the void; and again there is nothing: all existence seems suspended infinitely. Then, vaguely, there is a live human voice crying somewhere. One sees, with a shock, a mountain peak shewing faintly against a lighter background. The sky has returned from afar; and we suddenly remember where we were. The cry becomes distinct and urgent: it says Automobile, Automobile. *The complete reality comes back with a rush: in a moment it is full morning in the Sierra; and the* BRIGANDS *are scrambling to their feet and making for the road as the* GOATHERD *runs down from the hill, warning them of the approach of another motor.* TANNER *and* MENDOZA *rise amazedly and stare at one another with scattered wits.* STRAKER *sits up to yawn for a moment before he gets on his feet, making it a point of honor not to shew any undue interest in the excitement of the bandits.* MENDOZA *gives a quick look to see that his followers are attending to the alarm; then exchanges a private word with* TANNER.

MENDOZA. Did you dream?

TANNER. Damnably. Did you?

MENDOZA. Yes. I forget what. You were in it.

TANNER. So were you. Amazing!

MENDOZA. I warned you. (*A shot is heard from the road.*) Dolts! they will play with that gun. (*The* BRIGANDS *come running back scared.*) Who fired that shot? (*To* DUVAL.) Was it you?

DUVAL (*breathless*). I have not shoot. Dey shoot first.

ANARCHIST. I told you to begin by abolishing the State. Now we are all lost.

THE ROWDY SOCIAL-DEMOCRAT (*stampeding across the amphitheatre*). Run, everybody.

MENDOZA (*collaring him; throwing him on his back; and drawing a knife*). I stab the man who stirs. (*He blocks the way. The stampede is checked.*) What has happened?

THE SULKY SOCIAL-DEMOCRAT. A motor —

THE ANARCHIST. Three men —

DUVAL. Deux femmes —

MENDOZA. Three men and two women! Why have you not brought them here? Are you afraid of them?

THE ROWDY ONE (*getting up*). Thyve a hescort. Ow, de-ooh luts ook it, Mendowza.

THE SULKY ONE. Two armored cars full o soldiers at the ed o the valley.

ANARCHIST. The shot was fired in the air. It was a signal.

STRAKER *whistles his favorite air, which falls on the ears of the* BRIGANDS *like a funeral march.*

TANNER. It is not an escort, but an expedition to capture you. We were advised to wait for it; but I was in a hurry.

THE ROWDY ONE (*in an agony of apprehension*). And Ow my good Lord, ere we are, wytin for em! Luts tike to the mahntns.

MENDOZA. Idiot, what do you know about the mountains? Are you a Spaniard? You would be given up by the first shepherd you met. Besides, we are already within range of their rifles.

THE ROWDY ONE. Bat —

MENDOZA. Silence. Leave this to me. (*To* TANNER.) Comrade: you will not betray us.

STRAKER. Oo are you callin comrade?

MENDOZA. Last night the advantage was with me. The robber of the poor was at the mercy of the robber of the rich. You offered your hand: I took it.

TANNER. I bring no charge against you, comrade. We have spent a pleasant evening with you: that is all.

STRAKER. I gev my and to nobody, see?

MENDOZA (*turning on him impressively*). Young man, if I am tried, I shall plead guilty, and explain what drove me from England, home and duty. Do you wish to have the respectable name of Straker dragged through the mud of a Spanish criminal court? The police will search me. They will find

Man and Superman

Louisa's portrait. It will be published in the illustrated papers. You blench. It will be your doing, remember.

STRAKER (*with baffled rage*). I dont care about the court. It's avin our name mixed up with yours that I object to, you blackmailin swine, you.

MENDOZA. Language unworthy of Louisa's brother! But no matter: you are muzzled: that is enough for us. (*He turns to face his own men, who back uneasily across the amphitheatre towards the cave to take refuge behind him, as a fresh party, muffled for motoring, comes from the road in riotous spirits.* ANN, *who makes straight for* TANNER, *comes first; then* VIOLET, *helped over the rough ground by* HECTOR *holding her right hand and* RAMSDEN *her left.* MENDOZA *goes to his presidential block and seats himself calmly with his rank and file grouped behind him, and his Staff, consisting of* DUVAL *and the* ANARCHIST *on his right and the two* SOCIAL-DEMOCRATS *on his left, supporting him in flank.*)

ANN. It's Jack!

TANNER. Caught!

HECTOR. Why, certainly it is. I said it was you, Tanner. Weve just been stopped by a puncture: the road is full of nails.

VIOLET. What are you doing here with all these men?

ANN. Why did you leave us without a word of warning?

HECTOR. I wawnt that bunch of roses, Miss Whitefield. (*To* TANNER.) When we found you were gone, Miss Whitefield bet me a bunch of roses my car would not overtake yours before you reached Monte Carlo.

TANNER. But this is not the road to Monte Carlo.

HECTOR. No matter. Miss Whitefield tracked you at every stopping place: she is a regular Sherlock Holmes.

TANNER. The Life Force! I am lost.

OCTAVIUS (*bounding gaily down from the road into the amphitheatre, and coming between* TANNER *and* STRAKER). I am so glad you are safe, old chap. We were afraid you had been captured by brigands.

RAMSDEN (*who has been staring at* MENDOZA). I seem to remember the face of your friend here. (MENDOZA *rises politely and advances with a smile between* ANN *and* RAMSDEN.)

HECTOR. Why, so do I.

OCTAVIUS. I know you perfectly well, sir; but I cant think where I have met you.

MENDOZA (*to* VIOLET). Do you remember me, madam?

VIOLET. Oh, quite well; but I am so stupid about names.

MENDOZA. It was at the Savoy Hotel. (*To* HECTOR.) You, sir, used to come with this lady [*Violet*] to lunch. (*To* OCTAVIUS.) You, sir, often brought this lady [*Ann*] and her mother to dinner on your way to the Lyceum Theatre. (*To* RAMSDEN.) You, sir, used to come to supper, with (*dropping his voice to a confidential but perfectly audible whisper*) several different ladies.

RAMSDEN (*angrily*). Well, what is that to you, pray?

OCTAVIUS. Why, Violet, I thought you hardly knew one another before this trip, you and Malone!

VIOLET (*vexed*). I suppose this person was the manager.

MENDOZA. The waiter, madam. I have a grateful recollection of you all. I gathered from the bountiful way in which you treated me that you all enjoyed your visits very much.

VIOLET. What impertinence! (*She turns her back on him, and goes up the hill with* HECTOR.)

RAMSDEN. That will do, my friend. You do not expect these ladies to treat you as an acquaintance, I suppose, because you have waited on them at table.

MENDOZA. Pardon me: it was you who claimed my acquaintance. The ladies followed your example. However, this display of the unfortunate manners of your class closes the incident. For the future, you will please address me with the respect due to a stranger and fellow traveller. (*He turns haughtily away and resumes his presidential seat.*)

TANNER. There! I have found one man on my journey capable of reasonable conversation; and you all instinctively insult him. Even the New Man is as bad as any of you. Enry: you have behaved just like a miserable gentleman.

STRAKER. Gentleman! Not me.

RAMSDEN. Really, Tanner, this tone —

ANN. Dont mind him, Granny: you ought to know him by this time. (*She takes his arm and coaxes him away to the hill to join* VIOLET *and* HECTOR. OCTAVIUS *follows her, doglike.*)

VIOLET (*calling from the hill*). Here are the soldiers. They are getting out of their motors.

DUVAL (*panic stricken*). Oh, nom de Dieu!

THE ANARCHIST. Fools: the State is about to crush you because you spared it at the prompting of the political hangers-on of the bourgeoisie.

THE SULKY SOCIAL-DEMOCRAT (*argumentative to the last*). On the contrary, only by capturing the State machine —

THE ANARCHIST. It is going to capture you.

THE ROWDY SOCIAL DEMOCRAT (*his anguish culminating*). Ow, chack it. Wot are we ere for? Wot are we wytin for?

MENDOZA (*between his teeth*). Go on. Talk politics, you idiots: nothing sounds more respectable. Keep it up, I tell you.

> *The* SOLDIERS *line the road, commanding the amphitheatre with their rifles. The* BRIGANDS, *struggling with an overwhelming impulse to hide behind one another, look as unconcerned as they can.* MENDOZA *rises superbly, with undaunted front. The* OFFICER *in command steps down from the road into the amphitheatre; looks hard at the* BRIGANDS; *and then inquiringly at* TANNER.

THE OFFICER. Who are these men, Señor Ingles?

TANNER. My escort.

MENDOZA, *with a Mephistophelean smile, bows profoundly. An irrepressible grin runs from face to face among the* BRIGANDS. *They touch their hats, except the* ANARCHIST, *who defies the State with folded arms.*

ACT FOUR

The garden of a villa in Granada. Whoever wishes to know what it is like must go to Granada to see. One may prosaically specify a group of hills dotted with villas, the Alhambra on the top of one of the hills, and a considerable town in the valley, approached by dusty white roads in which the children, no matter what they are doing or thinking about, automatically whine for halfpence and reach out little clutching brown palms for them; but there is nothing in this description except the Alhambra, the begging, and the color of the roads, that does not fit Surrey as well as Spain. The difference is that the Surrey hills are comparatively small and ugly, and should properly be called the Surrey Protuberances; but these Spanish hills are of mountain stock: the amenity which conceals their size does not compromise their dignity.

This particular garden is on a hill opposite the Alhambra; and the villa is as expensive and pretentious as a villa must be if it is to be let furnished by the week to opulent American and English visitors. If we stand on the lawn at the foot of the garden and look uphill, our horizon is the stone balustrade of a flagged platform on the edge of infinite space at the top of the hill. Between us and this platform is a flower garden with a circular basin and fountain in the centre, surrounded by geometrical flower beds, gravel paths, and clipped yew trees in the genteelest order. The garden is higher than our lawn; so we reach it by a few steps in the middle of its embankment. The platform is higher again than the garden, from which we mount a couple more steps to look over the balustrade at a fine view of the town up the valley and of the hills that stretch away beyond it to where, in the remotest distance, they become mountains. On our left is the villa, accessible by steps from the left hand corner of the garden. Returning from the platform through the garden and down again to the lawn (a movement which leaves the villa behind us on our right) we find evidence of literary interests on the part of the tenants in the fact that there is no tennis net nor set of croquet hoops, but, on our left, a little iron garden table with books on it, mostly yellow-backed, and a chair beside it. A chair on the right has also a couple of open books upon it. There are no newspapers, a circumstance which, with the absence of games, might lead an intelligent spectator to the most far reaching conclusions as to the sort of people who live in the villa. Such speculations are checked, however, on this delightfully fine afternoon, by the appearance at a little gate in a paling on our left, of HENRY STRAKER *in his professional costume. He opens the gate for an elderly gentleman, and follows him on to the lawn.*

This elderly gentleman defies the Spanish sun in a black frock coat, tall silk hat, trousers in which narrow stripes of dark grey and lilac blend into a highly respectable color, and a black necktie tied into a bow over spotless linen. Probably therefore a man whose social position needs constant and scrupulous affirmation without regard to climate: one who would dress thus for the middle of the Sahara or the top of Mont Blanc. And since he has not the stamp of the class which accepts as its life-mission the advertising and maintenance of first rate tailoring and millinery, he looks vulgar in his finery, though in a working dress of any kind he would look dignified enough. He is a bullet cheeked man with a red complexion, stubbly hair, smallish eyes, a hard mouth that folds down at the corners, and a dogged chin. The looseness of skin that comes with age has attacked his throat and the laps of his cheeks; but he is still hard as an apple above the mouth; so that the upper half of his face looks younger than the lower. He has the self-confidence of one who has made money, and something of the truculence of one who has made it in a brutalizing struggle, his civility having under it a perceptible menace that he has other methods in reserve if necessary. Withal, a man to be rather pitied when he is not to be feared; for there is something pathetic about him at times, as if the huge commercial machine which has worked him into his frock coat had allowed him very little of his own way and left his affections hungry and baffled. At the first word that falls from him it is clear that he is an Irishman whose native intonation has clung to him through many changes of place and rank. One can only guess that the original material of his speech was perhaps the surly Kerry brogue; but the degradation of speech that occurs in London, Glasgow, Dublin and big cities generally has been at work on it so long that nobody but an arrant cockney would dream of calling it a brogue now; for its music is almost gone, though its surliness is still perceptible. STRAKER, *being a very obvious cockney, inspires him with implacable contempt, as a stupid Englishman who cannot even speak his own language properly.* STRAKER, *on the other hand, regards the old gentleman's accent as a joke thoughtfully provided by Providence expressly for the amusement of the British race, and treats him normally with the indulgence due to an inferior and unlucky species, but occasionally with indignant alarm when the old gentleman shews signs of intending his Irish nonsense to be taken seriously.*

STRAKER. I'll go tell the young lady. She said youd prefer to stay here. (*He turns to go up through the garden to the villa.*)

THE IRISHMAN (*who has been looking round him with lively curiosity*). The young lady? Thats Miss Violet, eh?

STRAKER (*stopping on the steps with sudden suspicion*). Well, you know, dont you?

THE IRISHMAN. Do I?

STRAKER (*his temper rising*). Well, do you or dont you?

THE IRISHMAN. What business is that of yours?

STRAKER,*now highly indignant, comes back from the steps and confronts the visitor.*

STRAKER. I'll tell you what business it is of mine. Miss Robinson —

THE IRISHMAN (*interrupting*). Oh, her name is Robinson, is it? Thank you.

STRAKER. Why, you dont know even her name?

THE IRISHMAN. Yes I do, now that youve told me.

STRAKER (*after a moment of stupefaction at the old man's readiness in repartee*). Look here: what do you mean by gittin into my car and lettin me bring you here if youre not the person I took that note to?

THE IRISHMAN. Who else did you take it to, pray?

STRAKER. I took it to Mr. Ector Malone, at Miss Robinson's request, see? Miss Robinson is not my principal: I took it to oblige her. I know Mr. Malone; and he aint you, not by a long chalk. At the hotel they told me that your name is Ector Malone —

MALONE. Hector Malone.

STRAKER (*with calm superiority*). Hector in your own country: thats what comes o livin in provincial places like Ireland and America. Over here youre Ector: if you avnt noticed it before you soon will.

The growing strain of the conversation is here relieved by VIOLET,*who has sallied from the villa and through the garden to the steps, which she now descends, coming very opportunely between* MALONE *and* STRAKER.

VIOLET (*to* STRAKER). Did you take my message?

STRAKER. Yes, miss. I took it to the hotel and sent it up, expecting to see young Mr. Malone. Then out walks this gent, and says it's all right and he'll come with me. So as the hotel people said he was Mr. Ector Malone, I fetched him. And now he goes back on what he said. But if he isnt the gentleman you meant, say the word: it's easy enough to fetch him back again.

MALONE. I should esteem it a great favor if I might have a short conversation with you, madam. I am Hector's father, as this bright Britisher would have guessed in the course of another hour or so.

STRAKER (*coolly defiant*). No, not in another year or so. When weve ad you as long to polish up as weve ad im, perhaps youll begin to look a little bit up to is mark. At present you fall a long way short. Youve got too many aitches, for one thing. (*To* VIOLET, *amiably.*) All right, Miss: you want to talk to him: I shant intrude. (*He nods affably to* MALONE *and goes out through the little gate in the paling.*)

VIOLET (*very civilly*). I am so sorry, Mr. Malone, if that man has been rude to you. But what can we do? He is our chauffeur.

MALONE. Your hwat?

VIOLET. The driver of our automobile. He can drive a motor car at seventy miles an hour, and mend it when it breaks down. We are dependent on our motor cars; and our motor cars are dependent on him; so of course we are dependent on him.

MALONE. Ive noticed, madam, that every thousand dollars an Englishman gets seems to add one to the number of people he's dependent on. However, you neednt apologize for your man: I made him talk on purpose. By doing so I learnt that youre staying here in Grannida with a party of English, including my son Hector.

VIOLET (*conversationally*). Yes. We intended to go to Nice; but we had to follow a rather eccentric member of our party who started first and came here. Wont you sit down? (*She clears the nearest chair of the two books on it.*)

MALONE (*impressed by this attention*). Thank you. (*He sits down, examining her curiously as she goes to the iron table to put down the books. When she turns to him again, he says*) Miss Robinson, I believe?

VIOLET (*sitting down*). Yes.

MALONE (*taking a letter from his pocket*). Your note to Hector runs as follows. (VIOLET *is unable to repress a start. He pauses quietly to take out and put on his spectacles, which have gold rims.*) "Dearest: they have all gone to the Alhambra for the afternoon. I have shammed headache and have the garden all to myself. Jump into Jack's motor: Straker will rattle you here in a jiffy. Quick, quick, quick. Your loving Violet." (*He looks at her; but by this time she has recovered herself, and meets his spectacles with perfect composure. He continues slowly.*) Now I dont know on hwat terms young people associate in English society; but in America that note would be considered to imply a very considerable degree of affectionate intimacy between the parties.

VIOLET. Yes: I know your son very well, Mr. Malone. Have you any objection?

MALONE (*somewhat taken aback*). No, no objection exactly. Provided it is understood that my son is altogether dependent on me, and that I have to be consulted in any important step he may propose to take.

VIOLET. I am sure you would not be unreasonable with him, Mr. Malone.

MALONE. I hope not, Miss Robinson; but at your age you might think many things unreasonable that dont seem so to me.

VIOLET (*with a little shrug*). Oh well, I suppose theres no use our playing at cross purposes, Mr. Malone. Hector wants to marry me.

MALONE. I inferred from your note that he might. Well, Miss Robinson, he is his own master; but if he marries you he shall not have a rap from me. (*He takes off his spectacles and pockets them with the note.*)

VIOLET (*with some severity*). That is not very complimentary to me, Mr. Malone.

MALONE. I say nothing against you, Miss Robinson: I daresay you are an amiable and excellent young lady. But I have other views for Hector.

VIOLET. Hector may not have other views for himself, Mr. Malone.

MALONE. Possibly not. Then he does without me: thats all. I daresay you are prepared for that. When a young lady writes to a young man to come to her quick, quick, quick, money seems nothing and love seems everything.

VIOLET (*sharply*). I beg your pardon, Mr. Malone: I do not think anything so foolish. Hector must have money.

MALONE (*staggered*). Oh, very well, very well. No doubt he can work for it.

VIOLET. What is the use of having money if you have to work for it? (*She rises impatiently.*) It's all nonsense, Mr. Malone: you *must* enable your son to keep up his position. It is his right.

MALONE (*grimly*). I should not advise you to marry him on the strength of that right, Miss Robinson.

> VIOLET, *who has almost lost her temper, controls herself with an effort; unclenches her fingers; and resumes her seat with studied tranquillity and reasonableness.*

VIOLET. What objection have you to me, pray? My social position is as good as Hector's, to say the least. He admits it.

MALONE (*shrewdly*). You tell him so from time to time, eh? Hector's social position in England, Miss Robinson, is just what I choose to buy for him. I have made him a fair offer. Let him pick out the most historic house, castle or abbey that England contains. The day that he tells me he wants it for a wife worthy of its traditions, I buy it for him, and give him the means of keeping it up.

VIOLET. What do you mean by a wife worthy of its traditions? Cannot any well bred woman keep such a house for him?

MALONE. No: she must be born to it.

VIOLET. Hector was not born to it, was he?

MALONE. His granmother was a barefooted Irish girl that nursed me by a turf fire. Let him marry another such, and I will not stint her marriage portion. Let him raise himself socially with my money or raise somebody else: so long as there is a social profit somewhere, I'll regard my expenditure as justified. But there must be a profit for someone. A marriage with you would leave things just where they are.

VIOLET. Many of my relations would object very much to my marrying the grandson of a common woman, Mr. Malone. That may be prejudice; but so is your desire to have him marry a title prejudice.

MALONE (*rising, and approaching her with scrutiny in which there is a good deal of reluctant respect*). You seem a pretty straightforward downright sort of a young woman.

VIOLET. I do not see why I should be made miserably poor because I cannot make profits for you. Why do you want to make Hector unhappy?

MALONE. He will get over it all right enough. Men thrive better on disappointments in love than on disappointments in money. I daresay you think that sordid; but I know what I'm talking about. My father died of starvation in Ireland in the black 47. Maybe youve heard of it.

VIOLET. The Famine?

MALONE (*with smouldering passion*). No, the starvation. When a country is full o food, and exporting it, there can be no famine. Me father was starved dead; and I was starved out to America in me mother's arms. English rule drove me and mine out of Ireland. Well, you can keep Ireland. I and me like are coming back to buy England; and we'll buy the best of it. I want no middle class properties and no middle class women for Hector. Thats straightforward, isnt it, like yourself?

VIOLET (*icily pitying his sentimentality*). Really, Mr. Malone, I am astonished to hear a man of your age and good sense talking in that romantic way. Do you suppose English noblemen will sell their places to you for the asking?

MALONE. I have the refusal of two of the oldest family mansions in England. One historic owner cant afford to keep all the rooms dusted: the other cant afford the death duties. What do you say now?

VIOLET. Of course it is very scandalous; but surely you know that the Government will sooner or later put a stop to all these Socialistic attacks on property.

MALONE (*grinning*). D'y' think theyll be able to get that done before I buy the house — or rather the abbey? Theyre both abbeys.

VIOLET (*putting that aside rather impatiently*). Oh, well, let us talk sense, Mr. Malone. You must feel that we havnt been talking sense so far.

MALONE. I cant say I do. I mean all I say.

VIOLET. Then you dont know Hector as I do. He is romantic and faddy — he gets it from you, I fancy — and he wants a certain sort of wife to take care of him. Not a faddy sort of person, you know.

MALONE. Somebody like you, perhaps?

VIOLET (*quietly*). Well, yes. But you cannot very well ask me to undertake this with absolutely no means of keeping up his position.

MALONE (*alarmed*). Stop a bit, stop a bit. Where are we getting to? I'm not aware that I'm asking you to undertake anything.

VIOLET. Of course, Mr. Malone, you can make it very difficult for me to speak to you if you choose to misunderstand me.

MALONE (*half bewildered*). I dont wish to take any unfair advantage; but we seem to have got off the straight track somehow.

STRAKER, *with the air of a man who has been making haste, opens the little gate, and admits* HECTOR, *who, snorting with indignation, comes upon the lawn, and is making for his father when* VIOLET, *greatly dismayed, springs up and intercepts him.* STRAKER *does not wait; at least he does not remain visibly within earshot.*

VIOLET. Oh, how unlucky! Now please, Hector, say nothing. Go away until I have finished speaking to your father.

HECTOR (*inexorably*). No, Violet: I mean to have this thing out, right away. (*He puts her aside; passes her by; and faces his father, whose cheeks darken as his Irish blood begins to simmer.*) Dad: youve not played this hand straight.

MALONE. Hwat d'y'mean?

HECTOR. Youve opened a letter addressed to me. Youve impersonated me and stolen a march on this lady. Thats disawnerable.

MALONE (*threateningly*). Now you take care what youre saying, Hector. Take care, I tell you.

HECTOR. I have taken care. I am taking care. I'm taking care of my honor and my position in English society.

MALONE (*hotly*). Your position has been got by my money: do you know that?

HECTOR. Well, youve just spoiled it all by opening that letter. A letter from an English lady, not addressed to you — a cawnfidential letter! a dullicate letter! a private letter! opened by my father! Thats a sort of thing a man cant struggle against in England. The sooner we go back together the better. (*He appeals mutely to the heavens to witness the shame and anguish of two outcasts.*)

VIOLET (*snubbing him with an instinctive dislike for scene making*). Dont be unreasonable, Hector. It was quite natural for Mr. Malone to open my letter: his name was on the envelope.

MALONE. There! Youve no common sense, Hector. I thank you, Miss Robinson.

HECTOR. I thank you, too. It's very kind of you. My father knows no better.

MALONE (*furiously clenching his fists*). Hector —

HECTOR (*with undaunted moral force*). Oh, it's no use hectoring me. A private letter's a private letter, dad: you cant get over that.

MALONE (*raising his voice*). I wont be talked back to by you, d'y'hear?

VIOLET. Ssh! please, please. Here they all come.

Father and son, checked, glare mutely at one another as TANNER *comes in through the little gate with* RAMSDEN, *followed by* OCTAVIUS *and* ANN.

VIOLET. Back already!

TANNER. The Alhambra is not open this afternoon.

VIOLET. What a sell!

TANNER *passes on, and presently finds himself between* HECTOR *and a strange elder, both apparently on the verge of personal combat. He looks from one to the other for an explanation. They sulkily avoid his eye, and nurse their wrath in silence.*

RAMSDEN. Is it wise for you to be out in the sunshine with such a headache, Violet?

TANNER. Have you recovered too, Malone?

VIOLET. Oh, I forgot. We have not all met before. Mr. Malone: wont you introduce your father?

HECTOR (*with Roman firmness*). No, I will not. He is no father of mine.

MALONE (*very angry*). You disown your dad before your English friends, do you?

VIOLET. Oh, please dont make a scene.

ANN *and* OCTAVIUS, *lingering near the gate, exchange an astonished glance, and discreetly withdraw up the steps to the garden, where they can enjoy the disturbance without intruding. On their way to the steps* ANN *sends a little grimace of mute sympathy to* VIOLET, *who is standing with her back to the little table, looking on in helpless annoyance as her husband soars to higher and higher moral eminences without the least regard to the old man's millions.*

HECTOR. I'm very sorry, Miss Rawbnsn; but I'm contending for a principle. I am a son, and, I hope, a dutiful one; but before everything I'm a Mahn! ! ! And when dad treats my private letters as his own, and takes it on himself to say that I shant marry you if I am happy and fortunate enough to gain your consent, then I just snap my fingers and go my own way.

TANNER. Marry Violet!

RAMSDEN. Are you in your senses?

TANNER. Do you forget what we told you?

HECTOR (*recklessly*). I dont care what you told me.

RAMSDEN (*scandalized*). Tut tut , sir! Monstrous! (*He flings away towards the gate, his elbows quivering with indignation.*)

TANNER. Another madman! These men in love should be locked up. (*He gives* HECTOR *up as hopeless, and turns away towards the garden; but* MALONE, *taking offence in a new direction, follows him and compels him, by the aggressiveness of his tone, to stop.*)

MALONE. I dont understand this. Is Hector not good enough for this lady, pray?

TANNER. My dear sir, the lady is married already. Hector knows it; and yet he persists in his infatuation. Take him home and lock him up.

MALONE (*bitterly*). So this is the high-born social tone Ive spoilt be me ignorant, uncultivated behavior! Makin love to a married woman! (*He comes angrily between* HECTOR *and* VIOLET, *and almost bawls into* HECTOR's *left ear.*) Youve picked up that habit of the British aristocracy, have you?

HECTOR. Thats all right. Dont you trouble yourself about that. I'll answer for the morality of what I'm doing.

TANNER (*coming forward to* HECTOR's *right hand with flashing eyes*). Well said, Malone! You also see that mere marriage laws are not morality! I agree with you; but unfortunately Violet does not.

MALONE. I take leave to doubt that, sir. (*Turning on* VIOLET.) Let me tell you, Mrs. Robinson, or whatever your right name is, you had no right to send that letter to my son when you were the wife of another man.

HECTOR (*outraged*). This is the last straw. Dad: you have insulted my wife.

MALONE. Your wife!

TANNER. *You* the missing husband! Another moral impostor! (*He smites his brow, and collapses into* MALONE's *chair.*)

MALONE. Youve married without my consent!

RAMSDEN. You have deliberately humbugged us, sir!

HECTOR. Here: I have had just about enough of being badgered. Violet and I are married: thats the long and the short of it. Now what have you got to say — any of you?

MALONE. I know what Ive got to say. She's married a beggar.

HECTOR. No; she's married a Worker. (*His American pronunciation imparts an overwhelming intensity to this simple and unpopular word.*) I start to earn my own living this very afternoon.

MALONE (*sneering angrily*). Yes: youre very plucky now, because you got your remittance from me yesterday or this morning, I reckon. Waitl it's spent. You wont be so full of cheek then.

HECTOR (*producing a letter from his pocketbook*). Here it is. (*Thrusting it on his father.*) Now you just take your remittance and yourself out of my life. I'm done with remittances; and I'm done with you. I dont sell the privilege of insulting my wife for a thousand dollars.

MALONE (*deeply wounded and full of concern*). Hector: you dont know what poverty is.

HECTOR (*fervidly*). Well, I wawnt to know what it is. I wawnt'be a Mahn. Violet: you come along with me, to your own home: I'll see you through.

OCTAVIUS (*jumping down from the garden to the lawn and running to* HECTOR's *left hand*). I hope youll shake hands with me before you go, Hector. I admire and respect you more than I can say. (*He is affected almost to tears as they shake hands.*)

VIOLET (*also almost in tears, but of vexation*). Oh dont be an idiot, Tavy. Hector's about as fit to become a workman as you are.

TANNER (*rising from his chair on the other side of* HECTOR). Never fear: theres no question of his becoming a navvy, Mrs. Malone. (*To* HECTOR.) Theres really no difficulty about capital to start with. Treat me as a friend: draw on me.

OCTAVIUS (*impulsively*). Or on me.

MALONE (*with fierce jealousy*). Who wants your durty money? Who should he draw on but his own father? (TANNER *and* OCTAVIUS *recoil,* OCTAVIUS *rather hurt,* TANNER *consoled by the solution of the money difficulty.* VIOLET *looks up hopefully.*) Hector: dont be rash, my boy. I'm sorry for what I said: I never meant to insult Violet: I take it all back. She's just the wife you want: there!

HECTOR (*patting him on the shoulder*). Well, thats all right, dad. Say no more: we're friends again. Only, I take no money from anybody.

MALONE (*pleading abjectly*). Dont be hard on me, Hector. I'd rather you quarrelled and took the money than made friends and starved. You dont know what the world is: I do.

HECTOR. No, no, NO. Thats fixed: thats not going to change. (*He passes his father inexorably by, and goes to* VIOLET.) Come, Mrs. Malone: youve got to move to the hotel with me, and take your proper place before the world.

VIOLET. But I must go in, dear, and tell Davis to pack. Wont you go on and make them give you a room overlooking the garden for me? I'll join you in half an hour.

HECTOR. Very well. Youll dine with us, Dad, wont you?

MALONE (*eager to conciliate him*). Yes, yes.

HECTOR. See you all later. (*He waves his hand to* ANN, *who has now been joined by* TANNER, OCTAVIUS, *and* RAMSDEN *in the garden, and goes out through the little gate, leaving his father and* VIOLET *together on the lawn.*)

MALONE. Youll try to bring him to his senses, Violet: I know you will.

VIOLET. I had no idea he could be so headstrong. If he goes on like that, what can I do?

MALONE. Dont be discurridged: domestic pressure may be slow; but it's sure. Youll wear him down. Promise me you will.

VIOLET. I will do my best. Of course I think it's the greatest nonsense deliberately making us poor like that.

MALONE. Of course it is.

VIOLET (*after a moment's reflection*). You had better give me the remittance. He will want it for his hotel bill. I'll see whether I can induce him to accept it. Not now, of course, but presently.

MALONE (*eagerly*). Yes, yes, yes: thats just the thing. (*He hands her the thousand dollar bill, and adds cunningly.*) Y'understand that this is only a bachelor allowance.

VIOLET (*coolly*). Oh, quite. (*She takes it.*). Thank you. By the way, Mr. Malone, those two houses you mentioned — the abbeys.

MALONE. Yes?

VIOLET. Dont take one of them until Ive seen it. One never knows what may be wrong with these places.

MALONE. I wont. I'll do nothing without consulting you, never fear.

VIOLET (*politely, but without a ray of gratitude*). Thanks: that will be much the best way. (*She goes calmly back to the villa, escorted obsequiously by* MALONE *to the upper end of the garden.*)

TANNER (*drawing* RAMSDEN'S *attention to* MALONE'S *cringing attitude as he takes leave of* VIOLET). And that poor devil is a billionaire! one of the master spirits of the age! Led in a string like a pug dog by the first girl who takes the trouble to despise him. I wonder will it ever come to that with me. (*He comes down to the lawn.*)

RAMSDEN (*following him*). The sooner the better for you.

MALONE (*slapping his hands as he returns through the garden*). That'll be a grand woman for Hector. I wouldnt exchange her for ten duchesses. (*He descends to the lawn and comes between* TANNER *and* RAMSDEN.)

RAMSDEN (*very civil to the billionaire*). It's an unexpected pleasure to find you in this corner of the world, Mr. Malone. Have you come to buy up the Alhambra?

MALONE. Well, I dont say I mightnt. I think I could do better with it than the Spanish government. But thats not what I came about. To tell you the truth, about a month ago I overheard a deal between two men over a bundle of shares. They differed about the price: they were young and greedy, and didnt know that if the shares were worth what was bid for them they must be worth what was asked, the margin being too small to be of any account, you see. To amuse meself, I cut in and bought the shares. Well, to this day I havnt found out what the business is. The office is in this town; and the name is Mendoza, Limited. Now whether Mendoza's a mine, or a steamboat line, or a bank, or a patent article —

TANNER. He's a man. I know him: his principles are thoroughly commercial. Let us take you round the town in our motor, Mr. Malone, and call on him on the way.

MALONE. If youll be so kind, yes. And may I ask who —

TANNER. Mr. Roebuck Ramsden, a very old friend of your daughter-in-law.

MALONE. Happy to meet you, Mr. Ramsden.

RAMSDEN. Thank you. Mr. Tanner is also one of our circle.

MALONE. Glad to know you also, Mr. Tanner.

TANNER. Thanks. (MALONE *and* RAMSDEN *go out very amicably through the little gate.* TANNER *calls to* OCTAVIUS, *who is wandering in the garden with* ANN.) Tavy! (TAVY *comes to the steps,* TANNER *whispers loudly to him.*) Violet's father-in-law is a financier of brigands. (TANNER *hurries away to overtake* MALONE *and* RAMSDEN. ANN *strolls to the steps with an idle impulse to torment* OCTAVIUS.)

ANN. Wont you go with them, Tavy?

OCTAVIUS (*tears suddenly flushing his eyes*). You cut me to the heart, Ann, by wanting me to go. (*He comes down on the lawn to hide his face from her. She follows him caressingly.*)

ANN. Poor Ricky Ticky Tavy! Poor heart!

OCTAVIUS. It belongs to you, Ann. Forgive me: I must speak of it. I love you. You know I love you.

ANN. Whats the good, Tavy? You know that my mother is determined that I shall marry Jack.

OCTAVIUS (*amazed*). Jack!

ANN. It seems absurd, doesnt it?

OCTAVIUS (*with growing resentment*). Do you mean to say that Jack has been playing with me all this time? That he has been urging me not to marry you because he intends to marry you himself?

ANN (*alarmed*). No, no: you mustnt lead him to believe that I said that: I dont for a moment think that Jack knows his own mind. But it's clear from my father's will that he wished me to marry Jack. And my mother is set on it.

OCTAVIUS. But you are not bound to sacrifice yourself always to the wishes of your parents.

ANN. My father loved me. My mother loves me. Surely their wishes are a better guide than my own selfishness.

OCTAVIUS. Oh, I know how unselfish you are, Ann. But believe me — though I know I am speaking in my own interest — there is another side to this question. Is it fair to Jack to marry him if you do not love him? Is it fair to destroy my happiness as well as your own if you can bring yourself to love me?

ANN (*looking at him with a faint impulse of pity*). Tavy, my dear, you are a nice creature — a good boy.

OCTAVIUS (*humiliated*). Is that all?

ANN (*mischievously in spite of her pity*). Thats a great deal, I assure you. You would always worship the ground I trod on, wouldnt you?

OCTAVIUS. I do. It sounds ridiculous; but it's no exaggeration. I do; and I always shall.

ANN. Always is a long word, Tavy. You see, I shall have to live up always to your idea of my divinity; and I dont think I could do that if we were married. But if I marry Jack, youll never be disillusioned — at least not until I grow too old.

OCTAVIUS. I too shall grow old, Ann. And when I am eighty, one white hair of the woman I love will make me tremble more than the thickest gold tress from the most beautiful young head.

ANN (*quite touched*). Oh, thats poetry, Tavy, real poetry. It gives me that strange sudden sense of an echo from a former existence which always seems to me such a striking proof that we have immortal souls.

OCTAVIUS. Do you believe that it is true?

ANN. Tavy: if it is to come true, you must lose me as well as love me.

OCTAVIUS. Oh! (*He hastily sits down at the little table and covers his face with his hands.*)

ANN (*with conviction*). Tavy: I wouldnt for worlds destroy your illusions. I can neither take you nor let you go. I can see exactly what will suit you. You must be a sentimental old bachelor for my sake.

OCTAVIUS (*desperately*). Ann: I'll kill myself.

ANN. Oh no, you wont: that wouldnt be kind. You wont have a bad time. You will be very nice to women; and you will go a good deal to the opera. A broken heart is a very pleasant complaint for a man in London if he has a comfortable income.

OCTAVIUS (*considerably cooled, but believing that he is only recovering his self-control*). I know you mean to be kind, Ann. Jack has persuaded you that cynicism is a good tonic for me. (*He rises with quiet dignity.*)

ANN (*studying him slyly*). You see, I'm disillusionizing you already. Thats what I dread.

OCTAVIUS. You do not dread disillusionizing Jack.

ANN (*her face lighting up with mischievous ecstasy — whispering*). I cant:

Man and Superman

he has no illusions about me. I shall surprise Jack the other way. Getting over an unfavorable impression is ever so much easier than living up to an ideal. Oh, I shall enrapture Jack sometimes!

OCTAVIUS (*resuming the calm phase of despair, and beginning to enjoy his broken heart and delicate attitude without knowing it*). I dont doubt that. You will enrapture him always. And he — the fool! — thinks you would make him wretched.

ANN. Yes: thats the difficulty, so far.

OCTAVIUS (*heroically*). Shall I tell him that you love him?

ANN (*quickly*). Oh no: he'd run away again.

OCTAVIUS (*shocked*). Ann: would you marry an unwilling man?

ANN. What a queer creature you are, Tavy! Theres no such thing as a willing man when you really go for him. (*She laughs naughtily.*) I'm shocking you, I suppose. But you know you are really getting a sort of satisfaction already in being out of danger yourself.

OCTAVIUS (*startled*). Satisfaction! (*Reproachfully.*) You say that to me!

ANN. Well, if it were really agony, would you ask for more of it?

OCTAVIUS. Have I asked for more of it?

ANN. You have offered to tell Jack that I love him. Thats self-sacrifice, I suppose; but there must be some satisfaction in it. Perhaps it's because youre a poet. You are like the bird that presses its breast against the sharp thorn to make itself sing.

OCTAVIUS. It's quite simple. I love you; and I want you to be happy. You dont love me; so I cant make you happy myself; but I can help another man to do it.

ANN. Yes: it seems quite simple. But I doubt if we ever know why we do things. The only really simple thing is to go straight for what you want and grab it. I suppose I dont love you, Tavy; but sometimes I feel as if I should like to make a man of you somehow. You are very foolish about women.

OCTAVIUS (*almost coldly*). I am content to be what I am in that respect.

ANN. Then you must keep away from them, and only dream about them. I wouldnt marry you for worlds, Tavy.

OCTAVIUS. I have no hope, Ann: I accept my ill luck. But I dont think you quite know how much it hurts.

ANN. You are so softhearted! It's queer that you should be so different from Violet. Violet's as hard as nails.

OCTAVIUS. Oh no. I am sure Violet is thoroughly womanly at heart.

ANN (*with some impatience*). Why do you say that? Is it unwomanly to be thoughtful and businesslike and sensible? Do you want Violet to be an idiot — or something worse, like me?

OCTAVIUS. Something worse — like you! What do you mean, Ann?

ANN. Oh well, I dont mean that, of course. But I have a great respect for Violet. She gets her own way always.

OCTAVIUS (*sighing*). So do you.

ANN. Yes; but somehow she gets it without coaxing — without having to make people sentimental about her.

OCTAVIUS (*with brotherly callousness*). Nobody could get very sentimental about Violet, I think, pretty as she is.

ANN. Oh yes they could, if she made them.

OCTAVIUS. But surely no really nice woman would deliberately practise on men's instincts in that way.

ANN (*throwing up her hands*). Oh Tavy, Tavy, Ricky Ticky Tavy, heaven help the woman who marries you!

OCTAVIUS (*his passion reviving at the name*). Oh why, why, why do you say that? Dont torment me. I dont understand.

ANN. Suppose she were to tell fibs, and lay snares for men?

OCTAVIUS. Do you think I could marry such a woman — I, who have known and loved you?

ANN. Hm! Well, at all events, she wouldnt let you if she were wise. So thats settled. And now I cant talk any more. Say you forgive me, and that the subject is closed.

OCTAVIUS. I have nothing to forgive; and the subject is closed. And if the wound is open, at least you shall never see it bleed.

ANN. Poetic to the last, Tavy. Goodbye, dear. (*She pats his cheek; has an impulse to kiss him and then another impulse of distaste which prevents her; finally runs away through the garden and into the villa.*)

> OCTAVIUS *again takes refuge at the table, bowing his head on his arms and sobbing softly.* MRS. WHITEFIELD, *who has been pottering round the Granada shops, and has a net full of little parcels in her hand, comes in through the gate and sees him.*

MRS. WHITEFIELD (*running to him and lifting his head*). Whats the matter, Tavy? Are you ill?

OCTAVIUS. No, nothing, nothing.

MRS. WHITEFIELD (*still holding his head, anxiously*). But youre crying. Is it about Violet's marriage?

OCTAVIUS. No, no. Who told you about Violet?

MRS. WHITEFIELD (*restoring the head to its owner*). I met Roebuck and that awful old Irishman. Are you sure youre not ill? Whats the matter?

OCTAVIUS (*affectionately*). It's nothing — only a man's broken heart. Doesnt that sound ridiculous?

MRS. WHITEFIELD. But what is it all about? Has Ann been doing anything to you?

OCTAVIUS. It's not Ann's fault. And dont think for a moment that I blame you.

MRS. WHITEFIELD (*startled*). For what?

OCTAVIUS (*pressing her hand consolingly*). For nothing. I said I didnt blame you.

MRS. WHITEFIELD. But I havnt done anything. Whats the matter?

OCTAVIUS (*smiling sadly*). Cant you guess? I daresay you are right to prefer Jack to me as a husband for Ann; but I love Ann; and it hurts rather. (*He rises and moves away from her towards the middle of the lawn.*)

MRS. WHITEFIELD (*following him hastily*). Does Ann say that I want her to marry Jack?

OCTAVIUS. Yes: she has told me.

MRS. WHITEFIELD (*thoughtfully*). Then I'm very sorry for you, Tavy. It's only her way of saying *she* wants to marry Jack. Little she cares what *I* say or what *I* want!

OCTAVIUS. But she would not say it unless she believed it. Surely you dont suspect Ann of — of *deceit*!!

MRS. WHITEFIELD. Well, never mind, Tavy. I dont know which is best for a young man: to know too little, like you, or too much, like Jack.

TANNER *returns*.

TANNER. Well, Ive disposed of old Malone. Ive introduced him to Mendoza, Limited; and left the two brigands together to talk it out. Hullo, Tavy! anything wrong?

OCTAVIUS. I must go wash my face, I see. (*To* MRS. WHITEFIELD.) Tell him what you wish. (*To* TANNER). You may take it from me, Jack, that Ann approves of it.

TANNER (*puzzled by his manner*). Approves of what?

OCTAVIUS. Of what Mrs. Whitefield wishes. (*He goes his way with sad dignity to the villa.*)

TANNER (*to* MRS. WHITEFIELD). This is very mysterious. What is it you wish? It shall be done, whatever it is.

MRS. WHITEFIELD (*with snivelling gratitude*). Thank you, Jack. (*She sits down.* TANNER *brings the other chair from the table and sits close to her with his elbows on his knees, giving her his whole attention.*) I dont know why it is that other people's children are so nice to me, and that my own have so little consideration for me. It's no wonder I dont seem able to care for Ann and Rhoda as I do for you and Tavy and Violet. It's a very queer world. It used to be so straightforward and simple; and now nobody seems to think and feel as they ought. Nothing has been right since that speech that Professor Tyndall made at Belfast.

TANNER. Yes: life is more complicated than we used to think. But what am I to do for you?

MRS. WHITEFIELD. Thats just what I want to tell you. Of course youll marry Ann whether I like it or not —

TANNER (*starting*). It seems to me that I shall presently be married to Ann whether I like it myself or not.

MRS. WHITEFIELD (*peacefully*). Oh, very likely you will: you know what she is when she has set her mind on anything. But dont put it on me: thats all I ask. Tavy has just let out that she's been saying that I am making her marry you; and the poor boy is breaking his heart about it; for he is in love with her himself, though what he sees in her so wonderful, goodness knows: I dont. It's no use telling Tavy that Ann puts things into people's heads by telling them that I want them when the thought of them never crossed my mind. It only sets Tavy against me. But you know better than that. So if you marry her, dont put the blame on me.

TANNER (*emphatically*). I havnt the slightest intention of marrying her.

MRS. WHITEFIELD (*slyly*). She'd suit you better than Tavy. She'd meet her match in you, Jack. I'd like to see her meet her match.

TANNER. No man is a match for a woman, except with a poker and a pair of hobnailed boots. Not always even then. Anyhow, I cant take the poker to her. I should be a mere slave.

MRS. WHITEFIELD. No: she's afraid of you. At all events, you would tell her the truth about herself. She wouldnt be able to slip out of it as she does with me.

TANNER. Everybody would call me a brute if I told Ann the truth about herself in terms of her own moral code. To begin with, Ann says things that are not strictly true.

MRS. WHITEFIELD. I'm glad somebody sees she is not an angel.

TANNER. In short — to put it as a husband would put it when exasperated to the point of speaking out — she is a liar. And since she has plunged Tavy head over ears in love with her without any intenton of marrying him, she is a coquette, according to the standard definition of a coquette as a woman who rouses passions she has no intention of gratifying. And as she has now reduced you to the point of being willing to sacrifice me at the altar for the mere satisfaction of getting me to call her a liar to her face, I may conclude that she is a bully as well. She cant bully men as she bullies women; so she habitually and unscrupulously uses her personal fascination to make men give her whatever she wants. That makes her almost something for which I know no polite name.

MRS. WHITEFIELD (*in mild expostulation*). Well, you cant expect perfection, Jack.

TANNER. I dont. But what annoys me is that Ann does. I know perfectly well that all this about her being a liar and a bully and a coquette and so forth is a trumped-up moral indictment which might be brought against anybody. We all lie; we all bully as much as we dare; we all bid for admiration without the least intention of earning it; we all get as much rent as we can out of our powers of fascination. If Ann would admit this I shouldnt quarrel with her. But she wont. If she has children she'll take advantage of their telling lies to amuse herself by whacking them. If another woman makes eyes at me, she'll refuse to know a coquette. She will do just what she likes herself whilst insisting on everybody else doing what the conventional code prescribes. In short, I can stand everything except her confounded hypocrisy. Thats what beats me.

Man and Superman

MRS. WHITEFIELD (*carried away by the relief of hearing her own opinion so eloquently expressed*). Oh, she is a hypocrite. She is: she is. Isnt she?

TANNER. Then why do you want to marry me to her?

MRS. WHITEFIELD (*querulously*). There now! put it on me, of course. I never thought of it until Tavy told me she said I did. But, you know, I'm very fond of Tavy: he's a sort of son to me; and I dont want him to be trampled on and made wretched.

TANNER. Whereas I dont matter, I suppose.

MRS. WHITEFIELD. Oh, you are different, somehow: you are able to take care of yourself. Youd serve her out. And anyhow, she must marry somebody.

TANNER. Aha! there speaks the life instinct. You detest her; but you feel that you must get her married.

MRS. WHITEFIELD (*rising, shocked*). Do you mean that I detest my own daughter! Surely you dont believe me to be so wicked and unnatural as that, merely because I see her faults.

TANNER (*cynically*). You love her, then?

MRS. WHITEFIELD. Why, of course I do. What queer things you say, Jack! We cant help loving our own blood relations.

TANNER. Well, perhaps it saves unpleasantness to say so. But for my part, I suspect that the tables of consanguinity have a natural basis in a natural repugnance. (*He rises.*)

MRS. WHITEFIEELD. You shouldnt say things like that, Jack. I hope you wont tell Ann that I have been speaking to you. I only wanted to set myself right with you and Tavy. I couldnt sit mumchance and have everything put on me.

TANNER (*politely*). Quite so.

MRS. WHITEFIELD (*dissatisfied*). And now Ive only made matters worse. Tavy's angry with me because I dont worship Ann. And when it's been put into my head that Ann ought to marry you, what can I say except that it would serve her right?

TANNER. Thank you.

MRS. WHITEFIELD. Now dont be silly and twist what I say into something I dont mean. I ought to have fair play —

ANN *comes from the villa, followed presently by* VIOLET, *who is dressed for driving.*

ANN (*coming to her mother's right hand with threatening suavity*). Well, mamma darling, you seem to be having a delightful chat with Jack. We can hear you all over the place.

MRS. WHITEFIELD (*appalled*). Have you overheard —

TANNER. Never fear: Ann is only — well, we were discussing that habit of hers just now. She hasnt heard a word.

MRS. WHITEFIELD (*stoutly*). I dont care whether she has or not: I have a right to say what I please.

VIOLET (*arriving on the lawn and coming between* MRS. WHITEFIELD *and* TANNER). Ive come to say goodbye. I'm off for my honeymoon.

MRS. WHITEFIELD (*crying*). Oh dont say that, Violet. And no wedding, no breakfast, no clothes, nor anything.

VIOLET (*petting her*). It wont be for long.

MRS. WHITEFIELD. Dont let him take you to America. Promise me that you wont.

VIOLET (*very decidedly*). I should think not, indeed. Dont cry, dear: I'm only going to the hotel.

MRS. WHITEFIELD. But going in that dress, with your luggage, makes one realize — (*She chokes, and then breaks out again.*) How I wish you were my daughter, Violet!

VIOLET (*soothing her*). There, there: so I am. Ann will be jealous.

MRS. WHITEFIELD. Ann doesnt care a bit for me.

ANN. Fie, mother! Come, now: you mustnt cry any more: you know Violet doesnt like it. (MRS. WHITEFIELD *dries her eyes, and subsides.*)

VIOLET. Goodbye, Jack.

TANNER. Goodbye, Violet.

VIOLET. The sooner you get married too, the better. You will be much less misunderstood.

TANNER (*restively*). I quite expect to get married in the course of the afternoon. You all seem to have set your minds on it.

VIOLET. You might do worse. (*To* MRS. WHITEFIELD: *putting her arm round her.*) Let me take you to the hotel with me: the drive will do you good. Come in and get a wrap. (*She takes her towards the villa.*)

MRS. WHITEFIELD (*as they go up through the garden*). I dont know what I shall do when you are gone, with no one but Ann in the house; and she always occupied with the men! It's not to be expected that your husband will care to be bothered with an old woman like me. Oh, you neednt tell me: politeness is all very well; but I know what people think — (*She talks herself and* VIOLET *out of sight and hearing.*)

> ANN, *alone with* TANNER, *watches him and waits. He makes an irresolute movement towards the gate; but some magnetism in her draws him to her, a broken man.*

ANN. Violet is quite right. You ought to get marired.

TANNER (*explosively*). Ann: I will not marry you. Do you hear? I wont, wont, wont, wont, WONT marry you.

ANN (*placidly*). Well, nobody axd you, sir she said, sir she said, sir she said. So thats settled.

TANNER. Yes, nobody has asked me; but everybody treats the thing as settled. It's in the air. When we meet, the others go away on absurd pretexts to leave us alone together. Ramsden no longer scowls at me: his eye beams, as if he were already giving you away to me in church. Tavy refers me to your mother and gives me his blessing. Straker openly treats you as his future employer: it was he who first told me of it.

ANN. Was that why you ran away?

TANNER. Yes, only to be stopped by a lovesick brigand and run down like a truant schoolboy.

ANN. Well, if you dont want to be married, you neednt be. (*She turns away from him and sits down, much at her ease.*)

TANNER (*following her*). Does any man want to be hanged? Yet men let themselves be hanged without a struggle for life, though they could at least give the chaplain a black eye. We do the world's will, not our own. I have a frightful feeling that I shall let myself be married because it is the world's will that you should have a husband.

ANN. I daresay I shall, someday.

TANNER. But why me — me of all men? Marriage is to me apostasy, profanation of the sanctuary of my soul, violation of my manhood, sale of my birthright, shameful surrender, ignominious capitulation, acceptance of defeat. I shall decay like a thing that has served its purpose and is done with; I shall change from a man with a future to a man with a past; I shall see in the greasy eyes of all the other husbands their relief at the arrival of a new prisoner to share their ignominy. The young men will scorn me as one who has sold out: to the young women I, who have always been an enigma and a possibility, shall be merely somebody else's property — and damaged goods at that: a secondhand man at best.

ANN. Well, your wife can put on a cap and make herself ugly to keep you in countenance, like my grandmother.

TANNER. So that she may make her triumph more insolent by publicly throwing away the bait the moment the trap snaps on the victim!

ANN. After all, though, what difference would it make? Beauty is all very well at first sight; but who ever looks at it when it has been in the house three days? I thought our pictures very lovely when papa bought them; but I havnt looked at them for years. You never bother about my looks: you are too well used to me. I might be the umbrella stand.

TANNER. You lie, you vampire: you lie.

ANN. Flatterer. Why are you trying to fascinate me, Jack, if you dont want to marry me?

TANNER. The Life Force. I am in the grip of the Life Force.

ANN. I dont understand in the least: it sounds like the Life Guards.

TANNER. Why dont you marry Tavy? He is willing. Can you not be satisfied unless your prey struggles?

ANN (*turning to him as if to let him into a secret*). Tavy will never marry. Havnt you noticed that that sort of man never marries?

TANNER. What! a man who idolizes women! who sees nothing in nature but romantic scenery for love duets! Tavy, the chivalrous, the faithful, the tenderhearted and true! Tavy never marry! Why, he was born to be swept up by the first pair of blue eyes he meets in the street.

ANN. Yes, I know. All the same, Jack, men like that always live in comfortable bachelor lodgings with broken hearts, and are adored by their landladies, and never get married. Men like you always get married.

TANNER (*smiting his brow*). How frightfully, horribly true! It has been staring me in the face all my life; and I never saw it before.

ANN. Oh, it's the same with women. The poetic temperament's a very nice temperament, very amiable, very harmless and poetic, I daresay; but it's an old maid's temperament.

TANNER. Barren. The Life Force passes it by.

ANN. If thats what you mean by the life Force, yes.

TANNER. You dont care for Tavy?

ANN (*looking round carefully to make sure that* TAVY *is not within earshot*). No.

TANNER. And you do care for me?

ANN (*rising quietly and shaking her finger at him*). Now Jack! Behave yourself.

TANNER. Infamous, abandoned woman! Devil!

ANN. Boa-constrictor! Elephant!

TANNER. Hypocrite!

ANN (*softly*). I must be, for my future husband's sake.

TANNER. For mine! (*Correcting himself savagely*). I mean for his.

ANN (*ignoring the correction*). Yes, for yours. You had better marry what you call a hypocrite, Jack. Women who are not hypocrites go about in rational dress and are insulted and get into all sorts of hot water. And then their husbands get dragged in too, and live in continual dread of fresh complications. Wouldnt you prefer a wife you could depend on?

TANNER. No, a thousand times no: hot water is the revolutionist's element. You clean men as you clean milkpails, by scalding them.

ANN. Cold water has its uses too. It's healthy.

TANNER (*despairingly*). Oh, you are witty: at the supreme moment the Life Force endows you with every quality. Well, I too can be a hypocrite. Your father's will appointed me your guardian, not your suitor. I shall be faithful to my trust.

ANN (*in low siren tones*). He asked me who would I have as my guardian before he made that will. I chose you!

TANNER. The will is yours then! The trap was laid from the beginning.

ANN (*concentrating all her magic*). From the beginning — from our childhood — for both of us — by the Life Force.

TANNER. I will not marry you. I will not marry you.

ANN. Oh, you will, you will.

TANNER. I tell you, no, no, no.

ANN. I tell you, yes, yes, yes.

TANNER. No.

ANN (*coaxing — imploring — almost exhausted*). Yes. Before it is too late for repentance. Yes.

TANNER (*struck by the echo from the past*). When did all this happen to me before? Are we two dreaming?

ANN (*suddenly losing her courage, with an anguish that she does not conceal*). No. We are awake; and you have said no: that is all.

TANNER (*brutally*). Well?

ANN. Well, I made a mistake: you do not love me.

TANNER (*seizing her in his arms*). It is false: I love you. The Life Force enchants me: I have the whole world in my arms when I clasp you. But I am fighting for my freedom, for my honor, for my self, one and indivisible.

ANN. Your happiness will be worth them all.

TANNER. You would sell freedom and honor and self for happiness?

ANN. It will not be all happiness for me. Perhaps death.

TANNER (*groaning*). Oh, that clutch holds and hurts. What have you grasped in me? Is there a father's heart as well as a mother's?

ANN. Take care, Jack: if anyone comes while we are like this, you will have to marry me.

TANNER. If we two stood now on the edge of a precipice, I would hold you tight and jump.

ANN (*panting, failing more and more under the strain*). Jack: let me go. I have dared so frightfully — it is lasting longer than I thought. Let me go: I cant bear it.

TANNER. Nor I. Let it kill us.

ANN. Yes: I dont care. I am at the end of my forces. I dont care. I think I am going to faint.

> At this moment VIOLET *and* OCTAVIUS *come from the villa with* MRS. WHITEFIELD, *who is wrapped up for driving. Simultaneously* MALONE *and* RAMSDEN, *followed by* MENDOZA *and* STRAKER, *come in through the little gate in the paling.* TANNER *shamefacedly releases* ANN, *who raises her hand giddily to her forehead.*

MALONE. Take care. Something's the matter with the lady.

RAMSDEN. What does this mean?

VIOLET (*running between* ANN *and* TANNER). Are you ill?

ANN (*reeling, with a supreme effort*). I have promised to marry Jack. (*She swoons.* VIOLET *kneels by her and chafes her hand.* TANNER *runs round to her other hand, and tries to lift her head.* OCTAVIUS *goes to* VIOLET'S *assistance, but does not know what to do.* MRS. WHITEFIELD *hurries back into the villa.* OCTAVIUS, MALONE *and* RAMSDEN *run to* ANN *and crowd round her, stooping to assist.* STRAKER *coolly comes to* ANN'S *feet, and* MENDOZA *to her head, both upright and self-possessed.*)

STRAKER. Now then, ladies and gentlemen: she dont want a crowd round her: she wants air — all the air she can git. If you please, gents — (MALONE *and* RAMSDEN *allow him to drive them gently past* ANN *and up the lawn towards the garden, where* OCTAVIUS, *who has already become conscious of his uselessness, joins them.* STRAKER, *following them up, pauses for a moment to instruct* TANNER.) Dont lift er ed, Mr. Tanner: let it go flat so's the blood can run back into it.

MENDOZA. He is right, Mr. Tanner. Trust to the air of the Sierra. (*He withdraws delicately to the garden steps.*)

TANNER (*rising*). I yield to your superior knowledge of physiology, Henry. (*He withdraws to the corner of the lawn; and* OCTAVIUS *immediately hurries down to him.*)

TAVY (*aside to* TANNER, *grasping his hand*). Jack: be very happy.

TANNER (*aside to* TAVY). I never asked her. It is a trap for me. (*He goes up the lawn towards the garden.* OCTAVIUS *remains petrified.*)

MENDOZA (*intercepting* MRS. WHITEFIELD, *who comes from the villa with a glass of brandy*). What is this, madam? (*He takes it from her.*)

MRS. WHITEFIELD. A little brandy.

MENDOZA. The worst thing you could give her. Allow me. (*He swallows it.*) Trust to the air of the Sierra, madam.

For a moment the men all forget ANN *and stare at* MENDOZA.

ANN (*in* VIOLET'S *ear, clutching her round the neck*). Violet: did Jack say anything when I fainted?

VIOLET. No.

ANN. Ah! (*With a sigh of intense relief she relapses.*)

MRS. WHITEFIELD. Oh, she's fainted again.

They are about to rush back to her; but MENDOZA *stops them with a warning gesture.*

ANN (*supine*). No, I havnt. I'm quite happy.

TANNER (*suddenly walking determinedly to her, and snatching her hand from* VIOLET *to feel her pulse*). Why, her pulse is positively bounding. Come, get up. What nonsense! Up with you. (*He gets her up summarily.*)

ANN. Yes: I feel strong enough now. But you very nearly killed me, Jack, for all that.

MALONE. A rough wooer, eh? Theyre the best sort, Miss Whitefield. I congratulate Mr. Tanner; and I hope to meet you and him as frequent guests at the abbey.

ANN. Thank you. (*She goes past* MALONE *to* OCTAVIUS.) Ricky Ticky Tavy: congratulate me. (*Aside to him.*) I want to make you cry for the last time.

TAVY (*steadfastly*). No more tears. I am happy in your happiness. And I believe in you in spite of everything.

RAMSDEN (*coming between* MALONE *and* TANNER). You are a happy man, Jack Tanner. I envy you.

MENDOZA (*advancing between* VIOLET *and* TANNER). Sir: there are two tragedies in life. One is to lose your heart's desire. The other is to gain it. Mine and yours, sir.

TANNER. Mr. Mendoza: I have no heart's desires. Ramsden: it is very easy for you to call me a happy man: you are only a spectator. I am one of the principals; and I know better. Ann: stop tempting Tavy, and come back to me.

ANN (*complying*). You are absurd, Jack. (*She takes his proffered arm.*)

TANNER (*continuing*). I solemnly say that I am not a happy man. Ann looks happy; but she is only triumphant, successful, victorious. That is not happiness, but the price for which the strong sell their happiness. What we have both done this afternoon is to renounce happiness, renounce freedom, renounce tranquillity, above all, renounce the romantic possibilities of an unknown future, for the cares of a household and a family. I beg that no man may seize the occasion to get half drunk and utter imbecile speeches and coarse pleasantries at my expense. We propose to furnish our own house according to our own taste; and I hereby give notice that the seven or eight travelling clocks, the four or five dressing cases, the salad bowls, the carvers and fish slicers, the copies of Patmore's Angel In The House in extra morocco, and all the other articles you are preparing to heap upon us, will be instantly sold, and the proceeds devoted to circulating free copies of the Revolutionist's Handbook. The wedding will take place three days after our return to England, by special license, at the office of the district superintendent registrar, in the presence of my solicitor and his clerk, who, like his clients, will be in ordinary walking dress —

VIOLET (*with intense conviction*). You are a brute, Jack.

ANN (*looking at him with fond pride and caressing his arm*). Never mind her, dear. Go on talking.

TANNER. Talking!

Universal laughter.

THE REVOLUTIONIST'S HANDBOOK AND POCKET COMPANION

By John Tanner, M.I.R.C.
(*Member of the Idle Rich Class*).

PREFACE TO THE REVOLUTIONIST'S HANDBOOK

"No one can contemplate the present condition of the masses of the people without desiring something like a revolution for the better." *Sir Robert Giffen*. Essays in Finance, vol. ii. p. 393.

FOREWORD

A revolutionist is one who desires to discard the existing social order and try another.

The constitution of England is revolutionary. To a Russian or Anglo-Indian bureaucrat, a general election is as much a revolution as a referendum or plebiscite in which the people fight instead of voting. The French Revolution overthrew one set of rulers and substituted another with different interests and different views. That is what a general election enables the people to do in England every seven years if they choose. Revolution is therefore a national institution in England; and its advocacy by an Englishman needs no apology.

Every man is a revolutionist concerning the thing he understands. For example, every person who has mastered a profession is a sceptic concerning it, and consequently a revolutionist.

Every genuinely religious person is a heretic and therefore a revolutionist.

All who achieve real distinction in life begin as revolutionists. The most distinguished persons become more revolutionary as they grow older, though they are commonly supposed to become more conservative owing to their loss of faith in conventional methods of reform.

Any person under the age of thirty, who, having any knowledge of the existing social order, is not a revolutionist, is an inferior.

AND YET

Revolutions have never lightened the burden of tyranny: they have only shifted it to another shoulder.

John Tanner.

THE REVOLUTIONIST'S HANDBOOK

I. ON GOOD BREEDING

If there were no God, said the eighteenth century Deist, it would be necessary to invent Him. Now this eighteenth century god was *deus ex machina*, the god who helped those who could not help themselves, the god of the lazy and incapable. The nineteenth century decided that there is indeed no such god; and now Man must take in hand all the work that he used to shirk with an idle prayer. He must, in effect, change himself into the political Providence which he formerly conceived as god; and such change is not only possible, but the only sort of change that is real. The mere transfigurations of institutions, as from military and priestly dominance to commercial and scientific dominance, from commercial dominance to proletarian democracy, from slavery to serfdom, from serfdom to capitalism, from monarchy to republicanism, from polytheism to monotheism, from monotheism to atheism, from atheism to pantheistic humanitarianism, from general illiteracy to general literacy, from romance to realism, from realism to mysticism, from metaphysics to physics, are all but changes from Tweedledum to Tweedledee: "*plus ça change, plus c'est la même chose.*" But the changes from the crab apple to the pippin, from the wolf and fox to the house dog, from the charger of Henry V to the brewer's draught horse and the race horse, are real; for here Man has played the god, subduing Nature to his intention, and ennobling or debasing Life for a set purpose. And what can be done with a wolf can be done with a man. If such monsters as the tramp and the gentleman can appear as mere by-products of Man's individual greed and folly, what might we hope for as a main product of his universal aspiration?

This is no new conclusion. The despair of institutions, and the inexorable "ye must be born again," with Mrs. Poyser's stipulation, "and born different," recurs in every generation. The cry for the Superman did not begin with Nietzsche, nor will it end with his vogue. But it has always been silenced by the same question: what kind of person is this Superman to be? You do not ask for a super-apple, but for an eatable apple; nor for a super-horse, but for a horse of greater draught or velocity. Neither is it of any use to ask for a Superman: you must furnish a specification of the sort of man you want. Unfortunately you do not know what sort of man you want. Some sort of goodlooking philosopher-athlete, with a handsome healthy woman for his mate, perhaps.

Vague as this is, it is a great advance on the popular demand for a perfect gentleman and a perfect lady. And, after all, no market demand in the world takes the form of exact technical specification of the article required. Excellent poultry and potatoes are produced to satisfy the demand of housewives who do not know the technical differences between a tuber and a chicken. They will tell you that the proof of the pudding is in the eating; and they are right. The proof of the Superman will be in the living; and we shall find out how to produce him by the old method of trial and error, and not by waiting for a completely convincing prescription of his ingredients.

Certain common and obvious mistakes may be ruled out from the beginning. For example, we agree that we want superior mind; but we need not fall into the football club folly of counting on this as a product of superior body. Yet if we recoil so far as to conclude that superior mind consists in being the dupe of our ethical classifications of virtues and vices, in short, of conventional morality, we shall fall out of the frying pan of the football club into the fire of the Sunday School. If we must choose between a race of athletes and a race of "good" men, let us have the athletes: better Samson and Milo than Calvin and Robespierre. But neither alternative is worth changing for: Samson is no more a Superman than Calvin. What then are we to do?

II. PROPERTY AND MARRIAGE

Let us hurry over the obstacles set up by property and marriage. Revolutionists make too much of them. No doubt it is easy to demonstrate that property will destroy society unless society destroys it. No doubt, also, property has hitherto held its own and destroyed all the empires. But that was because the superficial objection to it (that it distributes social wealth and the social labor burden in a grotesquely inequitable manner) did not threaten the existence of the race, but only the individual happiness of its units, and finally the maintenance of some irrelevant political form or other, such as a nation, an empire, or the like. Now as happiness never matters to Nature, as she neither recognizes flags and frontiers nor cares a straw whether the economic system adopted by a society is feudal, capitalistic or collectivist, provided it keeps the race afoot (the hive and the anthill being as acceptable to her as Utopia), the demonstrations of Socialists, though irrefutable, will never make any serious impression on property. The knell of that overrated institution will not sound until it is felt to conflict with some more vital matter than mere personal inequities in industrial economy. No such conflict was perceived whilst society had not yet grown beyond national communities too small and simple to disastrously overtax Man's limited political capacity. But we have now reached the stage of international organization. Man's political capacity and magnanimity are clearly beaten by the vastness and complexity of the problems forced on him. And it is at this anxious moment that he finds, when he looks upward for a mightier mind to help him, that the heavens are empty. He will presently see that his discarded formula that Man is the Temple of the Holy Ghost happens to be precisely true, and that it is only through his own brain and hand that this Holy Ghost, formerly the most nebulous person in the Trinity, and now become its sole survivor as it has always been its real Unity, can help him in any way. And so, if the Superman is to come, he must be born of Woman by Man's intentional and well-considered contrivance. Conviction of this will smash everything that opposes it. Even Property and Marriage, which laugh at the laborer's petty complaint that he is defrauded of "surplus value," and at the domestic miseries of the slaves of the wedding ring, will themselves be laughed aside as the lightest of trifles if they cross this conception when it becomes a fully realized vital purpose of the race.

That they must cross it becomes obvious the moment we acknowledge the futility of breeding men for special qualities as we breed cocks for game, greyhounds for speed, or sheep for mutton. What is really important in Man is the part of him that we do not yet understand. Of much of it we are not even conscious, just as we are not normally conscious of keeping up our circulation by our heart-pump, though if we neglect it we die. We are therefore driven to the conclusion that when we have carried selection as far as we can by rejecting from the list of eligible parents all persons who are uninteresting, unpromising, or blemished without any set-off, we shall still have to trust to the guidance of fancy (*alias* Voice of Nature), both in the breeders and the parents, for that superiority in the unconscious self which will be the true characteristic of the Superman.

At this point we perceive the importance of giving fancy the widest possible field. To cut humanity up into small cliques, and effectively limit the selection of the individual to his own clique, is to postpone the Superman for eons, if not for ever. Not only should every person be nourished and trained as a possible parent, but there should be no possibility of such an obstacle to natural selection as the objection of a countess to a navvy or of a duke to a charwoman. Equality is essential to good breeding; and equality, as all economists know, is incompatible with property.

Besides, equality is an essential condition of bad breeding also; and bad breeding is indispensable to the weeding out of the human race. When the conception of heredity took hold of the scientific imagination in the middle of last century, its devotees announced that it was a crime to marry the lunatic to the lunatic or the consumptive to the consumptive. But pray are we to try to correct our diseased stocks by infecting our healthy stocks with them? Clearly the attraction which disease has for diseased people is beneficial to the race. If two really unhealthy people get married, they will, as likely as not, have a great number of children who will all die before they reach maturity.

This is a far more satisfactory arrangement than the tragedy of a union between a healthy and an unhealthy person. Though more costly than sterilization of the unhealthy, it has the enormous advantage that in the event of our notions of health and unhealth being erroneous (which to some extent they most certainly are), the error will be corrected by experience instead of confirmed by evasion.

One fact must be faced resolutely, in spite of the shrieks of the romantic. There is no evidence that the best citizens are the offspring of congenial marriages, or that a conflict of temperament is not a highly important part of what breeders call crossing. On the contrary, it is quite sufficiently probable that good results may be obtained from parents who would be extremely unsuitable companions and partners, to make it certain that the experiment of mating them will sooner or later be tried purposely almost as often as it is now tried accidentally. But mating such couples must clearly not involve marrying them. In conjugation two complementary persons may supply one another's deficiencies: in the domestic partnership of marriage they only feel them and suffer from them. Thus the son of a robust, cheerful, eupeptic British country squire, with the tastes and range of his class, and of a clever, imaginative, intellectual, highly civilized Jewess, might be very superior to both his parents; but it is not likely that the Jewess would find the squire an interesting companion, or his habits, his friends, his place and mode of life congenial to her. Therefore marriage, whilst it is made an indispensable condition of mating, will delay the advent of the Superman as effectually as Property, and will be modified by the impulse towards him just as effectually.

The practical abrogation of Property and Marriage as they exist at present will occur without being much noticed. To the mass of men, the intelligent abolition of property would mean nothing except an increase in the quantity of food, clothing, housing and comfort at their personal disposal, as well as a greater control over their time and circumstances. Very few persons now make any distinction between virtually complete property and property held on such highly developed public conditions as to place its income on the same footing as that of a propertyless clergyman, officer, or civil servant. A landed proprietor may still drive men and women off his land, demolish their dwellings, and replace them with sheep or deer; and in the unregulated trades the private trader may still sponge on the regulated trades and sacrifice the life and health of the nation as lawlessly as the Manchester cotton manufacturers did at the beginning of last century. But though the Factory Code on the one hand, and Trade Union organization on the other, have, within the lifetime of men still living, converted the old unrestricted property of the cotton manufacturer in his mill and the cotton spinner in his labor into a mere permission to trade or work on stringent public or collective conditions, imposed in the interest of the general welfare without any regard for individual hard cases, people in Lancashire still speak of their "property" in the old terms, meaning nothing more by it than the things a thief can be punished for stealing. The total abolition of property, and the conversion of every citizen into a salaried functionary in the public service, would leave much more than 99 per cent of the nation quite unconscious of any greater change than now takes place when the son of a shipowner goes into the navy. They would still call their watches and umbrellas and back gardens their property.

Marriage also will persist as a name attached to a general custom long after the custom itself will have altered. For example, modern English marriage, as modified by divorce and by Married Women's Property Acts, differs more from early nineteenth century marriage than Byron's marriage did from Shakespear's. At the present moment marriage in England differs not only from marriage in France, but from marriage in Scotland. Marriage as modified by the divorce laws in South Dakota would be called mere promiscuity in Clapham. Yet the Americans, far from taking a profligate and cynical view of marriage, do homage to its ideals with a seriousness that seems old fashioned in Clapham. Neither in England nor America would a proposal to abolish marriage be tolerated for a moment; and yet nothing is more certain than that in both countries the progressive modification of the marriage contract will be continued until it is no more onerous nor irrevocable than any ordinary commercial deed of partnership. Were even this dispensed with, people would still call themselves husbands and wives; describe their companionships as marriages; and be for the most part unconscious that they were any less married than Henry VIII. For though a glance at the legal conditions of marriage in different Christian countries shews that marriage varies legally from frontier to frontier, domesticity varies so little that most people believe their own marriage laws to be universal. Consequently here again, as in the case of Property, the absolute confidence of the public in the stability of the institution's name, makes it all the easier to alter its substance.

However, it cannot be denied that one of the changes in public opinion demanded by the need for the Superman is a very unexpected one. It is nothing less than the dissolution of the present necessary association of marriage with conjugation, which most unmarried people regard as the very diagnostic of marriage. They are wrong, of course: it would be quite as near the truth to say that conjugation is the one purely accidental and incidental condition of marriage. Conjugation is essential to nothing but the propagation of the race; and the moment that paramount need is provided for otherwise than by marriage, conjugation, from Nature's creative point of view, ceases to be essential in marriage. But marriage does not thereupon cease to be so economical, convenient, and comfortable, that the Superman might safely bribe the matrimonomaniacs by offering to revive all the old inhuman stringency and irrevocability of marriage, to abolish divorce, to confirm the horrible bond which still chains decent people to drunkards, criminals and wasters, provided only the complete extrication of conjugation from it were conceded to him. For if people could form domestic companionships on no easier terms than these, they would still marry. The Roman Catholic, forbidden by his Church to avail himself of the divorce laws, marries as freely as the South Dakotan Presbyterians who can change partners with a facility that scandalizes the old world; and were his Church to dare a further step towards Christianity and enjoin celibacy on its laity as well as on its clergy, marriages would still be contracted for the sake of domesticity by perfectly obedient sons and daughters of the Church. One need not further pursue these hypotheses: they are only suggested here to help the reader to analyze marriage into its two functions of regulating conjugation and supplying a form of domesticity. These two functions are quite separable; and domesticity is the only one of the two which is essential to the existence of marriage, because conjugation without domesticity is not marriage at all, whereas domesticity without conjugation is still marriage: in fact it is necessarily the actual condition of all fertile marriages during a great part of their duration, and of some marriages during the whole of it.

Taking it, then, that Property and Marriage, by destroying Equality and thus hampering sexual selection with irrelevant conditions, are hostile to the evolution of the Superman, it is easy to understand why the only generally known modern experiment in breeding the human race took place in a community which discarded both institutions.

III. THE PERFECTIONIST EXPERIMENT AT ONEIDA CREEK

In 1848 the Oneida Community was founded in America to carry out a resolution arrived at by a handful of Perfectionist Communists "that we will devote ourselves exclusively to the establishment of the Kingdom of God." Though the American nation declared that this sort of thing was not to be tolerated in a Christian country, the Oneida Community held its own for over thirty years, during which period it seems to have produced healthier children and done and suffered less evil than any Joint Stock Company on record. It was, however, a highly selected community; for a genuine communist (roughly definable as an intensely proud person who proposes to enrich the common fund instead of to sponge on it) is superior to an ordinary joint stock capitalist precisely as an ordinary joint stock capitalist is superior to a pirate. Further, the Perfectionists were mightily shepherded by their chief Noyes, one of those chance attempts at the Superman which occur from time to time in spite of the interference of Man's blundering institutions. The existence of Noyes simplified the breeding problem for the Communists, the question as to what sort of man they should strive to breed being settled at once by the obvious desirability of breeding another Noyes.

But an experiment conducted by a handful of people, who, after thirty years of immunity from the unintentional child slaughter that goes on by ignorant parents in private homes, numbered only 300, could do very little except prove that the Communists, under the guidance of a Superman "devoted exclusively to the establishment of the Kingdom of God," and caring no more for property and marriage than a Camberwell minister cares for Hindoo Caste or Suttee, might make a much better job of their lives than ordinary folk under the harrow of both these institutions. Yet their Superman himself admitted that this apparent success was only part of the abnormal phenomenon of his own occurrence; for when he came to the end of his powers through age, he himself guided and organized the voluntary relapse of the Communists into marriage, capitalism, and customary private life, thus admitting that the real social solution was not what a casual Superman could persuade a picked company to do for him, but what a whole community of Supermen would do spontaneously. If Noyes had had to organize, not a few dozen Perfectionists, but the whole United States, America would have beaten him as completely as England beat Oliver Cromwell, France Napoleon, or Rome Julius Cæsar. Cromwell learnt by bitter experience that God himself cannot raise a people above its own level, and that even though you stir a nation to sacrifice all its appetites to its conscience, the result will still depend wholly on what sort of conscience the nation has got. Napoleon seems to have ended by regarding mankind as a troublesome pack of hounds only worth keeping for the sport of hunting with them. Cæsar's capacity for fighting without hatred or resentment was defeated by the determination of his soldiers to kill their enemies in the field instead of taking them prisoners to be spared by Cæsar; and his civil supremacy was purchased by colossal bribery of the citizens of Rome. What great rulers cannot do, codes and religions cannot do. Man reads his own nature into every ordinance: if you devise a superhuman commandment so cunningly that it cannot be misinterpreted in terms of his will, he will denounce it as seditious blasphemy, or else disregard it as either crazy or totally unintelligible. Parliaments and synods may tinker as much as they please with their codes and creeds as circumstances alter the balance of classes and their interests; and, as a result of the tinkering, there may be an occasional illusion of moral evolution, as when the victory of the commercial caste over the military caste leads to the substitution of social boycotting and pecuniary damages for duelling. At certain moments there may even be a considerable material advance, as when the conquest of political power by the working class produces a better distribution of wealth through the simple action of the selfishness of the new masters; but all this is mere readjustment and reformation: until the heart and mind of the people is changed the very greatest man will no more dare to govern on the assumption that all are as great as he than a drover dare leave his flock to find its way through the streets as he himself would. Until there is an England in which every man is a Cromwell, a France in which every man is a Napoleon, a Rome in which every man is a Cæsar, a Germany in which every man is a Luther plus a Goethe, the world will be no more improved by its heroes than a Brixton villa is improved by the pyramid of Cheops. The production of such nations is the only real change possible to us.

IV. MAN'S OBJECTION TO HIS OWN IMPROVEMENT

But would such a change be tolerated if Man must rise above himself to desire it? It would, through his misconception of its nature. Man does desire an ideal Superman with such energy as he can spare from his nutrition, and has in every age magnified the best living substitute for it he can find. His least incompetent general is set up as an Alexander; his king is the first gentleman in the world; his Pope is a saint. He is never without an array of human idols who are all nothing but sham Supermen. That the real Superman will snap his superfingers at all Man's present trumpery ideals of right, duty, honor, justice, religion, even decency, and accept moral obligations beyond present human endurance, is a thing that contemporary Man does not foresee: in fact he does not notice it when our casual Supermen do it in his very face. He actually does it himself every day without knowing it. He will therefore make no objection to the production of a race of what he calls Great Men or Heroes, because he will imagine them, not as true Supermen, but as himself endowed with infinite brains, infinite courage, and infinite money.

The most troublesome opposition will arise from the general fear of mankind that any interference with our conjugal customs will be an interference with our pleasures and our romance. This fear, by putting on airs of offended morality, has always intimidated people who have not measured its essential weakness; but it will prevail with those degenerates only in whom the instinct of fertility has faded into a mere itching for pleasure. The modern devices for combining pleasure with sterility, now universally known and accessible, enable these persons to weed themselves out of the race, a process already vigorously at work; and the consequent survival of the intelligently fertile means the survival of the partizans of the Superman; for what is proposed is nothing but the replacement of the old unintelligent, inevitable, almost unconscious fertility by an intelligently controlled, conscious fertility, and the elimination of the mere voluptuary from the evolutionary process.[1] Even if this selective agency had not been invented, the purpose of the race would still shatter the opposition of individual instincts. Not only do the bees and the ants satisfy their reproductive and parental instincts vicariously; but marriage itself successfully imposes celibacy on millions of unmarried normal men

---

[1] The part played in evolution by the voluptuary will be the same as that already played by the glutton. The glutton, as the man with the strongest motive for nourishing himself, will always take more pains than his fellows to get food. When food is so difficult to get that only great exertions can secure a sufficient supply of it, the glutton's appetite develops his cunning and enterprise to the utmost; and he becomes not only the best fed but the ablest man in the community. But in more hospitable climates, or where the social organization of the food supply makes it easy for a man to overeat, then the glutton eats himself out of health and finally out of existence. All other voluptuaries prosper and perish in the same way; and this is why the survival of the fittest means finally the survival of the self-controlled, because they alone can adapt themselves to the perpetual shifting of conditions produced by industrial progress.

and women. In short, the individual instinct in this matter, overwhelming as it is thoughtlessly supposed to be, is really a finally negligible one.

V. THE POLITICAL NEED FOR THE SUPERMAN

The need for the Superman is, in its most imperative aspect, a political one. We have been driven to Proletarian Democracy by the failure of all the alternative systems; for these depended on the existence of Supermen acting as despots or oligarchs; and not only were these Supermen not always or even often forthcoming at the right moment and in an eligible social position, but when they were forthcoming they could not, except for a short time and by morally suicidal coercive methods, impose superhumanity on those whom they governed; so by mere force of "human nature," government by consent of the governed has supplanted the old plan of governing the citizen as a public-schoolboy is governed.

Now we have yet to see the man who, having any practical experience of Proletarian Democracy, has any belief in its capacity for solving great political problems, or even for doing ordinary parochial work intelligently and economically. Only under despotism and oligarchies has the Radical faith in "universal suffrage" as a political panacea arisen. It withers the moment it is exposed to practical trial, because Democracy cannot rise above the level of the human material of which its voters are made. Switzerland seems happy in comparison with Russia; but if Russia were as small as Switzerland, and had her social problems simplified in the same way by impregnable natural fortifications and a population educated by the same variety and intimacy of international intercourse, there might be little to choose between them. At all events Australia and Canada, which are virtually protected democratic republics, and France and the United States, which are avowedly independent democratic republics, are neither healthy, wealthy nor wise; and they would be worse instead of better if their popular ministers were not experts in the art of dodging popular enthusiasms and duping popular ignorance. The politician who once had to learn how to flatter kings has now to learn how to fascinate, amuse, coax, humbug, frighten or otherwise strike the fancy of the electorate; and though in advanced modern States, where the artisan is better educated than the king, it takes a much bigger man to be a successful demagogue than to be a successful courtier, yet he who holds popular convictions with prodigious energy is the man for the mob, whilst the frailer sceptic who is cautiously feeling his way towards the next century has no chance unless he happens by accident to have the specific artistic talent of the mountebank as well, in which case it is as a mountebank that he catches votes, and not as a meliorist. Consequently the demagogue, though he professes (and fails) to readjust matters in the interests of the majority of the electors, yet stereotypes mediocrity, organizes intolerance, disparages exhibitions of uncommon qualities, and glorifies conspicuous exhibitions of common ones. He manages a small job well: he muddles rhetorically through a large one. When a great political movement takes place, it is not consciously led or organized: the unconscious self in mankind breaks its way through the problem as an elephant breaks through a jungle; and the politicians make speeches about whatever happens in the process, which, with the best intentions, they do all in their power to prevent. Finally, when social aggregation arrives at a point demanding international organization before the demagogues and electorates have learnt how to manage even a country parish properly much less internationalize Constantinople, the whole political business goes to smash; and presently we have Ruins of Empires, New Zealanders sitting on a broken arch of London Bridge, and so forth.

To that recurrent catastrophe we shall certainly come again unless we can have a Democracy of Supermen; and the production of such a Democracy is the only change that is now hopeful enough to nerve us to the effort that Revolution demands.

VI. PRUDERY EXPLAINED

Why the bees should pamper their mothers whilst we pamper only our operatic prima donnas is a question worth reflecting on. Our notion of treating a mother is, not to increase her supply of food, but to cut it off by forbidding her to work in a factory for a month after her confinement. Everything that can make birth a misfortune to the parents as well as a danger to the mother is conscientiously done. When a great French writer, Emile Zola, alarmed at the sterilization of his nation, wrote an eloquent and powerful book to restore the prestige of parentage, it was at once assumed in England that a work of this character, with such a title as *Fecundity*, was too abominable to be translated, and that any attempt to deal with the relations of the sexes from any other than the voluptuary or romantic point of view must be sternly put down. Now if this assumption were really founded on public opinion, it would indicate an attitude of disgust and resentment towards the Life Force that could only arise in a diseased and moribund community in which Ibsen's Hedda Gabler would be the typical woman. But it has no vital foundation at all. The prudery of the newspapers is, like the prudery of the dinner table, a mere difficulty of education and language. We are not taught to think decently on these subjects, and consequently we have no language for them except indecent language. We therefore have to declare them unfit for public discussion, because the only terms in which we can conduct the discussion are unfit for public use. Physiologists, who have a technical vocabulary at their disposal, find no difficulty; and masters of language who think decently can write popular stories like Zola's *Fecundity* or Tolstoy's *Resurrection* without giving the smallest offence to readers who can also think decently. But the ordinary modern journalist, who has never discussed such matters except in ribaldry, cannot write a simple comment on a divorce case without a conscious shamefulness or a furtive facetiousness that makes it impossible to read the comment aloud in company. All this ribaldry and prudery (the two are the same) does not mean that people do not feel decently on the subject: on the contrary, it is just the depth and seriousness of our feeling that makes its desecration by vile language and coarse humor intolerable; so that at last we cannot bear to have it spoken of at all because only one in a thousand can speak of it without wounding our self-respect, especially the self-respect of women. Add to the horrors of popular language the horrors of popular poverty. In crowded populations poverty destroys the possibility of cleanliness; and in the absence of cleanliness many of the natural conditions of life become offensive and noxious, with the result that at last the association of uncleanliness with these natural conditions becomes so overpowering that among civilized people (that is, people massed in the labyrinths of slums we call cities), half their bodily life becomes a guilty secret, unmentionable except to the doctor in emergencies; and Hedda Gabler shoots herself because maternity is so unladylike. In short, popular prudery is only a mere incident of popular squalor: the subjects which it taboos remain the most interesting and earnest of subjects in spite of it.

VII. PROGRESS AN ILLUSION

Unfortunately the earnest people get drawn off the track of evolution by the illusion of progress. Any Socialist can convince us easily that the difference between Man as he is and Man as he might become, without further evolution, under millennial conditions of nutrition, environment, and training, is enormous. He can shew that inequality and iniquitous distribution of wealth and allotment of labor have arisen through an unscientific economic system, and that Man, faulty as he is, no more intended to establish any such ordered disorder than a moth intends to be burnt when it flies into a candle flame. He can shew that the difference between the grace and strength of the acrobat and the bent back of the rheumatic field laborer is a difference produced by conditions, not by nature. He can shew that many of the most detestable human vices are not radical, but are mere reactions of our institutions on our very virtues. The Anarchist, the Fabian, the Salvationist, the Vegetarian, the doctor, the lawyer, the parson, the professor of ethics, the gymnast, the soldier, the sportsman, the inventor, the political program-maker, all have some prescription for bettering us; and almost all their remedies are physically possible and aimed at admitted evils. To them the limit of progress is, at worst, the completion of all the suggested reforms and the levelling up of all men to the point attained already by the most highly nourished and cultivated in mind and body.

Here, then, as it seems to them, is an enormous field for the energy of the reformer. Here are many noble goals attainable by many of those paths up the Hill Difficulty along which great spirits love to aspire. Unhappily, the hill will never be climbed by Man as we know him. It need not be denied that if we all struggled bravely to the end of the reformer's paths we should improve the world prodigiously. But there is no more hope in that If than in the equally plausible assurance that if the sky falls we shall all catch larks. We are not going to tread those paths: we have not sufficient energy. We do not desire the end enough: indeed in most cases we do not effectively desire it at all. Ask any man would he like to be a better man; and he will say yes, most piously. Ask him would he like to have a million of money; and he will say yes, most sincerely. But the pious citizen who would like to be a better man goes on behaving just as he did before. And the tramp who would like the million does not take the trouble to earn ten shillings: multitudes of men and women, all eager to accept a legacy of a million, live and die without having ever possessed five pounds at one time, although beggars have died in rags on mattresses stuffed with gold which they accumulated because they desired it enough to nerve them to get it and keep it. The economists who discovered that demand created supply soon had to limit the proposition to "effective demand," which turned out, in the final analysis, to mean nothing more than supply itself; and this holds good in politics, morals, and all other departments as well: the actual supply is the measure of the effective demand; and the mere aspirations and professions produce nothing. No community has ever yet passed beyond the initial phases in which its pugnacity and fanaticism enabled it to found a nation, and its cupidity to establish and develop a commercial civilization. Even these stages have never been attained by public spirit, but always by intolerant wilfulness and brute force. Take the Reform Bill of 1832 as an example of a conflict between two sections of educated Englishmen concerning a political measure which was as obviously necessary and inevitable as any political measure has ever been or is ever likely to be. It was not passed until the gentlemen of Birmingham had made arrangements to cut the throats of the gentlemen of St. James's parish in due military form. It would not have been passed to this day if there had been no force behind it except the logic and public conscience of the Utilitarians. A despotic ruler with as much sense as Queen Elizabeth would have done better than the mob of grown-up Eton boys who governed us then by privilege, and who, since the introduction of practically Manhood Suffrage in 1884, now govern us at the request of proletarian Democracy.

At the present time we have, instead of the Utilitarians, the Fabian Society, with its peaceful, constitutional, moral, economical policy of Socialism, which needs nothing for its bloodless and benevolent realization except that the English people shall understand it and approve of it. But why are the Fabians well spoken of in circles where thirty years ago the word Socialist was understood as equivalent to cut-throat and incendiary? Not because the English have the smallest intention of studying or adopting the Fabian policy, but because they believe that the Fabians, by eliminating the element of intimidation from the Socialist agitation, have drawn the teeth of insurgent poverty and saved the existing order from the only method of attack it really fears. Of course, if the nation adopted the Fabian policy, it would be carried out by brute force exactly as our present property system is. It would become the law; and those who resisted it would be fined, sold up, knocked on the head by policemen, thrown into prison, and in the last resort "executed" just as they are when they break the present law. But as our proprietary class has no fear of that conversion taking place, whereas it does fear sporadic cutthroats and gunpowder plots, and strives with all its might to hide the fact that there is no moral difference whatever between the methods by which it enforces its proprietary rights and the method by which the dynamitard asserts his conception of natural human rights, the Fabian Society is patted on the back just as the Christian Social Union is, whilst the Socialist who says bluntly that a Social revolution can be made only as all other revolutions have been made, by the people who want it killing, coercing and intimidating the people who dont want it, is denounced as a misleader of the people, and imprisoned with hard labor to shew him how much sincerity there is in the objection of his captors to physical force.

Are we then to repudiate Fabian methods, and return to those of the barricader, or adopt those of the dynamitard and the assassin? On the contrary, we are to recognize that both are fundamentally futile. It seems easy for the dynamitard to say "Have you not just admitted that nothing is ever conceded except to physical force? Did not Gladstone admit that the Irish Church was disestablished, not by the spirit of Liberalism, but by the explosion which wrecked Clerkenwell prison?" Well, we need not foolishly and timidly deny it. Let it be fully granted. Let us grant, further, that all this lies in the nature of things; that the most ardent Socialist, if he owns property, can by no means do otherwise than Conservative proprietors until property is forcibly abolished by the whole nation; nay, that ballots and parliamentary divisions, in spite of their vain ceremony of discussion, differ from battles only as the bloodless surrender of an outnumbered force in the field differs from Waterloo or Trafalgar. I make a present of all these admissions to the Fenian who collects money from thoughtless Irishmen in America to blow up Dublin Castle; to the detective who persuades foolish young workmen to order bombs from the nearest ironmonger and then delivers them up to penal servitude; to our military and naval commanders who believe, not in preaching, but in an ultimatum backed by plenty of lyddite; and, generally, to all whom it may concern. But of what use is it to substitute the will of reckless and bloodyminded Progressives for cautious and humane ones? Is England any the better for the wreck of Clerkenwell prison, or Ireland for the disestablishment of the Irish Church? Is there the smallest reason to suppose that the nation which sheepishly let Charles and Laud and Strafford coerce it, gained anything because it afterwards, still more sheepishly, let a few strongminded Puritans, inflamed by the masterpieces of Jewish revolutionary literature, cut off the heads of the three? Suppose the Gunpowder plot had succeeded, and a Fawkes dynasty were at present on the throne, would it have made any difference to the present state of the nation? The guillotine was used in France up to the limit of human endurance, both on Girondins and Jacobins. Fouquier-Tinville followed Marie Antoinette to the scaffold; and Marie Antoinette might have asked the crowd, just as pointedly as Fouquier did, whether their bread would be any cheaper when her head was off. And what came of it all? The Imperial France of the Rougon-Macquart family, and the Republican France of the Panama scandal and the Dreyfus case. Was the difference worth the guillotining of all those unlucky ladies and gentlemen, useless and mischievous as many of them were? Would any sane man guillotine a mouse to bring about such a result? Turn to Republican America. America has no Star Chamber, and no feudal barons. But it has Trusts; and it has millionaires whose factories, fenced in by live electric wires and defended by Pinkerton retainers with magazine rifles, would have made a Radical of Reginald Front de Boeuf. Would Washington or Franklin have lifted a finger in the cause of American Independence if they had foreseen its reality?

No: what Cæsar, Cromwell and Napoleon could not do with all the physical force and moral prestige of the State in their mighty hands, cannot be done by enthusiastic criminals and lunatics. Even the Jews, who, from Moses to Marx and Lassalle, have inspired all the revolutions, have had to confess that, after all, the dog will return to his vomit and the sow that was washed to her wallowing in the mire; and we may as well make up our minds that Man will return to his idols and his cupidities, in spite of all "movements" and all revolutions, until his nature is changed. Until then, his early successes in building commercial civilizations (and such civilizations, Good Heavens!) are but preliminaries to the inevitable later stage, now threatening us, in which the passions which built the civilization become fatal instead of productive, just as the same qualities which make the lion king in the forest ensure his destruction when he enters a city. Nothing can save society then except the clear head and the wide purpose: war and competition, potent instruments of selection and evolution in one epoch, become ruinous instruments of degeneration in the next. In the breeding of animals and plants, varieties which have arisen by selection through many generations relapse precipitously into the wild type in a generation or two when selection ceases; and in the same way a civilization in which lusty pugnacity and greed have ceased to act as selective agents and have begun to obstruct and destroy, rushes downwards and backwards with a suddenness that enables an observer to see with consternation the upward steps of many centuries retraced in a single lifetime. This has often occurred even within the period covered by history; and in every instance the turning point has been reached long before the attainment, or even the general advocacy on paper, of the levelling-up of the mass to the highest point attainable by the best nourished and cultivated normal individuals.

Man and Superman: The Revolutionist's Handbook 365

We must therefore frankly give up the notion that Man as he exists is capable of net progress. There will always be an illusion of progress, because wherever we are conscious of an evil we remedy it, and therefore always seem to ourselves to be progressing, forgetting that most of the evils we see are the effects, finally become acute, of long-unnoticed retrogressions, that our compromising remedies seldom fully recover the lost ground; above all, that on the lines along which we are degenerating, good has become evil in our eyes, and is being undone in the name of progress precisely as evil is undone and replaced by good on the lines along which we are evolving. This is indeed the Illusion of Illusions; for it gives us infallible and appalling assurance that if our political ruin is to come, it will be effected by ardent reformers and supported by enthusiastic patriots as a series of necessary steps in our progress. Let the Reformer, the Progressive, the Meliorist then reconsider himself and his eternal ifs and ans which never become pots and pans. Whilst Man remains what he is, there can be no progress beyond the point already attained and fallen headlong from at every attempt at civilization; and since even that point is but a pinnacle to which a few people cling in giddy terror above an abyss of squalor, mere progress should no longer charm us.

VIII. THE CONCEIT OF CIVILIZATION

After all, the progress illusion is not so very subtle. We begin by reading the satires of our fathers' contemporaries; and we conclude (usually quite ignorantly) that the abuses exposed by them are things of the past. We see also that reforms of crying evils are frequently produced by the sectional shifting of political power from oppressors to oppressed. The poor man is given a vote by the Liberals in the hope that he will cast it for his emancipators. The hope is not fulfilled; but the lifelong imprisonment of penniless men for debt ceases; Factory Acts are passed to mitigate swearing; schooling is made free and compulsory; sanitary by-laws are multiplied; public steps are taken to house the masses decently; the bare-footed get boots; rags become rare; and bathrooms and pianos, smart tweeds and starched collars, reach numbers of people who once, as "the unsoaped," played the Jew's harp or the accordion in moleskins and belchers. Some of these changes are gains: some of them are losses. Some of them are not changes at all: all of them are merely the changes that money makes. Still, they produce an illusion of bustling progress; and the reading class infers from them that the abuses of the early Victorian period no longer exist except as amusing pages in the novels of Dickens. But the moment we look for a reform due to character and not to money, to statesmanship and not to interest or mutiny, we are disillusioned. For example, we remembered the maladministration and incompetence revealed by the Crimean War as part of a bygone state of things until the South African war shewed that the nation and the War Office, like those poor Bourbons who have been so impudently blamed for a universal characteristic, had learnt nothing and forgotten nothing. We had hardly recovered from the fruitless irritation of this discovery when it transpired that the officers' mess of our most select regiment included a flogging club presided over by the senior subaltern. The disclosure provoked some disgust at the details of this schoolboyish debauchery, but no surprise at the apparent absence of any conception of manly honor and virtue, of personal courage and self-respect, in the front rank of our chivalry. In civil affairs we had assumed that the sycophancy and idolatry which encouraged Charles I to undervalue the Puritan revolt of the seventeenth century had been long outgrown; but it has needed nothing but favorable circumstances to revive, with added abjectness to compensate for its lost piety. We have relapsed into disputes about transubstantiation at the very moment when the discovery of the wide prevalence of theophagy as a tribal custom has deprived us of the last excuse for believing that our official religious rites differ in essentials from those of barbarians. The Christian doctrine of the uselessness of punishment and the wickedness of revenge has not, in spite of its simple common sense, found a single convert among the nations: Christianity means nothing to the masses but a sensational public execution which is made an excuse for other executions. In its name we take ten years of a thief's life minute by minute in the slow misery and degradation of modern reformed imprisonment with as little remorse as Laud and his Star Chamber clipped the ears of Bastwick and Burton. We dug up and mutilated the remains of the Mahdi the other day exactly as we dug up and mutilated the remains of Cromwell two centuries ago. We have demanded the decapitation of the Chinese Boxer princes as any Tartar would have done; and our military and naval expeditions to kill, burn, and destroy tribes and villages for knocking an Englishman on the head are so common a part of our Imperial routine that the last dozen of them has not elicited as much sympathy as can be counted on by any lady criminal. The judicial use of torture to extort confession is supposed to be a relic of darker ages; but whilst these pages are being written an English judge has sentenced a forger to twenty years penal servitude with an open declaration that the sentence will be carried out in full unless he confesses where he has hidden the notes he forged. And no comment whatever is made either on this or on a telegram from the seat of war in Somaliland mentioning that certain information has been given by a prisoner of war "under punishment." Even if these reports were false, the fact that they are accepted without protest as indicating a natural and proper course of public conduct shows that we are still as ready to resort to torture as Bacon was. As to vindictive cruelty, an incident in the South African war, when the relatives and friends of a prisoner were forced to witness his execution, betrayed a baseness of temper and character which hardly leaves us the right to plume ourselves on our superiority to Edward III at the surrender of Calais. And the democratic American officer indulges in torture in the Philippines just as the aristocratic English officer did in South Africa. The incidents of the white invasion of Africa in search of ivory, gold, diamonds and sport, have proved that the modern European is the same beast of prey that formerly marched to the conquest of new worlds under Alexander, Antony, and Pizarro. Parliaments and vestries are just what they were when Cromwell suppressed them and Dickens ridiculed them. The democratic politician remains exactly as Plato described him; the physician is still the credulous impostor and petulant scientific coxcomb whom Molière ridiculed; the schoolmaster remains at best a pedantic child farmer and at worst a flagellomaniac; arbitrations are more dreaded by honest men than lawsuits; the philanthropist is still a parasite on misery as the doctor is on disease; the miracles of priestcraft are none the less fraudulent and mischievous because they are now called scientific experiments and conducted by professors; witchcraft, in the modern form of patent medicines and prophylactic inoculations, is rampant; the landowner who is no longer powerful enough to set the mantrap of Rhampsinitis improves on it by barbed wire; the modern gentleman who is too lazy to daub his face with vermilion as a symbol of bravery employs a laundress to daub his shirt with starch as a symbol of cleanliness; we shake our heads at the dirt of the Middle Ages in cities made grimy with soot and foul and disgusting with shameless tobacco smoking; holy water, in its latest form of disinfectant fluid, is more widely used and believed in than ever; public health authorities deliberately go through incantations with burning sulphur (which they know to be useless) because the people believe in it as devoutly as the Italian peasant believes in the liquefaction of the blood of St. Januarius; and straightforward public lying has reached gigantic developments, there being nothing to choose in this respect between the pickpocket at the police station and the minister on the treasury bench, the editor in the newspaper office, the city magnate advertising bicycle tires that do not sideslip, the clergyman subscribing the thirty-nine articles, and the vivisector who pledges his knightly honor that no animal operated on in the physiological laboratory suffers the slightest pain. Hypocrisy is at its worst; for we not only persecute bigotedly but sincerely in the name of the cure-mongering witchcraft we do believe in, but callously and hypocritically in the name of the Evangelical creed that our rulers privately smile at as the Italian patricians of the fifth century smiled at Jupiter and Venus. Sport is, as it has always been, murderous excitement: the impulse to slaughter is universal; and museums are set up throughout the country to encourage little children and elderly gentlemen to make collections of corpses preserved in alcohol, and to steal birds' eggs and keep them as the red Indian used to keep scalps. Coercion with the lash is as natural to an Englishman as it was to Solomon spoiling Rehoboam: indeed, the comparison is unfair to the Jews in view of the facts that the Mosaic law forbade more than forty lashes in the name of humanity, and that floggings of a thousand lashes were inflicted on English soldiers in the eighteenth and nineteenth centuries, and would be inflicted still but for the change in the balance of political power between the military caste and the commercial classes and the proletariat. In spite of that change, flogging is still an institution in the public school, in the military prison, on the training ship, and in that school of littleness called the home. The lascivious clamor of the flagellomaniac for more of it, constant as the clamor for more insolence, more war, and lower rates, is tolerated and even gratified because, having no moral ends in view, we have sense enough to see that nothing but brute coercion can impose our selfish will on others. Cowardice is universal: patriotism, public opinion, parental duty, discipline, religion, morality, are only fine names for intimidation; and cruelty, gluttony, and credulity keep cowardice in countenance. We cut the throat of a calf and hang it up by the heels to bleed to death so that our veal cutlet may be white; we nail geese to a board and cram them with food because we like the taste of liver disease; we tear birds to pieces to decorate our women's hats; we mutilate domestic animals for no reason at all except to follow an instinctively cruel fashion; and we connive at the most abominable tortures in the hope of discovering some magical cure for our own diseases by them.

Now please observe that these are not exceptional developments of our admitted vices, deplored and prayed against by all good men. Not a word has been said here of the excesses of our Neros, of whom we have the full usual percentage. With the exception of the few military examples, which are mentioned mainly to shew that the education and standing of a gentleman, reinforced by the strongest conventions of honor, *esprit de corps,* publicity and responsibility, afford no better guarantees of conduct than the passions of a mob, the illustrations given above are commonplaces taken from the daily practices of our best citizens, vehemently defended in our newspapers and in our pulpits. The very humanitarians who abhor them are stirred to murder by them: the dagger of Brutus and Ravaillac is still active in the hands of Caserio and Luccheni; and the pistol has come to its aid in the hands of Guiteau and Czolgosz. Our remedies are still limited to endurance or assassination; and the assassin is still judicially assassinated on the principle that two blacks make a white. The only novelty is in our methods: through the discovery of dynamite the overloaded musket of Hamilton of Bothwellhaugh has been superseded by the bomb; but Ravachol's heart burns just as Hamilton's did. The world will not bear thinking of to those who know what it is, even with the largest discount for the restraints of poverty on the poor and cowardice on the rich.

All that can be said for us is that people must and do live and let live up to a certain point. Even the horse, with his docked tail and bitted jaw, finds his slavery mitigated by the fact that a total disregard of his need for food and rest would put his master to the expense of buying a new horse every second day; for you cannot work a horse to death and then pick up another one for nothing, as you can a laborer. But this natural check on inconsiderate selfishness is itself checked, partly by our shortsightedness, and partly by deliberate calculation; so that beside the man who, to his own loss, will shorten his horse's life in mere stinginess, we have the tramway company which discovers actuarially that though a horse may live from 24 to 40 years, yet it pays better to work him to death in 4 and then replace him by a fresh victim. And human slavery, which has reached its worst recorded point within our own time in the form of free wage labor, has encountered the same personal and commercial limits to both its aggravation and its mitigation. Now that the freedom of wage labor has produced a scarcity of it, as in South Africa, the leading English newspaper and the leading English weekly review have openly and without apology demanded a return to compulsory labor: that is, to the methods by which, as we believe, the Egyptians built the pyramids. We know now that the crusade against chattel slavery in the nineteenth century succeeded solely because chattel slavery was neither the most effective nor the least humane method of labor exploitation; and the world is now feeling its way towards a still more effective system which shall abolish the freedom of the worker without again making his exploiter responsible for him as a chattel.

Still, there is always some mitigation: there is the fear of revolt; and there are the effects of kindliness and affection. Let it be repeated therefore that no indictment is here laid against the world on the score of what its criminals and monsters do. The fires of Smithfield and of the Inquisition were lighted by earnestly pious people, who were kind and good as kindness and goodness go. And when a Negro is dipped in kerosene and set on fire in America at the present time, he is not a good man lynched by ruffians: he is a criminal lynched by crowds of respectable, charitable, virtuously indignant, highminded citizens, who, though they act outside the law, are at least more merciful than the American legislators and judges who not so long ago condemned men to solitary confinement for periods, not of five months, as our own practice is, but of five years and more. The things that our moral monsters do may be left out of account with St. Bartholomew massacres and other momentary outbursts of social disorder. Judge us by the admitted and respected practice of our most reputable circles; and, if you know the facts and are strong enough to look them in the face, you must admit that unless we are replaced by a more highly evolved animal — in short, by the Superman — the world must remain a den of dangerous animals among whom our few accidental supermen, our Shakespears, Goethes, Shelleys and their like, must live as precariously as lion tamers do, taking the humor of their situation, and the dignity of their superiority, as a setoff to the horror of the one and the loneliness of the other.

IX. THE VERDICT OF HISTORY

It may be said that though the wild beast breaks out in Man and casts him back momentarily into barbarism under the excitement of war and crime, yet his normal life is higher than the normal life of his forefathers. This view is very acceptable to Englishmen, who always lean sincerely to virtue's side as long as it costs them nothing either in money or in thought. They feel deeply the injustice of foreigners, who allow them no credit for this conditional highmindedness. But there is no reason to suppose that our ancestors were less capable of it than we are. To all such claims for the existence of a progressive moral evolution operating visibly from grandfather to grandson, there is the conclusive reply that a thousand years of such evolution would have produced enormous social changes, of which the historical evidence would be overwhelming. But not Macaulay himself, the most confident of Whig meliorists, can produce any such evidence that will bear cross-examination. Compare our conduct and our codes with those mentioned contemporarily in such ancient scriptures and classics as have come down to us, and you will find no jot of ground for the belief that any moral progress whatever has been made in historic time, in spite of all the romantic attempts of historians to reconstruct the past on that assumption. Within that time it has happened to nations as to private families and individuals that they have flourished and decayed, repented and hardened their hearts, submitted and protested, acted and reacted, oscillated between natural and artificial sanitation (the oldest house in the world, unearthed the other day in Crete, has quite modern sanitary arrangements), and rung a thousand changes on the different scales of income and pressure of population, firmly believing all the time that mankind was advancing by leaps and bounds because men were constantly busy. And the mere chapter of accidents has left a small accumulation of chance discoveries, such as the wheel, the arch, the safety pin, gunpowder, the magnet, the Voltaic pile and so forth: things which, unlike the gospels and philosophic treatises of the sages, can be usefully understood and applied by common men; so that steam locomotion is possible without a nation of Stephensons, although national Christianity is impossible without a nation of Christs. But does any man seriously believe that the *chauffeur* who drives a motor car from Paris to Berlin is a more highly evolved man than the charioteer of Achilles, or that a modern Prime Minister is a more enlightened ruler than Cæsar because he rides a tricycle, writes his dispatches by the electric light, and instructs his stockbroker through the telephone?

Enough, then, of this goose-cackle about Progress: Man, as he is, never will nor can add a cubit to his stature by any of its quackeries, political, scientific, educational, religious, or artistic. What is likely to happen when this conviction gets into the minds of the men whose present faith in these illusions is the cement of our social system, can be imagined only by those who know how suddenly a civilization which has long ceased to think (or in the old phrase, to watch and pray) can fall to pieces when the vulgar belief in its hypocrisies and impostures can no longer hold out against its failures and scandals. When religious and ethical formulae become so obsolete that no man of strong mind can believe them, they have also reached the point at which no man of high character will profess them; and from that moment until they are formally disestablished, they stand at the door of every profession and every public office to keep out every able man who is not a sophist or a liar. A nation which revises its parish councils once in three years, but will not revise its articles of religion once in three hundred, even when those articles avowedly began as a political compromise dictated by Mr. Facing-Both-Ways, is a nation that needs remaking.

Our only hope, then, is in evolution. We must replace the Man by the Superman. It is frightful for the citizen, as the years pass him, to see his own contemporaries so exactly reproduced by the younger generation, that his companions of thirty years ago have their counterparts in every city crowd; so that he has to check himself repeatedly in the act of saluting as an old friend some young man to whom he is only an elderly stranger. All hope of advance dies in his bosom as he watches them: he knows that they will do just what their fathers did, and that the few voices which will still, as always before, exhort them to do something else and be something better, might as well spare their breath to cool their porridge (if they can get any). Men like Ruskin and Carlyle will preach to Smith and Brown for the sake of preaching, just as St. Francis preached to the birds and St. Anthony to the fishes. But Smith and Brown, like the fishes and birds, remain as they are; and poets who plan Utopias and prove that nothing is necessary for their realization but that Man should will them, perceive at last, like Richard Wagner, that the fact to be faced is that Man does not effectively will them. And he never will until he becomes Superman.

And so we arrive at the end of the Socialist's dream of "the socialization of the means of production and exchange," of the Positivist's dream of moralizing the capitalist, and of the ethical professor's, legislator's, educator's dream of putting commandments and codes and lessons and examination marks on a man as harness is put on a horse, ermine on a judge, pipeclay on a soldier, or a wig on an actor, and pretending that his nature has been changed. The only fundamental and possible Socialism is the socialization of the selective breeding of Man: in other terms, of human evolution. We must eliminate the Yahoo, or his vote will wreck the commonwealth.

X. THE METHOD

As to the method, what can be said as yet except that where there is a will, there is a way? If there be no will, we are lost. That is a possibility for our crazy little empire, if not for the universe; and as such possibilities are not to be entertained without despair, we must, whilst we survive, proceed on the assumption that we have still energy enough to not only will to live, but to will to live better. That may mean that we must establish a State Department of Evolution, with a seat in the Cabinet for its chief, and a revenue to defray the cost of direct State experiments and provide inducements to private persons to achieve successful results. It may mean a private society or a chartered company for the improvement of human live stock. But for the present it is far more likely to mean a blatant repudiation of such proposals as indecent and immoral, with, nevertheless, a general secret pushing of the human will in the repudiated direction; so that all sorts of institutions and public authorities will under some pretext or other feel their way furtively towards the Superman. Mr. Graham Wallas has already ventured to suggest, as Chairman of the School Management Committee of the London School Board, that the accepted policy of the Sterilization of the Schoolmistress, however administratively convenient, is open to criticism from the national stock-breeding point of view; and this is as good an example as any of the way in which the drift towards the Superman may operate in spite of all our hypocrisies. One thing at least is clear to begin with. If a woman can, by careful selection of a father, and nourishment of herself, produce a citizen with efficient senses, sound organs and a good digestion, she should clearly be secured a sufficient reward for that natural service to make her willing to undertake and repeat it. Whether she be financed in the undertaking by herself, or by the father, or by a speculative capitalist, or by a new department of, say, the Royal Dublin Society, or (as at present) by the War Office maintaining her "on the strength" and authorizing a particular soldier to marry her, or by a local authority under a by-law directing that women may under certain circumstances have a year's leave of absence on full salary, or by the central government, does not matter provided the result be satisfactory.

It is a melancholy fact that as the vast majority of women and their husbands have, under existing circumstances, not enough nourishment, no capital, no credit, and no knowledge of science or business, they would, if the State would pay for birth as it now pays for death, be exploited by joint stock companies for dividends, just as they are in ordinary industries. Even a joint stock human stud farm (piously disguised as a reformed Foundling Hospital or something of that sort) might well, under proper inspection and regulation, produce better results than our present reliance on promiscuous marriage. It may be objected that when an ordinary contractor produces stores for sale to the Government, and the Government rejects them as not up to the required standard, the condemned goods are either sold for what they will fetch or else scrapped: that is, treated as waste material; whereas if the goods consisted of human beings, all that could be done would be to let them loose or send them to the nearest workhouse. But there is nothing new in private enterprise throwing its human refuse on the cheap labor market and the workhouse; and the refuse of the new industry would presumably be better bred than the staple product of ordinary poverty. In our present happy-go-lucky industrial disorder, all the human products, successful or not, would have to be thrown on the labor market; but the unsuccessful ones would not entitle the company to a bounty and so would be a dead loss to it. The practical commercial difficulty would be the uncertainty and the cost in time and money of the first experiments. Purely commercial capital would not touch such heroic operations during the experimental stage; and in any case the strength of mind needed for so momentous a new departure could not be fairly expected from the Stock Exchange. It will have to be handled by statesmen with character enough to tell our democracy and plutocracy that statecraft does not consist in flattering their follies or applying their suburban standards of propriety to the affairs of four continents. The matter must be taken up either by the State or by some organization strong enough to impose respect upon the State.

The novelty of any such experiment, however, is only in the scale of it. In one conspicuous case, that of royalty, the State does already select the parents on purely political grounds; and in the peerage, though the heir to a dukedom is legally free to marry a dairymaid, yet the social pressure on him to confine his choice to politically and socially eligible mates is so overwhelming that he is really no more free to marry the dairymaid than George IV was to marry Mrs. Fitzherbert; and such a marriage could only occur as a result of extraordinary strength of character on the part of the dairymaid acting upon extraordinary weakness on the part of the duke. Let those who think the whole conception of intelligent breeding absurd and scandalous ask themselves why George IV was not allowed to choose his own wife whilst any tinker could marry whom he pleased? Simply because it did not matter a rap politically whom the tinker married, whereas it mattered very much whom the king married. The way in which all considerations of the king's personal rights, of the claims of the heart, of the sanctity of the marriage oath, and of romantic morality crumpled up before this political need shews how negligible all these apparently irresistible prejudices are when they come into conflict with the demand for quality in our rulers. We learn the same lesson from the case of the soldier, whose marriage, when it is permitted at all, is despotically controlled with a view solely to military efficiency.

Well, nowadays it is not the king that rules, but the tinker. Dynastic wars are no longer feared, dynastic alliances no longer valued. Marriages in royal families are becoming rapidly less political, and more popular, domestic and romantic. If all the kings in Europe were made as free tomorrow as King Cophetua, nobody but their aunts and chamberlains would feel a moment's anxiety as to the consequences. On the other hand a sense of the social importance of the tinker's marriage has been steadily growing. We have made a public matter of his wife's health in the month after her confinement. We have taken the minds of his children out of his hands and put them into those of our State schoolmaster. We shall presently make their bodily nourishment independent of him. But they are still riff-raff; and to hand the country over to riff-raff is national suicide, since riff-raff can neither govern nor will let anyone else govern except the highest bidder of bread and circuses. There is no public enthusiast alive of twenty years practical democratic experience who believes in the political adequacy of the electorate or of the bodies it elects. The overthrow of the aristocrat has created the necessity for the Superman.

Englishmen hate Liberty and Equality too much to understand them. But every Englishman loves and desires a pedigree. And in that he is right. King Demos must be bred like all other kings; and with Must there is no arguing.

It is idle for an individual writer to carry so great a matter further in a pamphlet. A conference on the subject is the next step needed. It will be attended by men and women who, no longer believing that they can live for ever, are seeking for some immortal work into which they can build the best of themselves before their refuse is thrown into that arch dust destructor, the cremation furnace.

MAXIMS FOR REVOLUTIONISTS

THE GOLDEN RULE

Do not do unto others as you would that they should do unto you. Their tastes may not be the same.

Never resist temptation: prove all things: hold fast that which is good.

Do not love your neighbor as yourself. If you are on good terms with yourself it is an impertinence: if on bad, an injury.

The golden rule is that there are no golden rules.

IDOLATRY

The art of government is the organization of idolatry.

The bureaucracy consists of functionaries; the aristocracy, of idols; the democracy, of idolaters.

The populace cannot understand the bureaucracy: it can only worship the national idols.

The savage bows down to idols of wood and stone: the civilized man to idols of flesh and blood.

A limited monarchy is a device for combining the inertia of a wooden idol with the credibility of a flesh and blood one.

When the wooden idol does not answer the peasant's prayer, he beats it: when the flesh and blood idol does not satisfy the civilized man, he cuts its head off.

He who slays a king and he who dies for him are alike idolaters.

ROYALTY

Kings are not born: they are made by artificial hallucination. When the process is interrupted by adversity at a critical age, as in the case of Charles II, the subject becomes sane and never completely recovers his kingliness.

The Court is the servant's hall of the sovereign.

Vulgarity in a king flatters the majority of the nation.

The flunkeyism propagated by the throne is the price we pay for its political convenience.

DEMOCRACY

If the lesser mind could measure the greater as a footrule can measure a pyramid, there would be finality in universal suffrage. As it is, the political problem remains unsolved.

Democracy substitutes election by the incompetent many for appointment by the corrupt few.

Democratic republics can no more dispense with national idols than monarchies with public functionaries.

Government presents only one problem: the discovery of a trustworthy anthropometric method.

IMPERIALISM

Excess of insularity makes a Briton an Imperialist.

Excess of local self-assertion makes a colonist an Imperialist.

A colonial Imperialist is one who raises colonial troops, equips a colonial squadron, claims a Federal Parliament sending its measures to the Throne instead of to the Colonial Office, and, being finally brought by this means into insoluble conflict with the insular British Imperialist, "cuts the painter" and breaks up the Empire.

LIBERTY AND EQUALITY

He who confuses political liberty with freedom and political equality with similarity has never thought for five minutes about either.

Nothing can be unconditional: consequently nothing can be free.

Liberty mean responsibility. That is why most men dread it.

The duke inquires contemptuously whether his gamekeeper is the equal of the Astronomer Royal; but he insists that they shall both be hanged equally if they murder him.

The notion that the colonel need be a better man than the private is as confused as the notion that the keystone need be stronger than the coping stone.

Where equality is undisputed, so also is subordination.

Equality is fundamental in every department of social organization.

The relation of superior to inferior excludes good manners.

EDUCATION

When a man teaches something he does not know to somebody else who has no aptitude for it, and gives him a certificate of proficiency, the latter has completed the education of a gentleman.

A fool's brain digests philosophy into folly, science into superstition, and art into pedantry. Hence University education.

The best brought-up children are those who have seen their parents as they are. Hypocrisy is not the parent's first duty.

The vilest abortionist is he who attempts to mould a child's character.

At the University every great treatise is postponed until its author attains impartial judgment and perfect knowledge. If a horse could wait as long for its shoes and would pay for them in advance, our blacksmiths would all be college dons.

He who can, does. He who cannot, teaches.

A learned man is an idler who kills time with study. Beware of his false knowledge: it is more dangerous than ignorance.

Activity is the only road to knowledge.

Every fool believes what his teachers tell him, and calls his credulity science or morality as confidently as his father called it divine revelation.

No man fully capable of his own language ever masters another.

No man can be a pure specialist without being in the strict sense an idiot.

Do not give your children moral and religious instruction unless you are quite sure they will not take it too seriously. Better be the mother of Henri Quatre and Nell Gwynne than of Robespierre and Queen Mary Tudor.

MARRIAGE

Marriage is popular because it combines the maximum of temptation with the maximum of opportunity.

Marriage is the only legal contract which abrogates as between the parties all the laws that safeguard the particular relation to which it refers.

The essential function of marriage is the continuance of the race, as stated in the Book of Common Prayer.

The accidental function of marriage is the gratification of the amoristic sentiment of mankind.

The artificial sterilization of marriage makes it possible for marriage to fulfil its accidental function whilst neglecting its essential one.

The most revolutionary invention of the nineteenth century was the artificial sterilization of marriage.

Any marriage system which condemns a majority of the population to celibacy will be violently wrecked on the pretext that it outrages morality.

Polygamy, when tried under modern democratic conditions, as by the Mormons, is wrecked by the revolt of the mass of inferior men who are condemned to celibacy by it; for the maternal instinct leads a woman to prefer a tenth share in a first rate man to the exclusive possession of a third rate one. Polyandry has not been tried under these conditions.

The minimum of national celibacy (ascertained by dividing the number of males in the community by the number of females, and taking the quotient as the number of wives or husbands permitted to each person) is secured in England (where the quotient is 1) by the institution of monogamy.

The modern sentimental term for the national minimum of celibacy is Purity.

Marriage, or any other form of promiscuous amoristic monogamy, is fatal to large States because it puts its ban on the deliberate breeding of man as a political animal.

CRIME AND PUNISHMENT

All scoundrelism is summed up in the phrase "*Que Messieurs les Assassins commencent!*"

The man who has graduated from the flogging block at Eton to the bench from which he sentences the garotter to be flogged is the same social product as the garotter who has been kicked by his father and cuffed by his mother until he has grown strong enough to throttle and rob the rich citizen whose money he desires.

Imprisonment is as irrevocable as death.

Criminals do not die by the hands of the law. They die by the hands of other men.

The assassin Czolgosz made President McKinley a hero by assassinating him. The United States of America made Czolgosz a hero by the same process.

Assassination on the scaffold is the worst form of assassination, because there it is invested with the approval of society.

It is the deed that teaches, not the name we give it. Murder and capital punishment are not opposites that cancel one another, but similars that breed their kind.

Crime is only the retail department of what, in wholesale, we call penal law.

When a man wants to murder a tiger he calls it sport: when the tiger wants to murder him he calls it ferocity. The distinction between Crime and Justice is no greater.

Whilst we have prisons it matters little which of us occupy the cells.

The most anxious man in a prison is the governor.

It is not necessary to replace a guillotined criminal: it is necessary to replace a guillotined social system.

TITLES

Titles distinguish the mediocre, embarrass the superior, and are disgraced by the inferior.

Great men refuse titles because they are jealous of them.

HONOR

There are no perfectly honorable men; but every true man has one main point of honor and a few minor ones.

You cannot believe in honor until you have achieved it. Better keep yourself clean and bright: you are the window through which you must see the world.

Your word can never be as good as your bond, because your memory can never be as trustworthy as your honor.

PROPERTY

Property, said Proudhon, is theft. This is the only perfect truism that has been uttered on the subject.

SERVANTS

When domestic servants are treated as human beings it is not worth while to keep them.

The relation of master and servant is advantageous only to masters who do not scruple to abuse their authority, and to servants who do not scruple to abuse their trust.

The perfect servant, when his master makes humane advances to him, feels that his existence is threatened, and hastens to change his place.

Masters and servants are both tyrannical; but the masters are the more dependent of the two.

A man enjoys what he uses, not what his servants use.

Man is the only animal which esteems itself rich in proportion to the number and voracity of its parasites.

Ladies and gentlemen are permitted to have friends in the kennel, but not in the kitchen.

Domestic servants, by making spoiled children of their masters, are forced to intimidate them in order to be able to live with them.

In a slave state, the slaves rule: in Mayfair, the tradesman rules.

HOW TO BEAT CHILDREN

If you strike a child, take care that you strike it in anger, even at the risk of maiming it for life. A blow in cold blood neither can nor should be forgiven.

If you beat children for pleasure, avow your object frankly, and play the game according to the rules, as a foxhunter does; and you will do comparatively little harm. No foxhunter is such a cad as to pretend that he hunts the fox to teach it not to steal chickens, or that he suffers more acutely than the fox at the death. Remember that even in childbeating there is the sportsman's way and the cad's way.

RELIGION

Beware of the man whose god is in the skies.

What a man believes may be ascertained, not from his creed, but from the assumptions on which he habitually acts.

VIRTUES AND VICES

No specific virtue or vice in a man implies the existence of any other specific virtue or vice in him, however closely the imagination may associate them.

Virtue consists, not in abstaining from vice, but in not desiring it.

Self-denial is not a virtue: it is only the effect of prudence on rascality.

Obedience simulates subordination as fear of the police simulates honesty.

Disobedience, the rarest and most courageous of the virtues, is seldom distinguished from neglect, the laziest and commonest of the vices.

Vice is waste of life. Poverty, obedience and celibacy are the canonical vices.

Economy is the art of making the most of life.

The love of economy is the root of all virtue.

FAIRPLAY

The love of fairplay is a spectator's virtue, not a principal's.

GREATNESS

Greatness is only one of the sensations of littleness.

In heaven an angel is nobody in particular.

Greatness is the secular name for Divinity: both mean simply what lies beyond us.

If a great man could make us understand him, we should hang him.

We admit that when the divinity we worshipped made itself visible and comprehensible we crucified it.

To a mathematician the eleventh means only a single unit: to the bushman who cannot count further than his ten fingers it is an incalculable myriad.

The difference between the shallowest routineer and the deepest thinker appears, to the latter, trifling; to the former, infinite.

In a stupid nation the man of genius becomes a god: everybody worships him and nobody does his will.

BEAUTY AND HAPPINESS, ART AND RICHES

Happiness and Beauty are by-products.

Folly is the direct pursuit of Happiness and Beauty.

Riches and Art are spurious receipts for the production of Happiness and Beauty.

He who desires a lifetime of happiness with a beautiful woman desires to enjoy the taste of wine by keeping his mouth always full of it.

The most intolerable pain is produced by prolonging the keenest pleasure.

The man with toothache thinks everyone happy whose teeth are sound. The poverty-stricken man makes the same mistake about the rich man.

The more a man possesses over and above what he uses, the more careworn he becomes.

The tyranny that forbids you to make the road with pick and shovel is worse than that which prevents you from lolling along it in a carriage and pair.

In an ugly and unhappy world the richest man can purchase nothing but ugliness and unhappiness.

In his efforts to escape from ugliness and unhappiness the rich man intensifies both. Every new yard of West End creates a new acre of East End.

The nineteenth century was the Age of Faith in Fine Art. The results are before us.

THE PERFECT GENTLEMAN

The fatal reservation of the gentleman is that he sacrifices everything to his honor except his gentility.

A gentleman of our days is one who has money enough to do what every fool would do if he could afford it: that is, consume without producing.

The true diagnostic of modern gentility is parasitism.

No elaboration of physical or moral accomplishment can atone for the sin of parasitism.

A modern gentleman is necessarily the enemy of his country. Even in war he does not fight to defend it, but to prevent his power of preying on it from passing to a foreigner. Such combatants are patriots in the same sense as two dogs fighting for a bone are lovers of animals.

The North American Indian was a type of the sportsman warrior gentleman. The Periclean Athenian was a type of the intellectually and artistically cultivated gentleman. Both were political failures. The modern gentleman, without the hardihood of the one or the culture of the other, has the appetite of both put together. He will not succeed where they failed.

He who believes in education, criminal law, and sport, needs only property to make him a perfect modern gentleman.

MODERATION

Moderation is never applauded for its own sake.

A moderately honest man with a moderately faithful wife, moderate drinkers both, in a moderately healthy house: that is the true middle class unit.

THE UNCONSCIOUS SELF

The unconscious self is the real genius. Your breathing goes wrong the moment your conscious self meddles with it.

Except during the nine months before he draws his first breath, no man manages his affairs as well as a tree does.

REASON

The reasonable man adapts himself to the world: the unreasonable one persists in trying to adapt the world to himself. Therefore all progress depends on the unreasonable man.

The man who listens to Reason is lost: Reason enslaves all whose minds are not strong enough to master her.

DECENCY

Decency is Indecency's Conspiracy of Silence.

EXPERIENCE

Men are wise in proportion, not to their experience, but to their capacity for experience.

If we could learn from mere experience, the stones of London would be wiser than its wisest men.

TIME'S REVENGES

Those whom we called brutes had their revenge when Darwin shewed us that they were our cousins.

The thieves had their revenge when Marx convicted the bourgeoisie of theft.

GOOD INTENTIONS

Hell is paved with good intentions, not with bad ones.
All men mean well.

NATURAL RIGHTS

The Master of Arts, by proving that no man has any natural rights, compels himself to take his own for granted.

The right to live is abused whenever it is not constantly challenged.

FAUTE DE MIEUX

In my childhood I demurred to the description of a certain young lady as "the pretty Miss So and So." My aunt rebuked me by saying "Remember always that the least homely sister is the family beauty."

No age or condition is without its heroes. The least incapable general in a nation is its Cæsar, the least imbecile statesman its Solon, the least confused thinker its Socrates, the least commonplace poet its Shakespear.

CHARITY

Charity is the most mischievous sort of pruriency.

Those who minister to poverty and disease are accomplices in the two worst of all crimes.

He who gives money he has not earned is generous with other people's labor.

Every genuinely benevolent person loathes almsgiving and mendicity.

FAME

Life levels all men: death reveals the eminent.

DISCIPLINE

Mutiny Acts are needed only by officers who command without authority. Divine right needs no whip.

WOMEN IN THE HOME

Home is the girl's prison and the woman's workhouse.

CIVILIZATION

Civilization is a disease produced by the practice of building societies with rotten material.

Those who admire modern civilization usually identify it with the steam engine and the electric telegraph.

Those who understand the steam engine and the electric telegraph spend their lives in trying to replace them with something better.

The imagination cannot conceive a viler criminal than he who should build another London like the present one, nor a greater benefactor than he who should destroy it.

GAMBLING

The most popular method of distributing wealth is the method of the roulette table.

The roulette table pays nobody except him who keeps it. Nevertheless a passion for gaming is common, though a passion for keeping roulette tables is unknown.

Gambling promises the poor what Property performs for the rich: that is why the bishops dare not denounce it fundamentally.

THE SOCIAL QUESTION

Do not waste your time on Social Questions. What is the matter with the poor is Poverty: what is the matter with the Rich is Uselessness.

STRAY SAYINGS

We are told that when Jehovah created the world he saw that it was good. What would he say now?

The conversion of a savage to Christianity is the conversion of Christianity to savagery.

No man dares say so much of what he thinks as to appear to himself an extremist.

Mens sana in corpore sano is a foolish saying. The sound body is a product of the sound mind.

Decadence can find agents only when it wears the mask of progress.

In moments of progress the noble succeed, because things are going their way: in moments of decadence the base succeed for the same reason: hence the world is never without the exhilaration of contemporary success.

The reformer for whom the world is not good enough finds himself shoulder to shoulder with him that is not good enough for the world.

Every man over forty is a scoundrel.

Youth, which is forgiven everything, forgives itself nothing: age, which forgives itself everything, is forgiven nothing.

When we learn to sing that Britons never will be masters we shall make an end of slavery.

Do not mistake your objection to defeat for an objection to fighting, your objection to being a slave for an objection to slavery, your objection to not being as rich as your neighbor for an objection to poverty. The cowardly, the insubordinate, and the envious share your objections.

Take care to get what you like or you will be forced to like what you get. Where there is no ventilation fresh air is declared unwholesome. Where there is no religion hypocrisy becomes good taste. Where there is no knowledge ignorance calls itself science.

If the wicked flourish and the fittest survive, Nature must be the God of rascals.

If history repeats itself, and the unexpected always happens, how incapable must Man be of learning from experience!

Compassion is the fellow-feeling of the unsound.

Those who understand evil pardon it: those who resent it destroy it.

Acquired notions of propriety are stronger than natural instincts. It is easier to recruit for monasteries and convents than to induce an Arab woman to uncover her mouth in public, or a British officer to walk through Bond Street in a golfing cap on an afternoon in May.

It is dangerous to be sincere unless you are also stupid.

The Chinese tame fowls by clipping their wings, and women by deforming their feet. A petticoat round the ankles serves equally well.

Political Economy and Social Economy are amusing intellectual games; but Vital Economy is the Philosopher's Stone.

When a heretic wishes to avoid martyrdom he speaks of "Orthodoxy, True and False" and demonstrates that the True is his heresy.

Beware of the man who does not return your blow: he neither forgives you nor allows you to forgive yourself.

If you injure your neighbor, better not do it by halves.

Sentimentality is the error of supposing that quarter can be given or taken in moral conflicts.

Two starving men cannot be twice as hungry as one; but two rascals can be ten times as vicious as one.

Make your cross your crutch; but when you see another man do it, beware of him.

SELF-SACRIFICE

Self-sacrifice enables us to sacrifice other people without blushing.

If you begin by sacrificing yourself to those you love, you will end by hating those to whom you have sacrificed yourself.

THE END

VERSE DRAMA

William Butler Yeats

ON BAILE'S STRAND

[1903]

William Butler Yeats [1865-1939]

As the Irish poet Padraic Colum once said in a television interview, "Words, words, words: the rediscovery of language is the key to the Irish renaissance." Colum is of course right, and William Butler Yeats, perhaps the most widely praised poet in English in the twentieth century, is unquestionably the fountainhead of this renaissance. It was Yeats along with Lady Augusta Gregory and several others who organized the (Irish) National Literary Society in 1892, and later the Irish Literary Theatre in 1899. It was Yeats who contributed moving, beautifully phrased, penetrating essays to the official publications of the various literary organizations, thus furnishing the revival of interest in Celtic lore and history with manifestoes and detailed critical statements. And it was Yeats the poet but also the playwright who wrote *The Countess Cathleen* in 1892, *The Land of Heart's Desire* in 1894, *Cathleen Ni Houlihan* in 1902, *On Baile's Strand* in 1903, and *Deirdre* in 1907: all of them plays dramatizing mythical figures of the Irish past. With Yeats the movement to restore verse drama to the modern stage has its real beginnings.

It would be inaccurate to suggest that verse drama in the late nineteenth and the twentieth centuries has held the boards to any great extent: it has not. However, numerous critics have discussed the value of verse drama, and several playwrights have written in verse. The subject has not been dead, but modern drama whether

Yeats and Verse Drama

on the Continent, in the British Isles, or in America has produced relatively few plays in verse.

The basic reason is not far to seek. Although poetic drama has a long line of descent from the drama of ancient Greece, and although the dramatic art of Europe was predominantly a poetic one through the seventeenth century, with the tradition persisting, especially in serious plays, well into the nineteenth century, it was essentially a form that sought to idealize experience, not to reproduce it in the observable, factual terms of everyday life. With the development of the realistic temper in literature and the other arts in the late nineteenth century, and the view of realism as a "slice of life" as bodied forth by Ibsen in the drama, poetic expression on the stage came to be viewed as artificial and untrue to the "real-life" situations now being presented. With this view of reality prevailing, and of the role of the drama in presenting it, verse drama has not generally been viable in the modern theater.

However, verse drama has much to recommend it and many feel that its absence from our stage reveals a poverty in the modern drama. For one thing, the feelings engendered by verse are often more profound than those created by prose. It is no accident that much of the great drama, particularly the tragic drama, of the past has been in verse. The subtleties of the mind often find their most suggestive expression in the most subtle and complex use of lan-

Yeats and Verse Drama

guage; that is, in poetry. The highest flights of the imagination seem more appropriate and are more fully expressed in verse than in prose. Verse, through its greater degree of formality than prose, pleases the mind in the way that all highly formal works of art do. The sense of ordered beauty is more immediate in verse than in prose. As Yeats said in his essay "The Theatre," "The theatre began in ritual, and it cannot come to its greatness again without recalling words to their ancient sovereignty." Dramatic poetry can create a degree of intensity which is hard to produce with prose. One point should be made clear, however: a good verse drama is not a good prose play rewritten in verse. A good verse drama is one which could not have been written in prose; the form (poetry) is the appropriate expression of the idea. Since 1930 several verse dramatists have appeared: Maxwell Anderson, Federico Garcia Lorca, T. S. Eliot, and Christopher Fry; but despite their examples and their theorizing, good poetry in the theater has remained rare.

Though his urgent call to restore the sovereignty of words in the theater has not generally been heeded, Yeats exerted a quickening influence on modern drama through his leading role in the literary movement known as the Celtic or Irish renaissance. His *The Countess Cathleen,* together with a play by Edward Martyn, opened the Irish Literary Theatre in 1899; and *On Baile's Strand* inaugurated the illustrious Abbey Theatre on December 27, 1904. In love with words, as he urged Irish writers to be, Yeats gives dramatic form to the old story of the death of Cuchulain, the great hero of the Ulster cycle of the Irish sagas. Cuchulain, the passionate man, is at the vortex of the tragedy. (Yeats wrote, "The subject of all art is passion.") He finds himself opposed to Conchubar, with his prudential wisdom, living in an age which has no time for heroes of Cuchulain's cast. He is a kind of Irish Achilles, unwilling to be ruled by the concerns of statecraft. In order to underline this fundamental conflict, Yeats uses minor characters to mirror the theme metaphorically. To say, as the First Woman says, that "life drifts between a fool and a blind man," is to speak nonsense — unless one is using the language of poetry. Like Cuchulain and Conchubar, the Fool and the Blind Man are polar opposites; thus a degree of formality exists in *On Baile's Strand* which may not be apparent upon first reading. As one reflects, however, he is led to ask himself about the function of the two parallel characters from the lower levels of the society, and their relationship to the nobler figures in the drama. They speak in prose, but the kings speak in verse, the language of passion and elevated feeling; the Blind Man and the Fool are intent upon the fowl in the ovens, while the two kings weigh kingdoms and heroic deeds. Questions which arise out of the play are such as these: Why must Cuchulain die? And why in the particular way that he does? Are feeling, words and actions adequately related? Is the play successful as a verse drama?

THE REFORM OF THE THEATRE*

by William Butler Yeats

I think the theatre must be reformed in its plays, its speaking, its acting, and its scenery. That is to say, I think there is nothing good about it at present.

First. We have to write or find plays that will make the theatre a place of intellectual excitement — a place where the mind goes to be liberated as it was liberated by the theatres of Greece and England and France at certain great moments of their history, and as it is liberated in Scandinavia today. If we are to do this we must learn that beauty and truth are always justified of themselves, and that their creation is a greater service to our country than writing that compromises either in the seeming service of a cause. We will, doubtless, come more easily to truth and beauty because we love some cause with all but all our heart; but we must remember when truth and beauty open their mouths to speak, that all other mouths should be as silent as Finn bade the Son of Lugaidh be in the houses of the great. Truth and beauty judge and are above judgement. They justify and have no need of justification.

Such plays will require, both in writers and in audiences, a stronger feeling for beautiful and appropriate language than one finds in the ordinary theatre. Sainte-Beuve has said that there is nothing immortal in literature except style, and it is precisely this sense of style, once common among us, that is hardest for us to recover. I do not mean by style words with an air of literature about them, what is ordinarily called eloquent writing. The speeches of Falstaff are as perfect in their style as the soliloquies of Hamlet. One must be able to make a king of faery or an old countryman or a modern lover speak that language which is his and nobody else's, and speak it with so much of emotional subtlety that the hearer may find it hard to know whether it is the thought or the word that has moved him, or whether these could be separated at all.

If we do not know how to construct, if we cannot arrange much complicated life into a single action, our work will not hold the attention or linger in the memory, but if we are not in love with words it will lack the delicate

* From *Plays and Controversies* (New York: The Macmillan Company, 1924), pp. 45–49.

movement of living speech that is the chief garment of life; and because of this lack the great realists seem to the lovers of beautiful art to be wise in this generation, and for the next generation, perhaps, but not for all generations that are to come.

Second. But if we are to restore words to their sovereignty we must make speech even more important than gesture upon the stage.

I have been told that I desire a monotonous chant, but that is not true, for though a monotonous chant may be a safer beginning for an actor than the broken and prosaic speech of ordinary recitation, it puts me to sleep none the less. The sing-song in which a child says a verse is a right beginning, though the child grows out of it. An actor should understand how so to discriminate cadence from cadence, and so to cherish the musical lineaments of verse or prose that he delights the ear with a continually varied music. Certain passages of lyrical feeling, or where one wishes, as in the Angel's part in *The Hour-Glass,* to make a voice sound like the voice of an immortal, may be spoken upon pure notes which are carefully recorded and learned as if they were the notes of a song. Whatever method one adopts, one must always be certain that the work of art, as a whole, is masculine and intellectual, in its sound as in its form.

Third. We must simplify acting, especially in poetical drama, and in prose drama that is remote from real life like my *Hour-Glass.* We must get rid of everything that is restless, everything that draws the attention away from the sound of the voice, or from the few moments of intense expression, whether that expression is through the voice or through the hands; we must from time to time substitute for the movements that the eye sees the nobler movements that the heart sees, the rhythmical movements that seem to flow up into the imagination from some deeper life than that of the individual soul.

Fourth. Just as it is necessary to simplify gesture that it may accompany speech without being its rival, it is necessary to simplify both the form and the color of scenery and costume. As a rule the background should be but a single color, so that the persons in the play, wherever they stand, may harmonize with it and preoccupy our attention. In other words, it should be thought out not as one thinks out a landscape, but as if it were the background of a portrait, and this is especially necessary on a small stage where the moment the stage is filled the painted forms of the background are broken up and lost. Even when one has to represent trees or hills they should be treated in most cases decoratively, they should be little more than an unobtrusive pattern. There must be nothing unnecessary, nothing that will distract the attention from speech and movement. An art is always at its greatest when it is most human. Greek acting was great because it did all but everything with voice and movement. But an art which smothers these things with bad painting, with innumerable garish colors, with continual restless mimicries of the surface of life, is an art of fading humanity, a decaying art.

From THE PLAY, THE PLAYER, AND THE SCENE*

by William Butler Yeats

... Our plays [of the Irish National Theatre] must be literature or written in the spirit of literature. The modern theatre has died away to what it is because the writers have thought of their audiences instead of their subject. An old writer saw his hero, if it was a play of character, or some dominant passion, if it was a play of passion, like *Phèdre* or *Andromaque*, moving before him, living with a life he did not endeavor to control. The persons acted upon one another as they were bound by their natures to act, and the play was dramatic, not because he had sought out dramatic situations for their own sake, but because will broke itself upon will and passion upon passion. Then the imagination began to cool, the writer began to be less alive, to seek external aids, remembered situations, tricks of the theatre, that had proved themselves again and again. His persons no longer will have a particular character, but he knows that he can rely upon the incidents, and he feels himself fortunate when there is nothing in his play that has not succeeded a thousand times before the curtain has risen. Perhaps he has even read a certain guide-book to the stage published in France, and called *The Thirty-Six Situations of Drama*. The costumes will be magnificent, the actresses will be beautiful, the Castle in Spain will be painted by an artist upon the spot. We will come from his play excited if we are foolish, or can condescend to the folly of others, but knowing nothing new about ourselves, and seeing life with no new eyes and hearing it with no new ears. The whole movement of theatrical reform in our day has been a struggle to get rid of this kind of play, and the sincere play, the logical play, that we would have in its place, will always seem, when we hear it for the first time, undramatic, unexciting. It has to stir the heart in a long-disused way, it has to awaken the intellect to a pleasure that ennobles and wearies. I was at the first performance of an Ibsen play given in England. It was *The Doll's House*, and at the fall of the curtain I heard an old dramatic critic say, "It is but a series of

* From *Plays and Controversies* (New York: The Macmillan Company, 1924), pp. 117–124.

conversations terminated by an accident." So far, we here in Dublin mean the same thing as do Mr. Max Beerbohm, Mr. Walkley, and Mr. Archer, who are seeking to restore sincerity to the English stage, but I am not certain that we mean the same thing all through. The utmost sincerity, the most unbroken logic, give me, at any rate, but an imperfect pleasure if there is not a vivid and beautiful language. Ibsen has sincerity and logic beyond any writer of our time, and we are all seeking to learn them at his hands; but is he not a good deal less than the greatest of all times, because he lacks beautiful and vivid language? "Well, well, give me time and you shall hear all about it. If only I had Peter here now," is very like life, is entirely in its place where it comes, and when it is united to other sentences exactly like itself, one is moved, one knows not how, to pity and terror, and yet not moved as if the words themselves could sing and shine. Mr. Max Beerbohm wrote once that a play cannot have style because the people must talk as they talk in daily life. He was thinking, it is obvious, of a play made out of that typically modern life where there is no longer vivid speech. Blake says that a work of art must be minutely articulated by God or man, and man has too little help from that occasional collaborateur when he writes of people whose language has become abstract and dead. Falstaff gives one the sensation of reality, and when one remembers the abundant vocabulary of a time when all but everything present to the mind was present to the senses, one imagines that his words were but little magnified from the words of such a man in real life. Language was still alive then, alive as it is in Gaelic today, as it is in English-speaking Ireland where the Schoolmaster or the newspaper has not corrupted it. I know that we are at the mere beginning, laboriously learning our craft, trying our hands in little plays for the most part, that we may not venture too boldly in our ignorance; but I never hear the vivid, picturesque, ever-varied language of Mr. Synge's persons without feeling that the great collaborateur has his finger in our business. May it not be that the only realistic play that will live as Shakespeare has lived, as Calderon has lived, as the Greeks have lived, will arise out of the common life, where language is as much alive as if it were new come out of Eden? After all, is not the greatest play not the play that gives the sensation of an external reality but the play in which there is the greatest abundance of life itself, of the reality that is in our minds? Is it possible to make a work of art, which needs every subtlety of expression if it is to reveal what hides itself continually, out of a dying, or at any rate a very ailing, language? and all language but that of the poets and of the poor is already bedridden. We have, indeed, persiflage, the only speech of educated men that expresses a deliberate enjoyment of words: but persiflage is not a true language. It is impersonal; it is not in the midst but on the edge of life; it covers more character than it discovers: and yet, such as it is, all our comedies are made out of it.

What the ever-moving, delicately molded flesh is to human beauty, vivid musical words are to passion. Somebody has said that every nation begins with poetry and ends with algebra, and passion has always refused to express itself in algebraical terms.

Have we not been in error in demanding from our playwrights personages who do not transcend our common actions any more than our common speech? If we are in the right, all antiquity has been in error. The scholars of a few generations ago were fond of deciding that certain persons were unworthy of the dignity of art. They had, it may be, an over-abounding preference for kings and queens, but we are, it may be, very stupid in thinking that the average man is a fit subject at all for the finest art. Art delights in the exception, for it delights in the soul expressing itself according to its own laws and arranging the world about it in its own pattern, as sand strewn upon a drum will change itself into different patterns, according to the notes of music that are sung or played to it. But the average man is average because he has not attained to freedom. Habit, routine, fear of public opinion, fear of punishment here or hereafter, a myriad of things that are "something other than human life," something less than flame, work their will upon his soul and trundle his body here and there. At the first performance of *Ghosts* I could not escape from an illusion unaccountable to me at the time. All the characters seemed to be less than life-size; the stage, though it was but the little Royalty stage, seemed larger than I had ever seen it. Little whimpering puppets moved here and there in the middle of that great abyss. Why did they not speak out with louder voices or move with freer gestures? What was it that weighed upon their souls perpetually? Certainly they were all in prison, and yet there was no prison. In India there are villages so obedient that all the jailer has to do is to draw a circle upon the ground with his staff, and to tell his thief to stand there so many hours; but what law had these people broken that they had to wander round that narrow circle all their lives? May not such art, terrible, satirical, inhuman, be the medicine of great cities, where nobody is ever alone with his own strength? Nor is Maeterlinck very different, for his persons "inquire after Jerusalem in the regions of the grave, with weak voices almost inarticulate, wearying repose." Is it the mob that has robbed those angelic persons of the energy of their souls? Will not our next art be rather of the country, of great open spaces, of the soul rejoicing in itself? Will not the generations to come begin again to have an over-abounding faith in kings and queens, in masterful spirits, whatever names we call them by? I had Molière with me on my way to America, and as I read I seemed to be at home in Ireland listening to that conversation of the people which is so full of riches because so full of leisure, or to those old stories of the folk which were made by men who believed so much in the soul, and so little in anything else, that they were never entirely certain that the earth was solid under the foot-sole. What is there left for us, that have seen the newly discovered stability of things changed from an enthusiasm to a weariness, but to labor with a high heart, though it may be with weak hands, to rediscover an art of the theatre that shall be joyful, fantastic, extravagant, whimsical, beautiful, resonant, and altogether reckless? The arts are at their greatest when they seek for a life growing always more scornful of everything that is not itself and passing into its own fullness, as it were, ever more completely as all that is created out of the passing mode of society slips from it; and attaining that fullness, perfectly it may be — and from this is tragic joy and the perfectness of tragedy — when the world itself has slipped away in death. We, who are believers, cannot see reality anywhere but in the soul itself, and seeing it there we cannot do other than rejoice in every energy, whether of gesture, or of action, or of speech, coming out of the personality, the soul's image, even though the very laws of nature seem as unimportant in comparison as did the laws of Rome to Coriolanus when his pride was upon him. Has not the long decline of the arts been but the shadow of declining faith in an unseen reality?

> If the sun and moon would doubt,
> They'd immediately go out.

On Baile's Strand

TO WILLIAM FAY
because of the beautiful fantasy of his playing
in the character of the Fool

PERSONS IN THE PLAY

A FOOL

A BLIND MAN

CUCHULAIN, *King of Muirthemne*

CONCHUBAR, *High King of Uladh*

A YOUNG MAN, *son of Cuchulain*

KINGS *and* SINGING WOMEN

A great hall at Dundealgan, not "Cuchulain's great ancient house" but an assembly-house nearer to the sea. A big door at the back, and through the door misty light as of sea-mist. There are many chairs and one long bench. One of these chairs, which is towards the front of the stage, is bigger than the others. Somewhere at the back is a table with flagons of ale upon it and drinking-horns. There is a small door at one side of the hall. A FOOL *and* BLIND MAN, *both ragged, and their features made grotesque and extravagant by masks, come in through the door at the back. The* BLIND MAN *leans upon a staff.*

FOOL. What a clever man you are though you are blind! There's nobody with two eyes in his head that is as clever as you are. Who but you could have thought that the henwife sleeps every day a little at noon? I would never be able to steal anything if you didn't tell me where to look for it. And what a good cook you are! You take the fowl out of my hands after I have stolen it and plucked it, and you put it into the big pot at the fire there, and I can go out and run races with the witches at the edge of the waves and get an appetite, and when I've got it, there's the hen waiting inside for me, done to the turn.

BLIND MAN (*who is feeling about with his stick*). Done to the turn.

FOOL (*putting his arm round* BLIND MAN's *neck*). Come now, I'll have a leg and you'll have a leg, and we'll draw lots for the wish-bone. I'll be praising you, I'll be praising you while we're eating it, for your good plans and for your good cooking. There's nobody in the world like you, Blind Man. Come, come. Wait a minute. I shouldn't have closed the door. There are some that look for me, and I wouldn't like them not to find me. Don't tell it to anybody, Blind Man. There are some that follow me. Boann herself out of the river and Fand out of the deep sea. Witches they are, and they come by in the wind, and they cry, "Give a kiss, Fool, give a kiss," that's what they cry. That's wide enough. All the witches can come in now. I wouldn't have them beat at the door and say, "Where is the Fool? Why has he put a lock on the door?" Maybe they'll hear the bubbling of the pot and come in and sit on the ground. But we won't give them any of the fowl. Let them go back to the sea, let them go back to the sea.

BLIND MAN (*feeling legs of big chair with his hands*). Ah! (*Then, in a louder voice as he feels the back of it.*) Ah — ah —

FOOL. Why do you say "Ah-ah"?

BLIND MAN. I know the big chair. It is to-day the High King Conchubar is coming. They have brought out his chair. He is going to be Cuchulain's master in earnest from this day out. It is that he's coming for.

FOOL. He must be a great man to be Cuchulain's master.

BLIND MAN. So he is. He is a great man. He is over all the rest of the kings of Ireland.

FOOL. Cuchulain's master! I thought Cuchulain could do anything he liked.

BLIND MAN. So he did, so he did. But he ran too wild, and Conchubar is coming to-day to put an oath upon him that will stop his rambling and make him as biddable as a house-dog and keep him always at his hand. He will sit in this chair and put the oath upon him.

FOOL. How will he do that?

BLIND MAN. You have no wits to understand such things. (*The* BLIND MAN *has got into the chair.*) He will sit up in this chair and he'll say: "Take the oath, Cuchulain. I bid you take the oath. Do as I tell you. What are your wits compared with mine, and what are your riches compared with mine? And what sons have you to pay your debts and to put a stone over you when you die? Take the oath, I tell you. Take a strong oath."

FOOL (*crumpling himself up and whining*). I will not. I'll take no oath. I want my dinner.

BLIND MAN. Hush, hush! It is not done yet.

FOOL. You said it was done to a turn.

BLIND MAN. Did I, now? Well, it might be done, and not done. The wings might be white, but the legs might be red. The flesh might stick hard to the bones and not come away in the teeth. But, believe me, Fool, it will be well done before you put your teeth in it.

FOOL. My teeth are growing long with the hunger.

BLIND MAN. I'll tell you a story — the kings have story-tellers while they are waiting for their dinner — I will tell you a story with a fight in it, a story with a champion in it, and a ship and a queen's son that has his mind set on killing somebody that you and I know.

FOOL. Who is that? Who is he coming to kill?

BLIND MAN. Wait, now, till you hear. When you were stealing the fowl, I was lying in a hole in the sand, and I heard three men coming with a shuffling sort of noise. They were wounded and groaning.

FOOL. Go on. Tell me about the fight.

BLIND MAN. There had been a fight, a great fight, a tremendous great fight. A young man had landed on the shore, the guardians of the shore had asked his name, and he had refused to tell it, and he had killed one, and others had run away.

FOOL. That's enough. Come on now to the fowl. I wish it was bigger. I wish it was as big as a goose.

BLIND MAN. Hush! I haven't told you all. I know who that young man is. I heard the men who were running away say he had red hair, that he had come from Aoife's country, that he was coming to kill Cuchulain.

FOOL. Nobody can do that.

(To a tune)
Cuchulain has killed kings,
Kings and sons of kings,
Dragons out of the water,
And witches out of the air,
Banachas and Bonachas and people of the woods.

BLIND MAN. Hush! hush!

FOOL *(still singing)*.
Witches that steal the milk,
Fomor that steal the children,
Hags that have heads like hares,
Hares that have claws like witches,
All riding a-cock-horse
(Spoken)
Out of the very bottom of the bitter black North.

BLIND MAN. Hush, I say!

FOOL. Does Cuchulain know that he is coming to kill him?

BLIND MAN. How would he know that with his head in the clouds? He

On Baile's Strand

doesn't care for common fighting. Why would he put himself out, and nobody in it but that young man? Now if it were a white fawn that might turn into a queen before morning —

FOOL. Come to the fowl. I wish it was as big as a pig; a fowl with goose grease and pig's crackling.

BLIND MAN. No hurry, no hurry. I know whose son it is. I wouldn't tell anybody else, but I will tell you, — a secret is better to you than your dinner. You like being told secrets.

FOOL. Tell me the secret.

BLIND MAN. That young man is Aoife's son. I am sure it is Aoife's son, it flows in upon me that it is Aoife's son. You have often heard me talking of Aoife, the great woman-fighter Cuchulain got the mastery over in the North?

FOOL. I know, I know. She is one of those cross queens that live in hungry Scotland.

BLIND MAN. I am sure it is her son. I was in Aoife's country for a long time.

FOOL. That was before you were blinded for putting a curse upon the wind.

BLIND MAN. There was a boy in her house that had her own red colour on him, and everybody said he was to be brought up to kill Cuchulain, that she hated Cuchulain. She used to put a helmet on a pillar-stone and call it Cuchulain and set him casting at it. There is a step outside — Cuchulain's step.

CUCHULAIN *passes by in the mist outside the big door.*

FOOL. Where is Cuchulain going?

BLIND MAN. He is going to meet Conchubar that has bidden him to take the oath.

FOOL. Ah, an oath, Blind Man. How can I remember so many things at once? Who is going to take an oath?

BLIND MAN. Cuchulain is going to take an oath to Conchubar who is High King.

FOOL. What a mix-up you make of everything, Blind Man! You were telling me one story, and now you are telling me another story. . . . How can I get the hang of it at the end if you mix everything at the beginning? Wait till I settle it out. There now, there's Cuchulain (*he points to one foot*), and there is the young man (*he points to the other foot*) that is coming to kill him, and Cuchulain doesn't know. But where's Conchubar? (*Takes bag from side.*) That's Conchubar with all his riches — Cuchulain, young man, Conchubar. — And where's Aoife? (*Throws up cap.*) There is Aoife, high up on the mountains in high hungry Scotland. Maybe it is not true after all. Maybe it was your own making up. It's many a time you cheated me before with your lies. Come to the cooking-pot, my stomach is pinched and rusty. Would you have it to be creaking like a gate?

BLIND MAN. I tell you it's true. And more than that is true. If you listen to what I say, you'll forget your stomach.

FOOL. I won't.

BLIND MAN. Listen. I know who the young man's father is, but I won't say. I would be afraid to say. Ah, Fool, you would forget everything if you could know who the young man's father is.

FOOL. Who is it? Tell me now quick, or I'll shake you. Come, out with it, or I'll shake you.

A murmur of voices in the distance.

BLIND MAN. Wait, wait. There's somebody coming. . . . It is Cuchulain is coming. He's coming back with the High King. Go and ask Cuchulain. He'll tell you. It's little you'll care about the cooking-pot when you have asked Cuchulain that . . .

BLIND MAN *goes out by side door.*

FOOL. I'll ask him. Cuchulain will know. He was in Aoife's country. (*Goes up stage.*) I'll ask him. (*Turns and goes down stage.*) But, no, I won't ask him, I would be afraid. (*Going up again.*) Yes, I will ask him. What harm in asking? The Blind Man said I was to ask him. (*Going down.*) No, no. I'll not ask him. He might kill me. I have but killed hens and geese and pigs. He has killed kings. (*Goes up again almost to big door.*) Who says I'm afraid? I'm not afraid. I'm no coward. I'll ask him. No, no, Cuchulain, I'm not going to ask you.

>He has killed kings,
>Kings and the sons of kings,
>Dragons out of the water,
>And witches out of the air,
>Banachas and Bonachas and people of the woods.

FOOL *goes out by side door, the last words being heard outside.* CUCHULAIN *and* CONCHUBAR *enter through the big door at the back. While they are still outside,* CUCHULAIN'S *voice is heard raised in anger. He is a dark man, something over forty years of age.* CONCHUBAR *is much older and carries a long staff, elaborately carved or with an elaborate gold handle.*

CUCHULAIN. Because I have killed men without your bidding
And have rewarded others at my own pleasure,
Because of half a score of trifling things,
You'd lay this oath upon me, and now — and now
You add another pebble to the heap,
And I must be your man, well-nigh your bondsman,
Because a youngster out of Aoife's country
Has found the shore ill-guarded.
    CONCHUBAR.   He came to land
While you were somewhere out of sight and hearing,
Hunting or dancing with your wild companions.
    CUCHULAIN. He can be driven out. I'll not be bound.

I'll dance or hunt, or quarrel or make love,
Wherever and whenever I've a mind to.
If time had not put water in your blood,
You never would have thought it.
  CONCHUBAR.   I would leave
A strong and settled country to my children.
  CUCHULAIN. And I must be obedient in all things;
Give up my will to yours; go where you please;
Come when you call; sit at the council-board
Among the unshapely bodies of old men;
I whose mere name has kept this country safe,
I that in early days have driven out
Maeve of Cruachan and the northern pirates,
The hundred kings of Sorcha, and the kings
Out of the Garden in the East of the World.
Must I, that held you on the throne when all
Had pulled you from it, swear obedience
As if I were some cattle-raising king?
Are my shins speckled with the heat of the fire,
Or have my hands no skill but to make figures
Upon the ashes with a stick? Am I
So slack and idle that I need a whip
Before I serve you?
  CONCHUBAR.   No, no whip, Cuchulain,
But every day my children come and say:
"This man is growing harder to endure.
How can we be at safety with this man
That nobody can buy or bid or bind?
We shall be at his mercy when you are gone;
He burns the earth as if he were a fire,
And time can never touch him."
  CUCHULAIN.   And so the tale
Grows finer yet; and I am to obey
Whatever child you set upon the throne,
As if it were yourself!
  CONCHUBAR.   Most certainly.
I am High King, my son shall be High King;
And you for all the wildness of your blood,
And though your father came out of the sun,
Are but a little king and weigh but light
In anything that touches government,
If put into the balance with my children.
  CUCHULAIN. It's well that we should speak our minds out plainly,
For when we die we shall be spoken of

In many countries. We in our young days
Have seen the heavens like a burning cloud
Brooding upon the world, and being more
Than men can be now that cloud's lifted up,
We should be the more truthful. Conchubar,
I do not like your children — they have no pith,
No marrow in their bones, and will lie soft
Where you and I lie hard.
  CONCHUBAR. You rail at them
Because you have no children of your own.
  CUCHULAIN. I think myself most lucky that I leave
No pallid ghost or mockery of a man
To drift and mutter in the corridors
Where I have laughed and sung.
  CONCHUBAR. That is not true,
For all your boasting of the truth between us;
For there is no man having house and lands,
That have been in the one family, called
By that one family's name for centuries,
But is made miserable if he know
They are to pass into a stranger's keeping,
As yours will pass.
  CUCHULAIN. The most of men feel that,
But you and I leave names upon the harp.
  CONCHUBAR. You play with arguments as lawyers do,
And put no heart in them. I know your thoughts,
For we have slept under the one cloak and drunk
From the one wine-cup. I know you to the bone,
I have heard you cry, aye, in your very sleep,
"I have no son," and with such bitterness
That I have gone upon my knees and prayed
That it might be amended.
  CUCHULAIN. For you thought
That I should be as biddable as others
Had I their reason for it; but that's not true;
For I would need a weightier argument
Than one that marred me in the copying,
As I have that clean hawk out of the air
That, as men say, begot this body of mine
Upon a mortal woman.
  CONCHUBAR. Now as ever
You mock at every reasonable hope,
And would have nothing, or impossible things.
What eye has ever looked upon the child

On Baile's Strand

Would satisfy a mind like that?
    CUCHULAIN.   I would leave
My house and name to none that would not face
Even myself in battle.
    CONCHUBAR.   Being swift of foot,
And making light of every common chance,
You should have overtaken on the hills
Some daughter of the air, or on the shore
A daughter of the Country-under-Wave.
    CUCHULAIN. I am not blasphemous.
    CONCHUBAR.   Yet you despise
Our queens, and would not call a child your own,
If one of them had borne him.
    CUCHULAIN.   I have not said it.
    CONCHUBAR. Ah! I remember I have heard you boast,
When the ale was in your blood, that there was one
In Scotland, where you had learnt the trade of war,
That had a stone-pale cheek and red-brown hair;
And that although you had loved other women,
You'd sooner that fierce woman of the camp
Bore you a son than any queen among them.
    CUCHULAIN. You call her a "fierce woman of the camp,"
For, having lived among the spinning-wheels,
You'd have no woman near that would not say,
"Ah! how wise!" "What will you have for supper?"
"What shall I wear that I may please you, sir?"
And keep that humming through the day and night
For ever. A fierce woman of the camp!
But I am getting angry about nothing.
You have never seen her. Ah! Conchubar, had you seen her
With that high, laughing, turbulent head of hers
Thrown backward, and the bowstring at her ear,
Or sitting at the fire with those grave eyes
Full of good counsel as it were with wine,
Or when love ran through all the lineaments
Of her wild body — although she had no child,
None other had all beauty, queen or lover,
Or was so fitted to give birth to kings.
    CONCHUBAR. There's nothing I can say but drifts you farther
From the one weighty matter. That very woman —
For I know well that you are praising Aoife —
Now hates you and will leave no subtlety
Unknotted that might run into a noose
About your throat, no army in idleness

That might bring ruin on this land you serve.
  CUCHULAIN. No wonder in that, no wonder at all in that.
I never have known love but as a kiss
In the mid-battle, and a difficult truce
Of oil and water, candles and dark night,
Hillside and hollow, the hot-footed sun
And the cold, sliding, slippery-footed moon —
A brief forgiveness between opposites
That have been hatreds for three times the age
Of this long-'stablished ground
  CONCHUBAR.   Listen to me.
Aoife makes war on us, and every day
Our enemies grow greater and beat the walls
More bitterly, and you within the walls
Are every day more turbulent; and yet,
When I would speak about these things, your fancy
Runs as it were a swallow on the wind.
> *Outside the door in the blue light of the sea-mist are many old and young* KINGS; *amongst them are three* WOMEN, *two of whom carry a bowl of fire. The third, in what follows, puts from time to time fragrant herbs into the fire so that it flickers up into brighter flame.*

Look at the door and what men gather there —
Old counsellors that steer the land with me,
And younger kings, the dancers and harp-players
That follow in your tumults, and all these
Are held there by the one anxiety.
Will you be bound into obedience
And so make this land safe for them and theirs?
You are but half a king and I but half;
I need your might of hand and burning heart,
And you my wisdom.
  CUCHULAIN (*going near to door*). Nestlings of a high nest,
Hawks that have followed me into the air
And looked upon the sun, we'll out of this
And sail upon the wind once more. This king
Would have me take an oath to do his will,
And having listened to his tune from morning,
I will no more of it. Run to the stable
And set the horses to the chariot-pole,
And send a messenger to the harp-players.
We'll find a level place among the woods,
And dance awhile.
  A YOUNG KING. Cuchulain, take the oath.
There is none here that would not have you take it.
  CUCHULAIN. You'd have me take it? Are you of one mind?

On Baile's Strand

THE KINGS. All, all, all, all!
A YOUNG KING. Do what the High King bids you.
CONCHUBAR. There is not one but dreads this turbulence
Now that they're settled men.
CUCHULAIN. Are you so changed,
Or have I grown more dangerous of late?
But that's not it. I understand it all.
It's you that have changed. You've wives and children now,
And for that reason cannot follow one
That lives like a bird's flight from tree to tree. —
It's time the years put water in my blood
And drowned the wildness of it, for all's changed,
But that unchanged. — I'll take what oath you will:
The moon, the sun, the water, light, or air,
I do not care how binding.
CONCHUBAR. On this fire
That has been lighted from your hearth and mine;
The older men shall be my witnesses,
The younger, yours. The holders of the fire
Shall purify the thresholds of the house
With waving fire, and shut the outer door,
According to the custom; and sing rhyme
That has come down from the old law-makers
To blow the witches out. Considering
That the wild will of man could be oath-bound,
But that a woman's could not, they bid us sing
Against the will of woman at its wildest
In the Shape-Changers that run upon the wind.

CONCHUBAR *has gone on to his throne.*

THE WOMEN (*they sing in a very low voice after the first few words so that the others all but drown their words*).
May this fire have driven out
The Shape-Changers that can put
Ruin on a great king's house
Until all be ruinous.
Names whereby a man has known
The threshold and the hearthstone,
Gather on the wind and drive
The women none can kiss and thrive,
For they are but whirling wind,
Out of memory and mind.
They would make a prince decay
With light images of clay
Planted in the running wave;

Or, for many shapes they have,
They would change them into hounds
Until he had died of his wounds,
Though the change were but a whim;
Or they'd hurl a spell at him,
That he follow with desire
Bodies that can never tire
Or grow kind, for they anoint
All their bodies, joint by joint,
With a miracle-working juice
That is made out of the grease
Of the ungoverned unicorn.
But the man is thrice forlorn,
Emptied, ruined, wracked, and lost,
That they followed, for at most
They will give him kiss for kiss
While they murmur, "After this
Hatred may be sweet to the taste."
Those wild hands that have embraced
All his body can but shove
At the burning wheel of love
Till the side of hate comes up.
Therefore in this ancient cup
May the sword-blades drink their fill
Of the home-brew there, until
They will have for masters none
But the threshold and hearthstone.

    CUCHULAIN (*speaking, while they are singing*). I'll take and keep this oath, and from this day
I shall be what you please, my chicks, my nestlings.
Yet I had thought you were of those that praised
Whatever life could make the pulse run quickly,
Even though it were brief, and that you held
That a free gift was better than a forced. —
But that's all over. — I will keep it, too;
I never gave a gift and took it again.
If the wild horse should break the chariot-pole,
It would be punished. Should that be in the oath?

    Two of the WOMEN, *still singing, crouch in front of him holding the bowl over their heads. He spreads his hands over the flame.*

I swear to be obedient in all things
To Conchubar, and to uphold his children.

    CONCHUBAR. We are one being, as these flames are one:
I give my wisdom, and I take your strength.
Now thrust the swords into the flame, and pray

On Baile's Strand

That they may serve the threshold and the hearthstone
With faithful service.

> *The* KINGS *kneel in a semicircle before the two* WOMEN *and* CUCHULAIN, *who thrusts his sword into the flame. They all put the points of their swords into the flame. The third* WOMAN *is at the back near the big door.*

CUCHULAIN.   O pure, glittering ones
That should be more than wife or friend or mistress,
Give us the enduring will, the unquenchable hope,
The friendliness of the sword! —

> *The song grows louder, and the last words ring out clearly. There is a loud knocking at the door, and a cry of "Open! open!"*

CONCHUBAR. Some king that has been loitering on the way.
Open the door, for I would have all know
That the oath's finished and Cuchulain bound,
And that the swords are drinking up the flame.

> *The door is opened by the third* WOMAN, *and a* YOUNG MAN *with a drawn sword enters.*

YOUNG MAN. I am of Aoife's country.

> *The* KINGS *rush towards him.* CUCHULAIN *throws himself between.*

CUCHULAIN.   Put up your swords.
He is but one. Aoife is far away.
   YOUNG MAN. I have come alone into the midst of you
To weigh this sword against Cuchulain's sword.
   CONCHUBAR. And are you noble? for if of common seed,
You cannot weigh your sword against his sword
But in mixed battle.
   YOUNG MAN.   I am under bonds
To tell my name to no man; but it's noble.
   CONCHUBAR. But I would know your name and not your bonds.
You cannot speak in the Assembly House,
If you are not noble.
   FIRST OLD KING.   Answer the High King!
   YOUNG MAN. I will give no other proof than the hawk gives
That it's no sparrow!

> *He is silent for a moment, then speaks to all.*

                Yet look upon me, kings.
I, too, am of that ancient seed, and carry
The signs about this body and in these bones.
   CUCHULAIN. To have shown the hawk's grey feather is enough,

And you speak highly, too. Give me that helmet.
I'd thought they had grown weary sending champions.
That sword and belt will do. This fighting's welcome.
The High King there has promised me his wisdom;
But the hawk's sleepy till its well-beloved
Cries out amid the acorns, or it has seen
It's enemy like a speck upon the sun.
What's wisdom to the hawk, when that clear eye
Is burning nearer up in the high air?
> *Looks hard at* YOUNG MAN; *then comes down steps and grasps* YOUNG MAN *by shoulder.*

Hither into the light.
(*To* CONCHUBAR)   The very tint
Of her that I was speaking of but now.
Not a pin's difference.
(*To* YOUNG MAN)   You are from the North,
Where there are many that have that tint of hair —
Red-brown, the light red-brown. Come nearer, boy,
For I would have another look at you.
There's more likeness — a pale, a stone-pale cheek.
What brought you, boy? Have you no fear of death?
> YOUNG MAN. Whether I live or die is in the gods' hands.
> CUCHULAIN. That is all words, all words; a young man's talk.

I am their plough, their harrow, their very strength;
For he that's in the sun begot this body
Upon a mortal woman, and I have heard tell
It seemed as if he had outrun the moon
That he must follow always through waste heaven,
He loved so happily. He'll be but slow
To break a tree that was so sweetly planted.
Let's see that arm. I'll see it if I choose.
That arm had a good father and a good mother,
But it is not like this.
> YOUNG MAN.   You are mocking me;

You think I am not worthy to be fought.
But I'll not wrangle but with this talkative knife.
> CUCHULAIN. Put up your sword, I am not mocking you.

I'd have you for my friend, but if it's not
Because you have a hot heart and a cold eye,
I cannot tell the reason.
(*To* CONCHUBAR)   He has got her fierceness,
And nobody is as fierce as those pale women.
But I will keep him with me, Conchubar,
That he may set my memory upon her

On Baile's Strand

When the day's fading. — You will stop with us,
And we will hunt the deer and the wild bulls;
And, when we have grown weary, light our fires
Between the wood and water, or on some mountain
Where the Shape-Changers of the morning come.
The High King there would make a mock of me
Because I did not take a wife among them.
Why do you hang your head? It's a good life:
The head grows prouder in the light of the dawn,
And friendship thickens in the murmuring dark
Where the spare hazels meet the wool-white foam.
But I can see there's no more need for words
And that you'll be my friend from this day out.

  CONCHUBAR. He has come hither not in his own name
But in Queen Aoife's, and has challenged us
In challenging the foremost man of us all.

  CUCHULAIN. Well, well, what matter?

  CONCHUBAR.   You think it does not matter,
And that a fancy lighter than the air,
A whim of the moment, has more matter in it.
For, having none that shall reign after you,
You cannot think as I do, who would leave
A throne too high for insult.

  CUCHULAIN.   Let your children
Re-mortar their inheritance, as we have,
And put more muscle on. — I'll give you gifts,
But I'd have something too — that arm-ring, boy.
We'll have this quarrel out when you are older.

  YOUNG MAN. There is no man I'd sooner have my friend
Than you, whose name has gone about the world
As if it had been the wind; but Aoife'd say
I had turned coward.

  CUCHULAIN.   I will give you gifts
That Aoife'll know, and all her people know,
To have come from me. (*Showing cloak.*) My father gave me this.
He came to try me, rising up at dawn
Out of the cold dark of the rich sea.
He challenged me to battle, but before
My sword had touched his sword, told me his name,
Gave me this cloak, and vanished. It was woven
By women of the Country-under-Wave
Out of the fleeces of the sea. O! tell her
I was afraid, or tell her what you will.
No; tell her that I heard a raven croak

On the north side of the house, and was afraid.
   CONCHUBAR. Some witch of the air has troubled Cuchulain's mind.
   CUCHULAIN. No witchcraft. His head is like a woman's head
I had a fancy for.
   CONCHUBAR.   A witch of the air
Can make a leaf confound us with memories.
They run upon the wind and hurl the spells
That make us nothing, out of the invisible wind.
They have gone to school to learn the trick of it.
   CUCHULAIN. No, no — there's nothing out of common here;
The winds are innocent. — That arm-ring, boy.
   A KING. If I've your leave I'll take this challenge up.
   ANOTHER KING. No, give it me, High King, for this wild Aoife
Has carried off my slaves.
   ANOTHER KING.   No, give it me,
For she has harried me in house and herd.
   ANOTHER KING. I claim this fight.
   OTHER KINGS (*together*).   And I! And I! And I!
   CUCHULAIN. Back! back! Put up your swords! Put up your swords!
There's none alive that shall accept a challenge
I have refused. Laegaire, put up your sword!
   YOUNG MAN. No, let them come. If they've a mind for it,
I'll try it out with any two together.
   CUCHULAIN. That's spoken as I'd have spoken it at your age.
But you are in my house. Whatever man
Would fight with you shall fight it out with me.
They're dumb, they're dumb. How many of you would meet (*draws sword*)
This mutterer, this old whistler, this sand-piper,
This edge that's greyer than the tide, this mouse
That's gnawing at the timbers of the world,
This, this — Boy, I would meet them all in arms
If I'd a son like you. He would avenge me
When I have withstood for the last time the men
Whose fathers, brothers, sons, and friends I have killed
Upholding Conchubar, when the four provinces
Have gathered with the ravens over them.
But I'd need no avenger. You and I
Would scatter them like water from a dish.
   YOUNG MAN. We'll stand by one another from this out.
   Here is the ring.
   CUCHULAIN. No, turn and turn about.
But my turn's first because I am the older. (*Spreading out cloak.*)
Nine queens out of the Country-under-Wave
Have woven it with the fleeces of the sea

On Baile's Strand

And they were long embroidering at it. — Boy,
If I had fought my father, he'd have killed me,
As certainly as if I had a son
And fought with him, I should be deadly to him;
For the old fiery fountains are far off
And every day there is less heat o' the blood.
  CONCHUBAR (*in a loud voice*). No more of this. I will not have this friendship.
Cuchulain is my man, and I forbid it.
He shall not go unfought, for I myself —
  CUCHULAIN. I will not have it.
  CONCHUBAR.   You lay commands on me?
  CUCHULAIN (*seizing* CONCHUBAR). You shall not stir, High King. I'll hold you there.
  CONCHUBAR. Witchcraft has maddened you.
  THE KINGS (*shouting*).   Yes, witchcraft! witchcraft!
  FIRST OLD KING. Some witch has worked upon your mind, Cuchulain.
The head of that young man seemed like a woman's
You'd had a fancy for. Then of a sudden
You laid your hands on the High King himself!
  CUCHULAIN. And laid my hands on the High King himself?
  CONCHUBAR. Some witch is floating in the air above us.
  CUCHULAIN. Yes, witchcratf! witchcraft! Witches of the air!
(*To* YOUNG MAN) Why did you? Who was it set you to this work?
Out, out; I say, for now it's sword on sword!
  YOUNG MAN. But . . . but I did not.
  CUCHULAIN.   Out, I say, out, out!

> YOUNG MAN *goes out followed by* CUCHULAIN. *The* KINGS *follow them out with confused cries, and words one can hardly hear because of the noise. Some cry,* "Quicker, quicker!" "Why are you so long at the door?" "We'll be too late!" "Have they begun to fight?" "Can you see if they are fighting?" *and so on. Their voices drown each other. The three* WOMEN *are left alone.*

  FIRST WOMAN. I have seen, I have seen!
  SECOND WOMAN.   What do you cry aloud?
  FIRST WOMAN. The Ever-living have shown me what's to come.
  THIRD WOMAN. How? Where?
  FIRST WOMAN.   In the ashes of the bowl.
  SECOND WOMAN. While you were holding it between your hands?
  THIRD WOMAN. Speak quickly!
  FIRST WOMAN.   I have seen Cuchulain's roof-tree
Leap into fire, and the walls split and blacken.
  SECOND WOMAN. Cuchulain has gone out to die.

THIRD WOMAN. O! O!

SECOND WOMAN. Who could have thought that one so great as he
Should meet his end at this unnoted sword!

FIRST WOMAN. Life drifts between a fool and a blind man
To the end, and nobody can know his end.

SECOND WOMAN. Come, look upon the quenching of this greatness.

The other two go to the door, but they stop for a moment upon the threshold and wail.

FIRST WOMAN. No crying out, for there'll be need of cries
And rending of the hair when it's all finished.

The WOMEN *go out. There is the sound of clashing swords from time to time during what follows.*

Enter the FOOL, *dragging the* BLIND MAN.

FOOL. You have eaten it, you have eaten it! You have left me nothing but the bones. (*He throws* BLIND MAN *down by big chair.*)

BLIND MAN. O, that I should have to endure such a plague! O, I ache all over! O, I am pulled to pieces! This is the way you pay me all the good I have done you.

FOOL. You have eaten it! You have told me lies. I might have known you had eaten it when I saw your slow, sleepy walk. Lie there till the kings come. O, I will tell Conchubar and Cuchulain and all the kings about you!

BLIND MAN. What would have happened to you but for me, and you without your wits? If I did not take care of you, what would you do for food and warmth?

FOOL. You take care of me? You stay safe, and send me into every kind of danger. You sent me down the cliff for gulls' eggs while you warmed your blind eyes in the sun; and then you ate all that were good for food. You left me the eggs that were neither egg nor bird. (BLIND MAN *tries to rise;* FOOL *makes him lie down again.*) Keep quiet now, till I shut the door. There is some noise outside — a high vexing noise, so that I can't be listening to myself. (*Shuts the big door.*) Why can't they be quiet? Why can't they be quiet? (BLIND MAN *tries to get away.*) Ah! you would get away, would you? (*Follows* BLIND MAN *and brings him back.*). Lie there! lie there! No, you won't get away! Lie there till the kings come. I'll tell them all about you. I will tell it all. How you sit warming yourself, when you have made me light a fire of sticks, while I sit blowing it with my mouth. Do you not always make me take the windy side of the bush when it blows, and the rainy side when it rains?

BLIND MAN. O, good Fool! listen to me. Think of the care I have taken of you. I have brought you to many a warm hearth, where there was a good welcome for you, but you would not stay there; you were always wandering about.

FOOL. The last time you brought me in, it was not I who wandered away, but you that got put out because you took the crubeen out of the pot when nobody was looking. Keep quiet, now!

CUCHULAIN (*rushing in*). Witchcraft! There is no witchcraft on the earth, or among the witches of the air, that these hands cannot break.

FOOL. Listen to me, Cuchulain. I left him turning the fowl at the fire. He ate it all, though I had stolen it. He left me nothing but the feathers.

CUCHULAIN. Fill me a horn of ale!

BLIND MAN. I gave him what he likes best. You do not know how vain this Fool is. He likes nothing so well as a feather.

FOOL. He left me nothing but the bones and feathers. Nothing but the feathers, though I had stolen it.

CUCHULAIN. Give me that horn. Quarrels here, too! (*Drinks.*) What is there between you two that is worth a quarrel? Out with it!

BLIND MAN. Where would he be but for me? I must be always thinking — thinking to get food for the two of us, and when we've got it, if the moon is at the full or the tide on the turn, he'll leave the rabbit in the snare till it is full of maggots, or let the trout slip back through his hands into the stream.

The FOOL *has begun singing while the* BLIND MAN *is speaking.*

FOOL (*singing*).
> When you were an acorn on the tree-top,
> Then was I an eagle-cock;
> Now that you are a withered old block,
> Still am I an eagle-cock.

BLIND MAN. Listen to him, now. That's the sort of talk I have to put up with day out, day in.

The FOOL *is putting the feathers into his hair.* CUCHULAIN *takes a handful of feathers out of a heap the* FOOL *has on the bench beside him, and out of the* FOOL'S *hair, and begins to wipe the blood from his sword with them.*

FOOL. He has taken my feathers to wipe his sword. It is blood that he is wiping from his sword.

CUCHULAIN (*goes up to door at back and throws away feathers*). They are standing about his body. They will not awaken him, for all his witchcraft.

BLIND MAN. It is that young champion that he has killed. He that came out of Aoife's country.

CUCHULAIN. He thought to have saved himself with witchcraft.

FOOL. That Blind Man there said he would kill you. He came from Aoife's country to kill you. That Blind Man said they had taught him every kind of weapon that he might do it. But I always knew that you would kill him.

CUCHULAIN (*to the* BLIND MAN). You knew him, then?

BLIND MAN. I saw him, when I had my eyes, in Aoife's country.

CUCHULAIN. You were in Aoife's country?

BLIND MAN. I knew him and his mother there.

CUCHULAIN. He was about to speak of her when he died.

BLIND MAN. He was a queen's son.

CUCHULAIN. What queen? what queen? (*Seizes* BLIND MAN, *who is now sitting upon the bench.*) Was it Scathach? There were many queens. All the rulers there were queens.

BLIND MAN. No, not Scathach.

CUCHULAIN. It was Uathach, then? Speak! speak!

BLIND MAN. I cannot speak; you are clutching me too tightly. (CUCHULAIN *lets him go.*) I cannot remember who it was. I am not certain. It was some queen.

FOOL. He said a while ago that the young man was Aoife's son.

CUCHULAIN. She? No, no! She had no son when I was there.

FOOL. That Blind Man there said that she owned him for her son.

CUCHULAIN. I had rather he had been some other woman's son. What father had he? A soldier out of Alba? She was an amorous woman — a proud, pale, amorous woman.

BLIND MAN. None knew whose son he was.

CUCHULAIN. None knew! Did you know, old listener at doors?

BLIND MAN. No, no; I knew nothing.

FOOL. He said a while ago that he heard Aoife boast that she'd never but the one lover, and he the only man that had overcome her in battle. (*Pause.*)

BLIND MAN. Somebody is trembling, Fool! The bench is shaking. Why are you trembling? Is Cuchulain going to hurt us? It was not I who told you, Cuchulain.

FOOL. It is Cuchulain who is trembling. It is Cuchulain who is shaking the bench.

BLIND MAN. It is his own son he has slain.

CUCHULAIN. 'Twas they that did it, the pale windy people.
Where? where? where? My sword against the thunder!
But no, for they have always been my friends;
And though they love to blow a smoking coal
Till it's all flame, the wars they blow aflame
Are full of glory, and heart-uplifting pride,
And not like this. The wars they love awaken
Old fingers and the sleepy strings of harps.
Who did it then? Are you afraid? Speak out!
For I have put you under my protection,
And will reward you well. Dubthach the Chafer?
He'd an old grudge. No, for he is with Maeve.
Laegaire did it! Why do you not speak?
What is this house? (*Pause.*) Now I remember all.

Comes before CONCHUBAR's *chair, and strikes out with his sword, as if* CONCHUBAR *was sitting upon it.*

'Twas you who did it — you who sat up there
With your old rod of kingship, like a magpie
Nursing a stolen spoon. No, not a magpie,
A maggot that is eating up the earth!
Yes, but a magpie, for he's flown away.
Where did he fly to?

BLIND MAN. He is outside the door.

CUCHULAIN. Outside the door?

BLIND MAN. Between the door and the sea.

CUCHULAIN. Conchubar, Conchubar! the sword into your heart!

He rushes out. Pause. FOOL *creeps up to the big door and looks after him.*

FOOL. He is going up to King Conchubar. They are all about the young man. No, no, he is standing still. There is a great wave going to break, and he is looking at it. Ah! now he is running down to the sea, but he is holding up his sword as if he were going into a fight. (*Pause.*) Well struck! well struck!

BLIND MAN. What is he doing now?

FOOL. O! he is fighting the waves!

BLIND MAN. He sees King Conchubar's crown on every one of them.

FOOL. There, he has struck at a big one! He has struck the crown off it; he has made the foam fly. There again, another big one!

BLIND MAN. Where are the kings? What are the kings doing?

FOOL. They are shouting and running down to the shore, and the people are running out of the houses. They are all running.

BLIND MAN. You say they are running out of the houses? There will be nobody left in the houses. Listen, Fool!

FOOL. There, he is down! He is up again. He is going out in the deep water. There is a big wave. It has gone over him. I cannot see him now. He has killed kings and giants, but the waves have mastered him, the waves have mastered him!

BLIND MAN. Come here, Fool!

FOOL. The waves have mastered him.

BLIND MAN. Come here!

FOOL. The waves have mastered him.

BLIND MAN. Come here, I say.

FOOL (*coming towards him, but looking backwards towards the door*). What is it?

BLIND MAN. There will be nobody in the houses. Come this way; come quickly! The ovens will be full. We will put our hands into the ovens. (*They go out.*)

FOLK DRAMA

John Millington Synge

THE PLAYBOY OF THE WESTERN WORLD

[1907]

John Millington Synge [1871–1909]

John Millington Synge's career in the theater was brief, as was his life. After graduating from Trinity College, Dublin, in 1892, he studied on the Continent, spent several summers in the Aran Islands off the west coast of Ireland, and came to his association with the Irish literary renaissance in 1903. He wrote all of his six plays between 1902 and 1909, the year of his death from cancer. Synge's plays mark a high point in the return to the soil and to the folk for the inspiration for literature.

Some have called the essence of the Irish literary movement of the 1890's and later "anti-modern" since it was a "renaissance," a turning back to revive beauties of the past. The founders of this literary movement, mainly William Butler Yeats, sought to create an interest in and love for the culture and lore of an old and now-forgotten Ireland: its myths, its art, its language. Though J. M. Synge was not an antiquarian, and was not of the folk, he found congenial to his spirit the return to the simple life of rural Irish peasants, vagrants, and fishermen. He rejected as raw material for his dramas the modern world of the industrial, scientific, and social revolutions, and looked minutely at the small dramas in the lives of the uneducated and unsophisticated. He wrote, "There is nothing so great and sacred as what is most simple in life." With this statement he signals his break with the mainstream of modern literature and, incidentally, with the later Yeats and his somewhat precious devotion to coterie art.

The folk drama movement (as it has come to be called) began with the Irish plays of Lady Augusta Gregory and Synge. In general one may say that the folk drama consists of regional plays which draw much of their individuality and emphasis, as well as much of their meaning, from conditions which are local. The folk plays are not written by the folk themselves, but by sophisticated

Synge and Folk Drama

writers. They recapture in a literary form the essence of a time and place in which a culture is in its youth, "where the springtime of the local life has [not] been forgotten," as Synge himself said. The Irish folk plays of Synge and his colleagues have inspired an extremely large number of regional plays in America; the late 1920's especially, with the plays of Paul Green, Lynn Riggs, and others, was the seed and harvest time of the regional play here. While the regional or folk play has inherent in it the strength which comes from its direct roots in a vital life, it also carries with it built-in limitations; it may fail to transcend its own time and place in some significant way and so become a literary curiosity, a play written about interesting people and local color, but nothing more. Obviously, the best of the folk plays are not *merely* regional.

When *The Playboy of the Western World* was first produced at the Abbey Theatre, Dublin, in 1907, it was so deeply resented that rioting broke out. Is the play indeed a slander on the Irish people? Is it offensive in any way? The response which it evoked indicates that to many who were close enough to see themselves mirrored in some way, *The Playboy of the Western World* was repellent; most modern readers, however, will probably wonder why. They will be struck (if they have an ear to hear) by the rich prose which borders on poetry, and by the bold characterization of the play. Christy Mahon, especially, emerges as a grand figure. Someone has said that the characters bless and curse too well for the language to be authentic, but Synge himself has answered this charge in his beautifully written preface. Language, one of the most important features of this play, may be natural and at the same time poetic — if the characters portrayed are poetic speakers. Synge was blessed by the opportunity to write richly because his characters found genuine joy in the music of words.

PREFACE TO

THE PLAYBOY OF THE WESTERN WORLD

In writing *The Playboy of the Western World*, as in my other plays, I have used one or two words only that I have not heard among the country people of Ireland, or spoken in my own nursery before I could read the newspapers. A certain number of the phrases I employ I have heard also from herds and fishermen along the coast from Kerry to Mayo, or from beggar-women and ballad-singers nearer Dublin; and I am glad to acknowledge how much I owe to the folk-imagination of these fine people. Anyone who has lived in real intimacy with the Irish peasantry will know that the wildest sayings and ideas in this play are tame indeed, compared with the fancies one may hear in any little hillside cabin in Geesala, or Carraroe, or Dingle Bay. All art is a collaboration; and there is little doubt that in the happy ages of literature, striking and beautiful phrases were as ready to the story-teller's or the playwright's hand, as the rich cloaks and dresses of his time. It is probable that when the Elizabethan dramatist took his ink-horn and sat down to his work he used many phrases that he had just heard, as he sat at dinner, from his mother or his children. In Ireland, those of us who know the people have the same privilege. When I was writing *The Shadow of the Glen*, some years ago, I got more aid than any learning could have given me from a chink in the floor of the old Wicklow house where I was staying, that let me hear what was being said by the servant girls in the kitchen. This matter, I think, is of importance, for in countries where the imagination of the people, and the language they use, is rich and living, it is possible for a writer to be rich and copious in his words, and at the same time to give the reality, which is the root of all poetry, in a comprehensive and natural form. In the modern literature of towns, however, richness is found only in sonnets, or prose poems, or in one or two elaborate books that are far away from the profound and common interests of life. One has, on one side, Mallarmé and Huysmans producing this literature; and on the other, Ibsen and Zola dealing with the reality of life in joyless and pallid words. On the stage one must have reality, and one must have joy; and that is why the intellectual modern drama has failed, and people have grown sick of the false joy of the musical comedy, that has been given them in place of the rich joy found only in what is superb and wild in reality. In a good play every speech should be as fully flavoured as a nut or apple, and such speeches cannot be written by anyone who works among people who have shut their lips on poetry. In Ireland, for a few years more, we have a popular imagination that is fiery and magnificent, and tender; so that those of us who wish to write start with a chance that is not given to writers in places where the springtime of the local life has been forgotten, and the harvest is a memory only, and the straw has been turned into bricks.

J. M. S.

January 21, 1907

The Playboy of the Western World

A PLAY IN THREE ACTS

PERSONS IN THE PLAY

CHRISTOPHER MAHON
OLD MAHON, *his father, a squatter*
MICHAEL JAMES FLAHERTY, called MICHAEL JAMES, *a publican*
MARGARET FLAHERTY, called PEGEEN MIKE, *his daughter*
WIDOW QUIN, *a woman of about thirty*
SHAWN KEOGH, *her cousin, a young farmer*
PHILLY CULLEN and JIMMY FARRELL, *small farmers*
SARA TANSEY
SUSAN BRADY } *village girls*
HONOR BLAKE
NELLY
A BELLMAN
SOME PEASANTS

The action takes place near a village, on a wild coast of Mayo. The first Act passes on an evening of autumn, the other two Acts on the following day.

ACT I

Scene. Country public-house or shebeen, very rough and untidy. There is a sort of counter on the right with shelves, holding many bottles and jugs, just seen above it. Empty barrels stand near the counter. At back, a little to left of counter, there is a door into the open air, then, more to the left, there is a settle with shelves above it, with more jugs, and a table beneath a window. At the left there is a large open fire-place, with turf fire, and a small door into inner room. PEGEEN, *a wild-looking but fine girl, of about twenty, is writing at table. She is dressed in the usual peasant dress.*

PEGEEN (*slowly as she writes*). Six yards of stuff for to make a yellow gown. A pair of lace boots with lengthy heels on them and brassy eyes. A hat is suited for a wedding-day. A fine tooth comb. To be sent with three barrels of porter in Jimmy Farrell's creel cart on the evening of the coming Fair to Mister Michael James Flaherty. With the best compliments of this season. Margaret Flaherty.

SHAWN KEOGH (*a fat and fair young man comes in as she signs, looks round awkwardly, when he sees she is alone*). Where's himself?

PEGEEN (*without looking at him*). He's coming. (*She directs the letter.*) To Mister Sheamus Mulroy, Wine and Spirit Dealer, Castlebar.

SHAWN (*uneasily*). I didn't see him on the road.

PEGEEN. How would you see him (*licks stamp and puts it on letter*) and it dark night this half hour gone by?

SHAWN (*turning towards the door again*). I stood a while outside wondering would I have a right to pass on or to walk in and see you, Pegeen Mike (*comes to fire*), and I could hear the cows breathing, and sighing in the stillness of the air, and not a step moving any place from this gate to the bridge.

PEGEEN (*putting letter in envelope*). It's above at the cross-roads he is, meeting Philly Cullen; and a couple more are going along with him to Kate Cassidy's wake.

SHAWN (*looking at her blankly*). And he's going that length in the dark night?

PEGEEN (*impatiently*). He is surely, and leaving me lonesome on the scruff of the hill. (*She gets up and puts envelope on dresser, then winds clock.*) Isn't it long the nights are now, Shawn Keogh, to be leaving a poor girl with her own self counting the hours to the dawn of day?

SHAWN (*with awkward humour*). If it is, when we're wedded in a short while you'll have no call to complain, for I've little will to be walking off to wakes or weddings in the darkness of the night.

PEGEEN (*with rather scornful good humour*). You're making mighty certain, Shaneen, that I'll wed you now.

SHAWN. Aren't we after making a good bargain, the way we're only waiting these days on Father Reilly's dispensation from the bishops, or the Court of Rome.

PEGEEN (*looking at him teasingly, washing up at dresser*). It's a wonder, Shaneen, the Holy Father'd be taking notice of the likes of you; for if I was him I wouldn't bother with this place where you'll meet none but Red Linahan, has a squint in his eye, and Patcheen is lame in his heel, or the mad Mulrannies were driven from California and they lost in their wits. We're a queer lot these times to go troubling the Holy Father on his sacred seat.

SHAWN (*scandalized*). If we are, we're as good this place as another, maybe, and as good these times as we were for ever.

PEGEEN (*with scorn*). As good, is it? Where now will you meet the like of Daneen Sullivan knocked the eye from a peeler, or Marcus Quin, God rest him, got six months for maiming ewes, and he a great warrant to tell stories of holy Ireland till he'd have the old women shedding down tears about their feet. Where will you find the like of them, I'm saying?

SHAWN (*timidly*). If you don't, it's a good job, maybe; for (*with peculiar emphasis on the words*) Father Reilly has small conceit to have that kind walking around and talking to the girls.

PEGEEN (*impatiently, throwing water from basin out of the door*). Stop tormenting me with Father Reilly (*imitating his voice*) when I'm asking only what way I'll pass these twelve hours of dark, and not take my death with the fear.

Looking out of door.

SHAWN (*timidly*). Would I fetch you the Widow Quin, maybe?

PEGEEN. Is it the like of that murderer? You'll not, surely.

SHAWN (*going to her, soothingly*). Then I'm thinking himself will stop along with you when he sees you taking on, for it'll be a long night-time with great darkness, and I'm after feeling a kind of fellow above in the furzy ditch, groaning wicked like a maddening dog, the way it's good cause you have, maybe, to be fearing now.

PEGEEN (*turning on him sharply*). What's that? Is it a man you seen?

SHAWN (*retreating*). I couldn't see him at all; but I heard him groaning out, and breaking his heart. It should have been a young man from his words speaking.

PEGEEN (*going after him*). And you never went near to see was he hurted or what ailed him at all?

SHAWN. I did not, Pegeen Mike. It was a dark, lonesome place to be hearing the like of him.

PEGEEN. Well, you're a daring fellow, and if they find his corpse stretched above in the dews of dawn, what'll you say then to the peelers, or the Justice of the Peace?

SHAWN (*thunderstruck*). I wasn't thinking of that. For the love of God, Pegeen Mike, don't let on I was speaking of him. Don't tell your father and the men is coming above; for if they heard that story, they'd have great blabbing this night at the wake.

PEGEEN. I'll maybe tell them, and I'll maybe not.

SHAWN. They are coming at the door. Will you whisht, I'm saying?

PEGEEN. Whisht yourself.

She goes behind counter. MICHAEL JAMES, *fat jovial publican, comes in followed by* PHILLY CULLEN, *who is thin and mistrusting, and* JIMMY FARRELL, *who is fat and amorous, about forty-five.*

MEN (*together*). God bless you. The blessing of God on this place.

PEGEEN. God bless you kindly.

MICHAEL (*to men who go to the counter*). Sit down now, and take your rest. (*Crosses to* SHAWN *at the fire.*) And how is it you are, Shawn Keogh? Are you coming over the sands to Kate Cassidy's wake?

SHAWN. I am not, Michael James. I'm going home the short cut to my bed.

PEGEEN (*speaking across the counter*). He's right too, and have you no shame, Michael James, to be quitting off for the whole night, and leaving myself lonesome in the shop?

MICHAEL (*good-humouredly*). Isn't it the same whether I go for the whole night or a part only? and I'm thinking it's a queer daughter you are if you'd have me crossing backward through the Stooks of the Dead Women, with a drop taken.

PEGEEN. If I am a queer daughter, it's a queer father'd be leaving me lonesome these twelve hours of dark, and I piling the turf with the dogs barking, and the calves mooing, and my own teeth rattling with the fear.

JIMMY (*flatteringly*). What is there to hurt you, and you a fine, hardy girl would knock the head of any two men in the place?

PEGEEN (*working herself up*). Isn't there the harvest boys with their tongues red for drink, and the ten tinkers is camped in the east glen, and the thousand militia — bad cess to them! — walking idle through the land. There's lots surely to hurt me, and I won't stop alone in it, let himself do what he will.

MICHAEL. If you're that afeard, let Shawn Keogh stop along with you. It's the will of God, I'm thinking, himself should be seeing to you now.

They all turn on SHAWN.

SHAWN (*in horrified confusion*). I would and welcome, Michael James, but I'm afeard of Father Reilly; and what at all would the Holy Father and the Cardinals of Rome be saying if they heard I did the like of that?

MICHAEL (*with contempt*). God help you! Can't you sit in by the hearth with the light lit and herself beyond in the room? You'll do that surely, for I've heard tell there's a queer fellow above, going mad or getting his death, maybe, in the gripe of the ditch, so she'd be safer this night with a person here.

SHAWN (*with plaintive despair*). I'm afeard of Father Reilly, I'm saying. Let you not be tempting me, and we near married itself.

PHILLY (*with cold contempt*). Lock him in the west room. He'll stay then and have no sin to be telling to the priest.

MICHAEL (*to* SHAWN, *getting between him and the door*). Go up now.

SHAWN (*at the top of his voice*). Don't stop me, Michael James. Let me out of the door, I'm saying, for the love of the Almighty God. Let me out. (*Trying to dodge past him.*) Let me out of it, and may God grant you His indulgence in the hour of need.

MICHAEL (*loudly*). Stop your noising, and sit down by the hearth.

Gives him a push and goes to counter laughing.

SHAWN (*turning back, wringing his hands*). Oh, Father Reilly and the saints of God, where will I hide myself to-day? Oh, St. Joseph and St. Patrick and St. Brigid, and St. James, have mercy on me now!

SHAWN *turns round, sees door clear, and makes a rush for it.*

MICHAEL (*catching him by the coat-tail*). You'd be going, is it?

SHAWN (*screaming*). Leave me go, Michael James, leave me go, you old Pagan, leave me go, or I'll get the curse of the priests on you, and of the scarlet-coated bishops of the courts of Rome.

With a sudden movement he pulls himself out of his coat, and disappears out of the door, leaving his coat in MICHAEL's *hands.*

MICHAEL (*turning round, and holding up coat*). Well, there's the coat of a Christian man. Oh, there's sainted glory this day in the lonesome west; and by the will of God I've got you a decent man, Pegeen, you'll have no call to be spying after if you've a score of young girls, maybe, weeding in your fields.

PEGEEN (*taking up the defence of her property*). What right have you to be making game of a poor fellow for minding the priest, when it's your own the fault is, not paying a penny pot-boy to stand along with me and give me courage in the doing of my work?

She snaps the coat away from him, and goes behind counter with it.

MICHAEL (*taken aback*). Where would I get a pot-boy? Would you have me send the bellman screaming in the streets of Castlebar?

SHAWN (*opening the door a chink and putting in his head, in a small voice*). Michael James!

MICHAEL (*imitating him*). What ails you?

SHAWN. The queer dying fellow's beyond looking over the ditch. He's come up, I'm thinking, stealing your hens. (*Looks over his shoulder.*) God help me, he's following me now (*he runs into room*), and if he's heard what I said, he'll be having my life, and I going home lonesome in the darkness of the night.

For a perceptible moment they watch the door with curiosity. Someone coughs outside. Then CHRISTY MAHON, *a slight young man, comes in very tired and frightened and dirty.*

CHRISTY (*in a small voice*). God save all here!

MEN. God save you kindly.

CHRISTY (*going to the counter*). I'd trouble you for a glass of porter, woman of the house.

He puts down coin.

PEGEEN (*serving him*). You're one of the tinkers, young fellow, is beyond camped in the glen?

CHRISTY. I am not; but I'm destroyed walking.

MICHAEL (*patronizingly*). Let you come up then to the fire. You're looking famished with the cold.

CHRISTY. God reward you. (*He takes up his glass and goes a little way across to the left, then stops and looks about him.*) Is it often the police do be coming into this place, master of the house?

MICHAEL. If you'd come in better hours, you'd have seen "Licensed for the sale of Beer and Spirits, to be consumed on the premises," written in white letters above the door, and what would the polis want spying on me, and not a decent house within four miles, the way every living Christian is a bona fide, saving one widow alone?

CHRISTY (*with relief*). It's a safe house, so.

He goes over to the fire, sighing and moaning. Then he sits down, putting his glass beside him and begins gnawing a turnip, too miserable to feel the others staring at him with curiosity.

MICHAEL (*going after him*). Is it yourself is fearing the polis? You're wanting, maybe?

CHRISTY. There's many wanting.

MICHAEL. Many surely, with the broken harvest and the ended wars. (*He picks up some stockings, etc., that are near the fire, and carries them away furtively.*) It should be larceny, I'm thinking?

CHRISTY (*dolefully*). I had it in my mind it was a different word and a bigger.

PEGEEN. There's a queer lad. Were you never slapped in school, young fellow, that you don't know the name of your deed?

CHRISTY (*bashfully*). I'm slow at learning, a middling scholar only.

MICHAEL. If you're a dunce itself, you'd have a right to know that larceny's robbing and stealing. Is it for the like of that you're wanting?

CHRISTY (*with a flash of family pride*). And I the son of a strong farmer (*with a sudden qualm*), God rest his soul, could have bought up the whole of your old house a while since, from the butt of his tailpocket, and not have missed the weight of it gone.

MICHAEL (*impressed*). If it's not stealing, it's maybe something big.

CHRISTY (*flattered*). Aye; it's maybe something big.

JIMMY. He's a wicked-looking young fellow. Maybe he followed after a young woman on a lonesome night.

CHRISTY (*shocked*). Oh, the saints forbid, mister; I was all times a decent lad.

PHILLY (*turning on* JIMMY). You're a silly man, Jimmy Farrell. He said his father was a farmer a while since, and there's himself now in a poor state. Maybe the land was grabbed from him, and he did what any decent man would do.

MICHAEL (*to* CHRISTY, *mysteriously*). Was it bailiffs?

CHRISTY. The divil a one.

MICHAEL. Agents?

CHRISTY. The divil a one.

MICHAEL. Landlords?

CHRISTY (*peevishly*). Ah, not at all, I'm saying. You'd see the like of them stories on any little paper of a Munster town. But I'm not calling to mind any person, gentle, simple, judge or jury, did the like of me.

They all draw nearer with delighted curiosity.

PHILLY. Well, that lad's a puzzle-the-world.

JIMMY. He'd beat Dan Davies' circus, or the holy missioners making sermons on the villainy of man. Try him again, Philly.

PHILLY. Did you strike golden guineas out of solder, young fellow, or shilling coins itself?

CHRISTY. I did not, mister, not sixpence nor a farthing coin.

JIMMY. Did you marry three wives maybe? I'm told there's a sprinkling have done that among the holy Luthers of the preaching north.

CHRISTY (*shyly*). I never married with one, let alone with a couple or three.

PHILLY. Maybe he went fighting for the Boers, the like of the man beyond, was judged to be hanged, quartered and drawn. Were you off east, young fellow, fighting bloody wars for Kruger and the freedom of the Boers?

CHRISTY. I never left my own parish till Tuesday was a week.

PEGEEN (*coming from counter*). He's done nothing, so. (*To* CHRISTY.) If you didn't commit murder or a bad, nasty thing, or false coining, or robbery, or butchery, or the like of them, there isn't anything that would be worth your troubling for to run from now. You did nothing at all.

CHRISTY (*his feelings hurt*). That's an unkindly thing to be saying to a poor orphaned traveller, has a prison behind him, and hanging before, and hell's gap gaping below.

PEGEEN (*with a sign to the men to be quiet*). You're only saying it. You did nothing at all. A soft lad the like of you wouldn't slit the windpipe of a screeching sow.

CHRISTY (*offended*). You're not speaking the truth.

PEGEEN (*in mock rage*). Not speaking the truth, is it? Would you have me knock the head of you with the butt of the broom?

CHRISTY (*twisting round on her with a sharp cry of horror*). Don't strike me. I killed my poor father, Tuesday was a week, for doing the like of that.

PEGEEN (*with blank amazement*). Is it killed your father?

CHRISTY (*subsiding*). With the help of God I did surely, and that the Holy Immaculate Mother may intercede for his soul.

PHILLY (*retreating with Jimmy*). There's a daring fellow.

JIMMY. Oh, glory be to God!

MICHAEL (*with great respect*). That was a hanging crime, mister honey. You should have had good reason for doing the like of that.

CHRISTY (*in a very reasonable tone*). He was a dirty man, God forgive him, and he getting old and crusty, the way I couldn't put up with him at all.

PEGEEN. And you shot him dead?

CHRISTY (*shaking his head*). I never used weapons. I've no license, and I'm a law-fearing man.

MICHAEL. It was with a hilted knife maybe? I'm told, in the big world it's bloody knives they use.

CHRISTY (*loudly, scandalized*). Do you take me for a slaughter-boy?

PEGEEN. You never hanged him, the way Jimmy Farrell hanged his dog from the license, and had it screeching and wriggling three hours at the butt of a string, and himself swearing it was a dead dog, and the peelers swearing it had life?

CHRISTY. I did not then. I just riz the loy and let fall the edge of it on the ridge of his skull, and he went down at my feet like an empty sack, and never let a grunt or groan from him at all.

MICHAEL (*making a sign to* PEGEEN *to fill* CHRISTY's *glass*). And what way weren't you hanged, mister? Did you bury him then?

CHRISTY (*considering*). Aye. I buried him then. Wasn't I digging spuds in the field?

MICHAEL. And the peelers never followed after you the eleven days that you're out?

CHRISTY (*shaking his head*). Never a one of them, and I walking forward facing hog, dog, or divil on the highway of the road.

PHILLY (*nodding wisely*). It's only with a common week-day kind of a murderer them lads would be trusting their carcase, and that man should be a great terror when his temper's roused.

MICHAEL. He should then. (*To* CHRISTY.) And where was it, mister honey, that you did the deed?

CHRISTY (*looking at him with suspicion*). Oh, a distant place, master of the house, a windy corner of high, distant hills.

PHILLY (*nodding with approval*). He's a close man, and he's right, surely.

PEGEEN. That'd be a lad with the sense of Solomon to have for a pot-boy, Michael James, if it's the truth you're seeking one at all.

PHILLY. The peelers is fearing him, and if you'd that lad in the house there isn't one of them would come smelling around if the dogs itself were lapping poteen from the dung-pit of the yard.

JIMMY. Bravery's a treasure in a lonesome place, and a lad would kill his father, I'm thinking, would face a foxy divil with a pitchpike on the flags of hell.

PEGEEN. It's the truth they're saying, and if I'd that lad in the house, I wouldn't be fearing the looséd kharki cut-throats, or the walking dead.

CHRISTY (*swelling with surprise and triumph*). Well, glory be to God!

MICHAEL (*with deference*). Would you think well to stop here and be pot-boy, mister honey, if we gave you good wages, and didn't destroy you with the weight of work?

SHAWN (*coming forward uneasily*). That'd be a queer kind to bring into a decent quiet household with the like of Pegeen Mike.

PEGEEN (*very sharply*). Will you whisht? Who's speaking to you?

SHAWN (*retreating*). A bloody-handed murderer the like of . . .

PEGEEN (*snapping at him*). Whisht I am saying; we'll take no fooling from your like at all. (*To* CHRISTY *with a honeyed voice*.) And you, young fellow, you'd have a right to stop, I'm thinking, for we'd do our all and utmost to content your needs.

CHRISTY (*overcome with wonder*). And I'd be safe in this place from the searching law?

MICHAEL. You would, surely. If they're not fearing you, itself, the peelers in this place is decent droughty poor fellows, wouldn't touch a cur dog and not give warning in the dead of night.

PEGEEN (*very kindly and persuasively*). Let you stop a short while anyhow. Aren't you destroyed walking with your feet in bleeding blisters, and your whole skin needing washing like a Wicklow sheep.

CHRISTY (*looking round with satisfaction*). It's a nice room, and if it's not humbugging me you are, I'm thinking that I'll surely stay.

JIMMY (*jumps up*). Now, by the grace of God, herself will be safe this night, with a man killed his father holding danger from the door, and let you come on, Michael James, or they'll have the best stuff drunk at the wake.

MICHAEL (*going to the door with men*). And begging your pardon, mister, what name will we call you, for we'd like to know?

CHRISTY. Christopher Mahon.

MICHAEL. Well, God bless you, Christy, and a good rest till we meet again when the sun'll be rising to the noon of day.

CHRISTY. God bless you all.

MEN. God bless you.

They go out except SHAWN, *who lingers at door.*

SHAWN (*to* PEGEEN). Are you wanting me to stop along with you and keep you from harm?

PEGEEN (*gruffly*). Didn't you say you were fearing Father Reilly?

SHAWN. There'd be no harm staying now, I'm thinking, and himself in it too.

PEGEEN. You wouldn't stay when there was need for you, and let you step off nimble this time when there's none.

SHAWN. Didn't I say it was Father Reilly . . .

PEGEEN. Go on, then, to Father Reilly (*in a jeering tone*), and let him put you in the holy brotherhoods, and leave that lad to me.

SHAWN. If I meet the Widow Quin . . .

PEGEEN. Go on, I'm saying, and don't be waking this place with your noise. (*She hustles him out and bolts the door.*) That lad would wear the spirits from the saints of peace. (*Bustles about, then takes off her apron and pins it up in the window as a blind.* CHRISTY *watching her timidly. Then she comes to him and speaks with bland good-humour.*) Let you stretch out now by the fire, young fellow. You should be destroyed travelling.

CHRISTY (*shyly again, drawing off his boots*). I'm tired, surely, walking wild eleven days, and waking fearful in the night.

He holds up one of his feet, feeling his blisters, and looking at them with compassion.

PEGEEN (*standing beside him, watching him with delight*). You should have had great people in your family, I'm thinking, with the little, small feet you have, and you with a kind of a quality name, the like of what you'd find on the great powers and potentates of France and Spain.

CHRISTY (*with pride*). We were great surely, with wide and windy acres of rich Munster land.

PEGEEN. Wasn't I telling you, and you a fine, handsome young fellow with a noble brow?

CHRISTY (*with a flash of delighted surprise*). Is it me?

PEGEEN. Aye. Did you never hear that from the young girls where you come from in the west or south?

CHRISTY (*with venom*). I did not then. Oh, they're bloody liars in the naked parish where I grew a man.

PEGEEN. If they are itself, you've heard it these days, I'm thinking, and you walking the world telling out your story to young girls or old.

CHRISTY. I've told my story no place till this night, Pegeen Mike, and it's foolish I was here, maybe, to be talking free, but you're decent people, I'm thinking, and yourself a kindly woman, the way I wasn't fearing you at all.

PEGEEN (*filling a sack with straw*). You've said the like of that, maybe, in every cot and cabin where you've met a young girl on your way.

CHRISTY (*going over to her, gradually raising his voice*). I've said it nowhere till this night, I'm telling you, for I've seen none the like of you the eleven long days I am walking the world, looking over a low ditch or a high ditch on my north or my south, into stony scattered fields, or scribes of bog, where you'd see young, limber girls, and fine prancing women making laughter with the men.

PEGEEN. If you weren't destroyed travelling, you'd have as much talk and streeleen, I'm thinking, as Owen Roe O'Sullivan or the poets of the Dingle Bay, and I've heard all times it's the poets are your like, fine fiery fellows with great rages when their temper's roused.

CHRISTY (*drawing a little nearer to her*). You've a power of rings, God bless you, and would there be any offence if I was asking are you single now?

PEGEEN. What would I want wedding so young?

CHRISTY (*with relief*). We're alike, so.

PEGEEN (*she puts sack on settle and beats it up*). I never killed my father. I'd be afeared to do that, except I was the like of yourself with blind rages tearing me within, for I'm thinking you should have had great tussling when the end was come.

CHRISTY (*expanding with delight at the first confidential talk he has ever had with a woman*). We had not then. It was a hard woman was come over the hill, and if he was always a crusty kind when he'd a hard woman setting him on, not the divil himself or his four fathers could put up with him at all.

PEGEEN (*with curiosity*). And isn't it a great wonder that one wasn't fearing you?

CHRISTY (*very confidentially*). Up to the day I killed my father, there wasn't a person in Ireland knew the kind I was, and I there drinking, waking, eating, sleeping, a quiet, simple poor fellow with no man giving me heed.

PEGEEN (*getting a quilt out of the cupboard and putting it on the sack*). It was the girls were giving you heed maybe, and I'm thinking it's most conceit you'd have to be gaming with their like.

CHRISTY (*shaking his head, with simplicity*). Not the girls itself, and I won't tell you a lie. There wasn't anyone heeding me in that place saving only the dumb beasts of the field.

He sits down at fire.

PEGEEN (*with disappointment*). And I thinking you should have been living the like of a king of Norway or the Eastern world.

She comes and sits beside him after placing bread and mug of milk on the table.

CHRISTY (*laughing piteously*). The like of a king, is it? And I after toiling, moiling, digging, dodging from the dawn till dusk with never a sight of joy or sport saving only when I'd be abroad in the dark night poaching rabbits on hills, for I was a divil to poach, God forgive me, (*very naïvely*) and I near got six months for going with a dung fork and stabbing a fish.

PEGEEN. And it's that you'd call sport, is it, to be abroad in the darkness with yourself alone?

CHRISTY. I did, God help me, and there I'd be as happy as the sunshine of St. Martin's Day, watching the light passing the north or the patches of fog, till I'd hear a rabbit starting to screech and I'd go running in the furze. Then when I'd my full share I'd come walking down where you'd see the ducks and geese stretched sleeping on the highway of the road, and before I'd pass the dunghill, I'd hear himself snoring out, a loud lonesome snore he'd be making all times, the while he was sleeping, and he a man 'd be raging all times, the while he was waking, like a gaudy officer you'd hear cursing and damning and swearing oaths.

PEGEEN. Providence and Mercy, spare us all!

CHRISTY. It's that you'd say surely if you seen him and he after drinking for weeks, rising up in the red dawn, or before it maybe, and going out into the yard as naked as an ash tree in the moon of May, and shying clods against the visage of the stars till he'd put the fear of death into the banbhs and the screeching sows.

PEGEEN. I'd be well-nigh afeard of that lad myself, I'm thinking. And there was no one in it but the two of you alone?

CHRISTY. The divil a one, though he'd sons and daughters walking all great states and territories of the world, and not a one of them, to this day, but would say their seven curses on him, and they rousing up to let a cough or sneeze, maybe, in the deadness of the night.

PEGEEN (*nodding her head*). Well, you should have been a queer lot. I never cursed my father the like of that, though I'm twenty and more years of age.

CHRISTY. Then you'd have cursed mine, I'm telling you, and he a man never gave peace to any, saving when he'd get two months or three, or be locked in the asylums for battering peelers or assaulting men (*with depression*) the way it was a bitter life he led me till I did up a Tuesday and halve his skull.

PEGEEN (*putting her hand on his shoulder*). Well, you'll have peace in this place, Christy Mahon, and none to trouble you, and it's near time a fine lad like you should have your good share of the earth.

CHRISTY. It's time surely, and I a seemly fellow with great strength in me and bravery of . . .

Someone knocks.

CHRISTY (*clinging to* PEGEEN). Oh, glory! it's late for knocking, and this last while I'm in terror of the peelers, and the walking dead.

Knocking again.

PEGEEN. Who's there?

VOICE (*outside*). Me.

PEGEEN. Who's me?

VOICE. The Widow Quin.

PEGEEN (*jumping up and giving him the bread and milk*). Go on now with your supper, and let on to be sleepy, for if she found you were such a warrant to talk, she'd be stringing gabble till the dawn of day. (*He takes bread and sits shyly with his back to the door.*)

PEGEEN (*opening door, with temper*). What ails you, or what is it you're wanting at his hour of the night?

WIDOW QUIN (*coming in a step and peering at* CHRISTY). I'm after meeting Shawn Keogh and Father Reilly below, who told me of your curiosity man, and they fearing by this time he was maybe roaring, romping on your hands with drink.

PEGEEN (*pointing to* CHRISTY). Look now is he roaring, and he stretched away drowsy with his supper and his mug of milk. Walk down and tell that to Father Reilly and to Shaneen Keogh.

WIDOW QUIN (*coming forward*). I'll not see them again, for I've their word to lead that lad forward for to lodge with me.

PEGEEN (*in blank amazement*). This night, is it?

WIDOW QUIN (*going over*). This night. "It isn't fitting," says the priesteen, "to have his likeness lodging with an orphaned girl." (*To* CHRISTY.) God save you, mister!

CHRISTY (*shyly*). God save you kindly.

WIDOW QUIN (*looking at him with half-amazed curiosity*). Well, aren't you a little smiling fellow? It should have been great and bitter torments did rouse your spirits to a deed of blood.

CHRISTY (*doubtfully*). It should, maybe.

WIDOW QUIN. It's more than "maybe" I'm saying, and it'd soften my heart to see you sitting so simple with your cup and cake, and you fitter to be saying your catechism than slaying your da.

PEGEEN (*at counter, washing glasses*). There's talking when any'd see he's fit to be holding his head high with the wonders of the world. Walk on from this, for I'll not have him tormented and he destroyed travelling since Tuesday was a week.

WIDOW QUIN (*peaceably*). We'll be walking surely when his supper's done, and you'll find we're great company, young fellow, when it's of the like of you and me you'd hear the penny poets singing in an August Fair.

CHRISTY (*innocently*). Did you kill your father?

PEGEEN (*contemptuously*). She did not. She hit himself with a worn pick, and the rusted poison did corrode his blood the way he never overed it, and died after. That was a sneaky kind of murder did win small glory with the boys itself.

She crosses to Christy's left.

WIDOW QUIN (*with good-humour*). If it didn't, maybe all knows a widow woman has buried her children and destroyed her man is a wiser comrade for a young lad than a girl, the like of you, who'd go helter-skeltering after any man would let you a wink upon the road.

PEGEEN (*breaking out into wild rage*). And you'll say that, Widow Quin, and you gasping with the rage you had racing the hill beyond to look on his face.

WIDOW QUIN (*laughing derisively*). Me, is it? Well, Father Reilly has cuteness to divide you now. (*She pulls* CHRISTY *up.*) There's great temptation in a man did slay his da, and we'd best be going, young fellow; so rise up and come with me.

PEGEEN (*seizing his arm*). He'll not stir. He's pot-boy in this place, and I'll not have him stolen off and kidnabbed while himself's abroad.

WIDOW QUIN. It'd be a crazy pot-boy'd lodge him in the shebeen where he works by day, so you'd have a right to come on, young fellow, till you see my little houseen, a perch off on the rising hill.

PEGEEN. Wait till morning, Christy Mahon. Wait till you lay eyes on her leaky thatch is growing more pasture for her buck goat than her square of fields, and she without a tramp itself to keep in order her place at all.

WIDOW QUIN. When you see me contriving in my little gardens, Christy Mahon, you'll swear the Lord God formed me to be living lone, and that there isn't my match in Mayo for thatching, or mowing, or shearing a sheep.

PEGEEN (*with noisy scorn*). It's true the Lord God formed you to contrive indeed. Doesn't the world know you reared a black lamb at your own breast, so that the Lord Bishop of Connaught felt the elements of a Christian, and he eating it after in a kidney stew? Doesn't the world know you've been seen shaving the foxy skipper from France for a threepenny bit and a sop of grass tobacco would wring the liver from a mountain goat you'd meet leaping the hills?

WIDOW QUIN (*with amusement*). Do you hear her now, young fellow? Do you hear the way she'll be rating at your own self when a week is by?

PEGEEN (*to* CHRISTY). Don't heed her. Tell her to go into her pigsty and not plague us here.

WIDOW QUIN. I'm going; but he'll come with me.

PEGEEN (*shaking him*). Are you dumb, young fellow?

CHRISTY (*timidly, to* WIDOW QUIN). God increase you; but I'm pot-boy in this place, and it's here I'd liefer stay.

PEGEEN (*triumphantly*). Now you have heard him, and go on from this.

WIDOW QUIN (*looking round the room*). It's lonesome this hour crossing the hill, and if he won't come along with me, I'd have a right maybe to stop this night with yourselves. Let me stretch out on the settle, Pegeen Mike; and himself can lie by the hearth.

PEGEEN (*short and fiercely*). Faith, I won't. Quit off or I will send you now.

WIDOW QUIN (*gathering her shawl up*). Well, it's a terror to be aged a score. (*To* CHRISTY.) God bless you now, young fellow, and let you be wary, or there's right torment will await you here if you go romancing with her like, and she waiting only, as they bade me say, on a sheepskin parchment to be wed with Shawn Keogh of Killakeen.

CHRISTY (*going to* PEGEEN *as she bolts the door*). What's that she's after saying?

PEGEEN. Lies and blather, you've no call to mind. Well, isn't Shawn Keogh an impudent fellow to send up spying on me? Wait till I lay hands on him. Let him wait, I'm saying.

CHRISTY. And you're not wedding him at all?

PEGEEN. I wouldn't wed him if a bishop came walking for to join us here.

CHRISTY. That God in glory may be thanked for that.

PEGEEN. There's your bed now. I've put a quilt upon you I'm after quilting a while since with my own two hands, and you'd best stretch out now for your sleep, and may God give you a good rest till I call you in the morning when the cocks will crow.

CHRISTY (*as she goes to inner room*). May God and Mary and St. Patrick bless you and reward you, for your kindly talk. (*She shuts the door behind her. He settles his bed slowly, feeling the quilt with immense satisfaction.*) Well, it's a clean bed and soft with it, and it's great luck and company I've won me in the end of time — two fine women fighting for the likes of me — till I'm thinking this night wasn't I a foolish fellow not to kill my father in the years gone by.

CURTAIN

ACT II

Scene, as before. Brilliant morning light. CHRISTY, *looking bright and cheerful, is cleaning a girl's boots.*

CHRISTY (*to himself, counting jugs on dresser*). Half a hundred beyond. Ten there. A score that's above. Eighty jugs. Six cups and a broken one. Two plates. A power of glasses. Bottles, a school-master'd be hard set to count, and enough in them, I'm thinking, to drunken all the wealth and wisdom of the County Clare. (*He puts down the boot carefully.*) There's her boots now, nice and decent for her evening use, and isn't it grand brushes she has? (*He puts them down and goes by degrees to the looking-glass.*)

Well, this'd be a fine place to be my whole life talking out with swearing Christians, in place of my old dogs and cat, and I stalking around, smoking my pipe and drinking my fill, and never a day's work but drawing a cork an odd time, or wiping a glass, or rinsing out a shiny tumbler for a decent man. (*He takes the looking-glass from the wall and puts it on the back of a chair; then sits down in front of it and begins washing his face.*) Didn't I know rightly I was handsome, though it was the divil's own mirror we had beyond, would twist a squint across an angel's brow; and I'll be growing fine from this day, the way I'll have a soft lovely skin on me and won't be the like of the clumsy young fellows do be ploughing all times in the earth and dung. (*He starts.*) Is she coming again? (*He looks out.*) Stranger girls. God help me, where'll I hide myself away and my long neck naked to the world? (*He looks out.*) I'd best go to the room maybe till I'm dressed again.

> *He gathers up his coat and the looking-glass, and runs into the inner room. The door is pushed open, and* SUSAN BRADY *looks in, and knocks on door.*

SUSAN. There's nobody in it.

Knocks again.

NELLY (*pushing her in and following her, with* HONOR BLAKE *and* SARA TANSEY). It'd be early for them both to be out walking the hill.

SUSAN. I'm thinking Shawn Keogh was making game of us and there's no such man in it at all.

HONOR (*pointing to straw and quilt*). Look at that. He's been sleeping there in the night. Well, it'll be a hard case if he's gone off now, the way we'll never set our eyes on a man killed his father, and we after rising early and destroying ourselves running fast on the hill.

NELLY. Are you thinking them's his boots?

SARA (*taking them up*). If they are, there should be his father's track on them. Did you never read in the papers the way murdered men do bleed and drip?

SUSAN. Is that blood there, Sara Tansey?

SARA (*smelling it*). That's bog water, I'm thinking, but it's his own they are surely, for I never seen the like of them for whity mud, and red mud, and turf on them, and the fine sands of the sea. That man's been walking, I'm telling you.

> *She goes down right, putting on one of his boots.*

SUSAN (*going to window*). Maybe he's stolen off to Belmullet with the boots of Michael James, and you'd have a right so to follow after him, Sara Tansey, and you the one yoked the ass cart and drove ten miles to set your eyes on the man bit the yellow lady's nostril on the northern shore.

> *She looks out.*

SARA (*running to window with one boot on*). Don't be talking, and we fooled to-day. (*Putting on other boot.*) There's a pair do fit me well, and I'll be keeping them for walking to the priest, when you'd be ashamed this place, going up winter and summer with nothing worth while to confess at all.

HONOR (*who has been listening at the door*). Whisht! there's someone inside the room. (*She pushes door a chink open.*) It's a man.

    SARA *kicks off boots and puts them where they were. They all stand in a line looking through chink.*

SARA. I'll call him. Mister! Mister! (*He puts in his head.*) Is Pegeen within?

CHRISTY (*coming in as meek as a mouse, with the looking-glass held behind his back*). She's above on the cnuceen, seeking the nanny goats, the way she'd have a sup of goat's milk for to colour my tea.

SARA. And asking your pardon, is it you's the man killed his father?

CHRISTY (*sidling toward the nail where the glass was hanging*). I am, God help me!

SARA (*taking eggs she has brought*). Then my thousand welcomes to you, and I've run up with a brace of duck's eggs for your food to-day. Pegeen's ducks is no use, but these are the real rich sort. Hold out your hand and you'll see it's no lie I'm telling you.

CHRISTY (*coming forward shyly, and holding out his left hand*). They're a great and weighty size.

SUSAN. And I run up with a pat of butter, for it'd be a poor thing to have you eating your spuds dry, and you after running a great way since you did destroy your da.

CHRISTY. Thank you kindly.

HONOR. And I brought you a little cut of cake, for you should have a thin stomach on you, and you that length walking the world.

NELLY. And I brought you a little laying pullet — boiled and all she is — was crushed at the fall of night by the curate's car. Feel the fat of that breast, mister.

CHRISTY. It's bursting, surely.

    He feels it with the back of his hand, in which he holds the presents.

SARA. Will you pinch it? Is your right hand too sacred for to use at all? (*She slips round behind him.*) It's a glass he has. Well, I never seen to this day a man with a looking-glass held on his back. Them that kills their fathers is a vain lot surely.

    Girls giggle.

CHRISTY (*smiling innocently and piling presents on glass*). I'm very thankful to you all to-day . . .

WIDOW QUIN (*coming in quickly, at door*). Sara Tansey, Susan Brady, Honor Blake! What in glory has you here at this hour of day?

GIRLS (*giggling*). That's the man killed his father.

WIDOW QUIN (*coming to them*). I know well it's the man; and I'm after putting him down in the sports below for racing, leaping, pitching, and the Lord knows what.

SARA (*exuberantly*). That's right, Widow Quin. I'll bet my dowry that he'll lick the world.

WIDOW QUIN. If you will, you'd have a right to have him fresh and nourished in place of nursing a feast. (*Taking presents.*) Are you fasting or fed, young fellow?

CHRISTY. Fasting, if you please.

WIDOW QUIN (*loudly*). Well, you're the lot. Stir up now and give him his breakfast. (*To* CHRISTY.) Come here to me (*she puts him on bench beside her while the girls make tea and get his breakfast*) and let you tell us your story before Pegeen will come, in place of grinning your ears off like the moon of May.

CHRISTY (*beginning to be pleased*). It's a long story; you'd be destroyed listening.

WIDOW QUIN. Don't be letting on to be shy, a fine, gamey, treacherous lad the like of you. Was it in your house beyond you cracked his skull?

CHRISTY (*shy but flattered*). It was not. We were digging spuds in his cold, sloping, stony, divil's patch of a field.

WIDOW QUIN. And you went asking money of him, or making talk of getting a wife would drive him from his farm?

CHRISTY. I did not, then; but there I was, digging and digging, and "You squinting idiot," says he, "let you walk down now and tell the priest you'll wed the Widow Casey in a score of days."

WIDOW QUIN. And what kind was she?

CHRISTY (*with horror*). A walking terror from beyond the hills, and she two score and five years, and two hundredweights and five pounds in the weighing scales, with a limping leg on her, and a blinded eye, and she a woman of noted misbehaviour with the old and young.

GIRLS (*clustering round him, serving him*). Glory be.

WIDOW QUIN. And what did he want driving you to wed with her?

She takes a bit of the chicken.

CHRISTY (*eating with growing satisfaction*). He was letting on I was wanting a protector from the harshness of the world, and he without a thought the whole while but how he'd have her hut to live in and her gold to drink.

WIDOW QUIN. There's maybe worse than a dry hearth and a widow woman and your glass at night. So you hit him then?

CHRISTY (*getting almost excited*). I did not. "I won't wed her," says I, "when all know she did suckle me for six weeks when I came into the world, and she a hag this day with a tongue on her has the crows and seabirds scattered, the way they wouldn't cast a shadow on her garden with the dread of her curse."

WIDOW QUIN (*teasingly*). That one should be right company.

SARA (*eagerly*). Don't mind her. Did you kill him then?

CHRISTY. "She's too good for the like of you," says he, "and go on now or I'll flatten you out like a crawling beast has passed under a dray." "You will not if I can help it," says I. "Go on," says he, "or I'll have the divil making garters of your limbs to-night." "You will not if I can help it," says I.

He sits up, brandishing his mug.

SARA. You were right surely.

CHRISTY (*impressively*). With that the sun came out between the cloud and the hill, and it shining green in my face. "God have mercy on your soul," says he, lifting a scythe; "or on your own," says I, raising the loy.

SUSAN. That's a grand story.

HONOR. He tells it lovely.

CHRISTY (*flattered and confident, waving bone*). He gave a drive with the scythe, and I gave a lep to the east. Then I turned around with my back to the north, and I hit a blow on the ridge of his skull, laid him stretched out, and he split to the knob of his gullet.

He raises the chicken bone to his Adam's apple.

GIRLS (*together*). Well, you're a marvel! Oh, God bless you! You're the lad surely!

SUSAN. I'm thinking the Lord God sent him this road to make a second husband to the Widow Quin, and she with a great yearning to be wedded, though all dread her here. Lift him on her knee, Sara Tansey.

WIDOW QUIN. Don't tease him.

SARA (*going over to dresser and counter very quickly, and getting two glasses and porter*). You're heroes surely, and let you drink a supeen with your arms linked like the outlandish lovers in the sailor's song. (*She links their arms and gives them the glasses.*) There now. Drink a health to the wonders of the western world, the pirates, preachers, poteen-makers, with the jobbing jockies; parching peelers, and the juries fill their stomachs selling judgments of the English law.

Brandishing the bottle.

WIDOW QUIN. That's a right toast, Sara Tansey. Now Christy.

They drink with their arms linked, he drinking with his left hand, she with her right. As they are drinking, PEGEEN MIKE *comes in with a milk can and stands aghast. They all spring away from* CHRISTY. *He goes down left.* WIDOW QUIN *remains seated.*

PEGEEN (*angrily, to* SARA). What is it you're wanting?

SARA (*twisting her apron*). An ounce of tobacco.

PEGEEN. Have you tuppence?

SARA. I've forgotten my purse.

PEGEEN. Then you'd best be getting it and not fooling us here. (*To the* WIDOW QUIN, *with more elaborate scorn.*) And what is it you're wanting, Widow Quin?

WIDOW QUIN (*insolently*). A penn'orth of starch.

PEGEEN (*breaking out*). And you without a white shift or a shirt in your whole family since the drying of the flood. I've no starch for the like of you, and let you walk on now to Killamuck.

WIDOW QUIN (*turning to* CHRISTY, *as she goes out with the girls*). Well, you're mighty huffy this day, Pegeen Mike, and, you young fellow, let you not forget the sports and racing when the noon is by.

They go out.

PEGEEN (*imperiously*). Fling out that rubbish and put them cups away. (CHRISTY *tidies away in great haste.*) Shove in the bench by the wall. (*He does so.*) And hang that glass on the nail. What disturbed it at all?

CHRISTY (*very meekly*). I was making myself decent only, and this a fine country for young lovely girls.

PEGEEN (*sharply*). Whisht your talking of girls.

Goes to counter — right.

CHRISTY. Wouldn't any wish to be decent in a place . . .

PEGEEN. Whisht I'm saying.

CHRISTY (*looks at her face for a moment with great misgivings, then as a last effort, takes up a loy, and goes towards her, with feigned assurance*). It was with a loy the like of that I killed my father.

PEGEEN (*still sharply*). You've told me that story six times since the dawn of day.

CHRISTY (*reproachfully*). It's a queer thing you wouldn't care to be hearing it and them girls after walking four miles to be listening to me now.

PEGEEN (*turning round astonished*). Four miles.

CHRISTY (*apologetically*). Didn't himself say there were only four bona fides living in the place?

PEGEEN. It's bona fides by the road they are, but that lot came over the river lepping the stones. It's not three perches when you go like that, and I was down this morning looking on the papers the post-boy does have in his bag. (*With meaning and emphasis.*) For there was great news this day, Christopher Mahon.

She goes into room left.

CHRISTY (*suspiciously*). Is it news of my murder?

PEGEEN (*inside*). Murder, indeed.

CHRISTY (*loudly*). A murdered da?

PEGEEN (*coming in again and crossing right*). There was not, but a story filled half a page of the hanging of a man. Ah, that should be a fearful end, young fellow, and it worst of all for a man who destroyed his da, for the like of him would get small mercies, and when it's dead he is, they'd put him in a narrow grave, with cheap sacking wrapping him round, and pour down quicklime on his head, the way you'd see a woman pouring any frish-frash from a cup.

CHRISTY (*very miserably*). Oh, God help me. Are you thinking I'm safe? You were saying at the fall of night, I was shut of jeopardy and I here with yourselves.

PEGEEN (*severely*). You'll be shut of jeopardy no place if you go talking with a pack of wild girls the like of them do be walking abroad with the peelers, talking whispers at the fall of night.

CHRISTY (*with terror*). And you're thinking they'd tell?

PEGEEN (*with mock sympathy*). Who knows, God help you.

CHRISTY (*loudly*). What joy would they have to bring hanging to the likes of me?

PEGEEN. It's queer joys they have, and who knows the thing they'd do, if it'd make the green stones cry itself to think of you swaying and swiggling at the butt of a rope, and you with a fine, stout neck, God bless you! the way you'd be a half an hour, in great anguish, getting your death.

CHRISTY (*getting his boots and putting them on*). If there's that terror of them, it'd be best, maybe, I went on wandering like Esau or Cain and Abel on the sides of Neifin or the Erris plain.

PEGEEN (*beginning to play with him*). It would, maybe, for I've heard the Circuit Judges this place is a heartless crew.

CHRISTY (*bitterly*). It's more than Judges this place is a heartless crew. (*Looking up at her.*) And isn't it a poor thing to be starting again and I a lonesome fellow will be looking out on women and girls the way the needy fallen spirits do be looking on the Lord?

PEGEEN. What call have you to be that lonesome when there's poor girls walking Mayo in their thousands now?

CHRISTY (*grimly*). It's well you know what call I have. It's well you know it's a lonesome thing to be passing small towns with the lights shining sideways when the night is down, or going in strange places with a dog noising before you and a dog noising behind, or drawn to the cities where you'd hear a voice kissing and talking deep love in every shadow of the ditch, and you passing on with an empty, hungry stomach failing from your heart.

PEGEEN. I'm thinking you're an odd man, Christy Mahon. The oddest walking fellow I ever set my eyes on to this hour to-day.

CHRISTY. What would any be but odd men and they living lonesome in the world?

PEGEEN. I'm not odd, and I'm my whole life with my father only.

CHRISTY (*with infinite admiration*). How would a lovely handsome woman the like of you be lonesome when all men should be thronging around to hear the sweetness of your voice, and the little infant children should be pestering your steps I'm thinking, and you walking the roads.

PEGEEN. I'm hard set to know what way a coaxing fellow the like of yourself should be lonesome either.

CHRISTY. Coaxing?

PEGEEN. Would you have me think a man never talked with the girls would have the words you've spoken today? It's only letting on you are to be lonesome, the way you'd get around me now.

CHRISTY. I wish to God I was letting on; but I was lonesome all times, and born lonesome, I'm thinking, as the moon of dawn.

Going to the door.

PEGEEN (*puzzled by his talk*). Well, it's a story I'm not understanding at all why you'd be worse than another, Christy Mahon, and you a fine lad with the great savagery to destroy your da.

CHRISTY. It's little I'm understanding myself, saving only that my heart's scalded this day, and I going off stretching out the earth between us, the way I'll not be waking near you another dawn of the year till the two of us do arise to hope or judgment with the saints of God, and now I'd best be going with my wattle in my hand, for hanging is a poor thing (*turning to go*), and it's little welcome only is left me in this house to-day.

PEGEEN (*sharply*). Christy! (*He turns round.*) Come here to me. (*He goes towards her.*) Lay down that switch and throw some sods on the fire. You're pot-boy in this place, and I'll not have you mitch off from us now.

CHRISTY. You were saying I'd be hanged if I stay.

PEGEEN (*quite kindly at last*). I'm after going down and reading the fearful crimes of Ireland for two weeks or three, and there wasn't a word of your murder. (*Getting up and going over to the counter.*) They've likely not found the body. You're safe so with ourselves.

CHRISTY (*astonished, slowly*). It's making game of me you were (*following her with fearful joy*), and I can stay so, working at your side, and I not lonesome from this mortal day.

PEGEEN. What's to hinder you from staying, except the widow woman or the young girls would inveigle you off?

CHRISTY (*with rapture*). And I'll have your words from this day filling my ears, and that look is come upon you meeting my two eyes, and I watching you loafing around in the warm sun, or rinsing your ankles when the night is come.

PEGEEN (*kindly, but a little embarrassed*). I'm thinking you'll be a loyal young lad to have working around, and if you vexed me a while since with your leaguing with the girls, I wouldn't give a thraneen for a lad hadn't a mighty spirit in him and a gamey heart.

SHAWN KEOGH *runs in carrying a cleeve on his back, followed by the* WIDOW QUIN.

SHAWN (*to* PEGEEN). I was passing below, and I seen your mountainy sheep eating cabbages in Jimmy's field. Run up or they'll be bursting surely.

PEGEEN. Oh, God mend them!

She puts a shawl over her head and runs out.

CHRISTY (*looking from one to the other. Still in high spirits*). I'd best go to her aid maybe. I'm handy with ewes.

WIDOW QUIN (*closing the door*). She can do that much, and there is Shaneen has long speeches for to tell you now.

She sits down with an amused smile.

SHAWN (*taking something from his pocket and offering it to* CHRISTY). Do you see that, mister?

CHRISTY (*looking at it*). The half of a ticket to the Western States!

SHAWN (*trembling with anxiety*). I'll give it to you and my new hat (*pulling it out of hamper*); and my breeches with the double seat (*pulling it off*); and my new coat is woven from the blackest shearings for three miles around *(giving him the coat)*; I'll give you the whole of them, and my blessing, and the blessing of Father Reilly itself, maybe, if you'll quit from this and leave us in the peace we had till last night at the fall of dark.

CHRISTY *(with a new arrogance)*. And for what is it you're wanting to get shut of me?

SHAWN *(looking to the* WIDOW *for help)*. I'm a poor scholar with middling faculties to coin a lie, so I'll tell you the truth, Christy Mahon. I'm wedding with Pegeen beyond, and I don't think well of having a clever fearless man the like of you dwelling in her house.

CHRISTY *(almost pugnaciously)*. And you'd be using bribery for to banish me?

SHAWN *(in an imploring voice)*. Let you not take it badly, mister honey, isn't beyond the best place for you where you'll have golden chains and shiny coats and you riding upon hunters with the ladies of the land.

He makes an eager sign to the WIDOW QUIN *to come to help him.*

WIDOW QUIN *(coming over)*. It's true for him, and you'd best quit off and not have that poor girl setting her mind on you, for there's Shaneen thinks she wouldn't suit you though all is saying that she'll wed you now.

CHRISTY *beams with delight.*

SHAWN *(in terrified earnest)*. She wouldn't suit you, and she with the divil's own temper the way you'd be strangling one another in a score of days. *(He makes the movement of strangling with his hands.)* It's the like of me only that she's fit for, a quiet simple fellow wouldn't raise a hand upon her if she scratched itself.

WIDOW QUIN *(putting* SHAWN'S *hat on* CHRISTY*)*. Fit them clothes on you anyhow, young fellow, and he'd maybe loan them to you for the sports. *(Pushing him towards inner door.)* Fit them on and you can give your answer when you have them tried.

CHRISTY *(beaming, delighted with the clothes)*. I will then. I'd like herself to see me in them tweeds and hat.

He goes into room and shuts the door.

SHAWN *(in great anxiety)*. He'd like herself to see them. He'll not leave us, Widow Quin. He's a score of divils in him the way it's well nigh certain he will wed Pegeen.

WIDOW QUIN *(jeeringly)*. It's true all girls are fond of courage and do hate the like of you.

SHAWN *(walking about in desperation)*. Oh, Widow Quin, what'll I be doing now? I'd inform again him, but he'd burst from Kilmainham and he'd be sure and certain to destroy me. If I wasn't so God-fearing, I'd near have courage to come behind him and run a pike into his side. Oh, it's a hard case to be an orphan and not to have your father that you're used to, and you'd easy kill and make yourself a hero in the sight of all. *(Coming up to her.)* Oh, Widow Quin, will you find me some contrivance when I've promised you a ewe?

WIDOW QUIN. A ewe's a small thing, but what would you give me if I did wed him and did save you so?

SHAWN (*with astonisment*). You?

WIDOW QUIN. Aye. Would you give me the red cow you have and the mountainy ram, and the right of way across your rye path, and a load of dung at Michaelmas, and turbary upon the western hill?

SHAWN (*radiant with hope*). I would surely, and I'd give you the wedding-ring I have, and the loan of a new suit, the way you'd have him decent on the wedding-day. I'd give you two kids for your dinner, and a gallon of poteen, and I'd call the piper on the long car to your wedding from Crossmolina or from Ballina. I'd give you . . .

WIDOW QUIN. That'll do so, and let you whisht, for he's coming now again.

CHRISTY *comes in very natty in the new clothes.* WIDOW QUIN *goes to him admiringly.*

WIDOW QUIN. If you seen yourself now, I'm thinking you'd be too proud to speak to us at all, and it'd be a pity surely to have your like sailing from Mayo to the Western World.

CHRISTY (*as proud as a peacock*). I'm not going. If this is a poor place itself, I'll make myself contented to be lodging here.

WIDOW QUIN *makes a sign to* SHAWN *to leave them.*

SHAWN. Well, I'm going measuring the race-course while the tide is low, so I'll leave you the garments and my blessing for the sports to-day. God bless you!

He wriggles out.

WIDOW QUIN (*admiring* CHRISTY). Well, you're mighty spruce, young fellow. Sit down now while you're quiet till you talk with me.

CHRISTY (*swaggering*). I'm going abroad on the hillside for to seek Pegeen.

WIDOW QUIN. You'll have time and plenty for to seek Pegeen, and you heard me saying at the fall of night the two of us should be great company.

CHRISTY. From this out I'll have no want of company when all sorts is bringing me their food and clothing (*he swaggers to the door, tightening his belt*), the way they'd set their eyes upon a gallant orphan cleft his father with one blow to the breeches belt. (*He opens door, then staggers back.*) Saints of glory! Holy angels from the throne of light!

WIDOW QUIN (*going over*). What ails you?

CHRISTY. It's the walking spirit of my murdered da!

WIDOW QUIN (*looking out*). Is it that tramper?

CHRISTY (*wildly*). Where'll I hide my poor body from that ghost of hell?

The door is pushed open, and OLD MAHON *appears on threshold.* CHRISTY *darts in behind door.*

WIDOW QUIN (*in great amusement*). God save you, my poor man.

MAHON (*gruffly*). Did you see a young lad passing this way in the early morning or the fall of night?

WIDOW QUIN. You're a queer kind to walk in not saluting at all.

MAHON. Did you see the young lad?

WIDOW QUIN (*stiffly*). What kind was he?

MAHON. An ugly young streeler with a murderous gob on him, and a little switch in his hand. I met a tramper seen him coming this way at the fall of night.

WIDOW QUIN. There's harvest hundreds do be passing these days for the Sligo boat. For what is it you're wanting him, my poor man?

MAHON. I want to destroy him for breaking the head on me with the clout of a loy. (*He takes off a big hat, and shows his head in a mass of bandages and plaster, with some pride.*) It was he did that, and amn't I a great wonder to think I've traced him ten days with that rent in my crown?

WIDOW QUIN (*taking his head in both hands and examining it with extreme delight*). That was a great blow. And who hit you? A robber maybe?

MAHON. It was my own son hit me, and he the divil a robber, or anything else, but a dirty, stuttering lout.

WIDOW QUIN (*letting go his skull and wiping her hands in her apron*). You'd best be wary of a mortified scalp, I think they call it, lepping around with that wound in the splendour of the sun. It was a bad blow surely, and you should have vexed him fearful to make him strike that gash in his da.

MAHON. Is it me?

WIDOW QUIN (*amusing herself*). Aye. And isn't it a great shame when the old and hardened do torment the young?

MAHON (*raging*). Torment him is it? And I after holding out with the patience of a martyred saint till there's nothing but destruction on, and I'm driven out in my old age with none to aid me.

WIDOW QUIN (*greatly amused*). It's a sacred wonder the way that wickedness will spoil a man.

MAHON. My wickedness, is it? Amn't I after saying it is himself has me destroyed, and he a liar on walls, a talker of folly, a man you'd see stretched the half of the day in the brown ferns with his belly to the sun.

WIDOW QUIN. Not working at all?

MAHON. The divil a work, or if he did itself, you'd see him raising up a haystack like the stalk of a rush, or driving our last cow till he broke her leg at the hip, and when he wasn't at that he'd be fooling over little birds he had — finches and felts — or making mugs at his own self in the bit of a glass we had hung on the wall.

WIDOW QUIN (*looking at* CHRISTY). What way was he so foolish? It was running wild after the girls may be?

MAHON (*with a shout of derision*). Running wild, is it? If he seen a red petticoat coming swinging over the hill, he'd be off to hide in the sticks, and you'd see him shooting out his sheep's eyes between the little twigs and the leaves, and his two ears rising like a hare looking out through a gap. Girls, indeed!

WIDOW QUIN. It was drink maybe?

MAHON. And he a poor fellow would get drunk on the smell of a pint. He'd a queer rotten stomach, I'm telling you, and when I gave him three pulls from my pipe a while since, he was taken with contortions till I had to send him in the ass cart to the females' nurse.

WIDOW QUIN (*clasping her hands*). Well, I never till this day heard tell of a man the like of that!

MAHON. I'd take a mighty oath you didn't surely, and wasn't he the laughing joke of every female woman where four baronies meet, the way the girls would stop their weeding if they seen him coming the road to let a roar at him, and call him the looney of Mahon's.

WIDOW QUIN. I'd give the world and all to see the like of him. What kind was he?

MAHON. A small low fellow.

WIDOW QUIN. And dark?

MAHON. Dark and dirty.

WIDOW QUIN (*considering*). I'm thinking I seen him.

MAHON (*eagerly*). An ugly young blackguard.

WIDOW QUIN. A hideous, fearful villain, and the spit of you.

MAHON. What way is he fled?

WIDOW QUIN. Gone over the hills to catch a coasting steamer to the north or south.

MAHON. Could I pull up on him now?

WIDOW QUIN. If you'll cross the sands below where the tide is out, you'll be in it as soon as himself, for he had to go round ten miles by the top of the bay. (*She points to the door.*) Strike down by the head beyond and then follow on the roadway to the north and east.

MAHON *goes abruptly.*

WIDOW QUIN (*shouting after him*). Let you give him a good vengeance when you come up with him, but don't put yourself in the power of the law, for it'd be a poor thing to see a judge in his black cap reading out his sentence on a civil warrior the like of you.

She swings the door and looks at CHRISTY, *who is cowering in terror, for a moment, then she bursts into a laugh.*

WIDOW QUIN. Well, you're the walking Playboy of the Western World, and that's the poor man you had divided to his breeches belt.

CHRISTY (*looking out: then, to her*). What'll Pegeen say when she hears that story? What'll she be saying to me now?

WIDOW QUIN. She'll knock the head of you, I'm thinking, and drive you from the door. God help her to be taking you for a wonder, and you a little schemer making up the story you destroyed your da.

CHRISTY (*turning to the door, nearly speechless with rage, half to himself*). To be letting on he was dead, and coming back to his life, and following after me like an old weazel tracing a rat, and coming in here laying desolation between my own self and the fine women of Ireland, and he a kind of carcase that you'd fling upon the sea . . .

The Playboy of the Western World

WIDOW QUIN (*more soberly*). There's talking for a man's one only son.

CHRISTY (*breaking out*). His one son, is it? May I meet him with one tooth and it aching, and one eye to be seeing seven and seventy divils in the twists of the road, and one old timber leg on him to limp into the scalding grave. (*Looking out.*) There he is now crossing the strands, and that the Lord God would send a high wave to wash him from the world.

WIDOW QUIN (*scandalized*). Have you no shame? (*Putting her hand on his shoulder and turning him round.*) What ails you? Near crying, is it?

CHRISTY (*in despair and grief*). Amn't I after seeing the love-light of the star of knowledge shining from her brow, and hearing words would put you thinking on the holy Brigid speaking to the infant saints, and now she'll be turning again, and speaking hard words to me, like an old woman with a spavindy ass she'd have, urging on a hill.

WIDOW QUIN. There's poetry talk for a girl you'd see itching and scratching, and she with a stale stink of poteen on her from selling in the shop.

CHRISTY (*impatiently*). It's her like is fitted to be handling merchandise in the heavens above, and what'll I be doing now, I ask you, and I a kind of wonder was jilted by the heavens when a day was by.

There is a distant noise of girls' voices. WIDOW QUIN *looks from window and comes to him, hurriedly.*

WIDOW QUIN. You'll be doing like myself, I'm thinking, when I did destroy my man, for I'm above many's the day, odd times in great spirits, abroad in the sunshine, darning a stocking or stitching a shift; and odd times again looking out on the schooners, hookers, trawlers is sailing the sea, and I thinking on the gallant hairy fellows are drifting beyond, and myself long years living alone.

CHRISTY (*interested*). You're like me, so.

WIDOW QUIN. I am your like, and it's for that I'm taking a fancy to you, and I with my little houseen above where there'd be myself to tend you, and none to ask were you a murderer or what at all.

CHRISTY. And what would I be doing if I left Pegeen?

WIDOW QUIN. I've nice jobs you could be doing, gathering shells to make a whitewash for our hut within, building up a little goose-house, or stretching a new skin on an old curragh I have, and if my hut is far from all sides, it's there you'll meet the wisest old men, I tell you, at the corner of my wheel, and it's there yourself and me will have great times whispering and hugging....

VOICES (*outside, calling far away*). Christy! Christy Mahon! Christy!

CHRISTY. Is it Pegeen Mike?

WIDOW QUIN. It's the young girls, I'm thinking, coming to bring you to the sports below, and what is it you'll have me to tell them now?

CHRISTY. Aid me for to win Pegeen. It's herself only that I'm seeking now. (WIDOW QUIN *gets up and goes to window.*) Aid me for to win her, and I'll be asking God to stretch a hand to you in the hour of death, and lead you short cuts through the Meadows of Ease, and up the floor of Heaven to the Footstool of the Virgin's Son.

WIDOW QUIN. There's praying.

VOICES (*nearer*). Christy! Christy Mahon!

CHRISTY (*with agitation*). They're coming. Will you swear to aid and save me for the love of Christ?

WIDOW QUIN (*looks at him for a moment*). If I aid you, will you swear to give me a right of way I want, and a mountainy ram, and a load of dung at Michaelmas, the time that you'll be master here?

CHRISTY. I will, by the elements and stars of night.

WIDOW QUIN. Then we'll not say a word of the old fellow, the way Pegeen won't know your story till the end of time.

CHRISTY. And if he chances to return again?

WIDOW QUIN. We'll swear he's a maniac and not your da. I could take an oath I seen him raving on the sands to-day.

Girls run in.

SUSAN. Come on to the sports below. Pegeen says you're to come.

SARA TANSEY. The lepping's beginning, and we've a jockey's suit to fit upon you for the mule race on the sands below.

HONOR. Come on, will you?

CHRISTY. I will then if Pegeen's beyond.

SARA TANSEY. She's in the boreen making game of Shaneen Keogh.

CHRISTY. Then I'll be going to her now.

He runs out followed by the girls.

WIDOW QUIN. Well, if the worst comes in the end of all, it'll be great game to see there's none to pity him but a widow woman, the like of me, has buried her children and destroyed her man.

She goes out.

CURTAIN

ACT III

Scene, as before. Later in the day. Jimmy comes in, slightly drunk.

JIMMY (*calls*). Pegeen! (*Crosses to inner door.*) Pegeen Mike! (*Comes back again into the room.*) Pegeen! (PHILLY *comes in in the same state.*) (*To* PHILLY.) Did you see herself?

PHILLY. I did not; but I sent Shawn Keogh with the ass cart for to bear him home. (*Trying cupboards which are locked.*) Well, isn't he a nasty man to get into such staggers at a morning wake? and isn't herself the divil's daughter for locking, and she so fussy after that young gaffer, you might take your death with drought and none to heed you?

JIMMY. It's little wonder she'd be fussy, and he after bringing bankrupt ruin on the roulette man, and the trick-o'-the-loop man, and breaking the nose of the cockshot-man, and winning all in the sports below, racing, lepping, dancing, and the Lord knows what! He's right luck, I'm telling you.

PHILLY. If he has, he'll be rightly hobbled yet, and he not able to say ten words without making a brag of the way he killed his father, and the great blow he hit with the loy.

JIMMY. A man can't hang by his own informing, and his father should be rotten by now.

OLD MAHON *passes window slowly.*

PHILLY. Supposing a man's digging spuds in that field with a long spade, and supposing he flings up the two halves of that skull, what'll be said then in the papers and the courts of law?

JIMMY. They'd say it was an old Dane, maybe, was drowned in the flood. (OLD MAHON *comes in and sits down near door listening.*) Did you never hear tell of the skulls they have in the city of Dublin, ranged out like blue jugs in a cabin of Connaught?

PHILLY. And you believe that?

JIMMY (*pugnaciously*). Didn't a lad see them and he after coming from harvesting in the Liverpool boat? "They have them there," says he, "making a show of the great people there was one time walking the world. White skulls and yellow skulls, and some with full teeth, and some haven't only but one."

PHILLY. It was no lie, maybe, for when I was a young lad there was a graveyard beyond the house with the remnants of a man who had thighs as long as your arm. He was a horrid man, I'm telling you, and there was many a fine Sunday I'd put him together for fun, and he with shiny bones, you wouldn't meet the like of these days in the cities of the world.

MAHON (*getting up*). You wouldn't, is it? Lay your eyes on that skull, and tell me where and when there was another the like of it, is splintered only from the blow of a loy.

PHILLY. Glory be to God! And who hit you at all?

MAHON (*triumphantly*). It was my own son hit me. Would you believe that?

JIMMY. Well, there's wonders hidden in the heart of man!

PHILLY (*suspiciously*). And what way was it done?

MAHON (*wandering about the room*). I'm after walking hundreds and long scores of miles, winning clean beds and the fill of my belly four times in the day, and I doing nothing but telling stories of that naked truth. (*He comes to them a little aggressively.*) Give me a supeen and I'll tell you now.

WIDOW QUIN *comes in and stands aghast behind him. He is facing* JIMMY *and* PHILLY, *who are on the left.*

JIMMY. Ask herself beyond. She's the stuff hidden in her shawl.

WIDOW QUIN (*coming to* MAHON *quickly*). You here, is it? You didn't go far at all?

MAHON. I seen the coasting steamer passing, and I got a drought upon me and a cramping leg, so I said, "The divil go along with him," and turned again. (*Looking under her shawl.*) And let you give me a supeen, for I'm destroyed travelling since Tuesday was a week.

WIDOW QUIN (*getting a glass, in a cajoling tone*). Sit down then by the fire and take your ease for a space. You've a right to be destroyed indeed, with your walking, and fighting, and facing the sun. (*Giving him poteen from a stone jar she has brought in.*) There now is a drink for you, and may it be to your happiness and length of life.

MAHON (*taking glass greedily and sitting down by fire*). God increase you!

WIDOW QUIN (*taking men to the right stealthily*). Do you know what? That man's raving from his wound to-day, for I met him a while since telling a rambling tale of a tinker had him destroyed. Then he heard of Christy's deed, and he up and says it was his son had cracked his skull. O isn't madness a fright, for he'll go killing someone yet, and he thinking it's the man has struck him so?

JIMMY (*entirely convinced*). It's a fright, surely. I knew a party was kicked in the head by a red mare, and he went killing horses a great while, till he eat the insides of a clock and died after.

PHILLY (*with suspicion*). Did he see Christy?

WIDOW QUIN. He didn't. (*With a warning gesture.*) Let you not be putting him in mind of him, or you'll be likely summoned if there's murder done. (*Looking round at* MAHON.) Whisht! He's listening. Wait now till you hear me taking him easy and unravelling all. (*She goes to* MAHON.) And what way are you feeling, mister? Are you in contentment now?

MAHON (*slightly emotional from his drink*). I'm poorly only, for it's a hard story the way I'm left to-day, when it was I did tend him from his hour of birth, and he a dunce never reached his second book, the way he'd come from school, many's the day, with his legs lamed under him, and he blackened with his beatings like a tinker's ass. It's a hard story, I'm saying, the way some do have their next and nighest raising up a hand of murder on them, and some is lonesome getting their death with lamentation in the dead of night.

WIDOW QUIN (*not knowing what to say*). To hear you talking so quiet, who'd know you were the same fellow we seen pass to-day?

MAHON. I'm the same surely. The wrack and ruin of three score years; and it's a terror to live that length, I tell you, and to have your sons going to the dogs against you, and you wore out scolding them, and skelping them, and God knows what.

PHILLY (*to* JIMMY). He's not raving. (*To* WIDOW QUIN.) Will you ask him what kind was his son?

WIDOW QUIN (*to* MAHON, *with a peculiar look*). Was your son that hit you a lad of one year and a score maybe, a great hand at racing and lepping and licking the world?

MAHON (*turning on her with a roar of rage*). Didn't you hear me say he

The Playboy of the Western World 451

was the fool of men, the way from this out he'll know the orphan's lot with old and young making game of him and they swearing, raging, kicking at him like a mangy cur.

A great burst of cheering outside, some way off.

MAHON (*putting his hands to his ears*). What in the name of God do they want roaring below?

WIDOW QUIN (*with the shade of a smile*). They're cheering a young lad, the champion Playboy of the Western World.

More cheering.

MAHON (*going to window*). It'd split my heart to hear them, and I with pulses in my brain-pan for a week gone by. Is it racing they are?

JIMMY (*looking from door*). It is then. They are mounting him for the mule race will be run upon the sands. That's the playboy on the winkered mule.

MAHON (*puzzled*). That lad, is it? If you said it was a fool he was, I'd have laid a mighty oath he was the likeness of my wandering son. (*Uneasily, putting his hand to his head.*) Faith, I'm thinking I'll go walking for to view the race.

WIDOW QUIN (*stopping him, sharply*). You will not. You'd best take the road to Belmullet, and not be dilly-dallying in this place where there isn't a spot you could sleep.

PHILLY (*coming forward*). Don't mind her. Mount there on the bench and you'll have a view of the whole. They're hurrying before the tide will rise, and it'd be near over if you went down the pathway through the crags below.

MAHON (*mounts on bench,* WIDOW QUIN *beside him*). That's a right view again the edge of the sea. They're coming now from the point. He's leading. Who is he at all?

WIDOW QUIN. He's the champion of the world, I tell you, and there isn't a hop'orth isn't falling lucky to his hands to-day.

PHILLY (*looking out, interested in the race*). Look at that. They're pressing him now.

JIMMY. He'll win it yet.

PHILLY. Take your time, Jimmy Farrell. It's too soon to say.

WIDOW QUIN (*shouting*). Watch him taking the gate. There's riding.

JIMMY (*cheering*). More power to the young lad!

MAHON. He's passing the third.

JIMMY. He'll lick them yet!

WIDOW QUIN. He'd lick them if he was running races with a score itself.

MAHON. Look at the mule he has, kicking the stars.

WIDOW QUIN. There was a lep! (*Catching hold of* MAHON *in her excitement.*) He's fallen! He's mounted again! Faith, he's passing them all!

JIMMY. Look at him skelping her!

PHILLY. And the mountain girls hooshing him on!

JIMMY. It's the last turn! The post's cleared for them now!

MAHON. Look at the narrow place. He'll be into the bogs! (*With a yell.*) Good rider! He's through it again!

JIMMY. He neck and neck!

MAHON. Good boy to him! Flames, but he's in!

Great cheering, in which all join.

MAHON (*with hesitation*). What's that? They're raising him up. They're coming this way. (*With a roar of rage and astonishment.*) It's Christy! by the stars of God! I'd know his way of spitting and he astride the moon.

He jumps down and makes for the door, but WIDOW QUIN *catches him and pulls him back.*

WIDOW QUIN. Stay quiet, will you. That's not your son. (*To* JIMMY.) Stop him, or you'll get a month for the abetting of manslaughter and be fined as well.

JIMMY. I'll hold him.

MAHON (*struggling*). Let me out! Let me out, the lot of you! till I have my vengeance on his head to-day.

WIDOW QUIN (*shaking him, vehemently*). That's not your son. That's a man is going to make a marriage with the daughter of this house, a place with fine trade, with a license, and with poteen too.

MAHON (*amazed*). That man marrying a decent and a moneyed girl! Is it mad yous are? Is it in a crazy-house for females that I'm landed now?

WIDOW QUIN. It's mad yourself is with the blow upon your head. That lad is the wonder of the Western World.

MAHON. I seen it's my son.

WIDOW QUIN. You seen that you're mad. (*Cheering outside.*) Do you hear them cheering him in the zig-zags of the road? Aren't you after saying that your son's a fool, and how would they be cheering a true idiot born?

MAHON (*getting distressed*). It's maybe out of reason that that man's himself. (*Cheering again.*) There's none surely will go cheering him. Oh, I'm raving with a madness that would fright the world! (*He sits down with his hand to his head.*) There was one time I seen ten scarlet divils letting on they'd cork my spirit in a gallon can; and one time I seen rats as big as badgers sucking the life blood from the butt of my lug; but I never till this day confused that dribbling idiot with a likely man. I'm destroyed surely.

WIDOW QUIN. And who'd wonder when it's your brain-pan that is gaping now?

MAHON. Then the blight of the sacred drought upon myself and him, for I never went mad to this day, and I not three weeks with the Limerick girls drinking myself silly, and parlatic from the dusk to dawn. (*To* WIDOW QUIN, *suddenly.*) Is my visage astray?

WIDOW QUIN. It is then. You're a sniggering maniac, a child could see.

MAHON (*getting up more cheerfully*). Then I'd best be going to the union beyond, and there'll be a welcome before me, I tell you (*with great pride*), and I a terrible and fearful case, the way that there I was one time, screeching in a straitened waistcoat, with seven doctors writing out my sayings in a printed book. Would you believe that?

WIDOW QUIN. If you're a wonder itself, you'd best be hasty, for them lads caught a maniac one time and pelted the poor creature till he ran out, raving and foaming, and was drowned in the sea.

MAHON (*with philosophy*). It's true mankind is the divil when your head's astray. Let me out now and I'll slip down the boreen, and not see them so.

WIDOW QUIN (*showing him out*). That's it. Run to the right, and not a one will see.

He runs off.

PHILLY (*wisely*). You're at some gaming, Widow Quin; but I'll walk after him and give him his dinner and a time to rest, and I'll see then if he's raving or as sane as you.

WIDOW QUIN (*annoyed*). If you go near that lad, let you be wary of your head, I'm saying. Didn't you hear him telling he was crazed at times?

PHILLY. I heard him telling a power; and I'm thinking we'll have right sport, before night will fall.

He goes out.

JIMMY. Well, Philly's a conceited and foolish man. How could that madman have his senses and his brainpan slit? I'll go after them and see him turn on Philly now.

He goes; WIDOW QUIN *hides poteen behind counter. Then hubbub outside.*

VOICES. There you are! Good jumper! Grand lepper! Darlint boy! He's the racer! Bear him on, will you!

CHRISTY *comes in, in Jockey's dress, with* PEGEEN MIKE, SARA, *and other girls, and men.*

PEGEEN (*to crowd*). Go on now and don't destroy him and he drenching with sweat. Go along, I'm saying, and have your tug-of-warring till he's dried his skin.

CROWD. Here's his prizes! A bagpipes! A fiddle was played by a poet in the years gone by! A flat and three-thorned blackthorn would lick the scholars out of Dublin town!

CHRISTY (*taking prizes from the men*). Thank you kindly, the lot of you. But you'd say it was little only I did this day if you'd seen me a while since striking my one single blow.

TOWN CRIER (*outside, ringing a bell*). Take notice, last event of this day! Tug-of-warring on the green below! Come on, the lot of you! Great achievements for all Mayo men!

PEGEEN. Go on, and leave him for to rest and dry. Go on, I tell you, for he'll do no more. (*She hustles crowd out;* WIDOW QUIN *following them.*)

MEN (*going*). Come on then. Good luck for the while!

PEGEEN (*radiantly, wiping his face with her shawl*). Well, you're the lad, and you'll have great times from this out when you could win that wealth of prizes, and you swearing in the heat of noon!

CHRISTY (*looking at her with delight*). I'll have great times if I win the crowning prize I'm seeking now, and that's your promise that you'll wed me in a fortnight, when our banns is called.

PEGEEN (*backing away from him*). You've right daring to go ask me that, when all knows you'll be starting to some girl in your own townland, when your father's rotten in four months, or five.

CHRISTY (*indignantly*). Starting from you, is it? (*He follows her.*) I will not, then, and when the airs is warming in four months, or five, it's then yourself and me should be pacing Neifin in the dews of night, the times sweet smells do be rising, and you'd see a little shiny new moon, maybe, sinking on the hills.

PEGEEN (*looking at him playfully*). And it's that kind of a poacher's love you'd make, Christy Mahon, on the sides of Neifin, when the night is down?

CHRISTY. It's little you'll think if my love's a poacher's, or an earl's itself, when you'll feel my two hands stretched around you, and I squeezing kisses on your puckered lips, till I'd feel a kind of pity for the Lord God is all ages sitting lonesome in his golden chair.

PEGEEN. That'll be right fun, Christy Mahon, and any girl would walk her heart out before she'd meet a young man was your like for eloquence, or talk, at all.

CHRISTY (*encouraged*). Let you wait, to hear me talking, till we're astray in Erris, when Good Friday's by, drinking a sup from a well, and making mighty kisses with our wetted mouths, or gaming in a gap or sunshine, with yourself stretched back unto your necklace, in the flowers of the earth.

PEGEEN (*in a lower voice, moved by his tone*). I'd be nice so, is it?

CHRISTY (*with rapture*). If the mitred bishops seen you that time, they'd be the like of the holy prophets, I'm thinking, do be straining the bars of Paradise to lay eyes on the Lady Helen of Troy, and she abroad, pacing back and forward, with a nosegay in her golden shawl.

PEGEEN (*with real tenderness*). And what is it I have, Christy Mahon, to make me fitting entertainment for the like of you, that has such poet's talking, and such bravery of heart?

CHRISTY (*in a low voice*). Isn't there the light of seven heavens in your heart alone, the way you'll be an angel's lamp to me from this out, and I abroad in the darkness, spearing salmons in the Owen, or the Carrowmore?

PEGEEN. If I was your wife, I'd be along with you those nights, Christy Mahon, the way you'd see I was a great hand at coaxing bailiffs, or coining funny nick-names for the stars of night.

CHRISTY. You, is it? Taking your death in the hailstones, or in the fogs of dawn.

PEGEEN. Yourself and me would shelter easy in a narrow bush, (*with a qualm of dread*) but we're only talking, maybe, for this would be a poor, thatched place to hold a fine lad is the like of you.

CHRISTY (*putting his arm round her*). If I wasn't a good Christian, it's on my naked knees I'd be saying my prayers and paters to every jackstraw you have roofing your head, and every stony pebble is paving the laneway to your door.

PEGEEN (*radiantly*). If that's the truth, I'll be burning candles from this out to the miracles of God that have brought you from the south to-day, and I, with my gowns bought ready, the way that I can wed you, and not wait at all.

CHRISTY. It's miracles, and that's the truth. Me there toiling a long while, and walking a long while, not knowing at all I was drawing all times nearer to this holy day.

PEGEEN. And myself, a girl, was tempted often to go sailing the seas till I'd marry a Jew-man, with ten kegs of gold, and I not knowing at all there was the like of you drawing nearer, like the stars of God.

CHRISTY. And to think I'm long years hearing women talking that talk, to all bloody fools, and this the first time I've heard the like of your voice talking sweetly for my own delight.

PEGEEN. And to think it's me is talking sweetly, Christy Mahon, and I the fright of seven townlands for my biting tongue. Well, the heart's a wonder; and, I'm thinking, there won't be our like in Mayo, for gallant lovers, from this hour, to-day. (*Drunken singing is heard outside.*) There's my father coming from the wake, and when he's had his sleep we'll tell him, for he's peaceful then.

They separate.

MICHAEL (*singing outside*).

> The jailor and the turnkey
> They quickly ran us down,
> And brought us back as prisoners
> Once more to Cavan town.

He comes in supported by SHAWN.

> There we lay bewailing
> All in a prison bound....

He sees CHRISTY. *Goes and shakes him drunkenly by the hand, while* PEGEEN *and* SHAWN *talk on the left.*

MICHAEL (*to* CHRISTY). The blessings of God and the holy angels on your head, young fellow. I hear tell you're after winning all in the sports below; and wasn't it a shame I didn't bear you along with me to Kate Cassidy's wake, a fine, stout lad, the like of you, for you'd never see the match of it for flows of drink, the way when we sunk her bones at noonday in her narrow grave, there were five men, aye, and six men, stretched out retching speechless on the holy stones.

CHRISTY (*uneasily, watching* PEGEEN). Is that the truth?

MICHAEL. It is then, and aren't you a louty schemer to go burying your father unbeknownst when you'd a right to throw him on the crupper of a Kerry mule and drive him westwards, like holy Joseph in the days gone by, the way we could have given him a decent burial, and not have him rotting beyond, and not a Christian drinking a smart drop to the glory of his soul?

CHRISTY (*gruffly*). It's well enough he's lying, for the likes of him.

MICHAEL (*slapping him on the back*). Well, aren't you a hardened slayer? It'll be a poor thing for the household man where you go sniffing for a female wife; and (*pointing to* SHAWN) look beyond at that shy and decent Christian I have chosen for my daughter's hand, and I after getting the gilded dispensation this day for to wed them now.

CHRISTY. And you'll be wedding them this day, is it?

MICHAEL (*drawing himself up*). Aye. Are you thinking, if I'm drunk itself, I'd leave my daughter living single with a little frisky rascal is the like of you?

PEGEEN (*breaking away from* SHAWN). Is it the truth the dispensation's come?

MICHAEL (*triumphantly*). Father Reilly's after reading it in gallous Latin, and "It's come in the nick of time," says he; "so I'll wed them in a hurry, dreading that young gaffer who'd capsize the stars."

PEGEEN (*fiercely*). He's missed his nick of time, for it's that lad, Christy Mahon, that I'm wedding now.

MICHAEL (*loudly with horror*). You'd be making him a son to me, and he wet and crusted with his father's blood?

PEGEEN. Aye. Wouldn't it be a bitter thing for a girl to go marrying the like of Shaneen, and he a middling kind of a scarecrow, with no savagery or fine words in him at all?

MICHAEL (*gasping and sinking on a chair*). Oh, aren't you a heathen daughter to go shaking the fat of my heart, and I swamped and drownded with the weight of drink? Would you have them turning on me the way that I'd be roaring to the dawn of day with the wind upon my heart? Have you not a word to aid me, Shaneen? Are you not jealous at all?

SHANEEN (*in great misery*). I'd be afeard to be jealous of a man did slay his da.

PEGEEN. Well, it'd be a poor thing to go marrying your like. I'm seeing there's a word of peril for an orphan girl, and isn't it a great blessing I didn't wed you, before himself came walking from the west or south?

SHAWN. It's a queer story you'd go picking a dirty tramp up from the highways of the world.

PEGEEN (*playfully*). And you think you're a likely beau to go straying along with, the shiny Sundays of the opening year, when it's sooner on a bullock's liver you'd put a poor girl thinking than on the lily or the rose?

SHAWN. And have you no mind of my weight of passion, and the holy dispensation, and the drift of heifers I am giving, and the golden ring?

PEGEEN. I'm thinking you're too fine for the like of me, Shawn Keogh of Killakeen, and let you go off till you'd find a radiant lady with droves of bullocks on the plains of Meath, and herself bedizened in the diamond jewelleries of Pharaoh's ma. That'd be your match, Shaneen. So God save you now!

She retreats behind CHRISTY.

SHAWN. Won't you hear me telling you . . . ?

CHRISTY (*with ferocity*). Take yourself from this, young fellow, or I'll maybe add a murder to my deeds to-day.

MICHAEL (*springing up with a shriek*). Murder is it? Is it mad yous are? Would you go making murder in this place, and it piled with poteen for our drink to-night? Go on to the foreshore if it's fighting you want, where the rising tide will wash all traces from the memory of man.

Pushing SHAWN *towards* CHRISTY.

SHAWN (*shaking himself free, and getting behind* MICHAEL). I'll not fight him, Michael James. I'd liefer live a bachelor, simmering in passions to the end of time, than face a lepping savage the like of him has descended from the Lord knows where. Strike him yourself, Michael James, or you'll lose my drift of heifers and my blue bull from Sneem.

MICHAEL. Is it me fight him, when it's father-slaying he's bred to now? (*Pushing* SHAWN.) Go on you fool and fight him now.

SHAWN (*coming forward a little*). Will I strike him with my hand?

MICHAEL. Take the loy is on your western side.

SHAWN. I'd be afeard of the gallows if I struck him with that.

CHRISTY (*taking up the loy*). Then I'll make you face the gallows or quit off from this.

SHAWN *flies out of the door.*

CHRISTY. Well, fine weather be after him, (*going to* MICHAEL, *coaxingly*) and I'm thinking you wouldn't wish to have that quaking blackguard in your house at all. Let you give us your blessing and hear her swear her faith to me, for I'm mounted on the springtide of the stars of luck, the way it'll be good for any to have me in the house.

PEGEEN (*at the other side of* MICHAEL). Bless us now, for I swear to God I'll wed him, and I'll not renege.

MICHAEL (*standing up in the centre, holding on to both of them*). It's the will of God, I'm thinking, that all should win an easy or a cruel end, and it's the will of God that all should rear up lengthy families for the nurture of the earth. What's a single man, I ask you, eating a bit in one house and drinking a sup in another, and he with no place of his own, like an old braying jackass strayed upon the rocks? (*To* CHRISTY.) It's many would be in dread to bring your like into their house for to end them, maybe, with a sudden end; but I'm a decent man of Ireland, and I liefer face the grave untimely and I seeing a score of grandsons growing up little gallant swearers by the name of God, than go peopling my bedside with puny weeds the like of what you'd breed, I'm thinking, out of Shaneen Keogh. (*He joins their hands.*) A daring fellow is the jewel of the world, and a man did split his father's middle with a single clout, should have the bravery of ten, so may God and Mary and St. Patrick bless you, and increase you from this mortal day.

CHRISTY AND PEGEEN. Amen, O Lord!

Hubbub outside. OLD MAHON *rushes in, followed by all the crowd, and* WIDOW QUIN. *He makes a rush at* CHRISTY, *knocks him down, and begins to beat him.*

PEGEEN (*dragging back his arm*). Stop that, will you. Who are you at all?

MAHON. His father, God forgive me!

PEGEEN (*drawing back*). Is it rose from the dead?

MAHON. Do you think I look so easy quenched with the tap of a loy?

Beats CHRISTY *again.*

PEGEEN (*glaring at* CHRISTY). And it's lies you told, letting on you had him slitted, and you nothing at all.

CHRISTY (*catching* MAHON's *stick*). He's not my father. He's a raving maniac would scare the world. (*Pointing to* WIDOW QUIN.) Herself knows it is true.

CROWD. You're fooling Pegeen! The Widow Quin seen him this day, and you likely knew! You're a liar!

CHRISTY (*dumbfounded*). It's himself was a liar, lying stretched out with an open head on him, letting on he was dead.

MAHON. Weren't you off racing the hills before I got my breath with the start I had seeing you turn on me at all?

PEGEEN. And to think of the coaxing glory we had given him, and he after doing nothing but hitting a soft blow and chasing northward in a sweat of fear. Quit off from this.

CHRISTY (*piteously*). You've seen my doings this day, and let you save me from the old man; for why would you be in such a scorch of haste to spur me to destruction now?

PEGEEN. It's there your treachery is spurring me, till I'm hard set to think you're the one I'm after lacing in my heart-strings half-an-hour gone by. (*To* MAHON.) Take him on from this, for I think bad the world should see me raging for a Munster liar, and the fool of men.

MAHON. Rise up now to retribution, and come on with me.

CROWD (*jeeringly*). There's the playboy! There's the lad thought he'd rule the roost in Mayo. Slate him now, mister.

CHRISTY (*getting up in shy terror*). What is it drives you to torment me here, when I'd asked the thunders of the might of God to blast me if I ever did hurt to any saving only that one single blow.

MAHON (*loudly*). If you didn't, you're a poor good-for-nothing, and isn't it by the like of you the sins of the whole world are committed?

CHRISTY (*raising his hands*). In the name of the Almighty God....

MAHON. Leave troubling the Lord God. Would you have him sending down droughts, and fevers, and the old hen and the cholera morbus?

CHRISTY (*to* WIDOW QUIN). Will you come between us and protect me now?

WIDOW QUIN. I've tried a lot, God help me, and my share is done.

CHRISTY (*looking round in desperation*). And I must go back into my torment is it, or run off like a vagabond straying through the Unions with the dusts of August making mudstains in the gullet of my throat, or the winds of March blowing on me till I'd take an oath I felt them making whistles of my ribs within?

SARA. Ask Pegeen to aid you. Her like does often change.

CHRISTY. I will not then, for there's torment in the splendour of her like, and she a girl any moon of midnight would take pride to meet, facing southwards on the heaths of Keel. But what did I want crawling forward to scorch my understanding at her flaming brow?

PEGEEN (*to* MAHON, *vehemently, fearing she will break into tears*). Take him on from this or I'll set the young lads to destroy him here.

MAHON (*going to him, shaking his stick*). Come on now if you wouldn't have the company to see you skelped.

PEGEEN (*half laughing, through her tears*). That's it, now the world will see him pandied, and he an ugly liar was playing off the hero, and the fright of men.

CHRISTY (*to* MAHON, *very sharply*). Leave me go!

CROWD. That's it. Now Christy. If them two set fighting, it will lick the world.

MAHON (*making a grab at* CHRISTY). Come here to me.

CHRISTY (*more threateningly*). Leave me go, I'm saying.

MAHON. I will maybe, when your legs is limping, and your back is blue.

CROWD. Keep it up, the two of you. I'll back the old one. Now the playboy.

CHRISTY (*in low and intense voice*). Shut your yelling, for if you're after making a mighty man of me this day by the power of a lie, you're setting me now to think if it's a poor thing to be lonesome, it's worse maybe to go mixing with the fools of earth.

MAHON *makes a movement towards him.*

CHRISTY (*almost shouting*). Keep off . . . lest I do show a blow unto the lot of you would set the guardian angels winking in the clouds above.

He swings round with a sudden rapid movement and picks up a loy.

CROWD (*half frightened, half amused*). He's going mad! Mind yourselves! Run from the idiot!

CHRISTY. If I am an idiot, I'm after hearing my voice this day saying words would raise the topknot on a poet in a merchant's town. I've won your racing, and your lepping, and . . .

MAHON. Shut your gullet and come on with me.

CHRISTY. I'm going, but I'll stretch you first.

He runs at OLD MAHON *with the loy, chases him out of the door, followed by crowd and* WIDOW QUIN. *There is a great noise outside, then a yell, and dead silence for a moment.* CHRISTY *comes in, half dazed, and goes to fire.*

WIDOW QUIN (*coming in, hurriedly, and going to him*). They're turning again you. Come on, or you'll be hanged, indeed.

CHRISTY. I'm thinking, from this out, Pegeen'll be giving me praises the same as in the hours gone by.

WIDOW QUIN (*impatiently*). Come by the back-door. I'd think bad to have you stifled on the gallows tree.

CHRISTY (*indignantly*). I will not, then. What good'd be my life-time, if I left Pegeen?

WIDOW QUIN. Come on, and you'll be no worse than you were last night; and you with a double murder this time to be telling to the girls.

CHRISTY. I'll not leave Pegeen Mike.

WIDOW QUIN (*impatiently*). Isn't there the match of her in every parish public, from Binghamstown unto the plain of Meath? Come on, I tell you, and I'll find you finer sweethearts at each waning moon.

CHRISTY. It's Pegeen I'm seeking only, and what'd I care if you brought me a drift of chosen females, standing in their shifts itself, maybe, from this place to the Eastern World?

SARA (*runs in, pulling off one of her petticoats*). They're going to hang him. (*Holding out petticoat and shawl.*) Fit these upon him, and let him run off to the east.

WIDOW QUIN. He's raving now; but we'll fit them on him, and I'll take him, in the ferry, to the Achill boat.

CHRISTY (*struggling feebly*). Leave me go, will you? when I'm thinking of my luck to-day, for she will wed me surely, and I a proven hero in the end of all.

They try to fasten petticoat round him.

WIDOW QUIN. Take his left hand, and we'll pull him now. Come on, young fellow.

CHRISTY (*suddenly starting up*). You'll be taking me from her? You're jealous, is it, of her wedding me? Go on from this.

He snatches up a stool, and threatens them with it.

WIDOW QUIN (*going*). It's in the mad-house they should put him, not in jail, at all. We'll go by the back-door, to call the doctor, and we'll save him so.

She goes out, with SARA, *through inner room. Men crowd in the doorway.* CHRISTY *sits down again by the fire.*

MICHAEL (*in a terrified whisper*). Is the old lad killed surely?

PHILLY. I'm after feeling the last gasps quitting his heart.

They peer in at CHRISTY.

MICHAEL (*with a rope*). Look at the way he is. Twist a hangman's knot on it, and slip it over his head, while he's not minding at all.

PHILLY. Let you take it, Shaneen. You're the soberest of all that's here.

SHAWN. Is it me to go near him, and he the wickedest and worst with me? Let you take it, Pegeen Mike.

PEGEEN. Come on, so.

She goes forward with the others, and they drop the double hitch over his head.

CHRISTY. What ails you?

SHAWN (*triumphantly, as they pull the rope tight on his arms*). Come on to the peelers, till they stretch you now.

CHRISTY. Me!

MICHAEL. If we took pity on you, the Lord God would, maybe, bring us ruin from the law to-day, so you'd best come easy, for hanging is an easy and a speedy end.

CHRISTY. I'll not stir. (*To* PEGEEN.) And what is it you'll say to me, and I after doing it this time in the face of all?

PEGEEN. I'll say, a strange man is a marvel, with his mighty talk; but what's a squabble in your back-yard, and the blow of a loy, have taught me that there's a great gap between a gallous story and a dirty deed. (*To men.*) Take him on from this, or the lot of us will be likely put on trial for his deed to-day.

CHRISTY (*with horror in his voice*). And it's yourself will send me off, to have a horny-fingered hangman hitching his bloody slip-knots at the butt of my ear.

MEN (*pulling rope*). Come on, will you?

He is pulled down on the floor.

CHRISTY (*twisting his legs round the table*). Cut the rope, Pegeen, and I'll quit the lot of you, and live from this out, like the madmen of Keel, eating muck and green weeds, on the faces of the cliffs.

PEGEEN. And leave us to hang, is it, for a saucy liar, the like of you? (*To men.*) Take him on, out from this.

SHAWN. Pull a twist on his neck, and squeeze him so.

PHILLY. Twist yourself. Sure he cannot hurt you, if you keep your distance from his teeth alone.

SHAWN. I'm afeard of him. (*To* PEGEEN.) Lift a lighted sod, will you, and scorch his leg.

PEGEEN (*blowing the fire, with a bellows*). Leave go now, young fellow, or I'll scorch your shins.

CHRISTY. You're blowing for to torture me. (*His voice rising and growing stronger.*) That's your kind, is it? Then let the lot of you be wary, for, if I've to face the gallows, I'll have a gay march down, I tell you, and shed the blood of some of you before I die.

SHAWN (*in terror*). Keep a good hold, Philly. Be wary, for the love of God. For I'm thinking he would liefest wreak his pains on me.

CHRISTY (*almost gaily*). If I do lay my hands on you, it's the way you'll be at the fall of night, hanging as a scarecrow for the fowls of hell. Ah, you'll have a gallous jaunt I'm saying, coaching out through Limbo with my father's ghost.

SHAWN (*to* PEGEEN). Make haste, will you? Oh, isn't he a holy terror, and isn't it true for Father Reilly, that all drink's a curse that has the lot of you so shaky and uncertain now?

CHRISTY. If I can wring a neck among you, I'll have a royal judgment looking on the trembling jury in the courts of law. And won't there be crying out in Mayo the day I'm stretched upon the rope with ladies in their silks and satins snivelling in their lacy kerchiefs, and they rhyming songs and ballads on the terror of my fate?

He squirms round on the floor and bites SHAWN's *leg*.

SHAWN (*shrieking*). My leg's bit on me. He's the like of a mad dog, I'm thinking, the way that I will surely die.

CHRISTY (*delighted with himself*). You will then, the way you can shake out hell's flags of welcome for my coming in two weeks or three, for I'm thinking Satan hasn't many have killed their da in Kerry, and in Mayo too.

OLD MAHON *comes in behind on all fours and looks on unnoticed*.

MEN (*to* PEGEEN). Bring the sod, will you?

PEGEEN (*coming over*). God help him so. (*Burns his leg*.)

CHRISTY (*kicking and screaming*). O, glory be to God!

He kicks loose from the table, and they all drag him towards the door.

JIMMY (*seeing* OLD MAHON). Will you look what's come in?

They all drop CHRISTY *and run left*.

CHRISTY (*scrambling on his knees face to face with* OLD MAHON). Are you coming to be killed a third time, or what ails you now?

MAHON. For what is it they have you tied?

CHRISTY. They're taking me to the peelers to have me hanged for slaying you.

MICHAEL (*apologetically*). It is the will of God that all should guard their little cabins from the treachery of law, and what would my daughter be doing if I was ruined or was hanged itself?

MAHON (*grimly, loosening* CHRISTY). It's little I care if you put a bag on her back, and went picking cockles till the hour of death; but my son and myself will be going our own way, and we'll have great times from this out telling stories of the villainy of Mayo, and the fools is here. (*To* CHRISTY, *who is freed*.) Come on now.

CHRISTY. Go with you, is it? I will then, like a gallant captain with his heathen slave. Go on now and I'll see you from this day stewing my oatmeal and washing my spuds, for I'm master of all fights from now. (*Pushing* MAHON.) Go on, I'm saying.

MAHON. Is it me?

CHRISTY. Not a word out of you. Go on from this.

MAHON (*walking out and looking back at* CHRISTY *over his shoulder*). Glory be to God! (*With a broad smile.*) I am crazy again!

Goes.

CHRISTY. Ten thousand blessings upon all that's here, for you've turned me a likely gaffer in the end of all, the way I'll go romancing through a romping lifetime from this hour to the dawning of the judgment day.

He goes out.

MICHAEL. By the will of God, we'll have peace now for our drinks. Will you draw the porter, Pegeen?

SHAWN (*going up to her*). It's a miracle Father Reilly can wed us in the end of all, and we'll have none to trouble us when his vicious bite is healed.

PEGEEN (*hitting him a box on the ear*). Quit my sight. (*Putting her shawl over her head and breaking out into wild lamentations.*) Oh my grief, I've lost him surely. I've lost the only Playboy of the Western World.

CURTAIN

THE THEATER OF
THE GROTESQUE

Luigi Pirandello

SIX CHARACTERS IN SEARCH
OF AN AUTHOR

[1921]

Luigi Pirandello [1867–1936]

Unquestionably the most brilliant and successful playwright of southern Europe in the twentieth century has been Luigi Pirandello. Winner of the Nobel Prize for literature in 1934, he was the writer of poems, stories, novels, and plays. Beginning late as a playwright with the composition of one-act plays in 1910, by 1916 Pirandello was writing full-length plays, and writing them rapidly. From that time on, he was prolific and influential in the modern drama. He dramatized repeatedly the conflicts between illusion and reality, between falsity and truth, between Life and Art; and he was preoccupied with the problem of identity of personality. As Walter Starkie, his biographer, writes, "No writer has ever been so obsessed by this problem [of identity] as Pirandello." In his concern with this last subject, Pirandello entitled all of his volumes of plays *Naked Masks* to suggest the ways in which men daily make believe.

The first modern European playwright to dramatize the distance between the appearance and the reality in an arresting manner was Luigi Chiarelli. In 1913 he wrote *The Mask and the Face*, a "grotesque comedy" in which at the end of the play a man is in danger of imprisonment because he did *not* kill his wife when he had given testimony that he did and been exonerated. This reversal of the ordinary state of affairs leads one of the characters to observe grimly: "In life next to the most grotesque buffoonery burn the most terrible tragedies; the grin of the most obscene mask covers the most searing passions." The view of life implicit in this play was congenial to Pirandello, and his plays follow in the same tradition of the grotesque; he, too, usually calls his plays comedies. Thomas Mann has written:

Pirandello and the Grotesque

> The striking feature of modern art is that it has ceased to recognize the categories of tragic and comic, or the dramatic classifications, tragedy and comedy. It sees life as tragicomedy, with the result that the grotesque is its most genuine style.

Mann's description of modern art aptly describes the theater of the grotesque, because in reality the so-called comedies are too bitter and too ironic to be comic to the principals. If they are not tragedies, it is because the category of the tragic no longer makes sense. Rather, men's experiences are preposterous, ridiculous, absurd.

The *teatro del grottesco* tended to be theatricalist in method, sometimes relying upon plot tricks and stage effects to the point that some have questioned the seriousness and sincerity of the writers of the school, notably Pirandello. On one level, the grotesque theater is strongly anti-romantic; but some of the plays, such as *Six Characters in Search of an Author*, also reveal the limits of the realistic theater. As Raymond Williams writes:

> A competent analysis of naturalism could be outlined by attention to this play alone. As drama, it is perhaps best described as a brilliant aside on a method of play writing which, as it moved further into the area of serious experience, was increasingly demonstrating its inadequacy.

In Pirandello there is a fresh use of the theater and a distinctive view of the nature of man.

Although Pirandello had written full-length plays before *Six Characters in Search of an Author*, notably the one with the characteristically Pirandellian title, *It Is So (If You Think It Is)*, this play with its conflict, as Pirandello says, between life and form, and its sensationally fresh method, is a landmark in the modern drama. *Six Characters in Search of an Author* is the play which Bernard Shaw called "the most original dramatic production of any people in any age." Pirandello has taken Jacques' metaphorical generalization in *As You Like It*, "All the world's a stage,/And all the men and women merely players," and applied it literally and with a vengeance. If the world's a stage, characters (those created expressly for the stage) must be more real than ordinary men and women. Or at least their existence may have an order and a form to it which is lacking in the lives of "real" people. At any rate, this is the beginning of the problem which one finds himself trying to solve in *Six Characters*.

As the Six Characters enter, "a tenuous light surrounds them — the faint breath of their fantastic reality"; in a 1925 edition of the play Pirandello suggests that the Characters wear masks to differentiate them and their level of reality from that of the Actors — who are also characters in the play. The Characters are puppets of a sort, twice removed from human experience, not the kinds of characters in a play with whom one can identify himself. Since these Characters are frozen in a form which cannot change, they lack the dynamism of real life. Pirandello says that he is dramatizing the difference between Life and Art. But in using Art (form) to show us this difference, is he really only showing us the difference between two levels of artistic imagination? When we consider the play as a formal dramatization of a vision (view) of life or as a commentary on art as a portrayal of life, what implications do we find?

PREFACE TO

SIX CHARACTERS IN SEARCH OF AN AUTHOR*

It seems like yesterday but is actually many years ago that a nimble little maidservant entered the service of my art. However, she always comes fresh to the job.

She is called Fantasy.

A little puckish and malicious, if she likes to dress in black no one will wish to deny that she is often positively bizarre and no one will wish to believe that she always does everything in the same way and in earnest. She sticks her hand in her pocket, pulls out a cap and bells, sets it on her head, red as a cock's comb, and dashes away. Here today, there tomorrow. And she amuses herself by bringing to my house — since I derive stories and novels and plays from them — the most disgruntled tribe in the world, men, women, children, involved in strange adventures which they can find no way out of; thwarted in their plans; cheated in their hopes; with whom, in short, it is often torture to deal.

Well, this little maidservant of mine, Fantasy, several years ago, had the bad inspiration or ill-omened caprice to bring a family into my house. I wouldn't know where she fished them up or how, but, according to her, I could find in them the subject for a magnificent novel.

I found before me a man about fifty years old, in a dark jacket and light trousers, with a frowning air and ill-natured, mortified eyes; a poor woman in widow's weeds leading by one hand a little girl of four and by the other a boy of rather more than ten; a cheeky and "sexy" girl, also clad in black but with an equivocal and brazen pomp, all atremble with a lively, biting contempt for the mortified old man and for a young fellow of twenty who stood on one side closed in on himself as if he despised them all. In short, the six characters who are seen coming on stage at the beginning of the play. Now one of them and now another — often beating down one another —embarked on the sad story of their adventures, each shouting his own reasons, and projecting in my face his disordered passions, more or less as they do in the play to the unhappy Manager.

What author will be able to say how and why a character was born in his fantasy? The mystery of artistic creation is the same as that of birth. A woman who loves may desire to become a mother; but the desire by itself,

* 1925; translated by Eric Bentley, 1950.

however intense, cannot suffice. One fine day she will find herself a mother without having any precise intimation when it began. In the same way an artist imbibes very many germs of life and can never say how and why, at a certain moment, one of these vital germs inserts itself into his fantasy, there to become a living creature on a plane of life superior to the changeable existence of every day.

I can only say that, without having made any effort to seek them out, I found before me, alive — you could touch them and even hear them breathe — the six characters now seen on the stage. And they stayed there in my presence, each with his secret torment and all bound together by the one common origin and mutual entanglement of their affairs, while I had them enter the world of art, constructing from their persons, their passions, and their adventures a novel, a drama, or at least a story.

Born alive, they wished to live.

To me it was never enough to present a man or a woman and what is special and characteristic about them simply for the pleasure of presenting them; to narrate a particular affair, lively or sad, simply for the pleasure of narrating it; to describe a landscape simply for the pleasure of describing it.

There are some writers (and not a few) who do feel this pleasure and, satisfied, ask no more. They are, to speak more precisely, historical writers.

But there are others who, beyond such pleasure, feel a more profound spiritual need on whose account they admit only figures, affairs, landscapes which have been soaked, so to speak, in a particular sense of life and acquire from it a universal value. These are, more precisely, philosophical writers.

I have the misfortune to belong to these last.

I hate symbolic art in which the presentation loses all spontaneous movement in order to become a machine, an allegory — a vain and misconceived effort because the very fact of giving an allegorical sense to a presentation clearly shows that we have to do with a fable which by itself has no truth either fantastic or direct; it was made for the demonstration of some moral truth. The spiritual need I speak of cannot be satisfied — or seldom, and that to the end of a superior irony, as for example in Ariosto — by such allegorical symbolism. This latter starts from a concept, and from a concept which creates or tries to create for itself an image. The former on the other hand seeks in the image — which must remain alive and free throughout — a meaning to give it value.

Now, however much I sought, I did not succeed in uncovering this meaning in the six characters. And I concluded therefore that it was no use making them live.

I thought to myself: "I have already afflicted my readers with hundreds and hundreds of stories. Why should I afflict them now by narrating the sad entanglements of these six unfortunates?"

And, thinking thus, I put them away from me. Or rather I did all I could to put them away.

But one doesn't give life to a character for nothing.

Creatures of my spirit, these six were already living a life which was their own and not mine any more, a life which it was not in my power any more to deny them.

Thus it is that while I persisted in desiring to drive them out of my spirit, they, as if completely detached from every narrative support, characters from a novel miraculously emerging from the pages of the book that contained them, went on living on their own, choosing certain moments of the day to reappear before me in the solitude of my study and coming — now one, now the other, now two together — to tempt me, to propose that I present or describe this scene or that, to explain the effects that could be secured with them, the new interest which a certain unusual situation could provide, and so forth.

For a moment I let myself be won over. And this condescension of mine, thus letting myself go for a while, was enough, because they drew from it a new increment of life, a greater degree of clarity and addition, consequently a greater degree of persuasive power over me. And thus as it became gradually harder and harder for me to go back and free myself from them, it became easier and easier for them to come back and tempt me. At a certain point I actually became obsessed with them. Until, all of a sudden, a way out of the difficulty flashed upon me.

"Why not," I said to myself, "present this highly strange fact of an author who refuses to let some of his characters live though they have been born in his fantasy, and the fact that these characters, having by now life in their veins, do not resign themselves to remaining excluded from the world of art? They are detached from me; live on their own; have acquired voice and movement; have by themselves — in this struggle for existence that they have had to wage with me — become dramatic characters, characters that can move and talk on their own initiative; already see themselves as such; have learned to defend themselves against me; will even know how to defend themselves against others. And so let them go where dramatic characters do go to have life: on a stage. And let us see what will happen."

That's what I did. And, naturally, the result was what it had to be: a mixture of tragic and comic, fantastic and realistic, in a humorous situation that was quite new and infinitely complex, a drama which is conveyed by means of the characters, who carry it within them and suffer it, a drama, breathing, speaking, self-propelled, which seeks at all costs to find the means of its own presentation; and the comedy of the vain attempt at an improvised realization of the drama on stage. First, the surprise of the poor actors in a theatrical company rehearsing a play by day on a bare stage (no scenery, no flats). Surprise and incredulity at the sight of the six characters announcing themselves as such in search of an author. Then, immediately afterwards, through that sudden fainting fit of the Mother veiled in black, their instinctive interest in the drama of which they catch a glimpse in her and in the other members of the strange family, an obscure, ambiguous drama, coming about so unexpectedly on a stage that is empty and unprepared to receive it. And gradually the growth of this interest to the bursting forth of the contrasting passions of Father, of Step-Daughter, of Son, of that poor Mother, passions seeking, as I said, to overwhelm each other with a tragic, lacerating fury.

And here is the universal meaning at first vainly sought in the six characters, now that, going on stage of their own accord, they succeed in finding it within themselves in the excitement of the desperate struggle which each wages against the other and all wage against the Manager and the actors, who do not understand them.

Without wanting to, without knowing it, in the strife of their bedevilled souls, each of them, defending himself against the accusations of the others, expresses as his own living passion and torment the passion and torment which for so many years have been the pangs of my spirit: the deceit of mutual understanding irremediably founded on the empty abstraction of the words, the multiple personality of everyone corresponding to the possibilities of being to be found in each of us, and finally the inherent tragic conflict between life (which is always moving and changing) and form (which fixes it, immutable).

Two above all among the six characters, the Father and the Step-Daughter, speak of that outrageous unalterable fixity of their form in which he and she see their essential nature expressed permanently and immutably, a nature that for one means punishment and for the other revenge; and they defend it against the factitious affectations and unaware volatility of the actors, and they try to impose it on the vulgar Manager who would like to change it and adapt it to the so-called exigencies of the theatre.

If the six characters don't all seem to exist on the same plane, it is not because some are figures of first rank and others of the second, that is, some are main characters and others minor ones — the elementary perspective necessary to all scenic or narrative art — nor is it that any are not completely created — for their purpose. They are all six at the same point of artistic realization and on the same level of reality, which is the fantastic level of the whole play. Except that the Father, the Step-Daughter, and also the Son are realized as mind; the Mother as nature; the Boy as a presence watching and performing a gesture and the Baby unaware of it all. This fact creates among them a perspective of a new sort. Unconsciously I had had the impression that some of them needed to be fully realized (artistically speaking), others less so, and others merely sketched in as elements in a narrative or presentational sequence: the most alive, the most completely created, are the Father and the Step-Daughter who naturally stand out more and lead the way, dragging themselves along beside the almost dead weight of the others — first, the Son, holding back; second, the Mother, like a victim resigned to her fate, between the two children who have hardly any substance beyond their appearance and who need to be led by the hand.

Six Characters in Search of an Author: Preface

And actually! actually they had each to appear in that stage of creation which they had attained in the author's fantasy at the moment when he wished to drive them away.

If I now think about these things, about having intuited that necessity, having unconsciously found the way to resolve it by means of a new perspective, and about the way in which I actually obtained it, they seem like miracles. The fact is that the play was really conceived in one of those spontaneous illuminations of the fantasy when by a miracle all the elements of the mind answer to each other's call and work in divine accord. No human brain, working "in the cold," however stirred up it might be, could ever have succeeded in penetrating far enough, could ever have been in a position to satisfy all the exigencies of the play's form. Therefore the reasons which I will give to clarify the values of the play must not be thought of as intentions that I conceived beforehand when I prepared myself for the job and which I now undertake to defend, but only as discoveries which I have been able to make afterwards in tranquillity.

I wanted to present six characters seeking an author. Their play does not manage to get presented — precisely because the author whom they seek is missing. Instead is presented the comedy of their vain attempt with all that it contains of tragedy by virtue of the fact that the six characters have been rejected.

But can one present a character while rejecting him? Obviously, to present him one needs, on the contrary, to receive him into one's fantasy before one can express him. And I have actually accepted and realized the six characters: I have, however, accepted and realized them as rejected: in search of *another* author.

What have I rejected of them? Not themselves, obviously, but their drama, which doubtless is what interests them above all but which did not interest me — for the reasons already indicated.

And what is it, for a character — his drama?

Every creature of fantasy and art, in order to exist, must have his drama, that is, a drama in which he may be a character and for which he *is* a character. This drama is the character's *raison d'être*, his vital function, necessary for his existence.

In these six, then, I have accepted the "being" without the reason for being. I have taken the organism and entrusted to it, not its own proper function, but another more complex function into which its own function entered, if at all, only as a datum. A terrible and desperate situation especially for the two — Father and Step-Daughter — who more than the others crave life and more than the others feel themselves to be characters, that is, absolutely need a drama and therefore their own drama — the only one which they can envisage for themselves yet which meantime they see rejected: an "impossible" situation from which they feel they must escape at whatever cost; it is a matter of life and death. True, I have given them another *raison d'être*, another function: precisely that "impossible" situation, the drama of being in search of an author and rejected. But that this should be a *raison d'être*, that it should have become their real function, that it should be necessary, that it should suffice, they can hardly suppose; for they have a life of their own. If someone were to tell them, they wouldn't believe him. It is not possible to believe that the sole reason for our living should lie in a torment that seems to us unjust and inexplicable.

I cannot imagine, therefore, why the charge was brought against me that the character of the Father was not what it should have been because it stepped out of its quality and position as a character and invaded at times the author's province and took it over. I who understand those who don't quite understand me see that the charge derives from the fact that the character expresses and makes his own a torment of spirit which is recognized as mine. Which is entirely natural and of absolutely no significance. Aside from the fact that this torment of spirit in the character of the Father derives from causes, and is suffered and lived for reasons, that have nothing to do with the drama of my personal experience, a fact which alone removes all substance from the criticism, I want to make it clear that the inherent torment of my spirit is one thing, a torment which I can legitimately — provided that it be organic — reflect in a character, and that the activity of my spirit as revealed in the realized work, the activity that succeeds in forming a drama out of the six characters in search of an author is another thing. If the Father participated in this latter activity, if he competed in forming the drama of the six characters without an author, then and only then would it by all means be justified to say that he was at times the author himself and therefore not the man he should be. But the Father suffers and does not create his existence as a character in search of an author. He suffers it as an inexplicable fatality and as a situation which he tries with all his powers to rebel against, which he tries to remedy: hence it is that he is a character in search of an author and nothing more, even if he expresses as his own the torment of my spirit. If he, so to speak, assumed some of the author's responsibilities, the fatality would be completely explained. He would, that is to say, see himself accepted, if only as a rejected character, accepted in the poet's heart of hearts, and he would no longer have any reason to suffer the despair of not finding someone to construct and affirm his life as a character. I mean that he would quite willingly accept the *raison d'être* which the author gives him and without regrets would forego his own, throwing over the Manager and the actors to whom in fact he runs as his only recourse.

There is one character, that of the Mother, who on the other hand does not care about being alive (considering being alive as an end in itself). She hasn't the least suspicion that she is *not* alive. It has never occurred to her to ask how and why and in what manner she lives. In short, she is not aware of being a character, inasmuch as she is never, even for a moment, detached from her role. She doesn't know she has a role.

This makes her perfectly organic. Indeed, her role of Mother does not of itself, in its natural essence, embrace mental activity. And she does not exist as a mind. She lives in an endless continuum of feeling, and therefore she cannot acquire awareness of her life — that is, of her existence as a character. But with all this, even she, in her own way and for her own ends, seeks an author, and at a certain stage seems happy to have been brought before the Manager. Because she hopes to take life from him, perhaps? No: because she hopes the Manager will have her present a scene with the Son in which she would put so much of her own life. But it is a scene which does not exist, which never has and never could take place. So unaware is she of being a character, that is, of the life that is possible to her, all fixed and determined, moment by moment, in every action, every phrase.

She appears on stage with the other characters but without understanding what the others make her do. Obviously, she imagines that the itch for life with which the husband and the daughter are afflicted and for which she herself is to be found on stage is no more than one of the usual incomprehensible extravagances of this man who is both tortured and torturer and — horrible, most horrible — a new equivocal rebellion on the part of that poor erring girl. The Mother is completely passive. The events of her own life and the values they assume in her eyes, her very character, are all things which are "said" by the others and which she only once contradicts, and that because the maternal instinct rises up and rebels within her to make it clear that she didn't at all wish to abandon either the son or the husband: the Son was taken from her and the husband forced her to abandon him. She is only correcting data; she explains and knows nothing.

In short, she is nature. Nature fixed in the figure of a mother.

This character gave me a satisfaction of a new sort, not to be ignored. Nearly all my critics, instead of defining her, after their habit, as "unhuman" — which seems to be the peculiar and incorrigible characteristic of all my creatures without exception — had the goodness to note "with real pleasure" that at last a *very human* figure had emerged from my fantasy. I explain this praise to myself in the following way: since my poor Mother is entirely limited to the natural attitude of a Mother with no possibility of free mental activity, being, that is, little more than a lump of flesh completely alive in all its functions — procreation, lactation, caring for and loving its young — without any need therefore of exercising her brain, she realizes in her person the true and complete "human type." That must be how it is, since in a human organism nothing seems more superfluous than the mind.

But the critics have tried to get rid of the Mother with this praise without bothering to penetrate the nucleus of poetic values which the character in the play represents. A very human figure, certainly, because mindless, that is, unaware of being what she is or not caring to explain it to herself. But not knowing that she is a character doesn't prevent her from being one. That is her drama in my play. And the most living expression of it comes spurting out in her cry to the Manager who wants her to think all these things have happened already and therefore cannot now be a reason for renewed lamentations: "No, it's happening now, it's happening always! My torture is not a pretence, signore! I am alive and present, always, in every moment of my torture: it is renewed, alive and present, always!" This she *feels*, without being conscious of it, and feels it therefore as something inexplicable: but she feels it so terribly that she doesn't think it *can* be something to explain either to herself or to others. She feels it and that is that. She feels it as pain, and this pain is immediate; she cries it out. Thus she reflects the growing fixity of life in a form — the same thing, which in another way, tortures the Father and the Step-Daughter. In them, mind. In her, nature. The mind rebels and, as best it may, seeks an advantage; nature, if not aroused by sensory stimuli, weeps.

Conflict between life-in-movement and form is the inexorable condition not only of the mental but also of the physical order. The life which in order to exist has become fixed in our corporeal form little by little kills that form. The tears of a nature thus fixed lament the irreparable, continuous aging of our bodies. Hence the tears of the Mother are passive and perpetual. Revealed in three faces, made significant in three distinct and simultaneous dramas, this inherent conflict finds in the play its most complete expression. More: the Mother declares also the particular value of artistic form — a form which does not delimit or destroy its own life and which life does not consume — in her cry to the Manager. If the Father and Step-Daughter began their scene a hundred thousand times in succession, always, at the appointed moment, at the instant when the life of the work of art must be expressed with that cry, it would always be heard, unaltered and unalterable in its form, not as a mechanical repetition, not as a return determined by external necessities, but on the contrary, alive every time and as new, suddenly born *thus forever!* embalmed alive in its incorruptible form. Hence, always, as we open the book, we shall find Francesca alive and confessing to Dante her sweet sin, and if we turn to the passage a hundred thousand times in succession, a hundred thousand times in succession Francesca will speak her words, never repeating them mechanically, but saying them as though each time were the first time with such living and sudden passion that Dante every time will turn faint. All that lives, by the fact of living, has a form, and by the same token must die — except the work of art which lives forever in so far as it *is* form.

The birth of a creature of human fantasy, a birth which is a step across the threshold between nothing and eternity, can also happen suddenly, occasioned by some necessity. An imagined drama needs a character who does or says a certain necessary thing; accordingly this character is born and is precisely what he had to be. In this way Madame Pace is born among the six characters and seems a miracle, even a trick, realistically portrayed on the stage. It is no trick. The birth is real. The new character is alive not because she was alive already but because she is now happily born as is required by the fact of her being a character — she is obliged to be as she is. There is a break here, a sudden change in the level of reality of the scene, because a character can be born in this way only in the poet's fancy and not on the boards of a stage. Without anyone's noticing it, I have all of a sudden changed the scene: I have gathered it up again into my own fantasy without removing it from the spectator's eyes. That is, I have shown them, instead of the stage, my own fantasy in the act of creating — my own fantasy in the form of this same stage. The sudden and uncontrollable changing of a visual phenomenon from one level of reality to another is a miracle comparable to those of the saint who sets his own statue in motion: it is neither wood nor stone at such a moment. But the miracle is not arbitrary. The stage — a stage which accepts the fantastic reality of the six characters — is no fixed, immutable datum. Nothing in this play exists as given and preconceived. Everything is in the making, is in motion, is a sudden experiment: even the place in which this unformed life, reaching after its own form, changes and changes again contrives to shift position organically. The level of reality changes. When I had the idea of bringing Madame Pace to birth right there on the stage, I felt I could do it and I did it. Had I noticed that this birth was unhinging and silently, unnoticed, in a second, giving another shape, another reality to my scene, I certainly wouldn't have brought it about. I would have been afraid of the apparent lack of logic. And I would have committed an ill-omened assault on the beauty of my work. The fervor of my mind saved me from doing so. For, despite appearances, with their specious logic, this fantastic birth is sustained by a real necessity in mysterious, organic relation with the whole life of the work.

That someone now tells me it hasn't all the value it could have because its expression is not constructed but chaotic, because it smacks of romanticism, makes me smile.

I understand why this observation was made to me: because in this work of mine the presentation of the drama in which the six characters are involved appears tumultuous and never proceeds in an orderly manner. There is no logical development, no concatenation of the events. Very true. Had I hunted it with a lamp I couldn't have found a more disordered, crazy, arbitrary, complicated, in short, romantic way of presenting "the drama in which the six characters are involved." Very true. But I have not presented that drama. I have presented another — and I won't undertake to say again what! — in which, among the many fine things that everyone, according to his tastes, can find, there is a discreet satire on romantic procedures: in the six characters thus excited to the point where they stifle themselves in the roles which each of them plays in a certain drama while I present them as characters in another play which they don't know and don't suspect the existence of, so that this inflamation of their passions — which belongs to the realm of romantic procedures — is humorously "placed," located in the void. And the drama of the six characters presented not as it would have been organized by my fantasy had it been accepted but in this way, as a rejected drama, could not exist in the work except as a "situation," with some little development, and could not come out except in indications, stormily, disorderedly, in violent foreshortenings, in a chaotic manner: continually interrupted, sidetracked, contradicted (by one of its characters), denied, and (by two others) not even seen.

There is a character indeed — he who denies the drama which makes him a character, the Son — who draws all his importance and value from being a character not of the comedy in the making — which as such hardly appears — but from the presentation that I made of it. In short, he is the only one who lives solely as "a character in search of an author" — inasmuch as the author he seeks is not a dramatic author. Even this could not be otherwise. The character's attitude is an organic product of my conception, and it is logical that in the situation it should produce greater confusion and disorder and another element of romantic contrast.

But I had precisely to *present* this organic and natural chaos. And to present a chaos is not at all to present chaotically, that is, romantically. That my presentation is the reverse of confused, that it is quite simple, clear, and orderly, is proved by the clarity which the intrigue, the characters, the fantastic and realistic, dramatic and comic levels of the work have had for every public in the world and by the way in which, for those with more searching vision, the unusual values enclosed within it come out.

Great is the confusion of tongues among men if criticisms thus made find words for their expression. No less great than this confusion is the intimate law of order which, obeyed in all points, makes this work of mine classical and typical and at its catastrophic close forbids the use of words. Though the audience eventually understands that one does not create life by artifice and that the drama of the six characters cannot be presented without an author to give them value with his spirit, the Manager remains vulgarly anxious to know how the thing turned out, and the "ending" is remembered by the Son in its sequence of actual moments, but without any sense and therefore not needing a human voice for its expression. It happens stupidly, uselessly, with the going-off of a mechanical weapon on stage. It breaks up and disperses the sterile experiment of the characters and the actors, which has apparently been made without the assistance of the poet.

The poet, unknown to them, as if looking on at a distance during the whole period of the experiment, was at the same time busy creating — with it and of it — his own play.

English version by Edward Storer

Six Characters in Search of an Author

A COMEDY IN THE MAKING

CHARACTERS OF THE COMEDY IN THE MAKING

THE FATHER
THE MOTHER
THE STEP-DAUGHTER
THE SON
THE BOY
THE CHILD
(*The last two do not speak*)
MADAME PACE

ACTORS OF THE COMPANY

THE MANAGER
LEADING LADY
LEADING MAN
SECOND LADY
LEAD
L'INGÉNUE
JUVENILE LEAD
OTHER ACTORS AND ACTRESSES
PROPERTY MAN
PROMPTER
MACHINIST
MANAGER'S SECRETARY
DOOR-KEEPER
SCENE-SHIFTERS

Daytime. The Stage of a Theatre

N.B. The Comedy is without acts or scenes. The performance is interrupted once, without the curtain being lowered, when the manager and the chief characters withdraw to arrange the scenario. A second interruption of the action takes place when, by mistake, the stage hands let the curtain down.

ACT I

The spectators will find the curtain raised and the stage as it usually is during the day time. It will be half dark, and empty, so that from the beginning the public may have the impression of an impromptu performance.

Prompter's box and a small table and chair for the manager.

Two other small tables and several chairs scattered about as during rehearsals.

The ACTORS and ACTRESSES of the company enter from the back of the stage:
first one, then another, then two together; nine or ten in all. They are about to rehearse a Pirandello play: Mixing It Up.* Some of the company move off towards their dressing rooms. The PROMPTER who has the "book" under his arm, is waiting for the manager in order to begin the rehearsal.

The ACTORS and ACTRESSES, some standing, some sitting, chat and smoke. One perhaps reads a paper; another cons his part.

Finally, the MANAGER enters and goes to the table prepared for him. His SECRETARY brings him his mail, through which he glances. The PROMPTER takes his seat, turns on a light, and opens the "book."

THE MANAGER (*throwing a letter down on the table*). I can't see. (*To* PROPERTY MAN.) Let's have a little light, please!

PROPERTY MAN. Yes sir, yes, at once. (*A light comes down on to the stage.*)

THE MANAGER (*clapping his hands*). Come along! Come along! Second act of "Mixing It Up." (*Sits down.*)

The ACTORS and ACTRESSES go from the front of the stage to the wings, all except the three who are to begin the rehearsal.

THE PROMPTER (*reading the "book"*). "Leo Gala's house. A curious room serving as dining-room and study."

THE MANAGER (*to* PROPERTY MAN). Fix up the old red room.

PROPERTY MAN (*noting it down*). Red set. All right!

THE PROMPTER (*continuing to read from the "book"*). "Table already laid and writing desk with books and papers. Book-shelves. Exit rear to Leo's bedroom. Exit left to kitchen. Principal exit to right."

THE MANAGER (*energetically*). Well, you understand: The principal exit over there; here, the kitchen. (*Turning to actor who is to play the part of* SOCRATES.) You make your entrances and exits here. (*To* PROPERTY MAN.) The baize doors at the rear, and curtains.

PROPERTY MAN (*noting it down*). Right!

PROMPTER (*reading as before*). "When the curtain rises, Leo Gala, dressed in cook's cap and apron is busy beating an egg in a cup. Philip, also dressed as a cook, is beating another egg. Guido Venanzi is seated and listening."

LEADING MAN (*to* MANAGER). Excuse me, but must I absolutely wear a cook's cap?

THE MANAGER (*annoyed*). I imagine so. It says so there anyway. (*Pointing to the "book."*)

LEADING MAN. But it's ridiculous!

* i.e. Il giuoco delle parti.

THE MANAGER (*jumping up in a rage*). Ridiculous? Ridiculous? Is it my fault if France won't send us any more good comedies, and we are reduced to putting on Pirandello's works, where nobody understands anything, and where the author plays the fool with us all? (*The* ACTORS *grin. The* MANAGER *goes to* LEADING MAN *and shouts.*) Yes sir, you put on the cook's cap and beat eggs. Do you suppose that with all this egg-beating business you are on an ordinary stage? Get that out of your head. You represent the shell of the eggs you are beating! (*Laughter and comments among the* ACTORS.) Silence! and listen to my explanations, please! (*To* LEADING MAN.) "The empty form of reason without the fullness of instinct, which is blind." — You stand for reason, your wife is instinct. It's a mixing up of the parts, according to which you who act your own part become the puppet of yourself. Do you understand?

LEADING MAN. I'm hanged if I do.

THE MANAGER. Neither do I. But let's get on with it. It's sure to be a glorious failure anyway. (*Confidentially.*) But I say, please face three-quarters. Otherwise, what with the abstruseness of the dialogue, and the public that won't be able to hear you, the whole thing will go to hell. Come on! come on!

PROMPTER. Pardon sir, may I get into my box? There's a bit of a draught.

THE MANAGER. Yes, yes, of course!

At this point, the DOOR-KEEPER *has entered from the stage door and advances towards the manager's table, taking off his braided cap. During this manoeuvre, the* SIX CHARACTERS *enter, and stop by the door at back of stage, so that when the* DOOR-KEEPER *is about to announce their coming to the* MANAGER, *they are already on the stage. A tenuous light surrounds them, almost as if irradiated by them — the faint breath of their fantastic reality.*

This light will disappear when they come forward towards the actors. They preserve, however, something of the dream lightness in which they seem almost suspended; but this does not detract from the essential reality of their forms and expressions.

He who is known as THE FATHER *is a man of about 50: hair, reddish in colour, thin at the temples; he is not bald, however; thick moustaches, falling over his still fresh mouth, which often opens in an empty and uncertain smile. He is fattish, pale; with an especially wide forehead. He has blue, oval-shaped eyes, very clear and piercing. Wears light trousers and a dark jacket. He is alternatively mellifluous and violent in his manner.*

THE MOTHER *seems crushed and terrified as if by an intolerable weight of shame and abasement. She is dressed in modest black and wears a thick widow's veil of crêpe. When she lifts this, she reveals a wax-like face. She always keeps her eyes downcast.*

THE STEP-DAUGHTER, *is dashing, almost impudent, beautiful. She wears mourning too, but with great elegance. She shows contempt for the timid half-frightened manner of the wretched* BOY (*14 years old, and also dressed in black*); *on the other hand, she displays a lively tenderness for her little sister,* THE CHILD (*about four*), *who is dressed in white, with a black silk sash at the waist.*

   THE SON (22) *tall, severe in his attitude of contempt for* THE FATHER, *supercilious and indifferent to* THE MOTHER. *He looks as if he had come on the stage against his will.*

DOOR-KEEPER (*cap in hand*). Excuse me, sir . . .

THE MANAGER (*rudely*). Eh? What is it?

DOOR-KEEPER (*timidly*). These people are asking for you, sir.

THE MANAGER (*furious*). I am rehearsing, and you know perfectly well no one's allowed to come in during rehearsals! (*Turning to the* CHARACTERS.) Who are you, please? What do you want?

THE FATHER (*coming forward a little, followed by the others who seem embarrassed*). As a matter of fact . . . we have come here in search of an author . . .

THE MANAGER (*half angry, half amazed*). An author? What author?

THE FATHER. Any author, sir.

THE MANAGER. But there's no author here. We are not rehearsing a new piece.

THE STEP-DAUGHTER (*vivaciously*). So much the better, so much the better! We can be your new piece.

AN ACTOR (*coming forward from the others*). Oh, do you hear that?

THE FATHER (*to* STEP-DAUGHTER). Yes, but if the author isn't here . . . (*To* MANAGER.) Unless you would be willing . . .

THE MANAGER. You are trying to be funny.

THE FATHER. No, for Heaven's sake, what are you saying? We bring you a drama, sir.

THE STEP-DAUGHTER. We may be your fortune.

THE MANAGER. Will you oblige me by going away? We haven't time to waste with mad people.

THE FATHER (*mellifluously*). Oh sir, you know well that life is full of infinite absurdities, which, strangely enough, do not even need to appear plausible, since they are true.

THE MANAGER. What the devil is he talking about?

THE FATHER. I say that to reverse the ordinary process may well be considered a madness: that is, to create credible situations, in order that they may appear true. But permit me to observe that if this be madness, it is the sole *raison d'être* of your profession, gentlemen. (*The* ACTORS *look hurt and perplexed.*)

THE MANAGER (*getting up and looking at him*). So our profession seems to you one worthy of madmen then?

THE FATHER. Well, to make seem true that which isn't true . . . without any need . . . for a joke as it were . . . Isn't that your mission, gentlemen: to give life to fantastic characters on the stage?

THE MANAGER (*interpreting the rising anger of the company*). But I would beg you to believe, my dear sir, that the profession of the comedian is a noble one. If today, as things go, the playwrights give us stupid comedies to play and puppets to represent instead of men, remember we are proud to have given life to immortal works here on these very boards! (*The* ACTORS, *satisfied, applaud their* MANAGER.)

THE FATHER (*interrupting furiously*). Exactly, perfectly, to living beings more alive than those who breathe and wear clothes: beings less real perhaps, but truer! I agree with you entirely. (*The* ACTORS *look at one another in amazement.*)

THE MANAGER. But what do you mean? Before, you said . . .

THE FATHER. No, excuse me, I meant it for you, sir, who were crying out that you had no time to lose with madmen, while no one better than yourself knows that nature uses the instrument of human fantasy in order to pursue her high creative purpose.

THE MANAGER. Very well, — but where does all this take us?

THE FATHER. Nowhere! It is merely to show you that one is born to life in many forms, in many shapes, as tree, or as stone, as water, as butterfly, or as woman. So one may also be born a character in a play.

THE MANAGER (*with feigned comic dismay*). So you and these other friends of yours have been born characters?

THE FATHER. Exactly, and alive as you see! (MANAGER *and* ACTORS *burst out laughing.*)

THE FATHER (*hurt*). I am sorry you laugh, because we carry in us a drama, as you can guess from this woman here veiled in black.

THE MANAGER (*losing patience at last and almost indignant*). Oh, chuck it! Get away please! Clear out of here! (*To* PROPERTY MAN.) For Heaven's sake, turn them out!

THE FATHER (*resisting*). No, no, look here, we . . .

THE MANAGER (*roaring*). We come here to work, you know.

LEADING ACTOR. One cannot let oneself be made such a fool of.

THE FATHER (*determined, coming forward*). I marvel at your incredulity, gentlemen. Are you not accustomed to see the characters created by an author spring to life in yourself and face each other? Just because there is no "book" (*Pointing to the prompter's box.*) which contains us, you refuse to believe . . .

THE STEP-DAUGHTER (*advances towards* MANAGER, *smiling and coquettish*). Believe me, we are really six most interesting characters, sir; side-tracked however.

THE FATHER. Yes, that is the word! (*To* MANAGER *all at once.*) In the sense, that is, that the author who created us alive no longer wished, or was no longer able, materially to put us into a work of art. And this was a real crime, sir; because he who has had the luck to be born a character can laugh even at death. He cannot die. The man, the writer, the instrument of the creation will die, but his creation does not die. And to live for ever, it does not need to have extraordinary gifts or to be able to work wonders. Who was Sancho Panza? Who was Don Abbondio? Yet they live eternally because — live germs as they were — they had the fortune to find a fecundating matrix, a fantasy which could raise and nourish them: make them live for ever!

THE MANAGER. That is quite all right. But what do you want here, all of you?

THE FATHER. We want to live.

THE MANAGER (*ironically*). For Eternity?

THE FATHER. No, sir, only for a moment . . . in you.

AN ACTOR. Just listen to him!

LEADING LADY. They want to live, in us . . . !

JUVENILE LEAD (*pointing to the* STEP-DAUGHTER). I've no objection, as far as that one is concerned!

THE FATHER. Look here! look here! The comedy has to be made. (*To the* MANAGER.) But if you and your actors are willing, we can soon concert it among ourselves.

THE MANAGER (*annoyed*). But what do you want to concert? We don't go in for concerts here. Here we play dramas and comedies!

THE FATHER. Exactly! That is just why we have come to you.

THE MANAGER. And where is the "book"?

THE FATHER. It is in us! (*The* ACTORS *laugh*.) The drama is in us, and we are in the drama. We are impatient to play it. Our inner passion drives us on to this.

THE STEP-DAUGHTER (*disdainful, alluring, treacherous, full of impudence*). My passion, sir! Ah, if you only knew! My passion for him! (*Points to the* FATHER *and makes a pretence of embracing him. Then she breaks out into a loud laugh.*)

THE FATHER (*angrily*). Behave yourself! And please don't laugh in that fashion.

THE STEP-DAUGHTER. With your permission, gentlemen, I, who am a two months' orphan, will show you how I can dance and sing. (*Sings and then dances* Prenez garde à Tchou-Tchin-Tchou.)

>Les chinois sont un peuple malin,
>De Shangaï à Pekin,
>Ils ont mis des écriteaux partout:
>Prenez garde à Tchou-Tchin-Tchou.

ACTORS AND ACTRESSES. Bravo! Well done! Tip-top!

THE MANAGER. Silence! This isn't a café concert, you know! (*Turning to the* FATHER *in consternation.*) Is she mad?

THE FATHER. Mad? No, she's worse than mad.

THE STEP-DAUGHTER (*to* MANAGER). Worse? Worse? Listen! Stage this drama for us at once! Then you will see that at a certain moment I . . . when this little darling here . . . (*Takes the* CHILD *by the hand and leads her to the* MANAGER.) Isn't she a dear? (*Takes her up and kisses her.*) Darling! Darling! (*Puts her down again and adds feelingly.*) Well, when God suddenly takes this dear little child away from that poor mother there; and this imbecile here (*seizing hold of the* BOY *roughly and pushing him forward*) does the stupidest things, like the fool he is, you will see me run away. Yes, gentlemen, I shall be off. But the moment hasn't arrived yet. After what has taken place between him and me (*indicates the* FATHER *with a horrible wink*), I can't remain any longer in this society, to have to witness the anguish of this mother here for that fool . . . (*indicates the* SON.) Look at him! Look at him! See how indifferent, how frigid he is, because he is the legitimate son. He despises me, despises him (*pointing to the* BOY), despises this baby here; because . . . we are bastards. (*Goes to the* MOTHER *and embraces her.*) And he doesn't want to recognize her as his mother — she who is the common mother of us all. He looks down upon her as if she were only the mother of us three bastards. Wretch! (*She says all this very rapidly, excitedly. At the word "bastards" she raises her voice, and almost spits out the final "Wretch!"*)

THE MOTHER (*to the* MANAGER, *in anguish*). In the name of these two little children, I beg you . . . (*She grows faint and is about to fall.*) Oh God!

THE FATHER (*coming forward to support her as do some of the* ACTORS). Quick, a chair, a chair for this poor widow!

THE ACTORS. Is it true? Has she really fainted?

THE MANAGER. Quick, a chair! Here!

One of the actors brings a chair, the others proffer assistance. The MOTHER tries to prevent the FATHER from lifting the veil which covers her face.

THE FATHER. Look at her! Look at her!

THE MOTHER. No, no; stop it please!

THE FATHER (*raising her veil*). Let them see you!

THE MOTHER (*rising and covering her face with her hands, in desperation*). I beg you, sir, to prevent this man from carrying out his plan which is loathsome to me.

THE MANAGER (*dumbfounded*). I don't understand at all. What is the situation? Is this lady your wife? (*To the* FATHER.)

THE FATHER. Yes, gentlemen: my wife!

THE MANAGER. But how can she be a widow if you are alive? (*The* ACTORS *find relief for their astonishment in a loud laugh.*)

THE FATHER. Don't laugh! Don't laugh like that, for Heaven's sake. Her drama lies just here in this: she has had a lover, a man who ought to be here.

THE MOTHER (*with a cry*). No! No!

THE STEP-DAUGHTER. Fortunately for her, he is dead. Two months ago as I said. We are in mourning, as you see.

THE FATHER. He isn't here you see, not because he is dead. He isn't here

— look at her a moment and you will understand — because her drama isn't a drama of the love of two men for whom she was incapable of feeling anything except possibly a little gratitude — gratitude not for me but for the other. She isn't a woman, she is a mother, and her drama — powerful sir, I assure you — lies, as a matter of fact, all in these four children she has had by two men.

THE MOTHER. I had them? Have you got the courage to say that I wanted them? (*To the company.*) It was his doing. It was he who gave me that other man, who forced me to go away with him.

THE STEP-DAUGHTER. It isn't true.

THE MOTHER (*startled*). Not true, isn't it?

THE STEP-DAUGHTER. No, it isn't true, it just isn't true.

THE MOTHER. And what can you know about it?

THE STEP-DAUGHTER. It isn't true. Don't believe it. (*To* MANAGER.) Do you know why she says so? For that fellow there. (*Indicates the* SON.) She tortures herself, destroys herself on account of the neglect of that son there; and she wants him to believe that if she abandoned him when he was only two years old, it was because he (*indicates the* FATHER) made her do so.

THE MOTHER (*vigorously*). He forced me to it, and I call God to witness it. (*To the* MANAGER.) Ask him (*indicates* HUSBAND) if it isn't true. Let him speak. You (*to* DAUGHTER) are not in a position to know anything about it.

THE STEP-DAUGHTER. I know you lived in peace and happiness with my father while he lived. Can you deny it?

THE MOTHER. No, I don't deny it . . .

THE STEP-DAUGHTER. He was always full of affection and kindness for you. (*To the* BOY, *angrily.*) It's true, isn't it? Tell them! Why don't you speak, you little fool?

THE MOTHER. Leave the poor boy alone. Why do you want to make me appear ungrateful, daughter? I don't want to offend your father. I have answered him that I didn't abandon my house and my son through any fault of mine, nor from any wilful passion.

THE FATHER. It is true. It was my doing.

LEADING MAN (*to the company*). What a spectacle!

LEADING LADY. We are the audience this time.

JUVENILE LEAD. For once, in a way.

THE MANAGER (*beginning to get really interested*). Let's hear them out. Listen!

THE SON. Oh yes, you're going to hear a fine bit now. He will talk to you of the Demon of Experiment.

THE FATHER. You are a cynical imbecile. I've told you so already a hundred times. (*To the* MANAGER.) He tries to make fun of me on account of this expression which I have found to excuse myself with.

THE SON (*with disgust*). Yes, phrases! phrases!

THE FATHER. Phrases! Isn't everyone consoled when faced with a trouble or fact he doesn't understand, by a word, some simple word, which tells us nothing and yet calms us?

THE STEP-DAUGHTER. Even in the case of remorse. In fact, especially then.

THE FATHER. Remorse? No, that isn't true. I've done more than use words to quieten the remorse in me.

THE STEP-DAUGHTER. Yes, there was a bit of money too. Yes, yes, a bit of money. There were the hundred lire he was about to offer me in payment, gentlemen . . .

Sensation of horror among the ACTORS.

THE SON (*to the* STEP-DAUGHTER). This is vile.

THE STEP-DAUGHTER. Vile? There they were in a pale blue envelope on a little mahogany table in the back of Madame Pace's shop. You know Madame Pace — one of those ladies who attract poor girls of good family into their ateliers, under the pretext of their selling *robes et manteaux*.

THE SON. And he thinks he has bought the right to tyrannize over us all with those hundred lire he was going to pay; but which, fortunately — note this, gentlemen — he had no chance of paying.

THE STEP-DAUGHTER. It was a near thing, though, you know! (*Laughs ironically.*)

THE MOTHER (*protesting*). Shame, my daughter, shame!

THE STEP-DAUGHTER. Shame indeed! This is my revenge! I am dying to live that scene . . . The room . . . I see it . . . Here is the window with the mantles exposed, there the divan, the looking-glass, a screen, there in front of the window the little mahogany table with the blue envelope containing one hundred lire. I see it. I see it. I could take hold of it . . . But you, gentlemen, you ought to turn your backs now: I am almost nude, you know. But I don't blush: I leave that to him. (*Indicating* FATHER.)

THE MANAGER. I don't understand this at all.

THE FATHER. Naturally enough. I would ask you, sir, to exercise your authority a little here, and let me speak before you believe all she is trying to blame me with. Let me explain.

THE STEP-DAUGHTER. Ah yes, explain it in your own way.

THE FATHER. But don't you see that the whole trouble lies here. In words, words. Each one of us has within him a whole world of things, each man of us his own special world. And how can we ever come to an understanding if I put in the words I utter the sense and value of things as I see them; while you who listen to me must inevitably translate them according to the conception of things each one of you has within himself. We think we understand each other, but we never really do. Look here! This woman (*indicating the* MOTHER) takes all my pity for her as a specially ferocious form of cruelty.

THE MOTHER. But you drove me away.

THE FATHER. Do you hear her? I drove her away! She believes I really sent her away.

THE MOTHER. You know how to talk, and I don't; but, believe me, sir (*to*

MANAGER), after he had married me . . . who knows why? . . . I was a poor insignificant woman . . .

THE FATHER. But, good Heavens! it was just for your humility that I married you. I loved this simplicity in you. (*He stops when he sees she makes signs to contradict him, opens his arms wide in sign of desperation, seeing how hopeless it is to make himself understood.*) You see she denies it. Her mental deafness, believe me, is phenomenal, the limit: (*touches his forehead*) deaf, deaf, mentally deaf; She has plenty of feeling. Oh yes, a good heart for the children; but the brain — deaf, to the point of desperation —!

THE STEP-DAUGHTER. Yes, but ask him how his intelligence has helped us.

THE FATHER. If we could see all the evil that may spring from good, what should we do? (*At this point the* LEADING LADY *who is biting her lips with rage at seeing the* LEADING MAN *flirting with the* STEP-DAUGHTER, *comes forward and says to the* MANAGER.)

LEADING LADY. Excuse me, but are we going to rehearse today?

MANAGER. Of course, of course; but let's hear them out.

JUVENILE LEAD. This is something quite new.

L'INGÉNUE. Most interesting!

LEADING LADY. Yes, for the people who like that kind of thing. (*Casts a glance at* LEADING MAN.)

THE MANAGER (*to* FATHER). You must please explain yourself quite clearly. (*Sits down.*)

THE FATHER. Very well then: listen! I had in my service a poor man, a clerk, a secretary of mine, full of devotion, who became friends with her. (*Indicating the* MOTHER.) They understood one another, were kindred souls in fact, without, however, the least suspicion of any evil existing. They were incapable even of thinking of it.

THE STEP-DAUGHTER. So he thought of it — for them!

THE FATHER. That's not true. I meant to do good to them — and to myself, I confess, at the same time. Things had come to the point that I could not say a word to either of them without their making a mute appeal, one to the other, with their eyes. I could see them silently asking each other how I was to be kept in countenance, how I was to be kept quiet. And this, believe me, was just about enough of itself to keep me in a constant rage, to exasperate me beyond measure.

THE MANAGER. And why didn't you send him away then — this secretary of yours?

THE FATHER. Precisely what I did, sir. And then I had to watch this poor woman drifting forlornly about the house like an animal without a master, like an animal one has taken in out of pity.

THE MOTHER. Ah yes . . . !

THE FATHER (*suddenly turning to the* MOTHER). It's true about the son anyway, isn't it?

THE MOTHER. He took my son away from me first of all.

THE FATHER. But not from cruelty. I did it so that he should grow up healthy and strong by living in the country.

THE STEP-DAUGHTER (*pointing to him ironically*). As one can see.

THE FATHER (*quickly*). Is it my fault if he has grown up like this? I sent him to a wet nurse in the country, a peasant, as *she* did not seem to me strong enough, though she is of humble origin. That was, anyway, the reason I married her. Unpleasant all this may be, but how can it be helped? My mistake possibly, but there we are! All my life I have had these confounded aspirations towards a certain moral sanity. (*At this point the* STEP-DAUGHTER *bursts into a noisy laugh.*) Oh, stop it! Stop it! I can't stand it.

THE MANAGER. Yes, please stop it, for Heaven's sake.

THE STEP-DAUGHTER. But imagine moral sanity from him, if you please — the client of certain ateliers like that of Madame Pace!

THE FATHER. Fool! That is the proof that I am a man! This seeming contradiction, gentlemen, is the strongest proof that I stand here a live man before you. Why, it is just for this very incongruity in my nature that I have had to suffer what I have. I could not live by the side of that woman (*indicating the* MOTHER) any longer; but not so much for the boredom she inspired me with as for the pity I felt for her.

THE MOTHER. And so he turned me out —.

THE FATHER. — well provided for! Yes, I sent her to that man, gentlemen ... to let her go free of me.

THE MOTHER. And to free himself.

THE FATHER. Yes, I admit it. It was also a liberation for me. But great evil has come of it. I meant well when I did it; and I did it more for her sake than mine. I swear it. (*Crosses his arms on his chest; then turns suddenly to the* MOTHER.) Did I ever lose sight of you until that other man carried you off to another town, like the angry fool he was? And on account of my pure interest in you ... my pure interest, I repeat, that had no base motive in it ... I watched with the tenderest concern the new family that grew up around her. She can bear witness to this. (*Points to the* STEP-DAUGHTER.)

THE STEP-DAUGHTER. Oh yes, that's true enough. When I was a kiddie, so so high, you know, with plaits over my shoulders and knickers longer than my skirts, I used to see him waiting outside the school for me to come out. He came to see how I was growing up.

THE FATHER. This is infamous, shameful!

THE STEP-DAUGHTER. No. Why?

THE FATHER. Infamous! infamous! (*Then excitedly to* MANAGER *explaining.*) After she (*indicating* MOTHER) went away, my house seemed suddenly empty. She was my incubus, but she filled my house. I was like a dazed fly alone in the empty rooms. This boy here (*indicating the* SON) was educated away from home, and when he came back, he seemed to me to be no more mine. With no mother to stand between him and me, he grew up entirely for himself, on his own, apart, with no tie of intellect or affection binding him to me. And then — strange but true — I was driven, by curiosity at first and then by some tender sentiment, towards her family, which had come into being through my will. The thought of her began gradually to fill up the emptiness I felt all around me. I wanted to know if she were happy in living out the simple daily duties of life. I wanted to think of her as fortunate and happy because far away from the complicated torments of my spirit. And so, to have proof of this, I used to watch that child coming out of school.

THE STEP-DAUGHTER. Yes, yes. True. He used to follow me in the street and smiled at me, waved his hand, like this. I would look at him with interest, wondering who he might be. I told my mother, who guessed at once. (*The* MOTHER *agrees with a nod.*) Then she didn't want to send me to school for some days; and when I finally went back, there he was again — looking so ridiculous — with a paper parcel in his hands. He came close to me, caressed me, and drew out a fine straw hat from the parcel, with a bouquet of flowers — all for me!

THE MANAGER. A bit discursive this, you know!

THE SON (*contemptuously*). Literature! Literature!

THE FATHER. Literature indeed! This is life, this is passion!

THE MANAGER. It may be, but it won't act.

THE FATHER. I agree. This is only the part leading up. I don't suggest this should be staged. She (*pointing to the* STEP-DAUGHTER), as you see, is no longer the flapper with plaits down her back —

THE STEP-DAUGHTER. — and the knickers showing below the skirt!

THE FATHER. The drama is coming now, sir; something new, complex, most interesting.

THE STEP-DAUGHTER. As soon as my father died . . .

THE FATHER. — there was absolute misery for them. They came back here, unknown to me. Through her stupidity! (*Pointing to the* MOTHER.) It is true she can barely write her own name; but she could anyhow have got her daughter to write to me that they were in need . . .

THE MOTHER. And how was I to divine all this sentiment in him?

THE FATHER. That is exactly your mistake, never to have guessed any of my sentiments.

THE MOTHER. After so many years apart, and all that had happened . . .

THE FATHER. Was it my fault if that fellow carried you away? It happened quite suddenly; for after he had obtained some job or other, I could find no trace of them; and so, not unnaturally, my interest in them dwindled. But the drama culminated unforeseen and violent on their return, when I was impelled by my miserable flesh that still lives . . . Ah! what misery, what wretchedness is that of the man who is alone and disdains debasing *liaisons*! Not old enough to do without women, and not young enough to go and look for one without shame. Misery? It's worse than misery; it's a horror; for no woman can any longer give him love; and when a man feels this ... One ought to do without, you say? Yes, yes, I know. Each of us when he appears before his fellows is clothed in a certain dignity. But every man knows what unconfessable things pass within the secrecy of his own heart. One gives way to the temptation, only to rise from it again, afterwards, with a great eagerness to re-establish one's dignity, as if it were a tombstone to place on the grave of one's shame, and a monument to hide and sign the memory of our weaknesses. Everybody's in the same case. Some folks haven't the courage to say certain things, that's all!

THE STEP-DAUGHTER. All appear to have the courage to do them though.

THE FATHER. Yes, but in secret. Therefore, you want more courage to say these things. Let a man but speak these things out, and folks at once label him a cynic. But it isn't true. He is like all the others, better indeed, because he isn't afraid to reveal with the light of the intelligence the red shame of human bestiality on which most men close their eyes so as not to see it.

Woman — for example, look at her case! She turns tantalizing inviting glances on you. You seize her. No sooner does she feel herself in your grasp than she closes her eyes. It is the sign of her mission, the sign by which she says to man: "Blind yourself, for I am blind."

THE STEP-DAUGHTER. Sometimes she can close them no more: when she no longer feels the need of hiding her shame to herself, but dry-eyed and dispassionately, sees only that of the man who has blinded himself without love. Oh, all these intellectual complications make me sick, disgust me — all this philosophy that uncovers the beast in man, and then seeks to save him, excuse him ... I can't stand it, sir. When a man seeks to "simplify" life bestially, throwing aside every relic of humanity, every chaste aspiration, every pure feeling, all sense of ideality, duty, modesty, shame ... then nothing is more revolting and nauseous than a certain kind of remorse — crocodiles' tears, that's what it is.

THE MANAGER. Let's come to the point. This is only discussion.

THE FATHER. Very good, sir! But a fact is like a sack which won't stand up when it is empty. In order that it may stand up, one has to put into it the reason and sentiment which have caused it to exist. I couldn't possibly know that after the death of that man, they had decided to return here, that they were in misery, and that she (*pointing to the* MOTHER) had gone to work as a modiste, and at a shop of the type of that of Madame Pace.

THE STEP-DAUGHTER. A real high-class modiste, you must know, gentlemen. In appearance, she works for the leaders of the best society; but she arranges matters so that these elegant ladies serve her purpose ... without prejudice to other ladies who are ... well ... only so so.

THE MOTHER. You will believe me, gentlemen, that it never entered my mind that the old hag offered me work because she had her eye on my daughter.

THE STEP-DAUGHTER. Poor mamma! Do you know, sir, what that woman did when I brought her back the work my mother had finished? She would point out to me that I had torn one of my frocks, and she would give it back to my mother to mend. It was I who paid for it, always I; while this poor creature here believed she was sacrificing herself for me and these two children here, sitting up at night sewing Madame Pace's robes.

THE MANAGER. And one day you met there . . .

THE STEP-DAUGHTER. Him, him. Yes sir, an old client. There's a scene for you to play! Superb!

THE FATHER. She, the Mother arrived just then . . .

THE STEP-DAUGHTER (*treacherously*). Almost in time!

THE FATHER (*crying out*). No, in time! in time! Fortunately I recognized her . . . in time. And I took them back home with me to my house. You can imagine now her position and mine; she, as you see her; and I who cannot look her in the face.

THE STEP-DAUGHTER. Absurd! How can I possibly be expected — after that — to be a modest young miss, a fit person to go with his confounded aspirations for "a solid moral sanity"?

THE FATHER. For the drama lies all in this — in the conscience that I have, that each one of us has. We believe this conscience to be a single thing, but it is manysided. There is one for this person, and another for that. Diverse consciences. So we have this illusion of being one person for all, of having a personality that is unique in all our acts. But it isn't true. We perceive this when, tragically perhaps, in something we do, we are as it were, suspended, caught up in the air on a kind of hook. Then we perceive that all of us was not in that act, and that it would be an atrocious injustice to judge us by that action alone, as if all our existence were summed up in that one deed. Now do you understand the perfidy of this girl? She surprised me in a place, where she ought not to have known me, just as I could not exist for her; and she now seeks to attach to me a reality such as I should have to assume for her in a shameful and fleeting moment of my life. I feel this above all else. And the drama, you will see, acquires a tremendous value from this point. Then there is the position of the others . . . his . . . (*Indicating the* SON.)

THE SON (*shrugging his shoulders scornfully*). Leave me alone! I don't come into this.

THE FATHER. What? You don't come into this?

THE SON. I've got nothing to do with it, and don't want to have; because you know well enough I wasn't made to be mixed up in all this with the rest of you.

THE STEP-DAUGHTER. We are only vulgar folk! He is the fine gentleman. You may have noticed, Mr. Manager, that I fix him now and again with a look of scorn while he lowers his eyes — for he knows the evil he has done me.

THE SON (*scarcely looking at her*). I?

THE STEP-DAUGHTER. You! you! I owe my life on the streets to you. Did you or did you not deny us, with your behaviour, I won't say the intimacy of home, but even that mere hospitality which makes guests feel at their ease? We were intruders who had come to disturb the kingdom of your legitimacy. I should like to have you witness, Mr. Manager, certain scenes between him and me. He says I have tyrannized over everyone. But it was just his behaviour which made me insist on the reason for which I had come into the house, — this reason he calls "vile" — into his house, with my mother who is his mother too. And I came as mistress of the house.

THE SON. It's easy for them to put me always in the wrong. But imagine, gentlemen, the position of a son, whose fate it is to see arrive one day at his home a young woman of impudent bearing, a young woman who inquires for his father, with whom who knows what business she has. This young man has then to witness her return bolder than ever, accompanied by that child there. He is obliged to watch her treat his father in an equivocal and confidential manner. She asks money of him in a way that lets one suppose he must give it her, *must*, do you understand, because he has every obligation to do so.

THE FATHER. But I have, as a matter of fact, this obligation. I owe it to your mother.

THE SON. How should I know? When had I ever seen or heard of her? One day there arrive with her (*indicating* STEP-DAUGHTER) that lad and this baby here. I am told: "This is *your* mother too, you know." I divine from her manner (*indicating* STEP-DAUGHTER *again*) why it is they have come home. I had rather not say what I feel and think about it. I shouldn't even care to confess to myself. No action can therefore be hoped for from me in this affair. Believe me, Mr. Manager, I am an "unrealized" character, dramatically speaking; and I find myself not at all at ease in their company. Leave me out of it, I beg you.

THE FATHER. What? It is just because you are so that . . .

THE SON. How do you know what I am like? When did you ever bother your head about me?

THE FATHER. I admit it. I admit it. But isn't that a situation in itself? This aloofness of yours which is so cruel to me and to your mother, who returns home and sees you almost for the first time grown up, who doesn't recognize you but knows you are her son . . . (*Pointing out the* MOTHER *to the* MANAGER.) See, she's crying!

THE STEP-DAUGHTER (*angrily, stamping her foot*). Like a fool!

THE FATHER (*indicating* STEP-DAUGHTER). She can't stand him you know. (*Then referring again to the* SON.) He says he doesn't come into the affair, whereas he is really the hinge of the whole action. Look at that lad who is always clinging to his mother, frightened and humiliated. It is on account of this fellow here. Possibly his situation is the most painful of all. He feels himself a stranger more than the others. The poor little chap feels mortified, humiliated at being brought into a home out of charity as it were. (*In confidence.*) He is the image of his father. Hardly talks at all. Humble and quiet.

THE MANAGER. Oh, we'll cut him out. You've no notion what a nuisance boys are on the stage . . .

THE FATHER. He disappears soon, you know. And the baby too. She is the first to vanish from the scene. The drama consists finally in this: when that mother re-enters my house, her family born outside of it, and shall we say superimposed on the original, ends with the death of the little girl, the tragedy of the boy and the flight of the elder daughter. It cannot go on, because it is foreign to its surroundings. So after much torment, we three remain: I, the mother, that son. Then, owing to the disappearance of that extraneous family, we too find ourselves strange to one another. We find we are living in an atmosphere of mortal desolation which is the revenge, as he (*indicating* SON) scornfully said of the Demon of Experiment, that unfortunately hides in me. Thus, sir, you see when faith is lacking, it becomes impossible to create certain states of happiness, for we lack the necessary humility. Vaingloriously, we try to substitute ourselves for this faith, creating thus for the rest of the world a reality which we believe after their fashion, while, actually, it doesn't exist. For each one of us has his own reality to be respected before God, even when it is harmful to one's very self.

THE MANAGER. There is something in what you say. I assure you all this interests me very much. I begin to think there's the stuff for a drama in all this, and not a bad drama either.

THE STEP-DAUGHTER (*coming forward*). When you've got a character like me.

THE FATHER (*shutting her up, all excited to learn the decision of the* MANAGER). You be quiet!

THE MANAGER (*reflecting, heedless of interruption*). It's new . . . hem . . . yes . . .

THE FATHER. Absolutely new!

THE MANAGER. You've got a nerve though, I must say, to come here and fling it at me like this . . .

THE FATHER. You will understand, sir, born as we are for the stage . . .

THE MANAGER. Are you amateur actors then?

THE FATHER. No. I say born for the stage, because . . .

THE MANAGER. Oh, nonsense. You're an old hand, you know.

THE FATHER. No sir, no. We act that rôle for which we have been cast, that rôle which we are given in life. And in my own case, passion itself, as usually happens, becomes a trifle theatrical when it is exalted.

THE MANAGER. Well, well, that will do. But you see, without an author . . . I could give you the address of an author if you like . . .

THE FATHER. No, no. Look here! You must be the author.

THE MANAGER. I? What are you talking about?

THE FATHER. Yes, you, you! Why not?

THE MANAGER. Because I have never been an author: that's why.

THE FATHER. Then why not turn author now? Everybody does it. You don't want any special qualities. Your task is made much easier by the fact that we are all here alive before you . . .

THE MANAGER. It won't do.

THE FATHER. What? When you see us live our drama . . .

THE MANAGER. Yes, that's all right. But you want someone to write it.

THE FATHER. No, no. Someone to take it down, possibly, while we play it, scene by scene! It will be enough to sketch it out at first, and then try it over.

THE MANAGER. Well . . . I am almost tempted. It's a bit of an idea. One might have a shot at it.

THE FATHER. Of course. You'll see what scenes will come out of it. I can give you one, at once . . .

THE MANAGER. By Jove, it tempts me. I'd like to have a go at it. Let's try it out. Come with me to my office. (*Turning to the* ACTORS.) You are at liberty for a bit, but don't step out of the theatre for long. In a quarter of an hour, twenty minutes, all back here again! (*To the* FATHER.) We'll see what can be done. Who knows if we don't get something really extraordinary out of it?

THE FATHER. There's no doubt about it. They (*indicating the* CHARACTERS) had better come with us too, hadn't they?

THE MANAGER. Yes, yes. Come on! come on! (*Moves away and then turning to the* ACTORS.) *Be punctual, please!* (MANAGER *and the* SIX CHARACTERS *cross the stage and go off. The other* ACTORS *remain, looking at one another in astonishment.*)

LEADING MAN. Is he serious? What the devil does he want to do?

JUVENILE LEAD. This is rank madness.

THIRD ACTOR. Does he expect to knock up a drama in five minutes?

JUVENILE LEAD. Like the improvisers!

LEADING LADY. If he thinks I'm going to take part in a joke like this . . .

JUVENILE LEAD. I'm out of it anyway.

FOURTH ACTOR. I should like to know who they are. (*Alludes to* CHARACTERS).

THIRD ACTOR. What do you suppose? Madmen or rascals!

JUVENILE LEAD. And he takes them seriously!

L'INGÉNUE. Vanity! He fancies himself as an author now.

LEADING MAN. It's absolutely unheard of. If the stage has come to this . . . well I'm . . .

FIFTH ACTOR. It's rather a joke.

THIRD ACTOR. Well, we'll see what's going to happen next.

> *Thus talking, the* ACTORS *leave the stage; some going out by the little door at the back; others retiring to their dressing-rooms.*
>
> *The curtain remains up.*
>
> *The action of the play is suspended for twenty minutes.*

ACT II

The stage call-bells ring to warn the company that the play is about to begin again.

The STEP-DAUGHTER *comes out of the* MANAGER's *office along with the* CHILD *and the* BOY. *As she comes out of the office, she cries:—*

Nonsense! nonsense! Do it yourselves! I'm not going to mix myself up in this mess. (*Turning to the* CHILD *and coming quickly with her on to the stage.*) Come on, Rosetta, let's run!

The BOY *follows them slowly, remaining a little behind and seeming perplexed.*

THE STEP-DAUGHTER (*stops, bends over the* CHILD *and takes the latter's face between her hands*). My little darling! You're frightened, aren't you? You don't know where we are, do you? (*Pretending to reply to a question of the* CHILD.) What is the stage? It's a place, baby, you know, where people play at being serious, a place where they act comedies. We've got to act a comedy now, dead serious, you know; and you're in it also, little one. (*Embraces her, pressing the little head to her breast, and rocking the* CHILD *for a moment.*) Oh darling, darling, what a horrid comedy you've got to play! What a wretched part they've found for you! A garden ... a fountain ... look ... just suppose, kiddie, it's here. Where, you say? Why, right here in the middle. It's all pretence you know. That's the trouble, my pet: it's all make-believe here. It's better to imagine it though, because if they fix it up for you, it'll only be painted cardboard, painted cardboard for the rockery, the water, the plants ... Ah, but I think a baby like this one would sooner have a make-believe fountain than a real one, so she could play with it. What a joke it'll be for the others! But for you, alas! not quite such a joke: you who are real, baby dear, and really play by a real fountain that is big and green and beautiful, with ever so many bamboos around it that are reflected in the water, and a whole lot of little ducks swimming about ... No, Rosetta, no, your mother doesn't bother about you on account of that wretch of a son there. I'm in the devil of a temper, and as for that lad ... (*Seizes* BOY *by the arm to force him to take one of his hands out of his pockets.*) What have you got there? What are you hiding? (*Pulls his hand out of his pocket, looks into it and catches the glint of a revolver.*) Ah! where did you get this? (*The* BOY, *very pale in the face, looks at her, but does not answer*). Idiot! If I'd been in your place, instead of killing myself, I'd have shot one of those two, or both of them: father and son.

The FATHER *enters from the office, all excited from his work. The* MANAGER *follows him.*

THE FATHER. Come on, come on dear! Come here for a minute! We've arranged everything. It's all fixed up.

THE MANAGER (*also excited*). If you please, young lady, there are one or two points to settle still. Will you come along?

THE STEP-DAUGHTER (*following him towards the office*). Ouff! what's the good, if you've arranged everything.

The FATHER, MANAGER *and* STEP-DAUGHTER *go back into the office again (off) for a moment. At the same time, the* SON *followed by the* MOTHER, *comes out.*

THE SON (*looking at the three entering office*). Oh this is fine, fine! And to think I can't even get away!

The MOTHER *attempts to look at him, but lowers her eyes immediately when he turns away from her. She then sits down. The* BOY *and the* CHILD *approach her. She casts a glance again at the* SON, *and speaks with humble tones, trying to draw him into conversation.*

THE MOTHER. And isn't my punishment the worst of all? (*Then seeing from the* SON's *manner that he will not bother himself about her.*) My God! Why are you so cruel? Isn't it enough for one person to support all this torment? Must you then insist on others seeing it also?

THE SON (*half to himself, meaning the* MOTHER *to hear, however*). And they want to put it on the stage! If there was at least a reason for it! He thinks he has got at the meaning of it all. Just as if each one of us in every circumstance of life couldn't find his own explanation of it! (*Pauses.*) He complains he was discovered in a place where he ought not to have been seen, in a moment of his life which ought to have remained hidden and kept out of the reach of that convention which he has to maintain for other people. And what about my case? Haven't I had to reveal what no son ought ever to reveal: how father and mother live and are man and wife for themselves quite apart from that idea of father and mother which we give them? When this idea is revealed, our life is then linked at one point only to that man and that woman; and as such it should shame them, shouldn't it?

The MOTHER *hides her face in her hands. From the dressing-rooms and the little door at the back of the stage the* ACTORS *and* STAGE MANAGER *return, followed by the* PROPERTY MAN, *and the* PROMPTER. *At the same moment, the* MANAGER *comes out of his office, accompanied by the* FATHER *and the* STEP-DAUGHTER.

THE MANAGER. Come on, come on, ladies and gentlemen! Heh! you there, machinist!

MACHINIST. Yes sir?

THE MANAGER. Fix up the white parlor with the floral decorations. Two wings and a drop with a door will do. Hurry up!

The MACHINIST *runs off at once to prepare the scene, and arranges it while the* MANAGER *talks with the* STAGE MANAGER, *the* PROPERTY MAN, *and the* PROMPTER *on matters of detail.*

THE MANAGER (*to* PROPERTY MAN). Just have a look, and see if there isn't a sofa or divan in the wardrobe . . .

PROPERTY MAN. There's the green one.

THE STEP-DAUGHTER. No no! Green won't do. It was yellow, ornamented with flowers — very large! and most comfortable!

PROPERTY MAN. There isn't one like that.

THE MANAGER. It doesn't matter. Use the one we've got.

THE STEP-DAUGHTER. Doesn't matter? It's most important!

THE MANAGER. We're only trying it now. Please don't interfere. (*To* PROPERTY MAN.) See if we've got a shop window — long and narrowish.

THE STEP-DAUGHTER. And the little table! The little mahogany table for the pale blue envelope!

PROPERTY MAN (*to* MANAGER). There's that little gilt one.

THE MANAGER. That'll do fine.

THE FATHER. A mirror.

THE STEP-DAUGHTER. And the screen! We must have a screen. Otherwise how can I manage?

PROPERTY MAN. That's all right, Miss. We've got any amount of them.

THE MANAGER (*to the* STEP-DAUGHTER). We want some clothes pegs too, don't we?

THE STEP-DAUGHTER. Yes, several, several!

THE MANAGER. See how many we've got and bring them all.

PROPERTY MAN. All right!

The PROPERTY MAN *hurries off to obey his orders. While he is putting the things in their places, the* MANAGER *talks to the* PROMPTER *and then with the* CHARACTERS *and the* ACTORS.

THE MANAGER (*to* PROMPTER). Take your seat. Look here: this is the outline of the scenes, act by act. (*Hands him some sheets of paper.*) And now I'm going to ask you to do something out of the ordinary.

PROMPTER. Take it down in shorthand?

THE MANAGER (*pleasantly surprised*). Exactly! Can you do shorthand?

PROMPTER. Yes, a little.

THE MANAGER. Good! (*Turning to a* STAGE HAND.) Go and get some paper from my office, plenty, as much as you can find.

The STAGE HAND *goes off, and soon returns with a handful of paper which he gives to the* PROMPTER.

THE MANAGER (*to* PROMPTER). You follow the scenes as we play them, and try and get the points down, at any rate the most important ones. (*Then addressing the* ACTORS.) Clear the stage, ladies and gentlemen! Come over here (*Pointing to the left.*) and listen attentively.

LEADING LADY. But, excuse me, we . . .

THE MANAGER (*guessing her thought*). Don't worry! You won't have to improvise.

LEADING MAN. What have we to do then?

THE MANAGER. Nothing. For the moment you just watch and listen. Everybody will get his part written out afterwards. At present we're going to try the thing as best we can. They're going to act now.

THE FATHER (*as if fallen from the clouds into the confusion of the stage*). We? What do you mean, if you please, by a rehearsal?

THE MANAGER. A rehearsal for them. (*Points to the* ACTORS.)

THE FATHER. But since we are the characters . . .

THE MANAGER. All right: "characters" then, if you insist on calling yourselves such. But here, my dear sir, the characters don't act. Here the actors do the acting. The characters are there, in the "book" (*pointing towards prompter's box*) — when there is a "book"!

THE FATHER. I won't contradict you; but excuse me, the actors aren't the characters. They want to be, they pretend to be, don't they? Now if these gentlemen here are fortunate enough to have us alive before them . . .

THE MANAGER. Oh this is grand! You want to come before the public yourselves then?

THE FATHER. As we are . . .

THE MANAGER. I can assure you it would be a magnificent spectacle!

LEADING MAN. What's the use of us here anyway then?

THE MANAGER. You're not going to pretend that you can act? It makes me laugh! (*The* ACTORS *laugh*.) There, you see, they are laughing at the notion. But, by the way, I must cast the parts. That won't be difficult. They cast themselves. (*To the* SECOND LADY LEAD.) You play the Mother. (*To the* FATHER.) We must find her a name.

THE FATHER. Amalia, sir.

THE MANAGER. But that is the real name of your wife. We don't want to call her by her real name.

THE FATHER. Why ever not, if it is her name? . . . Still, perhaps, if that lady must . . . (*Makes a slight motion of the hand to indicate the* SECOND LADY LEAD.) I see this woman here (*means the* MOTHER) as Amalia. But do as you like. (*Gets more and more confused.*) I don't know what to say to you. Already, I begin to hear my own words ring false, as if they had another sound . . .

THE MANAGER. Don't you worry about it. It'll be our job to find the right tones. And as for her name, if you want her Amalia, Amalia it shall be; and if you don't like it, we'll find another! For the moment though, we'll call the characters in this way: (*To* JUVENILE LEAD.) You are the Son. (*To the* LEADING LADY.) You naturally are the Step-Daughter . . .

THE STEP-DAUGHTER (*excitedly*). What? what? I, that woman there? (*Bursts out laughing.*)

THE MANAGER (*angry*). What is there to laugh at?

LEADING LADY (*indignant*). Nobody has ever dared to laugh at me. I insist on being treated with respect; otherwise I go away.

THE STEP-DAUGHTER. No, no, excuse me . . . I am not laughing at you . . .

THE MANAGER (*to* STEP-DAUGHTER). You ought to feel honored to be played by . . .

LEADING LADY (*at once, contemptuously*). "That woman there" . . .

THE STEP-DAUGHTER. But I wasn't speaking of you, you know. I was speaking of myself — whom I can't see at all in you! That is all. I don't know . . . but . . . you . . . aren't the least like me . . .

THE FATHER. True. Here's the point. Look here, sir, our temperaments, our souls . . .

THE MANAGER. Temperament, soul, be hanged! Do you suppose the spirit of the piece is in you? Nothing of the kind!

THE FATHER. What, haven't we our own temperaments, our own souls?

THE MANAGER. Not at all. Your soul or whatever you like to call it takes shape here. The actors give body and form to it, voice and gesture. And my actors — I may tell you — have given expression to much more lofty material than this little drama of yours, which may or may not hold up on the stage. But if it does, the merit of it, believe me, will be due to my actors.

THE FATHER. I don't dare contradict you, sir; but, believe me, it is a terrible suffering for us who are as we are, with these bodies of ours, these features to see . . .

THE MANAGER (*cutting him short and out of patience*). Good heavens! The make-up will remedy all that, man, the make-up . . .

THE FATHER. Maybe. But the voice, the gestures . . .

THE MANAGER. Now, look here! On the stage, you as yourself, cannot exist. The actor here acts you, and that's an end to it!

THE FATHER. I understand. And now I think I see why our author who conceived us as we are, all alive, didn't want to put us on the stage after all. I haven't the least desire to offend your actors. Far from it! But when I think that I am to be acted by . . . I don't know by whom . . .

LEADING MAN (*on his dignity*). By me, if you've no objection!

THE FATHER (*humbly, mellifluously*). Honored, I assure you, sir. (*Bows.*) Still, I must say that try as this gentleman may, with all his good will and wonderful art, to absorb me into himself . . .

LEADING MAN. Oh chuck it! "Wonderful art!" Withdraw that, please!

THE FATHER. The performance he will give, even doing his best with make-up to look like me . . .

LEADING MAN. It will certainly be a bit difficult! (*The* ACTORS *laugh.*)

THE FATHER. Exactly! It will be difficult to act me as I really am. The effect will be rather — apart from the make-up — according as to how he supposes I am, as he senses me — if he does sense me — and not as I inside of myself feel myself to be. It seems to me then that account should be taken of this by everyone whose duty it may become to criticize us . . .

THE MANAGER. Heavens! The man's starting to think about the critics now! Let them say what they like. It's up to us to put on the play if we can. (*Looking around.*) Come on! come on! Is the stage set? (*To the* ACTORS *and* CHARACTERS.) Stand back — stand back! Let me see, and don't let's lose any more time! *To the* STEP-DAUGHTER.) Is it all right as it is now?

THE STEP-DAUGHTER. Well, to tell the truth, I don't recognize the scene.

THE MANAGER. My dear lady, you can't possibly suppose that we can construct that shop of Madame Pace piece by piece here? (*To the* FATHER.) You said a white room with flowered wall paper, didn't you?

THE FATHER. Yes.

THE MANAGER. Well then. We've got the furniture right more or less. Bring that little table a bit further forward. (*The* STAGE HANDS *obey the order. To* PROPERTY MAN.) You go and find an envelope, if possible, a pale blue one; and give it to that gentleman. (*Indicates* FATHER.)

PROPERTY MAN. An ordinary envelope?

MANAGER AND FATHER. Yes, yes, an ordinary envelope.

PROPERTY MAN. At once, sir. (*Exit.*)

THE MANAGER. Ready, everyone! First scene — the Young Lady. (*The* LEADING LADY *comes forward.*) No, no. you must wait. I meant her (*Indicating the* STEP-DAUGHTER.) You just watch —

THE STEP-DAUGHTER (*adding at once*). How I shall play it, how I shall live it! . . .

Leading Lady (*offended*). I shall live it also, you may be sure, as soon as I begin!

THE MANAGER (*with his hands to his head*). Ladies and gentlemen, if you please! No more useless discussions! Scene I: the young lady with Madame Pace: Oh! (*Looks around as if lost.*) And this Madame Pace, where is she?

THE FATHER. She isn't with us, sir.

THE MANAGER. Then what the devil's to be done?

THE FATHER. But she is alive too.

THE MANAGER. Yes, but where is she?

THE FATHER. One minute. Let me speak! (*Turning to the* ACTRESSES.) If these ladies would be so good as to give me their hats for a moment . . .

THE ACTRESSES (*half surprised, half laughing, in chorus*). What? Why? Our hats? What does he say?

THE MANAGER. What are you going to do with the ladies' hats? (*The* ACTORS *laugh.*)

THE FATHER. Oh nothing. I just want to put them on these pegs for a moment. And one of the ladies will be so kind as to take off her mantle . . .

THE ACTORS. Oh, what d'you think of that? Only the mantle? He must be mad.

SOME ACTRESSES. But why? Mantles as well?

THE FATHER. To hang them up here for a moment. Please be so kind, will you?

THE ACTRESSES (*taking off their hats, one or two also their cloaks, and going to hang them on the racks*). After all, why not?

There you are!
This is really funny.
We've got to put them on show.

THE FATHER. Exactly; just like that, on show.

THE MANAGER. May we know why?

THE FATHER. I'll tell you. Who knows if, by arranging the stage for her, she does not come here herself, attracted by the very articles of her trade? (*Inviting the* ACTORS *to look towards the exit at back of stage.*) Look! Look!

> *The door at the back of stage opens and* MADAME PACE *enters and takes a few steps forward. She is a fat, oldish woman with puffy oxygenated hair. She is rouged and powdered, dressed with a comical elegance in black silk. Round her waist is a long silver chain from which hangs a pair of scissors. The* STEP-DAUGHTER *runs over to her at once amid the stupor of the actors.*

THE STEP-DAUGHTER (*turning towards her*). There she is! There she is!

THE FATHER (*radiant*). It's she! I said so, didn't I? There she is!

THE MANAGER (*conquering his surprise, and then becoming indignant*). What sort of a trick is this?

LEADING MAN (*almost at the same time*). What's going to happen next?

JUVENILE LEAD. Where does *she* come from?

L'INGÉNUE. They've been holding her in reserve, I guess.

LEADING LADY. A vulgar trick!

THE FATHER (*dominating the protests*). Excuse me, all of you! Why are you so anxious to destroy in the name of a vulgar, commonplace sense of truth, this reality which comes to birth attracted and formed by the magic of the stage itself, which has indeed more right to live here than you, since it is much truer than you — if you don't mind my saying so? Which is the actress among you who is to play Madame Pace? Well, here is Madame Pace herself. And you will allow, I fancy, that the actress who acts her will be less true than this woman here, who is herself in person. You see my daughter recognized her and went over to her at once. Now you're going to witness the scene!

> *But the scene between the* STEP-DAUGHTER *and* MADAME PACE *has already begun despite the protest of the actors and the reply of the* FATHER. *It has begun quietly, naturally, in a manner impossible for the stage. So when the actors, called to attention by the* FATHER, *turn round and see* MADAME PACE, *who has placed one hand under the* STEP-DAUGHTER'S *chin to raise her head, they observe her at first with great attention, but hearing her speak in an unintelligible manner their interest begins to wane.*

THE MANAGER. Well? well?

LEADING MAN. What does she say?

LEADING LADY. One can't hear a word.

JUVENILE LEAD. Louder! Louder please!

Six Characters in Search of an Author

THE STEP-DAUGHTER (*leaving* MADAME PACE, *who smiles a Sphinx-like smile, and advancing towards the actors*). Louder? Louder? What are you talking about? These aren't matters which can be shouted at the top of one's voice. If I have spoken them out loud, it was to shame him and have my revenge. (*Indicates* FATHER.) But for Madame it's quite a different matter.

THE MANAGER. Indeed? indeed? But here, you know, people have got to make themselves heard, my dear. Even we who are on the stage can't hear you. What will it be when the public's in the theatre? And anyway, you can very well speak up now among yourselves, since we shan't be present to listen to you as we are now. You've got to pretend to be alone in a room at the back of a shop where no one can hear you.

The STEP-DAUGHTER *coquettishly and with a touch of malice makes a sign of disagreement two or three times with her finger.*

THE MANAGER. What do you mean by no?

THE STEP-DAUGHTER (*sotto voce, mysteriously*). There's someone who will hear us if she (*indicating* MADAME PACE) speaks out loud.

THE MANAGER (*in consternation*). What? Have you got someone else to spring on us now? (*The* ACTORS *burst out laughing.*)

THE FATHER. No, no sir. She is alluding to me. I've got to be here — there behind that door, in waiting; and Madame Pace knows it. In fact, if you will allow me, I'll go there at once, so I can be quite ready. (*Moves away.*)

THE MANAGER (*stopping him*). No! Wait! wait! We must observe the conventions of the theatre. Before you are ready . . .

THE STEP-DAUGHTER (*interrupting him*). No, get on with it at once! I'm just dying, I tell you, to act this scene. If he's ready, I'm more than ready.

THE MANAGER (*shouting*). But, my dear young lady, first of all, we must have the scene between you and this lady . . . (*Indicates* MADAME PACE.) Do you understand? . . .

THE STEP-DAUGHTER. Good Heavens! She's been telling me what you know already: that mamma's work is badly done again, that the material's ruined; and that if I want her to continue to help us in our misery I must be patient . . .

MADAME PACE (*coming forward with an air of great importance*). Yes indeed, sir, I no wanta take advantage of her, I no wanta be hard . . .

Note. MADAME PACE *is supposed to talk in a jargon half Italian, half English.*

THE MANAGER (*alarmed*). What? What? She talks like that? (*The* ACTORS *burst out laughing again.*)

THE STEP-DAUGHTER (*also laughing*). Yes yes, that's the way she talks, half English, half Italian! Most comical it is!

MADAME PACE. Itta seem not verra polite gentlemen laugha atta me eef I trya best speaka English.

THE MANAGER. *Diamine!* Of course! Of course! Let her talk like that! Just what we want. Talk just like that, Madame, if you please! The effect will be certain. Exactly what was wanted to put a little comic relief into the crudity of the situation. Of course she talks like that! Magnificent!

THE STEP-DAUGHTER. Magnificent? Certainly! When certain suggestions are made to one in language of that kind, the effect is certain, since it seems almost a joke. One feels inclined to laugh when one hears her talk about an "old signore" "who wanta talka nicely with you." Nice old signore, eh, Madame?

MADAME PACE. Not so old my dear, not so old! And even if you no lika him, he won't make any scandal!

THE MOTHER (*jumping up amid the amazement and consternation of the actors who had not been noticing her. They move to restrain her*). You old devil! You murderess!

THE STEP-DAUGHTER (*running over to calm her* MOTHER). Calm yourself, Mother, calm yourself! Please don't . . .

THE FATHER (*going to her also at the same time*). Calm yourself! Don't get excited! Sit down now!

THE MOTHER. Well then, take that woman away out of my sight!

THE STEP-DAUGHTER (*to* MANAGER). It is impossible for my mother to remain here.

THE FATHER (to MANAGER). They can't be here together. And for this reason, you see: that woman there was not with us when we came . . . If they are on together, the whole thing is given away inevitably, as you see.

THE MANAGER. It doesn't matter. This is only a first rough sketch — just to get an idea of the various points of the scene, even confusedly . . . (*Turning to the* MOTHER *and leading her to her chair*.) Come along, my dear lady, sit down now, and let's get on with the scene . . .

    Meanwhile, *the* STEP-DAUGHTER, *coming forward again, turns to* MADAME PACE.

THE STEP-DAUGHTER. Come on, Madame, come on!

MADAME PACE (*offended*). No, no, *grazie*. I not do anything witha your mother present.

THE STEP-DAUGHTER. Nonsense! Introduce this "old signore" who wants to talk nicely to me. (*Addressing the company imperiously*.) We've got to do this scene one way or another, haven't we? Come on! (*To* MADAME PACE.) You can go!

MADAME PACE. Ah yes! I go'way! I go'way! Certainly! (*Exits furious*.)

THE STEP-DAUGHTER (*to the* FATHER). Now you make your entry. No, you needn't go over here. Come here. Let's suppose you've already come in. Like that, yes! I'm here with bowed head, modest like. Come on! Out with your voice! Say "Good morning, Miss" in that peculiar tone, that special tone . . .

THE MANAGER. Excuse me, but are you the Manager, or am I? (*To the* FATHER, *who looks undecided and perplexed*.) Get on with it, man! Go down there to the back of the stage. You needn't go off. Then come right forward here.

> *The* FATHER *does as he is told, looking troubled and perplexed at first. But as soon as he begins to move, the reality of the action affects him, and he begins to smile and to be more natural. The* ACTORS *watch intently.*

THE MANAGER (*sotto voce, quickly to the* PROMPTER *in his box*). Ready! ready? Get ready to write now.

THE FATHER (*coming forward and speaking in a different tone*). Good afternoon, Miss!

THE STEP-DAUGHTER (*head bowed down slightly, with restrained disgust*). Good afternoon!

THE FATHER (*looks under her hat which partly covers her face. Perceiving she is very young, he makes an exclamation, partly of surprise, partly of fear lest he compromise himself in a risky adventure*). Ah . . . but . . . ah . . . I say . . . this is not the first time that you have come here, is it?

THE STEP-DAUGHTER (*modestly*). No sir.

THE FATHER. You've been here before, eh? (*Then seeing her nod agreement.*) More than once? (*Waits for her to answer, looks under her hat, smiles, and then says.*) Well then, there's no need to be so shy, is there? May I take off your hat?

THE STEP-DAUGHTER (*anticipating him and with veiled disgust*). No sir . . . I'll do it myself. (*Takes it off quickly.*)

> *The* MOTHER, *who watches the progress of the scene with the* SON *and the other two children who cling to her, is on thorns; and follows with varying expressions of sorrow, indignation, anxiety, and horror the words and actions of the other two. From time to time she hides her face in her hands and sobs.*

THE MOTHER. Oh, my God, my God!

THE FATHER (*playing his part with a touch of gallantry*). Give it to me! I'll put it down. (*Takes hat from her hands.*) But a dear little head like yours ought to have a smarter hat. Come and help me choose one from the stock, won't you?

L'INGÉNUE (*interrupting*). I say . . . those are our hats you know.

THE MANAGER (*furious*). Silence! silence! Don't try and be funny, if you please . . . We're playing the scene now I'd have you notice. (*To the* STEP-DAUGHTER.) Begin again, please!

THE STEP-DAUGHTER (*continuing*). No thank you, sir.

THE FATHER. Oh, come now. Don't talk like that. You must take it. I shall be upset if you don't. There are some lovely little hats here; and then — Madame will be pleased. She expects it, anyway, you know.

THE STEP-DAUGHTER. No, no! I couldn't wear it!

THE FATHER. Oh, you're thinking about what they'd say at home if they saw you come in with a new hat? My dear girl, there's always a way round these little matters, you know.

THE STEP-DAUGHTER (*all keyed up*). No, it's not that. I couldn't wear it because I am . . . as you see . . . you might have noticed . . . (*Showing her black dress.*)

THE FATHER. . . . in mourning! Of course: I beg your pardon: I'm frightfully sorry . . .

THE STEP-DAUGHTER (*forcing herself to conquer her indignation and nausea*). Stop! Stop! It's I who must thank you. There's no need for you to feel mortified or specially sorry. Don't think any more of what I've said. (*Tries to smile.*) I must forget that I am dressed so . . .

THE MANAGER (*interrupting and turning to the* PROMPTER). Stop a minute! Stop! Don't write that down. Cut out that last bit. (*Then to the* FATHER *and* STEP-DAUGHTER.) Fine! it's going fine! (*To the* FATHER *only.*) And now you can go on as we arranged. (*To the* ACTORS.) Pretty good that scene, where he offers her the hat, eh?

THE STEP-DAUGHTER. The best's coming now. Why can't we go on?

THE MANAGER. Have a little patience! (*To the* ACTORS.) Of course, it must be treated rather lightly.

LEADING MAN. Still, with a bit of go in it!

LEADING LADY. Of course! It's easy enough! (*To* LEADING MAN.) Shall you and I try it now?

LEADING MAN. Why, yes! I'll prepare my entrance. (*Exit in order to make his entrance.*)

THE MANAGER (*to* LEADING LADY). See here! The scene between you and Madame Pace is finished. I'll have it written out properly after. You remain here . . . oh, where are you going?

LEADING LADY. One minute. I want to put my hat on again. (*Goes over to hat-rack and puts her hat on her head.*)

THE MANAGER. Good! You stay here with your head bowed down a bit.

THE STEP-DAUGHTER. But she isn't dressed in black.

LEADING LADY. But I shall be, and much more effectively than you.

THE MANAGER (*to* STEP-DAUGHTER). Be quiet please, and watch! You'll be able to learn something. (*Clapping his hands.*) Come on! come on! Entrance, please!

> *The door at rear of stage opens, and the* LEADING MAN *enters with the lively manner of an old gallant. The rendering of the scene by the* ACTORS *from the very first words is seen to be quite a different thing, though it has not in any way the air of a parody. Naturally, the* STEP-DAUGHTER *and the* FATHER, *not being able to recognize themselves in the* LEADING LADY *and the* LEADING MAN, *who deliver their words in different tones and with a different psychology, express, sometimes with smiles, sometimes with gestures, the impression they receive.*

LEADING MAN. Good afternoon, Miss . . .

THE FATHER (*at once unable to contain himself*). No! no!
The STEP-DAUGHTER *noticing the way the* LEADING MAN *enters, bursts out laughing.*

THE MANAGER (*furious*). Silence! And you please just stop that laughing. If we go on like this, we shall never finish.

THE STEP-DAUGHTER. Forgive me, sir, but it's natural enough. This lady (*indicating* LEADING LADY) stands there still; but if she is supposed to be me, I can assure you that if I heard anyone say "Good afternoon" in that manner and in that tone, I should burst out laughing as I did.

THE FATHER. Yes, yes, the manner, the tone . . .

THE MANAGER. Nonsense! Rubbish! Stand aside and let me see the action.

LEADING MAN. If I've got to represent an old fellow who's coming into a house of an equivocal character . . .

THE MANAGER. Don't listen to them, for Heaven's sake! Do it again! It goes fine. (*Waiting for the* ACTORS *to begin again.*) Well?

LEADING MAN. Good afternoon, Miss.

LEADING LADY. Good afternoon.

LEADING MAN (*imitating the gesture of the* FATHER *when he looked under the hat, and then expressing quite clearly first satisfaction and then fear*). Ah, but . . . I say . . . this is not the first time that you have come here, is it?

THE MANAGER. Good, but not quite so heavily. Like this. (*Acts himself.*) "This isn't the first time that you have come here" . . . (*To* LEADING LADY.) And you say: "No, sir."

LEADING LADY. No, sir.

LEADING MAN. You've been here before, more than once.

THE MANAGER. No, no, stop! Let her nod "yes" first. "You've been here before, eh?" (*The* LEADING LADY *lifts up her head slightly and closes her eyes as though in disgust. Then she inclines her head twice.*)

THE STEP-DAUGHTER (*unable to contain herself*). Oh my God! (*Puts a hand to her mouth to prevent herself from laughing.*)

THE MANAGER (*turning round*). What's the matter?

THE STEP-DAUGHTER. Nothing, nothing!

THE MANAGER (*to* LEADING MAN). Go on!

LEADING MAN. You've been here before, eh? Well then, there's no need to be so shy, is there? May I take off your hat?

The LEADING MAN *says this last speech in such a tone and with such gestures that the* STEP-DAUGHTER, *though she has her hand to her mouth, cannot keep from laughing.*

LEADING LADY (*indignant*). I'm not going to stop here to be made a fool of by that woman there.

LEADING MAN. Neither am I! I'm through with it!

THE MANAGER (*shouting to* STEP-DAUGHTER). Silence! for once and all, I tell you!

THE STEP-DAUGHTER. Forgive me! forgive me!

THE MANAGER. You haven't any manners: that's what it is! You go too far.

THE FATHER (*endeavouring to intervene*). Yes, it's true, but excuse her . . .

THE MANAGER. Excuse what? It's absolutely disgusting.

THE FATHER. Yes, sir, but believe me, it has such a strange effect when . . .

THE MANAGER. Strange? Why strange? Where is it strange?

THE FATHER. No, sir; I admire your actors — this gentleman here, this lady; but they are certainly not us!

THE MANAGER. I should hope not. Evidently they cannot be you, if they are actors.

THE FATHER. Just so: actors! Both of them act our parts exceedingly well. But, believe me, it produces quite a different effect on us. They want to be us, but they aren't, all the same.

THE MANAGER. What is it then anyway?

THE FATHER. Something that is . . . that is theirs — and no longer ours . . .

THE MANAGER. But naturally, inevitably. I've told you so already.

THE FATHER. Yes, I understand . . . I understand . . .

THE MANAGER. Well then, let's have no more of it! (*Turning to the* ACTORS.) We'll have the rehearsals by ourselves, afterwards, in the ordinary way. I never could stand rehearsing with the author present. He's never satisfied! (*Turning to* FATHER *and* STEP-DAUGHTER.) Come on! Let's get on with it again; and try and see if you can't keep from laughing.

THE STEP-DAUGHTER. Oh, I shan't laugh any more. There's a nice little bit coming for me now: you'll see.

THE MANAGER. Well then: when she says "Don't think any more of what I've said. I must forget, etc.," you (*addressing the* FATHER) come in sharp with "I understand, I understand"; and then you ask her . . .

THE STEP-DAUGHTER (*interrupting*). What?

THE MANAGER. Why she is in mourning.

THE STEP-DAUGHTER. Not at all! See here: when I told him that it was useless for me to be thinking about my wearing mourning, do you know how he answered me? "Ah well," he said, "then let's take off this little frock."

THE MANAGER. Great! Just what we want, to make a riot in the theatre!

THE STEP-DAUGHTER. But it's the truth!

THE MANAGER. What does that matter? Acting in our business here. Truth up to a certain point, but no further.

THE STEP-DAUGHTER. What do you want to do then?

THE MANAGER. You'll see, you'll see! Leave it to me.

THE STEP-DAUGHTER. No sir! What you want to do is to piece together a little romantic sentimental scene out of my disgust, out of all the reasons, each more cruel and viler than the other, why I am what I am. He is to ask me why I'm in mourning; and I'm to answer with tears in my eyes, that it is just two months since papa died. No sir, no! He's got to say to me; as **he** did say: "Well, let's take off this little dress at once." And I, with my two months' mourning in my heart, went there behind that screen, and with these fingers tingling with shame . . .

THE MANAGER (*running his hands through his hair*). For Heaven's sake! What are you saying?

THE STEP-DAUGHTER (*crying out excitedly*). The truth! The truth!

THE MANAGER. It may be. I don't deny it, and I can understand all your horror; but you must surely see that you can't have this kind of thing on the stage. It won't go.

THE STEP-DAUGHTER. Not possible, eh? Very well! I'm much obliged to you — but I'm off!

THE MANAGER. Now be reasonable! Don't lose your temper!

THE STEP-DAUGHTER. I won't stop here! I won't! I can see you've fixed it all up with him in your office. All this talk about what is possible for the stage . . . I understand! He wants to get at his complicated "cerebral drama," to have his famous remorses and torments acted; but I want to act my part, *my part!*

THE MANAGER (*annoyed, shaking his shoulders*). Ah! Just *your* part! But, if you will pardon me, there are other parts than yours: His (*indicating the* FATHER) and hers! (*Indicating the* MOTHER.) On the stage you can't have a character becoming too prominent and overshadowing all the others. The thing is to pack them all into a neat little framework and then act what is actable. I am aware of the fact that everyone has his own interior life which he wants very much to put forward. But the difficulty lies in this fact: to set out just so much as is necessary for the stage, taking the other characters into consideration, and at the same time hint at the unrevealed interior life of each. I am willing to admit, my dear young lady, that from your point of view it would be a fine idea if each character could tell the public all his troubles in a nice monologue or a regular one hour lecture. (*Good humoredly.*) You must restrain yourself, my dear, and in your own interest, too; because this fury of yours, this exaggerated disgust you show, may make a bad impression, you know. After you have confessed to me that there were others before him at Madame Pace's and more than once . . .

THE STEP-DAUGHTER (*bowing her head, impressed*). It's true. But remember those others mean him for me all the same.

THE MANAGER (*not understanding*). What? The others? What do you mean?

THE STEP-DAUGHTER. For one who has gone wrong, sir, he who was responsible for the first fault is responsible for all that follow. He is responsible for my faults, was, even before I was born. Look at him, and see if it isn't true!

THE MANAGER. Well, well! And does the weight of so much responsibility seem nothing to you! Give him a chance to act it, to get it over!

THE STEP-DAUGHTER. How? How can he act all his "noble remorses," all his "moral torments," if you want to spare him the horror of being discovered one day — after he had asked her what he did ask her — in the arms of her, that already fallen woman, that child, sir, that child he used to watch come out of school? (*She is moved.*)

> The MOTHER *at this point is overcome with emotion, and breaks out into a fit of crying. All are touched. A long pause.*

THE STEP-DAUGHTER (*as soon as the* MOTHER *becomes a little quieter, adds resolutely and gravely*). At present, we are unknown to the public. Tomorrow, you will act us as you wish, treating us in your own manner. But do you really want to see drama, do you want to see it flash out as it really did?

THE MANAGER. Of course! That's just what I do want, so I can use as much of it as is possible.

THE STEP-DAUGHTER. Well then, ask that Mother there to leave us.

THE MOTHER (*changing her low plaint into a sharp cry*). No! No! Don't permit it, sir, don't permit it!

THE MANAGER. But it's only to try it.

THE MOTHER. I can't bear it. I can't.

THE MANAGER. But since it has happened already . . . I don't understand!

THE MOTHER. It's taking place now. It happens all the time. My torment isn't a pretended one. I live and feel every minute of my torture. Those two children there — have you heard them speak? They can't speak any more. They cling to me to keep up my torment actual and vivid for me. But for themselves, they do not exist, they aren't any more. And she (*indicating the* STEP-DAUGHTER) has run away, she has left me, and is lost. If I now see her here before me, it is only to renew for me the tortures I have suffered for her too.

THE FATHER. The eternal moment! She (*indicating the* STEP-DAUGHTER) is here to catch me, fix me, and hold me eternally in the stocks for that one fleeting and shameful moment of my life. She can't give it up! And you sir, cannot either fairly spare me it.

THE MANAGER. I never said I didn't want to act it. It will form, as a matter of fact, the nucleus of the whole first act right up to her surprise. (*Indicates the* MOTHER.)

THE FATHER. Just so! This is my punishment: the passion in all of us that must culminate in her final cry.

THE STEP-DAUGHTER. I can hear it still in my ears. It's driven me mad, that cry! — You can put me on as you like; it doesn't matter. Fully dressed, if you like — provided I have at least the arm bare; because, standing like this (*she goes close to the* FATHER *and leans her head on his breast*) with my head so, and my arms round his neck, I saw a vein pulsing in my arm here; and then, as if that live vein had awakened disgust in me, I closed my eyes like this, and let my head sink on his breast. (*Turning to the* MOTHER.) Cry out mother! Cry out! (*Buries head in* FATHER's *breast, and with her shoulders raised as if to prevent her hearing the cry, adds in tones of intense emotion.)* Cry out as you did then!

THE MOTHER *(coming forward to separate them).* No! My daughter, my daughter! *(And after having pulled her away from him.)* You brute! you brute! She is my daughter! Don't you see she's my daughter?

THE MANAGER *(walking backwards towards footlights).* Fine! fine! Damned good! And then, of course — curtain!

THE FATHER *(going towards him excitedly).* Yes, of course, because that's the way it really happened.

THE MANAGER *(convinced and pleased).* Oh, yes, no doubt about it. Curtain here, curtain!

At the reiterated cry of the MANAGER, *the* MACHINIST *lets the curtain down, leaving the* MANAGER *and the* FATHER *in front of it before the footlights.*

THE MANAGER. The darned idiot! I said "curtain" to show the act should end there, and he goes and lets it down in earnest. *(To the* FATHER, *while he pulls the curtain back to go on to the stage again.)* Yes, yes, it's all right. Effect certain! That's the right ending. I'll guarantee the first act at any rate.

ACT III

When the curtain goes up again, it is seen that the stage hands have shifted the bit of scenery used in the last part, and have rigged up instead at the back of the stage a drop, with some trees, and one or two wings. A portion of a fountain basin is visible. The MOTHER *is sitting on the right with the two children by her side. The* SON *is on the same side, but away from the others. He seems bored, angry, and full of shame. The* FATHER *and the* STEP-DAUGHTER *are also seated towards the right front. On the other side (left) are the* ACTORS, *much in the positions they occupied before the curtain was lowered. Only the* MANAGER *is standing up in the middle of the stage, with his hand closed over his mouth in the act of meditating.*

THE MANAGER *(shaking his shoulders after a brief pause).* Ah yes: the second act! Leave it to me, leave it all to me as we arranged, and you'll see! It'll go fine!

THE STEP-DAUGHTER. Our entry into his house *(indicates* FATHER*)* in spite of him . . . *(Indicates the* SON.*)*

THE MANAGER *(out of patience).* Leave it to me, I tell you!

THE STEP-DAUGHTER. Do let it be clear, at any rate, that it is in spite of my wishes.

THE MOTHER (*from her corner, shaking her head*). For all the good that's come of it . . .

THE STEP-DAUGHTER (*turning towards her quickly*). It doesn't matter. The more harm done us, the more remorse for him.

THE MANAGER (*impatiently*). I understand! Good Heavens! I understand! I'm taking it into account.

THE MOTHER (*supplicatingly*). I beg you, sir, to let it appear quite plain that for conscience' sake I did try in every way . . .

THE STEP-DAUGHTER (*interrupting indignantly and continuing for the* MOTHER). . . . to pacify me, to dissuade me from spiting him. (*To* MANAGER.) Do as she wants: satisfy her, because it is true! I enjoy it immensely. Anyhow, as you can see, the meeker she is, the more she tries to get at his heart, the more distant and aloof does he become.

THE MANAGER. Are we going to begin this second act or not?

THE STEP-DAUGHTER. I'm not going to talk any more now. But I must tell you this: you can't have the whole action take place in the garden, as you suggest. It isn't possible!

THE MANAGER. Why not?

THE STEP-DAUGHTER. Because he (*indicates the* SON *again*) is always shut up alone in his room. And then there's all the part of that poor dazed-looking boy there which takes place indoors.

THE MANAGER. Maybe! On the other hand, you will understand — we can't change scenes three or four times in one act.

THE LEADING MAN. They used to once.

THE MANAGER. Yes, when the public was up to the level of that child there.

THE LEADING LADY. It makes the illusion easier.

THE FATHER (*irritated*). The illusion! For Heaven's sake, don't say illusion. Please don't use that word, which is particularly painful for us.

THE MANAGER (*astounded*). And why, if you please?

THE FATHER. It's painful, cruel, really cruel; and you ought to understand that.

THE MANAGER. But why? What ought we to say then? The illusion, I tell you, sir, which we've got to create for the audience . . .

THE LEADING MAN. With our acting.

THE MANAGER. The illusion of a reality.

THE FATHER. I understand; but you, perhaps, do not understand us. Forgive me! You see . . . here for you and your actors, the thing is only — and rightly so . . . a kind of game . . .

THE LEADING LADY (*interrupting indignantly*). A game! We're not children here, if you please! We are serious actors.

THE FATHER. I don't deny it. What I mean is the game, or play, of your art, which has to give, as the gentleman says, a perfect illusion of reality.

THE MANAGER. Precisely — !

THE FATHER. Now, if you consider the fact that we (*indicates himself and the other five* CHARACTERS), as we are, have no other reality outside of this illusion . . .

THE MANAGER (*astonished, looking at his* ACTORS, *who are also amazed*). And what does this mean?

THE FATHER (*after watching them for a moment with a wan smile*). As I say, sir, that which is a game of art for you is our sole reality. (*Brief pause. He goes a step or two nearer the* MANAGER *and adds.*) But not only for us, you know, by the way. Just you think it over well. (*Looks him in the eyes.*) Can you tell me who you are?

THE MANAGER (*perplexed, half smiling*). What? Who am I? I am myself.

THE FATHER. And if I were to tell you that that isn't true, because you and I . . . ?

THE MANAGER. I should say you were mad — ! (*The* ACTORS *laugh.*)

THE FATHER. You're quite right to laugh: because we are all making believe here. (*To* MANAGER.) And you can therefore object that it's only for a joke that that gentleman there (*indicates the* LEADING MAN), who naturally is himself, has to be me, who am on the contrary myself — this thing you see here. You see I've caught you in a trap! (*The* ACTORS *laugh.*)

THE MANAGER (*annoyed*). But we've had all this over once before. Do you want to begin again?

THE FATHER. No, no! That wasn't my meaning! In fact, I should like to request you to abandon this game of art (*looking at the* LEADING LADY *as if anticipating her*) which you are accustomed to play here with your actors, and to ask you seriously once again: who are you?

THE MANAGER (*astonished and irritated, turning to his* ACTORS). If this fellow here hasn't got a nerve! A man who calls himself a character comes and asks me who I am!

THE FATHER (*with dignity, but not offended*). A character, sir, may always ask a man who he is. Because a character has really a life of his own, marked with his especial characteristics; for which reason he is always "somebody." But a man — I'm not speaking of you now — may very well be "nobody."

THE MANAGER. Yes, but you are asking these questions of me, the boss, the manager! Do you understand?

THE FATHER. But only in order to know if you, as you really are now, see yourself as you once were with all the illusions that were yours then, with all the things both inside and outside of you as they seemed to you — as they were then indeed for you. Well, sir, if you think of all those illusions that mean nothing to you now, of all those things which don't even *seem* to you to exist any more, while once they *were* for you, don't you feel that — I won't say these boards — but the very earth under your feet is sinking away from you when you reflect that in the same way this *you* as you feel it today — all this present reality of yours — is fated to seem a mere illusion to you tomorrow?

THE MANAGER (*without having understood much, but astonished by the specious argument*). Well, well! And where does all this take us anyway?

THE FATHER. Oh, nowhere! It's only to show you that if we (*indicating the* CHARACTERS) have no other reality beyond the illusion, you too must not count overmuch on your reality as you feel it today, since, like that of yesterday, it may prove an illusion for you tomorrow.

THE MANAGER (*determining to make fun of him*). Ah, excellent! Then you'll be saying next that you, with this comedy of yours that you brought here to act, are truer and more real than I am.

THE FATHER (*with the greatest seriousness*). But of course; without doubt!

THE MANAGER. Ah, really?

THE FATHER. Why, I thought you'd understand that from the beginning.

THE MANAGER. More real than I?

THE FATHER. If your reality can change from one day to another . . .

THE MANAGER. But everyone knows it can change. It is always changing, the same as anyone else's.

THE FATHER (*with a cry*). No, sir, not ours! Look here! That is the very difference! Our reality doesn't change: it can't change! It can't be other than what it is, because it is already fixed for ever. It's terrible. Ours is an immutable reality which should make you shudder when you approach us if you are really conscious of the fact that your reality is a mere transitory and fleeting illusion, taking this form today and that tomorrow, according to the conditions, according to your will, your sentiments, which in turn are controlled by an intellect that shows them to you today in one manner and tomorrow . . . who knows how? . . . Illusions of reality represented in this fatuous comedy of life that never ends, nor can ever end! Because if tomorrow it were to end . . . then why, all would be finished.

THE MANAGER. Oh for God's sake, will you *at least* finish with this philosophizing and let us try and shape this comedy which you yourself have brought me here? You argue and philosophize a bit too much, my dear sir. You know you seem to me almost, almost . . . (*Stops and looks him over from head to foot.*) Ah, by the way, I think you introduced yourself to me as a — what shall . . . we say — a "character," created by an author who did not afterward care to make a drama of his own creations.

THE FATHER. It is the simple truth, sir.

THE MANAGER. Nonsense! Cut that out, please! None of us believes it, because it isn't a thing, as you must recognize yourself, which one can believe seriously. If you want to know, it seems to me you are trying to imitate the manner of a certain author whom I heartily detest — I warn you — although I have unfortunately bound myself to put on one of his works. As a matter of fact, I was just starting to rehearse it, when you arrived. (*Turning to the* ACTORS.) And this is what we've gained — out of the frying-pan into the fire!

THE FATHER. I don't know to what author you may be alluding, but believe me I feel what I think; and I seem to be philosophizing only for those who do not think what they feel, because they blind themselves with their own sentiment. I know that for many people this self-blinding seems much more "human"; but the contrary is really true. For man never reasons so much and becomes so introspective as when he suffers; since he is anxious to get at the cause of his sufferings, to learn who has produced them, and whether it is just or unjust that he should have to bear them. On the other hand, when he is happy, he takes his happiness as it comes and doesn't analyze it, just as if happiness were his right. The animals suffer without reasoning about their sufferings. But take the case of a man who suffers and begins to reason about it. Oh no! it can't be allowed! Let him suffer like an animal, and then — ah yet, he is "human"!

THE MANAGER. Look here! Look here! You're off again, philosophizing worse than ever.

THE FATHER. Because I suffer, sir! I'm not philosophizing: I'm crying aloud the reason of my sufferings.

THE MANAGER (*makes brusque movement as he is taken with a new idea*). I should like to know if anyone has ever heard of a character who gets right out of his part and perorates and speechifies as you do. Have you ever heard of a case? I haven't.

THE FATHER. You have never met such a case, sir, because authors, as a rule, hide the labour of their creations. When the characters are really alive before their author, the latter does nothing but follow them in their action, in their words, in the situations which they suggest to him; and he has to will them the way they will themselves — for there's trouble if he doesn't. When a character is born, he acquires at once such an independence, even of his own author, that he can be imagined by everybody even in many other situations where the author never dreamed of placing him; and so he acquires for himself a meaning which the author never thought of giving him.

THE MANAGER. Yes, yes, I know this.

THE FATHER. What is there then to marvel at in us? Imagine such a misfortune for characters as I have described to you: to be born of an author's fantasy, and be denied life by him; and then answer me if these characters left alive, and yet without life, weren't right in doing what they did do and are doing now, after they have attempted everything in their power to persuade him to give them their stage life. We've all tried him in turn, I, she (*indicating the* STEP-DAUGHTER) and she (*indicating the* MOTHER).

THE STEP-DAUGHTER. It's true. I too have sought to tempt him, many, many times, when he has been sitting at his writing table, feeling a bit melancholy, at the twilight hour. He would sit in his armchair too lazy to switch on the light, and all the shadows that crept into his room were full of our presence coming to tempt him. (*As if she saw herself still there by the writing table, and was annoyed by the presence of the* ACTORS.) Oh, if you would only go away, go away and leave us alone — mother here with that son of hers — I with that Child — that Boy there always alone — and then I with him (*just hints at the* FATHER) — and then I alone, alone ... in those shadows! (*Makes a sudden movement as if in the vision she has of herself illuminating those shadows she wanted to seize hold of herself.*) Ah! my life! my life! Oh, what scenes we proposed to him — and I tempted him more than any of the others!

THE FATHER. Maybe. But perhaps it was your fault that he refused to give us life: because you were too insistent, too troublesome.

THE STEP-DAUGHTER. Nonsense! Didn't he make me so himself? (*Goes close to the* MANAGER *to tell him as if in confidence.*) In my opinion he abandoned us in a fit of depression, of disgust for the ordinary theatre as the public knows it and likes it.

THE SON. Exactly what it was, sir; exactly that!

THE FATHER. Not at all! Don't believe it for a minute. Listen to me! You'll be doing quite right to modify, as you suggest, the excesses both of this girl here, who wants to do too much, and of this young man, who won't do anything at all.

THE SON. No, nothing!

THE MANAGER. You too get over the mark occasionally, my dear sir, if I may say so.

THE FATHER. I? When? Where?

THE MANAGER. Always! Continuously! Then there's this insistence of yours in trying to make us believe you are a character. And then too, you must really argue and philosophize less, you know, much less.

THE FATHER. Well, if you want to take away from me the possibility of representing the torment of my spirit which never gives me peace, you will be suppressing me: that's all. Every true man, sir, who is a little above the level of the beasts and plants does not live for the sake of living, without knowing how to live; but he lives so as to give a meaning and a value of his own to life. For me this is *everything*. I cannot give up this, just to represent a mere fact as she (*indicating the* STEP-DAUGHTER) wants. It's all very well for her, since her "vendetta" lies in the "fact." I'm not going to do it. It destroys my *raison d'être*.

THE MANAGER. Your *raison d'être*! Oh, we're going ahead fine! First she starts off, and then you jump in. At this rate, we'll never finish.

THE FATHER. Now, don't be offended! Have it your own way — provided, however, that within the limits of the parts you assign us each one's sacrifice isn't too great.

THE MANAGER. You've got to understand that you can't go on arguing at your own pleasure. Drama is action, sir, action and not confounded philosophy.

THE FATHER. All right. I'll do just as much arguing and philosophizing as everybody does when he is considering his own torments.

THE MANAGER. If the drama permits! But for Heaven's sake, man, let's get along and come to the scene.

THE STEP-DAUGHTER. It seems to me we've got too much action with our coming into his house. (*Indicating* FATHER.) You said, before, you couldn't change the scene every five minutes.

THE MANAGER. Of course not. What we've got to do is to combine and group up all the facts in one simultaneous, close-knit, action. We can't have it as you want, with your little brother wandering like a ghost from room to room, hiding behind doors and meditating a project which — what did you say it did to him?

THE STEP-DAUGHTER. Consumes him, sir, wastes him away!

THE MANAGER. Well, it may be. And then at the same time, you want the little girl there to be playing in the garden . . . one in the house, and the other in the garden: isn't that it?

THE STEP-DAUGHTER. Yes, in the sun, in the sun! That is my only pleasure: to see her happy and careless in the garden after the misery and squalor of the horrible room where we all four slept together. And I had to sleep with her — I, do you understand? — with my vile contaminated body next to hers; with her holding me fast in her loving little arms. In the garden, whenever she spied me, she would run to take me by the hand. She didn't care for the big flowers, only the little ones; and she loved to show me them and pet me.

THE MANAGER. Well then, we'll have it in the garden. Everything shall happen in the garden; and we'll group the other scenes there. (*Calls a* STAGE HAND.) Here, a backcloth with trees and something to do as a fountain basin. (*Turning round to look at the back of the stage.*) Ah, you've fixed it up. Good! (*To* STEP-DAUGHTER.) This is just to give an idea, of course. The Boy, instead of hiding behind the doors, will wander about here in the garden, hiding behind the trees. But it's going to be rather difficult to find a child to do that scene with you where she shows you the flowers. (*Turning to the* BOY.) Come forward a little, will you please? Let's try it now! Come along! come along! (*Then seeing him come shyly forward, full of fear and looking lost.*) It's a nice business, this lad here. What's the matter with him? We'll have to give him a word or two to say. (*Goes close to him, puts a hand on his shoulders, and leads him behind one of the trees.*) Come on! come on! Let me see you a little! Hide here . . . yes, like that. Try and show your head just a little as if you were looking for someone . . . (*Goes back to observe the effect, when the* BOY *at once goes through the action.*) Excellent! fine! (*Turning to* STEP-DAUGHTER.) Suppose the little girl there were to surprise him as he looks round, and run over to him, so we could give him a word or two to say?

THE STEP-DAUGHTER. It's useless to hope he will speak, as long as that fellow there is here . . . (*Indicates the* SON.) You must send him away first.

THE SON (*jumping up*). Delighted! Delighted! I don't ask for anything better. (*Begins to move away.*)

THE MANAGER (*at once stopping him*). No! No! Where are you going? Wait a bit!

The MOTHER *gets up alarmed and terrified at the thought that he is really about to go away. Instinctively she lifts her arms to prevent him, without, however, leaving her seat.*

THE SON (*to* MANAGER *who stops him*). I've got nothing to do with this affair. Let me go please! Let me go!

THE MANAGER. What do you mean by saying you've got nothing to do with this?

THE STEP-DAUGHTER (*calmly, with irony*). Don't bother to stop him: he won't go away.

THE FATHER. He has to act the terrible scene in the garden with his mother.

THE SON (*suddenly resolute and with dignity*). I shall act nothing at all. I've said so from the very beginning. (*To the* MANAGER.) Let me go!

THE STEP-DAUGHTER (*going over to the* MANAGER). Allow me? (*Puts down the* MANAGER'S *arm which is restraining the* SON.) Well, go away then, if you want to! (*The* SON *looks at her with contempt and hatred. She laughs and says.*) You see, he can't, he can't go away! He is obliged to stay here, indissolubly bound to the chain. If I, who fly off when that happens which has to happen, because I can't bear him — if I am still here and support that face and expression of his, you can well imagine that he is unable to move. He has to remain here, has to stop with that nice father of his, and that mother whose only son he is. (*Turning to the* MOTHER.) Come on, mother, come along! (*Turning to* MANAGER *to indicate her.*) You see, she was getting up to keep him back. (*To the* MOTHER, *beckoning her with her hand.*) Come on! come on! (*Then to* MANAGER.) You can imagine how little she wants to show these actors of yours what she really feels; but so eager is she to get near him that . . . There, you see? She is willing to act her part. (*And in fact, the* MOTHER *approaches him; and as soon as the* STEP-DAUGHTER *has finished speaking, opens her arms to signify that she consents.*)

THE SON (*suddenly*). No! no! If I can't go away, then I'll stop here; but I repeat: I act nothing!

THE FATHER (*to* MANAGER *excitedly*). You can force him, sir.

THE SON. Nobody can force me.

THE FATHER. I can.

THE STEP-DAUGHTER. Wait a minute, wait . . . First of all, the baby has to go to the fountain . . . (*Runs to take the* CHILD *and leads her to the fountain.*)

THE MANAGER. Yes, yes of course; that's it. Both at the same time.

The second LADY LEAD *and the* JUVENILE LEAD *at this point separate themselves from the group of* ACTORS. *One watches the* MOTHER *attentively; the other moves about studying the movements and manner of the* SON *whom he will have to act.*

THE SON (*to* MANAGER). What do you mean by both at the same time? It isn't right. There was no scene between me and her. (*Indicates the* MOTHER.) Ask her how it was!

THE MOTHER. Yes, it's true. I had come into his room . . .

THE SON. Into my room, do you understand? Nothing to do with the garden.

THE MANAGER. It doesn't matter. Haven't I told you we've got to group the action?

THE SON (*observing the* JUVENILE LEAD *studying him*). What do you want?

THE JUVENILE LEAD. Nothing! I was just looking at you.

THE SON (*turning towards the second* LADY LEAD). Ah! she's at it too: to re-act her part! (*Indicating the* MOTHER.)

THE MANAGER. Exactly! And it seems to me that you ought to be grateful to them for their interest.

THE SON. Yes, but haven't you yet perceived that it isn't possible to live in front of a mirror which not only freezes us with the image of ourselves, but throws our likeness back at us with a horrible grimace?

THE FATHER. That is true, absolutely true. You must see that.

THE MANAGER (*to second* LADY LEAD *and* JUVENILE LEAD). He's right! Move away from them!

THE SON. Do as you like. I'm out of this!

THE MANAGER. Be quiet, you, will you? And let me hear your mother! (*To* MOTHER.) You were saying you had entered . . .

THE MOTHER. Yes, into his room, because I couldn't stand it any longer. I went to empty my heart to him of all the anguish that tortures me . . . But as soon as he saw me come in . . .

THE SON. Nothing happened! There was no scene. I went away, that's all! I don't care for scenes!

THE MOTHER. It's true, true. That's how it was.

THE MANAGER. Well now, we've got to do this bit between you and him. It's indispensable.

THE MOTHER. I'm ready . . . when you are ready. If you could only find a chance for me to tell him what I feel here in my heart.

THE FATHER (*going to* SON *in a great rage*). You'll do this for your mother, for your mother, do you understand?

THE SON (*quite determined*). I do nothing!

THE FATHER (*taking hold of him and shaking him*). For God's sake, do as I tell you! Don't you hear your mother asking you for a favor? Haven't you even got the guts to be a son?

THE SON (*taking hold of the* FATHER). No! No! And for God's sake stop it, or else . . . (*General agitation. The* MOTHER, *frightened, tries to separate them.*)

THE MOTHER (*pleading*). Please! please!

THE FATHER (*not leaving hold of the* SON). You've got to obey, do you hear?

THE SON (*almost crying from rage*). What does it mean, this madness you've got? (*They separate.*) Have you no decency, that you insist on showing everyone our shame? I won't do it! I won't! And I stand for the will of our author in this. He didn't want to put us on the stage, after all!

THE MANAGER. Man alive! You came here . . .

THE SON (*indicating* FATHER). *He* did! I didn't!

THE MANAGER. Aren't you here now?

THE SON. It was his wish, and he dragged us along with him. He's told you not only the things that did happen, but also things that have never happened at all.

THE MANAGER. Well, tell me then what did happen. You went out of your room without saying a word?

THE SON. Without a word, so as to avoid a scene!

THE MANAGER. And then what did you do?

THE SON. Nothing . . . walking in the garden . . . (*Hesitates for a moment with expression of gloom.*)

THE MANAGER (*coming closer to him, interested by his extraordinary reserve*). Well, well . . . walking in the garden . . .

THE SON (*exasperated*). Why on earth do you insist? It's horrible! (*The* MOTHER *trembles, sobs, and looks towards the fountain.*)

THE MANAGER (*slowly observing the glance and turning towards the* SON *with increasing apprehension*). The baby?

THE SON. There in the fountain . . .

THE FATHER (*pointing with tender pity to the* MOTHER). She was following him at the moment . . .

THE MANAGER (*to the* SON *anxiously*). And then you . . .

THE SON. I ran over to her; I was jumping in to drag her out when I saw something that froze my blood . . . the boy standing stock still, with eyes like a madman's, watching his little drowned sister, in the fountain! (*The* STEPDAUGHTER *bends over the fountain to hide the* CHILD. *She sobs.*) Then . . . (*A revolver shot rings out behind the trees where the* BOY *is hidden.*)

THE MOTHER (*with a cry of terror runs over in that direction together with several of the* ACTORS *amid general confusion*). My son! My son! (*Then amid the cries and exclamations one hears her voice.*) Help! Help!

THE MANAGER (*pushing the* ACTORS *aside while they lift up the* BOY *and carry him off.*) Is he really wounded?

SOME ACTORS. He's dead! dead!

OTHER ACTORS. No, no, it's only make believe, it's only pretence!

THE FATHER (*with a terrible cry*). Pretence? Reality, sir, reality!

THE MANAGER. Pretence? Reality? To hell with it all! Never in my life has such a thing happened to me. I've lost a whole day over these people, a whole day!

CURTAIN

EPIC THEATER

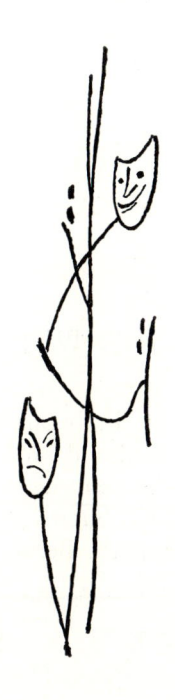

Bertolt Brecht

THE GOOD WOMAN OF SETZUAN

[1941]

Bertolt Brecht [1898–1956]

Although Bertolt Brecht began writing plays in 1918, and was having them published and produced in the early 1920's, it was not until 1928 and the great success of *The Threepenny Opera* that he became well known. Shortly after he became established as one of the major writers in the Berlin of the Weimar Republic, Hitler came to power, and Brecht (Jewish and Marxist) left the country to live in exile until 1948. While his theatrical career was in some measure interrupted by his forced expatriation, his writing career continued; and to the period of his exile in Denmark, Sweden, Finland, and the United States (1933–1948) we owe the plays of Brecht's maturity, among them *Mother Courage and Her Children, Galileo, The Good Woman of Setzuan,* and *The Caucasian Chalk Circle.* From the 1940's we can date Brecht's international fame and influence. Strangely enough, after Brecht returned to East Berlin in 1948 and had his own theater, the Berlin Ensemble, under Communist auspices, he did not write many more plays. Although he was a Marxist from the 1920's (but not a Party member), his plays with their marked deviation from official Party prescriptions for art have never been widely performed in most Soviet-dominated countries.

The term "epic theater" in approximately its present meaning was first used by Brecht and others around 1926. The theory was put into practice and developed in *The Threepenny Opera* and the production notes for that and other Brecht plays of the period, and was more or less complete by 1930 — when Brecht published his *Versuche* (*Experiments* or *Attempts*). Brecht's theory and practice have always had a reciprocal relationship, and it was not until after the writing and production of all of his major plays that

Brecht and Epic Theater

he composed a reconsidered summary of his ideas on epic theater, "A Short Organum for the Theater" (1948).

Though in its ordinary English usage, "epic" suggests grandness of scale and the heroic, in Brecht's use it indicates a narrative (as opposed to a "dramatic") form. John Willet, one of the best-informed students of Brecht and his theater, defines epic theater as "a sequence of incidents or events, narrated without artificial restrictions as to time, place, or relevance to a formal 'plot.'" And Mordecai Gorelik, in "An Epic Theatre Catechism," says that epic theater "should describe individuals in relation to the social, historical, and political circumstances under which they live." These two definitions, one emphasizing form and the other emphasizing content, indicate two salient features of epic theater, but neither of them defines it sharply. The reason is, simply, that the epic theater itself is not clearly delimited. There are qualities which we recognize as "epic" and mannerisms of production identified with the epic theater, but no single, definitive epic style and content exist.

Epic theater (called "epic realism" by Gorelik and "narrative realism" by Eric Bentley) is likely to present a disjointed, fragmentary, episodic, picaresque chronicle. Epic theory decries socially irrelevant plays and emotional plays in which the spectator is invited to lose himself through some kind of identification with the figures of the drama. Epic plays dramatize man in society, and in a society which is to be changed as a result of a clearheaded, not an emotional, understanding of the problems set forth on the stage. (One can understand why Brecht admired Shaw with his emphasis on problem as the staple of the drama.) In the presen-

523

tation (as against representation), anti-illusionist techniques are used: film sequences, projected scene titles, half-curtains, direct address to the audience, and use of the stage as a platform characterize epic productions. The acting is even self-consciously detached, quite different from the identification with the characters which naturalistic acting demands. The aim of this deliberate avoidance of the illusion of everyday actuality is to create the effect of *Verfremdung* (variously translated *alienation, estrangement,* and *distancing*). According to Brecht, the somewhat detached spectator can assume what he calls the attitude of "watching while smoking," and can thus catch the full significance of the didactic play which he is watching. (Notice throughout the emphasis on theater and spectator, not drama and reader.) Certainly Brecht espouses chiefly a theater of social action, and he thinks of his plays as instruments of instruction, as well as of entertainment.

One critic of Brecht has said that "all the plays of Brecht's maturity are merely parables designed to illustrate [the Marxist] doctrine." It is not surprising, then, to find *The Good Woman of Setzuan* in a volume of two plays by Brecht entitled *Parables for the Theatre*. This openly didactic play is highly characteristic of epic theater in many ways. In plot, conflict, theme, characters and characterization, we see Brecht's use of epic form. We must imagine ourselves as spectators watching the play unfold in order to pass judgment on its effectiveness as a theater piece. As we consider it, can we see any direct evidence of Brecht's Marxist doctrine? If we remain emotionally detached from the play, are we likely to be moved to action? Is the play too coldly rational? Are the issues, like those in the old morality plays, too clearly drawn?

THE ALIENATION EFFECT IN CHINESE ACTING*

by Bertolt Brecht

In the following paper something will be said about the use of "alienation" in Chinese acting. The "alienation effect" has been used in Germany in plays of a non-Aristotelian kind, that is, in plays which are not based on empathy (*einfuehlung*). I refer to various attempts to act in such a manner that the spectator is prevented from feeling his way into the characters. Acceptance or rejection of the characters' words is thus placed in the conscious realm, not, as hitherto, in the spectator's subconscious.

The attempt to "alienate" the events being presented from the audience was made in a primitive way in the theatrical and pictorial displays of old fairs. We also find it in the circus clown's manner of speech and in the way in which so-called "panoramas"[1] are painted. The reproduction of the painting *The Flight of Charles the Bold After the Battle of Murten*, often to be found on German fairgrounds, was always inadequately painted. Yet the copyist achieved an alienation effect not to be found in the original; and one can scarcely blame this on his inadequacy. The fleeing general, his horse, his retinue, and the landscape are quite consciously painted to give the impression of an *extra*-ordinary occasion, a forbidding catastrophe. Despite his inadequacy the painter admirably produces the effect of the unexpected; astonishment guides his brush. This *effect of estrangement* is also known to the Chinese actor, who uses it in a very subtle manner.

(Everyone knows that the Chinese theatre makes use of many symbols. A general wears little ribbons on his shoulders, as many, in fact, as the regiments he commands. Poverty is indicated by sewing irregular patches onto silk robes, the patches being also of silk, though of a different color. The personages of a play are characterized by a particular kind of make-up, that is, simply by paint. Certain gestures with both hands represent the forcible opening of a door, and so forth. The stage stays unchanged though articles of furniture are brought on during the play. All this has been known for a

---

* Translated by Eric Bentley. Reprinted by permission from *Furioso*, Autumn, 1949, pp. 68–77.

[1] A "panorama" is a series of pictures used by a ballad singer as an accompaniment to his songs.

525

long time and can scarcely be taken over by us *in toto*. And one is accustomed to regard an artistic phenomenon *in toto* — as a whole. However, if you want to study one particular effect among many you have to break with this custom.)

In the Chinese theatre the alienation effect is achieved in the following way. The Chinese performer does not act as if, in addition to the three walls around him there were also a fourth wall. *He makes it clear that he knows he is being looked at*. Thus, one of the illusions of the European stage is set aside. The audience forfeits the illusion of being unseen spectators at an event which is really taking place. The European stage has worked out an elaborate technique by which the fact that scenes are so arranged as to be easily seen by the audience is concealed. The Chinese approach renders this technique superfluous. As openly as acrobats the actors can choose those positions which show them off to best advantage.

Another expedient is this: *the actor looks at himself*. Presenting, let us say, a cloud, its unsuspected appearance, its gentle yet strong development, its speedy yet gradual transformation; from time to time he looks at the spectator as if to say: Isn't it just like that? But he also looks at his own arms and legs, guiding them, examining them, in the end, perhaps praising them. If he glances at the floor or measures the space available for his act, he sees nothing in this procedure that could disturb the illusion. In this way the performer separates mimicry[2] (presenting the act of observation) from gesture[3] (presenting the cloud) but the latter loses nothing thereby, for the attitude of the body reacts back upon the face, gives to the face, as it were, its own expression. An expression now of complete reservation, now of utter triumph. The performer has used his face as an empty sheet of paper that can be written on by bodily movement.

The performer wishes to appear alien to the spectator. Alien to the point of arousing surprise. This he manages by seeing himself and his performance as alien. In this way the things he does on the stage become astonishing. By this craft everyday things are removed from the realm of the self-evident.

A young woman, a fisherman's daughter, is shown on the stage, rowing a boat. She stands up and steers the (non-existent) boat with a little oar that hardly comes down to her knees. The current runs faster. Now it is harder for her to keep her balance. Now she is in a bay and rows more quietly. Well, that's the way to row a boat. But this voyage has an historic quality, as if it had been sung in many songs, a most unusual voyage, known to everyone. Each of this famous girl's movements has been preserved in pictures. Every bend in the river was an adventure that one knows about. The bend she is now approaching is well-known. This feeling in the spectator is called forth by the performer's attitude. It is she who confers fame on the voyage. (The scene reminds us of the march to Budweis in Piscator's production of

[2] *Mimik*.
[3] *Gestik*.

The Good Soldier Schweik. Schweik's three day march under sun and moon to the front, which, curiously enough, he never reaches, was seen in a completely historical way, as something just as worth thinking about as Napoleon's journey to Russia in 1812.)

To look at himself is for the performer an artful and artistic act of self-estrangement. Any empathy on the spectator's part is thereby prevented from becoming total, that is, from being a complete self-surrender. An admirable distance from the events portrayed is achieved. This is not to say that the spectator experiences no empathy whatsoever. He feels his way into the actor as into an observer. In this manner an observing, watching attitude is cultivated.

In many ways the art of the Chinese actor seems to the western actor cold. Not that the Chinese theatre renounces the presentation of feelings! The actor presents events of considerable passionateness, but his delivery remains unimpassioned. At moments when the presented character is deeply excited, the performer takes a strand of hair between his lips and bites it. That is pretty much of a rite; there is nothing eruptive about it. Clearly it is a matter of the repetition of an event by another man, a *rendering* (artistic, certainly). The performer shows that *this man is beside himself* and he indicates the outward signs of such a state of mind. This is the proper way to express being beside oneself. (It may be improper too, but not for the stage.) Anyway a few special symptoms are chosen out of many — obviously with great deliberation. Anger is naturally distinguished from fury, hate from dislike, love from sympathy, but the various movements of feeling are sparingly presented. The pervading coolness arises from the fact that the individual is not so much the center of interest as in western theatre. True, the cult of the star has gone further in Asia than perhaps anywhere else. The spectator's eyes positively hang on the star. The other roles give him the cue to the star, place obstacles in his way, show him off. Nevertheless, the star places himself at a distance from the role he plays in the manner just described. He guards against making the audience feel exactly what the character is feeling. Nobody will be raped by the individual he presents. This individual is not the spectator but his neighbor.

The western performer does all he can to bring the spectator as close as possible to the events and the character being presented. To this end he gets him to feel his way into him, the actor. He spends all his strength on transforming himself as completely as possible into another type of person, the type being presented. When this complete transformation is achieved, his art is pretty much exhausted. Once he *is* the bank clerk, the doctor, the general, he needs just as little art as the bank clerk, the doctor or the general need in real life. The act of completely transforming oneself takes a lot of trouble to accomplish. Stanislavski provides a whole list of devices, a whole *system* of devices, by means of which this "creative mood" can be produced afresh at each performance. Usually the actor does not succeed for long in really feeling like the other person. He soon begins, in his exhaustion, to copy certain external features of his carriage or tone of voice, and thereby the effect on the audience is appallingly weakened. Doubtless the reason is that the creation of the Other Man was an intuitive act taking place in the subconscious. The subconscious is very hard to regulate. It has, so to speak, a bad memory.

The Chinese performer knows nothing of these difficulties. He eschews complete transformation He confines himself at the outset to merely *quoting* the character. But with how much art he does this! He requires only a minimum of illusion. What he shows is worth seeing even to those who are not out of their senses. What western actor, with the exception of a comedian or so, could do what the Chinese actor Mei-Lan-Fang does — show the elements of his craft clad in evening dress in a room with no special lights before an audience of professionals? The scene of Lear's division of his kingdom, let us say, or Othello and the handkerchief? He'd be like a conjurer at a fairground showing his magical tricks, which no one would want to see a second time. He would merely show how one *dissembles*. The hypnosis would pass and there would remain a couple of pounds of badly beaten-up mimicry, a commodity quickly thrown together for sale in the dark to customers who are in a hurry. Naturally, no western actor would arrange such a performance. Isn't art sacrosanct? Isn't theatrical metamorphosis a mystical process? He lays store by the fact that what he does is unconscious; it has more value for him that way. A comparison with Asiatic acting shows how deeply parsonic our art still is.

Certainly it gets harder all the time for our actors to consummate the mystery of complete transformation. Their subconscious mind's memory is getting weaker all the time. And even when the actor is a genius it is hard to create truth out of the adulterated intuition of a member of a class society.

It is difficult for the actor to generate certain emotions and moods in himself every evening and comparatively easy to render the outward signs that accompany and denote these emotions. Certainly the transference of these emotions to the spectator, the emotional contagion, does not take place automatically. The "alienation effect" enters in at this point, not in the form of emotionlessness, but in the form of emotions which do not have to be identical with those of the presented character. The spectator can feel joy at the sight of sorrow, disgust at the sight of anger. We speak of rendering the outward signs of emotions as a way of effecting alienation. This procedure may, however, fail to do so. The actor can so render these signs and select these signs that, on the contrary, emotional contagion follows, because the actor *has*, while rendering the signs, generated in himself the emotions to be presented. The actor can easily stir up anger within himself by letting his voice swell and by holding his breath, also by drawing his throat muscles together so that the blood flows to his head. In this case, alienation is out of the question. On the other hand, alienation does occur when at a particular point and without transition the actor displays a deadly pale face which he has acquired artificially. (He held his face in his hands, and in his hands was some white grease paint.) If the actor exhibits at the same time an apparently undisturbed nature, his fright at this point in the play (occasioned by a piece of news or a discovery) will produce the alienation effect. To act in this manner is more healthy and, it seems to us, more worthy of a thinking being. It calls for a considerable knowledge of men, a considerable general intelligence, and a keen grasp of what is socially important. Obviously a creative process is going on here too. And one of a higher sort, since it belongs to the sphere of consciousness.

Obviously the alienation effect in no way presupposes an unnatural style of acting. One must at all costs not think of what is called Stylization. On the contrary the success of the alienation effect is dependent on the lightness and naturalness of the whole procedure. And when the actor comes to examine the truth of this performance — a necessary operation, which gives Stanislavski a lot of trouble — he is not merely thrown back on his natural sensibility. He can always be corrected by reference to reality. Does an angry man really speak like that? Does a guilty man sit like that? He can be corrected, that is, from without, by other people. His style is such that nearly every sentence could be *judged* by the audience. Nearly every gesture is submitted to the approval of the audience.

The Chinese actor is in no trance. He can be interrupted at any moment. There is no question of his "coming to." After an interruption he will take up his performance at the exact place where he was interrupted. We disturb him at no mystic moment of creation. He had finished "creating" before he came on the stage. If scene building is going on while he is acting, he doesn't mind. Stagehands hand him whatever he needs for his work quite openly. During a death scene played by Mei-Lan-Fang a spectator sitting near me let out a startled cry at one of the actor's gestures. Several spectators in front of us turned indignantly around and hissed: *Sh!* They conducted themselves as at the death of some real girl. Perhaps their behavior was right for a European production, but it was unspeakably ridiculous in a Chinese theatre. The alienation effect had misfired.

It is not altogether easy to regard the alienation effect of Chinese acting as something that can be shaken loose from the Chinese theatre and exported. The Chinese theatre seems to us uncommonly precious, its presentation of human passions merely schematic, its conception of society rigid and false. At first sight nothing in this great art seems useful in a realistic and revolutionary theatre. The motives and aims of the alienation effect are alien and suspect.

In the first place it is difficult, when watching the Chinese act, to rid ourselves of the feeling of strangeness that they arouse in us because we are Europeans. One must be able to imagine they achieve the alienation effect also in their Chinese spectators. But, and this is more difficult, we must not allow ourselves to be disturbed at the fact that the Chinese performer creates an impression of mystery for a quite different purpose from any that we can envisage. If one has learned to think dialectically one can find it possible that a technique which is taken from the realm of magic can be used to combat magic with. The Chinese performer may intend to use the alienation effect to make the events on stage mysterious, incomprehensible, and uncontrollable to the audience. And yet this effect can be used to make the events mundane, comprehensible, and controllable.

The attitude of the scientist, who at first views the object of his investigation with astonishment, may resemble the attitude of a magician. Yet these apparently identical attitudes have a precisely opposite function. Whoever finds the formula $2 \times 2 = 4$ obvious is no mathematician; neither is the man who doesn't know what the formula means. The man who viewed a lamp swinging on a rope with astonishment at first and found it not obvious but very remarkable that the lamp swung thus and not otherwise — such a man approached the understanding of the phenomenon and, with this, the mastery of the phenomenon. It won't do to exclaim that this attitude is appropriate to science alone and not to art. Why shouldn't art try (by its own means, of course) to contribute to the great social task of mastering life?

A technical feature like the alienation effect in Chinese acting can be studied with profit only by those who *need* such a feature for particular social purposes. As charm, novelty, finesse, and formalistic frivolity it could never become significant.

Moreover, in the experiments of the new German theatre, the alienation effect was developed quite independently. The influence of Asiatic acting was nil.

In the German epic theatre the alienation effect was employed not only through the actors but also through the music (choruses and solos) and the décor (placards, film, etc.). The aim was the *historification* of the events presented. Under this head the following is meant.

The bourgeois theatre (this is everything that we think of when we speak of theatre in general) sifts out from its materials the timeless element. The presentation of the human being stops with the so-called Eternally Human. By a certain ordering of the plot or fable, general situations are created in which Man — the man of all periods and every color — can express himself. Events on stage are all one long cue, the cue for the Eternal Answer, the inevitable, usual, natural, human answer. Here is an example. The black man loves in the same way as the white man. But only when the plot extorts the same reaction from him as the white man gives (the formula presumably works in reverse too) is the result called Art. The peculiar and distinct elements may have a place in the cue; the answer is the same for both; and in the answer there is nothing peculiar and distinct.

Such a philosophy may acknowledge the existence of history but it is an unhistorical philosophy. Certain circumstances may be changed; milieus are transformed; but man does not change. History is valid for the milieu; but

The Alienation Effect in Chinese Acting

not for man. The milieu is so essentially unimportant, is understood just as the *occasion* for things. A variable quantity, and essentially inhuman, it really exists without man. It confronts him as a closed unity. And *he* is forever unchanged, a fixed quantity. To regard man as a variable which, moreover, controls the milieu, to conceive of the liquidation of the milieu in relationships between men — these notions spring from a new mode of thought, historical thought. An example will cut short this historical-philosophical excursion.

The following is to be presented on the stage. A girl leaves her family to take a job in a big city. (Dreiser's *American Tragedy*, which was adapted to the stage by Piscator.) For the bourgeois theatre the idea is a pretty limited one. It constitutes only the beginning of a story, the bit of information we must have if we are to understand or be excited by what follows. The actor's imagination can hardly be set in motion at all by this. In a way the event is general: girls do take jobs. And in this case one can be excited at the thought of what in particular will happen to her. The event is also peculiar: this girl leaves home; had she stayed, the following would not have occurred. The important thing is what kind of girl she is. What is her character? That her family lets her go is not a subject for investigation. It is credible. Motives are "credible."

For our history-making theatre it is otherwise. It seizes on the special, the particular, on what needs investigation in this everyday event. What? The family lets one of its members leave the paternal roof? To live quite independently and earn her living without assistance? Can she do it? Will what she has learned in the family help her to earn her living? Can families not keep their children any more? Are they a burden? Is this so in all families? Was it always so? Is this the way of the world and not to be affected? "When the fruit is ripe, it falls from the tree:" does the proverb apply? If children always and at all times make themselves independent, if this is something biological, does it always happen in the same way, for the same reason, with the same results?

These are the questions — or some of them — that the actors have to answer if they want to present the event as a unique historical one, if they want to point to it as a custom which provides a key to the whole social structure of a particular, transitory period. How can such an event be presented so that its historical character comes out? How can the confusion of our unhappy age be made to stand out while a mother, amid warnings and moral demands, packs her daughter's bag, which is a very small bag? So many demands and so little underwear? Warnings for a lifetime and bread for five hours? How is this to be put on the stage? When she hands the small bag to her daughter the mother says: "Well, I think that'll be enough." How can the actress playing the role speak this sentence so that it will be understood as an historical expression? It can only be done if the alienation effect is brought off. The actress must not make of this sentence an affair of her own. She must hand it over for criticism. She must make it possible for the audience to understand the motives behind it. She must make protest possible.

In the Artef Players Collective in New York (1935), I saw a stage version of Samuel Ornitz' *Haunch, Paunch and Jowl*, which showed how an east-side boy rose to be a corrupt lawyer. The theatre could not play the piece. And yet scenes like this were in it. Sitting in the street in front of his house, the young lawyer gives legal advice at very low prices. A young woman comes with the complaint that her leg had been damaged in a traffic accident. But the case was bungled. Her claim for compensation has not yet been handed in. In despair she points at her leg and shouts: "It's healing already!" Working without the alienation effect, this theatre could not adequately display the horror of a bloody age in this extraordinary scene. Few people in the auditorium paid any attention to it. Few of them, even if they read these lines, would remember the woman's cry. The actress spoke it as something obvious. But precisely the fact that such a complaint seems obvious to the poor woman the actress should have reported to the audience as an outraged messenger returning from the lowest of hells. In this she would have needed to be helped by a special technique to underline the historical nature of a given social condition. Only the alienation effect makes this possible.

In bringing forward new artistic principles and in working out new methods of presentation we must proceed from the imperative demands of an age of transition. It seems possible and necessary to rebuild society. All events in the human realm are being examined. Everything must be seen from the social standpoint. Among other effects, a new theatre will find the alienation effect necessary for the criticism of society and for historical reporting on changes already accomplished.

English Version by Eric Bentley

The Good Woman of Setzuan

CHARACTERS

WONG, *a water seller*
THREE GODS
SHEN TE, *a prostitute, later a shopkeeper*
MRS. SHIN, *former owner of Shen Te's shop*
A FAMILY OF EIGHT (*husband, wife, brother, sister-in-law, grandfather, nephew, niece, boy*)
AN UNEMPLOYED MAN
A CARPENTER
MRS. MI TZU, *Shen Te's landlady*
YANG SUN, *an unemployed pilot, later a factory manager*
AN OLD WHORE
A POLICEMAN
AN OLD MAN
AN OLD WOMAN, *his wife*
MR. SHU FU, *a barber*
MRS. YANG, *mother of Yang Sun*
GENTLEMEN, VOICES, CHILDREN (*three*), *etc.*

PROLOGUE

At the gates of the half-Westernized city of Setzuan.* Evening. WONG *the Water Seller introduces himself to the audience.*

WONG. I sell water here in the city of Setzuan. It isn't easy. When water is scarce, I have long distances to go in search of it, and when it is plentiful, I have no income. But in our part of the world there is nothing unusual about poverty. Many people think only the gods can save the situation. And I hear from a cattle merchant — who travels a lot — that some of the highest gods are on their way here at this very moment. Informed sources

---

* Thus the first MS of the play. Brecht later learned that Setzuan (Szechwan) is not a city but a province, and changed the script accordingly. But, as often, the solecism seems more appropriate than the fact. E.B.

have it that heaven is quite disturbed at all the complaining. I've been coming out here to the city gates for three days now to bid these gods welcome. I want to be the first to greet them. What about those fellows over there? No, no, they *work*. And that one there has ink on his fingers, he's no god, he must be a clerk from the cement factory. *Those* two are another story. They look as though they'd like to beat you. But gods don't need to beat you, do they? (THREE GODS *appear*.) What about those three? Old-fashioned clothes — dust on their feet — they *must* be gods! (*He throws himself at their feet.*) Do with me what you will, illustrious ones!

FIRST GOD (*with an ear trumpet*). Ah! (*He is pleased.*) So we were expected?

WONG (*giving them water*). Oh, yes. And I *knew* you'd come.

FIRST GOD. We need somewhere to stay the night. You know of a place?

WONG. The whole town is at your service, illustrious ones! What sort of a place would you like?

The GODS *eye each other.*

FIRST GOD. Just try the first house you come to, my son.

WONG. That would be Mr. Fo's place.

FIRST GOD. Mr. Fo.

WONG. One moment! (*He knocks at the first house.*)

VOICE FROM MR. FO'S. No!

WONG *returns a little nervously.*

WONG. It's too bad. Mr. Fo isn't in. And his servants don't dare do a thing without his consent. He'll have a fit when he finds out who they turned away, won't he?

FIRST GOD (*smiling*). He will, won't he?

WONG. One moment! The next house is Mr. Cheng's. Won't he be thrilled!

FIRST GOD. Mr. Cheng.

WONG *knocks*.

VOICE FROM MR. CHENG'S. Keep your gods. We have our own troubles!

WONG (*back with the* GODS). Mr. Cheng is very sorry, but he has a houseful of relations. I think some of them are a bad lot, and naturally, he wouldn't like you to see them.

THIRD GOD. Are we so terrible?

WONG. Well, only with bad people, of course. Everyone knows the province of Kwan is always having floods.

SECOND GOD. Really? How's that?

WONG. Why, because they're so irreligious.

SECOND GOD. Rubbish. It's because they neglected the dam.

FIRST GOD (*to* SECOND). Sh! (*To* WONG.) You're still in hopes, aren't you, you, my son?

WONG. Certainly. All Setzuan is competing for the honor! What happened up to now is pure coincidence. I'll be back. (*He walks away, but then stands undecided.*)

The Good Woman of Setzuan

SECOND GOD. What did I tell you?

THIRD GOD. It *could* be pure coincidence.

SECOND GOD. The same coincidence in Shun, Kwan, and Setzuan? People just aren't religious any more, let's face the fact. Our mission has failed!

FIRST GOD. Oh come, we might run into a good person any minute.

THIRD GOD. How did the resolution read? (*Unrolling a scroll and reading from it.*) "The world can stay as it is if enough people are found (*at the word "found" he unrolls it a little more*) living lives worthy of human beings." Good people, that is. Well, what about this Water Seller himself? *He's* good, or I'm very much mistaken.

SECOND GOD. You're very much mistaken. When he gave us a drink, I had the impression there was something odd about the cup. Well, look! (*He shows the cup to the* FIRST GOD.)

FIRST GOD. A false bottom!

SECOND GOD. The man is a swindler.

FIRST GOD. Very well, count *him* out. That's one man among millions. And as a matter of fact, we only need one on *our* side. These atheists are saying, "The world must be changed because no one can *be* good and *stay* good." No one, eh? I say: let us find one — just one — and we have those fellows where we want them!

THIRD GOD (*to* WONG). Water Seller, is it so hard to find a place to stay?

WONG. Nothing could be easier. It's just me. I don't go about it right.

THIRD GOD. Really?

He returns to the others. A GENTLEMAN *passes by.*

WONG. Oh dear, they're catching on. (*He accosts the* GENTLEMAN.) Excuse the intrusion, dear sir, but three gods have just turned up. Three of the very highest. They need a place for the night. Seize this rare opportunity — to have real gods as your guests!

GENTLEMAN (*laughing*). A new way of finding free rooms for a gang of crooks. (*Exit* GENTLEMAN.)

WONG (*shouting at him*). Godless rascal! Have you no religion, gentlemen of Setzuan? (*Pause.*) Patience, illustrious ones! (*Pause.*) There's only one person left. Shen Te, the prostitute. She *can't* say no. (*Calls up to a window.*) Shen Te!

SHEN TE *opens the shutters and looks out.*

WONG. Shen Te, it's Wong. *They're* here, and nobody wants them. Will you take them?

SHEN TE. Oh, no, Wong, I'm expecting a gentleman.

WONG. Can't you forget about him for tonight?

SHEN TE. The rent has to be paid by tomorrow or I'll be out on the street.

WONG. This is no time for calculation, Shen Te.

SHEN TE. Stomachs rumble even on the Emperor's birthday, Wong.

WONG. Setzuan is one big dung hill!

SHEN TE. Oh, very well! I'll hide till my gentleman has come and gone. Then I'll take them. (*She disappears.*)

WONG. They mustn't see her gentleman or they'll know what she is.

FIRST GOD (*who hasn't heard any of this*). I think it's hopeless.

They approach WONG.

WONG (*jumping, as he finds them behind him*). A room has been found, illustrious ones! (*He wipes sweat off his brow.*)

SECOND GOD. Oh, good.

THIRD GOD. Let's see it.

WONG (*nervously*). Just a minute. It has to be tidied up a bit.

THIRD GOD. Then we'll sit down here and wait.

WONG (*still more nervous*). No, no! (*Holding himself back.*) Too much traffic, you know.

THIRD GOD (*with a smile*). Of course, if you *want* us to move.

They retire a little. They sit on a doorstep. WONG *sits on the ground.*

WONG (*after a deep breath*). You'll be staying with a single girl — the finest human being in Setzuan!

THIRD GOD. That's nice.

WONG (*to the audience*). They gave me such a look when I picked up my cup just now.

THIRD GOD. You're worn out, Wong.

WONG. A little, maybe.

FIRST GOD. Do people here have a hard time of it?

WONG. The good ones do.

FIRST GOD. What about yourself?

WONG. You mean I'm not good. That's true. And I don't have an easy time either!

During this dialogue, a GENTLEMAN *has turned up in front of* SHEN TE'S *house, and has whistled several times. Each time* WONG *has given a start.*

THIRD GOD (*to* WONG, *softly*). Psst! I think he's gone now.

WONG (*confused and surprised*). Ye-e-es.

The GENTLEMAN *has left now, and* SHEN TE *has come down to the street.*

SHEN TE (*softly*). Wong!

Getting no answer, she goes off down the street. WONG *arrives just too late, forgetting his carrying pole.*

WONG (*softly*). Shen Te! Shen Te! (*To himself.*) So she's gone off to earn the rent. Oh dear, I can't go to the gods *again* with no room to offer them. Having failed in the services of the gods, I shall run to my den in the sewer pipe down by the river and hide from their sight!

He rushes off. SHEN TE *returns, looking for him, but finding the* GODS. *She stops in confusion.*

SHEN TE. You are the illustrious ones? My name is Shen Te. It would please me very much if my simple room could be of use to you.

THIRD GOD. Where is the Water Seller, Miss . . . Shen Te?

SHEN TE. I missed him, somehow.

FIRST GOD. Oh, he probably thought you weren't coming, and was afraid of telling us.

THIRD GOD (*picking up the carrying pole*). We'll leave this with you. He'll be needing it.

Led by SHEN TE, *they go into the house. It grows dark, then light. Dawn. Again escorted by* SHEN TE, *who leads them through the half-light with a little lamp, the* GODS *take their leave.*

FIRST GOD. Thank you, thank you, dear Shen Te, for your elegant hospitality! We shall not forget! And give our thanks to the Water Seller — he showed us a good human being.

SHEN TE. Oh, I'm not good. Let me tell you something: when Wong asked me to put you up, I hesitated.

FIRST GOD. It's all right to hesitate if you then go ahead! And in giving us that room you did much more than you knew. You proved that good people still exist, a point that has been disputed of late — even in heaven. Farewell!

SECOND GOD. Farewell!

THIRD GOD. Farewell!

SHEN TE. Stop, illustrious ones! I'm not sure you're right. I'd like to be good, it's true, but there's the rent to pay. And that's not all: I sell myself for a living. Even so I can't make ends meet, there's too much competition. I'd like to honor my father and mother and speak nothing but the truth and not covet my neighbor's house. I should love to stay with one man. But how? How is it done? Even breaking a few of your commandments, I can hardly manage.

FIRST GOD (*clearing his throat*). These thoughts are but, um, the misgivings of an unusually good woman!

THIRD GOD. Good-bye, Shen Te! Give our regards to the Water Seller!

SECOND GOD. And above all: be good! Farewell!

FIRST GOD. Farewell!

THIRD GOD. Farewell!

They start to wave good-bye.

SHEN TE. But everything is so expensive, I don't feel sure I can do it!

SECOND GOD. That's not in our sphere. We never meddle with economics.

THIRD GOD. One moment. (*They stop.*) Isn't it true she might do better if she had more money?

SECOND GOD. Come, come! How could we ever account for it Up Above?

FIRST GOD. Oh, there are ways. (*They put their heads together and confer in dumb show. To* SHEN TE, *with embarrassment.*) As you say you can't pay your rent, well, um, we're not paupers, so of course we *insist* on paying for our room. (*Awkwardly thrusting money into her hands.*) There! (*Quickly.*) But don't tell anyone! The incident is open to misinterpretation.

SECOND GOD. It certainly is!

FIRST GOD (*defensively*). But there's no law against it! It was never decreed that a god mustn't pay hotel bills!

The GODS *leave.*

1

A small tobacco shop. The shop is not as yet completely furnished and hasn't started doing business.

SHEN TE (*to the audience*). It's three days now since the gods left. When they said they wanted to pay for the room, I looked down at my hand, and there was more than a thousand silver dollars! I bought a tobacco shop with the money, and moved in yesterday. I don't own the building, of course, but I can pay the rent, and I hope to do a lot of good here. Beginning with Mrs. Shin, who's just coming across the square with her pot. She had the shop before me, and yesterday she dropped in to ask for rice for her children. (*Enter* MRS. SHIN. *Both women bow.*) How do you do, Mrs. Shin.

MRS. SHIN. How do you do, Miss Shen Te. You like your new home?

SHEN TE. Indeed, yes. Did your children have a good night?

MRS. SHIN. In that hovel? The youngest is coughing already.

SHEN TE. Oh, dear!

MRS. SHIN. You're going to learn a thing or two in these slums.

SHEN TE. Slums? That's not what you said when you sold me the shop!

MRS. SHIN. Now don't start nagging! Robbing me and my innocent children of their home and then calling it a slum! That's the limit! (*She weeps.*)

SHEN TE (*tactfully*). I'll get your rice.

MRS. SHIN. And a little cash while you're at it.

SHEN TE. I'm afraid I haven't sold anything yet.

MRS. SHIN (*screeching*). I've got to have it. Strip the clothes from my back and then cut my throat, will you? I know what I'll do: I'll dump my children on your doorstep! (*She snatches the pot out of* SHEN TE'S *hands.*)

SHEN TE. Please don't be angry. You'll spill the rice.

Enter an elderly HUSBAND *and* WIFE *with their shabbily dressed* NEPHEW.

WIFE. Shen Te, dear! You've come into money, they tell me. And we haven't a roof over our heads! A tobacco shop. We had one too. But it's gone. Could we spend the night here, do you think?

NEPHEW (*appraising the shop*). Not bad!

WIFE. He's our nephew. We're inseparable!

MRS. SHIN. And who are these . . . ladies and gentlemen?

SHEN TE. They put me up when I first came in from the country. (*To the audience.*) Of course, when my small purse was empty, they put me out on the street, and they may be afraid I'll do the same to them. (*To the newcomers, kindly.*) Come in, and welcome, though I've only one little room for you — it's behind the shop.

HUSBAND. That'll do. Don't worry.

WIFE (*bringing* SHEN TE *some tea*). We'll stay over here, so we won't be in your way. Did you make it a tobacco shop in memory of your first real home? We can certainly give you a hint or two! That's one reason we came.

MRS. SHIN (*to* SHEN TE). Very nice! As long as you have a few customers too!

HUSBAND. Sh! A customer!

Enter an UNEMPLOYED MAN, *in rags.*

UNEMPLOYED MAN. Excuse me. I'm unemployed.

MRS. SHIN *laughs.*

SHEN TE. Can I help you?

UNEMPLOYED MAN. Have you any damaged cigarettes? I thought there might be some damage when you're unpacking.

WIFE. What nerve, begging for tobacco! (*Rhetorically.*) Why don't they ask for bread?

UNEMPLOYED MAN. Bread is expensive. One cigarette butt and I'll be a new man.

SHEN TE (*giving him cigarettes*). That's very important — to be a new man. You'll be my first customer and bring me luck.

The UNEMPLOYED MAN *quickly lights a cigarette, inhales, and goes off coughing.*

WIFE. Was that right, Shen Te, dear?

MRS. SHIN. If this is the opening of a shop, you can hold the closing at the end of the week.

HUSBAND. I bet he had money on him.

SHEN TE. Oh, no, he said he hadn't!

NEPHEW. How d'you know he wasn't lying?

SHEN TE (*angrily*). How do you know he was?

WIFE (*wagging her head*). You're too good, Shen Te, dear. If you're going to keep this shop, you'll have to learn to say no.

HUSBAND. Tell them the place isn't yours to dispose of. Belongs to . . . some relative who insists on all accounts being strictly in order . . .

MRS. SHIN. That's right! What do you think you are — a philanthropist?

SHEN TE (*laughing*). Very well, suppose I ask you for my rice back, Mrs. Shin?

WIFE (*combatively, at* MRS. SHIN). So that's *her* rice?

Enter the CARPENTER, *a small man.*

MRS. SHIN (*who, at the sight of him, starts to hurry away*). See you tomorrow, Miss Shen Te! (*Exit* MRS. SHIN.)

CARPENTER. Mrs. Shin, it's you I want!

WIFE (*to* SHEN TE). Has she some claim on you?

SHEN TE. She's hungry. That's a claim.

CARPENTER. Are you the new tenant? And filling up the shelves already? Well, they're not yours till they're paid for, ma'am. I'm the carpenter, so I should know.

SHEN TE. I took the shop "furnishings included."

CARPENTER. You're in league with that Mrs. Shin, of course. All right. I demand my hundred silver dollars.

SHEN TE. I'm afraid I haven't got a hundred silver dollars.

CARPENTER. Then you'll find it. Or I'll have you arrested.

WIFE (*whispering to* SHEN TE). That relative: make it a cousin.

SHEN TE. Can't it wait till next month?

CARPENTER. No!

SHEN TE. Be a little patient, Mr. Carpenter, I can't settle all claims at once.

CARPENTER. Who's patient with me? (*He grabs a shelf from the wall.*) Pay up — or I take the shelves back!

WIFE. Shen Te! Dear! Why don't you let your . . . cousin settle this affair? (*To* CARPENTER.) Put your claim in writing. Shen Te's cousin will see you get paid.

CARPENTER (*derisively*). Cousin, eh?

HUSBAND. Cousin, yes.

CARPENTER. I know these cousins!

NEPHEW. Don't be silly. He's a personal friend of mine.

HUSBAND. What a man! Sharp as a razor!

CARPENTER. All right. I'll put my claim in writing. (*Puts shelf on the floor, sits on it, writes out bill.*)

WIFE (*to* SHEN TE). He'd tear the dress off your back to get his shelves. Never recognize a claim! That's my motto.

SHEN TE. He's done a job, and wants something in return. It's shameful that I can't give it to him. What will the gods say?

HUSBAND. You did your bit when you took *us* in.

Enter the BROTHER, *limping, and the* SISTER-IN-LAW, *pregnant.*

BROTHER (*to* HUSBAND *and* WIFE). So this is where you're hiding out! There's family feeling for you! Leaving us on the corner!

WIFE (*embarrassed, to* SHEN TE). It's my brother and his wife. (*To them.*) Now stop grumbling, and sit quietly in that corner. (*To* SHEN TE.) It can't be helped. She's in her fifth month.

SHEN TE. Oh yes. Welcome!

WIFE (*to the couple*). Say thank you. (*They mutter something.*) The cups are there. (*To* SHEN TE.) Lucky you bought this shop when you did!

SHEN TE (*laughing and bringing tea*). Lucky indeed!

Enter MRS. MI TZU, *the landlady.*

MRS. MI TZU. Miss Shen Te? I am Mrs. Mi Tzu, your landlady. I hope our relationship will be a happy one. I like to think I give my tenants modern, personalized service. Here is your lease. (*To the others, as* SHEN TE *reads the lease.*) There's nothing like the opening of a little shop, is there? A moment of true beauty! (*She is looking around.*) Not very much on the shelves, of course. But everything in the gods' good time! Where are your references, Miss Shen Te?

SHEN TE. Do I *have* to have references?

MRS. MI TZU. After all, I haven't a notion who you are!

HUSBAND. Oh, *we'd* be glad to vouch for Miss Shen Te! We'd go through fire for her!

MRS. MI TZU. And who may *you* be?

HUSBAND (*stammering*). Ma Fu, tobacco dealer.

MRS. MI TZU. Where is your shop, Mr. . . . Ma Fu?

HUSBAND. Well, um, I haven't got a shop — I've just sold it.

MRS. MI TZU. I see. (*To* SHEN TE.) Is there no one else that knows you?

WIFE (*whispering to* SHEN TE). Your cousin! Your cousin!

MRS. MI TZU. This is a respectable house, Miss Shen Te. I never sign a lease without certain assurances.

SHEN TE (*slowly, her eyes downcast*). I have . . . a cousin.

MRS. MI TZU. On the square? Let's go over and see him. What does he do?

SHEN TE (*as before*). He lives . . . in another city.

WIFE (*prompting*). Didn't you say he was in Shung?

SHEN TE. That's right. Shung.

HUSBAND (*prompting*). I had his name on the tip of my tongue. Mr. . . .

SHEN TE (*with an effort*). Mr. . . . Shui . . . Ta.

HUSBAND. That's it! Tall, skinny fellow!

SHEN TE. Shui Ta!

NEPHEW (*to* CARPENTER). *You* were in touch with him, weren't you? About the shelves?

CARPENTER (*surlily*). Give him this bill. (*He hands it over.*) I'll be back in the morning. (*Exit* CARPENTER.)

NEPHEW (*calling after him, but with his eyes on* MRS. MI TZU). Don't worry! Mr. Shui Ta pays on the nail!

MRS. MI TZU (*looking closely at* SHEN TE). I'll be happy to make his acquaintance, Miss Shen Te. (*Exit* MRS. MI TZU.)

Pause.

WIFE. By tomorrow morning she'll know more about you than you do yourself.

SISTER-IN-LAW (*to* NEPHEW). This thing isn't built to last.

Enter GRANDFATHER.

WIFE. It's Grandfather! (*To* SHEN TE.) Such a good old soul!

The BOY *enters.*

BOY (*over his shoulder*). Here they are!

WIFE. And the boy, how he's grown! But he always could eat enough for ten.

Enter the NIECE.

WIFE (*to* SHEN TE). Our little niece from the country. There are more of us now than in your time. The less we had, the more there were of us; the more there were of us, the less we had. Give me the key. We must protect ourselves from unwanted guests. (*She takes the key and locks the door.*) Just make yourself at home. I'll light the little lamp.

NEPHEW (*a big joke*). I hope her cousin doesn't drop in tonight! The strict Mr. Shui Ta!

SISTER-IN-LAW *laughs*.

BROTHER (*reaching for a cigarette*). One cigarette more or less . . .

HUSBAND. One cigarette more or less.

They pile into the cigarettes. The BROTHER *hands a jug of wine round.*

NEPHEW. Mr. Shui Ta'll pay for it!

GRANDFATHER (*gravely, to* SHEN TE). How do you do?

SHEN TE, *a little taken aback by the belatedness of the greeting, bows. She has the* CARPENTER'S *bill in one hand, the landlady's lease in the other.*

WIFE. How about a bit of a song? To keep Shen Te's spirits up?

NEPHEW. Good idea. Grandfather: you start!

SONG OF THE SMOKE

GRANDFATHER.
    I used to think (before old age beset me)
      That brains could fill the pantry of the poor.
    But where did all my cerebration get me?
      I'm just as hungry as I was before.
        So what's the use?
          See the smoke float free
      Into ever colder coldness!
        It's the same with me.

HUSBAND.
    The straight and narrow path leads to disaster
      And so the crooked path I tried to tread.
    That got me to disaster even faster
      (They say we shall be happy when we're dead.)
        So what's the use?
          See the smoke float free
      Into ever colder coldness!
        It's the same with me.

NIECE.
    You older people, full of expectation,
      At any moment now you'll walk the plank!
    The future's for the younger generation!
      Yes, even if that future is a blank.
        So what's the use?
          See the smoke float free
      Into ever colder coldness!
        It's the same with me.

NEPHEW (*to the* BROTHER). Where'd you get that wine?

SISTER-IN-LAW (*answering for the* BROTHER). He pawned the sack of tobacco.

HUSBAND (*stepping in*). What? That tobacco was all we had to fall back on! You pig!

BROTHER. You'd call a man a pig because your wife was frigid! Did you refuse to drink it?

They fight. The shelves fall over.

SHEN TE (*imploringly*). Oh don't! Don't break everything! Take it, take it all, but don't destroy a gift from the gods!

WIFE (*disparagingly*). This shop isn't big enough. I should never have mentioned it to Uncle and the others. When *they* arrive, it's going to be disgustingly overcrowded.

SISTER-IN-LAW. And did you hear our gracious hostess? She cools off quick!

Voices outside. Knocking at the door.

UNCLE'S VOICE. Open the door!

WIFE. Uncle? Is that you, Uncle?

UNCLE'S VOICE. Certainly, it's me. Auntie says to tell you she'll have the children here in ten minutes.

WIFE (*to* SHEN TE). I'll have to let him in.

SHEN TE (*who scarcely hears her*).
> The little lifeboat is swiftly sent down
> Too many men too greedily
> Hold on to it as they drown.

— 1a —

WONG'S *den in a sewer pipe.*

WONG (*crouching there*). All quiet! It's four days now since I left the city. The gods passed this way on the second day. I heard their steps on the bridge over there. They must be a long way off by this time, so I'm safe. (*Breathing a sigh of relief, he curls up and goes to sleep. In his dream the pipe becomes transparent, and the* GODS *appear. Raising an arm, as if in self-defense:*) I know, I know, illustrious ones! I found no one to give you a room — not in all Setzuan! There, it's out. Please continue on your way!

FIRST GOD (*mildly*). But you did find someone. Someone who took us in for the night, watched over us in our sleep, and in the early morning lighted us down to the street with a lamp.

WONG. It was . . . Shen Te that took you in?

THIRD GOD. Who else?

WONG. And I ran away! "She isn't coming," I thought, "she just can't afford it."

GODS (*singing*):

O you feeble, well-intentioned, and yet feeble chap
Where there's need the fellow thinks there is no goodness!
When there's danger he thinks courage starts to ebb away!
Some people only see the seamy side!
What hasty judgment! What premature desperation!

WONG. I'm *very* ashamed, illustrious ones.

FIRST GOD. Do us a favor, Water Seller. Go back to Setzuan. Find Shen Te, and give us a report on her. We hear that she's come into a little money. Show interest in her goodness — for no one can be good for long if goodness is not in demand. Meanwhile we shall continue the search, and find other good people. After which, the idle chatter about the impossibility of goodness will stop!

The GODS *vanish.*

2

A knocking.

WIFE. Shen Te! Someone at the door. Where is she anyway?

NEPHEW. She must be getting the breakfast. Mr. Shui Ta will pay for it.

The WIFE *laughs and shuffles to the door. Enter* MR. SHUI TA *and the* CARPENTER.

WIFE. Who is it?

SHUI TA. I am Miss Shen Te's cousin.

WIFE. What??

SHUI TA. My name is Shui Ta.

WIFE. Her cousin?

NEPHEW. Her cousin?

NIECE. But that was a joke. She hasn't got a cousin.

HUSBAND. So early in the morning?

BROTHER. What's all the noise?

SISTER-IN-LAW. This fellow says he's her cousin.

BROTHER. Tell him to prove it.

NEPHEW. Right. If you're Shen Te's cousin, prove it by getting the breakfast.

SHUI TA (*whose regime begins as he puts out the lamp to save oil; loudly, to all present, asleep or awake*). Would you all please get dressed! Customers will be coming! I wish to open my shop!

HUSBAND. *Your* shop? Doesn't it belong to our good friend Shen Te?

SHUI TA *shakes his head.*

SISTER-IN-LAW. So we've been cheated. Where *is* the little liar?

SHUI TA. Miss Shen Te has been delayed. She wishes me to tell you there will be nothing she can do — now that I am here.

WIFE (*bowled over*). I thought she was good!

The Good Woman of Setzuan

NEPHEW. Do you have to believe *him?*

HUSBAND. I don't.

NEPHEW. Then do something.

HUSBAND. Certainly! I'll send out a search party at once. You, you, you, and you, go out and look for Shen Te. (*As the* GRANDFATHER *rises and makes for the door:*) Not you, Grandfather, you and I will hold the fort.

SHUI TA. You won't find Miss Shen Te. She has suspended her hospitable activity for an unlimited period. There are too many of you. She asked me to say: this is a tobacco shop, not a gold mine.

HUSBAND. Shen Te never said a thing like that. Boy, food! There's a bakery on the corner. Stuff your shirt full when they're not looking!

SISTER-IN-LAW. Don't overlook the raspberry tarts.

HUSBAND. And don't let the policeman see you.

The BOY *leaves.*

SHUI TA. Don't you depend on this shop now? Then why give it a bad name by stealing from the bakery?

NEPHEW. Don't listen to him. Let's find Shen Te. She'll give him a piece of her mind.

SISTER-IN-LAW. Don't forget to leave us some breakfast.

BROTHER, SISTER-IN-LAW *and* NEPHEW *leave.*

SHUI TA (*to the* CARPENTER). You see, Mr. Carpenter, nothing has changed since the poet, eleven hundred years ago, penned these lines:

> A governor was asked what was needed
> To save the freezing people in the city.
> He replied:
> "A blanket ten thousand feet long
> To cover the city and all its suburbs."

He starts to tidy up the shop.

CARPENTER. Your cousin owes me money. I've got witnesses. For the shelves.

SHUI TA. Yes, I have your bill. (*He takes it out of his pocket.*) Isn't a hundred silver dollars rather a lot?

CARPENTER. No deductions! I have a wife and children.

SHUI TA. How many children?

CARPENTER. Three.

SHUI TA. I'll make you an offer. Twenty silver dollars.

The HUSBAND *laughs.*

CARPENTER. You're crazy. Those shelves are real walnut.

SHUI TA. Very well. Take them away.

CARPENTER. What?

SHUI TA. They cost too much. Please take them away.

WIFE. Not bad! (*And she, too, is laughing.*)

CARPENTER (*a little bewildered*). Call Shen Te, someone! (*To* SHUI TA.) She's *good!*

SHUI TA. Certainly. She's ruined.

CARPENTER (*provoked into taking some of the shelves*). All right, you can keep your tobacco on the floor.

SHUI TA (*to the* HUSBAND). Help him with the shelves.

HUSBAND (*grins and carries one shelf over to the door where the* CARPENTER *now is*). Good-bye, shelves!

CARPENTER (*to the* HUSBAND). You dog! You want my family to starve?

SHUI TA. I repeat my offer. I have no desire to keep my tobacco on the floor. Twenty silver dollars.

CARPENTER (*with desperate aggressiveness*). One hundred!

SHUI TA *shows indifference, looks through the window. The* HUSBAND *picks up several shelves.*

CARPENTER (*to* HUSBAND). You needn't smash them against the doorpost, you idiot! (*To* SHUI TA.) These shelves were made to measure. They're no use anywhere else!

SHUI TA. Precisely.

The WIFE *squeals with pleasure.*

CARPENTER (*giving up, sullenly*). Take the shelves. Pay what you want to pay.

SHUI TA (*smoothly*). Twenty silver dollars.

He places two large coins on the table. The CARPENTER *picks them up.*

HUSBAND (*bringing the shelves back in*). And quite enough too!

CARPENTER (*slinking off*). Quite enough to get drunk on.

HUSBAND (*happily*). Well, we got rid of *him*!

WIFE (*weeping with fun, gives a rendition of the dialogue just spoken*). "Real walnut," says he. "Very well, take them away," says his lordship. "I have three children," says he. "Twenty silver dollars," says his lordship. "They're no use anywhere else," says he. "Pre-cisely," said his lordship! (*She dissolves into shrieks of merriment.*)

SHUI TA. And now: go!

HUSBAND. What's that?

SHUI TA. You're thieves, parasites. I'm giving you this chance. Go!

HUSBAND (*summoning all his ancestral dignity*). That sort deserves no answer. Besides, one should never shout on an empty stomach.

WIFE. Where's that boy?

SHUI TA. Exactly. The boy. I want no stolen goods in this shop. (*Very loudly.*) I strongly advise you to leave! (*But they remain seated, noses in the air. Quietly.*) As you wish. (SHUI TA *goes to the door. A* POLICEMAN *appears.* SHUI TA *bows.*) I am addressing the officer in charge of this precinct?

POLICEMAN. That's right, Mr., um, what was the name, sir?

SHUI TA. Mr. Shui Ta.

POLICEMAN. Yes, of course, sir.

They exchange a smile.

SHUI TA. Nice weather we're having.

The Good Woman of Setzuan

POLICEMAN. A little on the warm side, sir.

SHUI TA. Oh, a little on the warm side.

HUSBAND (*whispering to the* WIFE). If he keeps it up till the boy's back, we're done for. (*Tries to signal* SHUI TA.)

SHUI TA (*ignoring the signal*). Weather, of course, is one thing indoors, another out on the dusty street!

POLICEMAN. Oh, quite another, sir!

WIFE (*to the* HUSBAND). It's all right as long as he's standing in the doorway — the boy will see him.

SHUI TA. Step inside for a moment! It's quite cool indoors. My cousin and I have just opened the place. And we attach the greatest importance to being on good terms with the, um, authorities.

POLICEMAN (*entering*). Thank you, Mr. Shui Ta. It *is* cool!

HUSBAND (*whispering to the* WIFE). And now the boy *won't* see him.

SHUI TA (*showing* HUSBAND *and* WIFE *to the* POLICEMAN). Visitors. I think my cousin knows them. They were just leaving.

HUSBAND (*defeated*). Ye-e-es, we were . . . just leaving.

SHUI TA. I'll tell my cousin you couldn't wait.

Noise from the street. Shouts of "Stop, Thief!"

POLICEMAN. What's that?

The BOY *is in the doorway with cakes and buns and rolls spilling out of his shirt. The* WIFE *signals desperately to him to leave. He gets the idea.*

POLICEMAN. No, you don't! (*He grabs the* BOY *by the collar.*) Where's all this from?

BOY (*vaguely pointing*). Down the street.

POLICEMAN (*grimly*). So that's it. (*Prepares to arrest the* BOY.)

WIFE (*stepping in*). And *we* knew nothing about it. (*To the* BOY.) Nasty little thief!

POLICEMAN (*dryly*). Can you clarify the situation, Mr. Shui Ta?

SHUI TA *is silent.*

POLICEMAN (*who understands silence*). Aha. You're all coming with me — to the station.

SHUI TA. I can hardly say how sorry I am that *my* establishment . . .

THE WIFE. Oh, he saw the boy leave not ten minutes ago!

SHUI TA. And to conceal the theft asked a policeman in?

POLICEMAN. Don't listen to her, Mr. Shui Ta, I'll be happy to relieve you of their presence one and all! (*To all three.*) Out!

(*He drives them before him.*)

GRANDFATHER (*leaving last, gravely*). Good morning!

POLICEMAN. Good morning!

SHUI TA, *left alone, continues to tidy up.* MRS. MI TZU *breezes in.*

MRS. MI TZU. You're her cousin, are you? Then have the goodness to explain what all this means — police dragging people from a respectable house!

By what right does your Miss Shen Te turn my property into a house of assignation? — Well, as you see, I know all!

SHUI TA. Yes. My cousin has the worst possible reputation: that of being poor.

MRS. MI TZU. No sentimental rubbish, Mr. Shui Ta. Your cousin was a common. . . .

SHUI TA. Pauper. Let's use the uglier word.

MRS. MI TZU. I'm speaking of her conduct, not her earnings. But there must have *been* earnings, or how did she buy all this? Several elderly gentlemen took care of it, I suppose. I repeat: this is a respectable house! I have tenants who prefer not to live under the same roof with such a person.

SHUI TA (*quietly*). How much do you want?

MRS. MI TZU (*he is ahead of her now*). I beg your pardon.

SHUI TA. To reassure yourself. To reassure your tenants. How much will it cost?

MRS. MI TZU. You're a cool customer.

SHUI TA (*picking up the lease*). The rent is high. (*He reads on.*) I assume it's payable by the month?

MRS. MI TZU. Not in her case.

SHUI TA (*looking up*). What?

MRS. MI TZU. Six months rent payable in advance. Two hundred silver dollars.

SHUI TA. Six . . . ! Sheer usury! And where am I to find it?

MRS. MI TZU. You should have thought of that before.

SHUI TA. Have you no heart, Mrs. Mi Tzu? It's true Shen Te acted foolishly, being kind to all those people, but she'll improve with time. I'll see to it she does. She'll work her fingers to the bone to pay her rent, and all the time be as quiet as a mouse, as humble as a fly.

MRS. MI TZU. Her social background . . .

SHUI TA. Out of the depths! She came out of the depths! And before she'll go back there, she'll work, sacrifice, shrink from nothing. . . . Such a tenant is worth her weight in gold, Mrs. Mi Tzu.

MRS. MI TZU. It's silver we were talking about, Mr. Shui Ta. Two hundred silver dollars or . . .

Enter the POLICEMAN.

POLICEMAN. Am I intruding, Mr. Shui Ta?

MRS. MI TZU. This tobacco shop is well-known to the police, I see.

POLICEMAN. Mr. Shui Ta has done us a service, Mrs. Mi Tzu. I am here to present our official felicitations!

MRS. MI TZU. That means less than nothing to me, sir. Mr. Shui Ta, all I can say is: I hope your cousin will find my terms acceptable. Good day, gentlemen. (*Exit.*)

SHUI TA. Good day, ma'am.

Pause.

POLICEMAN. Mrs. Mi Tzu a bit of a stumbling block, sir?

SHUI TA. She wants six months' rent in advance.

POLICEMAN. And you haven't got it, eh? (SHUI TA *is silent.*) But surely you can get it, sir? A man like you?

SHUI TA. What about a woman like Shen Te?

POLICEMAN. You're not staying, sir?

SHUI TA: No, and I won't be back. Do you smoke?

POLICEMAN (*taking two cigars, and placing them both in his pocket*). Thank you, sir — I see your point. Miss Shen Te — let's mince no words — Miss Shen Te lived by selling herself. "What else could she have done?" you ask. "How else was she to pay the rent?" True. But the fact remains, Mr. Shui Ta, it is not respectable. Why not? A very deep question. But, in the first place, love — love isn't bought and sold like cigars, Mr. Shui Ta. In the second place, it isn't respectable to go waltzing off with someone that's paying his way, so to speak — it must be for love! Thirdly and lastly, as the proverb has it: not for a handful of rice but for love! (*Pause. He is thinking hard.*) "Well," you may say, "and what good is all this wisdom if the milk's already spilt?" Miss Shen Te is what she is. Is *where* she is. We have to face the fact that if she doesn't get hold of six months' rent pronto, she'll be back on the streets. The question then as I see it — everything in this world is a matter of opinion — the question as I see it is: *how* is she to get hold of this rent? How? Mr. Shui Ta: I don't know. (*Pause.*) I take that back, sir. It's just come to me. A husband. We must find her a husband!

Enter a little OLD WOMAN.

OLD WOMAN. A good cheap cigar for my husband, we'll have been married forty years tomorrow and we're having a little celebration.

SHUI TA. Forty years? And you still want to celebrate?

OLD WOMAN. As much as we can afford to. We have the carpet shop across the square. We'll be good neighbors, I hope?

SHUI TA. I hope so too.

POLICEMAN (*who keeps making discoveries*). Mr. Shui Ta, you know what we need? We need capital. And how do we acquire capital? We get married.

SHUI TA (*to* OLD WOMAN). I'm afraid I've been pestering this gentleman with my personal worries.

POLICEMAN (*lyrically*). We can't pay six months' rent, so what do we do? We marry money.

SHUI TA. That might not be easy.

POLICEMAN. Oh, I don't know. She's a good match. Has a nice, growing business. (*To the* OLD WOMAN.) What do you think?

OLD WOMAN (*undecided*). Well —

POLICEMAN. Should she put an ad in the paper?

OLD WOMAN (*not eager to commit herself*). Well, if *she* agrees —

POLICEMAN. I'll write it for her. You lend us a hand, and we write an ad for you! (*He chuckles away to himself, takes out his notebook, wets the stump of a pencil between his lips, and writes away.*)

SHUI TA (*slowly*). Not a bad idea.

POLICEMAN. "What . . . *respectable* . . . man . . . with small capital . . . widower . . . not excluded . . . desires . . . marriage . . . into flourishing . . . tobacco shop?" And now let's add: "Am . . . pretty . . ." No! . . . "Prepossessing appearance."

SHUI TA. If you don't think that's an exaggeration?

OLD WOMAN. Oh, not a bit. I've seen her.

The POLICEMAN *tears the page out of his notebook, and hands it over to* SHUI TA.

SHUI TA *(with horror in his voice)*. How much luck we need to keep our heads above water! How many ideas! How many friends! *(To the* POLICEMAN.*)* Thank you, sir. I think I see my way clear.

3

Evening in the municipal park. Noise of a plane overhead. YANG SUN, *a young man in rags, is following the plane with his eyes: one can tell that the machine is describing a curve above the park.* YANG SUN *then takes a rope out of his pocket, looking anxiously about him as he does so. He moves toward a large willow. Enter two prostitutes, one old, the other the* NIECE *whom we have already met.*

NIECE. Hello. Coming with me?

YANG SUN *(taken aback)*. If you'd like to buy me a dinner.

OLD WHORE. Buy you a dinner! *(To the* NIECE.*)* Oh, we know him — it's the unemployed pilot. Waste no time on him!

NIECE. But he's the only man left in the park. And it's going to rain.

OLD WHORE. Oh, how do you know?

And they pass by. YANG SUN *again looks about him, again takes his rope, and this time throws it round a branch of the willow tree. Again he is interrupted. It is the two prostitutes returning — and in such a hurry they don't notice him.*

NIECE. It's going to pour!

Enter SHEN TE.

OLD WHORE. There's that *gorgon* Shen Te! That *drove* your family out into the cold!

NIECE. It wasn't her. It was that cousin of hers. She offered to pay for the cakes. I've nothing against her.

OLD WHORE. I have, though. *(So that* SHEN TE *can hear.)* Now where could the little lady be off to? She may be rich now but that won't stop her snatching our young men, will it?

SHEN TE. I'm going to the tearoom by the pond.

NIECE. Is it true what they say? You're marrying a widower — with three children?

The Good Woman of Setzuan

SHEN TE. Yes. I'm just going to see him.

YANG SUN (*his patience at breaking point*). Move on there! This is a park, not a whorehouse!

OLD WHORE. Shut your mouth!

But the two prostitutes leave.

YANG SUN. Even in the farthest corner of the park, even when it's raining, you can't get rid of them! (*He spits.*)

SHEN TE (*overhearing this*). And what right have you to scold them? (*But at this point she sees the rope.*) Oh!

YANG SUN. Well, what are you staring at?

SHEN TE. That rope. What is it for?

YANG SUN. Think! Think! I haven't a penny. Even if I had, I wouldn't spend it on you. I'd buy a drink of water.

The rain starts.

SHEN TE (*still looking at the rope*). What is the rope for? You mustn't!

YANG SUN. What's it to you? Clear out!

SHEN TE (*irrelevantly*). It's raining.

YANG SUN. Well, don't try to come under this tree.

SHEN TE. Oh, no. (*She stays in the rain.*)

YANG SUN. Now go away. (*Pause.*) For one thing, I don't like your looks, you're bowlegged.

SHEN TE (*indignantly*). That's not true!

YANG SUN. Well, don't show 'em to me. Look, it's raining. You better come under this tree.

Slowly, she takes shelter under the tree.

SHEN TE. Why did you want to do it?

YANG SUN. You really want to know? (*Pause.*) To get rid of you! (*Pause.*) You know what a flyer is?

SHEN TE. Oh yes, I've met a lot of pilots. At the tearoom.

YANG SUN. You call *them* flyers? Think they know what a machine is? Just 'cause they have leather helmets? They gave the airfield director a bribe, that's the way *those* fellows got up in the air! Try one of them out sometime. "Go up to two thousand feet," tell him, "then let it fall, then pick it up again with a flick of the wrist at the last moment." Know what he'll say to that? "It's not in my contract." Then again, there's the landing problem. It's like landing on your own backside. It's no different, planes are human. Those fools don't understand. (*Pause.*) And I'm the biggest fool for reading the book on flying in the Peking school and skipping the page where it says: "We've got enough flyers and we don't need you." I'm a mail pilot with no mail. You understand that?

SHEN TE (*shyly*). Yes. I do.

YANG SUN. No, you don't. You'd never understand that.

SHEN TE. When we were little we had a crane with a broken wing. He made friends with us and was very good-natured about our jokes. He would strut along behind us and call out to stop us going too fast for him. But every spring and autumn when the cranes flew over the villages in great swarms, he got quite restless. (*Pause.*) I understand that. (*She bursts out crying.*)

YANG SUN. Don't!

SHEN TE (*quieting down*). No.

YANG SUN. It's bad for the complexion.

SHEN TE (*sniffing*). I've stopped.

She dries her tears on her big sleeve. Leaning against the tree, but not looking at her, he reaches for her face.

YANG SUN. You can't even wipe your own face. (*He is wiping it for her with his handkerchief. Pause.*)

SHEN TE (*still sobbing*). I don't know *anything*!

YANG SUN. You interrupted me! What for?

SHEN TE. It's such a rainy day. You only wanted to do . . . *that* because it's such a rainy day.

(*To the audience.*)

>In our country
>The evenings should never be somber
>High bridges over rivers
>The grey hour between night and morning
>And the long, long winter:
>Such things are dangerous
>For, with all the misery,
>A very little is enough
>And men throw away an unbearable life.

Pause.

YANG SUN. Talk about yourself for a change.

SHEN TE. What about me? I have a shop.

YANG SUN (*incredulous*). You have a shop, have you? Never thought of walking the streets?

SHEN TE. I did walk the streets. Now I have a shop.

YANG SUN (*ironically*). A gift of the gods, I suppose!

SHEN TE. How did you know?

YANG SUN (*even more ironical*). One fine evening the gods turned up saying: here's some money!

SHEN TE (*quickly*). One fine morning.

YANG SUN (*fed up*). This isn't much of an entertainment.

Pause.

SHEN TE. I can play the zither a little. (*Pause.*) And I can mimic men. (*Pause.*) I got the shop, so the first thing I did was to give my zither away. I can be as stupid as a fish now, I said to myself, and it won't matter.

>I'm rich now, I said
>I walk alone, I sleep alone
>For a whole year, I said
>I'll have nothing to do with a man.

YANG SUN. And now you're marrying one! The one at the tearoom by the pond?

SHEN TE *is silent.*

YANG SUN. What do you know about love?

SHEN TE. Everything.

YANG SUN. Nothing. (*Pause.*) Or d'you just mean you enjoyed it?

SHEN TE. No.

YANG SUN (*again without turning to look at her, he strokes her cheek with his hand*). You like that?

SHEN TE. Yes.

YANG SUN (*breaking off*). You're easily satisfied, I must say. (*Pause.*) What a town!

SHEN TE. You have no friends?

YANG SUN (*defensively*). Yes, I have! (*Change of tone.*) But they don't want to hear I'm still unemployed. "What?" they ask. "Is there still water in the sea?" You have friends?

SHEN TE (*hesitating*). Just a . . . cousin.

YANG SUN. Watch him carefully.

SHEN TE. He only came once. Then he went away. He won't be back. (YANG SUN *is looking away.*) But to be without hope, they say, is to be without goodness!

Pause.

YANG SUN. Go on talking. A voice is a voice.

SHEN TE. Once, when I was a little girl, I fell, with a load of brushwood. An old man picked me up. He gave me a penny too. Isn't it funny how people who don't have very much like to give some of it away? They must like to show what they can do, and how could they show it better than by being kind? Being wicked is just like being clumsy. When we sing a song, or build a machine, or plant some rice, we're being kind. You're kind.

YANG SUN. You make it sound easy.

SHEN TE. Oh, no. (*Little pause.*) Oh! A drop of rain!

YANG SUN. Where'd you feel it?

SHEN TE. Between the eyes.

YANG SUN. Near the right eye? Or the left?

SHEN TE. Near the left eye.

YANG SUN. Oh, good. (*He is getting sleepy.*) So you're through with men, eh?

SHEN TE (*with a smile*). But I'm not bowlegged.

YANG SUN. Perhaps not.

SHEN TE. Definitely not.

Pause.

YANG SUN (*leaning wearily against the willow*). I haven't had a drop to drink all day, I haven't eaten anything for *two* days. I couldn't love you if I tried.

Pause.

SHEN TE. I like it in the rain.
Enter WONG *the Water Seller, singing.*

THE SONG OF THE WATER SELLER IN THE RAIN

"Buy my water," I am yelling
And my fury restraining
For no water I'm selling
'Cause it's raining, 'cause it's raining!
   I keep yelling: "Buy my water!"
   But no one's buying
   Athirst and dying
   And drinking and paying!
   Buy water!
   Buy water, you dogs!

Nice to dream of lovely weather!
Think of all the consternation
Were there no precipitation
Half a dozen years together!
   Can't you hear them shrieking. "Water!"
   Pretending they adore me?
   They all would go down on their knees before me!
   Down on your knees!
   Go down on your knees, you dogs!

What are lawns and hedges thinking?
What are fields and forests saying?
"At the cloud's breast we are drinking!
And we've no idea who's paying!"
   I keep yelling: "Buy my water!"
   But no one's buying
   Arthirst and dying
   And drinking and paying!
   Buy water!
   Buy water, you dogs!

The rain has stopped now. SHEN TE *sees* WONG *and runs toward him.*
SHEN TE. Wong! You're back! Your carrying pole's at the shop.
WONG. Oh, thank you, Shen Te. And how is life treating *you?*
SHEN TE. I've just met a brave and clever man. And I want to buy him a cup of your water.
WONG (*bitterly*). Throw back your head and open your mouth and you'll have all the water you need —

The Good Woman of Setzuan   555

    SHEN TE (*tenderly*).
        I want *your* water, Wong
        The water that has tired you so
        The water that you carried all this way
        The water that is hard to sell because it's been raining.

        I need it for the young man over there — he's a flyer!

        A flyer is a bold man:
        Braving the storms
        In company with the clouds
        He crosses the heavens
        And brings to friends in far-away lands
        The friendly mail!
    She pays WONG, *and runs over to* YANG SUN *with the cup. But* YANG SUN *is fast asleep.*
    SHEN TE (*calling to* WONG, *with a laugh*). He's fallen asleep! Despair and rain and I have worn him out!

— 3a —

    WONG'S *den. The sewer pipe is transparent, and the* GODS *again appear to* WONG *in a dream.*
    WONG (*radiant*). I've seen her, illustrious ones! And she hasn't changed!
    FIRST GOD. That's good to hear.
    WONG. She loves someone.
    FIRST GOD. Let's hope the experience gives her the strength to stay good!
    WONG. It does. She's doing good deeds all the time.
    FIRST GOD. Ah? What sort? What sort of good deeds, Wong?
    WONG. Well, she has a kind word for everybody.
    FIRST GOD (*eagerly*). And then?
    WONG. Hardly anyone leaves her shop without tobacco in his pocket — even if he can't pay for it.
    FIRST GOD. Not bad at all. Next?
    WONG. She's putting up a family of eight.
    FIRST GOD (*gleefully, to the* SECOND GOD). Eight! (*To* WONG.) And that's not all, of course!
    WONG. She bought a cup of water from me even though it was raining.
    FIRST GOD. Yes, yes, yes, all these smaller good deeds!
    WONG. Even they run into money. A little tobacco shop doesn't make so much.
    FIRST GOD (*sententiously*). A prudent gardener works miracles on the smallest plot.
    WONG. She hands out rice every morning. That eats up half her earnings.

FIRST GOD (*a little disappointed*). Well, as a beginning...

WONG. They call her the Angel of the Slums — whatever the Carpenter may say!

FIRST GOD. What's this? A carpenter speaks ill of her?

WONG. Oh, he only says her shelves weren't paid for in full.

SECOND GOD (*who has a bad cold and can't pronounce his n's and m's*). What's this? Not paying a carpenter? Why was that?

WONG. I suppose she didn't have the money.

SECOND GOD (*severely*). One pays what one owes, that's in our book of rules! First the letter of the law, then the spirit!

WONG. But it wasn't Shen Te, illustrious ones, it was her cousin. She called *him* in to help.

SECOND GOD. Then her cousin must never darken her threshold again!

WONG. Very well, illustrious ones! But in fairness to Shen Te, let me say that her cousin is a businessman.

FIRST GOD. Perhaps we should enquire what is customary? I find business quite unintelligible. But everybody's doing it. Business! Did the Seven Good Kings do business? Did Kung the Just sell fish?

SECOND GOD. In any case, such a thing must not occur again!

The GODS *start to leave.*

THIRD GOD. Forgive us for taking this tone with you, Wong, we haven't been getting enough sleep. The rich recommend us to the poor, and the poor tell us they haven't enough room.

SECOND GOD. Feeble, feeble, the best of them!

FIRST GOD. No great deeds! No heroic daring!

THIRD GOD. On such a *small* scale!

SECOND GOD. Sincere, yes, but what is actually *achieved*?

One can no longer hear them.

WONG (*calling after them*). I've thought of something, illustrious ones: Perhaps you shouldn't ask — too — much — all — at — once!

4

The square in front of SHEN TE'S *tobacco shop. Besides* SHEN TE'S *place, two other shops are seen: the carpet shop and a barber's. Morning. Outside* SHEN TE'S *the* GRANDFATHER, *the* SISTER-IN-LAW, *the* UNEMPLOYED MAN, *and* MRS. SHIN *stand waiting.*

SISTER-IN-LAW. She's been out all night again.

MRS. SHIN. No sooner did we get rid of that crazy cousin of hers than Shen Te herself starts carrying on! Maybe she does give us an ounce of rice now and then, but can you depend on her? Can you depend on her?

Loud voices from the Barber's.

VOICE OF SHU FU. What are you doing in my shop? Get out — at once!
VOICE OF WONG. But sir. They all let me sell...

WONG comes staggering out of the Barber's shop pursued by MR. SHU FU, *the Barber, a fat man carrying a heavy curling iron.*

SHU FU. Get out, I said! Pestering my customers with your slimy old water! Get out! Take your cup!

He holds out the cup. WONG *reaches out for it.* MR. SHU FU *strikes his hand with the curling iron, which is hot.* WONG *howls.*

SHU FU. You had it coming, my man!

Puffing, he returns to his shop. The UNEMPLOYED MAN *picks up the cup and gives it to* WONG.

UNEMPLOYED MAN. You can report that to the police.
WONG. My hand! It's smashed up!
UNEMPLOYED MAN. Any bones broken?
WONG. I can't move my fingers.
UNEMPLOYED MAN. Sit down. I'll put some water on it.
WONG *sits.*
MRS. SHIN. The water won't cost you anything.
SISTER-IN-LAW. You might have got a bandage from Miss Shen Te till she took to staying out all night. It's a scandal.
MRS. SHIN (*despondently*). If you ask me, she's forgotten we ever existed!

Enter SHEN TE *down the street, with a dish of rice.*

SHEN TE (*to the audience*). How wonderful to see Setzuan in the early morning! I always used to stay in bed with my dirty blanket over my head afraid to wake up. This morning I saw the newspapers being delivered by little boys, the streets being washed by strong men, and fresh vegetables coming in from the country on ox carts. It's a long walk from where Yang Sun lives, but I feel lighter at every step. They say you walk on air when you're in love, but it's even better walking on the rough earth, on the hard cement. In the early morning, the old city looks like a great heap of rubbish! Nice, though, with all its little lights. And the sky, so pink, so transparent, before the dust comes and muddies it! What a lot you miss if you never see your city rising from its slumbers like an honest old craftsman pumping his lungs full of air and reaching for his tools, as the poet says! (*Cheerfully, to her waiting guests.*) Good morning, everyone, here's your rice! (*Distributing the rice, she comes upon* WONG.) Good morning, Wong. I'm quite lightheaded today. On my way over, I looked at myself in all the shop windows. I'd love to be beautiful.

She slips into the carpet shop. MR. SHU FU *has just emerged from his shop.*

SHU FU (*to the audience*). It surprises me how beautiful Miss Shen Te is looking today! I never gave her a passing thought before. But now I've been gazing upon her comely form for exactly three minutes! I begin to suspect I am in love with her. She is overpoweringly attractive! (*Crossly, to* WONG.) Be off with you, rascal!

He returns to his shop. SHEN TE *comes back out of the carpet shop with the* OLD MAN, *its proprietor, and his wife — whom we have already met — the* OLD WOMAN. SHEN TE *is wearing a shawl. The* OLD MAN *is holding up a looking glass for her.*

OLD WOMAN. Isn't it lovely? We'll give you a reduction because there's a little hole in it.

SHEN TE (*looking at another shawl on the* OLD WOMAN's *arm*). The other one's nice too.

OLD WOMAN (*smiling*). Too bad there's no hole in that!

SHEN TE. That's right. My shop doesn't make very much.

OLD WOMAN. And your good deeds eat it all up! Be more careful, my dear....

SHEN TE (*trying on the shawl with the hole*). Just now, I'm light-headed! Does the color suit me?

OLD WOMAN. You'd better ask a man.

SHEN TE. (*to the* OLD MAN). Does the color suit me?

OLD MAN. You'd better ask your young friend.

SHEN TE. I'd like to have your opinion.

OLD MAN. It suits you very well. But wear it this way: the dull side out.

SHEN TE *pays up.*

OLD WOMAN. If you decide you don't like it, you can exchange it. (*She pulls* SHEN TE *to one side.*) Has he got money?

SHEN TE (*with a laugh*). Yang Sun? Oh, no.

OLD WOMAN. Then how're you going to pay your rent?

SHEN TE. I'd forgotten about that.

OLD WOMAN. And next Monday is the first of the month! Miss Shen Te, I've got something to say to you. After we (*indicating her husband*) got to know you, we had our doubts about that marriage ad. We thought it would be better if you'd let *us* help you. Out of our savings. We reckon we could lend you two hundred silver dollars. We don't need anything in writing — you could pledge us your tobacco stock.

SHEN TE. You're prepared to lend money to a person like me?

OLD WOMAN. It's folks like you that need it. We'd think twice about lending anything to your cousin.

OLD MAN (*coming up*). All settled, my dear?

SHEN TE. I wish the gods could have heard what your wife was just saying, Mr. Ma. They're looking for good people who're happy — and helping me makes you happy because you know it was love that got me into difficulties!

The OLD COUPLE *smile knowingly at each other.*

OLD MAN. And here's the money, Miss Shen Te.

He hands her an envelope. SHEN TE *takes it. She bows. They bow back. They return to their shop.*

SHEN TE (*holding up her envelope*). Look, Wong, here's six months' rent! Don't you believe in miracles now? And how do you like my new shawl?

WONG. For the young fellow I saw you with in the park?

The Good Woman of Setzuan

SHEN TE *nods*.

MRS. SHIN. Never mind all that. It's time you took a look at his hand!

SHEN TE. Have you hurt your hand?

MRS. SHIN. That barber smashed it with his hot curling iron. Right in front of our eyes.

SHEN TE (*shocked at herself*). And I never noticed! We must get you to a doctor this minute or who knows what will happen?

UNEMPLOYED MAN. It's not a doctor he should see, it's a judge. He can ask for compensation. The barber's filthy rich.

WONG. You think I have a chance?

MRS. SHIN (*with relish*). If it's really good and smashed. But is it?

WONG. I think so. It's very swollen. Could I get a pension?

MRS. SHIN. You'd need a witness.

WONG. Well, you all saw it. You could all testify.

He looks round. The UNEMPLOYED MAN, *the* GRANDFATHER, *and the* SISTER-IN-LAW *are all sitting against the wall of the shop eating rice. Their concentration on eating is complete.*

SHEN TE (*to* MRS. SHIN). You saw it yourself.

MRS. SHIN. I want nothing to do with the police. It's against my principles.

SHEN TE (*to* SISTER-IN-LAW). What about you?

SISTER-IN-LAW. Me? I wasn't looking.

SHEN TE (*to the* GRANDFATHER, *coaxingly*). Grandfather, *you'll* testify, won't you?

SISTER-IN-LAW. And a lot of good that will do. He's simple-minded.

SHEN TE (*to the* UNEMPLOYED MAN). You seem to be the only witness left.

UNEMPLOYED MAN. My testimony would only hurt him. I've been picked up twice for begging.

SHEN TE.
    Your brother is assaulted, and you shut your eyes?
    He is hit, cries out in pain, and you are silent?
    The beast prowls, chooses and seizes his victim, and you say:
    "Because we showed no displeasure, he has spared us."
If no one present will be a witness, I will. I'll say *I* saw it.

MRS. SHIN (*solemnly*). The name for that is perjury.

WONG. I don't know if I can accept that. Though maybe I'll have to. (*Looking at his hand.*) Is it swollen enough, do you think? The swelling's not going down?

UNEMPLOYED MAN. No, no, the swelling's holding up well.

WONG. Yes. It's *more* swollen if anything. Maybe my wrist is broken after all. I'd better see a judge at once.

Holding his hand very carefully, and fixing his eyes on it, he runs off. MRS. SHIN *goes quickly into the Barber's shop.*

UNEMPLOYED MAN (*seeing her*). She is getting on the right side of Mr. Shu Fu.

SISTER-IN-LAW. You and I can't change the world, Shen Te.

SHEN TE. Go away! Go away all of you!

The UNEMPLOYED MAN, *the* SISTER-IN-LAW, *and the* GRANDFATHER *stalk off, eating and sulking.*

(*To the audience.*)
>They've stopped answering
>They stay put
>They do as they're told
>They don't care
>Nothing can make them look up
>But the smell of food.

Enter MRS. YANG, YANG SUN's *mother, out of breath.*

MRS. YANG. Miss. Shen Te. My son has told me everything. I am Mrs. Yang, Sun's mother. Just think. He's got an offer. Of a job as a pilot. A letter has just come. From the director of the airfield in Peking!

SHEN TE. So he can fly again? Isn't that wonderful!

MRS. YANG (*less breathlessly all the time*). They won't give him the job for nothing. They want five hundred silver dollars.

SHEN TE. We can't let money stand in his way, Mrs. Yang!

MRS. YANG. If only you could help him out!

SHEN TE. I have the shop. I can try! (*She embraces* MRS. YANG.) I happen to have two hundred with me now. Take it. (*She gives her the* OLD COUPLE's *money.*) It was a loan but they said I could repay it with my tobacco stock.

MRS. YANG. And they were calling Sun the Dead Pilot of Setzuan! A friend in need!

SHEN TE. We must find another three hundred.

MRS. YANG. How?

SHEN TE. Let me think. (*Slowly.*) I know someone who can help. I didn't want to call on his services again, he's hard and cunning. But a flyer must fly. And I'll make this the last time.

Distant sound of a plane.

MRS. YANG. If the man you mentioned can do it. . . . Oh, look, there's the morning mail plane, heading for Peking!

SHEN TE. The pilot can see us, let's wave!

They wave. The noise of the engine is louder.

MRS. YANG. You know that pilot up there?

SHEN TE. Wave, Mrs. Yang! I know the pilot who will be up there. He gave up hope. But he'll do it now. One man to raise himself above the misery, above us all.

(*To the audience.*)
>Yang Sun, my lover:
>Braving the storms
>In company with the clouds
>Crossing the heavens

And bringing to friends in far-away lands
The friendly mail!

— 4a —

In front of the inner curtain. Enter SHEN TE, *carrying* SHUI TA'S *mask. She sings.*

THE SONG OF DEFENSELESSNESS

In our country
A useful man needs luck
Only if he finds strong backers
Can he prove himself useful.
The good can't defend themselves and
Even the gods are defenseless.

Oh, why don't the gods have their own ammunition
And launch against badness their own expedition
Enthroning the good and preventing sedition
And bringing the world to a peaceful condition?

Oh, why don't the gods do the buying and selling
Injustice forbidding, starvation dispelling
Give bread to each city and joy to each dwelling?
Oh, why don't the gods do the buying and selling?

She puts on SHUI TA'S *mask and sings in his voice.*

You can only help one of your luckless brothers
By trampling down a dozen others.

Why is it the gods do not feel indignation
And come down in fury to end exploitation
Defeat all defeat and forbid desperation
Refusing to tolerate such toleration?

Why is it?

5

SHEN TE's *tobacco shop. Behind the counter,* MR. SHUI TA, *reading the paper.* MRS. SHIN *is cleaning up. She talks and he takes no notice.*

MRS. SHIN. And when certain rumors get about, what *happens* to a little place like this? It goes to pot. *I* know. So, if you want my advice, Mr. Shui Ta, find out just what has been going on between Miss Shen Te and that Yang Sun from Yellow Street. And remember: a certain interest in Miss Shen Te has been expressed by the barber next door, a man with twelve houses and only one wife, who, for that matter, is likely to drop off at any time. A certain interest has been expressed. He was even enquiring about her means and, if *that* doesn't prove a man is getting serious, what would? (*Still getting no response, she leaves with her bucket*).

YANG SUN'S VOICE. Is that Miss Shen Te's tobacco shop?

MRS. SHIN'S VOICE. Yes, it is, but it's Mr. Shui Ta who's here today.

SHUI TA *runs to the mirror with the short, light steps of* SHEN TE, *and is just about to start primping, when he realizes his mistake, and turns away, with a short laugh. Enter* YANG SUN. MRS. SHIN *enters behind him and slips into the back room to eavesdrop.*

YANG SUN. I am Yang Sun. (SHUI TA *bows.*) Is Shen Te in?

SHUI TA. No.

YANG SUN. I guess you know our relationship? (*He is inspecting the stock.*) Quite a place! And I thought she was just talking big. I'll be flying again, all right. (*He takes a cigar, solicits and receives a light from* SHUI TA.) You think we can squeeze the other three hundred out of the tobacco stock?

SHUI TA. May I ask if it is your intention to sell at once?

YANG SUN. It was decent of her to come out with the two hundred but they aren't much use with the other three hundred still missing.

SHUI TA. Shen Te was overhasty promising so much. She might have to sell the shop itself to raise it. Haste, they say, is the wind that blows the house down.

YANG SUN. Oh, she isn't a girl to keep a man waiting. For one thing or the other, if you take my meaning.

SHUI TA. I take your meaning.

YANG SUN (*leering*). Uh, huh.

SHUI TA. Would you explain what the five hundred silver dollars are for?

YANG SUN. Want to sound me out? Very well. The director of the Peking airfield is a friend of mine from flying school. I give him five hundred: he gets me the job.

SHUI TA. The price is high.

The Good Woman of Setzuan

YANG SUN. Not as these things go. He'll have to fire one of the present pilots — for negligence. Only the man he has in mind isn't negligent. Not easy, you understand. You needn't mention that part of it to Shen Te.

SHUI TA (*looking intently at* YANG SUN). Mr. Yang Sun, you are asking my cousin to give up her possessions, leave her friends, and place her entire fate in your hands. I presume you intend to marry her?

YANG SUN. I'd be prepared to.

Slight pause.

SHUI TA. Those two hundred silver dollars would pay the rent here for six months. If you were Shen Te wouldn't you be tempted to continue in business?

YANG SUN. What? Can you imagine Yang Sun the Flyer behind a counter? (*In an oily voice.*) "A strong cigar or a mild one, worthy sir?" Not in this century!

SHUI TA. My cousin wishes to follow the promptings of her heart, and, from her own point of view, she may even have what is called the right to love. Accordingly, she has commissioned me to help you to this post. There is nothing here that I am not empowered to turn immediately into cash. Mrs. Mi Tzu, the landlady, will advise me about the sale.

Enter MRS. MI TZU.

MRS. MI TZU. Good morning, Mr. Shui Ta, you wish to see me about the rent? As you know it falls due the day after tomorrow.

SHUI TA. Circumstances have changed, Mrs. Mi Tzu: my cousin is getting married. Her future husband here, Mr. Yang Sun, will be taking her to Peking. I am interested in selling the tobacco stock.

MRS. MI TZU. How much are you asking, Mr. Shui Ta?

YANG SUN. Three hundred sil —

SHUI TA. Five hundred silver dollars.

MRS. MI TZU. How much did she pay for it, Mr. Shui Ta?

SHUI TA. A thousand. And very little has been sold.

MRS. MI TZU. She was robbed. But I'll make you a special offer if you'll promise to be out by the day after tomorrow. Three hundred silver dollars.

YANG SUN (*shrugging*). Take it, man, take it.

SHUI TA. It is not enough.

YANG SUN. Why not? Why not? Certainly, it's enough.

SHUI TA. Five hundred silver dollars.

YANG SUN. But why? We only need three!

SHUI TA (*to* MRS. MI TZU). Excuse me. (*Takes* YANG SUN *on one side.*) The tobacco stock is pledged to the old couple who gave my cousin the two hundred.

YANG SUN. Is it in writing?

SHUI TA. No.

YANG SUN (*to* MRS. MI TZU). Three hundred will do.

MRS. MI TZU. Of course, I need an assurance that Miss Shen Te is not in debt.

YANG SUN. Mr. Shui Ta?

SHUI TA. She is not in debt.

YANG SUN. When can you let us have the money?

MRS. MI TZU. The day after tomorrow. And remember: I'm doing this because I have a soft spot in my heart for young lovers! (*Exit.*)

YANG SUN (*calling after her*). Boxes, jars and sacks — three hundred for the lot and the pain's over! (*To* SHUI TA.) Where else can we raise money by the day after tomorrow?

SHUI TA. Nowhere. Haven't you enough for the trip and the first few weeks?

YANG SUN. Oh, certainly.

SHUI TA. How much, exactly?

YANG SUN. Oh, I'll dig it up, even if I have to steal it.

SHUI TA. I see.

YANG SUN. Well, don't fall off the roof. I'll get to Peking somehow.

SHUI TA. Two people can't travel for nothing.

YANG SUN (*not giving* SHUI TA *a chance to answer*). I'm leaving *her* behind. No millstones round *my* neck!

SHUI TA. Oh.

YANG SUN. Don't look at me like that!

SHUI TA. How precisely is my cousin to live?

YANG SUN. Oh, you'll think of something.

SHUI TA. A small request, Mr. Yang Sun. Leave the the two hundred silver dollars here until you can show me two tickets for Peking.

YANG SUN. You learn to mind your own business, Mr. Shui Ta.

SHUI TA. I'm afraid Miss Shen Te may not wish to sell the shop when she discovers that . . .

YANG SUN. You don't know women. She'll want to. Even then.

SHUI TA (*a slight outburst*). She is a human being, sir! And not devoid of common sense!

YANG SUN. Shen Te is a woman: she *is* devoid of common sense. I only have to lay my hand on her shoulder, and church bells ring.

SHUI TA (*with difficulty*). Mr. Yang Sun!

YANG SUN. Mr. Shui Whatever-it-is!

SHUI TA. My cousin is devoted to you . . . because . . .

YANG SUN. Because I have my hands on her breasts. Give me a cigar. (*He takes one for himself, stuffs a few more in his pocket, then changes his mind and takes the whole box.*) Tell her I'll marry her, then bring me the three hundred. Or let her bring it. One or the other. (*Exit.*)

MRS. SHIN (*sticking her head out of the back room*). Well, he has your cousin under his thumb, and doesn't care if all Yellow Street knows it!

SHUI TA (*crying out*). I've lost my shop! And he doesn't love me! (*He

The Good Woman of Setzuan

runs berserk through the room, repeating these lines incoherently. Then stops suddenly, and addresses MRS. SHIN.) Mrs. Shin, you grew up in the gutter, like me. Are we lacking in hardness? I doubt it. If you steal a penny from me, I'll take you by the throat till you spit it out! You'd do the same to me. The times are bad, this city is hell, but we're like ants, we keep coming, up and up the walls, however smooth! Till bad luck comes. Being in love, for instance. One weakness is enough, and love is the deadliest.

MRS. SHIN (*emerging from the back room*). You should have a little talk with Mr. Shu Fu the Barber. He's a real gentleman and just the thing for your cousin. (*She runs off.*)

SHUI TA.
        A caress becomes a stranglehold
        A sigh of love turns to a cry of fear
        Why are there vultures circling in the air?
        A girl is going to meet her lover.

SHUI TA *sits down and* MR. SHU FU *enters with* MRS. SHIN.

SHUI TA. Mr. Shu Fu?

SHU FU. Mr. Shui Ta.

They both bow.

SHUI TA. I am told that you have expressed a certain interest in my cousin Shen Te. Let me set aside all propriety and confess: she is at this moment in grave danger.

SHU FU. Oh, dear!

SHUI TA. She has lost her shop, Mr. Shu Fu.

SHU FU. The charm of Miss Shen Te, Mr. Shui Ta, derives from the goodness, not of her shop, but of her heart. Men call her the Angel of the Slums.

SHUI TA. Yet her goodness has cost her two hundred silver dollars in a single day: we must put a stop to it.

SHU FU. Permit me to differ, Mr. Shui Ta. Let us, rather, open wide the gates to such goodness! Every morning, with pleasure tinged by affection, I watch her charitable ministrations. For they are hungry, and she giveth them to eat! Four of them, to be precise. Why only four? I ask. Why not four hundred? I hear she has been seeking shelter for the homeless. What about my humble cabins behind the cattle run? They are at her disposal. And so forth. And so on. Mr. Shui Ta, do you think Miss Shen Te could be persuaded to listen to certain ideas of mine? Ideas like these?

SHUI TA. Mr. Shu Fu, she would be honored.

Enter WONG *and the* POLICEMAN. MR. SHU FU *turns abruptly away and studies the shelves.*

WONG. Is Miss Shen Te here?

SHUI TA. No.

WONG. I am Wong the Water Seller. You are Mr. Shui Ta?

SHUI TA. I am.

WONG. I am a friend of Shen Te's.

SHUI TA. An intimate friend, I hear.

WONG (*to the* POLICEMAN). You see? (*To* SHUI TA.) It's because of my hand.

POLICEMAN. He hurt his hand, sir, that's a fact.

SHUI TA (*quickly*). You need a sling, I see. (*He takes a shawl from the back room, and throws it to* WONG.)

WONG. But that's her new shawl!

SHUI TA. She has no more use for it.

WONG. But she bought it to please someone!

SHUI TA. It happens to be no longer necessary.

WONG (*making the sling*). She is my only witness.

POLICEMAN. Mr. Shui Ta, your cousin is supposed to have seen the Barber hit the Water Seller with a curling iron.

SHUI TA. I'm afraid my cousin was not present at the time.

WONG. But she was, sir! Just ask her! Isn't she in?

SHUI TA (*gravely*). Mr. Wong, my cousin has her own troubles. You wouldn't wish her to add to them by committing perjury?

WONG. But it was she that told me to go to the judge!

SHUI TA. Was the judge supposed to heal your hand?

MR. SHU FU *turns quickly around.* SHUI TA *bows to* SHU FU, *and vice versa.*

WONG (*taking the sling off, and putting it back*). I see how it is.

POLICEMAN. Well, I'll be on my way. (*To* WONG.) And you be careful. If Mr. Shu Fu wasn't a man who tempers justice with mercy, as the saying is, you'd be in jail for libel. Be off with you!

Exit WONG, *followed by* POLICEMAN.

SHUI TA. Profound apologies, Mr. Shu Fu.

SHU FU. Not at all, Mr. Shui Ta. (*Pointing to the shawl.*) The episode is over?

SHUI TA. It may take her time to recover. There are some fresh wounds.

SHU FU. We shall be discreet. Delicate. A short vacation could be arranged....

SHUI TA. First of course, you and she would have to talk things over.

MR. SHU FU. At a small supper in a small, but high-class, restaurant.

SHUI TA. I'll go and find her. (*Exit into back room.*)

MRS. SHIN (*sticking her head in again*). Time for congratulations, Mr. Shu Fu?

SHU FU. Ah, Mrs. Shin! Please inform Miss Shen Te's guests they may take shelter in the cabins behind the cattle run!

MRS. SHIN *nods, grinning.*

SHU FU (*to the audience*). Well? What do you think of me, ladies and gentlemen? What could a man do more? Could he be less selfish? More farsighted? A small supper in a small but . . . Does that bring rather vulgar and clumsy thoughts into your mind? Ts, ts, ts. Nothing of the sort will occur. She won't even be touched. Not even accidentally while passing the salt. An exchange of ideas only. Over the flowers on the table — white

The Good Woman of Setzuan

chrysanthemums, by the way (*he writes down a note of this*) — yes, over the white chrysanthemums, two young souls will . . . shall I say "find each other"? We shall NOT exploit the misfortune of others. Understanding? Yes. An offer of assistance? Certainly. But quietly. Almost inaudibly. Perhaps with single glance. A glance that could also — mean more.

MRS. SHIN (*coming forward*). Everything under control, Mr. Shu Fu?

SHU FU. Oh, Mrs. Shin, what do you know about this worthless rascal Yang Sun?

MRS. SHIN. Why, he's the most worthless rascal . . .

SHU FU. Is he really? You're sure? (*As she opens her mouth.*) From now on, he doesn't exist! Can't be found anywhere!

Enter YANG SUN.

YANG SUN. What's been going on here?

MRS. SHIN. Shall I call Mr. Shui Ta, Mr. Shu Fu? He wouldn't want strangers in here!

SHU FU. Mr. Shui Ta is in conference with Miss Shen Te. Not to be disturbed!

YANG SUN. Shen Te here? I didn't see her come in. What kind of conference?

SHU FU (*not letting him enter the back room*). Patience, dear sir! And if by chance I have an inkling who you are, pray take note that Miss Shen Te and I are about to announce our engagement.

YANG SUN. What?

MRS. SHIN. You didn't expect that, did you?

YANG SUN *is trying to push past the barber into the back room when* SHEN TE *comes out.*

SHU FU. My dear Shen Te, ten thousand apologies! Perhaps you . . .

YANG SUN. What is it, Shen Te? Have you gone crazy?

SHEN TE (*breathless*). My cousin and Mr. Shu Fu have come to an understanding. They wish me to hear Mr. Shu Fu's plans for helping the poor.

YANG SUN. Your cousin wants to part us.

SHEN TE. Yes.

YANG SUN. And you've agreed to it?

SHEN TE. Yes.

YANG SUN. They told you I was bad. (SHEN TE *is silent.*) And suppose I am. Does that make me need you less? I'm low, Shen Te, I have no money, I don't do the right thing but at least I put up a fight! (*He is near her now, and speaks in an undertone.*) Have you no eyes? Look at him. Have you forgotten already?

SHEN TE. No.

YANG SUN. How it was raining?

SHEN TE. No.

YANG SUN. How you cut me down from the willow tree? Bought me water? Promised me money to fly with?

SHEN TE (*shakily*). Yang Sun, what do you want?

YANG SUN. I want you to come with me.

SHEN TE (*in a small voice*). Forgive me, Mr. Shu Fu, I want to go with Mr. Yang Sun.

YANG SUN. We're lovers you know. Give me the key to the shop. (SHEN TE *takes the key from around her neck.* YANG SUN *puts it on the counter. To* MRS. SHIN.) Leave it under the mat when you're through. Let's go, Shen Te.

SHU FU. But this is rape! Mr. Shui Ta! !

YANG SUN (*to* SHEN TE). Tell him not to shout.

SHEN TE. Please don't shout for my cousin, Mr. Shu Fu. He doesn't agree with me, I know, but he's wrong.

(*To the audience.*)

> I want to go with the man I love
> I don't want to count the cost
> I don't want to consider if it's wise
> I don't want to know if he loves me
> I want to go with the man I love.

YANG SUN. That's the spirit.

And the couple leave.

— 5a —

In front of the inner curtain. SHEN TE *in her wedding clothes, on the way to her wedding.*

SHEN TE. Something terrible has happened. As I left the shop with Yang Sun, I found the old carpet dealer's wife waiting on the street, trembling all over. She told me her husband had taken to his bed — sick with all the worry and excitement over the two hundred silver dollars they lent me. She said it would be best if I gave it back now. Of course, I had to say I would. She said she couldn't quite trust my cousin Shui Ta or even my fiancé Yang Sun. There were tears in her eyes. With my emotions in an uproar, I threw myself into Yang Sun's arms, I couldn't resist him. The things he'd said to Shui Ta had taught Shen Te nothing. Sinking into his arms, I said to myself:

> To let no one perish, not even oneself
> To fill everyone with happiness, even oneself
> Is so good

How could I have forgotten those two old people? Yang Sun swept me away like a small hurricane. But he's not a bad man, and he loves me. He'd rather work in the cement factory than owe his flying to a crime. Though, of course, flying *is* a great passion with Sun. Now, on the way to my wedding, I waver between fear and joy.

6

The "private dining room" on the upper floor of a cheap restaurant in a poor section of town. With SHEN TE: *the* GRANDFATHER, *the* SISTER-IN-LAW, *the* NIECE, MRS. SHIN, *the* UNEMPLOYED MAN. *In a corner, alone, a* PRIEST. *A* WAITER *pouring wine. Downstage,* YANG SUN *talking to his* MOTHER. *He wears a dinner jacket.*

YANG SUN. Bad news, Mamma. She came right out and told me she can't sell the shop for me. Some idiot is bringing a claim because he lent her the two hundred she gave you.

MRS. YANG. What did you say? Of course, you can't marry her now.

YANG SUN. It's no use saying anything to *her*. I've sent for her cousin, Mr. Shui Ta. He said there was nothing in writing.

MRS. YANG. Good idea. I'll go out and look for him. Keep an eye on things.

Exit MRS. YANG. SHEN TE *has been pouring wine.*

SHEN TE (*to the audience, pitcher in hand*). I wasn't mistaken in him. He's bearing up well. Though it must have been an awful blow — giving up flying. I do love him so. (*Calling across the room to him.*) Sun, you haven't drunk a toast with the bride!

YANG SUN. What do we drink to?

SHEN TE. Why, to the future!

YANG SUN. When the bridegroom's dinner jacket won't be a hired one!

SHEN TE. But when the bride's dress will still get rained on sometimes!

YANG SUN. To everything we ever wished for!

SHEN TE. May all our dreams come true!

They drink.

YANG SUN (*with loud conviviality*). And now, friends, before the wedding gets under way, I have to ask the bride a few questions. I've no idea what kind of a wife she'll make, and it worries me. (*Wheeling on* SHEN TE.) For example. Can you make five cups of tea with three tea leaves?

SHEN TE. No.

YANG SUN. So I won't be getting very much tea. Can you sleep on a straw mattress the size of that book? (*He points to the large volume the* PRIEST *is reading.*)

SHEN TE. The two of us?

YANG SUN. The one of you.

SHEN TE. In that case, no.

YANG SUN. What a wife! I'm shocked!

While the audience is laughing, his MOTHER *returns. With a shrug of her shoulders, she tells* SUN *the expected guest hasn't arrived. The* PRIEST *shuts the book with a bang, and makes for the door.*

MRS. YANG. Where are *you* off to? It's only a matter of minutes.

PRIEST (*watch in hand*). Time goes on, Mrs. Yang, and I've another wedding to attend to. Also a funeral.

MRS. YANG (*irately*). D'you think we planned it this way? I was hoping to manage with one pitcher of wine, and we've run through two already. (*Points to empty pitcher. Loudly.*) My dear Shen Te, I don't know where your cousin can be keeping himself!

SHEN TE. My cousin?!

MRS. YANG. Certainly. I'm old-fashioned enough to think such a close relative should attend the wedding.

SHEN TE. Oh, Sun, is it the three hundred silver dollars?

YANG SUN (*not looking her in the eye*). Are you deaf? Mother says she's old-fashioned. And I say I'm considerate. We'll wait another fifteen minutes.

HUSBAND. Another fifteen minutes.

MRS. YANG (*addressing the company*). Now you all know, don't you, that my son is getting a job as a mail pilot?

SISTER-IN-LAW. In Peking, too, isn't it?

MRS. YANG. In Peking, too! The two of us are moving to Peking!

SHEN TE. Sun, tell your mother Peking is out of the question now.

YANG SUN. Your cousin'll tell her. If he agrees. I don't agree.

SHEN TE (*amazed, and dismayed*). Sun!

YANG SUN. I hate this godforsaken Setzuan. What people! Know what they look like when I half close my eyes? Horses! Whinnying, fretting, stamping, screwing their necks up! (*Loudly.*) And what is it the thunder says? They are su-per-flu-ous! (*He hammers out the syllables.*) They've run their last race! They can go trample themselves to death! (*Pause.*) I've got to get out of here.

SHEN TE. But I've promised the money to the old couple.

YANG SUN. And since you always do the wrong thing, it's lucky your cousin's coming. Have another drink.

SHEN TE (*quietly*). My cousin can't be coming.

YANG SUN. How d'you mean?

SHEN TE. My cousin can't be where I am.

YANG SUN. Quite a conundrum!

SHEN TE (*desperately*). Sun, I'm the one that loves you. Not my cousin. He was thinking of the job in Peking when he promised you the old couple's money —

YANG SUN. Right. And that's why he's bringing the three hundred silver dollars. Here — to my wedding.

SHEN TE. He is not bringing the three hundred silver dollars.

YANG SUN. Huh? What makes you think that?

SHEN TE (*looking into his eyes*). He says you only bought one ticket to Peking.

Short pause.

YANG SUN. That was yesterday. (*He pulls two tickets part way out of his inside pocket, making her look under his coat.*) Two tickets. I don't want Mother to know. She'll get left behind. I sold her furniture to buy these tickets, so you see . . .

SHEN TE. But what's to become of the old couple?

YANG SUN. What's to become of me? Have another drink. Or do you believe in moderation? If I drink, I fly again. And if you drink, you may learn to understand me.

SHEN TE. You want to fly. But I can't help you.

YANG SUN. "Here's a plane, my darling — but it's only got one wing!"

The WAITER *enters.*

WAITER. Mrs. Yang!

MRS. YANG. Yes?

WAITER. Another pitcher of wine, ma'am?

MRS. YANG. We have enough, thanks. Drinking makes me sweat.

WAITER. Would you mind paying, ma'am?

MRS. YANG (*to everyone*). Just be patient a few moments longer, everyone, Mr. Shui Ta is on his way over! (*To the* WAITER.) Don't be a spoilsport.

WAITER. I can't let you leave till you've paid your bill, ma'am.

MRS. YANG. But they know me here!

WAITER. That's just it.

PRIEST (*ponderously getting up*). I humbly take my leave. (*And he does.*)

MRS. YANG (*to the others, desperately*). Stay where you are, everybody! The priest says he'll be back in two minutes!

YANG SUN. It's no good, Mamma. Ladies and gentlemen, Mr. Shui Ta still hasn't arrived and the priest has gone home. We won't detain you any longer.

They are leaving now.

GRANDFATHER (*in the doorway, having forgotten to put his glass down*). To the bride! (*He drinks, puts down the glass, and follows the others.*)

Pause.

SHEN TE. Shall I go too?

YANG SUN. You? Aren't you the bride? Isn't this your wedding? (*He drags her across the room, tearing her wedding dress.*) If we can wait, you can wait. Mother calls me her falcon. She wants to see me in the clouds. But I think it may be St. Nevercome's Day before she'll go to the door and see my plane thunder by. (*Pause. He pretends the guests are still present.*) Why such a lull in the conversation, ladies and gentlemen? Don't you like it here? The ceremony is only slightly postponed — because an important guest is expected at any moment. Also because the bride doesn't know what love is. While we're waiting, the bridegroom will sing a little song. (*He does so.*)

THE SONG OF ST. NEVERCOME'S DAY

On a certain day, as is generally known,
    One and all will be shouting: Hooray, hooray!
For the beggar maid's son has a solid-gold throne
    And the day is St. Nevercome's Day
On St. Nevercome's, Nevercome's, Nevercome's Day
    He'll sit on his solid-gold throne

Oh, hooray, hooray! That day goodness will pay!
    That day badness will cost you your head!
And merit and money will smile and be funny
    While exchanging salt and bread
On St. Nevercome's, Nevercome's, Nevercome's Day
    While exchanging salt and bread

And the grass, oh, the grass will look down at the sky
    And the pebbles will roll up the stream
And all men will be good without batting an eye
    They will make of our earth a dream
On St. Nevercome's, Nevercome's, Nevercome's Day
    They will make of our earth a dream

And as for me, that's the day I shall be
    A flyer and one of the best
Unemployed man, you will have work to do
    Washerwoman, you'll get your rest
On St. Nevercome's, Nevercome's, Nevercome's Day
    Washerwoman, you'll get your rest

MRS. YANG. It looks like he's not coming.
The three of them sit looking at the door.

— 6a —

WONG'S *den. The sewer pipe is again transparent and again the* GODS *appear to* WONG *in a dream.*

WONG. I'm so glad you've come, illustrious ones. It's Shen Te. She's in great trouble from following the rule about loving thy neighbor. Perhaps she's *too* good for this world!

The Good Woman of Setzuan

FIRST GOD. Nonsense! You are eaten up by lice and doubts!

WONG. Forgive me, illustrious one, I only meant you might deign to intervene.

FIRST GOD. Out of the question! My colleague here intervened in some squabble or other only yesterday. (*He points to the* THIRD GOD *who has a black eye.*) The results are before us!

WONG. She had to call on her cousin again. But not even he could help. I'm afraid the shop is done for.

THIRD GOD (*a little concerned*). Perhaps we should help after all?

FIRST GOD. The gods help those that help themselves.

WONG. What if we *can't* help ourselves, illustrious ones?

Slight pause.

SECOND GOD. Try, anyway! Suffering ennobles!

FIRST GOD. Our faith in Shen Te is unshaken!

THIRD GOD. We certainly haven't found any *other* good people. You can see where we spend our nights from the straw on our clothes.

WONG. You might help her find her way by —

FIRST GOD. The good man finds his own way here below!

SECOND GOD. The good woman too.

FIRST GOD. The heavier the burden, the greater her strength!

THIRD GOD. We're only onlookers, you know.

FIRST GOD. And everything will be all right in the end, O ye of little faith!

They are gradually disappearing through these last lines.

7

The yard behind SHEN TE'S *shop. A few articles of furniture on a cart.* SHEN TE *and* MRS. SHIN *are taking the washing off the line.*

MRS. SHIN. If you ask me, you should fight tooth and nail to keep the shop.

SHEN TE. How can I? I have to sell the tobacco to pay back the two hundred silver dollars today.

MRS. SHIN. No husband, no tobacco, no house and home! What are you going to live on?

SHEN TE. I can work. I can sort tobacco.

MRS. SHIN. Hey, look, Mr. Shui Ta's trousers! He must have left here stark naked!

SHEN TE. Oh, he may have another pair, Mrs. Shin.

MRS. SHIN. But if he's gone for good as you say, why has he left his pants behind?

SHEN TE. Maybe he's thrown them away.

MRS. SHIN. Can I take them?

SHEN TE. Oh, no.

Enter MR. SHU FU, *running*.

SHU FU. Not a word! Total silence! I know all. You have sacrificed your own love and happiness so as not to hurt a dear old couple who had put their trust in you! Not in vain does this district — for all its malevolent tongues — call you the Angel of the Slums! That young man couldn't rise to your level, so you left him. And now, when I see you closing up the little shop, that veritable haven of rest for the multitude, well, I cannot, I cannot let it pass. Morning after morning I have stood watching in the doorway not unmoved — while you graciously handed out rice to the wretched. Is that never to happen again? Is the good woman of Setzuan to disappear? If only you would allow *me* to assist you! Now don't say anything! No assurances, no exclamations of gratitude! (*He has taken out his check book.*) Here! A blank check. (*He places it on the cart.*) Just my signature. Fill it out as you wish. Any sum in the world. I herewith retire from the scene, quietly, unobtrusively, making no claims, on tiptoe, full of veneration, absolutely selflessly . . . (*He has gone.*)

MRS. SHIN. Well! You're saved. There's always some idiot of a man. . . . Now hurry! Put down a thousand silver dollars and let me fly to the bank before he comes to his senses.

SHEN TE. I can pay you for the washing without any check.

MRS. SHIN. What? You're not going to cash it just because you might have to marry him? Are you crazy? Men like him *want* to be led by the nose! Are you still thinking of that flyer? All Yellow Street knows how he treated you!

SHEN TE. When I heard his cunning laugh, I was afraid
But when I saw the holes in his shoes, I loved him dearly.

MRS. SHIN. Defending that good-for-nothing after all that's happened!

SHEN TE (*staggering as she holds some of the washing*). Oh!

MRS. SHIN (*taking the washing from her, dryly*). So you feel dizzy when you stretch and bend? There couldn't be a little visitor on the way? If that's it, you can forget Mr. Shu Fu's blank check: it wasn't meant for a christening present!

She goes to the back with a basket. SHEN TE'S *eyes follow* MRS. SHIN *for a moment. Then she looks down at her own body, feels her stomach, and a great joy comes into her eyes.*

SHEN TE. O joy! A new human being is on the way. The world awaits him. In the cities the people say: he's got to be reckoned with, this new human being! (*She imagines a little boy to be present, and introduces him to the audience.*) This is my son, the well-known flyer!
Say: Welcome
To the conqueror of unknown mountains and unreachable regions
Who brings us our mail across the impassable deserts!

She leads him up and down by the hand.
Take a look at the world, my son. That's a tree. Tree, yes. Say: "Hello, tree!" And bow. Like this. (*She bows.*) Now you know each other. And,

look, here comes the Water Seller. He's a friend, give him your hand. A cup of fresh water for my little son, please. Yes, it *is* a warm day. (*Handing the cup.*) Oh dear, a policeman, we'll have to make a circle round *him*. Perhaps we can pick a few cherries over there in the rich Mr. Pung's garden. But we mustn't be seen. You want cherries? Just like children with fathers. No, no, you can't go straight at them like that. Don't pull. We must learn to be reasonable. Well, have it your own way. (*She has let him make for the cherries.*) Can you reach? Where to put them? Your mouth is the best place. (*She tries one herself.*) Mmm, they're good. But the policeman, we must run! (*They run.*) Yes, back to the street. Calm now, so no one will notice us. (*Walking the street with her child, she sings.*)

> Once a plum — 'twas in Japan —
> Made a conquest of a man
> But the man's turn soon did come
> For he gobbled up the plum

Enter WONG, *with a* CHILD *by the hand. He coughs.*

SHEN TE. Wong!

WONG. It's about the Carpenter, Shen Te. He's lost his shop, and he's been drinking. His children are on the streets. This is one. Can you help?

SHEN TE (*to the* CHILD). Come here, little man. (*Takes him down to the footlights. To the audience.*)

> You there! A man is asking you for shelter!
> A man of tomorrow says: what about today?
> His friend the conqueror, whom you know,
> Is his advocate!

(*To* WONG.) He can live in Mr. Shu Fu's cabins. I may have to go there myself. I'm going to have a baby. That's a secret — don't tell Yang Sun — we'd only be in his way. Can you find the Carpenter for me?

WONG. I knew you'd think of something. (*To the* CHILD.) Goodbye, son, I'm going for your father.

SHEN TE. What about your hand, Wong? I wanted to help, but my cousin . . .

WONG. Oh, I can get along with one hand, don't worry. (*He shows how he can handle his pole with his left hand alone.*)

SHEN TE. But your right hand! Look, take this cart, sell everything that's on it, and go to the doctor with the money . . .

WONG. She's still good. But first I'll bring the Carpenter. I'll pick up the cart when I get back. (*Exit* WONG.)

SHEN TE (*to the* CHILD). Sit down over here, son, till your father comes.

The CHILD *sits crosslegged on the ground. Enter the* HUSBAND *and* WIFE, *each dragging a large, full sack.*

WIFE (*furtively*). You're alone, Shen Te, dear?

SHEN TE *nods. The* WIFE *beckons to the* NEPHEW *off stage. He comes on with another sack.*

WIFE. Your cousin's away? (SHEN TE *nods.*) He's not coming back?

SHEN TE. No. I'm giving up the shop.

WIFE. That's why we're here. We want to know if we can leave these things in your new home. Will you do us this favor?

SHEN TE. Why, yes, I'd be glad to.

HUSBAND (*cryptically*). And if anyone asks about them, say they're yours.

SHEN TE. Would anyone ask?

WIFE (*with a glance back at her husband*). Oh, someone might. The police, for instance. They don't seem to like us. Where can we put it?

SHEN TE. Well, I'd rather not get in any more trouble . . .

WIFE. Listen to her! The good woman of Setzuan!

SHEN TE *is silent.*

HUSBAND. There's enough tobacco in those sacks to give us a new start in life. We could have our own tobacco factory!

SHEN TE (*slowly*). You'll have to put them in the back room.

The sacks are taken off stage, while the CHILD *is left alone. Shyly glancing about him, he goes to the garbage can, starts playing with the contents, and eating some of the scraps. The others return.*

WIFE. We're counting on you, Shen Te!

SHEN TE. Yes. (*She sees the* CHILD *and is shocked.*)

HUSBAND. We'll see you in Mr. Shu Fu's cabins.

NEPHEW. The day after tomorrow.

SHEN TE. Yes. Now, go. Go! I'm not feeling well.

Exeunt all three, virtually pushed off.

He is eating the refuse in the garbage can!
Only look at his little grey mouth!

Pause. Music.

As this is the world *my* son will enter
I will study to defend him.
To be good to you, my son,
I shall be a tigress to all others
If I have to.
And I shall have to.

She starts to go.

One more time, then. I hope really the last.

Exit SHEN TE, *taking* SHUI TA's *trousers.* MRS. SHIN *enters and watches her with marked interest. Enter the* SISTER-IN-LAW *and the* GRANDFATHER.

SISTER-IN-LAW. So it's true, the shop has closed down. And the furniture's in the back yard. It's the end of the road!

MRS. SHIN (*pompously*). The fruit of high living, selfishness, and sensuality! Down the primrose path to Mr. Shu Fu's cabins — with you!

SISTER-IN-LAW. Cabins? Rat holes! He gave them to us because his soap supplies only went moldy there!

Enter the UNEMPLOYED MAN.

UNEMPLOYED MAN. Shen Te is moving?

SISTER-IN-LAW. Yes. She was sneaking away.

MRS. SHIN. She's ashamed of herself, and no wonder!

UNEMPLOYED MAN. Tell her to call Mr. Shui Ta or she's done for this time!

SISTER-IN-LAW. Tell her to call Mr. Shui Ta or *we're* done for this time!

Enter WONG *and* CARPENTER, *the latter with a* CHILD *on each hand.*

CARPENTER. So we'll have a roof over our heads for a change!

MRS. SHIN. Roof? Whose roof?

CARPENTER. Mr. Shu Fu's cabins. And we have little Feng to thank for it. (*Feng, we find, is the name of the child already there; his father now takes him. To the other two.*) Bow to your little brother, you two!

The CARPENTER *and the* TWO NEW ARRIVALS *bow to Feng. Enter* SHUI TA.

UNEMPLOYED MAN. Sst! Mr. Shui Ta!

Pause.

SHUI TA. And what is this crowd here for, may I ask?

WONG. How do you do, Mr. Shui Ta. This is the Carpenter. Miss Shen Te promised him space in Mr. Shu Fu's cabins.

SHUI TA. That will not be possible.

CARPENTER. We can't go there after all?

SHUI TA. All the space is needed for other purposes.

SISTER-IN-LAW. You mean we have to get out? But we've got nowhere to go.

SHUI TA. Miss Shen Te finds it possible to provide employment. If the proposition interests you, you may stay in the cabins.

SISTER-IN-LAW (*with distaste*). You mean *work*? Work for Miss Shen Te?

SHUI TA. Making tobacco, yes. There are three bales here already. Would you like to get them?

SISTER-IN-LAW (*trying to bluster*). We have our own tobacco! We were in the tobacco business before you were born!

SHUI TA (*to the* CARPENTER *and the* UNEMPLOYED MAN). You *don't* have your own tobacco. What about you?

The CARPENTER *and the* UNEMPLOYED MAN *get the point, and go for the sacks. Enter* MRS. MI TZU.

MRS. MI TZU. Mr. Shui Ta? I've brought you your three hundred silver dollars.

SHUI TA. I'll sign your lease instead. I've decided not to sell.

MRS. MI TZU. What? You don't need the money for that flyer?

SHUI TA. No.

MRS. MI TZU. And you can pay six months' rent?

SHUI TA (*takes the Barber's blank check from the cart and fills it out*). Here is a check for ten thousand silver dollars. On Mr. Shu Fu's account. Look! (*He shows her the signature on the check.*) Your six months' rent will be in your hands by seven this evening. And now, if you'll excuse me.

MRS. MI TZU. So it's Mr. Shu Fu now. The flyer has been given his walking papers. These modern girls! In my day they'd have said she was flighty. That poor, deserted Mr. Yang Sun!

Exit MRS. MI TZU. *The* CARPENTER *and the* UNEMPLOYED MAN *drag the three sacks back on the stage.*

CARPENTER (*to* SHUI TA). I don't know why I'm doing this for you.

SHUI TA. Perhaps your children want to eat, Mr. Carpenter.

SISTER-IN-LAW (*catching sight of the sacks*). Was my brother-in-law here?

MRS. SHIN. Yes, he was.

SISTER-IN-LAW. I thought as much. I know those sacks! That's our tobacco!

SHUI TA. Really? I thought it came from my back room! Shall we consult the police on the point?

SISTER-IN-LAW (*defeated*). No.

SHUI TA. Perhaps you will show me the way to Mr. Shu Fu's cabins?

Taking FENG *by the hand,* SHUI TA *goes off, followed by the* CARPENTER *and his* TWO OLDER CHILDREN, *the* SISTER-IN-LAW, *the* GRANDFATHER, *and the* UNEMPLOYED MAN. *Each of the last three drags a sack. Enter* OLD MAN *and* OLD WOMAN.

MRS. SHIN. A pair of pants — missing from the clothes line one minute — and next minute on the honorable backside of Mr. Shui Ta.

OLD WOMAN. We thought Miss Shen Te was here.

MRS. SHIN (*preoccupied*). Well, she's not.

OLD MAN. There was something she was going to give us.

WONG. She was going to help me too. (*Looking at his hand.*) It'll be too late soon. But she'll be back. This cousin has never stayed long.

MRS. SHIN (*approaching a conclusion*). No, he hasn't, has he?

— 7a —

The Sewer Pipe: WONG *asleep. In his dream, he tell the* GODS *his fears. The* GODS *seem tired from all their travels. They stop for a moment and look over their shoulders at the Water Seller.*

WONG. Illustrious ones. I've been having a bad dream. Our beloved Shen Te was in great distress in the rushes down by the river — the spot where the bodies of suicides are washed up. She kept staggering and holding her head down as if she was carrying something and it was dragging her down into the mud. When I called out to her, she said she had to take your Book of Rules to the other side, and not get it wet, or the ink would all come off. You had talked to her about the virtues, you know, the time she gave you shelter in Setzuan.

THIRD GOD. Well, but what do you suggest, my dear Wong?

WONG. Maybe a little relaxation of the rules, Benevolent One, in view of the bad times.

THIRD GOD. As for instance?

The Good Woman of Setzuan

WONG. Well, um, good-will, for instance, might do instead of love?
THIRD GOD. I'm afraid that would create new problems.
WONG. Or, instead of justice, good sportsmanship?
THIRD GOD. That would only mean more work.
WONG. Instead of honor, outward propriety?
THIRD GOD. Still more work! No, no! The rules will have to stand, my dear Wong!

Wearily shaking their heads, all three journey on.

8

SHUI TA's *tobacco factory in* SHU FU's *cabins. Huddled together behind bars, several families, mostly women and children. Among these people the* SISTER-IN-LAW, *the* GRANDFATHER, *the* CARPENTER *and his* THREE CHILDREN. *Enter* MRS. YANG *followed by* YANG SUN.

MRS. YANG (*to the audience*). There's something I just *have* to tell you: strength and wisdom are wonderful things. The strong and wise Mr. Shui Ta has transformed my son from a dissipated good-for-nothing into a model citizen. As you may have heard, Mr. Shui Ta opened a small tobacco factory near the cattle runs. It flourished. Three months ago — I shall never forget it — I asked for an appointment, and Mr. Shui Ta agreed to see us — me and my son. I can see him now as he came through the door to meet us. . . .

Enter SHUI TA, *from a door.*

SHUI TA. What can I do for you, Mrs. Yang?
MRS. YANG. This morning the police came to the house. We find you've brought an action for breach of promise of marriage. In the name of Shen Te. You also claim that Sun came by two hundred silver dollars by improper means.
SHUI TA. That is correct.
MRS. YANG. Mr. Shui Ta, the money's all gone. When the Peking job didn't materialize, he ran through it all in three days. I know he's a good-for-nothing. He sold my furniture. He was moving to Peking without me. Miss Shen Te thought highly of him at one time.
SHUI TA. What do *you* say, Mr. Yang Sun?
YANG SUN. The money's gone.
SHUI TA (*to* MRS. YANG). Mrs. Yang, in consideration of my cousin's incomprehensible weakness for your son, I am prepared to give him another chance. He can have a job — here. The two hundred silver dollars will be taken out of his wages.
YANG SUN. So it's the factory or jail?
SHUI TA. Take your choice.

YANG SUN. May I speak with Shen Te?
SHUI TA. You may not.
Pause.
YANG SUN (*sullenly*). Show me where to go.
MRS. YANG. Mr. Shui Ta, you are kindness itself: the gods will reward you! (*To* YANG SUN.) And honest work will make a man of you, my boy. (YANG SUN *follows* SHUI TA *into the factory.* MRS. YANG *comes down again to the footlights.*) Actually, honest work didn't agree with him — at first. And he got no opportunity to distinguish himself till — in the third week — when the wages were being paid . . .

SHUI TA *has a bag of money. Standing next to his foreman — the former* UNEMPLOYED MAN — *he counts out the wages. It is* YANG SUN's *turn.*

UNEMPLOYED MAN (*reading*). Carpenter, six silver dollars. Yang Sun, six silver dollars.
YANG SUN (*quietly*). Excuse me, sir. I don't think it can be more than five. May I see? (*He takes the foreman's list.*) It says six working days. But that's a mistake, sir. I took a day off for court business. And I won't take what I haven't earned, however miserable the pay is!
UNEMPLOYED MAN. Yang Sun. Five silver dollars. (*To* SHUI TA.) A rare case, Mr. Shui Ta!
SHUI TA. How is it the book says six when it should say five?
UNEMPLOYED MAN. I must've made a mistake, Mr. Shui Ta. (*With a look at* YANG SUN.) It won't happen again.
SHUI TA (*taking* YANG SUN *aside*). You don't hold back, do you? You give your all to the firm. You're even honest. Do the foreman's mistakes always favor the workers?
YANG SUN. He does have . . . friends.
SHUI TA. Thank you. May I offer you any little recompense?
YANG SUN. Give me a trial period of one week, and I'll prove my intelligence is worth more to you than my strength.
MRS. YANG (*still down at the footlights*). Fighting words, fighting words! That evening, I said to Sun: "If you're a flyer, then fly, my falcon! Rise in the world!" And he got to be foreman. Yes, in Mr. Shui Ta's tobacco factory, he worked real miracles.

We see YANG SUN *with his legs apart standing behind the* WORKERS *who are handing along a basket of raw tobacco above their heads.*

YANG SUN. Faster! Faster! You, there, d'you think you can just stand around, now you're not foreman any more? It'll be your job to lead us in song. Sing!

UNEMPLOYED MAN *starts singing. The others join in the refrain.*

SONG OF THE EIGHTH ELEPHANT

Chang had seven elephants — all much the same —
   But then there was Little Brother
The seven, they were wild, Little Brother, he was tame
   And to guard them Chang chose Little Brother
      Run faster!
      Mr. Chang has a forest park
      Which must be cleared before tonight
      And already it's growing dark!

When the seven elephants cleared that forest park
   Mr. Chang rode high on Little Brother
While the seven toiled and moiled till dark
   On his big behind sat Little Brother
      Dig faster!
      Mr. Chang has a forest park
      Which must be cleared before tonight
      And already it's growing dark!

And the seven elephants worked many an hour
   Till none of them could work another
Old Chang, he looked sour, on the seven he did glower
   But gave a pound of rice to Little Brother
      What was that?
      Mr. Chang has a forest park
      Which must be cleared before tonight
      And already it's getting dark!

And the seven elephants hadn't any tusks
   The one that had the tusks was Little Brother
Seven are no match for one, if the one has a gun!
   How old Chang did laugh at Little Brother!
      Keep on digging!
      Mr. Chang has a forest park
      Which must be cleared before tonight
      And already it's growing dark!

Smoking a cigar, SHUI TA *strolls by.* YANG SUN, *laughing, has joined in the refrain of the third stanza and speeded up the tempo of the last stanza by clapping his hands.*

MRS. YANG. And that's why I say: strength and wisdom are wonderful things. It took the strong and wise Mr. Shui Ta to bring out the best in

Yang Sun. A real superior man is like a bell. If you ring it, it rings, and if you don't, it don't, as the saying is.

9

SHEN TE'S *shop, now an office with club chairs and fine carpets. It is raining.* SHUI TA, *now fat, is just dismissing the* OLD MAN *and* OLD WOMAN. MRS. SHIN, *in obviously new clothes, looks on, smirking.*

SHUI TA. No! I can NOT tell you when we expect her back.

OLD WOMAN. The two hundred silver dollars came today. In an envelope. There was no letter, but it must be from Shen Te. We want to write and thank her. May we have her address?

SHUI TA. I'm afraid I haven't got it.

OLD MAN (*pulling* OLD WOMAN'S *sleeve*). Let's be going.

OLD WOMAN. She's got to come back some time!

They move off, uncertainly, worried. SHUI TA *bows.*

MRS. SHIN. They lost the carpet shop because they couldn't pay their taxes. The money arrived too late.

SHUI TA. They could have come to me.

MRS. SHIN. People don't like coming to you.

SHUI TA (*sits suddenly, one hand to his head*). I'm dizzy.

MRS. SHIN. After all, you *are* in your seventh month. But old Mrs. Shin will be there in your hour of trial! (*She cackles feebly.*)

SHUI TA (*in stifled voice*). Can I count on that?

MRS. SHIN. We all have our price, and mine won't be too high for the great Mr. Shui Ta! (*She opens* SHUI TA'S *collar.*)

SHUI TA. It's for the child's sake. All of this.

MRS. SHIN. "All for the child," of course.

SHUI TA. I'm so fat. People must notice.

MRS. SHIN. Oh no, they think it's 'cause you're rich.

SHUI TA (*more feelingly*). What will happen to the child?

MRS. SHIN. You ask that nine times a day. Why, it'll have the best that money can buy!

SHUI TA. He must never see Shui Ta.

MRS. SHIN. Oh, no. Always Shen Te.

SHUI TA. What about the neighbors? There are rumors, aren't there?

MRS. SHIN. As long as Mr. Shu Fu doesn't find out, there's nothing to worry about. Drink this.

Enter YANG SUN *in a smart business suit, and carrying a businessman's briefcase.* SHUI TA *is more or less in* MRS. SHIN'S *arms.*

YANG SUN (*surprised*). I guess I'm in the way.

SHUI TA (*ignoring this, rises with an effort*). Till tomorrow, Mrs. Shin.

MRS. SHIN *leaves with a smile, putting her new gloves on.*

YANG SUN. Gloves now! She couldn't be fleecing you? And since when did *you* have a private life? (*Taking a paper from the briefcase.*) You haven't been at your best lately, and things are getting out of hand. The police want to close us down. They say that at the most they can only permit twice the lawful number of workers.

SHUI TA (*evasively*). The cabins are quite good enough.

YANG SUN. For the workers maybe, not for the tobacco. They're too damp. We must take over some of Mrs. Mi Tzu's buildings.

SHUI TA. Her price is double what I can pay.

YANG SUN. Not unconditionally. If she has me to stroke her knees she'll come down.

SHUI TA. I'll never agree to that.

YANG SUN. What's wrong? Is it the rain? You get so irritable whenever it rains.

SHUI TA. Never! I will never . . .

YANG SUN. Mrs. Mi Tzu'll be here in five minutes. *You* fix it. And Shu Fu will be with her. . . . What's all that noise?

During the above dialogue, WONG *is heard offstage, calling:* "The good Shen Te, where is she? Which of you has seen Shen Te, good people? Where is Shen Te?" *A knock. Enter* WONG.

WONG. Mr. Shui Ta, I've come to ask when Miss Shen Te will be back, it's six months now. . . . There are rumors. People say something's happened to her.

SHUI TA. I'm busy. Come back next week.

WONG (*excited*). In the morning there was always rice on her doorstep — for the needy. It's been there again lately!

SHUI TA. And what do people conclude from this?

WONG. That Shen Te is still in Setzuan! She's been . . . (*He breaks off.*)

SHUI TA. She's been what? Mr. Wong, if you're Shen Te's friend, talk a little less about her, that's my advice to you.

WONG. I don't want your advice! Before she disappeared, Miss Shen Te told me something very important — she's pregnant!

YANG SUN. What? What was that?

SHUI TA (*quickly*). The man is lying.

WONG. A good woman isn't so easily forgotten, Mr. Shui Ta.

He leaves. SHUI TA *goes quickly into the back room.*

YANG SUN (*to the audience*). Shen Te pregnant? So that's why. Her cousin sent her away, so I wouldn't get wind of it. I have a son, a Yang appears on the scene, and what happens? Mother and child vanish into thin air! That scoundrel, that unspeakable . . . (*The sound of sobbing is heard from the back room.*) What was that? Someone sobbing? Who was it? Mr. Shui Ta the Tobacco King doesn't weep his heart out. And where does the rice come from that's on the doorstep in the morning? (SHUI TA *returns. He goes on to the door and looks out into the rain.*) Where is she?

SHUI TA. Sh! It's nine o'clock. But the rain's so heavy, you can't hear a thing.

YANG SUN. What do you want to hear?

SHUI TA. The mail plane.

YANG SUN. What?!

SHUI TA. I've been told *you* wanted to fly at one time. Is that all forgotten?

YANG SUN. Flying mail is night work. I prefer the daytime. And the firm is very dear to me — after all it belongs to my ex-fiancée, even if she's not around. And she's not, is she?

SHUI TA. What do you mean by that?

YANG SUN. Oh, well, let's say I haven't altogether — lost interest.

SHUI TA. My cousin might like to know that.

YANG SUN. I might not be indifferent — if I found she was being kept under lock and key.

SHUI TA. By whom?

YANG SUN. By you.

SHUI TA. What could you do about it?

YANG SUN. I could submit for discussion — my position in the firm.

SHUI TA. You are now my Manager. In return for a more . . . appropriate position, you might agree to drop the enquiry into your ex-fiancée's whereabouts?

YANG SUN. I might.

SHUI TA. What position *would* be more appropriate?

YANG SUN. The one at the top.

SHUI TA. My own? (*Silence.*) And if I preferred to throw you out on your neck?

YANG SUN. I'd come back on my feet. With suitable escort.

SHUI TA. The police?

YANG SUN. The police.

SHUI TA. And when the police found no one?

YANG SUN. I might ask them not to overlook the back room. (*Ending the pretense.*) In short, Mr. Shui Ta, my interest in this young woman has not been officially terminated. I should like to see more of her. (*Into* SHUI TA's *face.*) Besides, she's pregnant and needs a friend. (*He moves to the door.*) I shall talk about it with the Water Seller.

> *Exit.* SHUI TA *is rigid for a moment, then he quickly goes into the back room. He returns with* SHEN TE's *belongings: underwear, etc. He takes a long look at the shawl of the previous scene. He then wraps the things in a bundle, which upon hearing a noise, he hides under the table. Enter* MRS. MI TZU *and* MR. SHU FU. *They put away their umbrellas and galoshes.*

MRS. MI TZU. I thought your Manager was here, Mr. Shui Ta. He combines charm with business in a way that can only be to the advantage of all of us.

SHU FU. You sent for us, Mr. Shui Ta?

SHUI TA. The factory is in trouble.

SHU FU. It always is.

SHUI TA. The police are threatening to close us down unless I can show that the extension of our facilities is imminent.

SHU FU. Mr. Shui Ta, I'm sick and tired of your constantly expanding projects. I place cabins at your cousin's disposal; you make a factory of them. I hand your cousin a check; you present it. Your cousin disappears: you find the cabins too small and start talking of yet more —

SHUI TA. Mr. Shu Fu, I'm authorized to inform you that Miss Shen Te's return is now imminent.

SHU FU. Imminent? It's becoming his favorite word.

MRS. MI TZU. Yes, what does it mean?

SHUI TA. Mrs. Mi Tzu, I can pay you exactly half what you asked for your buildings. Are you ready to inform the police that I am taking them over?

MRS. MI TZU. Certainly, if I can take over your manager.

SHU FU. What?

MRS. MI TZU. He's so efficient.

SHUI TA. I'm afraid I need Mr. Yang Sun.

MRS. MI TZU. So do I.

SHUI TA. He will call on you tomorrow.

SHU FU. So much the better. With Shen Te likely to turn up at any moment, the presence of that young man is hardly in good taste.

SHUI TA. So we have reached a settlement. In what was once the good Shen Te's little shop we are laying the foundations for the great Mr. Shui Ta's twelve magnificent super tobacco markets. You will bear in mind that though they call me the Tobacco King of Setzuan, it is my cousin's interests that have been served . . .

VOICES (*off*). The police, the police! Going to the tobacco shop! Something must have happened!

Enter YANG SUN, WONG, *and the* POLICEMAN.

POLICEMAN. Quiet there, quiet, quiet! (*They quiet down.*) I'm sorry, Mr. Shui Ta, but there's a report that you've been depriving Miss Shen Te of her freedom. Not that I believe all I hear, but the whole city's in an uproar.

SHUI TA. That's a lie.

POLICEMAN. Mr. Yang Sun has testified that he heard someone sobbing in the back room.

SHU FU. Mrs. Mi Tzu and myself will testify that no one here has been sobbing.

MRS. MI TZU. We have been quietly smoking our cigars.

POLICEMAN. Mr. Shui Ta, I'm afraid I shall have to take a look at that room. (*He does so. The room is empty.*) No one there, of course, sir.

YANG SUN. But I heard sobbing. What's that? (*He finds the clothes.*)

WONG. Those are Shen Te's things. (*To crowd.*) Shen Te's clothes are here!

VOICES (*off, in sequence*). Shen Te's clothes!
They've been found under the table!
Body of murdered girl still missing!
Tobacco King suspected!

POLICEMAN. Mr. Shui Ta, unless you can tell us where the girl is, I'll have to ask you to come along.

SHUI TA. I do not know.

POLICEMAN. I can't say how sorry I am, Mr. Shui Ta. (*He shows him the door.*)

MR. SHUI TA. Everything will be cleared up in no time. There are still judges in Setzuan.

YANG SUN. I heard sobbing!

— 9a —

WONG's *den. For the last time, the* GODS *appear to the Water Seller in his dream. They have changed and show signs of a long journey, extreme fatigue, and plenty of mishaps. The* FIRST *no longer has a hat; the* THIRD *has lost a leg; all three are barefoot.*

WONG. Illustrious ones, at last you're here. Shen Te's been gone for months and today her cousin's been arrested. They think he murdered her to get the shop. But I had a dream and in this dream Shen Te said her cousin was keeping her prisoner. You must find her for us, illustrious ones!

FIRST GOD. We've found very few good people anywhere, and even they didn't keep it up. Shen Te is still the only one that stayed good.

SECOND GOD. If she *has* stayed good.

WONG. Certainly she has. But she's vanished.

FIRST GOD. That's the last straw. All is lost!

SECOND GOD. A little moderation, dear colleague!

FIRST GOD (*plaintively*). What's the good of moderation now? If she can't be found, we'll have to resign! The world is a terrible place! Nothing but misery, vulgarity, and waste! Even the countryside isn't what it used to be. The trees are getting their heads chopped off by telephone wires, and there's such a noise from all the gunfire, and I can't stand those heavy clouds of smoke, and —

THIRD GOD. The place is absolutely unlivable! Good intentions bring people to the brink of the abyss, and good deeds push them over the edge. I'm afraid our book of rules is destined for the scrap heap —

SECOND GOD. It's people! They're a worthless lot!

THIRD GOD. The world is too cold!

SECOND GOD. It's people! They're too weak!

FIRST GOD. Dignity, dear colleagues, dignity! Never despair! As for this world, didn't we agree that we only have to find one human being who can stand the place? Well, we found her. True, we lost her again. We must find her again, that's all! And at once!

They disappear.

10

Courtroom. Groups: SHU FU *and* MRS. MI TZU; YANG SUN *and* MRS. YANG; WONG, *the* CARPENTER, *the* GRANDFATHER, *the* NIECE, *the* OLD MAN, *the* OLD WOMAN; MRS. SHIN, *the* POLICEMAN; *the* UNEMPLOYED MAN, *the* SISTER-IN-LAW.

OLD MAN. So much power isn't good for one man.

UNEMPLOYED MAN. And he's going to open twelve super tobacco markets!

WIFE. One of the judges is a friend of Mr. Shu Fu's.

SISTER-IN-LAW. Another one accepted a present from Mr. Shui Ta only last night. A great fat goose.

OLD WOMAN (*to* WONG). And Shen Te is nowhere to be found.

WONG. Only the gods will ever know the truth.

POLICEMAN. Order in the court! My lords the judges!

Enter the THREE GODS *in judges' robes. We overhear their conversation as they pass along the footlights to their bench.*

THIRD GOD. We'll never get away with it, our certificates were so badly forged.

SECOND GOD. My predecessor's "sudden indigestion" will certainly cause comment.

FIRST GOD. But he *had* just eaten a whole goose.

UNEMPLOYED MAN. Look at that! *New* judges!

WONG. New judges. And what good ones!

The THIRD GOD *hears this, and turns to smile at* WONG. *The* GODS *sit. The* FIRST GOD *beats on the bench with his gavel. The* POLICEMAN *brings in* SHUI TA *who walks with lordly steps. He is whistled at.*

POLICEMAN (*to* SHUI TA). Be prepared for a surprise. The judges have been changed.

SHUI TA *turns quickly round, looks at them, and staggers.*

NIECE. What's the matter now?

WIFE. The great Tobacco King nearly fainted.

HUSBAND. Yes, as soon as he saw the new judges.

WONG. Does *he* know who they are?

SHUI TA *picks himself up, and the proceedings open.*

FIRST GOD. Defendant Shui Ta, you are accused of doing away with your cousin Shen Te in order to take possession of her business. Do you plead guilty or not guilty?

SHUI TA. Not guilty, my lord.

FIRST GOD (*thumbing through the documents of the case*). The first witness is the Policeman. I shall ask him to tell us something of the respective reputations of Miss Shen Te and Mr. Shui Ta.

POLICEMAN. Miss Shen Te was a young lady who aimed to please, my lord. She liked to live and let live, as the saying goes. Mr. Shui Ta, on the other hand, is a man of principle. Though the generosity of Miss Shen Te forced him at times to abandon half measures, unlike the girl he was always on the side of the law, my lord. One time, he even unmasked a gang of thieves to whom his too trustful cousin had given shelter. The evidence, in short, my lord, proves that Mr. Shui Ta was *incapable* of the crime of which he stands accused!

FIRST GOD. I see. And are there others who could testify along, shall we say, the same lines?

SHU FU *rises.*

POLICEMAN (*whispering to* GODS). Mr. Shu Fu — a very important person.

FIRST GOD (*inviting him to speak*). Mr. Shu Fu!

SHU FU. Mr. Shui Ta is a businessman, my lord. Need I say more?

FIRST GOD. Yes.

SHU FU. Very well, I will. He is Vice President of the Council of Commerce and is about to be elected a Justice of the Peace.

He returns to his seat. MRS. MI TZU *rises.*

WONG. Elected! *He* gave him the job!

With a gesture the FIRST GOD *asks who* MRS. MI TZU *is.*

POLICEMAN. Another very important person. Mrs. Mi Tzu.

FIRST GOD (*inviting her to speak*). Mrs. Mi Tzu!

MRS. MI TZU. My lord, as Chairman of the Committee on Social Work, I wish to call attention to just a couple of eloquent facts: Mr. Shui Ta not only has erected a model factory with model housing in our city, he is a regular contributor to our home for the disabled. (*She returns to her seat.*)

POLICEMAN (*whispering*). And she's a great friend of the judge that ate the goose!

FIRST GOD (*to the* POLICEMAN). Oh, thank you. What next? (*To the Court, genially.*) Oh, yes. We should find out if any of the evidence is less favorable to the defendant.

WONG, *the* CARPENTER, *the* OLD MAN, *the* OLD WOMAN, *the* UNEMPLOYED MAN, *the* SISTER-IN-LAW, *and the* NIECE *come forward.*

POLICEMAN (*whispering*). Just the riffraff, my lord.

FIRST GOD (*addressing the "riffraff"*). Well, um, riffraff — do you know anything of the defendant, Mr. Shui Ta?

WONG. Too much, my lord.

UNEMPLOYED MAN. What don't we know, my lord.

CARPENTER. He ruined us.
SISTER-IN-LAW. He's a cheat.
NIECE. Liar.
WIFE. Thief.
BOY. Blackmailer.
BROTHER. Murderer.
FIRST GOD. Thank you. We should now let the defendant state his point of view.
SHUI TA. I only came on the scene when Shen Te was in danger of losing what I had understood was a gift from the gods. Because I did the filthy jobs which someone had to do, they hate me. My activities were restricted to the minimum, my lord.
SISTER-IN-LAW. He had us arrested!
SHUI TA. Certainly. You stole from the bakery!
SISTER-IN-LAW. Such concern for the bakery! You didn't want the shop for yourself, I suppose!
SHUI TA. I didn't want the shop overrun with parasites.
SISTER-IN-LAW. We had nowhere else to go.
SHUI TA. There were too many of you.
WONG. What about this old couple: Were *they* parasites?
OLD MAN. We lost our shop because of you!
SISTER-IN-LAW. And we gave your cousin money!
SHUI TA. My cousin's fiancé was a flyer. The money had to go to *him*.
WONG. Did you care whether he flew or not? Did you care whether she married him or not? You wanted her to marry someone else! (*He points at* SHU FU.)
SHUI TA. The flyer unexpectedly turned out to be a scoundrel.
YANG SUN (*jumping up*). Which was the reason you made him your Manager?
SHUI TA. Later on he improved.
WONG. And when he improved, you sold him to her? (*He points out* MRS. MI TZU.)
SHUI TA. She wouldn't let me have her premises unless she had him to stroke her knees!
MRS. MI TZU. What? The man's a pathological liar. (*To him.*) Don't mention my property to me as long as you live! Murderer! (*She rustles off, in high dudgeon.*)
YANG SUN (*pushing in*). My lord, I wish to speak for the defendant.
SISTER-IN-LAW. Naturally. He's your employer.
UNEMPLOYED MAN. And the worst slave driver in the country.
MRS. YANG. That's a lie! My lord, Mr. Shui Ta is a great man. He . . .
YANG SUN. He's this and he's that, but he is not a murderer, my lord. Just fifteen minutes before his arrest I heard Shen Te's voice in his own back room.
FIRST GOD. Oh? Tell us more!

YANG SUN. I heard sobbing, my lord!

FIRST GOD. But lots of women sob, we've been finding.

YANG SUN. Could I fail to recognize her voice?

SHU FU. No, you made her sob so often yourself, young man!

YANG SUN. Yes. But I also made her happy. Till he (*pointing at* SHUI TA) decided to sell her to you!

SHUI TA. Because you didn't love her.

WONG. Oh, no: it was for the money, my lord!

SHUI TA. And what was the money for, my lord? For the poor! And for Shen Te so she could go on being good!

WONG. For the poor? That he sent to his sweatshops? And why didn't you let Shen Te be good when you signed the big check?

SHUI TA. For the child's sake, my lord.

CARPENTER. What about *my* children? What did he do about them?

SHUI TA *is silent.*

WONG. The shop was to be a fountain of goodness. That was the gods' idea. You came and spoiled it!

SHUI TA. If I hadn't, it would have run dry!

MRS. SHIN. There's a lot in that, my lord.

WONG. What have you done with the good Shen Te, bad man? She *was* good, my lords, she was, I swear it! (*He raises his hand in an oath.*)

THIRD GOD. What's happened to your hand, Water Seller?

WONG (*pointing to* SHUI TA). It's all his fault, my lord, *she* was going to send me to a doctor — (*To* SHUI TA.) You were her worst enemy!

SHUI TA. I was her only friend!

WONG. Where is she then? Tell us where your good friend is!

The excitement of this exchange has run through the whole crowd.

ALL. Yes, where is she? Where is Shen Te? (*Etc.*)

SHUI TA. Shen Te . . . had to go.

WONG. Where? Where to?

SHUI TA. I cannot tell you! I cannot tell you!

ALL. Why? Why did she have to go away? (*Etc.*)

WONG (*into the din with the first words, but talking on beyond the others*). Why not, why not? Why did she have to go away?

SHUI TA (*shouting*). Because you'd all have torn her to shreds, that's why! My lords, I have a request. Clear the court! When only the judges remain, I will make a confession.

ALL (*except* WONG, *who is silent, struck by the new turn of events*). So he's guilty? He's confessing! (*Etc.*)

FIRST GOD (*using the gavel*). Clear the court!

POLICEMAN. Clear the court!

WONG. Mr. Shui Ta has met his match this time.

MRS. SHIN (*with a gesture toward the judges*). You're in for a little surprise.

The court is cleared. Silence.

SHUI TA. Illustrious ones!

The GODS *look at each other, not quite believing their ears.*
SHUI TA. Yes, I recognize you!
SECOND GOD (*taking matters in hand, sternly*). What have you done with our good woman of Setzuan?
SHUI TA. I have a terrible confession to make: I am she! (*He takes off his mask, and tears away his clothes.* SHEN TE *stands there.*)
SECOND GOD. Shen Te!
SHEN TE. Shen Te, yes. Shui Ta *and* Shen Te. Both.

> Your injunction
> To be good and yet to live
> Was a thunderbolt:
> It has torn me in two
> I can't tell how it was
> But to be good to others
> And myself at the same time
> I could not do it
> Your world is not an easy one, illustrious ones!
> When we extend our hand to a beggar, he tears it off for us
> When we help the lost, we are lost ourselves
> And so
> Since not to eat is to die
> Who can long refuse to be bad?
> As I lay prostrate beneath the weight of good intentions
> Ruin stared me in the face
> It was when I was unjust that I ate good meat
> And hobnobbed with the mighty
> Why?
> Why are bad deeds rewarded?
> Good ones punished?
> I enjoyed giving
> I truly wished to be the Angel of the Slums
> But washed by a foster-mother in the water of the gutter
> I developed a sharp eye
> The time came when pity was a thorn in my side
> And, later, when kind words turned to ashes in my mouth
> And anger took over
> I became a wolf
> Find me guilty, then, illustrious ones,
> But know:
> All that I have done I did
> To help my neighbor
> To love my lover
> And to keep my little one from want
> For your great, godly deeds, I was too poor, too small.

Pause.

FIRST GOD (*shocked*). Don't go on making yourself miserable, Shen Te! We're overjoyed to have found you!

SHEN TE. I'm telling you I'm the bad man who committed all those crimes!

FIRST GOD (*using — or failing to use — his ear trumpet*). The good woman who did all those good deeds?

SHEN TE. Yes, but the bad man too!

FIRST GOD (*as if something had dawned*). Unfortunate coincidences! Heartless neighbors!

THIRD GOD (*shouting in his ear*). But how is she to continue?

FIRST GOD. Continue? Well, she's a strong, healthy girl . . .

SECOND GOD. You didn't hear what she said!

FIRST GOD. I heard every word! She is confused, that's all! (*He begins to bluster.*) And what about this book of rules — we can't renounce our rules, can we? (*More quietly.*) Should the world be changed? How? By whom? The world should *not* be changed! (*At a sign from him, the lights turn pink, and music plays.*)

> And now the hour of parting is at hand.
> Dost thou behold, Shen Te, yon fleecy cloud?
> It is our chariot. At a sign from me
> 'Twill come and take us back from whence we came
> Above the azure vault and silver stars. . . .

SHEN TE. No! Don't go, illustrious ones!

FIRST GOD.
> Our cloud has landed now in yonder field
> From whence it will transport us back to heaven.
> Farewell, Shen Te, let not thy courage fail thee. . . .

Exeunt GODS.

SHEN TE. What about the old couple? They've lost their shop! What about the Water Seller and his hand? And I've got to defend myself against the Barber, because I don't love him! And against Sun, because I do love him! How? How?

> SHEN TE's *eyes follow the* GODS *as they are imagined to step into a cloud which rises and moves forward over the orchestra and up beyond the balcony.*

FIRST GOD (*from on high*). We have faith in you, Shen Te!

SHEN TE. There'll be a child. And he'll have to be fed. I can't stay here. Where shall I go?

FIRST GOD. Continue to be good, good woman of Setzuan!

SHEN TE. I need my bad cousin!

FIRST GOD. But not very often!

SHEN TE. Once a week at least!

FIRST GOD. Once a month will be quite enough!

SHEN TE (*shrieking*). No, no! Help!

But the cloud continues to recede as the GODS *sing:*

VALEDICTORY HYMN

What rapture, oh, it is to know
   A good thing when you see it
And having seen a good thing, oh,
   What rapture 'tis to flee it

Be good, sweet maid of Setzuan
   Let Shui Ta be clever
Departing, we forget the man
   Remember your endeavor

Because through all the length of days
   Her goodness faileth never
Sing hallelujah! Make Shen Te's
   Good name live on forever!

SHEN TE. Help!

ECLECTICISM

Arthur Miller

DEATH OF A SALESMAN

[1949]

Arthur Miller [1916-   ]

Arthur Miller writes in one of the main streams of American letters, perhaps *the* main stream. His one novel and his plays center upon the social fact. Such questions as "Who is my neighbor?" are dramatized in his plays. Whether the immediate subject is criminal war profiteering as in *All My Sons* (where Joe Keller comes to realize that U.S. service men were *all* his sons), or the witch hunt of Salem in 1692, the problem of a man's relationship with the larger world (and its relationship with him) is central.

While Miller's first play, *All My Sons* (1947), was a piece of straight realism *à la* Ibsen, his second play was a new departure. In *Death of a Salesman* Arthur Miller offered a synthesis of what might seem to be incompatible dramatic modes: realism and theatricalism. The main action is set in the present and within this framework the action and dialogue are realistic, though the set is skeletal, or stylized. However, as we move from time present to time past, following the vagaries of Willy Loman's mind, we are outside of stage realism and in the realm of theatrical effects where lights and music concretely suggest another world which is not the objective, external world. As Willy moves through walls (in both a figurative and a literal sense), our imagination follows him as it does not tend to in straight realistic drama. Yet when we see a father and a son struggling with their passions and abortive love, we are struck by the immediate force of the stark realism. In a sense, in this play we may experience something of two worlds. The playwright is not limited by any single convention but appropriates to his use the varied resources available to the modern dramatist: in a word, he is eclectic.

Among critics, *Death of a Salesman* has called forth perhaps more strongly divergent evaluations than any other recent play. In the days and weeks following its opening in 1949, one read such opinions as these: "By common consent, this is one of the finest dramas in the whole range of the American theater" (Brooks Atkinson); "[Mr. Miller's] play is the most poignant statement of man as he must face himself to have come out of our theater" (Joseph Wood Krutch); ". . . not tragedy at all but an ambitious piece of confusionism, . . . put across by purely technical skills not unlike those of a magician or an acrobat" (Eleanor Clark); ". . . play is wholly conceptualized, like the ads to which it gives a bitter retort. Parents, children, and neighbors are cut-out figures, types, . . . it strives to be tragedy and becomes instead confused and hortatory" (Mary McCarthy). The question one might ask is this: "Did all of these critics see the same production of the same play?" The answer is "Yes." The reasons for such opposing reactions are matter for serious consideration.

FROM THE INTRODUCTION TO
ARTHUR MILLER'S COLLECTED PLAYS*

... The first image that occurred to me which was to result in *Death of a Salesman* was of an enormous face the height of the proscenium arch which would appear and then open up, and we would see the inside of a man's head. In fact, *The Inside of His Head* was the first title. It was conceived half in laughter, for the inside of his head was a mass of contradictions. The image was in direct opposition to the method of *All My Sons* — a method one might call linear or eventual in that one fact or incident creates the necessity for the next. The *Salesman* image was from the beginning absorbed with the concept that nothing in life comes "next" but that everything exists together and at the same time within us; that there is no past to be "brought forward" in a human being, but that he is his past at every moment and that the present is merely that which his past is capable of noticing and smelling and reacting to.

I wished to create a form which, in itself as a form, would literally be the process of Willy Loman's way of mind. But to say "wished" is not accurate. Any dramatic form is an artifice, a way of transforming a subjective feeling into something that can be comprehended through public symbols. Its efficiency as a form is to be judged — at least by the writer — by how much of the original vision and feeling is lost or distorted by this transformation. I wished to speak of the salesman most precisely as I felt about him, to give no part of that feeling away for the sake of any effect or any dramatic necessity. What was wanted now was not a mounting line of tension, nor a gradually narrowing cone of intensifying suspense, but a bloc, a single chord presented as such at the outset, within which all the strains and melodies would already be contained. The strategy, as with *All My Sons*, was to appear entirely unstrategic but with a difference. This time, if I could, I would have told the whole story and set forth all the characters in one unbroken speech or even one sentence or a single flash of light. As I look at the play now its form seems the form of a confession, for that is how it is told, now speaking of what happened yesterday, then suddenly following some connection to a time twenty years ago, then leaping even further back and then returning to the present and even speculating about the future.

Where in *All My Sons* it had seemed necessary to prove the connections

* New York: The Viking Press, 1957; pp. 23–36, 38–39, 52–55.

Introduction to Collected Plays

between the present and the past, between events and moral consequences, between the manifest and the hidden, in this play all was assumed as proven to begin with. All I was doing was bringing things to mind. The assumption, also, was that everyone knew Willy Loman. I can realize this only now, it is true, but it is equally apparent to me that I took it somehow for granted then. There was still the attitude of the unveiler, but no bringing together of hitherto unrelated things; only pre-existing images, events, confrontations, moods, and pieces of knowledge. So there was a kind of confidence underlying this play which the form itself expresses, even a naïveté, a self-disarming quality that was in part born of my belief in the audience as being essentially the same as myself. If I had wanted, then, to put the audience reaction into words, it would not have been "What happens next and why?" so much as "Oh, God, of course!"

In one sense a play is a species of jurisprudence, and some part of it must take the advocate's role, something else must act in defense, and the entirety must engage the Law. Against my will, *All My Sons* states, and even proclaims, that it is a form and that a writer wrote it and organized it. In *Death of a Salesman* the original impulse was to make that same proclamation in an immeasurably more violent, abrupt, and openly conscious way. Willy Loman does not merely suggest or hint that he is at the end of his strength and of his justifications, he is hardly on the stage for five minutes when he says so; he does not gradually imply a deadly conflict with his son, an implication dropped into the midst of serenity and surface calm, he is avowedly grappling with that conflict at the outset. The ultimate matter with which the play will close is announced at the outset and is the matter of its every moment from the first. There is enough revealed in the first scene of *Death of a Salesman* to fill another kind of play which, in service to another dramatic form, would hold back and only gradually release it. I wanted to proclaim that an artist had made this play, but the nature of the proclamation was to be entirely "inartistic" and avowedly unstrategic; it was to hold back nothing, at any moment, which life would have revealed, even at the cost of suspense and climax. It was to forgo the usual preparations for scenes and to permit — and even seek — whatever in each character contradicted his position in the advocate-defense scheme of its jurisprudence. The play was begun with only one firm piece of knowledge and this was that Loman was to destroy himself. How it would wander before it got to that point I did not know and resolved not to care. I was convinced only that if I could make him remember enough he would kill himself, and the structure of the play was determined by what was needed to draw up his memories like a mass of tangled roots without end or beginning.

As I have said, the structure of events and the nature of its form are also the direct reflection of Willy Loman's way of thinking at this moment of his life. He was the kind of man you see muttering to himself on a subway, decently dressed, on his way home or to the office, perfectly integrated with his surroundings excepting that unlike other people he can no longer restrain the power of his experience from disrupting the superficial sociality of his behavior. Consequently he is working on two logics which often collide. For instance, if he meets his son Happy while in the midst of some memory in which Happy disappointed him, he is instantly furious at Happy, despite the fact that Happy at this particular moment deeply desires to be of use to him. He is literally at that terrible moment when the voice of the past is no longer distant but quite as loud as the voice of the present. In dramatic terms the form, therefore, *is* this process, instead of being a once-removed summation or indication if it.

The way of telling the tale, in this sense, is as mad as Willy and as abrupt and as suddenly lyrical. And it is difficult not to add that the subsequent imitations of the form had to collapse for this particular reason. It is not possible, in my opinion, to graft it onto a character whose psychology it does not reflect, and I have not used it since because it would be false to a more integrated — or less disintegrating — personality to pretend that the past and the present are so openly and vocally intertwined in his mind. The ability of people to down their past is normal, and without it we could have no comprehensible communication among men. In the hands of writers who see it as an easy way to elicit anterior information in a play it becomes merely a flashback. There are no flashbacks in this play but only a mobile concurrency of past and present, and this, again, because in his desperation to justify his life Willy Loman has destroyed the boundaries between now and then, just as anyone would do who, on picking up his telephone, discovered that this perfectly harmless act had somehow set off an explosion in his basement. The previously assumed and believed-in results of ordinary and accepted actions, and their abrupt and unforeseen — but apparently logical — effects, form the basic collision in this play, and, I suppose, its ultimate irony.

It may be in place to remark, in this connection, that while the play was sometimes called cinematographic in its structure, it failed as a motion picture. I believe that the basic reason — aside from the gross insensitivity permeating its film production — was that the dramatic tension of Willy's memories was destroyed by transferring him, literally, to the locales he had only imagined in the play. There is an inevitable horror in the spectacle of a man losing consciousness of his immediate surroundings to the point where he engages in conversations with unseen persons. The horror is lost — and drama becomes narrative — when the context actually becomes his imagined world. And the drama evaporates because psychological truth has been amended, a truth which depends not only on what images we recall but in what connections and contexts we recall them. The setting on the stage was never shifted, despite the many changes in locale, for the precise reason that, quite simply, the mere fact that a man forgets where he is does not mean that he has really moved. Indeed, his terror springs from his never-lost awareness of time and place. It did not need this play to teach me that the screen

Introduction to Collected Plays 601

is time-bound and earth-bound compared to the stage, if only because its preponderant emphasis is on the visual image, which, however rapidly it may be changed before our eyes, still displaces its predecessor, while scene-changing with words is instantaneous; and because of the flexibility of language, especially of English, a preceding image can be kept alive through the image that succeeds it. The movie's tendency is always to wipe out what has gone before, and it is thus in constant danger of transforming the dramatic into narrative. There is no swifter method of telling a "story" but neither is there a more difficult medium in which to keep a pattern of relationships constantly in being. Even in those sequences which retained the real backgrounds for Willy's imaginary confrontations the tension between now and then was lost. I suspect this loss was due to the necessity of shooting the actors close up — effectively eliminating awareness of their surroundings. The basic failure of the picture was a formal one. It did not solve, nor really attempt to find a resolution for, the problem of keeping the past constantly alive, and that friction, collision, and tension between past and present was the heart of the play's particular construction.

A great deal has been said and written about what *Death of a Salesman* is supposed to signify, both psychologically and from the socio-political viewpoints. For instance, in one periodical of the far Right it was called a "time bomb expertly placed under the edifice of Americanism," while the *Daily Worker* reviewer thought it entirely decadent. In Catholic Spain it ran longer than any modern play and it has been refused production in Russia but not, from time to time, in certain satellite countries, depending on the direction and velocity of the wind. The Spanish press, thoroughly controlled by Catholic orthodoxy, regarded the play as commendable proof of the spirit's death where there is no God. In America, even as it was being cannonaded as a piece of Communist propaganda, two of the largest manufacturing corporations in the country invited me to address their sales organizations in conventions assembled, while the road company was here and there picketed by the Catholic War Veterans and the American Legion. It made only a fair impression in London, but in the area of the Norwegian Arctic Circle fishermen whose only contact with civilization was the radio and the occasional visit of the government boat insisted on seeing it night after night — the same few people — believing it to be some kind of religious rite. One organization of salesmen raised me up nearly to patron-sainthood, and another, a national sales managers' group, complained that the difficulty of recruiting salesmen was directly traceable to the play. When the movie was made, the producing company got so frightened it produced a sort of trailer to be shown before the picture, a documentary short film which demonstrated how exceptional Willy Loman was; how necessary selling is to the economy; how secure the salesman's life really is; how idiotic, in short, was the feature film they had just spent more than a million dollars to produce. Fright does odd things to people.

On the psychological front the play spawned a small hill of doctoral theses explaining its Freudian symbolism, and there were innumerable letters asking if I was aware that the fountain pen which Biff steals is a phallic symbol. Some, on the other hand, felt it was merely a fountain pen and dismissed the whole play. I received visits from men over sixty from as far away as California who had come across the country to have me write the stories of their lives, because the story of Willy Loman was exactly like theirs. The letters from women made it clear that the central character of the play was Linda; sons saw the entire action revolving around Biff or Happy, and fathers wanted advice, in effect, on how to avoid parricide. Probably the most succinct reaction to the play was voiced by a man who, on leaving the theatre, said, "I always said that New England territory was no damned good." This, at least, was a fact.

That I have and had not the slightest interest in the selling profession is probably unbelievable to most people, and I very early gave up trying even to say so. And when asked what Willy was selling, what was in his bags, I could only reply, "Himself." I was trying neither to condemn a profession nor particularly to improve it, and, I will admit, I was little better than ignorant of Freud's teachings when I wrote it. There was no attempt to bring down the American edifice nor to raise it higher, to show up family relations or to cure the ills afflicting that inevitable institution. The truth, at least of my aim — which is all I can speak of authoritatively — is much simpler and more complex.

The play grew from simple images. From a little frame house on a street of little frame houses, which had once been loud with the noise of growing boys, and then was empty and silent and finally occupied by strangers. Strangers who could not know with what conquistadorial joy Willy and his boys had once reshingled the roof. Now it was quiet in the house, and the wrong people in the beds.

It grew from images of futility — the cavernous Sunday afternoons polishing the car. Where is that car now? And the chamois cloths carefully washed and put up to dry, where are the chamois cloths?

And the endless, convoluted discussions, wonderments, arguments, belittlements, encouragements, fiery resolutions, abdications, returns, partings, voyages out and voyages back, tremendous opportunities, and small, squeaking denouements — and all in the kitchen now occupied by strangers who cannot hear what the walls are saying.

The image of aging and so many of your friends already gone and strangers in the seats of the mighty who do not know you or your triumphs or your incredible value.

The image of the son's hard, public eye upon you, no longer swept by your myth, no longer rousable from his separateness, no longer knowing you have lived for him and have wept for him.

Introduction to Collected Plays

The image of ferocity when love has turned to something else and yet is there, is somewhere in the room if one could only find it.

The image of people turning into strangers who only evaluate one another.

Above all, perhaps, the image of a need greater than hunger or sex or thirst, a need to leave a thumbprint somewhere on the world. A need for immortality, and by admitting it, the knowing that one has carefully inscribed one's name on a cake of ice on a hot July day.

I sought the relatedness of all things by isolating their unrelatedness, a man superbly alone with his sense of not having touched, and finally knowing in his last extremity that the love which had always been in the room unlocated was now found.

The image of a suicide so mixed in motive as to be unfathomable and yet demanding statement. Revenge was in it and a power of love, a victory in that it would bequeath a fortune to the living and a flight from emptiness. With it an image of peace at the final curtain, the peace that is between wars, the peace leaving the issues aboveground and viable yet.

And always, throughout, the image of private man in a world full of strangers, a world that is not home nor even an open battleground but only galaxies of high promise over a fear of falling.

And the image of a man making something with his hands being a rock to touch and return to. "He was always so wonderful with his hands," says his wife over his grave, and I laughed when the line came, laughed with the artist-devil's laugh, for it had all come together in this line, she having been made by him though he did not know it or believe in it or receive it into himself. Only rank, height of power, the sense of having won he believed was real — the galaxy thrust up into the sky by projectors on the rooftops of the city he believed were real stars.

It came from structural images. The play's eye was to revolve from within Willy's head, sweeping endlessly in all directions like a light on the sea, and nothing that formed in the distant mist was to be left uninvestigated. It was thought of as having the density of the novel form in its interchange of viewpoints, so that while all roads led to Willy the other characters were to feel it was their play, a story about them and not him.

There were two undulating lines in mind, one above the other, the past webbed to the present moving on together in him and sometimes openly joined and once, finally, colliding in the showdown which defined him in his eyes at least — and so to sleep.

Above all, in the structural sense, I aimed to make a play with the veritable countenance of life. To make one the many, as in life, so that "society" is a power and a mystery of custom and inside the man and surrounding him, as the fish is in the sea and the sea inside the fish, his birthplace and burial ground, promise and threat. To speak commonsensically of social facts which every businessman knows and talks about but which are too prosaic to mention or are usually fancied up on the stage as philosophical problems. When a man gets old you fire him, you have to, he can't do the work. To speak and even to celebrate the common sense of businessmen, who love the personality that wins the day but know that you've got to have the right goods at the right price, handsome and well spoken as you are. (To some, these were scandalous and infamous arraignments of society when uttered in the context of art. But not to the businessmen themselves; they knew it was all true and I cherished their clear-eyed talk.)

The image of a play without transitional scenes was there in the beginning. There was too much to say to waste precious stage time with feints and preparations, in themselves agonizing "structural" bridges for a writer to work out since they are not why he is writing. There was a resolution, as in *All My Sons*, not to waste motion or moments, but in this case to shear through everything up to the meat of a scene; a resolution not to write an unmeant word for the sake of the form but to make the form give and stretch and contract for the sake of the thing to be said. To cling to the process of Willy's mind as the form the story would take.

The play was always heroic to me, and in later years the academy's charge that Willy lacked the "stature" for the tragic hero seemed incredible to me. I had not understood that these matters are measured by Greco-Elizabethan paragraphs which hold no mention of insurance payments, front porches, refrigerator fan belts, steering knuckles, Chevrolets, and visions seen not through the portals of Delphi but in the blue flame of the hot-water heater. How could "Tragedy" make people weep, of all things?

I set out not to "write a tragedy" in this play, but to show the truth as I saw it. However, some of the attacks upon it as a pseudo-tragedy contain ideas so misleading, and in some cases so laughable, that it might be in place here to deal with a few of them.

Aristotle having spoken of a fall from the heights, it goes without saying that someone of the common mold cannot be a fit tragic hero. It is now many centuries since Aristotle lived. There is no more reason for falling down in a faint before his *Poetics* than before Euclid's geometry, which has been amended numerous times by men with new insights; nor, for that matter, would I choose to have my illnesses diagnosed by Hippocrates rather than the most ordinary graduate of an American medical school, despite the Greek's genius. Things do change, and even a genius is limited by his time and the nature of his society.

I would deny, on grounds of simple logic, this one of Aristotle's contentions if only because he lived in a slave society. When a vast number of people are divested of alternatives, as slaves are, it is rather inevitable that one will not be able to imagine drama, let alone tragedy, as being possible for any but the higher ranks of society. There is a legitimate question of stature here, but none of rank, which is so often confused with it. So long as the hero may be said to have had alternatives of a magnitude to have materially

Introduction to Collected Plays

changed the course of his life, it seems to me that in this respect at least, he cannot be debarred from the heroic role.

The question of rank is significant to me only as it reflects the question of the social application of the hero's career. There is no doubt that if a character is shown on the stage who goes through the most ordinary actions, and is suddenly revealed to be the President of the United States, his actions immediately assume a much greater magnitude, and pose the possibilities of much greater meaning, than if he is the corner grocer. But at the same time, his stature as a hero is not so utterly dependent upon his rank that the corner grocer cannot outdistance him as a tragic figure — providing, of course, that the grocer's career engages the issues of, for instance, the survival of the race, the relationships of man to God — the questions, in short, whose answers define humanity and the right way to live so that the world is a home, instead of a battleground or a fog in which disembodied spirits pass each other in an endless twilight.

In this respect *Death of a Salesman* is a slippery play to categorize because nobody in it stops to make a speech objectively stating the great issues which I believe it embodies. If it were a worse play, less closely articulating its meanings with its actions, I think it would have more quickly satisfied a certain kind of criticism. But it was meant to be less a play than a fact; it refused admission to its author's opinions and opened itself to a revelation of process and the operations of an ethic, of social laws of action no less powerful in their effects upon individuals than any tribal law administered by gods with names. I need not claim that this play is a genuine solid gold tragedy for my opinions on tragedy to be held valid. My purpose here is simply to point out a historical fact which must be taken into account in any consideration of tragedy, and it is the sharp alteration in the meaning of rank in society between the present time and the distant past. More important to me is the fact that this particular kind of argument obscures much more relevant considerations.

One of these is the question of intensity. It matters not at all whether a modern play concerns itself with a grocer or a president if the intensity of the hero's commitment to his course is less than the maximum possible. It matters not at all whether the hero falls from a great height or a small one, whether he is highly conscious or only dimly aware of what is happening, whether his pride brings the fall or an unseen pattern written behind clouds; if the intensity, the human passion to surpass his given bounds, the fanatic insistence upon his self-conceived role — if these are not present there can only be an outline of tragedy but no living thing. I believe, for myself, that the lasting appeal of tragedy is due to our need to face the fact of death in order to strengthen ourselves for life, and that over and above this function of the tragic viewpoint there are and will be a great number of formal variations which no single definition will ever embrace.

Another issue worth considering is the so-called tragic victory, a question closely related to the consciousness of the hero. One makes nonsense of this if a "victory" means that the hero makes us feel some certain joy when, for instance, he sacrifices himself for a "cause," and unhappy and morose because he dies without one. To begin at the bottom, a man's death is and ought to be an essentially terrifying thing and ought to make nobody happy. But in a great variety of ways even death, the ultimate negative, can be, and appear to be, an assertion of bravery, and can serve to separate the death of man from the death of animals; and I think it is this distinction which underlies any conception of a victory in death. For a society of faith, the nature of the death can prove the existence of the spirit, and posit its immortality. For a secular society it is perhaps more difficult for such a victory to document itself and to make itself felt, but, conversely, the need to offer greater proofs of the humanity of man can make that victory more real. It goes without saying that in a society where there is basic disagreement as to the right way to live, there can hardly be agreement as to the right way to die, and both life and death must be heavily weighted with meaningless futility.

It was not out of any deference to a tragic definition that Willy Loman is filled with a joy, however brokenhearted, as he approaches his end, but simply that my sense of his character dictated his joy, and even what I felt was an exultation. In terms of his character, he has achieved a very powerful piece of knowledge, which is that he is loved by his son and has been embraced by him and forgiven. In this he is given his existence, so to speak — his fatherhood, for which he has always striven and which until now he could not achieve. That he is unable to take this victory thoroughly to his heart, that it closes the circle for him and propels him to his death, is the wage of his sin, which was to have committed himself so completely to the counterfeits of dignity and the false coinage embodied in his idea of success that he can prove his existence only by bestowing "power" on his posterity, a power deriving from the sale of his last asset, himself, for the price of his insurance policy.

I must confess here to a miscalculation, however. I did not realize while writing the play that so many people in the world do not see as clearly or would not admit, as I thought they must, how futile most lives are; so there could be no hope of consoling the audience for the death of this man. I did not realize either how few would be impressed by the fact that this man is actually a very brave spirit who cannot settle for half but must pursue his dream of himself to the end. Finally, I thought it must be clear, even obvious, that this was no dumb brute heading mindlessly to his catastrophe.

I have no need to be Willy's advocate before the jury which decides who is and who is not a tragic hero. I am merely noting that the lingering ponderousness of so many ancient definitions has blinded students and critics to the facts before them, and not only in regard to this play. Had Willy been unaware of his separation from values that endure he would have died contentedly while polishing his car, probably on a Sunday afternoon with the

Introduction to Collected Plays

ball game coming over the radio. But he was agonized by his awareness of being in a false position, so constantly haunted by the hollowness of all he had placed his faith in, so aware, in short, that he must somehow be filled in his spirit or fly apart, that he staked his very life on the ultimate assertion. That he had not the intellectual fluency to verbalize his situation is not the same thing as saying that he lacked awareness, even an overly intensified consciousness that the life he has made was without form and inner meaning.

To be sure, had he been able to know that he was as much the victim of his beliefs as their defeated exemplar, had he known how much of guilt he ought to bear and how much to shed from his soul, he would be more conscious. But it seems to me that there is of necessity a severe limitation of self-awareness in any character, even the most knowing, which serves to define him as a character, and more, that this very limit serves to complete the tragedy and, indeed, to make it at all possible. Complete consciousness is possible only in a play about forces, like *Prometheus*, but not in a play about people. I think that the point is whether there is a sufficient awareness in the hero's career to make the audience supply the rest. Had Oedipus, for instance, been more conscious and more aware of the forces at work upon him he must surely have said that he was not really to blame for having cohabited with his mother since neither he nor anyone else knew she was his mother. He must surely decide to divorce her, provide for their children, firmly resolve to investigate the family background of his next wife, and thus deprive us of a very fine play and the name for a famous neurosis. But he is conscious only up to a point, the point at which guilt begins. Now he is inconsolable and must tear out his eyes. What is tragic about this? Why is it not even ridiculous? How can we respect a man who goes to such extremities over something he could in no way help or prevent? The answer, I think, is not that we respect the man, but that we respect the Law he has so completely broken, wittingly or not, for it is that Law which, we believe, defines us as men. The confusion of some critics viewing *Death of a Salesman* in this regard is that they do not see that Willy Loman has broken a law without whose protection life is insupportable if not incomprehensible to him and to many others; it is the law which says that a failure in society and in business has no right to live. Unlike the law against incest, the law of success is not administered by statute or church, but it is very nearly as powerful in its grip upon men. The confusion increases because, while it is a law, it is by no means a wholly agreeable one even as it is slavishly obeyed, for to fail is no longer to belong to society, in his estimate. Therefore, the path is opened for those who wish to call Willy merely a foolish man even as they themselves are living in obedience to the same law that killed him. Equally, the fact that Willy's law — the belief, in other words, which administers guilt to him — is not a civilizing statute whose destruction menaces us all; it is, rather, a deeply believed and deeply suspect "good" which, when questioned as to its value, as it is in this play, serves more to raise our anxieties than to reassure us of the existence of an unseen but humane metaphysical system in the world. My attempt in the play was to counter this anxiety with an opposing system which, so to speak, is in a race for Willy's faith, and it is the system of love which is the opposite of the law of success. It is embodied in Biff Loman, but by the time Willy can perceive his love it can serve only as an ironic comment upon the life he sacrificed for power and for success and its tokens.

In the writing of *Death of a Salesman* I tried, of course, to achieve a maximum power of effect. But when I saw the devastating force with which it struck its audiences, something within me was shocked and put off. I had thought of myself as rather an optimistic man. I looked at what I had wrought and was forced to wonder whether I knew myself at all if this play, which I had written half in laughter and joy, was as morose and as utterly sad as its audiences found it. Either I was much tougher than they, and could stare at calamity with fewer terrors, or I was harboring within myself another man who was only tangentially connected with what I would have called my rather bright viewpoint about mankind. As I watched and saw tears in the eyes of the audience I felt a certain embarrassment at having, as I thought then, convinced so many people that life was not worth living — for so the play was widely interpreted. I hasten to add now that I ought not have been embarrassed, and that I am convinced the play is not a document of pessimism, a philosophy in which I do not believe.

Nevertheless, the emotionalism with which the play was received helped to generate an opposite impulse and an altered dramatic aim. This ultimately took shape in *The Crucible*, but before it became quite so definite and formed into idea, it was taking hold of my thoughts in a purely dramatic and theatrical context. Perhaps I can indicate its basic elements by saying that *Salesman* moves with its arms open wide, sweeping into itself by means of a subjective process of thought-connection a multitude of observations, feelings, suggestions, and shadings much as the mind does in its ordinary daily functionings. Its author chose its path, of course, but, once chosen, that path could meander as it pleased through a world that was well recognized by the audience. From the theatrical viewpoint that play desired the audience to forget it was in a theater even as it broke the bounds, I believe, of a long convention of realism. Its expressionistic elements were consciously used as such, but since the approach to Willy Loman's characterization was consistently and rigorously subjective, the audience would not ever be aware — if I could help it — that they were witnessing the use of a technique which had until then created only coldness, objectivity, and a highly styled sort of play. I had willingly employed expressionism but always to create a subjective truth, and this play, which was so manifestly "written," seemed as though nobody had written it at all but that it had simply "happened." I had always been attracted and repelled by the brilliance of German expressionism after World

Introduction to Collected Plays

War I, and one aim in *Salesman* was to employ its quite marvelous shorthand for humane, "felt" characterizations rather than for purposes of demonstration for which the Germans had used it.

... For myself, the theater is above all else an instrument of passion. However important considerations of style and form have been to me, they are only means, tools to pry up the well-worn, "inevitable" surfaces of experience behind which swarm the living thoughts and feelings whose expression is the essential purpose of art. I have stood squarely in conventional realism; I have tried to expand it with an imposition of various forms in order to speak more directly, even more abruptly and nakedly of what has moved me behind the visible façades of life. Critics have given me more praise than a writer can reasonably hope for, and more condemnation than one dares believe one has the power to survive. There are certain distillations which remain after the dross rises to the top and boils away, certain old and new commitments which, despite the heat applied to them and the turmoil that has threatened to sweep them away, nevertheless remain, some of them purified.

A play, I think, ought to make sense to common-sense people. I know what it is to have been rejected by them, even unfairly so, but the only challenge worth the effort is the widest one and the tallest one, which is the people themselves. It is their innate conservatism which, I think, is and ought to be the barrier to excess in experiment and the exploitation of the bizarre, even as it is the proper aim of drama to break down the limits of conventional unawareness and acceptance of outmoded and banal forms.

By whatever means it is accomplished, the prime business of a play is to arouse the passions of its audience so that by the route of passion may be opened up new relationships between a man and men, and between men and Man. Drama is akin to the other inventions of man in that it ought to help us to know more, and not merely to spend our feelings.

The ultimate justification for a genuine new form is the new and heightened consciousness it creates and makes possible — a consciousness of causation in the light of known but hitherto inexplicable effects.

Not only in the drama, but in sociology, psychology, psychiatry, and religion, the past half century has created an almost overwhelming documentation of man as a nearly passive creation of environment and family-created psychological drives. If only from the dramatic point of view, this dictum cannot be accepted as final and "realistic" any more than man's ultimate position can be accepted as his efficient use by state or corporate apparatus. It is no more "real," however, for drama to "liberate" itself from this vise by the route of romance and the spectacle of free will and a new heroic formula than it is "real" now to represent man's defeat as the ultimate implication of an overwhelming determinism.

Realism, heightened or conventional, is neither more nor less an artifice, a species of poetic symbolization, than any other form. It is merely more familiar in this age. If it is used as a covering of safety against the evaluation of life it must be overthrown, and for that reason above all the rest. But neither poetry nor liberation can come merely from a rearrangement of the lights or from leaving the skeletons of the flats exposed instead of covered by painted cloths; nor can it come merely from the masking of the human face or the transformation of speech into rhythmic verse, or from the expunging of common details of life's apparencies. A new poem on the stage is a new concept of relationships between the one and the many and the many and history, and to create it requires greater attention, not less, to the inexorable, common, pervasive conditions of existence in this time and this hour. Otherwise only a new self-indulgence is created, and it will be left behind, however poetic its surface.

A drama worthy of its time must first, knowingly or by instinctive means, recognize its major and most valuable traditions and where it has departed from them. Determinism, whether it is based on the iron necessities of economics or on psychoanalytic theory seen as a closed circle, is a contradiction of the idea of drama itself as drama has come down to us in its fullest developments. The idea of the hero, let alone the mere protagonist, is incompatible with a drama whose bounds are set in advance by the concept of an unbreakable trap. Nor is it merely that one wants arbitrarily to find a hero and victory. The history of man is a ceaseless process of overthrowing one determinism to make way for another more faithful to life's changing relationships. And it is a process inconceivable without the existence of the will of man. His will is as much a fact as his defeat. Any determinism, even the most scientific, is only that stasis, that seemingly endless pause, before the application of man's will administering a new insight into causation.

The analogy to physics may not be out of place. The once-irreducible elements of matter, whose behavior was seen as fixed and remorseless, disintegrated under the controlled bombardment of atomic particles until so fine a perception as the scale of atomic weights appears as a relatively gross concept on the road to man's manipulation of the material world. More to the point: even as the paths, the powers, and the behavior of smaller and smaller elements and forces in nature are brought into the fields of measurement, we are faced with the dialectical irony that the act of measurement itself changes the particle being measured, so that we can know only what it is at the moment when it receives the impact of our rays, not what it was before it was struck. The idea of realism has become wedded to the idea that man is at best the sum of forces working upon him and of given psychological forces within him. Yet an innate value, an innate will, does in fact posit itself as real not alone because it is devoutly to be wished, but because, however closely he is measured and systematically accounted for, he is more than the sum of his stimuli and is unpredictable beyond a certain point. A drama, like a history, which stops at this point, the point of conditioning, is not reflecting reality. What is wanted, therefore, is not a poetry of escape from process and determinism, like that mood play which stops where feeling ends or that inverted romanticism which would mirror all the world in the sado-masochistic relationship. Nor will the heightening of the intensity of language alone yield the prize. A new poem will appear because a new balance has been struck which embraces both determinism and the paradox of will. If there is one unseen goal toward which every play in this book strives, it is that very discovery and its proof — that we are made and yet are more than what made us.

Death of a Salesman

Certain private conversations in two acts and a requiem

The action takes place in Willy Loman's house and yard and in various places he visits in the New York and Boston of today. Throughout the play, in the stage directions, left and right mean stage left and stage right.

ACT ONE

A melody is heard, played upon a flute. It is small and fine, telling of grass and trees and the horizon. The curtain rises.

Before us is the Salesman's house. We are aware of towering, angular shapes behind it, surrounding it on all sides. Only the blue light of the sky falls upon the house and forestage; the surrounding area shows an angry glow of orange. As more light appears, we see a solid vault of apartment houses around the small, fragile-seeming home. An air of the dream clings to the place, a dream rising out of reality. The kitchen at center seems actual enough, for there is a kitchen table with three chairs, and a refrigerator. But no other fixtures are seen. At the back of the kitchen there is a draped entrance, which leads to the living-room.

To the right of the kitchen, on a level raised two feet, is a bedroom furnished only with a brass bedstead and a straight chair. On a shelf over the bed a silver athletic trophy stands. A window opens onto the apartment house at the side.

Behind the kitchen, on a level raised six and a half feet, is the boys' bedroom, at present barely visible. Two beds are dimly seen, and at the back of the room a dormer window. (This bedroom is above the unseen living-room.) At the left a stairway curves up to it from the kitchen.

The entire setting is wholly or, in some places, partially transparent. The roof-line of the house is one-dimensional; under and over it we see the apartment buildings. Before the house lies an apron, curving beyond the forestage into the orchestra. This forward area serves as the back yard as well as the locale of all WILLY's imaginings and of his city scenes. Whenever the action is in the present the actors observe the imaginary wall-lines, entering the house only through its door at the left. But in the scenes of the past these boundaries are broken, and characters enter or leave a room by stepping "through" a wall onto the forestage.

From the right, WILLY LOMAN, the Salesman, enters, carrying two large sample cases. The flute plays on. He hears but is not aware of it. He is past sixty years of age, dressed quietly. Even as he crosses the stage to the doorway of the house, his exhaustion is apparent. He unlocks the door, comes into the kitchen, and thankfully lets his burden down, feeling the soreness of his palms. A word-sigh escapes his lips — it might be "Oh, boy, oh, boy." He closes the door, then carries his cases out into the living-room, through the draped kitchen doorway.

LINDA, his wife, has stirred in her bed at the right. She gets out and puts on a robe, listening. Most often jovial, she has developed an iron repression of her exceptions to WILLY's behavior — she more than loves him, she admires him, as though his mercurial nature, his temper, his massive dreams and little cruelties, served her only as sharp reminders of the turbulent longings within him, longings which she shares but lacks the temperament to utter and follow to their end.

LINDA (*hearing* WILLY *outside the bedroom, calls with some trepidation*). Willy!
WILLY. It's all right. I came back.
LINDA. Why? What happened? (*Slight pause.*) Did something happen, Willy?
WILLY. No, nothing happened.
LINDA. You didn't smash the car, did you?
WILLY (*with casual irritation*). I said nothing happened. Didn't you hear me?
LINDA. Don't you feel well?
WILLY. I'm tired to the death. (*The flute has faded away. He sits on the bed beside her, a little numb.*) I couldn't make it. I just couldn't make it, Linda.
LINDA (*very carefully, delicately*). Where were you all day? You look terrible.
WILLY. I got as far as a little above Yonkers. I stopped for a cup of coffee. Maybe it was the coffee.
LINDA. What?
WILLY (*after a pause*). I suddenly couldn't drive any more. The car kept going off onto the shoulder, y'know?
LINDA (*helpfully*). Oh. Maybe it was the steering again. I don't think Angelo knows the Studebaker.
WILLY. No, it's me, it's me. Suddenly I realize I'm goin' sixty miles an

hour and I don't remember the last five minutes. I'm — I can't seem to — keep my mind to it.

LINDA. Maybe it's your glasses. You never went for your new glasses.

WILLY. No, I see everything. I came back ten miles an hour. It took me nearly four hours from Yonkers.

LINDA (*resigned*). Well, you'll just have to take a rest, Willy, you can't continue this way.

WILLY. I just got back from Florida.

LINDA. But you didn't rest your mind. Your mind is overactive, and the mind is what counts, dear.

WILLY. I'll start out in the morning. Maybe I'll feel better in the morning. (*She is taking off his shoes.*) These goddam arch supports are killing me.

LINDA. Take an aspirin. Should I get you an aspirin? It'll soothe you.

WILLY (*with wonder*). I was driving along, you understand? And I was fine. I was even observing the scenery. You can imagine, me looking at scenery, on the road every week of my life. But it's so beautiful up there, Linda, the trees are so thick, and the sun is warm. I opened the windshield and just let the warm air bathe over me. And then all of a sudden I'm goin' off the road! I'm tellin' ya, I absolutely forgot I was driving. If I'd've gone the other way over the white line I might've killed somebody. So I went on again — and five minutes later I'm dreamin' again, and I nearly — (*He presses two fingers against his eyes.*) I have such thoughts, I have such strange thoughts.

LINDA. Willy, dear. Talk to them again. There's no reason why you can't work in New York.

WILLY. They don't need me in New York. I'm the New England man. I'm vital in New England.

LINDA. But you're sixty years old. They can't expect you to keep traveling every week.

WILLY. I'll have to send a wire to Portland. I'm supposed to see Brown and Morrison tomorrow morning at ten o'clock to show the line. Goddammit, I could sell them! (*He starts putting on his jacket.*)

LINDA (*taking the jacket from him*). Why don't you go down to the place tomorrow and tell Howard you've simply got to work in New York? You're too accommodating, dear.

WILLY. If old man Wagner was alive I'd a been in charge of New York now! That man was a prince, he was a masterful man. But that boy of his, that Howard, he don't appreciate. When I went north the first time, the Wagner Company didn't know where New England was!

LINDA. Why don't you tell those things to Howard, dear?

WILLY (*encouraged*). I will, I definitely will. Is there any cheese?

LINDA. I'll make you a sandwich.

WILLY. No, go to sleep. I'll take some milk. I'll be up right away. The boys in?

LINDA. They're sleeping. Happy took Biff on a date tonight.

WILLY (*interested*). That so?

LINDA. It was so nice to see them shaving together, one behind the other, in the bathroom. And going out together. You notice? The whole house smells of shaving lotion.

WILLY. Figure it out. Work a lifetime to pay off a house. You finally own it, and there's nobody to live in it.

LINDA. Well, dear, life is a casting off. It's always that way.

WILLY. No, no, some people — some people accomplish something. Did Biff say anything after I went this morning?

LINDA. You shouldn't have criticized him, Willy, especially after he just got off the train. You mustn't lose your temper with him.

WILLY. When the hell did I lose my temper? I simply asked him if he was making any money. Is that a criticism?

LINDA. But, dear, how could he make any money?

WILLY (*worried and angered*). There's such an undercurrent in him. He became a moody man. Did he apologize when I left this morning?

LINDA. He was crestfallen, Willy. You know how he admires you. I think if he finds himself, then you'll both be happier and not fight any more.

WILLY. How can he find himself on a farm? Is that a life? A farmhand? In the beginning, when he was young, I thought, well, a young man, it's good for him to tramp around, take a lot of different jobs. But it's more than ten years now and he has yet to make thirty-five dollars a week!

LINDA. He's finding himself, Willy.

WILLY. Not finding yourself at the age of thirty-four is a disgrace!

LINDA. Shh!

WILLY. The trouble is he's lazy, goddammit!

LINDA. Willy, please!

WILLY. Biff is a lazy bum!

LINDA. They're sleeping. Get something to eat. Go on down.

WILLY. Why did he come home? I would like to know what brought him home.

LINDA. I don't know. I think he's still lost, Willy. I think he's very lost.

WILLY. Biff Loman is lost. In the greatest country in the world a young man with such — personal attractiveness, gets lost. And such a hard worker. There's one thing about Biff — he's not lazy.

LINDA. Never.

WILLY (*with pity and resolve*). I'll see him in the morning; I'll have a nice talk with him. I'll get him a job selling. He could be big in no time. My God! Remember how they used to follow him around in high school? When he smiled at one of them their faces lit up. When he walked down the street ... (*He loses himself in reminiscences.*)

LINDA (*trying to bring him out of it*). Willy, dear, I got a new kind of American-type cheese today. It's whipped.

WILLY. Why do you get American when I like Swiss?

LINDA. I just thought you'd like a change —

WILLY. I don't want a change! I want Swiss cheese. Why am I always being contradicted?

LINDA (*with a covering laugh*). I thought it would be a surprise.

WILLY. Why don't you open a window in here, for God's sake?

LINDA (*with infinite patience*). They're all open, dear.

WILLY. The way they boxed us in here. Bricks and windows, windows and bricks.

LINDA. We should've bought the land next door.

WILLY. The street is lined with cars. There's not a breath of fresh air in the neighborhood. The grass don't grow any more, you can't raise a carrot in the back yard. They should've had a law against apartment houses. Remember those two beautiful elm trees out there? When I and Biff hung the swing between them?

LINDA. Yeah, like being a million miles from the city.

WILLY. They should've arrested the builder for cutting those down. They massacred the neighborhood. (*Lost.*) More and more I think of those days, Linda. This time of year it was lilac and wisteria. And then the peonies would come out, and the daffodils. What fragrance in this room!

LINDA. Well, after all, people had to move somewhere.

WILLY. No, there's more people now.

LINDA. I don't think there's more people. I think —

WILLY. There's more people! That's what's ruining this country! Population is getting out of control. The competition is maddening! Smell the stink from that apartment house! And another one on the other side . . . How can they whip cheese?

On WILLY's *last line*, BIFF *and* HAPPY *raise themselves up in their beds, listening.*

LINDA. Go down, try it. And be quiet.

WILLY (*turning to* LINDA, *guiltily*). You're not worried about me, are you, sweetheart?

BIFF. What's the matter?

HAPPY. Listen!

LINDA. You've got too much on the ball to worry about.

WILLY. You're my foundation and my support, Linda.

LINDA. Just try to relax, dear. You make mountains out of molehills.

WILLY. I won't fight with him any more. If he wants to go back to Texas, let him go.

LINDA. He'll find his way.

WILLY. Sure. Certain men just don't get started till later in life. Like Thomas Edison, I think. Or B. F. Goodrich. One of them was deaf. (*He starts for the bedroom doorway.*) I'll put my money on Biff.

LINDA. And Willy — if it's warm Sunday we'll drive in the country. And we'll open the windshield, and take lunch.

WILLY. No, the windshields don't open on the new cars.

LINDA. But you opened it today.

Death of a Salesman 617

WILLY. Me? I didn't. (*He stops.*) Now isn't that peculiar! Isn't that a remarkable — (*He breaks off in amazement and fright as the flute is heard distantly.*)

LINDA. What, darling?

WILLY. That is the most remarkable thing.

LINDA. What, dear?

WILLY. I was thinking of the Chevvy. (*Slight pause.*) Nineteen twenty-eight . . . when I had that red Chevvy — (*Breaks off.*) That funny? I coulda sworn I was driving that Chevvy today.

LINDA. Well, that's nothing. Something must've reminded you.

WILLY. Remarkable. Ts. Remember those days? The way Biff used to simonize that car? The dealer refused to believe there was eighty thousand miles on it. (*He shakes his head.*) Heh! (*To* LINDA.) Close your eyes, I'll be right up. (*He walks out of the bedroom.*)

HAPPY (*to* BIFF). Jesus, maybe he smashed up the car again!

LINDA (*calling after* WILLY). Be careful on the stairs, dear! The cheese is on the middle shelf! (*She turns, goes over to the bed, takes his jacket, and goes out of the bedroom.*)

> *Light has risen on the boys' room. Unseen,* WILLY *is heard talking to himself, "Eighty thousand miles," and a little laugh.* BIFF *gets out of bed, comes downstage a bit, and stands attentively.* BIFF *is two years older than his brother* HAPPY, *well built, but in these days bears a worn air and seems less self-assured. He has succeeded less, and his dreams are stronger and less acceptable than* HAPPY's. HAPPY *is tall, powerfully made. Sexuality is like a visible color on him, or a scent that many women have discovered. He, like his brother, is lost, but in a different way, for he has never allowed himself to turn his face toward defeat and is thus more confused and hard-skinned, although seemingly more content.*

HAPPY (*getting out of bed*). He's going to get his license taken away if he keeps that up. I'm getting nervous about him, y'know, Biff?

BIFF. His eyes are going.

HAPPY. No, I've driven with him. He sees all right. He just doesn't keep his mind on it. I drove into the city with him last week. He stops at a green light and then it turns red and he goes. (*He laughs.*)

BIFF. Maybe he's color-blind.

HAPPY. Pop? Why he's got the finest eye for color in the business. You know that.

BIFF (*sitting down on his bed*). I'm going to sleep.

HAPPY. You're not still sour on Dad, are you, Biff?

BIFF. He's all right, I guess.

WILLY (*underneath them, in the living-room*). Yes, sir, eighty thousand miles — eighty-two thousand!

BIFF. You smoking?

HAPPY (*holding out a pack of cigarettes*). Want one?

BIFF (*taking a cigarette*). I can never sleep when I smell it.

WILLY. What a simonizing job, heh!

HAPPY (*with deep sentiment*). Funny, Biff, y'know? Us sleeping in here again? The old beds. (*He pats his bed affectionately.*) All the talk that went across those two beds, huh? Our whole lives.

BIFF. Yeah. Lotta dreams and plans.

HAPPY (*with a deep and masculine laugh*). About five hundred women would like to know what was said in this room.

They share a soft laugh.

BIFF. Remember that big Betsy something — what the hell was her name — over on Bushwick Avenue?

HAPPY (*combing his hair*). With the collie dog!

BIFF. That's the one. I got you in there, remember?

HAPPY. Yeah, that was my first time — I think. Boy, there was a pig! (*They laugh, almost crudely.*) You taught me everything I know about women. Don't forget that.

BIFF. I bet you forgot how bashful you used to be. Especially with girls.

HAPPY. Oh, I still am, Biff.

BIFF. Oh, go on.

HAPPY. I just control it, that's all. I think I got less bashful and you got more so. What happened, Biff? Where's the old humor, the old confidence? (*He shakes* BIFF's *knee.* BIFF *gets up and moves restlessly about the room.*) What's the matter?

BIFF. Why does Dad mock me all the time?

HAPPY. He's not mocking you, he —

BIFF. Everything I say there's a twist of mockery on his face. I can't get near him.

HAPPY. He just wants you to make good, that's all. I wanted to talk to you about Dad for a long time, Biff. Something's — happening to him. He — talks to himself.

BIFF. I noticed that this morning. But he always mumbled.

HAPPY. But not so noticeable. It got so embarrassing I sent him to Florida. And you know something? Most of the time he's talking to you.

BIFF. What's he say about me?

HAPPY. I can't make it out.

BIFF. What's he say about me?

HAPPY. I think the fact that you're not settled, that you're still kind of up in the air . . .

BIFF. There's one or two other things depressing him, Happy.

HAPPY. What do you mean?

BIFF. Never mind. Just don't lay it all to me.

HAPPY. But I think if you just got started — I mean — is there any future for you out there?

BIFF. I tell ya, Hap, I don't know what the future is. I don't know — what I'm supposed to want.

HAPPY. What do you mean?

BIFF. Well, I spent six or seven years after high school trying to work myself up. Shipping clerk, salesman, business of one kind or another. And it's a measly manner of existence. To get on that subway on the hot mornings in summer. To devote your whole life to keeping stock, or making phone calls, or selling or buying. To suffer fifty weeks of the year for the sake of a two-week vacation, when all you really desire is to be outdoors, with your shirt off. And always to have to get ahead of the next fella. And still — that's how you build a future.

HAPPY. Well, you really enjoy it on a farm? Are you content out there?

BIFF (*with rising agitation*). Hap, I've had twenty or thirty different kinds of jobs since I left home before the war, and it always turns out the same. I just realized it lately. In Nebraska when I herded cattle, and the Dakotas, and Arizona, and now in Texas. It's why I came home now, I guess, because I realized it. This farm I work on, it's spring there now, see? And they've got about fifteen new colts. There's nothing more inspiring or — beautiful than the sight of a mare and a new colt. And it's cool there now, see? Texas is cool now, and it's spring. And whenever spring comes to where I am, I suddenly get the feeling, my God, I'm not gettin' anywhere! What the hell am I doing, playing around with horses, twenty-eight dollars a week! I'm thirty-four years old, I oughta be makin' my future. That's when I come running home. And now, I get here, and I don't know what to do with myself. (*After a pause.*) I've always made a point of not wasting my life, and everytime I come back here I know that all I've done is to waste my life.

HAPPY. You're a poet, you know that, Biff? You're a — you're an idealist!

BIFF. No, I'm mixed up very bad. Maybe I oughta get married. Maybe I oughta get stuck into something. Maybe that's my trouble. I'm like a boy. I'm not married, I'm not in business, I just — I'm like a boy. Are you content, Hap? You're a success, aren't you? Are you content?

HAPPY. Hell, no!

BIFF. Why? You're making money, aren't you?

HAPPY (*moving about with energy, expressiveness*). All I can do now is wait for the merchandise manager to die. And suppose I get to be merchandise manager? He's a good friend of mine, and he just built a terrific estate on Long Island. And he lived there about two months and sold it, and now he's building another one. He can't enjoy it once it's finished. And I know that's just what I would do. I don't know what the hell I'm workin' for. Sometimes I sit in my apartment — all alone. And I think of the rent I'm paying. And it's crazy. But then, it's what I always wanted. My own apartment, a car, and plenty of women. And still, goddammit, I'm lonely.

BIFF (*with enthusiasm*). Listen, why don't you come out West with me?

HAPPY. You and I, heh?

BIFF. Sure, maybe we could buy a ranch. Raise cattle, use our muscles. Men built like we are should be working out in the open.

HAPPY (*avidly*). The Loman Brothers, heh?

BIFF (*with vast affection*). Sure, we'd be known all over the counties!

HAPPY (*enthralled*). That's what I dream about, Biff. Sometimes I want to just rip my clothes off in the middle of the store and outbox that goddam merchandise manager. I mean I can outbox, outrun, and outlift anybody in that store, and I have to take orders from those common, petty sons-of-bitches till I can't stand it any more.

BIFF. I'm tellin' you, kid, if you were with me I'd be happy out there.

HAPPY (*enthused*). See, Biff, everybody around me is so false that I'm constantly lowering my ideals . . .

BIFF. Baby, together we'd stand up for one another, we'd have someone to trust.

HAPPY. If I were around you —

BIFF. Hap, the trouble is we weren't brought up to grub for money. I don't know how to do it.

HAPPY. Neither can I!

BIFF. Then let's go!

HAPPY. The only thing is — what can you make out there?

BIFF. But look at your friend. Builds an estate and then hasn't the peace of mind to live in it.

HAPPY. Yeah, but when he walks into the store the waves part in front of him. That's fifty-two thousand dollars a year coming through the revolving door, and I got more in my pinky finger than he's got in his head.

BIFF. Yeah, but you just said —

HAPPY. I gotta show some of those pompous, self-important executives over there that Hap Loman can make the grade. I want to walk into the store the way he walks in. Then I'll go with you, Biff. We'll be together yet, I swear. But take those two we had tonight. Now weren't they gorgeous creatures?

BIFF. Yeah, yeah, most gorgeous I've had in years.

HAPPY. I get that any time I want, Biff. Whenever I feel disgusted. The only trouble is, it gets like bowling or something. I just keep knockin' them over and it doesn't mean anything. You still run around a lot?

BIFF. Naa. I'd like to find a girl — steady, somebody with substance.

HAPPY. That's what I long for.

BIFF. Go on! You'd never come home.

HAPPY. I would! Somebody with character, with resistance! Like Mom, y'know? You're gonna call me a bastard when I tell you this. That girl Charlotte I was with tonight is engaged to be married in five weeks. (*He tries on his new hat.*)

BIFF. No kiddin'!

HAPPY. Sure, the guy's in line for the vice-presidency of the store. I don't know what gets into me, maybe I just have an overdeveloped sense of competition or something, but I went and ruined her, and furthermore I can't get rid of her. And he's the third executive I've done that to. Isn't that a crummy characteristic? And to top it all, I go to their weddings! (*Indig-*

Death of a Salesman 621

nantly, but laughing.) Like I'm not supposed to take bribes. Manufacturers offer me a hundred-dollar bill now and then to throw an order their way. You know how honest I am, but it's like this girl, see. I hate myself for it. Because I don't want the girl, and, still, I take it and — I love it!

BIFF. Let's go to sleep.
HAPPY. I guess we didn't settle anything, heh?
BIFF. I just got one idea that I think I'm going to try.
HAPPY. What's that?
BIFF. Remember Bill Oliver?
HAPPY. Sure, Oliver is very big now. You want to work for him again?
BIFF. No, but when I quit he said something to me. He put his arm on my shoulder, and he said, "Biff, if you ever need anything, come to me."
HAPPY. I remember that. That sounds good.
BIFF. I think I'll go to see him. If I could get ten thousand or even seven or eight thousand dollars I could buy a beautiful ranch.
HAPPY. I bet he'd back you. 'Cause he thought highly of you, Biff. I mean, they all do. You're well liked, Biff. That's why I say to come back here, and we both have the apartment. And I'm telling' you, Biff, any babe you want . . .
BIFF. No, with a ranch I could do the work I like and still be something. I just wonder though. I wonder if Oliver still thinks I stole that carton of basketballs.
HAPPY. Oh, he probably forgot that long ago. It's almost ten years. You're too sensitive. Anyway, he didn't really fire you.
BIFF. Well, I think he was going to. I think that's why I quit. I was never sure whether he knew or not. I know he thought the world of me, though. I was the only one he'd let lock up the place.
WILLY (*below*). You gonna wash the engine, Biff?
HAPPY. Shh!

BIFF *looks at* HAPPY, *who is gazing down, listening.* WILLY *is mumbling in the parlor.*

HAPPY. You hear that?

They listen. WILLY *laughs warmly.*

BIFF (*growing angry*). Doesn't he know Mom can hear that?
WILLY. Don't get your sweater dirty, Biff!

A look of pain crosses BIFF's *face.*

HAPPY. Isn't that terrible? Don't leave again, will you? You'll find a job here. You gotta stick around. I don't know what to do about him, it's getting embarrassing.
WILLY. What a simonizing job!
BIFF. Mom's hearing that!
WILLY. No kiddin', Biff, you got a date? Wonderful!
HAPPY. Go on to sleep. But talk to him in the morning, will you?
BIFF (*reluctantly getting into bed*). With her in the house. Brother!
HAPPY (*getting into bed*). I wish you'd have a good talk with him.

The light on their room begins to fade.

BIFF (*to himself in bed*). That selfish, stupid...

HAPPY. Sh... Sleep, Biff.

Their light is out. Well before they have finished speaking, WILLY's *form is dimly seen below in the darkened kitchen. He opens the refrigerator, searches in there, and takes out a bottle of milk. The apartment houses are fading out, and the entire house and surroundings become covered with leaves. Music insinuates itself as the leaves appear........*

WILLY. Just wanna be careful with those girls, Biff, that's all. Don't make any promises. No promises of any kind. Because a girl, y'know, they always believe what you tell 'em, and you're very young, Biff, you're too young to be talking seriously to girls.

Light rises on the kitchen. WILLY, *talking, shuts the refrigerator door and comes downstage to the kitchen table. He pours milk into a glass. He is totally immersed in himself, smiling faintly.*

WILLY. Too young entirely, Biff. You want to watch your schooling first. Then when you're all set, there'll be plenty of girls for a boy like you. (*He smiles broadly at a kitchen chair.*) That so? The girls pay for you? (*He laughs.*) Boy, you must really be makin' a hit.

WILLY *is gradually addressing — physically — a point offstage, speaking through the wall of the kitchen, and his voice has been rising in volume to that of a normal conversation.*

WILLY. I been wondering why you polish the car so careful. Ha! Don't leave the hubcaps, boys. Get the chamois to the hubcaps. Happy, use newspaper on the windows, it's the easiest thing. Show him how to do it, Biff! You see, Happy? Pad it up, use it like a pad. That's it, that's it, good work. You're doin' all right, Hap. (*He pauses, then nods in approbation for a few seconds, then looks upward.*) Biff, first thing we gotta do when we get time is clip that big branch over the house. Afraid it's gonna fall in a storm and hit the roof. Tell you what. We get a rope and sling her around, and then we climb up there with a couple of saws and take her down. Soon as you finish the car, boys, I wanna see ya. I got a surprise for you, boys.

BIFF (*offstage*). Whatta ya got, Dad?

WILLY. No, you finish first. Never leave a job till you're finished — remember that. (*Looking toward the "big trees."*) Biff, up in Albany I saw a beautiful hammock. I think I'll buy it next trip, and we'll hang it right between those two elms. Wouldn't that be something? Just swingin' there under those branches. Boy, that would be...

YOUNG BIFF *and* YOUNG HAPPY *appear from the direction* WILLY *was addressing.* HAPPY *carries rags and a pail of water.* BIFF, *wearing a sweater with a block "S," carries a football.*

BIFF (*pointing in the direction of the car offstage*). How's that, Pop, professional?

WILLY. Terrific. Terrific job, boys. Good work, Biff.

HAPPY. Where's the surprise, Pop?

WILLY. In the back seat of the car.

HAPPY. Boy! (*He runs off.*)

BIFF. What is it, Dad? Tell me, what'd you buy?

WILLY (*laughing, cuffs him*). Never mind, something I want you to have.

BIFF (*turns and starts off*). What is it, Hap?

HAPPY (*offstage*). It's a punching bag!

BIFF. Oh, Pop!

WILLY. It's got Gene Tunney's signature on it!

   HAPPY *runs onstage with a punching bag.*

BIFF. Gee, how'd you know we wanted a punching bag?

WILLY. Well, it's the finest thing for the timing.

HAPPY (*lies down on his back and pedals with his feet*). I'm losing weight, you notice, Pop?

WILLY (*to* HAPPY). Jumping rope is good too.

BIFF. Did you see the new football I got?

WILLY (*examining the ball*). Where'd you get a new ball?

BIFF. The coach told me to practice my passing.

WILLY. That so? And he gave you the ball, heh?

BIFF. Well, I borrowed it from the locker room. (*He laughs confidentially.*)

WILLY (*laughing with him at the theft*). I want you to return that.

HAPPY. I told you he wouldn't like it!

BIFF (*angrily*). Well, I'm bringing it back!

WILLY (*stopping the incipient argument, to* HAPPY). Sure, he's gotta practice with a regulation ball, doesn't he? (*To* BIFF.) Coach'll probably congratulate you on your initiative!

BIFF. Oh, he keeps congratulating my initiative all the time Pop.

WILLY. That's because he likes you. If somebody else took that ball there'd be an uproar. So what's the report, boys, what's the report?

BIFF. Where'd you go this time, Dad? Gee we were lonesome for you.

WILLY (*pleased, puts an arm around each boy and they come down to the apron*). Lonesome, heh?

BIFF. Missed you every minute.

WILLY. Don't say? Tell you a secret, boys. Don't breathe it to a soul. Someday I'll have my own business, and I'll never have to leave home any more.

HAPPY. Like Uncle Charley, heh?

WILLY. Bigger than Uncle Charley! Because Charley is not — liked. He's liked, but he's not — well liked.

BIFF. Where'd you go this time, Dad?

WILLY. Well, I got on the road, and I went north to Providence. Met the Mayor.

BIFF. The Mayor of Providence!

WILLY. He was sitting in the hotel lobby.

BIFF. What'd he say?

WILLY. He said, "Morning!" And I said, "You got a fine city here, Mayor." And then he had coffee with me. And then I went to Waterbury. Waterbury is a fine city. Big clock city, the famous Waterbury clock. Sold a nice bill there. And then Boston — Boston is the cradle of the Revolution. A fine city. And a couple of other towns in Mass., and on to Portland and Bangor and straight home!

BIFF. Gee, I'd love to go with you sometime, Dad.

WILLY. Soon as summer comes.

HAPPY. Promise?

WILLY. You and Hap and I, and I'll show you all the towns. America is full of beautiful towns, and fine, upstanding people. And they know me, boys, they know me up and down New England. The finest people. And when I bring you fellas up, there'll be open sesame for all of us, 'cause one thing, boys: I have friends. I can park my car in any street in New England and the cops protect it like their own. This summer, heh?

BIFF and HAPPY (*together*). Yeah! You bet!

WILLY. We'll take our bathing suits.

HAPPY. We'll carry your bags, Pop!

WILLY. Oh, won't that be something! Me comin' into the Boston stores with you boys carryin' my bags. What a sensation!

BIFF *is prancing around, practicing passing the ball.*

WILLY. You nervous, Biff, about the game?

BIFF. Not if you're gonna be there.

WILLY. What do they say about you in school, now that they made you captain?

HAPPY. There's a crowd of girls behind him everytime the classes change.

BIFF (*taking* WILLY's *hand*). This Saturday, Pop, this Saturday — just for you, I'm going to break through for a touchdown.

HAPPY. You're supposed to pass.

BIFF. I'm takin' one play for Pop. You watch me, Pop, and when I take off my helmet, that means I'm breakin' out. Then you watch me crash through that line!

WILLY (*kisses* BIFF). Oh, wait'll I tell this in Boston!

BERNARD *enters in knickers. He is younger than* BIFF, *earnest and loyal, a worried boy.*

BERNARD. Biff, where are you? You're supposed to study with me today.

WILLY. Hey, looka Bernard. What're you lookin' so anemic about, Bernard?

BERNARD. He's gotta study, Uncle Willy. He's got Regents next week.

HAPPY (*tauntingly, spinning* BERNARD *around*). Let's box, Bernard!

BERNARD. Biff! (*He gets away from* HAPPY.) Listen, Biff, I heard Mr. Birnbaum say that if you don't start studyin' math he's gonna flunk you, and you won't graduate. I heard him!

WILLY. You better study with him, Biff. Go ahead now.

BERNARD. I heard him!

BIFF. Oh, Pop, you didn't see my sneakers! (*He holds up a foot for* WILLY *to look at.*)

WILLY. Hey, that's a beautiful job of printing!

BERNARD (*wiping his glasses*). Just because he printed University of Virginia on his sneakers doesn't mean they've got to graduate him, Uncle Willy!

WILLY (*angrily*). What're you talking about? With scholarships to three universities they're gonna flunk him?

BERNARD. But I heard Mr. Birnbaum say —

WILLY. Don't be a pest, Bernard! (*To his boys.*) What an anemic!

BERNARD. Okay, I'm waiting for you in my house, Biff.

BERNARD *goes off. The Lomans laugh.*

WILLY. Bernard is not well liked, is he?

BIFF. He's liked, but he's not well liked.

HAPPY. That's right, Pop.

WILLY. That's just what I mean. Bernard can get the best marks in school, y'understand, but when he gets out in the business world, y'understand, you are going to be five times ahead of him. That's why I thank Almighty God you're both built like Adonises. Because the man who makes an appearance in the business world, the man who creates personal interest, is the man who gets ahead. Be liked and you will never want. You take me, for instance. I never have to wait in line to see a buyer. "Willy Loman is here!" That's all they have to know, and I go right through.

BIFF. Did you knock them dead, Pop?

WILLY. Knocked 'em cold in Providence, slaughtered 'em in Boston.

HAPPY (*on his back, pedaling again*). I'm losing weight, you notice, Pop?

LINDA *enters, as of old, a ribbon in her hair, carrying a basket of washing.*

LINDA (*with youthful energy*). Hello, dear!

WILLY. Sweetheart!

LINDA. How'd the Chevvy run?

WILLY. Chevrolet, Linda, is the greatest car ever built. (*To the boys.*) Since when do you let your mother carry wash up the stairs?

BIFF. Grab hold there, boy!

HAPPY. Where to, Mom?

LINDA. Hang them up on the line. And you better go down to your friends, Biff. The cellar is full of boys. They don't know what to do with themselves.

BIFF. Ah, when Pop comes home they can wait!

WILLY (*laughs appreciatively*). You better go down and tell them what to do, Biff.

BIFF. I think I'll have them sweep out the furnace room.

WILLY. Good work, Biff.

BIFF (*goes through wall-line of kitchen to doorway at back and calls down.*) Fellas! Everybody sweep out the furnace room! I'll be right down!

VOICES. All right! Okay, Biff.

BIFF. George and Sam and Frank, come out back! We're hangin' up the wash! Come on, Hap, on the double! (*He and* HAPPY *carry out the basket.*)

LINDA. The way they obey him!

WILLY. Well, that's training, the training. I'm tellin' you, I was sellin' thousands and thousands, but I had to come home.

LINDA. Oh, the whole block'll be at that game. Did you sell anything?

WILLY. I did five hundred gross in Providence and seven hundred gross in Boston.

LINDA. No! Wait a minute, I've got a pencil. (*She pulls pencil and paper out of her apron pocket.*) That makes your commission . . . Two hundred — my God! Two hundred and twelve dollars!

WILLY. Well, I didn't figure it yet, but . . .

LINDA. How much did you do?

WILLY. Well, I — I did — about a hundred and eighty gross in Providence. Well, no — it came to — roughly two hundred gross on the whole trip.

LINDA (*without hesitation*). Two hundred gross. That's . . . (*She figures.*)

WILLY. The trouble was that three of the stores were half closed for inventory in Boston. Otherwise I woulda broke records.

LINDA. Well, it makes seventy dollars and some pennies. That's very good.

WILLY. What do we owe?

LINDA. Well, on the first there's sixteen dollars on the refrigerator —

WILLY. Why sixteen?

LINDA. Well, the fan belt broke, so it was a dollar eighty.

WILLY. But it's brand new.

LINDA. Well, the man said that's the way it is. Till they work themselves in, y'know.

They move through the wall-line into the kitchen.

WILLY. I hope we didn't get stuck on that machine.

LINDA. They got the biggest ads of any of them!

WILLY. I know, it's a fine machine. What else?

LINDA. Well, there's nine-sixty for the washing machine. And for the vacuum cleaner there's three and a half due on the fifteenth. Then the roof, you got twenty-one dollars remaining.

WILLY. It don't leak, does it?

LINDA. No, they did a wonderful job. Then you owe Frank for the carburetor.

WILLY. I'm not going to pay that man! That goddam Chevrolet, they ought to prohibit the manufacture of that car!

LINDA. Well, you owe him three and a half. And odds and ends, comes to around a hundred and twenty dollars by the fifteenth.

WILLY. A hundred and twenty dollars! My God, if business don't pick up I don't know what I'm gonna do!

LINDA. Well, next week you'll do better.

WILLY. Oh, I'll knock 'em dead next week. I'll go to Hartford. I'm very

Death of a Salesman

well liked in Hartford. You know, the trouble is, Linda, people don't seem to take to me.

They move onto the forestage.

LINDA. Oh, don't be foolish.

WILLY. I know it when I walk in. They seem to laugh at me.

LINDA. Why? Why would they laugh at you? Don't talk that way, Willy.

WILLY moves to the edge of the stage. LINDA goes into the kitchen and starts to darn stockings.

WILLY. I don't know the reason for it, but they just pass me by. I'm not noticed.

LINDA. But you're doing wonderful, dear. You're making seventy to a hundred dollars a week.

WILLY. But I gotta be at it ten, twelve hours a day. Other men — I don't know — they do it easier. I don't know why — I can't stop myself — I talk too much. A man oughta come in with a few words. One thing about Charley. He's a man of few words, and they respect him.

LINDA. You don't talk too much, you're just lively.

WILLY (*smiling*). Well, I figure, what the hell, life is short, a couple of jokes. (*To himself.*) I joke too much! (*The smile goes.*)

LINDA. Why? You're —

WILLY. I'm fat. I'm very — foolish to look at, Linda. I didn't tell you, but Christmas time I happened to be calling on F. H. Stewarts, and a salesman I know, as I was going in to see the buyer I heard him say something about — walrus. And I — I cracked him right across the face. I won't take that. I simply will not take that. But they do laugh at me. I know that.

LINDA. Darling . . .

WILLY. I gotta overcome it. I know I gotta overcome it. I'm not dressing to advantage, maybe.

LINDA. Willy, darling, you're the handsomest man in the world —

WILLY. Oh, no, Linda.

LINDA. To me you are. (*Slight pause.*) The handsomest.

From the darkness is heard the laughter of a woman. WILLY doesn't turn to it, but it continues through LINDA's lines.

LINDA. And the boys, Willy. Few men are idolized by their children the way you are.

Music is heard as behind a scrim, to the left of the house, The WOMAN, dimly seen, is dressing.

WILLY (*with great feeling*). You're the best there is, Linda, you're a pal, you know that? On the road — on the road I want to grab you sometimes and just kiss the life outa you.

The laughter is loud now, and he moves into a brightening area at the left, where the WOMAN has come from behind the scrim and is standing, putting on her hat, looking into a "mirror" and laughing.

WILLY. 'Cause I get so lonely — especially when business is bad and there's nobody to talk to. I get the feeling that I'll never sell anything again, that I won't make a living for you, or a business, a business for the boys. (*He talks through the* WOMAN's *subsiding laughter; the* WOMAN *primps at the "mirror."*) There's so much I want to make for—

THE WOMAN. Me? You didn't make me, Willy. I picked you.

WILLY (*pleased*). You picked me?

THE WOMAN (*who is quite proper-looking, Willy's age*). I did. I've been sitting at that desk watching all the salesmen go by, day in, day out. But you've got such a sense of humor, and we do have such a good time together, don't we?

WILLY. Sure, sure. (*He takes her in his arms.*) Why do you have to go now?

THE WOMAN. It's two o'clock . . .

WILLY. No, come on in! (*He pulls her.*)

THE WOMAN. . . . my sisters'll be scandalized. When'll you be back?

WILLY. Oh, two weeks about. Will you come up again?

THE WOMAN. Sure thing. You do make me laugh. It's good for me. (*She squeezes his arm, kisses him.*) And I think you're a wonderful man.

WILLY. You picked me, heh?

THE WOMAN. Sure. Because you're so sweet. And such a kidder.

WILLY. Well, I'll see you next time I'm in Boston.

THE WOMAN. I'll put you right through to the buyers.

WILLY (*slapping her bottom*). Right. Well, bottoms up!

THE WOMAN (*slaps him gently and laughs*). You just kill me, Willy. (*He suddenly grabs her and kisses her roughly.*) You kill me. And thanks for the stockings. I love a lot of stockings. Well, good night.

WILLY. Good night. And keep your pores open!

THE WOMAN. Oh, Willy!

The WOMAN *bursts out laughing, and* LINDA's *laughter blends in. The* WOMAN *disappears into the dark. Now the area at the kitchen table brightens.* LINDA *is sitting where she was at the kitchen table, but now is mending a pair of her silk stockings.*

LINDA. You are, Willy. The handsomest man. You've got no reason to feel that—

WILLY (*coming out of the* WOMAN's *dimming area and going over to* LINDA). I'll make it all up to you, Linda, I'll—

LINDA. There's nothing to make up, dear. You're doing fine, better than—

WILLY (*noticing her mending*). What's that?

LINDA. Just mending my stockings. They're so expensive—

WILLY (*angrily, taking them from her*). I won't have you mending stockings in this house! Now throw them out!

LINDA *puts the stockings in her pocket.*

BERNARD (*entering on the run*). Where is he? If he doesn't study!

WILLY (*moving to the forestage, with great agitation*). You'll give him the answers!

Death of a Salesman

BERNARD. I do, but I can't on a Regents! That's a state exam! They're liable to arrest me!

WILLY. Where is he? I'll whip him, I'll whip him!

LINDA. And he'd better give back that football, Willy, it's not nice.

WILLY. Biff! Where is he? Why is he taking everything?

LINDA. He's too rough with the girls, Willy. All the mothers are afraid of him!

WILLY. I'll whip him!

BERNARD. He's driving the car without a license!

The WOMAN's *laugh is heard.*

WILLY. Shut up!

LINDA. All the mothers —

WILLY. Shut up!

BERNARD (*backing quietly away and out*). Mr. Birnbaum say he's stuck up.

WILLY. Get outa here!

BERNARD. If he doesn't buckle down he'll flunk math! (*He goes off.*)

LINDA. He's right, Willy, you've gotta —

WILLY (*exploding at her*). There's nothing the matter with him! You want him to be a worm like Bernard? He's got spirit, personality . . .

As he speaks, LINDA, *almost in tears, exits into the living-room.* WILLY *is alone in the kitchen, wilting and staring. The leaves are gone. It is night again, and the apartment houses look down from behind.*

WILLY. Loaded with it. Loaded! What is he stealing? He's giving it back, isn't he? Why is he stealing? What did I tell him? I never in my life told him anything but decent things.

HAPPY *in pajamas has come down the stairs;* WILLY *suddenly becomes aware of* HAPPY's *presence.*

HAPPY. Let's go now, come on.

WILLY (*sitting down at the kitchen table*). Huh! Why did she have to wax the floors herself? Everytime she waxes the floors she keels over. She knows that!

HAPPY. Shh! Take it easy. What brought you back tonight?

WILLY. I got an awful scare. Nearly hit a kid in Yonkers. God! Why didn't I go to Alaska with my brother Ben that time! Ben! That man was a genius, that man was success incarnate! What a mistake! He begged me to go.

HAPPY. Well, there's no use in —

WILLY. You guys! There was a man started with the clothes on his back and ended up with diamond mines!

HAPPY. Boy, someday I'd like to know how he did it.

WILLY. What's the mystery? The man knew what he wanted and went out and got it! Walked into a jungle, and comes out, the age of twenty-one, and he's rich! The world is an oyster, but you don't crack it open on a mattress!

HAPPY. Pop, I told you I'm gonna retire you for life.

WILLY. You'll retire me for life on seventy goddam dollars a week? And your women and your car and your apartment, and you'll retire me for life! Christ's sake, I couldn't get past Yonkers today! Where are you guys, where are you? The woods are burning! I can't drive a car!

    CHARLEY *has appeared in the doorway. He is a large man, slow of speech, laconic, immovable. In all he says, despite what he says, there is pity, and, now, trepidation. He has a robe over pajamas, slippers on his feet. He enters the kitchen.*

CHARLEY. Everything all right?

HAPPY. Yeah, Charley, everything's . . .

WILLY. What's the matter?

CHARLEY. I heard some noise. I thought something happened. Can't we do something about the walls? You sneeze in here, and in my house hats blow off.

HAPPY. Let's go to bed, Dad. Come on.

    CHARLEY *signals to* HAPPY *to go.*

WILLY. You go ahead, I'm not tired at the moment.

HAPPY (*to* WILLY). Take it easy, huh? (*He exits.*)

WILLY. What're you doin' up?

CHARLEY (*sitting down at the kitchen table opposite* WILLY). Couldn't sleep good. I had a heartburn.

WILLY. Well, you don't know how to eat.

CHARLEY. I eat with my mouth.

WILLY. No, you're ignorant. You gotta know about vitamins and things like that.

CHARLEY. Come on, let's shoot. Tire you out a little.

WILLY (*hesitantly*). All right. You got cards?

CHARLEY (*taking a deck from his pocket*). Yeah, I got them. Someplace. What is it with those vitamins?

WILLY (*dealing*). They build up your bones. Chemistry.

CHARLEY. Yeah, but there's no bones in a heartburn.

WILLY. What are you talkin' about? Do you know the first thing about it?

CHARLEY. Don't get insulted.

WILLEY. Don't talk about something you don't know anything about.

    They are playing. Pause.

CHARLEY. What're you doin' home?

WILLY. A little trouble with the car.

CHARLEY. Oh. (*Pause.*) I'd like to take a trip to California.

WILLY. Don't say.

CHARLEY. You want a job?

WILLY. I got a job, I told you that. (*After a slight pause.*) What the hell are you offering me a job for?

CHARLEY. Don't get insulted.

WILLY. Don't insult me.

CHARLEY. I don't see no sense in it. You don't have to go on this way.

WILLY. I got a good job. (*Slight pause.*) What do you keep comin' in here for?

CHARLEY. You want me to go?

WILLY (*after a pause, withering*). I can't understand it. He's going back to Texas again. What the hell is that?

CHARLEY. Let him go.

WILLY. I got nothin' to give him, Charley, I'm clean, I'm clean.

CHARLEY. He won't starve. None a them starve. Forget about him.

WILLY. Then what have I got to remember?

CHARLEY. You take it too hard. To hell with it. When a deposit bottle is broken you don't get your nickel back.

WILLY. That's easy enough for you to say.

CHARLEY. That ain't easy for me to say.

WILLY. Did you see the ceiling I put up in the living-room?

CHARLEY. Yeah, that's a piece of work. To put up a ceiling is a mystery to me. How do you do it?

WILLY. What's the difference?

CHARLEY. Well, talk about it.

WILLY. You gonna put up a ceiling?

CHARLEY. How could I put up a ceiling?

WILLY. Then what the hell are you bothering me for?

CHARLEY. You're insulted again.

WILLY. A man who can't handle tools is not a man. You're disgusting.

CHARLEY. Don't call me disgusting, Willy.

> UNCLE BEN, *carrying a valise and an umbrella, enters the forestage from around the right corner of the house. He is a stolid man, in his sixties, with a mustache and an authoritative air. He is utterly certain of his destiny, and there is an aura of far places about him. He enters exactly as* WILLY *speaks.*

WILLY. I'm getting awfully tired, Ben.

> BEN'S *music is heard.* BEN *looks around at everything.*

CHARLEY. Good, keep playing; you'll sleep better. Did you call me Ben?

> BEN *looks at his watch.*

WILLY. That's funny. For a second there you reminded me of my brother Ben.

BEN. I only have a few minutes. (*He strolls, inspecting the place.* WILLY *and* CHARLEY *continue playing.*)

CHARLEY. You never heard from him again, heh? Since that time?

WILLY. Didn't Linda tell you? Couple of weeks ago we got a letter from his wife in Africa. He died.

CHARLEY. That so.

BEN (*chuckling*). So this is Brooklyn, eh?

CHARLEY. Maybe you're in for some of his money.

WILLEY. Naa, he had seven sons. There's just one opportunity I had with that man . . .

BEN. I must make a train, William. There are several properties I'm looking at in Alaska.

WILLY. Sure, sure! If I'd gone with him to Alaska that time, everything would've been totally different.

CHARLEY. Go on, you'd froze to death up there.

WILLY. What're you talking about?

BEN. Opportunity is tremendous in Alaska, William. Surprised you're not up there.

WILLY. Sure, tremendous.

CHARLEY. Heh?

WILLY. There was the only man I ever met who knew the answers.

CHARLEY. Who?

BEN. How are you all?

WILLY (*taking a pot, smiling*). Fine, fine.

CHARLEY. Pretty sharp tonight.

BEN. Is Mother living with you?

WILLY. No, she died a long time ago.

CHARLEY. Who?

BEN. That's too bad. Fine specimen of a lady, Mother.

WILLY (*to* CHARLEY). Heh?

BEN. I'd hoped to see the old girl.

CHARLEY. Who died?

BEN. Heard anything from Father, have you?

WILLY (*unnerved*). What do you mean, who died?

CHARLEY (*taking a pot*). What're you talkin' about?

BEN (*looking at his watch*). William, it's half-past eight!

WILLY (*as though to dispel his confusion he angrily stops* CHARLEY's *hand*). That's my build!

CHARLEY. I put the ace —

WILLY. If you don't know how to play the game I'm not gonna throw my money away on you!

CHARLEY (*rising*). It was my ace, for God's sake!

WILLY. I'm through, I'm through!

BEN. When did Mother die?

WILLY. Long ago. Since the beginning you never knew how to play cards.

CHARLEY (*picks up the cards and goes to the door*). All right! Next time I'll bring a deck with five aces.

WILLY. I don't play that kind of game!

CHARLEY (*turning to him*). You ought to be ashamed of yourself!

WILLY. Yeah?

CHARLEY. Yeah! (*He goes out.*)

WILLY (*slamming the door after him*). Ignoramus!

Death of a Salesman

BEN (*as* WILLY *comes toward him through the wall-line of the kitchen*). So you're William.

WILLY (*shaking* BEN'S *hand*). Ben! I've been waiting for you so long! What's the answer? How did you do it?

BEN. Oh, there's a story in that.

LINDA *enters the forestage, as of old, carrying the wash basket.*

LINDA. Is this Ben?

BEN (*gallantly*). How do you do, my dear.

LINDA. Where've you been all these years? Willy's always wondered why you —

WILLY (*pulling* BEN *away from her impatiently*). Where is Dad? Didn't you follow him? How did you get started?

BEN. Well, I don't know how much you remember.

WILLY. Well, I was just a baby, of course, only three or four years old —

BEN. Three years and eleven months.

WILLY. What a memory, Ben!

BEN. I have many enterprises, William, and I have never kept books.

WILLY. I remember I was sitting under the wagon in — was it Nebraska?

BEN. It was South Dakota, and I gave you a bunch of wild flowers.

WILLY. I remember you walking away down some open road.

BEN (*laughing*). I was going to find Father in Alaska.

WILLY. Where is he?

BEN. At that age I had a very faulty view of geography, William. I discovered after a few days that I was heading due south, so instead of Alaska, I ended up in Africa.

LINDA. Africa!

WILLY. The Gold Coast!

BEN. Principally diamond mines.

LINDA. Diamond mines!

BEN. Yes, my dear. But I've only a few minutes —

WILLY. No! Boys! Boys! (YOUNG BIFF *and* HAPPY *appear.*) Listen to this. This is your Uncle Ben, a great man! Tell my boys, Ben!

BEN. Why, boys, when I was seventeen I walked into the jungle, and when I was twenty-one I walked out. (*He laughs.*) And by God I was rich.

WILLY (*to the boys*). You see what I been talking about? The greatest things can happen!

BEN (*glancing at his watch*). I have an appointment in Ketchikan Tuesday week.

WILLY. No, Ben! Please tell about Dad. I want my boys to hear. I want them to know the kind of stock they spring from. All I remember is a man with a big beard, and I was in Mamma's lap, sitting around a fire, and some kind of high music.

BEN. His flute. He played the flute.

WILLY. Sure, the flute, that's right!

New music is heard, a high, rollicking tune.

BEN. Father was a very great and a very wild-hearted man. We would start in Boston, and he'd toss the whole family into the wagon, and then he'd drive the team right across the country; through Ohio, and Indiana, Michigan, Illinois, and all the Western states. And we'd stop in the towns and sell the flutes that he'd made on the way. Great inventor, Father. With one gadget he made more in a week than a man like you could make in a lifetime.

WILLY. That's just the way I'm bringing them up, Ben — rugged, well liked, all-around.

BEN. Yeah? (*To* BIFF.) Hit that, boy — hard as you can. (*He pounds his stomach.*)

BIFF. Oh, no, sir!

BEN (*taking boxing stance*). Come on, get to me! (*He laughs.*)

WILLY. Go to it, Biff! Go ahead, show him!

BIFF. Okay! (*He cocks his fists and starts in.*)

LINDA (*to* WILLY). Why must he fight, dear?

BEN (*sparring with* BIFF). Good boy! Good boy!

WILLY. How's that, Ben, heh?

HAPPY. Give him the left, Biff!

LINDA. Why are you fighting?

BEN. Good boy! (*Suddenly comes in, trips* BIFF, *and stands over him, the point of his umbrella poised over* BIFF's *eye.*)

LINDA. Look out, Biff!

BIFF. Gee!

BEN (*patting* BIFF's *knee*). Never fight fair with a stranger boy. You'll never get out of the jungle that way. (*Taking* LINDA's *hand and bowing.*) It was an honor and a pleasure to meet you, Linda.

LINDA (*withdrawing her hand coldly, frightened*). Have a nice — trip.

BEN (*to* WILLY). And good luck with your — what do you do?

WILLY. Selling.

BEN. Yes. Well . . . (*He raises his hand in farewell to all.*)

WILLY. No, Ben, I don't want you to think . . . (*He takes* BEN's *arm to show him.*) It's Brooklyn, I know, but we hunt too.

BEN. Really, now.

WILLY. Oh, sure, there's snakes and rabbits and — that's why I moved out here. Why, Biff can fell any one of these trees in no time! Boys! Go right over to where they're building the apartment house and get some sand. We're gonna rebuild the entire front stoop right now! Watch this, Ben!

BIFF. Yes, sir! On the double, Hap!

HAPPY (*as he and* BIFF *run off*). I lost weight, Pop, you notice?

CHARLEY *enters in knickers, even before the boys are gone.*

CHARLEY. Listen, if they steal any more from that building the watchman'll put the cops on them!

LINDA (*to* WILLY). Don't let Biff . . .

BEN *laughs lustily.*

WILLY. You shoulda seen the lumber they brought home last week. At least a dozen six-by-tens worth all kinds a money.

CHARLEY. Listen, if that watchman —

WILLY. I gave them hell, understand. But I got a couple of fearless characters there.

CHARLEY. Willy, the jails are full of fearless characters.

BEN (*clapping* WILLY *on the back, with a laugh at* CHARLEY). And the stock exchange, friend!

WILLY (*joining in* BEN's *laughter*). Where are the rest of your pants?

CHARLEY. My wife bought them.

WILLY. Now all you need is a golf club and you can go upstairs and go to sleep. (*To* BEN.) Great athlete! Between him and his son Bernard they can't hammer a nail!

BERNARD (*rushing in*). The watchman's chasing Biff!

WILLY (*angrily*). Shut up! He's not stealing anything!

LINDA (*alarmed, hurrying off left*). Where is he? Biff, dear! (*She exits.*)

WILLY (*moving toward the left, away from* BEN). There's nothing wrong. What's the matter with you?

BEN. Nervy boy. Good!

WILLY (*laughing*). Oh, nerves of iron, that Biff!

CHARLEY. Don't know what it is. My New England man comes back and he's bleedin', they murdered him up there.

WILLY. It's contacts, Charley, I got important contacts!

CHARLEY (*sarcastically*). Glad to hear it, Willy. Come in later, we'll shoot a little casino. I'll take some of your Portland money. (*He laughs at* WILLY *and exits.*)

WILLY (*turning to* BEN). Business is bad, it's murderous. But not for me, of course.

BEN. I'll stop by on my way back to Africa.

WILLY (*longingly*). Can't you stay a few days? You're just what I need, Ben, because I — I have a fine position here, but I — well, Dad left when I was such a baby and I never had a chance to talk to him and I still feel — kind of temporary about myself.

BEN. I'll be late for my train.

They are at opposite ends of the stage.

WILLY. Ben, my boys — can't we talk? They'd go into the jaws of hell for me, see, but I —

BEN. William, you're being first-rate with your boys. Outstanding, manly chaps!

WILLY (*hanging on to his words*). Oh, Ben, that's good to hear! Because sometimes I'm afraid that I'm not teaching them the right kind of — Ben, how should I teach them?

BEN (*giving great weight to each word, and with a certain vicious audacity*).

William, when I walked into the jungle, I was seventeen. When I walked out I was twenty-one. And, by God, I was rich! (*He goes off into darkness around the right corner of the house.*)

WILLY. . . . was rich! That's just the spirit I want to imbue them with! To walk into a jungle! I was right! I was right! I was right!

BEN *is gone, but* WILLY *is still speaking to him as* LINDA, *in nightgown and robe, enters the kitchen, glances around for* WILLY, *then goes to the door of the house, looks out and sees him. Comes down to his left. He looks at her.*

LINDA. Willy, dear? Willy?

WILLY. I was right!

LINDA. Did you have some cheese? (*He can't answer.*) It's very late, darling. Come to bed, heh?

WILLY (*looking straight up*). Gotta break your neck to see a star in this yard.

LINDA. You coming in?

WILLY. Whatever happened to that diamond watch fob? Remember? When Ben came from Africa that time? Didn't he give me a watch fob with a diamond in it?

LINDA. You pawned it, dear. Twelve, thirteen years ago. For Biff's radio correspondence course.

WILLY. Gee, that was a beautiful thing. I'll take a walk.

LINDA. But you're in your slippers.

WILLY (*starting to go around the house at the left*). I was right! I was! (*Half to* LINDA, *as he goes, shaking his head.*) What a man! There was a man worth talking to. I was right!

LINDA (*calling after* WILLY). But in your slippers, Willy!

WILLY *is almost gone when* BIFF, *in his pajamas, comes down the stairs and enters the kitchen.*

BIFF. What is he doing out there?

LINDA. Sh!

BIFF. God Almighty, Mom, how long has he been doing this?

LINDA. Don't, he'll hear you.

BIFF. What the hell is the matter with him?

LINDA. It'll pass by morning.

BIFF. Shouldn't we do anything?

LINDA. Oh, my dear, you should do a lot of things, but there's nothing to do, so go to sleep.

HAPPY *comes down the stairs and sits on the steps.*

HAPPY. I never heard him so loud, Mom.

LINDA. Well, come around more often; you'll hear him. (*She sits down at the table and mends the lining of* WILLY's *jacket.*)

BIFF. Why didn't you ever write me about this, Mom?

LINDA. How would I write to you? For over three months you had no address.

BIFF. I was on the move. But you know I thought of you all the time. You know that, don't you, pal?

LINDA. I know, dear, I know. But he likes to have a letter. Just to know that there's still a possibility for better things.

BIFF. He's not like this all the time, is he?

LINDA. It's when you come home he's always the worst.

BIFF. When I come home?

LINDA. When you write you're coming, he's all smiles, and talks about the future, and — he's just wonderful. And then the closer you seem to come, the more shaky he gets, and then, by the time you get here, he's arguing, and he seems angry at you. I think it's just that maybe he can't bring himself to — to open up to you. Why are you so hateful to each other? Why is that?

BIFF (*evasively*). I'm not hateful, Mom.

LINDA. But you no sooner come in that door than you're fighting!

BIFF. I don't know why. I mean to change. I'm tryin', Mom, you understand?

LINDA. Are you home to stay now?

BIFF. I don't know. I want to look around, see what's doin'.

LINDA. Biff, you can't look around all your life, can you?

BIFF. I just can't take hold, Mom. I can't take hold of some kind of a life.

LINDA. Biff, a man is not a bird, to come and go with the springtime.

BIFF. Your hair . . . (*He touches her hair.*) Your hair got so gray.

LINDA. Oh, it's been gray since you were in high school. I just stopped dyeing it, that's all.

BIFF. Dye it again, will ya? I don't want my pal looking old. (*He smiles.*)

LINDA. You're such a boy! You think you can go away for a year and . . . You've got to get it into your head now that one day you'll knock on this door and there'll be strange people here —

BIFF. What are you talking about? You're not even sixty, Mom.

LINDA. But what about your father?

BIFF (*lamely*). Well, I meant him too.

HAPPY. He admires Pop.

LINDA. Biff, dear, if you don't have any feeling for him, then you can't have any feeling for me.

BIFF. Sure I can, Mom.

LINDA. No. You can't just come to see me, because I love him. (*With a threat, but only a threat, of tears.*) He's the dearest man in the world to me, and I won't have anyone making him feel unwanted and low and blue. You've got to make up your mind now, darling, there's no leeway any more. Either he's your father and you pay him that respect, or else you're not to come here. I know he's not easy to get along with — nobody knows that better than me — but . . .

WILLY (*from the left, with a laugh*). Hey, hey, Biffo!

BIFF (*starting to go out after* WILLY). What the hell is the matter with him? (HAPPY *stops him.*)

LINDA. Don't — don't go near him!

BIFF. Stop making excuses for him! He always, always wiped the floor with you. Never had an ounce of respect for you.

HAPPY. He's always had respect for —

BIFF. What the hell do you know about it?

HAPPY (*surlily*). Just don't call him crazy!

BIFF. He's got no character — Charley wouldn't do this. Not in his own house — spewing out that vomit from his mind.

HAPPY. Charley never had to cope with what he's got to.

BIFF. People are worse off than Willy Loman. Believe me, I've seen them!

LINDA. Then make Charley your father, Biff. You can't do that, can you? I don't say he's a great man. Willy Loman never made a lot of money. His name was never in the paper. He's not the finest character that ever lived. But he's a human being, and a terrible thing is happening to him. So attention must be paid. He's not to be allowed to fall into his grave like an old dog. Attention, attention must be finally paid to such a person. You called him crazy —

BIFF. I didn't mean —

LINDA. No, a lot of people think he's lost his — balance. But you don't have to be very smart to know what his trouble is. The man is exhausted.

HAPPY. Sure!

LINDA. A small man can be just as exhausted as a great man. He works for a company thirty-six years this March, opens up unheard-of territories to their trademark, and now in his old age they take his salary away.

HAPPY (*indignantly*). I didn't know that, Mom.

LINDA. You never asked, my dear! Now that you get your spending money someplace else you don't trouble your mind with him.

HAPPY. But I gave you money last —

LINDA. Christmas time, fifty dollars! To fix the hot water it cost ninety-seven fifty! For five weeks he's been on straight commission, like a beginner, an unknown!

BIFF. Those ungrateful bastards!

LINDA. Are they any worse than his sons? When he brought them business, when he was young, they were glad to see him. But now his old friends, the buyers that loved him so and always found some order to hand him in a pinch — they're all dead, retired. He used to be able to make six, seven calls a day in Boston. Now he takes his valises out of the car and puts them back and takes them out again and he's exhausted. Instead of walking he talks now. He drives seven hundred miles, and when he gets there no one knows him any more, no one welcomes him. And what goes through a man's mind, driving seven hundred miles home without having earned a cent? Why shouldn't he talk to himself? Why? When he has to go to Charley and borrow fifty dollars a week and pretend to me that it's his pay? How long can that go on? How long? You see what I'm sitting here and waiting for?

And you tell me he has no character? The man who never worked a day but for your benefit? When does he get the medal for that? Is this his reward — to turn around at the age of sixty-three and find his sons, who he loved better than his life, one a philandering bum —

HAPPY. Mom!

LINDA. That's all you are, my baby! (*To* BIFF.) And you! What happened to the love you had for him? You were such pals! How you used to talk to him on the phone every night! How lonely he was till he could come home to you!

BIFF. All right, Mom. I'll live here in my room, and I'll get a job. I'll keep away from him, that's all.

LINDA. No, Biff. You can't stay here and fight all the time.

BIFF. He threw me out of this house, remember that.

LINDA. Why did he do that? I never knew why.

BIFF. Because I know he's a fake and he doesn't like anybody around who knows!

LINDA. Why a fake? In what way? What do you mean?

BIFF. Just don't lay it all at my feet. It's between me and him — that's all I have to say. I'll chip in from now on. He'll settle for half my pay check. He'll be all right. I'm going to bed. (*He starts for the stairs.*)

LINDA. He won't be all right.

BIFF (*turning on the stairs, furiously*). I hate this city and I'll stay here. Now what do you want?

LINDA. He's dying, Biff.

HAPPY *turns quickly to her, shocked.*

BIFF (*after a pause*). Why is he dying?

LINDA. He's been trying to kill himself.

BIFF (*with great horror*). How?

LINDA. I live from day to day.

BIFF. What're you talking about?

LINDA. Remember I wrote you that he smashed up the car again? In February?

BIFF. Well?

LINDA. The insurance inspector came. He said that they have evidence. That all these accidents in the last year — weren't — weren't — accidents.

HAPPY. How can they tell that? That's a lie.

LINDA. It seems there's a woman . . . (*She takes a breath as*)

BIFF (*sharply but contained*). What woman?

LINDA (*simultaneously*). . . . and this woman . . .

LINDA. What?

BIFF. Nothing. Go ahead.

LINDA. What did you say?

BIFF. Nothing. I just said what woman?

HAPPY. What about her?

LINDA. Well, it seems she was walking down the road and saw his car. She says that he wasn't driving fast at all, and that he didn't skid. She says he came to that little bridge, and then deliberately smashed into the railing, and it was only the shallowness of the water that saved him.

BIFF. Oh, no, he probably just fell asleep again.

LINDA. I don't think he fell asleep.

BIFF. Why not?

LINDA. Last month . . . (*With great difficulty.*) Oh, boys, it's so hard to say a thing like this! He's just a big stupid man to you, but I tell you there's more good in him than in many other people. (*She chokes, wipes her eyes.*) I was looking for a fuse. The lights blew out, and I went down the cellar. And behind the fuse box — it happened to fall out — was a length of rubber pipe — just short.

HAPPY. No kidding?

LINDA. There's a little attachment on the end of it. I knew right away. And sure enough, on the bottom of the water heater there's a new little nipple on the gas pipe.

HAPPY (*angrily*). That — jerk.

BIFF. Did you have it taken off?

LINDA. I'm — I'm ashamed to. How can I mention it to him? Every day I go down and take away that little rubber pipe. But, when he comes home, I put it back where it was. How can I insult him that way? I don't know what to do. I live from day to day, boys. I tell you, I know every thought in his mind. It sounds so old-fashioned and silly, but I tell you he put his whole life into you and you've turned your backs on him. (*She is bent over in the chair, weeping, her face in her hands.*) Biff, I swear to God! Biff, his whole life is in your hands!

HAPPY (*to* BIFF). How do you like that damned fool!

BIFF (*kissing her*). All right, pal, all right. It's all settled now. I've been remiss. I know that, Mom. But now I'll stay, and I swear to you, I'll apply myself. (*Kneeling in front of her, in a fever of self-reproach.*) It's just — you see, Mom, I don't fit in business. Not that I won't try. I'll try, and I'll make good.

HAPPY. Sure you will. The trouble with you in business was you never tried to please people.

BIFF. I know, I —

HAPPY. Like when you worked for Harrison's. Bob Harrison said you were tops, and then you go and do some damn fool thing like whistling whole songs in the elevator like a comedian.

BIFF (*against* HAPPY). So what? I like to whistle sometimes.

HAPPY. You don't raise a guy to a responsible job who whistles in the elevator!

LINDA. Well, don't argue about it now.

HAPPY. Like when you'd go off and swim in the middle of the day instead of taking the line around.

BIFF (*his resentment rising*). Well, don't you run off? You take off sometimes, don't you? On a nice summer day?

HAPPY. Yeah, but I cover myself!

LINDA. Boys!

HAPPY. If I'm going to take a fade the boss can call any number where I'm supposed to be and they'll swear to him that I just left. I'll tell you something that I hate to say, Biff, but in the business world some of them think you're crazy.

BIFF (*angered*). Screw the business world!

HAPPY. All right, screw it! Great, but cover yourself!

LINDA. Hap, Hap!

BIFF. I don't care what they think! They've laughed at Dad for years, and you know why? Because we don't belong in this nuthouse of a city! We should be mixing cement on some open plain, or — or carpenters. A carpenter is allowed to whistle!

WILLY *walks in from the entrance of the house, at left.*

WILLY. Even your grandfather was better than a carpenter. (*Pause. They watch him.*) You never grew up. Bernard does not whistle in the elevator, I assure you.

BIFF (*as though to laugh* WILLY *out of it*). Yeah, but you do, Pop.

WILLY. I never in my life whistled in an elevator! And who in the business world thinks I'm crazy?

BIFF. I didn't mean it like that, Pop. Now don't make a whole thing out of it, will ya?

WILLY. Go back to the West! Be a carpenter, a cowboy, enjoy yourself!

LINDA. Willy, he was just saying —

WILLY. I heard what he said!

HAPPY (*trying to quiet* WILLY). Hey, Pop, come on now . . .

WILLY (*continuing over* HAPPY's *line*). They laugh at me, heh? Go to Filene's, go to the Hub, go to Slattery's, Boston. Call out the name Willy Loman and see what happens! Big shot!

BIFF. All right, Pop.

WILLY. Big!

BIFF. All right!

WILLY. Why do you always insult me?

BIFF. I didn't say a word. (*To* LINDA.) Did I say a word?

LINDA. He didn't say anything, Willy.

WILLY (*going to the doorway of the living-room*). All right, good night, good night.

LINDA. Willy, dear, he just decided . . .

WILLY (*to* BIFF). If you get tired hanging around tomorrow, paint the ceiling I put up in the living-room.

BIFF. I'm leaving early tomorrow.

HAPPY. He's going to see Bill Oliver, Pop.

WILLY (*interestedly*). Oliver? For what?

BIFF (*with reserve, but trying, trying*). He always said he'd stake me. I'd like to go in business, so maybe I can take him up on it.

LINDA. Isn't that wonderful?

WILLY. Don't interrupt. What's wonderful about it? There's fifty men in the City of New York who'd stake him. (*To* BIFF.) Sporting goods?

BIFF. I guess so. I know something about it and —

WILLY. He knows something about it! You know sporting goods better than Spalding, for God's sake! How much is he giving you?

BIFF. I don't know, I didn't even see him yet, but —

WILLY. Then what're you talkin' about?

BIFF (*getting angry*). Well, all I said was I'm gonna see him, that's all!

WILLY (*turning away*). Ah, you're counting your chickens again.

BIFF (*starting left for the stairs*). Oh, Jesus, I'm going to sleep!

WILLY (*calling after him*). Don't curse in this house!

BIFF (*turning*). Since when did you get so clean?

HAPPY (*trying to stop them*). Wait a . . .

WILLY. Don't use that language to me! I won't have it!

HAPPY (*grabbing* BIFF, *shouts*). Wait a minute! I got an idea. I got a feasible idea. Come here, Biff, let's talk this over now, let's talk some sense here. When I was down in Florida last time, I thought of a great idea to sell sporting goods. It just came back to me. You and I, Biff — we have a line, the Loman Line. We train a couple of weeks, and put on a couple of exhibitions, see?

WILLY. That's an idea!

HAPPY. Wait! We form two basketball teams, see? Two water-polo teams. We play each other. It's a million dollars' worth of publicity. Two brothers, see? The Loman Brothers. Displays in the Royal Palms — all the hotels. And banners over the ring and the basketball court: "Loman Brothers." Baby, we could sell sporting goods!

WILLY. That is a one-million-dollar idea!

LINDA. Marvelous!

BIFF. I'm in great shape as far as that's concerned.

HAPPY. And the beauty of it is, Biff, it wouldn't be like a business. We'd be out playin' ball again . . .

BIFF (*enthused*). Yeah, that's . . .

WILLY. Million-dollar . . .

HAPPY. And you wouldn't get fed up with it, Biff. It'd be the family again. There'd be the old honor, and comradeship, and if you wanted to go off for a swim or somethin' — well, you'd do it! Without some smart cooky gettin' up ahead of you!

WILLY. Lick the world! You guys together could absolutely lick the civilized world.

BIFF. I'll see Oliver tomorrow. Hap, if we could work that out . . .

LINDA. Maybe things are beginning to —

WILLY (*wildly enthused, to* LINDA). Stop interrupting! (*To* BIFF.) But don't wear sport jacket and slacks when you see Oliver.

BIFF. No, I'll —

WILLY. A business suit, and talk as little as possible, and don't crack any jokes.

BIFF. He did like me. Always liked me.

LINDA. He loved you!

WILLY (*to* LINDA). Will you stop! (*To* BIFF.) Walk in very serious. You are not applying for a boy's job. Money is to pass. Be quiet, fine, and serious. Everybody likes a kidder, but nobody lends him money.

HAPPY. I'll try to get some myself, Biff. I'm sure I can.

WILLY. I see great things for you kids, I think your troubles are over. But remember, start big and you'll end big. Ask for fifteen. How much you gonna ask for?

BIFF. Gee, I don't know —

WILLY. And don't say "Gee." "Gee" is a boy's word. A man walking in for fifteen thousand dollars does not say "Gee!"

BIFF. Ten, I think, would be top though.

WILLY. Don't be so modest. You always started too low. Walk in with a big laugh. Don't look worried. Start off with a couple of your good stories to lighten things up. It's not what you say, it's how you say it — because personality always wins the day.

LINDA. Oliver always thought the highest of him —

WILLY. Will you let me talk?

BIFF. Don't yell at her, Pop, will ya?

WILLY (*angrily*). I was talking, wasn't I?

BIFF. I don't like you yelling at her all the time, and I'm tellin' you, that's all.

WILLY. What're you, takin' over this house?

LINDA. Willy —

WILLY (*turning on her*). Don't take his side all the time, goddammit!

BIFF (*furiously*). Stop yelling at her!

WILLY (*suddenly pulling on his cheek, beaten down, guilt ridden*). Give my best to Bill Oliver — he may remember me. (*He exits through the living-room doorway.*)

LINDA (*her voice subdued*). What'd you have to start that for? (BIFF *turns away.*) You see how sweet he was as soon as you talked hopefully? (*She goes over to* BIFF.) Come up and say good night to him. Don't let him go to bed that way.

HAPPY. Come on, Biff, let's buck him up.

LINDA. Please, dear. Just say good night. It takes so little to make him happy. Come. (*She goes through the living-room doorway, calling upstairs from within the living-room.*) Your pajamas are hanging in the bathroom, Willy!

HAPPY (*looking toward where* LINDA *went out*). What a woman! They broke the mold when they made her. You know that, Biff?

BIFF. He's off salary. My God, working on commission!

HAPPY. Well, let's face it: he's no hot-shot selling man. Except that sometimes, you have to admit, he's a sweet personality.

BIFF (*deciding*). Lend me ten bucks, will ya? I want to buy some new ties.

HAPPY. I'll take you to a place I know. Beautiful stuff. Wear one of my striped shirts tomorrow.

BIFF. She got gray. Mom got awful old. Gee, I'm gonna go in to Oliver tomorrow and knock him for a —

HAPPY. Come on up. Tell that to Dad. Let's give him a whirl. Come on.

BIFF (*steamed up*). You know, with ten thousand bucks, boy!

HAPPY (*as they go into the living-room*). That's the talk, Biff, that's the first time I've heard the old confidence out of you! (*From within the living-room, fading off.*) You gonna live with me, kid, and any babe you want just say the word . . . (*The last lines are hardly heard. They are mounting the stairs to their parents' bedroom.*)

LINDA (*entering her bedroom and addressing* WILLY, *who is in the bathroom. She is straightening the bed for him*). Can you do anything about the shower? It drips.

WILLY (*from the bathroom*). All of a sudden everything falls to pieces! Goddam plumbing, oughta be sued, those people. I hardly finished putting it in and the thing . . . (*His words rumble off.*)

LINDA. I'm just wondering if Oliver will remember him. You think he might?

WILLY (*coming out of the bathroom in his pajamas*). Remember him? What's the matter with you, you crazy? If he'd've stayed with Oliver he'd be on top by now! Wait'll Oliver gets a look at him. You don't know the average caliber any more. The average young man today — (*he is getting into bed*) — is got a caliber of zero. Greatest thing in the world for him was to bum around.

BIFF *and* HAPPY *enter the bedroom. Slight pause.*

WILLY (*stops short, looking at* BIFF). Glad to hear it, boy.

HAPPY. He wanted to say good night to you, sport.

WILLY (*to* BIFF). Yeah. Knock him dead, boy. What'd you want to tell me?

BIFF. Just take it easy, Pop. Good night. (*He turns to go.*)

WILLY (*unable to resist*). And if anything falls off the desk while you're talking to him — like a package or something — don't you pick it up. They have office boys for that.

LINDA. I'll make a big breakfast —

WILLY. Will you let me finish? (*To* BIFF.) Tell him you were in the business in the West. Not farm work.

BIFF. All right, Dad.

Death of a Salesman

LINDA. I think everything—

WILLY (*going right through her speech*). And don't undersell yourself. No less than fifteen thousand dollars.

BIFF (*unable to bear him*). Okay. Good night, Mom. (*He starts moving.*)

WILLY. Because you got a greatness in you, Biff, remember that. You got all kinds a greatness . . . (*He lies back, exhausted.* BIFF *walks out.*)

LINDA (*calling after* BIFF). Sleep well, darling!

HAPPY. I'm gonna get married, Mom. I wanted to tell you.

LINDA. Go to sleep, dear.

HAPPY (*going*). I just wanted to tell you.

WILLY. Keep up the good work. (HAPPY *exits.*) God . . . remember that Ebbets Field game? The championship of the city?

LINDA. Just rest. Should I sing to you?

WILLY. Yeah. Sing to me. (LINDA *hums a soft lullaby.*) When that team came out — he was the tallest, remember?

LINDA. Oh, yes. And in gold.

> BIFF *enters the darkened kitchen, takes a cigarette, and leaves the house. He comes downstage into a golden pool of light. He smokes, staring at the night.*

WILLY. Like a young god. Hercules — something like that. And the sun, the sun all around him. Remember how we waved to me? Right up from the field, with the representatives of three colleges standing by? And the buyers I brought, and the cheers when he came out — Loman, Loman, Loman! God Almighty, he'll be great yet. A star like that, magnificent, can never really fade away!

> *The light on* WILLY *is fading. The gas heater begins to glow through the kitchen wall, near the stairs, a blue flame beneath red coils.*

LINDA (*timidly*). Willy dear, what has he got against you?

WILLY. I'm so tired. Don't talk any more.

BIFF *slowly returns to the kitchen. He stops, stares toward the heater.*

LINDA. Will you ask Howard to let you work in New York?

WILLY. First thing in the morning. Everything'll be all right.

> BIFF *reaches behind the heater and draws out a length of rubber tubing. He is horrified and turns his head toward* WILLY'S *room, still dimly lit, from which the strains of* LINDA'S *desperate but monotonous humming rise.*

WILLY (*staring through the window into the moonlight*). Gee, look at the moon moving between the buildings!

BIFF *wraps the tubing around his hand and quickly goes up the stairs.*

CURTAIN

ACT TWO

Music is heard, gay and bright. The curtain rises as the music fades away. Willy, in his shirt sleeves, is sitting at the kitchen table, sipping coffee, his hat in his lap. Linda is filling his cup when she can.

WILLY. Wonderful coffee. Meal in itself.
LINDA. Can I make you some eggs?
WILLY. No. Take a breath.
LINDA. You look so rested, dear.
WILLY. I slept like a dead one. First time in months. Imagine, sleeping till ten on a Tuesday morning. Boys left nice and early, heh?
LINDA. They were out of here by eight o'clock.
WILLY. Good work!
LINDA. It was so thrilling to see them leaving together. I can't get over the shaving lotion in this house!
WILLY (*smiling*). Mmm —
LINDA. Biff was very changed this morning. His whole attitude seemed to be hopeful. He couldn't wait to get downtown to see Oliver.
WILLY. He's heading for a change. There's no question, there simply are certain men that take longer to get — solidified. How did he dress?
LINDA. His blue suit. He's so handsome in that suit. He could be a — anything in that suit!

   WILLY *gets up from the table.* LINDA *holds his jacket for him.*

WILLY. There's no question, no question at all. Gee, on the way home tonight I'd like to buy some seeds.
LINDA (*laughing*). That'd be wonderful. But not enough sun gets back there. Nothing'll grow any more.
WILLY. You wait, kid, before it's all over we're gonna get a little place out in the country, and I'll raise some vegetables, a couple of chickens . . .
LINDA. You'll do it yet, dear.

   WILLY *walks out of his jacket.* LINDA *follows him.*

WILLY. And they'll get married, and come for a weekend. I'd build a little guest house. 'Cause I got so many fine tools, all I'd need would be a little lumber and some peace of mind.
LINDA (*joyfully*). I sewed the lining . . .
WILLY. I could build two guest houses, so they'd both come. Did he decide how much he's going to ask Oliver for?
LINDA (*getting him into the jacket*). He didn't mention it, but I imagine ten or fifteen thousand. You going to talk to Howard today?
WILLY. Yeah. I'll put it to him straight and simple. He'll just have to take me off the road.

LINDA. And Willy, don't forget to ask for a little advance, because we've got the insurance premium. It's the grace period now.

WILLY. That's a hundred . . . ?

LINDA. A hundred and eight, sixty-eight. Because we're a little short again.

WILLY. Why are we short?

LINDA. Well, you had the motor job on the car . . .

WILLY. That goddam Studebaker!

LINDA. And you got one more payment on the refrigerator . . .

WILLY. But it just broke again!

LINDA. Well, it's old, dear.

WILLY. I told you we should've bought a well-advertised machine. Charley bought a General Electric and it's twenty years old and it's still good, that son-of-a-bitch.

LINDA. But, Willy —

WILLY. Whoever heard of a Hastings refrigerator? Once in my life I would like to own something outright before it's broken! I'm always in a race with the junkyard! I just finished paying for the car and it's on its last legs. The refrigerator consumes belts like a goddam maniac. They time those things. They time them so when you finally paid for them, they're used up.

LINDA (*buttoning up his jacket as he unbuttons it*). All told, about two hundred dollars would carry us, dear. But that includes the last payment on the mortgage. After this payment, Willy, the house belongs to us.

WILLY. It's twenty-five years!

LINDA. Biff was nine years old when we bought it.

WILLY. Well, that's a great thing. To weather a twenty-five year mortgage is —

LINDA. It's an accomplishment.

WILLY. All the cement, the lumber, the reconstruction I put in this house! There ain't a crack to be found in it any more.

LINDA. Well, it served its purpose.

WILLY. What purpose? Some stranger'll come along, move in, and that's that. If only Biff would take this house, and raise a family . . . (*He starts to go.*) Good-by, I'm late.

LINDA (*suddenly remembering*). Oh, I forgot! You're supposed to meet them for dinner.

WILLY. Me?

LINDA. At Frank's Chop House on Forty-eighth near Sixth Avenue.

WILLY. Is that so! How about you!

LINDA. No, just the three of you. They're gonna blow you to a big meal!

WILLY. Don't say! Who thought of that?

LINDA. Biff came to me this morning, Willy, and he said, "Tell Dad, we want to blow him to a big meal." Be there six o'clock. You and your two boys are going to have dinner.

WILLY. Gee whiz! That's really somethin'. I'm gonna knock Howard for a loop, kid. I'll get an advance, and I'll come home with a New York job. Goddammit, now I'm gonna do it!

LINDA. Oh, that's the spirit, Willy!

WILLY. I will never get behind a wheel the rest of my life!

LINDA. It's changing, Willy, I can feel it changing!

WILLY. Beyond a question. G'by, I'm late. (*He starts to go again.*)

LINDA (*calling after him as she runs to the kitchen table for a handkerchief*). You got your glasses?

WILLY (*feels for them, then comes back in*). Yeah, yeah, got my glasses.

LINDA (*giving him the handkerchief*). And a handkerchief.

WILLY. Yeah, handkerchief.

LINDA. And your saccharine?

WILLY. Yeah, my saccharine.

LINDA. Be careful on the subway stairs.

She kisses him, and a silk stocking is seen hanging from her hand. WILLY *notices it.*

WILLY. Will you stop mending stockings? At least while I'm in the house. It gets me nervous. I can't tell you. Please.

LINDA *hides the stocking in her hand as she follows* WILLY *across the forestage in front of the house.*

LINDA. Remember, Frank's Chop House.

WILLY (*passing the apron*). Maybe beets would grow out there.

LINDA (*laughing*). But you tried so many times.

WILLY. Yeah. Well, don't work hard today. (*He disappears around the right corner of the house.*)

LINDA. Be careful!

As WILLY *vanishes,* LINDA *waves to him. Suddenly the phone rings. She runs across the stage and into the kitchen and lifts it.*

LINDA. Hello? Oh, Biff! I'm so glad you called, I just . . . Yes, sure, I just told him. Yes, he'll be there for dinner at six o'clock, I didn't forget. Listen, I was just dying to tell you. You know that little rubber pipe I told you about? That he connected to the gas heater? I finally decided to go down the cellar this morning and take it away and destroy it. But it's gone! Imagine? He took it away himself, it isn't there! (*She listens.*) When? Oh, then you took it. Oh — nothing, it's just that I'd hoped he'd taken it away himself. Oh, I'm not worried, darling, because this morning he left in such high spirits, it was like the old days! I'm not afraid any more. Did Mr. Oliver see you? . . . Well, you wait there then. And make a nice impression on him, darling. Just don't perspire too much before you see him. And have a nice time with Dad. He may have big news too! . . . That's right, a New York job. And be sweet to him tonight, dear. Be loving to him. Because he's only a little boat looking for a harbor. (*She is trembling with sorrow and joy.*) Oh, that's wonderful, Biff, you'll save his life. Thanks, darling. Just put your arm around him when he comes into the restaurant. Give him a smile. That's the boy . . . Good-by, dear. . . . You got your comb? . . . That's fine. Good-by, Biff dear.

In the middle of her speech, HOWARD WAGNER, *thirty-six, wheels on a small typewriter table on which is a wire-recording machine and proceeds to plug it in. This is on the left forestage. Light slowly fades on* LINDA *as it rises on* HOWARD. HOWARD *is intent on threading the machine and only glances over his shoulder as* WILLY *appears.*

WILLY. Pst! Pst!

HOWARD. Hello, Willy, come in.

WILLY. Like to have a little talk with you, Howard.

HOWARD. Sorry to keep you waiting. I'll be with you in a minute.

WILLY. What's that, Howard?

HOWARD. Didn't you ever see one of these? Wire recorder.

WILLY. Oh. Can we talk a minute?

HOWARD. Records things. Just got delivery yesterday. Been driving me crazy, the most terrific machine I ever saw in my life. I was up all night with it.

WILLY. What do you do with it?

HOWARD. I bought it for dictation, but you can do anything with it. Listen to this. I had it home last night. Listen to what I picked up. The first one is my daughter. Get this. (*He flicks the switch and "Roll out the Barrel" is heard being whistled.*) Listen to that kid whistle.

WILLY. That is lifelike, isn't it?

HOWARD. Seven years old. Get that tone.

WILLY. Ts, ts. Like to ask a little favor if you . . .

The whistling breaks off, and the voice of HOWARD's *daughter is heard.*

HIS DAUGHTER. "Now you, Daddy."

HOWARD. She's crazy for me! (*Again the same song is whistled.*) That's me! Ha! (*He winks.*)

WILLY. You're very good!

The whistling breaks off again. The machine runs silent for a moment.

HOWARD. Sh! Get this now, this is my son.

HIS SON. "The capital of Alabama is Montgomery; the capital of Arizona is Phoenix; the capital of Arkansas is Little Rock; the capital of California is Sacramento . . ." (*And on, and on.*)

HOWARD (*holding up five fingers*). Five years old, Willy!

WILLY. He'll make an announcer some day!

HIS SON (*continuing*). "The capital . . ."

HOWARD. Get that — alphabetical order! (*The machine breaks off suddenly.*) Wait a minute. The maid kicked the plug out.

WILLY. It certainly is a —

HOWARD. Sh, for God's sake!

HIS SON. "It's nine o'clock, Bulova watch time. So I have to go to sleep."

WILLY. That really is —

HOWARD. Wait a minute! The next is my wife.

They wait.

HOWARD'S VOICE. "Go on, say something." (*Pause.*) "Well, you gonna talk?"

HIS WIFE. "I can't think of anything."

HOWARD'S VOICE. "Well, talk — it's turning."

HIS WIFE (*shyly, beaten*). "Hello." (*Silence.*) "Oh, Howard, I can't talk into this . . ."

HOWARD (*snapping the machine off*). That was my wife.

WILLY. That is a wonderful machine. Can we —

HOWARD. I tell you, Willy, I'm gonna take my camera, and my bandsaw, and all my hobbies, and out they go. This is the most fascinating relaxation I ever found.

WILLY. I think I'll get one myself.

HOWARD. Sure, they're only a hundred and a half. You can't do without it. Supposing you wanna hear Jack Benny, see? But you can't be at home at that hour. So you tell the maid to turn the radio on when Jack Benny comes on, and this automatically goes on with the radio . . .

WILLY. And when you come home you . . .

HOWARD. You can come home twelve o'clock, one o'clock, any time you like, and you get yourself a Coke and sit yourself down, throw the switch, and there's Jack Benny's program in the middle of the night!

WILLY. I'm definitely going to get one. Because lots of times I'm on the road, and I think to myself, what I must be missing on the radio!

HOWARD. Don't you have a radio in the car?

WILLY. Well, yeah, but who ever thinks of turning it on?

HOWARD. Say, aren't you supposed to be in Boston?

WILLY. That's what I want to talk to you about, Howard. You got a minute? (*He draws a chair in from the wing.*)

HOWARD. What happened? What're you doing here?

WILLY. Well . . .

HOWARD. You didn't crack up again, did you?

WILLY. Oh, no. No . . .

HOWARD. Geez, you had me worried there for a minute. What's the trouble?

WILLY. Well, tell you the truth, Howard. I've come to the decision that I'd rather not travel any more.

HOWARD. Not travel! Well, what'll you do?

WILLY. Remember, Christmas time, when you had the party here? You said you'd try to think of some spot for me here in town.

HOWARD. With us?

WILLY. Well, sure.

HOWARD. Oh, yeah, yeah. I remember. Well, I couldn't think of anything for you, Willy.

WILLY. I tell ya, Howard. The kids are all grown up, y'know. I don't need much any more. If I could take home — well, sixty-five dollars a week, I could swing it.

HOWARD. Yeah, but Willy, see I —

WILLY. I tell ya why, Howard. Speaking frankly and between the two of us, y'know — I'm just a little tired.

HOWARD. Oh, I could understand that, Willy. But you're a road man, Willy, and we do a road business. We've only got a half-dozen salesmen on the floor here.

WILLY. God knows, Howard, I never asked a favor of any man. But I was with the firm when your father used to carry you in here in his arms.

HOWARD. I know that, Willy, but —

WILLY. Your father came to me the day you were born and asked me what I thought of the name of Howard, may he rest in peace.

HOWARD. I appreciate that, Willy, but there just is no spot here for you. If I had a spot I'd slam you right in, but I just don't have a single solitary spot.

He looks for his lighter. WILLY *has picked it up and gives it to him. Pause.*

WILLY (*with increasing anger*). Howard, all I need to set my table is fifty dollars a week.

HOWARD. But where am I going to put you, kid?

WILLY. Look, it isn't a question of whether I can sell merchandise, is it?

HOWARD. No, but it's a business, kid, and everybody's gotta pull his own weight.

WILLY (*desperately*). Just let me tell you a story, Howard —

HOWARD. 'Cause you gotta admit, business is business.

WILLY (*angrily*). Business is definitely business, but just listen for a minute. You don't understand this. When I was a boy — eighteen, nineteen — I was already on the road. And there was a question in my mind as to whether selling had a future for me. Because in those days I had a yearning to go to Alaska. See, there were three gold strikes in one month in Alaska, and I felt like going out. Just for the ride, you might say.

HOWARD (*barely interested*). Don't say.

WILLY. Oh, yeah, my father lived many years in Alaska. He was an adventurous man. We've got quite a little streak of self-reliance in our family. I thought I'd go out with my older brother and try to locate him, and maybe settle in the North with the old man. And I was almost decided to go, when I met a salesman in the Parker House. His name was Dave Singleman. And he was eighty-four years old, and he'd drummed merchandise in thirty-one states. And old Dave, he'd go up to his room, y'understand, put on his green velvet slippers — I'll never forget — and pick up his phone and call the buyers, and without ever leaving his room, at the age of eighty-four, he made his living. And when I saw that, I realized that selling was the greatest career a man could want. 'Cause what could be more satisfying than to be able to go, at the age of eighty-four, into twenty or thirty different cities, and pick up a phone, and be remembered and loved and helped by so many different people? Do you know? when he died — and by the way he died the death of a salesman, in his green velvet slippers in the smoker of the New York, New Haven and Hartford, going into Boston — when he died, hundreds of salesmen and buyers were at his funeral. Things were sad on a lotta trains for months after that. (*He stands up.* HOWARD *has not looked at him.*) In those days there was personality in it, Howard. There was respect and comradeship, and gratitude in it. Today, it's all cut and dried, and there's no chance for bringing friendship to bear — or personality. You see what I mean? They don't know me any more.

HOWARD (*moving away, to the right*). That's just the thing, Willy.

WILLY. If I had forty dollars a week — that's all I'd need. Forty dollars, Howard.

HOWARD. Kid, I can't take blood from a stone, I —

WILLY (*desperation is on him now*). Howard, the year Al Smith was nominated, your father came to me and —

HOWARD (*starting to go off*). I've got to see some people, kid.

WILLY (*stopping him*). I'm talking about your father! There were promises made across this desk! You mustn't tell me you've got people to see — I put thirty-four years into this firm, Howard, and now I can't pay my insurance! You can't eat the orange and throw the peel away — a man is not a piece of fruit! (*After a pause.*) Now pay attention. Your father — in 1928 I had a big year. I averaged a hundred and seventy dollars a week in commissions.

HOWARD (*impatiently*). Now, Willy, you never averaged —

WILLY (*banging his hand on the desk*). I averaged a hundred and seventy dollars a week in the year of 1928! And your father came to me — or rather, I was in the office here — it was right over this desk — and he put his hand on my shoulder —

HOWARD (*getting up*). You'll have to excuse me, Willy, I gotta see some people. Pull yourself together. (*Going out.*) I'll be back in a little while.

On HOWARD's *exit, the light on his chair grows very bright and strange.*

WILLY. Pull myself together! What the hell did I say to him? My God, I was yelling at him! How could I! (WILLY *breaks off, staring at the light, which occupies the chair, animating it. He approaches this chair, standing across the desk from it.*) Frank, Frank, don't you remember what you told me that time? How you put your hand on my shoulder, and Frank . . . (*He leans on the desk and as he speaks the dead man's name he accidentally switches on the recorder, and instantly*)

HOWARD'S SON. ". . . of New York is Albany. The capital of Ohio is Cincinnati, the capital of Rhode Island is . . ." (*The recitation continues.*)

WILLY (*leaping away with fright, shouting*). Ha! Howard! Howard! Howard!

HOWARD (*rushing in*). What happened?

WILLY (*pointing at the machine, which continues nasally, childishly, with the capital cities*). Shut it off! Shut it off!

HOWARD (*pulling the plug out*). Look, Willy . . .

WILLY (*pressing his hands to his eyes*). I gotta get myself some coffee. I'll get some coffee . . .

WILLY *starts to walk out.* HOWARD *stops him.*

HOWARD (*rolling up the cord*). Willy, look . . .

WILLY. I'll go to Boston.

HOWARD. Willy, you can't go to Boston for us.

WILLY. Why can't I go?

HOWARD. I don't want you to represent us. I've been meaning to tell you for a long time now.

WILLY. Howard, are you firing me?

HOWARD. I think you need a good long rest, Willy.

WILLY. Howard —

HOWARD. And when you feel better, come back, and we'll see if we can work something out.

WILLY. But I gotta earn money, Howard. I'm in no position to —

HOWARD. Where are your sons? Why don't your sons give you a hand?

WILLY. They're working on a very big deal.

HOWARD. This is no time for false pride, Willy. You go to your sons and you tell them that you're tired. You've got two great boys, haven't you?

WILLY. Oh, no question, no question, but in the meantime . . .

HOWARD. Then that's that, heh?

WILLY. All right, I'll go to Boston tomorrow.

HOWARD. No, no.

WILLY. I can't throw myself on my sons. I'm not a cripple!

HOWARD. Look, kid, I'm busy this morning.

WILLY (*grasping Howard's arm*). Howard, you've got to let me go to Boston!

HOWARD (*hard, keeping himself under control*). I've got a line of people to see this morning. Sit down, take five minutes, and pull yourself together, and then go home, will ya? I need the office, Willy. (*He starts to go, turns, remembering the recorder, starts to push off the table holding the recorder.*) Oh, yeah. Whenever you can this week, stop by and drop off the samples. You'll feel better, Willy, and then come back and we'll talk. Pull yourself together, kid, there's people outside.

HOWARD *exits, pushing the table off left.* WILLY *stares into space, ex-*

hausted. Now the music is heard — BEN's music — first distantly, then closer, closer. As WILLY speaks, BEN enters from the right. He carries valise and umbrella.

WILLY. Oh, Ben, how did you do it? What is the answer? Did you wind up the Alaska deal already?

BEN. Doesn't take much time if you know what you're doing. Just a short business trip. Boarding ship in an hour. Wanted to say good-by.

WILLY. Ben, I've got to talk to you.

BEN (glancing at his watch). Haven't the time, William.

WILLY (crossing the apron to BEN). Ben, nothing's working out. I don't know what to do.

BEN. Now, look here, William. I've bought timberland in Alaska and I need a man to look after things for me.

WILLY. God, timberland! Me and my boys in those grand outdoors!

BEN. You've a new continent at your doorstep, William. Get out of these cities, they're full of talk and time payments and courts of law. Screw on your fists and you can fight for a fortune up there.

WILLY. Yes, yes! Linda, Linda!

LINDA enters as of old, with the wash.

LINDA. Oh, you're back?

BEN. I haven't much time.

WILLY. No, wait! Linda, he's got a proposition for me in Alaska.

LINDA. But you've got — (To BEN.) He's got a beautiful job here.

WILLY. But in Alaska, kid, I could —

LINDA. You're doing well enough, Willy!

BEN (to LINDA). Enough for what, my dear?

LINDA (frightened of BEN and angry at him). Don't say those things to him! Enough to be happy right here, right now. (To WILLY, while BEN laughs.) Why must everybody conquer the world? You're well liked, and the boys love you, and someday — (to BEN) — why, old man Wagner told him just the other day that if he keeps it up he'll be a member of the firm, didn't he, Willy?

WILLY. Sure, sure. I am building something with this firm, Ben, and if a man is building something he must be on the right track, mustn't he?

BEN. What are you building? Lay your hand on it. Where is it?

WILLY (hesitantly). That's true, Linda, there's nothing.

LINDA. Why? (To BEN.) There's a man eighty-four years old —

WILLY. That's right, Ben, that's right. When I look at that man I say, what is there to worry about?

BEN. Bah!

WILLY. It's true, Ben. All he has to do is go into any city, pick up the phone, and he's making his living and you know why?

BEN (picking up his valise). I've got to go.

WILLY (*holding* BEN *back*). Look at this boy!
  BIFF, *in his high school sweater, enters carrying suitcase.* HAPPY *carries* BIFF's *shoulder guards, gold helmet, and football pants.*
WILLY. Without a penny to his name, three great universities are begging for him, and from there the sky's the limit, because it's not what you do, Ben. It's who you know and the smile on your face! It's contacts, Ben, contacts! The whole wealth of Alaska passes over the lunch table at the Commodore Hotel, and that's the wonder, the wonder of this country, that a man can end with diamonds here on the basis of being liked! (*He turns to* BIFF.) And that's why when you get out on that field today it's important. Because thousands of people will be rooting for you and loving you. (*To* BEN, *who has again begun to leave.*) And Ben! when he walks into a business office his name will sound out like a bell and all the doors will open to him! I've seen it, Ben, I've seen it a thousand times! You can't feel it with your hand like timber, but it's there!
BEN. Good-by, William.
WILLY. Ben, am I right? Don't you think I'm right? I value your advice.
BEN. There's a new continent at your doorstep, William. You could walk out rich. Rich! (*He is gone.*)
WILLY. We'll do it here, Ben! You hear me? We're gonna do it here!
  YOUNG BERNARD *rushes in. The gay music of the* BOYS *is heard.*
BERNARD. Oh, gee, I was afraid you left already!
WILLY. Why? What time is it?
BERNARD. It's half-past one!
WILLY. Well, come on, everybody! Ebbets Field next stop! Where's the pennants? (*He rushes through the wall-line of the kitchen and out into the living-room.*)
LINDA (*to* BIFF). Did you pack fresh underwear?
BIFF (*who has been limbering up*). I want to go!
BERNARD. Biff, I'm carrying your helmet, ain't I?
HAPPY. No, I'm carrying the helmet.
BERNARD. Oh, Biff, you promised me.
HAPPY. I'm carrying the helmet.
BERNARD. How am I going to get in the locker room?
LINDA. Let him carry the shoulder guards. (*She puts her coat and hat on in the kitchen.*)
BERNARD. Can I, Biff? 'Cause I told everybody I'm going to be in the locker room.
HAPPY. In Ebbets Field it's the clubhouse.
BERNARD. I meant the clubhouse. Biff!
HAPPY. Biff!
BIFF (*grandly, after a slight pause*). Let him carry the shoulder guards.
HAPPY (*as he gives* BERNARD *the shoulder guards*). Stay close to us now.

WILLY *rushes in with the pennants.*

WILLY (*handing them out*). Everybody wave when Biff comes out on the field. (HAPPY *and* BERNARD *run off.*) You set now, boy?

The music has died away.

BIFF. Ready to go, Pop. Every muscle is ready.

WILLY (*at the edge of the apron*). You realize what this means?

BIFF. That's right, Pop.

WILLY (*feeling* BIFF's *muscles*). You're comin' home this afternoon captain of the All-Scholastic Championship Team of the City of New York.

BIFF. I got it, Pop. And remember, pal, when I take off my helmet, that touchdown is for you.

WILLY. Let's go! (*He is starting out, with his arm around* BIFF, *when* CHARLEY *enters, as of old, in knickers.*) I got no room for you, Charley.

CHARLEY. Room? For what?

WILLY. In the car.

CHARLEY. You goin' for a ride? I wanted to shoot some casino.

WILLY (*furiously*). Casino! (*Incredulously.*) Don't you realize what today is?

LINDA. Oh, he knows, Willy. He's just kidding you.

WILLY. That's nothing to kid about!

CHARLEY. No, Linda, what's goin' on?

LINDA. He's playing in Ebbets Field.

CHARLEY. Baseball in this weather?

WILLY. Don't talk to him. Come on, come on! (*He is pushing them out.*)

CHARLEY. Wait a minute, didn't you hear the news?

WILLY. What?

CHARLEY. Don't you listen to the radio? Ebbets Field just blew up.

WILLY. You go to hell! (CHARLEY *laughs. Pushing them out.*) Come on, come on! We're late.

CHARLEY (*as they go*). Knock a homer, Biff, knock a homer!

WILLY (*the last to leave, turning to* CHARLEY). I don't think that was funny, Charley. This is the greatest day of his life.

CHARLEY. Willy, when are you going to grow up?

WILLY. Yeah, heh? When this game is over, Charley, you'll be laughing out of the other side of your face. They'll be calling him another Red Grange. Twenty-five thousand a year.

CHARLEY (*kidding*). Is that so?

WILLY. Yeah, that's so.

CHARLEY. Well, then, I'm sorry, Willy. But tell me something.

WILLY. What?

CHARLEY. Who is Red Grange?

WILLY. Put up your hands. Goddam you, put up your hands!

CHARLEY, *chuckling, shakes his head and walks away, around the left corner of the stage.* WILLY *follows him. The music rises to a mocking frenzy.*

WILLY. Who the hell do you think you are, better than everybody else? You don't know everything, you big, ignorant, stupid . . . Put up your hands!

Light rises, on the right side of the forestage, on a small table in the reception room of CHARLEY's *office. Traffic sounds are heard.* BERNARD, *now mature, sits whistling to himself. A pair of tennis rackets and an overnight bag are on the floor beside him.*

WILLY (*offstage*). What are you walking away for? Don't walk away! If you're going to say something say it to my face! I know you laugh at me behind my back. You'll laugh out of the other side of your goddam face after this game. Touchdown! Touchdown! Eighty thousand people! Touchdown! Right between the goal posts.

BERNARD *is a quiet, earnest, but self-assured young man.* WILLY's *voice is coming from right upstage now.* BERNARD *lowers his feet off the table and listens.* JENNY, *his father's secretary, enters.*

JENNY (*distressed*). Say, Bernard, will you go out in the hall?

BERNARD. What is that noise? Who is it?

JENNY. Mr. Loman. He just got off the elevator.

BERNARD (*getting up*). Who's he arguing with?

JENNY. Nobody. There's nobody with him. I can't deal with him any more, and your father gets all upset everytime he comes. I've got a lot of typing to do, and your father's waiting to sign it. Will you see him?

WILLY (*entering*). Touchdown! Touch — (*He sees* JENNY.) Jenny, Jenny, good to see you. How're ya? Workin'? Or still honest?

JENNY. Fine. How've you been feeling?

WILLY. Not much any more, Jenny. Ha, ha! (*He is surprised to see the rackets.*)

BERNARD. Hello, Uncle Willy.

WILLY (*almost shocked*). Bernard! Well, look who's here! (*He comes quickly, guiltily, to* BERNARD *and warmly shakes his hand.*)

BERNARD. How are you? Good to see you.

WILLY. What are you doing here?

BERNARD. Oh, just stopped by to see Pop. Get off my feet till my train leaves. I'm going to Washington in a few minutes.

WILLY. Is he in?

BERNARD. Yes, he's in his office with the accountant. Sit down.

WILLY (*sitting down*). What're you going to do in Washington?

BERNARD. Oh, just a case I've got there, Willy.

WILLY. That so? (*Indicating the rackets.*) You going to play tennis there?

BERNARD. I'm staying with a friend who's got a court.

WILLY. Don't say. His own tennis court. Must be fine people, I bet.

BERNARD. They are, very nice. Dad tells me Biff's in town.

WILLY (*with a big smile*). Yeah, Biff's in. Working on a very big deal, Bernard.

BERNARD. What's Biff doing?

WILLY. Well, he's been doing very big things in the West. But he decided to establish himself here. Very big. We're having dinner. Did I hear your wife had a boy?

BERNARD. That's right. Our second.

WILLY. Two boys! What do you know!

BERNARD. What kind of a deal has Biff got?

WILLY. Well, Bill Oliver — very big sporting-goods man — he wants Biff very badly. Called him in from the West. Long distance, carte blanche, special deliveries. Your friends have their own private tennis court?

BERNARD. You still with the old firm, Willy?

WILLY (*after a pause*). I'm — I'm overjoyed to see how you made the grade, Bernard, overjoyed. It's an encouraging thing to see a young man really — really — Looks very good for Biff — very — (*He breaks off, then:*) Bernard — (*He is so full of emotion, he breaks off again.*)

BERNARD. What is it, Willy?

WILLY (*small and alone*). What — what's the secret?

BERNARD. What secret?

WILLY. How — how did you? Why didn't he ever catch on?

BERNARD. I wouldn't know that, Willy.

WILLY (*confidentially, desperately*). You were his friend, his boyhood friend. There's something I don't understand about it. His life ended after that Ebbets Field game. From the age of seventeen nothing good ever happened to him.

BERNARD. He never trained himself for anything.

WILLY. But he did, he did. After high school he took so many correspondence courses. Radio mechanics; television; God knows what, and never made the slightest mark.

BERNARD (*taking off his glasses*). Willy, do you want to talk candidly?

WILLY (*rising, faces* BERNARD). I regard you as a very brilliant man, Bernard. I value your advice.

BERNARD. Oh, the hell with the advice, Willy. I couldn't advise you. There's just one thing I've always wanted to ask you. When he was supposed to graduate, and the math teacher flunked him —

WILLY. Oh, that son-of-a-bitch ruined his life.

BERNARD. Yeah, but, Willy, all he had to do was go to summer school and make up that subject.

WILLY. That's right, that's right.

BERNARD. Did you tell him not to go to summer school?

WILLY. Me? I begged him to go. I ordered him to go!

BERNARD. Then why wouldn't he go?

WILLY. Why? Why! Bernard, that question has been trailing me like a ghost for the last fifteen years. He flunked the subject, and laid down and died like a hammer hit him

BERNARD. Take it easy, kid.

WILLY. Let me talk to you — I got nobody to talk to. Bernard, Bernard, was it my fault? Y'see? It keeps going around in my mind, maybe I did something to him. I got nothing to give him.

BERNARD. Don't take it so hard.

WILLY. Why did he lay down? What is the story there? You were his friend!

BERNARD. Willy, I remember, it was June, and our grades came out. And he'd flunked math.

WILLY. That son-of-a-bitch!

BERNARD. No, it wasn't right then. Biff just got very angry, I remember, and he was ready to enroll in summer school.

WILLY (*surprised*). He was?

BERNARD. He wasn't beaten by it at all. But then, Willy, he disappeared from the block for almost a month. And I got the idea that he'd gone up to New England to see you. Did he have a talk with you then?

WILLY *stares in silence.*

BERNARD. Willy?

WILLY (*with a strong edge of resentment in his voice*). Yeah, he came to Boston. What about it?

BERNARD. Well, just that when he came back — I'll never forget this, it always mystifies me. Because I'd thought so well of Biff, even though he'd always taken advantage of me. I loved him, Willy, y'know? And he came back after that month and took his sneakers — remember those sneakers with "University of Virginia" printed on them? He was so proud of those, wore them every day. And he took them down in the cellar, and burned them up in the furnace. We had a fist fight. It lasted at least half an hour. Just the two of us, punching each other down the cellar, and crying right through it. I've often thought of how strange it was that I knew he'd given up his life. What happened in Boston, Willy?

WILLY *looks at him as at an intruder.*

BERNARD. I just bring it up because you asked me.

WILLY (*angrily*). Nothing. What do you mean, "What happened?" What's that got to do with anything?

BERNARD. Well, don't get sore.

WILLY. What are you trying to do, blame it on me? If a boy lays down is that my fault?

BERNARD. Now, Willy, don't get —

WILLY. Well, don't — don't talk to me that way! What does that mean, "What happened?"

CHARLEY *enters. He is in his vest, and he carries a bottle of bourbon.*

CHARLEY. Hey, you're going to miss that train. (*He waves the bottle.*)

BERNARD. Yeah, I'm going. (*He takes the bottle.*) Thanks, Pop. (*He picks up his rackets and bag.*) Good-by, Willy, and don't worry about it. You know, "If at first you don't succeed . . ."

WILLY. Yes, I believe in that.

BERNARD. But sometimes, Willy, it's better for a man just to walk away.

WILLY. Walk away?

BERNARD. That's right.

WILLY. But if you can't walk away?

BERNARD (*after a slight pause*). I guess that's when it's tough. (*Extending his hand.*) Good-by, Willy.

WILLY (*shaking BERNARD's hand*). Good-by, boy.

CHARLEY (*an arm on BERNARD's shoulder*). How do you like this kid? Gonna argue a case in front of the Supreme Court.

BERNARD (*protesting*). Pop!

WILLY (*genuinely shocked, pained, and happy*). No! The Supreme Court!

BERNARD. I gotta run. 'By, Dad!

CHARLEY. Knock 'em dead, Bernard!

BERNARD *goes off.*

WILLY (*as CHARLEY takes out his wallet*). The Supreme Court! And he didn't even mention it!

CHARLEY (*counting out money on the desk*). He don't have to — he's gonna do it.

WILLY. And you never told him what to do, did you? You never took any interest in him.

CHARLEY. My salvation is that I never took any interest in anything. There's some money — fifty dollars. I got an accountant inside.

WILLY. Charley, look . . . (*With difficulty.*) I got my insurance to pay. If you can manage it — I need a hundred and ten dollars.

CHARLEY *doesn't reply for a moment; merely stops moving.*

WILLY. I'd draw it from my bank but Linda would know, and I . . .

CHARLEY. Sit down, Willy.

WILLY (*moving toward the chair*). I'm keeping an account of everything, remember. I'll pay every penny back. (*He sits.*)

CHARLEY. Now listen to me, Willy.

WILLY. I want you to know I appreciate . . .

CHARLEY (*sitting down on the table*). Willy, what're you doin'? What the hell is goin' on in your head?

WILLY. Why? I'm simply . . .

CHARLEY. I offered you a job. You can make fifty dollars a week. And I won't send you on the road.

WILLY. I've got a job.

CHARLEY. Without pay? What kind of a job is a job without pay? (*He rises.*) Now, look, kid, enough is enough. I'm no genius but I know when I'm being insulted.

WILLY. Insulted!

CHARLEY. Why don't you want to work for me?

WILLY. What's the matter with you? I've got a job.

CHARLEY. Then what're you walkin' in here every week for?

WILLY (*getting up*). Well, if you don't want me to walk in here —

CHARLEY. I am offering you a job.

WILLY. I don't want your goddam job!

CHARLEY. When the hell are you going to grow up?

WILLY (*furiously*). You big ignoramus, if you say that to me again I'll rap you one! I don't care how big you are! (*He's ready to fight.*)

Pause.

CHARLEY (*kindly, going to him*). How much do you need, Willy?

WILLY. Charley, I'm strapped, I'm strapped. I don't know what to do. I was just fired.

CHARLEY. Howard fired you?

WILLY. That snotnose. Imagine that? I named him. I named him Howard.

CHARLEY. Willy, when're you gonna realize that them things don't mean anything? You named him Howard, but you can't sell that. The only thing you got in this world is what you can sell. And the funny thing is that you're a salesman, and you don't know that.

WILLY. I've always tried to think otherwise, I guess. I always felt that if a man was impressive, and well liked, that nothing —

CHARLEY. Why must everybody like you? Who liked J. P. Morgan? Was he impressive? In a Turkish bath he'd look like a butcher. But with his pockets on he was very well liked. Now listen, Willy, I know you don't like me, and nobody can say I'm in love with you, but I'll give you a job because — just for the hell of it, put it that way. Now what do you say?

WILLY. I — I just can't work for you, Charley.

CHARLEY. What're you, jealous of me?

WILLY. I can't work for you, that's all, don't ask me why.

CHARLEY (*angered, takes out more bills*). You been jealous of me all your life, you damned fool! Here, pay your insurance. (*He puts the money in* WILLY's *hand.*)

WILLY. I'm keeping strict accounts.

CHARLEY. I've got some work to do. Take care of yourself. And pay your insurance.

WILLY (*moving to the right*). Funny, y'know? After all the highways, and the trains, and the appointments, and the years, you end up worth more dead than alive.

CHARLEY. Willy, nobody's worth nothin' dead. (*After a slight pause.*) Did you hear what I said?

WILLY *stands still, dreaming.*

CHARLEY. Willy!

WILLY. Apologize to Bernard for me when you see him. I didn't mean to argue with him. He's a fine boy. They're all fine boys, and they'll end up big — all of them. Someday they'll all play tennis together. Wish me luck, Charley. He saw Bill Oliver today.

CHARLEY. Good luck.

WILLY (*on the verge of tears*). Charley, you're the only friend I got. Isn't that a remarkable thing? (*He goes out.*)

CHARLEY. Jesus!

CHARLEY *stares after him a moment and follows. All light blacks out. Suddenly raucous music is heard, and a red glow rises behind the screen at right.* STANLEY, *a young waiter, appears, carrying a table, followed by* HAPPY, *who is carrying two chairs.*

STANLEY (*putting the table down*). That's all right, Mr. Loman, I can handle it myself. (*He turns and takes the chairs from* HAPPY *and places them at the table.*)

HAPPY (*glancing around*). Oh, this is better.

STANLEY. Sure, in the front there you're in the middle of all kinds a noise. Whenever you got a party, Mr. Loman, you just tell me and I'll put you back here. Y'know, there's a lotta people they don't like it private, because when they go out they like to see a lotta action around them because they're sick and tired to stay in the house by theirself. But I know you, you ain't from Hackensack. You know what I mean?

HAPPY (*sitting down*). So how's it coming, Stanley?

STANLEY. Ah, it's a dog's life. I only wish during the war they'd a took me in the Army. I coulda been dead by now.

HAPPY. My brother's back, Stanley.

STANLEY. Oh, he come back, heh? From the Far West.

HAPPY. Yeah, big cattle man, my brother, so treat him right. And my father's coming too.

STANLEY. Oh, your father too!

HAPPY. You got a couple of nice lobsters?

STANLEY. Hundred per cent, big.

HAPPY. I want them with the claws.

STANLEY. Don't worry, I don't give you no mice. (HAPPY *laughs.*) How about some wine? It'll put a head on the meal.

HAPPY. No. You remember, Stanley, that recipe I brought you from overseas? With the champagne in it?

STANLEY. Oh, yeah, sure. I still got it tacked up yet in the kitchen. But that'll have to cost a buck apiece anyways.

HAPPY. That's all right.

STANLEY. What'd you, hit a number or somethin'?

HAPPY. No, it's a little celebration. My brother is — I think he pulled off a big deal today. I think we're going into business together.

STANLEY. Great! That's the best for you. Because a family business, you know what I mean? — that's the best.

HAPPY. That's what I think.
STANLEY. 'Cause what's the difference? Somebody steals? It's in the family. Know what I mean? (*Sotto voce.*) Like this bartender here. The boss is goin' crazy what kinda leak he's got in the cash register. You put it in but it don't come out.
HAPPY (*raising his head*). Sh!
STANLEY. What?
HAPPY. You notice I wasn't lookin' right or left, was I?
STANLEY. No.
HAPPY. And my eyes are closed.
STANLEY. So what's the —?
HAPPY. Strudel's comin'.
STANLEY (*catching on, looks around*). Ah, no, there's no —
   He breaks off as a furred, lavishly dressed GIRL *enters and sits at the next table. Both follow her with their eyes.*
STANLEY. Geez, how'd ya know?
HAPPY. I got radar or something. (*Starring directly at her profile.*) Oooooooo . . . Stanley.
STANLEY. I think that's for you, Mr. Loman.
HAPPY. Look at that mouth. Oh, God. And the binoculars.
STANLEY. Geez, you got a life, Mr. Loman.
HAPPY. Wait on her.
STANLEY (*going to the* GIRL's *table*). Would you like a menu, ma'am?
GIRL. I'm expecting someone, but I'd like a —
HAPPY. Why don't you bring her — excuse me, miss, do you mind? I sell champagne, and I'd like you to try my brand. Bring her a champagne, Stanley.
GIRL. That's awfully nice of you.
HAPPY. Don't mention it. It's all company money. (*He laughs.*)
GIRL. That's a charming product to be selling, isn't it?
HAPPY. Oh, gets to be like everything else. Selling is selling, y'know.
GIRL. I suppose.
HAPPY. You don't happen to sell, do you?
GIRL. No, I don't sell.
HAPPY. Would you object to a compliment from a stranger? You ought to be on a magazine cover.
GIRL (*looking at him a little archly*). I have been.
   STANLEY *comes in with a glass of champagne.*
HAPPY. What'd I say before, Stanley? You see? She's a cover girl.
STANLEY. Oh, I could see, I could see.
HAPPY (*to the* GIRL). What magazine?
GIRL. Oh, a lot of them. (*She takes the drink.*) Thank you.
HAPPY. You know what they say in France, don't you? "Champagne is the drink of the complexion" — Hya, Biff!
   BIFF *has entered and sits with* HAPPY.

BIFF. Hello, kid. Sorry I'm late.

HAPPY. I just got here. Uh, Miss —?

GIRL. Forsythe.

HAPPY. Miss Forsythe, this is my brother.

BIFF. Is Dad here?

HAPPY. His name is Biff. You might've heard of him. Great football player.

GIRL. Really? What team?

HAPPY. Are you familiar with football?

GIRL. No, I'm afraid I'm not.

HAPPY. Biff is quarterback with the New York Giants.

GIRL. Well, that is nice, isn't it? (*She drinks.*)

HAPPY. Good health.

GIRL. I'm happy to meet you.

HAPPY. That's my name. Hap. It's really Harold, but at West Point they called me Happy.

GIRL (*now really impressed*). Oh, I see. How do you do? (*She turns her profile.*)

BIFF. Isn't Dad coming?

HAPPY. You want her?

BIFF. Oh, I could never make that.

HAPPY. I remember the time that idea would never come into your head. Where's the old confidence, Biff?

BIFF. I just saw Oliver —

HAPPY. Wait a minute. I've got to see that old confidence again. Do you want her? She's on call.

BIFF. Oh, no. (*He turns to look at the* GIRL.)

HAPPY. I'm telling you. Watch this. (*Turning to the* GIRL.) Honey? (*She turns to him.*) Are you busy?

GIRL. Well, I am . . . but I could make a phone call.

HAPPY. Do that, will you, honey? And see if you can get a friend. We'll be here for a while. Biff is one of the greatest football players in the country.

GIRL (*standing up*). Well, I'm certainly happy to meet you.

HAPPY. Come back soon.

GIRL. I'll try.

HAPPY. Don't try, honey, try hard.

The GIRL *exits.* STANLEY *follows, shaking his head in bewildered admiration.*

HAPPY. Isn't that a shame now? A beautiful girl like that? That's why I can't get married. There's not a good woman in a thousand. New York is loaded with them, kid!

BIFF. Hap, look —

HAPPY. I told you she was on call!

BIFF (*strangely unnerved*). Cut it out, will ya? I want to say something to you.

Death of a Salesman

HAPPY. Did you see Oliver?

BIFF. I saw him all right. Now look, I want to tell Dad a couple of things and I want you to help me.

HAPPY. What? Is he going to back you?

BIFF. Are you crazy? You're out of your goddam head, you know that?

HAPPY. Why? What happened?

BIFF (*breathlessly*). I did a terrible thing today, Hap. It's been the strangest day I ever went through. I'm all numb, I swear.

HAPPY. You mean he wouldn't see you?

BIFF. Well, I waited six hours for him, see? All day. Kept sending my name in. Even tried to date his secretary so she'd get me to him, but no soap.

HAPPY. Because you're not showin' the old confidence, Biff. He remembered you, didn't he?

BIFF (*stopping* HAPPY *with a gesture*). Finally, about five o'clock, he comes out. Didn't remember who I was or anything. I felt like such an idiot, Hap.

HAPPY. Did you tell him my Florida idea?

BIFF. He walked away. I saw him for one minute. I got so mad I could've torn the walls down! How the hell did I ever get the idea I was a salesman there? I even believed myself that I'd been a salesman for him! And then he gave me one look and — I realized what a ridiculous lie my whole life has been! We've been talking in a dream for fifteen years. I was a shipping clerk.

HAPPY. What'd you do?

BIFF (*with great tension and wonder*). Well, he left, see. And the secretary went out. I was all alone in the waiting-room. I don't know what came over me, Hap. The next thing I know I'm in his office — paneled walls, everything. I can't explain it. I — Hap, I took his fountain pen.

HAPPY. Geez, did he catch you?

BIFF. I ran out. I ran down all eleven flights. I ran and ran and ran.

HAPPY. That was an awful dumb — what'd you do that for?

BIFF (*agonized*). I don't know, I just — wanted to take something, I don't know. You gotta help me, Hap, I'm gonna tell Pop.

HAPPY. You crazy? What for?

BIFF. Hap, he's got to understand that I'm not the man somebody lends that kind of money to. He thinks I've been spiting him all these years and it's eating him up.

HAPPY. That's just it. You tell him something nice.

BIFF. I can't.

HAPPY. Say you got a lunch date with Oliver tomorrow.

BIFF. So what do I do tomorrow?

HAPPY. You leave the house tomorrow and come back at night and say Oliver is thinking it over. And he thinks it over for a couple of weeks, and gradually it fades away and nobody's the worse.

BIFF. But it'll go on forever!

HAPPY. Dad is never so happy as when he's looking forward to something!
WILLY *enters.*
HAPPY. Hello, scout!
WILLY. Gee, I haven't been here in years!
  STANLEY *has followed* WILLY *in and sets a chair for him.* STANLEY *starts off but* HAPPY *stops him.*
HAPPY. Stanley!
  STANLEY *stands by, waiting for an order.*
BIFF (*going to* WILLY *with guilt, as to an invalid*). Sit down, Pop. You want a drink?
WILLY. Sure, I don't mind.
BIFF. Let's get a load on.
WILLY. You look worried.
BIFF. N-no. (*To* STANLEY.) Scotch all around. Make it doubles.
STANLEY. Doubles, right. (*He goes.*)
WILLY. You had a couple already, didn't you?
BIFF. Just a couple, yeah.
WILLY. Well, what happened, boy? (*Nodding affirmatively, with a smile.*) Everything go all right?
BIFF (*takes a breath, then reaches out and grasps* WILLY's *hand*). Pal . . . (*He is smiling bravely, and* WILLY *is smiling too.*) I had an experience today.
HAPPY. Terrific, Pop.
WILLY. That so? What happened?
BIFF (*high, slightly alcoholic, above the earth*). I'm going to tell you everything from first to last. It's been a strange day. (*Silence. He looks around, composes himself as best as he can, but his breath keeps breaking the rhythm of his voice.*) I had to wait quite a while for him, and —
WILLY. Oliver?
BIFF. Yeah, Oliver. All day, as a matter of cold fact. And a lot of — instances — facts, Pop, facts about my life came back to me. Who was it, Pop? Who ever said I was a salesman with Oliver?
WILLY. Well, you were.
BIFF. No, Dad, I was a shipping clerk.
WILLY. But you were practically —
BIFF (*with determination*). Dad, I don't know who said it first, but I was never a salesman for Bill Oliver.
WILLY. What're you talking about?
BIFF. Let's hold on to the facts tonight, Pop. We're not going to get anywhere bullin' around. I was a shipping clerk.
WILLY (*angrily*). All right, now listen to me —
BIFF. Why don't you let me finish?
WILLY. I'm not interested in stories about the past or any crap of that kind because the woods are burning, boys, you understand? There's a big blaze going on all around. I was fired today.

BIFF (*shocked*). How could you be?

WILLY. I was fired, and I'm looking for a little good news to tell your mother, because the woman has waited and the woman has suffered. The gist of it is that I haven't got a story left in my head, Biff. So don't give me a lecture about facts and aspects. I am not interested. Now what've you got to say to me?

STANLEY *enters with three drinks. They wait until he leaves.*

WILLY. Did you see Oliver?

BIFF. Jesus, Dad!

WILLY. You mean you didn't go up there?

HAPPY. Sure he went up there.

BIFF. I did. I — saw him. How could they fire you?

WILLY (*on the edge of his chair*). What kind of a welcome did he give you?

BIFF. He won't even let you work on commission?

WILLY. I'm out! (*Driving.*) So tell me, he gave you a warm welcome?

HAPPY. Sure, Pop, sure!

BIFF (*driven*). Well, it was kind of —

WILLY. I was wondering if he'd remember you. (*To* HAPPY.) Imagine, man doesn't see him for ten, twelve years and gives him that kind of a welcome!

HAPPY. Damn right!

BIFF (*trying to return to the offensive*). Pop, look —

WILLY. You know why he remembered you, don't you? Because you impressed him in those days.

BIFF. Let's talk quietly and get this down to the facts, huh?

WILLY (*as though* BIFF *had been interrupting*). Well, what happened? It's great news, Biff. Did he take you into his office or'd you talk in the waiting-room?

BIFF. Well, he came in, see, and —

WILLY (*with a big smile*). What'd he say? Betcha he threw his arm around you.

BIFF. Well, he kinda —

WILLY. He's a fine man. (*To* HAPPY.) Very hard man to see, y'know.

HAPPY (*agreeing*). Oh, I know.

WILLY (*to* BIFF). Is that where you had the drinks?

BIFF. Yeah, he gave me a couple of — no, no!

HAPPY (*cutting in*). He told him my Florida idea.

WILLY. Don't interrupt. (*To* BIFF.) How'd he react to the Florida idea?

BIFF. Dad, will you give me a minute to explain?

WILLY. I've been waiting for you to explain since I sat down here! What happened? He took you into his office and what?

BIFF. Well — I talked. And — and he listened, see.

WILLY. Famous for the way he listens, y'know. What was his answer?

BIFF. His answer was — (*He breaks off, suddenly angry.*) Dad, you're not letting me tell you what I want to tell you!

WILLY (*accusing, angered*). You didn't see him, did you?

BIFF. I did see him!

WILLY. What'd you insult him or something? You insulted him, didn't you?

BIFF. Listen, will you let me out of it, will you just let me out of it!

HAPPY. What the hell!

WILLY. Tell me what happened!

BIFF (*to* HAPPY). I can't talk to him!

A single trumpet note jars the ear. The light of green leaves stains the house, which holds the air of night and a dream. YOUNG BERNARD *enters and knocks on the door of the house.*

YOUNG BERNARD (*frantically*). Mrs. Loman, Mrs. Loman!

HAPPY. Tell him what happened!

BIFF (*to* HAPPY). Shut up and leave me alone!

WILLY. No, no! You had to go and flunk math!

BIFF. What math? What're you talking about?

YOUNG BERNARD. Mrs. Loman, Mrs. Loman!

LINDA *appears in the house, as of old.*

WILLY (*wildly*). Math, math, math!

BIFF. Take it easy, Pop!

YOUNG BERNARD. Mrs. Loman!

WILLY (*furiously*). If you hadn't flunked you'd've been set by now!

BIFF. Now, look, I'm gonna tell you what happened, and you're going to listen to me.

YOUNG BERNARD. Mrs. Loman!

BIFF. I waited six hours —

HAPPY. What the hell are you saying?

BIFF. I kept sending in my name but he wouldn't see me. So finally he ... (*He continues unheard as light fades low on the restaurant.*)

YOUNG BERNARD. Biff flunked math!

LINDA. No!

YOUNG BERNARD. Birnbaum flunked him. They won't graduate him!

LINDA. But they have to. He's gotta go to the university. Where is he? Biff! Biff!

YOUNG BERNARD. No, he left. He went to Grand Central.

LINDA. Grand — You mean he went to Boston!

YOUNG BERNARD. Is Uncle Willy in Boston?

LINDA. Oh, maybe Willy can talk to the teacher. Oh, the poor, poor boy!

Light on house area snaps out.

BIFF (*at the table, now audible, holding up a gold fountain pen*). . . . so I'm washed up with Oliver, you understand? Are you listening to me?

WILLY (*at a loss*). Yeah, sure. If you hadn't flunked —

BIFF. Flunked what? What're you talking about?

WILLY. Don't blame everything on me! I didn't flunk math — you did! What pen?

HAPPY. That was awful dumb, Biff, a pen like that is worth —

WILLY (*seeing the pen for the first time*). You took Oliver's pen?

BIFF (*weakening*). Dad, I just explained it to you.

WILLY. You stole Bill Oliver's fountain pen!

BIFF. I didn't exactly steal it! That's just what I've been explaining to you!

HAPPY. He had it in his hand and just then Oliver walked in, so he got nervous and stuck it in his pocket!

WILLY. My God, Biff!

BIFF. I never intended to do it, Dad!

OPERATOR'S VOICE. Standish Arms, good evening!

WILLY (*shouting*). I'm not in my room!

BIFF (*frightened*). Dad, what's the matter? (*He and* HAPPY *stand up*.)

OPERATOR. Ringing Mr. Loman for you!

WILLY. I'm not there, stop it!

BIFF (*horrified, gets down on one knee before* WILLY). Dad, I'll make good, I'll make good. (WILLY *tries to get to his feet.* BIFF *holds him down.*) Sit down now.

WILLY. No, you're no good, you're no good for anything.

BIFF. I am, Dad, I'll find something else, you understand? Now don't worry about anything. (*He holds up* WILLY's *face.*) Talk to me, Dad.

OPERATOR. Mr. Loman does not answer. Shall I page him?

WILLY (*attempting to stand, as though to rush and silence the* OPERATOR). No, no, no!

HAPPY. He'll strike something, Pop.

WILLY. No, no . . .

BIFF (*desperately, standing over* WILLY). Pop, listen! Listen to me! I'm telling you something good. Oliver talked to his partner about the Florida idea. You listening? He — he talked to his partner, and he came to me . . . I'm going to be all right, you hear? Dad, listen to me, he said it was just a question of the amount!

WILLY. Then you . . . got it?

HAPPY. He's gonna be terrific, Pop!

WILLY (*trying to stand*). Then you got it, haven't you? You got it! You got it!

BIFF (*agonized, holds* WILLY *down*). No, no. Look, Pop. I'm supposed to have lunch with them tomorrow. I'm just telling you this so you'll know that I can still make an impression, Pop. And I'll make good somewhere, but I can't go tomorrow, see?

WILLY. Why not? You simply —

BIFF. But the pen, Pop!

WILLY. You give it to him and tell him it was an oversight!

HAPPY. Sure, have lunch tomorrow!
BIFF. I can't say that —
WILLY. You were doing a crossword puzzle and accidentally used his pen!
BIFF. Listen, kid, I took those balls years ago, now I walk in with his fountain pen? That clinches it, don't you see? I can't face him like that! I'll try elsewhere.
PAGE'S VOICE. Paging Mr. Loman!
WILLY. Don't you want to be anything?
BIFF. Pop, how can I go back?
WILLY. You don't want to be anything, is that what's behind it?
BIFF (*now angry at* WILLY *for not crediting his sympathy*). Don't take it that way! You think it was easy walking into that office after what I'd done to him? A team of horses couldn't have dragged me back to Bill Oliver!
WILLY. Then why'd you go?
BIFF. Why did I go? Why did I go! Look at you! Look at what's become of you!

Off left, the WOMAN *laughs.*

WILLY. Biff, you're going to that lunch tomorrow, or —
BIFF. I can't go. I've got no appointment!
HAPPY. Biff, for . . . !
WILLY. Are you spiting me?
BIFF. Don't take it that way! Goddammit!
WILLY (*strikes Biff and falters away from the table*). You rotten little louse! Are you spiting me?
THE WOMAN. Someone's at the door, Willy!
BIFF. I'm no good, can't you see what I am?
HAPPY (*separating them*). Hey, you're in a restaurant! Now cut it out, both of you! (*The girls enter.*) Hello, girls, sit down.

The WOMAN *laughs, off left.*

MISS FORSYTHE. I guess we might as well. This is Letta.
THE WOMAN. Willy, are you going to wake up?
BIFF (*ignoring* WILLY). How're ya, miss, sit down. What do you drink?
MISS FORSYTHE. Letta might not be able to stay long.
LETTA. I gotta get up very early tomorrow. I got jury duty. I'm so excited! Were you fellows ever on a jury?
BIFF. No, but I been in front of them! (*The girls laugh.*) This is my father.
LETTA. Isn't he cute? Sit down with us, Pop.
HAPPY. Sit him down, Biff!
BIFF (*going to him*). Come on, slugger, drink us under the table. To hell with it! Come on, sit down, pal.

On BIFF'S *last insistence,* WILLY *is about to sit.*

THE WOMAN (*now urgently*). Willy, are you going to answer the door!

The WOMAN'S *call pulls* WILLY *back. He starts right, befuddled.*

BIFF. Hey, where are you going?

WILLY. Open the door.
BIFF. The door?
WILLY. The washroom . . . the door . . . where's the door?
BIFF (*leading* WILLY *to the left*). Just go straight down.
   WILLY *moves left.*
THE WOMAN. Willy, Willy, are you going to get up, get up, get up, get up?
   WILLY *exits left.*
LETTA. I think it's sweet you bring your daddy along.
MISS FORSYTHE. Oh, he isn't really your father!
BIFF (*at left, turning to her resentfully*). Miss Forsythe, you've just seen a prince walk by. A fine, troubled prince. A hard-working, unappreciated prince. A pal, you understand? A good companion. Always for his boys.
LETTA. That's so sweet.
HAPPY. Well, girls, what's the program? We're wasting time. Come on, Biff. Gather round. Where would you like to go?
BIFF. Why don't you do something for him?
HAPPY. Me!
BIFF. Don't you give a damn for him, Hap?
HAPPY. What're you talking about? I'm the one who —
BIFF. I sense it, you don't give a good goddam about him. (*He takes the rolled-up hose from his pocket and puts it on the table in front of* HAPPY.) Look what I found in the cellar, for Christ's sake. How can you bear to let it go on?
HAPPY. Me? Who goes away? Who runs off and —
BIFF. Yeah, but he doesn't mean anything to you. You could help him — I can't! Don't you understand what I'm talking about? He's going to kill himself, don't you know that?
HAPPY. Don't I know it! Me!
BIFF. Hap, help him! Jesus . . . help him . . . Help me, help me, I can't bear to look at his face! (*Ready to weep, he hurries out, up right.*)
HAPPY (*starting after him*). Where are you going?
MISS FORSYTHE. What's he so mad about?
HAPPY. Come on, girls, we'll catch up with him.
MISS FORSYTHE (*as* HAPPY *pushes her out*). Say, I don't like that temper of his!
HAPPY. He's just a little overstrung, he'll be all right!
WILLY (*off left, as the* WOMAN *laughs*). Don't answer! Don't answer!
LETTA. Don't you want to tell your father —
HAPPY. No, that's not my father. He's just a guy. Come on, we'll catch Biff, and, honey, we're going to paint this town! Stanley, where's the check! Hey, Stanley!
   They exit. STANLEY *looks toward left.*
STANLEY (*calling to* HAPPY *indignantly*). Mr. Loman! Mr. Loman!
   STANLEY *picks up a chair and follows them off. Knocking is heard off left. The* WOMAN *enters, laughing.* WILLY *follows her. She is in a black*

slip; he is buttoning his shirt. Raw, sensuous music accompanies their speech.

WILLY. Will you stop laughing? Will you stop?

THE WOMAN. Aren't you going to answer the door? He'll wake the whole hotel.

WILLY. I'm not expecting anybody.

THE WOMAN. Whyn't you have another drink, honey, and stop being so damn self-centered?

WILLY. I'm so lonely.

THE WOMAN. You know you ruined me, Willy? From now on, whenever you come to the office, I'll see that you go right through to the buyers. No waiting at my desk any more, Willy. You ruined me.

WILLY. That's nice of you to say that.

THE WOMAN. Gee, you are self-centered! Why so sad? You are the saddest, self-centeredest soul I ever did see-saw. (*She laughs. He kisses her.*) Come on inside, drummer boy. It's silly to be dressing in the middle of the night. (*As knocking is heard.*) Aren't you going to answer the door?

WILLY. They're knocking on the wrong door.

THE WOMAN. But I felt the knocking. And he heard us talking in here. Maybe the hotel's on fire!

WILLY (*his terror rising*). It's a mistake.

THE WOMAN. Then tell him to go away!

WILLY. There's nobody there.

THE WOMAN. It's getting on my nerves, Willy. There's somebody standing out there and it's getting on my nerves!

WILLY (*pushing her away from him*). All right, stay in the bathroom here, and don't come out. I think there's a law in Massachusetts about it, so don't come out. It may be that new room clerk. He looked very mean. So don't come out. It's a mistake, there's no fire.

The knocking is heard again. He takes a few steps away from her, and she vanishes into the wing. The light follows him, and now he is facing YOUNG BIFF, *who carries a suitcase.* BIFF *steps toward him. The music is gone.*

BIFF. Why didn't you answer?

WILLY. Biff! What are you doing in Boston?

BIFF. Why didn't you answer? I've been knocking for five minutes, I called you on the phone—

WILLY. I just heard you. I was in the bathroom and had the door shut. Did anything happen home?

BIFF. Dad—I let you down.

WILLY. What do you mean?

BIFF. Dad...

WILLY. Biffo, what's this about? (*Putting his arm around* BIFF.) Come on, let's go downstairs and get you a malted.

BIFF. Dad, I flunked math.

WILLY. Not for the term?

BIFF. The term. I haven't got enough credits to graduate.

WILLY. You mean to say Bernard wouldn't give you the answers?

BIFF. He did, he tried, but I only got a sixty-one.

WILLY. And they wouldn't give you four points?

BIFF. Birnbaum refused absolutely. I begged him, Pop, but he won't give me those points. You gotta talk to him before they close the school. Because if he saw the kind of man you are, and you just talked to him in your way, I'm sure he'd come through for me. The class came right before practice, see, and I didn't go enough. Would you talk to him? He'd like you, Pop. You know the way you could talk.

WILLY. You're on. We'll drive right back.

BIFF. Oh, Dad, good work! I'm sure he'll change it for you!

WILLY. Go downstairs and tell the clerk I'm checkin' out. Go right down.

BIFF. Yes, sir! See, the reason he hates me, Pop — one day he was late for class so I got up at the blackboard and imitated him. I crossed my eyes and talked with a lithp.

WILLY (*laughing*). You did? The kids like it?

BIFF. They nearly died laughing!

WILLY. Yeah? What'd you do?

BIFF. The thquare root of thixty twee is . . . (WILLY *bursts out laughing;* BIFF *joins him.*) And in the middle of it he walked in!

WILLY *laughs and the* WOMAN *joins in offstage.*

WILLY (*without hesitation*). Hurry downstairs and —

BIFF. Somebody in there?

WILLY. No, that was next door.

The WOMAN *laughs offstage.*

BIFF. Somebody got in your bathroom!

WILLY. No, it's the next room, there's a party —

THE WOMAN (*enters, laughing. She lisps this*). Can I come in? There's something in the bathtub, Willy, and it's moving!

WILLY *looks at* BIFF, *who is staring open-mouthed and horrified at the* WOMAN.

WILLY. Ah — you better go back to your room. They must be finished painting by now. They're painting her room so I let her take a shower here. Go back, go back . . . *He pushes her.*

THE WOMAN (*resisting*). But I've got to get dressed, Willy, I can't —

WILLY. Get out of here! Go back, go back . . . (*Suddenly striving for the ordinary.*) This is Miss Francis, Biff, she's a buyer. They're painting her room. Go back, Miss Francis, go back . . .

THE WOMAN. But my clothes, I can't go out naked in the hall!

WILLY (*pushing her offstage*). Get outa here! Go back, go back!

BIFF *slowly sits down on his suitcase as the argument continues offstage.*

THE WOMAN. Where's my stockings? You promised me stockings, Willy!

WILLY. I have no stockings here!

THE WOMAN. You had two boxes of size nine sheers for me, and I want them!

WILLY. Here, for God's sake, will you get outa here!

THE WOMAN (*enters holding a box of stockings*). I just hope there's nobody in the hall. That's all I hope. (*To* BIFF.) Are you football or baseball?

BIFF. Football.

THE WOMAN (*angry, humiliated*). That's me too. G'night. (*She snatches her clothes from* WILLY, *and walks out.*)

WILLY (*after a pause*). Well, better get going. I want to get to the school first thing in the morning. Get my suits out of the closet. I'll get my valise. (BIFF *doesn't move.*) What's the matter? (BIFF *remains motionless, tears falling.*) She's a buyer. Buys for J. H. Simmons. She lives down the hall — they're painting. You don't imagine — (*He breaks off. After a pause.*) Now listen, pal, she's just a buyer. She sees merchandise in her room and they have to keep it looking just so . . . (*Pause. Assuming command.*) All right, get my suits. (BIFF *doesn't move.*) Now stop crying and do as I say. I gave you an order. Biff, I gave you an order! Is that what you do when I give you an order? How dare you cry! (*Putting his arm around* BIFF.) Now look, Biff, when you grow up you'll understand about these things. You mustn't — you mustn't overemphasize a thing like this. I'll see Birnbaum first thing in the morning.

BIFF. Never mind.

WILLY. (*getting down beside* BIFF). Never mind! He's going to give you those points. I'll see to it.

BIFF. He wouldn't listen to you.

WILLY. He certainly will listen to me. You need those points for the U. of Virginia.

BIFF. I'm not going there.

WILLY. Heh? If I can't get him to change that mark you'll make it up in summer school. You've got all summer to —

BIFF (*his weeping breaking from him*). Dad . . .

WILLY (*infected by it*). Oh, my boy . . .

BIFF. Dad . . .

WILLY. She's nothing to me, Biff. I was lonely, I was terribly lonely.

BIFF. You — you gave her Mama's stockings! (*His tears break through and he rises to go.*)

WILLY (*grabbing for* BIFF). I gave you an order!

BIFF. Don't touch me, you — liar!

WILLY. Apologize for that!

BIFF. You fake! You phony little fake! You fake! (*Overcome, he turns quickly and weeping fully goes out with his suitcase.* WILLY *is left on the floor on his knees.*)

WILLY. I gave you an order! Biff, come back here or I'll beat you! Come back here! I'll whip you!

Death of a Salesman

STANLEY *comes quickly in from the right and stands in front of* WILLY.

WILLY (*shouts at* STANLEY). I gave you an order . . .

STANLEY. Hey, let's pick it up, pick it up, Mr. Loman. (*He helps* WILLY *to his feet.*) Your boys left with the chippies. They said they'll see you home.

A second waiter watches some distance away.

WILLY. But we were supposed to have dinner together.

Music is heard, WILLY'S *theme.*

STANLEY. Can you make it?

WILLY. I'll — sure, I can make it. (*Suddenly concerned about his clothes.*) Do I — I look all right?

STANLEY. Sure, you look all right. (*He flecks a speck off* WILLY'S *lapel.*)

WILLY. Here — here's a dollar.

STANLEY. Oh, your son paid me. It's all right.

WILLY (*putting it in* STANLEY'S *hand*). No, take it. You're a good boy.

STANLEY. Oh, no, you don't have to . . .

WILLY. Here — here's some more, I don't need it any more. (*After a slight pause.*) Tell me — is there a seed store in the neighborhood?

STANLEY. Seeds? You mean like to plant?

As WILLY *turns,* STANLEY *slips the money back into his jacket pocket.*

WILLY. Yes. Carrots, peas . . .

STANLEY. Well, there's hardware stores on Sixth Avenue, but it may be too late now.

WILLY (*anxiously*). Oh, I'd better hurry. I've got to get some seeds. (*He starts off to the right.*) I've got to get some seeds, right away. Nothing's planted. I don't have a thing in the ground.

WILLY *hurries out as the light goes down.* STANLEY *moves over to the right after him, watches him off. The other waiter has been staring at* WILLY.

STANLEY (*to the waiter*): Well, whatta you looking at?

The waiter picks up the chairs and moves off right. STANLEY *takes the table and follows him. The light fades on this area. There is a long pause, the sound of the flute coming over. The light gradually rises on the kitchen, which is empty.* HAPPY *appears at the door of the house, followed by* BIFF. HAPPY *is carrying a large bunch of long-stemmed roses. He enters the kitchen, looks around for* LINDA. *Not seeing her, he turns to* BIFF, *who is just outside the house door, and makes a gesture with his hands, indicating "Not here, I guess." He looks into the living-room and freezes. Inside,* LINDA, *unseen, is seated,* WILLY'S *coat on her lap. She rises ominously and quietly and moves toward* HAPPY, *who backs up into the kitchen, afraid.*

HAPPY. Hey, what're you doing up? (LINDA *says nothing but moves toward him implacably.*) Where's Pop? (*He keeps backing to the right, and now* LINDA *is in full view in the doorway to the living-room.* Is he sleeping?

LINDA. Where were you?

HAPPY (*trying to laugh it off*). We met two girls, Mom, very fine types. Here, we brought you some flowers. (*Offering them to her.*) Put them in your room, Ma.

    She knocks them to the floor at BIFF's *feet. He has now come inside and closed the door behind him. She stares at* BIFF, *silent.*

HAPPY. Now what'd you do that for? Mom, I want you to have some flowers —

LINDA (*cutting* HAPPY *off, violently to* BIFF). Don't you care whether he lives or dies?

HAPPY (*going to the stairs*). Come upstairs, Biff.

BIFF (*with a flare of disgust, to* HAPPY). Go away from me! (*To* LINDA.) What do you mean, lives or dies? Nobody's dying around here, pal.

LINDA. Get out of my sight! Get out of here!

BIFF. I wanna see the boss.

LINDA. You're not going near him!

BIFF. Where is he? (*He moves into the living-room and* LINDA *follows.*)

LINDA (*shouting after* BIFF). You invite him for dinner. He looks forward to it all day — (BIFF *appears in his parents' bedroom, looks around, and exits*) — and then you desert him there. There's no stranger you'd do that to!

HAPPY. Why? He had a swell time with us. Listen, when I — (LINDA *comes back into the kitchen*) — desert him I hope I don't outlive the day!

LINDA. Get out of here!

HAPPY. Now look, Mom . . .

LINDA. Did you have to go to women tonight? You and your lousy rotten whores!

    BIFF *re-enters the kitchen.*

HAPPY. Mom, all we did was follow Biff around trying to cheer him up! (*To* BIFF.) Boy, what a night you gave me!

LINDA. Get out of here, both of you, and don't come back! I don't want you tormenting him any more. Go on now, get your things together! (*To* BIFF.) You can sleep in his apartment. (*She starts to pick up the flowers and stops herself.*) Pick up this stuff, I'm not your maid any more. Pick it up, you bum, you!

    HAPPY *turns his back to her in refusal.* BIFF *slowly moves over and gets down on his knees, picking up the flowers.*

LINDA. You're a pair of animals! Not one, not another living soul would have had the cruelty to walk out on that man in a restaurant!

BIFF (*not looking at her*). Is that what he said?

LINDA. He didn't have to say anything. He was so humiliated he nearly limped when he came in.

HAPPY. But, Mom, he had a great time with us —

BIFF (*cutting him off violently*). Shut up!

    Without another word, HAPPY *goes upstairs.*

LINDA. You! You didn't even go in to see if he was all right!

BIFF (*still on the floor in front of* LINDA, *the flowers in his hand; with self-*

Death of a Salesman

loathing). No. Didn't. Didn't do a damned thing. How do you like that, heh? Left him babbling in a toilet.

LINDA. You louse. You . . .

BIFF. Now you hit it on the nose! (*He gets up, throws the flowers in the wastebasket.*) The scum of the earth, and you're looking at him!

LINDA. Get out of here!

BIFF. I gotta talk to the boss, Mom. Where is he?

LINDA. You're not going near him. Get out of this house!

BIFF (*with absolute assurance, determination*). No. We're gonna have an abrupt conversation, him and me.

LINDA. You're not talking to him!

> Hammering is heard from outside the house, off right. BIFF *turns toward the noise.*

LINDA (*suddenly pleading*). Will you please leave him alone?

BIFF. What's he doing out there?

LINDA. He planting the garden!

BIFF (*quietly*). Now? Oh, my God!

> BIFF *moves outside,* LINDA *following. The light dies down on them and comes up on the center of the apron as* WILLY *walks into it. He is carrying a flashlight, a hoe, and a handful of seed packets. He raps the hoe sharply to fix it firmly, and then moves to the left, measuring off the distance with his foot. He holds the flashlight to look at the seed packets, reading off the instructions. He is in the blue of night.*

WILLY. Carrots . . . quarter-inch apart. Rows . . . one-foot rows. (*He measures it off.*) One foot. (*He puts down a package and measures off.*) Beets. (*He puts down another package and measures again.*) Lettuce. (*He reads the package, puts it down.*) One foot — (*He breaks off as* BEN *appears at the right and moves slowly down to him.*) What a proposition, ts, ts. Terrific, terrific. 'Cause she's suffered, Ben, the woman has suffered. You understand me? A man can't go out the way he came in, Ben, a man has got to add up to something. You can't, you can't — (BEN *moves toward him as though to interrupt.*) You gotta consider, now. Don't answer so quick. Remember, it's a guaranteed twenty-thousand-dollar proposition. Now look, Ben, I want you to go through the ins and outs of this thing with me. I've got nobody to talk to, Ben, and the woman has suffered, you hear me?

BEN (*standing still, considering*). What's the proposition?

WILLY. It's twenty thousand dollars on the barrelhead. Guaranteed, gilt-edged, you understand?

BEN. You don't want to make a fool of yourself. They might not honor the policy.

WILLY. How can they dare refuse? Didn't I work like a coolie to meet every premium on the nose? And now they don't pay off? Impossible!

BEN. It's called a cowardly thing, William.

WILLY. Why? Does it take more guts to stand here the rest of my life ringing up a zero?

BEN (*yielding*). That's a point, William. (*He moves, thinking, turns.*) And twenty thousand — that *is* something one can feel with the hand, it is there.

WILLY (*now assured, with rising power*). Oh, Ben, that's the whole beauty of it! I see it like a diamond, shining in the dark, hard and rough, that I can pick up and touch in my hand. Not like — like an appointment! This would not be another damned-fool appointment, Ben, and it changes all the aspects. Because he thinks I'm nothing, see, and so he spites me. But the funeral — (*Straightening up.*) Ben, that funeral will be massive! They'll come from Maine, Massachusetts, Vermont, New Hampshire! All the old-timers with the strange license plates — that boy will be thunder-struck, Ben, because he never realized — I am known! Rhode Island, New York, New Jersey — I am known, Ben, and he'll see it with his eyes once and for all. He'll see what I am, Ben! He's in for a shock, that boy!

BEN (*coming down to the edge of the garden*). He'll call you a coward.

WILLY (*suddenly fearful*). No, that would be terrible.

BEN. Yes. And a damned fool.

WILLY. No, no, he mustn't, I won't have that! (*He is broken and desperate.*)

BEN. He'll hate you, William.

The gay music of the BOYS *is heard.*

WILLY. Oh, Ben, how do we get back to all the great times? Used to be so full of light, and comradeship, the sleigh-riding in winter, and the ruddiness on his cheeks. And always some kind of good news coming up, always something nice coming up ahead. And never even let me carry the valises in the house, and simonizing, simonizing that little red car! Why, why can't I give him something and not have him hate me?

BEN. Let me think about it. (*He glances at his watch.*) I still have a little time. Remarkable proposition, but you've got to be sure you're not making a fool of yourself.

BEN *drifts off upstage and goes out of sight.* BIFF *comes down from the left.*

WILLY (*suddenly conscious of* BIFF, *turns and looks up at him, then begins picking up the packages of seeds in confusion*). Where the hell is that seed? (*Indignantly.*) You can't see nothing out here! They boxed in the whole goddam neighborhood!

BIFF. There are people all around here. Don't you realize that?

WILLY. I'm busy. Don't bother me.

BIFF (*taking the hoe from* WILLY). I'm saying good-by to you, Pop. (WILLY *looks at him, silent, unable to move.*) I'm not coming back any more.

WILLY. You're not going to see Oliver tomorrow?

BIFF. I've got no appointment, Dad.

WILLY. He put his arm around you, and you've got no appointment?

BIFF. Pop, get this now, will you? Everytime I've left it's been a fight that sent me out of here. Today I realized something about myself and I tried to explain it to you and I — I think I'm just not smart enough to make any sense out of it for you. To hell with whose fault it is or anything like that. (*He takes* WILLY'S *arm.*) Let's just wrap it up, heh? Come on in, we'll tell Mom. (*He gently tries to pull* WILLY *to left.*)

WILLY (*frozen, immobile, with guilt in his voice*). No, I don't want to see her.

BIFF. Come on! (*He pulls again, and* WILLY *tries to pull away.*)

WILLY (*highly nervous*). No, no, I don't want to see her.

BIFF (*tries to look into* WILLY'S *face, as if to find the answer there*). Why don't you want to see her?

WILLY (*more harshly now*). Don't bother me, will you?

BIFF. What do you mean, you don't want to see her? You don't want them calling you yellow, do you? This isn't your fault; it's me, I'm a bum. Now come inside! (WILLY *strains to get away.*) Did you hear what I said to you?

> WILLY *pulls away and quickly goes by himself into the house.* BIFF *follows.*

LINDA (*to* WILLY). Did you plant, dear?

BIFF (*at the door, to* LINDA). All right, we had it out. I'm going and I'm not writing any more.

LINDA (*going to* WILLY *in the kitchen*). I think that's the best way, dear. 'Cause there's no use drawing it out, you'll just never get along.

WILLY *doesn't respond.*

BIFF. People ask where I am and what I'm doing, you don't know, and you don't care. That way it'll be off your mind and you can start brightening up again. All right? That clears it, doesn't it? (WILLY *is silent, and* BIFF *goes to him.*) You gonna wish me luck, scout? (*He extends his hand.*) What do you say?

LINDA. Shake his hand, Willy.

WILLY (*turning to her, seething with hurt*). There's no necessity to mention the pen at all, y'know.

BIFF (*gently*). I've got no appointment, Dad.

WILLY (*erupting fiercely*). He put his arm around . . . ?

BIFF. Dad, you're never going to see what I am, so what's the use of arguing? If I strike oil I'll send you a check. Meantime forget I'm alive.

WILLY (*to* LINDA). Spite, see?

BIFF. Shake hands, Dad.

WILLY. Not my hand.

BIFF. I was hoping not to go this way.

WILLY. Well, this is the way you're going. Good-by.

> BIFF *looks at him a moment, then turns sharply and goes to the stairs.*

WILLY (*stops him with*). May you rot in hell if you leave this house!

BIFF (*turning*). Exactly what is it that you want from me?

WILLY. I want you to know, on the train, in the mountains, in the valleys, wherever you go, that you cut down your life for spite!

BIFF. No, no.

WILLY. Spite, spite, is the word of your undoing! And when you're down and out, remember what did it. When you're rotting somewhere beside the railroad tracks, remember, and don't you dare blame it on me!

BIFF. I'm not blaming it on you!

WILLY. I don't take the rap for this, you hear?

HAPPY *comes down the stairs and stands on the bottom step, watching.*

BIFF. That's just what I'm telling you!

WILLY (*sinking into a chair at the table, with full accusation*). You're trying to put a knife in me — don't think I don't know what you're doing!

BIFF. All right, phony! Then let's lay it on the line. (*He whips the rubber tube out of his pocket and puts it on the table.*)

HAPPY. You crazy —

LINDA. Biff! (*She moves to grab the hose, but* BIFF *holds it down with his hand.*)

BIFF. Leave it there! Don't move it!

WILLY (*not looking at it*). What is that?

BIFF. You know goddam well what that is.

WILLY (*caged, wanting to escape*). I never saw that.

BIFF. You saw it. The mice didn't bring it into the cellar What is this supposed to do, make a hero out of you? This supposed to make me sorry for you?

WILLY. Never heard of it.

BIFF. There'll be no pity for you, you hear it? No pity!

WILLY (*to* LINDA). You hear the spite!

BIFF. No, you're going to hear the truth — what you are and what I am!

LINDA. Stop it!

WILLY. Spite!

HAPPY (*coming down toward* BIFF). You cut it now!

BIFF (*to* HAPPY). The man don't know who we are! The man is gonna know! (*To* WILLY.) We never told the truth for ten minutes in this house!

HAPPY. We always told the truth!

BIFF (*turning on him*). You big blow, are you the assistant buyer? You're one of the two assistants to the assistant, aren't you?

HAPPY. Well, I'm practically —

BIFF. You're practically full of it! We all are! And I'm through with it. (*To* WILLY.) Now hear this, Willy, this is me.

WILLY. I know you!

BIFF. You know why I had no address for three months? I stole a suit in Kansas City and I was in jail. (*To* LINDA, *who is sobbing.*) Stop crying. I'm through with it.

LINDA *turns away from them, her hands covering her face.*

WILLY. I suppose that's my fault!
BIFF. I stole myself out of every good job since high school!
WILLY. And whose fault is that?
BIFF. And I never got anywhere because you blew me so full of hot air I could never stand taking orders from anybody! That's whose fault it is!
WILLY. I hear that!
LINDA. Don't, Biff!
BIFF. It's goddam time you heard that! I had to be boss big shot in two weeks, and I'm through with it!
WILLY. Then hang yourself! For spite, hang yourself!
BIFF. No! Nobody's hanging himself, Willy! I ran down eleven flights with a pen in my hand today. And suddenly I stopped, you hear me? And in the middle of that office building, do you hear this? I stopped in the middle of that building and I saw — the sky. I saw the things that I love in this world. The work and the food and time to sit and smoke. And I looked at the pen and said to myself, what the hell am I grabbing this for? Why am I trying to become what I don't want to be? What am I doing in an office, making a contemptuous, begging fool of myself, when all I want is out there, waiting for me the minute I say I know who I am! Why can't I say that, Willy? (*He tries to make* WILLY *face him, but* WILLY *pulls away and moves to the left.*)
WILLY (*with hatred, threateningly*). The door of your life is wide open!
BIFF. Pop! I'm a dime a dozen, and so are you!
WILLY (*turning on him now in an uncontrolled outburst*). I am not a dime a dozen! I am Willy Loman, and you are Biff Loman!

BIFF *starts for* WILLY, *but is blocked by* HAPPY. *In his fury,* BIFF *seems on the verge of attacking his father.*

BIFF. I am not a leader of men, Willy, and neither are you. You were never anything but a hard-working drummer who landed in the ash can like all the rest of them! I'm one dollar an hour, Willy! I tried seven states and couldn't raise it. A buck an hour! Do you gather my meaning? I'm not bringing home any prizes any more, and you're going to stop waiting for me to bring them home!
WILLY (*directly to* BIFF). You vengeful, spiteful mut!

BIFF *breaks from* HAPPY. WILLY, *in fright, starts up the stairs.* BIFF *grabs him.*

BIFF (*at the peak of his fury*). Pop, I'm nothing! I'm nothing, Pop. Can't you understand that? There's no spite in it any more. I'm just what I am, that's all.

BIFF'*s fury has spent itself, and he breaks down, sobbing, holding on to* WILLY, *who dumbly fumbles for* BIFF'*s face.*

WILLY (*astonished*). What're you doing? What're you doing? (*To* LINDA.) Why is he crying?
BIFF (*crying, broken*). Will you let me go, for Christ's sake? Will you

take that phony dream and burn it before something happens? (*Struggling to contain himself, he pulls away and moves to the stairs.*) I'll go in the morning. Put him — put him to bed. (*Exhausted,* BIFF *moves up the stairs to his room.*)

WILLY (*after a long pause, astonished, elevated*). Isn't that — isn't that remarkable? Biff — he likes me!

LINDA. He loves you, Willy!

HAPPY (*deeply moved*). Always did, Pop.

WILLY. Oh, Biff! (*Staring wildly.*) He cried! Cried to me. (*He is choking with his love, and now cries out his promise.*) That boy — that boy is going to be magnificent!

BEN *appears in the light just outside the kitchen.*

BEN. Yes, outstanding, with twenty thousand behind him.

LINDA (*sensing the racing of his mind, fearfully, carefully*). Now come to bed, Willy. It's all settled now.

WILLY (*finding it difficult not to rush out of the house*). Yes, we'll sleep. Come on. Go to sleep, Hap.

BEN. And it does take a great kind of a man to crack the jungle.

In accents of dread, BEN's *idyllic music starts up.*

HAPPY (*his arm around* LINDA). I'm getting married, Pop, don't forget it. I'm changing everything. I'm gonna run that department before the year is up. You'll see, Mom. (*He kisses her.*)

BEN. The jungle is dark but full of diamonds, Willy.

WILLY *turns, moves, listening to* BEN.

LINDA. Be good. You're both good boys, just act that way, that's all.

HAPPY. 'Night, Pop. *He goes upstairs.*

LINDA (*to* WILLY). Come, dear.

BEN (*with greater force*). One must go in to fetch a diamond out.

WILLY (*to* LINDA, *as he moves slowly along the edge of the kitchen, toward the door*). I just want to get settled down, Linda. Let me sit alone for a little.

LINDA (*almost uttering her fear*). I want you upstairs.

WILLY (*taking her in his arms*). In a few minutes, Linda. I couldn't sleep right now. Go on, you look awful tired. (*He kisses her.*)

BEN. Not like an appointment at all. A diamond is rough and hard to the touch.

WILLY. Go on now. I'll be right up.

LINDA. I think this is the only way, Willy.

WILLY. Sure, it's the best thing.

BEN. Best thing!

WILLY. The only way. Everything is gonna be — go on, kid, get to bed. You look so tired.

LINDA. Come right up.

WILLY. Two minutes.

Death of a Salesman

LINDA *goes into the living-room, then reappears in her bedroom.* WILLY *moves just outside the kitchen door.*

WILLY. Loves me. (*Wonderingly.*) Always loved me. Isn't that a remarkable thing? Ben, he'll worship me for it!

BEN (*with promise*). It's dark there, but full of diamonds.

WILLY. Can you imagine that magnificence with twenty thousand dollars in his pocket?

LINDA (*calling from her room*). Willy! Come up!

WILLY (*calling into the kitchen*). Yes! Yes. Coming! It's very smart, you realize that, don't you, sweetheart? Even Ben sees it. I gotta go, baby. 'By! 'By! (*Going over to* BEN, *almost dancing.*) Imagine? When the mail comes he'll be ahead of Bernard again!

BEN. A perfect proposition all around.

WILLY. Did you see how he cried to me? Oh, if I could kiss him, Ben!

BEN. Time, William, time!

WILLY. Oh, Ben, I always knew one way or another we were gonna make it, Biff and I!

BEN (*looking at his watch*). The boat. We'll be late. (*He moves slowly off into the darkness.*)

WILLY (*elegiacally, turning to the house*). Now when you kick off, boy, I want a seventy-yard boot, and get right down the field under the ball, and when you hit, hit low and hit hard, because it's important, boy. (*He swings around and faces the audience.*) There's all kinds of important people in the stands, and the first thing you know . . . (*Suddenly realizing he is alone.*) Ben! Ben, where do I . . . ? (*He makes a sudden movement of search.*) Ben, how do I . . . ?

LINDA (*calling*). Willy, you coming up?

WILLY (*uttering a gasp of fear, whirling about as if to quiet her*). Sh! (*He turns around as if to find his way; sounds, faces, voices, seem to be swarming in upon him and he flicks at them, crying,*) Sh! Sh! (*Suddenly music, faint and high, stops him. It rises in intensity, almost to an unbearable scream. He goes up and down on his toes, and rushes off around the house.*) Shhh!

LINDA. Willy?

There is no answer. LINDA *waits.* BIFF *gets up off his bed. He is still in his clothes.* HAPPY *sits up.* BIFF *stands listening.*

LINDA (*with real fear*). Willy, answer me! Willy!

There is the sound of a car starting and moving away at full speed.

LINDA. No!

BIFF (*rushing down the stairs*). Pop!

As the car speeds off, the music crashes down in a frenzy of sound, which becomes the soft pulsation of a single cello string. BIFF *slowly returns to his bedroom. He and* HAPPY *gravely don their jackets.* LINDA *slowly walks out of her room. The music has developed into a dead march.*

The leaves of day are appearing over everything. CHARLEY *and* BERNARD, *somberly dressed, appear and knock on the kitchen door.* BIFF *and* HAPPY *slowly descend the stairs to the kitchen as* CHARLEY *and* BERNARD *enter. All stop a moment when* LINDA, *in clothes of mourning, bearing a little bunch of roses, comes through the draped doorway into the kitchen. She goes to* CHARLEY *and takes his arm. Now all move toward the audience, through the wall-line of the kitchen. At the limit of the apron, Linda lays down the flowers, kneels, and sits back on her heels. All stare down at the grave.*

REQUIEM

CHARLEY. It's getting dark, Linda.

LINDA *doesn't react. She stares at the grave.*

BIFF. How about it, Mom? Better get some rest, heh? They'll be closing the gate soon.

LINDA *makes no move. Pause.*

HAPPY (*deeply angered*). He had no right to do that. There was no necessity for it. We would've helped him.

CHARLEY (*grunting*). Hmmm.

BIFF. Come along, Mom.

LINDA. Why didn't anybody come?

CHARLEY. It was a very nice funeral.

LINDA. But where are all the people he knew? Maybe they blame him.

CHARLEY. Naa. It's a rough world, Linda. They wouldn't blame him.

LINDA. I can't understand it. At this time especially. First time in thirty-five years we were just about free and clear. He only needed a little salary. He was even finished with the dentist.

CHARLEY. No man only needs a little salary.

LINDA. I can't understand it.

BIFF. There were a lot of nice days. When he'd come home from a trip; or on Sundays, making the stoop; finishing the cellar; putting on the new porch; when he built the extra bathroom; and put up the garage. You know something, Charley, there's more of him in that front stoop than in all the sales he ever made.

CHARLEY. Yeah. He was a happy man with a batch of cement.

LINDA. He was so wonderful with his hands.

BIFF. He had the wrong dreams. All, all, wrong.

HAPPY (*almost ready to fight* BIFF). Don't say that!

BIFF. He never knew who he was.

CHARLEY (*stopping* HAPPY's *movement and reply. To* BIFF). Nobody dast blame this man. You don't understand: Willy was a salesman. And for a salesman, there is no rock bottom to the life. He don't put a bolt to a nut, he don't tell you the law or give you medicine. He's a man way out there in the blue, riding on a smile and a shoeshine. And when they start not smiling back — that's an earthquake. And then you get yourself a couple of spots on your hat, and you're finished. Nobody dast blame this man. A salesman is got to dream, boy. It comes with the territory.

BIFF. Charley, the man didn't know who he was.

HAPPY (*infuriated*). Don't say that!

BIFF. Why don't you come with me, Happy?

HAPPY. I'm not licked that easily. I'm staying right in this city, and I'm gonna beat this racket! (*He looks at* BIFF, *his chin set.*) The Loman Brothers!

BIFF. I know who I am, kid.

HAPPY. All right, boy. I'm gonna show you and everybody else that Willy Loman did not die in vain. He had a good dream. It's the only dream you can have — to come out number-one man. He fought it out here, and this is where I'm gonna win it for him.

BIFF (*with a hopeless glance at* HAPPY, *bends toward his mother*). Let's go, Mom.

LINDA. I'll be with you in a minute. Go on, Charley. (*He hesitates.*) I want to, just for a minute. I never had a chance to say good-by.

> CHARLEY *moves away, followed by* HAPPY. BIFF *remains a slight distance up and left of* LINDA. *She sits there, summoning herself. The flute begins, not far away, playing behind her speech.*

LINDA. Forgive me, dear. I can't cry. I don't know what it is, but I can't cry. I don't understand it. Why did you ever do that? Help me, Willy, I can't cry. It seems to me that you're just on another trip. I keep expecting you. Willy, dear, I can't cry. Why did you do it? I search and search and I search, and I can't understand it, Willy. I made the last payment on the house today. Today, dear. And there'll be nobody home. (*A sob rises in her throat.*) We're free and clear. (*Sobbing more fully, released.*) We're free. (BIFF *comes slowly toward her.*) We're free . . . We're free . . .

> BIFF *lifts her to her feet and moves out up right with her in his arms.* LINDA *sobs quietly.* BERNARD *and* CHARLEY *come together and follow them, followed by* HAPPY. *Only the music of the flute is left on the darkening stage as over the house the hard towers of the apartment buildings rise into sharp focus, and*

THE CURTAIN FALLS

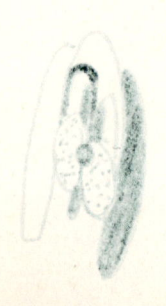

THE THEATER OF
THE ABSURD

Eugene Ionesco

THE BALD SOPRANO

[1950]

Eugene Ionesco [1912-   ]

Since the mid-1950's, Eugene Ionesco has been one of the most frequently produced and discussed playwrights in the world. Though he was born in Rumania, he spent most of his childhood in France, and French is his first language. After graduating from the University of Bucharest, he taught French in a Rumanian *lycée*; in 1938 he returned to France to do research for an advanced degree, and has lived there ever since. His first play, *The Bald Soprano*, was written in 1948 after Ionesco began to study English. When it was produced in 1950, it failed to attract critical notice. In 1951 *The Lesson* failed; and in 1952 *The Chairs* received predominantly unfavorable reviews. However, Ionesco kept on writing, and in 1954 a volume of six of his plays was published by France's leading publisher; by 1956, when *The Chairs* was revived, Ionesco had become a recognized playwright in France. In 1959–1960 *Rhinoceros* established him as a major figure in world drama.

Ionesco's plays have elicited extremes of praise and of condemnation: they are scarcely performances to which one can be indifferent. Simply to list some of the circumstances depicted in them is to indicate the nightmare world, meaningless in its horror and horrible in its meaninglessness, which he creates: a professor murders his fortieth pupil of the day as the climax of the lesson; an aged couple fill the room with invisible guests and then jump to their deaths, leaving a message to humanity to be delivered by an Orator — who turns out to be a deafmute who writes nonsense on a blackboard; a couple live in an apartment with a corpse which continues growing till it crashes through the walls and extends across the stage. This is the world which Eugene Ionesco

Ionesco and the Absurd

depicts in all its reality — but without using the techniques of realism. Although Ionesco shuns didacticism, his plays are urgent invitations to contemplate (among others) questions about the nature of reality, the meaning of existence, the laws of the universe, and the existence of causality.

The theater of the absurd, as it has come to be called, dates from the late 1940's and the early 1950's, and has centered in France. Jean Genet, Ionesco, and Samuel Beckett are the best known of the playwrights whose plays form the canon of the theater of the absurd. This new dramatic movement owes much to symbolism, surrealism, and expressionism, to the grotesque theater, and to post-World War II existentialism (again chiefly in France), to say nothing of much older theatrical traditions. However, through its peculiar composition and use of these earlier traditions and techniques, it has created a new theater.

The term *absurd* has in this context a philosophical meaning. In everyday usage *absurd* may mean *silly* or *ridiculous* in a superficial sense. Ionesco, however, defines the absurd as "that which is devoid of purpose" in any metaphysical sense. The author of the first detailed study of this dramatic movement generalizes thus: "[The] sense of metaphysical anguish at the absurdity of the human condition is, broadly speaking, the theme of the plays of Beckett, Adamov, Ionesco, [and] Genet." It happens that in the dramatization of the absurdities of the human condition, absurdities in the superficial sense occur. And thus we find some critics of this new drama dismissing it as nonsense (which it is in one way) and trivia (which it is not).

This "world of infinite coincidence," this "anti-theater," this

Ionesco and the Absurd

"drama of non-communication," makes special demands upon its audience, which is almost inevitably used to expecting logical sequences of events arranged in some cause-and-effect pattern. However, in the theater of the absurd, perhaps to an incomparable degree, form is identical with function. The notion of the absurdity of experience manifests itself in the *non sequiturs* of the drama. Discursive reasoning disappears, to be replaced by the illogical, the unreasonable, the inexplicable. And just there lies the "meaning" of the drama: in the language of paradox, the meaning is in its absurdity. It is a truism to say that no paraphrase or criticism is an adequate substitute for a work of art itself. Nonetheless, one can quite satisfactorily explain and discuss Ibsen or Shaw, since the intellectual content can, for purposes of analysis, be temporarily isolated from their plays. But with Beckett and Ionesco it is another matter. When Alice asked the Dodo, "What *is* a Caucus-race?" the Dodo replied, "Why, the best way to explain it is to do it." Similarly, the best way to say what Ionesco's plays mean is simply to show them. (If one recalls the meaninglessness of a Caucus-race, the analogy is even more apt.) To an unusual degree *The Bald Soprano* must be seen to be appreciated. It is of the theater.

Like most of Ionesco's other plays, *The Bald Soprano* is irrational — and serious. It is an "anti-play": a play which rejects the basis for all rational and realistic drama — language used as a means for communication. Further, it does not work from some beginning to a conclusion following logically from what has preceded. As Ionesco himself says, "A play is a structure that consists of a series of states of consciousness, or situations, which become intensified, grow more and more dense, then get entangled, either to be disentangled again or to end in unbearable inextricability." What then are we to understand from this circular play in which we find no psychological penetration of character, no character development, no plot in the ordinary sense of that term?

What begins as a cosy evening in the home of the Smiths ends as an orgy of nonsense in which words, ordinarily used to express meaning or feeling, have tyrannized the Smiths and the Martins. In the interim, personality, identity, and time have become meaningless, logic and reason have flown, and words have been used to convey — nothing. It is sheer fun to play with words, garbling meaning, making a plaything of language; in the theater of the absurd, however, this fantastic playfulness brings us up short when we see that it is also a dark and pessimistic inversion of meaning into meaninglessness: the joyous word play of Lewis Carroll goes sour in Ionesco.

Although it is somewhat dangerous to "hunt for meanings" in *The Bald Soprano*, that is precisely the activity toward which the rational, reasoning mind is inclined. However, Ionesco's play (like abstract painting) is not a series of logically related parts, but a composition which does not wish to explain or to be explained. It does not so much "say" something: it "is" something. The question is, what is it? Does it dramatize the shortcomings of the middle class? or the problems of communication? or marriage? What is the relationship between the words that appear on the printed page and the end effects of the play? Could this really happen? Or does it matter?

THE TRAGEDY OF LANGUAGE*

How an English Primer became my first Play

by Eugene Ionesco

In 1948, before writing my first play, *The Bald Soprano*, I had no idea of becoming a playwright. My only ambition, quite simply, was to learn English. The study of English does not necessarily lead to playwriting. On the contrary, it was because I had no luck with English that I turned to the stage. Nor did I write these plays to avenge my failure, although some have said that my *Bald Soprano* was a satire of the English bourgeoisie. If I had wanted to learn Italian, Russian or Turkish and not succeeded, they would have claimed, by the same token, that the play resulting from that futile effort was a satire of Italian, Russian or Turkish society. Perhaps I ought to explain. Here is what happened: nine or ten years ago, in order to learn English conversation, I bought a French-English Primer. I set to work. Conscientiously, I copied whole sentences from my Primer with the purpose of memorizing them. Rereading them attentively, I learned not English, but some astonishing truths: that, for example, there are seven days in the week, something, moreover, I already knew; that the floor is down, the ceiling is up, things I already knew as well perhaps, but which I had never seriously thought about or had forgotten and which seemed to me, suddenly, as stupefying as they were indisputably true.

I probably have enough of a philosophical bent to have realized that what I was copying into my notebook were not simple English sentences in French translation, but fundamental truths, profound observations. I didn't give up English quite yet. Fortunately so, because, after universal truths, the author of the Primer went on to disclose private ones; probably inspired by the Platonic method, he expressed them by means of dialogue. From the third lesson onward, two characters were presented whose real or fictive existence I am still not sure of: Mr. and Mrs. Smith, an English couple. To my great astonishment, Mrs. Smith informed her husband that they had several children, that they lived in the vicinity of London, that their name was Smith, that Mr. Smith was a clerk, that they had a servant, Mary, English like themselves, that for the past twenty years they have had friends by the name of

* Translated by Jack Undank. Reprinted by permission from *The Tulane Drama Review*, Spring, 1960, pp. 10–13.

Mr. and Mrs. Martin, that their house was a palace, for "the home of an Englishman is his true palace."

I really supposed that Mr. Smith was probably somewhat abreast of all this, but can one be sure; there are people that absent-minded. Moreover, it is wise to remind our fellow men of things they may forget or of which they are insufficiently conscious. Besides these permanent, private truths, there were other truths, truths of the moment, which became apparent: for example, the fact that the Smiths had just finished their dinner and that it was nine o'clock at night, according to the clock — English time.

I should like to point out the irrefutable, perfectly axiomatic character of Mrs. Smith's assertions as well as the entirely Cartesian manner of the author of my English Primer, for what was truly remarkable about it was its eminently methodical procedure in its quest for truth. In the fifth lesson, the Smith's friends, the Martins, arrive; the four of them begin to chat, and, starting from basic axioms, they build more complex truths: "the country is quieter than the big city," some of them contend; "yes, but the city is more heavily populated and there are also more shops," the others reply — which is equally true and proves, moreover, that opposing truths can very well coexist.

It was then that my idea came to me. Perfecting my knowledge of English was now out of the question. To concentrate on enriching my English vocabulary, to learn words, to translate into another language what I could just as well say in French, without bearing in mind the "content" of those words, what they revealed, would have been to stumble into that sin of formalism which our thought-directors of today rightly condemn. My ambition had become greater: to communicate to my contemporaries the essential truths of which the French-English Primer had made me aware. And what is more, the dialogues of the Smiths, the Martins, the Smiths and the Martins, were really theatre, theatre and dialogue being one and the same thing. I had only to put it into a play. That is how I came to write *The Bald Soprano*, a pointedly didactic, theatrical work. And why is this work called *The Bald Soprano* and not *English Without Toil*, the title I first thought of giving it, or *The English Hour*, a title I thought of subsequently? That is too long a story: one of the reasons why *The Bald Soprano* has its present title is that no soprano, bald or otherwise, appears in it. That ought to be sufficient comment. A good part of the play is composed of sentence fragments drawn from my English Primer and set end to end. The Smiths and Martins of the Primer are the Smiths and Martins of my play; they are one and the same, mouth the same maxims, perform the same actions or the same "inactions." In all "didactic theatre," you are not supposed to be original, to say what you yourself think: that would be a serious mishandling of objective *truth*; you have only to transmit, humbly, the instruction that has been transmitted to you, ideas that have been handed down. How could I take the slightest liberty with words expressing absolute truth in so edifying a fashion? My play, *authentically* didactic, was not meant to be original nor intended to show my talent to advantage.

. . . Nevertheless, the text of The Bald Soprano was a lesson (and an act of plagiarism) only at the start. A strange phenomenon took place, I don't know how: the text began imperceptibly to change before my eyes, and in spite of me. The very simple, luminously clear statements I had copied diligently into my schoolboy's notebook, left to themselves, fermented after a while, became denatured, expanded and overflowed. The repartee which I had, in careful and precise succession, copied from the Primer, became a jumble. Which is what happened to that certain, irrefutable truth: "the floor is down, the ceiling is up." Assertions — as categorical as they were solid: the seven days of the week are Monday, Tuesday, Wednesday, Thursday, Friday, Saturday, Sunday — collapsed, and Mr. Smith, my hero, now proposed that the week consisted of three days, namely: Tuesday, Thursday and Tuesday. My characters, my good bourgeois, the Martins, husband and wife, were suddenly afflicted with amnesia: although they continued to speak to and see one another every day, they no longer recognized each other. Other alarming things happened: the Smiths now told of the death of a certain Bobby Watson whose identity was unrecognizable because, as they mentioned elsewhere, three quarters of the town's inhabitants, men, women, children, cats and pseudo-philosophers were named Bobby Watson. A fifth character now unexpectedly burst upon the scene and added to the confusion of the couples' peaceable domesticity: the Fire Chief, who told stories which had something to do with a young bull supposedly giving birth to an enormous heifer, with a mouse giving birth to a mountain — then, the fireman went off to catch a fire which he had foreseen three days in advance (he had marked it on his calendar) and which was scheduled to break out at the other end of town. Whereupon the Smiths resumed their conversation. Alas! the wise and fundamental truths they exchanged, each carefully linked to the next, had gone wild, their language had become disjointed; the characters disintegrated: their words became meaningless absurdities; the entire cast ended up quarreling. It was impossible to grasp my heroes' motives in this quarrel. They didn't fling retorts at one another, not even sentence fragments or words; all they spoke were syllables, consonants and vowels! . . .

. . . It represented, for me, a kind of collapse of reality. Words had become empty, noisy shells without meaning; the characters as well, of course, had become psychologically empty. Everything appeared to me in an unfamiliar light, people moving in a timeless time, in a spaceless space. . .

While writing the play (for it had become a kind of play or anti-play, that is, a parody of a play, a comedy of comedy), I felt sick, dizzy, nauseous. I had to interrupt my work from time to time and, wondering all the while what demon was prodding me on, lie down on my couch for fear of seeing my work sink into nothingness, and me with it. All the same, once I had finished, I was very proud. I fancied myself having written something like *the tragedy of language!* . . . When it was staged, I was almost amazed to hear the audience laugh; they took it lightly (and still do), believing that it was a comedy, if not an outright farce. Some people (Jean Pouillon among them), those who sensed the uneasiness in it, were not fooled. Others noticed that I was poking fun at Bernstein's theatre and his actors. Nicolas Bataille's troupe was the first to notice this; they acted out the play (especially in its initial performances) as though it were a melodrama.

Serious and learned critics, analyzing the work later on, interpreted it as no more than a criticism of the Théâtre de Boulevard (popular theatre). I have just said that I believe that interpretation valid; however, in my mind, it is not a satire of petty bourgeois mentality associated with any particular society. It is, above all, concerned with a kind of universal petty bourgeoisie, the petty bourgeoisie being the personification of accepted ideas and slogans, the ubiquitous conformist. His automatic use of language is, of course, what gives him away. The text of *The Bald Soprano* or of the English (or Russian or Portuguese) Primer, composed of ready-made expressions and the most tired clichés, made me aware of the automatic quality of language and human behavior, "empty talk," speaking because there is nothing personal to say, the absence of inner life, the mechanical aspect of daily existence, man bathing in his social environment, becoming an indistinguishable part of it. The Smiths, the Martins, can no longer talk because they can no longer think; they can no longer think *because they can no longer be moved, can no longer feel passions*; they can no longer be, they can "become" anybody, anything, for, having lost their identity, they assume the identity of others, become part of the world of the impersonal; they are interchangeable: you can put Martin in place of Smith and vice versa, no one will notice. The tragic character does not change, he is crushed; he is himself, he is *real*. Comic characters, fools, are people who do not exist.

Translated by Donald M. Allen

The Bald Soprano

ANTI-PLAY

THE CHARACTERS

MR. SMITH
MRS. SMITH
MR. MARTIN
MRS. MARTIN
MARY, *the maid*
THE FIRE CHIEF

SCENE: *A middle-class English interior, with English armchairs. An English evening.* MR. SMITH, *an Englishman, seated in his English armchair and wearing English slippers, is smoking his English pipe and reading an English newspaper, near an English fire. He is wearing English spectacles and a small gray English mustache. Beside him, in another English armchair,* MRS. SMITH, *an Englishwoman, is darning some English socks. A long moment of English silence. The English clock strikes 17 English strokes.*

MRS. SMITH. There, it's nine o'clock. We've drunk the soup, and eaten the fish and chips, and the English salad. The children have drunk English water. We've eaten well this evening. That's because we live in the suburbs of London and because our name is Smith.

MR. SMITH (*continues to read, clicks his tongue*).

MRS. SMITH. Potatoes are very good fried in fat; the salad oil was not rancid. The oil from the grocer at the corner is better quality than the oil from the grocer across the street. It is even better than the oil from the grocer at the bottom of the street. However, I prefer not to tell them that their oil is bad.

MR. SMITH (*continues to read, clicks his tongue*).

MRS. SMITH. However, the oil from the grocer at the corner is still the best.

MR. SMITH (*continues to read, clicks his tongue*).

MRS. SMITH. Mary did the potatoes very well, this evening. The last time she did not do them well. I do not like them when they are well done.

MR. SMITH (*continues to read, clicks his tongue*).

The Bald Soprano

MRS. SMITH. The fish was fresh. It made my mouth water. I had two helpings. No, three helpings. That made me go to the w.c. You also had three helpings. However, the third time you took less than the first two times, while as for me, I took a great deal more. I eat better than you this evening. Why is that? Usually, it is you who eats more. It is not appetite you lack.

MR. SMITH *(clicks his tongue).*

MRS. SMITH. But still, the soup was perhaps a little too salt. It was saltier than you. Ha, ha, ha. It also had too many leeks and not enough onions. I regret I didn't advise Mary to add some aniseed stars. The next time I'll know better.

MR. SMITH *(continues to read, clicks his tongue).*

MRS. SMITH. Our little boy wanted to drink some beer; he's going to love getting tiddly. He's like you. At table did you notice how he stared at the bottle? But I poured some water from the jug into his glass. He was thirsty and he drank it. Helen is like me: she's a good manager, thrifty, plays the piano. She never asks to drink English beer. She's like our little daughter who drinks only milk and eats only porridge. It's obvious that she's only two. She's named Peggy. The quince and bean pie was marvelous. It would have been nice, perhaps, to have had a small glass of Australian Burgundy with the sweet, but I did not bring the bottle to the table because I did not wish to set the children a bad example of gluttony. They must learn to be sober and temperate.

MR. SMITH *(continues to read, clicks his tongue).*

MRS. SMITH. Mrs. Parker knows a Rumanian grocer by the name of Popesco Rosenfeld, who has just come from Constantinople. He is a great specialist in yogurt. He has a diploma from the school of yogurt-making in Adrianople. Tomorrow I shall buy a large pot of native Rumanian yogurt from him. One doesn't often find such things here in the suburbs of London.

MR. SMITH *(continues to read, clicks his tongue).*

MRS. SMITH. Yogurt is excellent for the stomach, the kidneys, the appendicitis, and apotheosis. It was Doctor Mackenzie-King who told me that, he's the one who takes care of the children of our neighbors, the Johns. He's a good doctor. One can trust him. He never prescribes any medicine that he's not tried out on himself first. Before operating on Parker, he had his own liver operated on first, although he was not the least bit ill.

MR. SMITH. But how does it happen that the doctor pulled through while Parker died?

MRS. SMITH. Because the operation was successful in the doctor's case and it was not in Parker's.

MR. SMITH. Then Mackenzie is not a good doctor. The operation should have succeeded with both of them or else both should have died.

MRS. SMITH. Why?

MR. SMITH. A conscientious doctor must die with his patient if they can't get well together. The captain of a ship goes down with his ship into the briny deep, he does not survive alone.

MRS. SMITH. One cannot compare a patient with a ship.

MR. SMITH. Why not? A ship has its diseases too; moreover, your doctor is as hale as a ship; that's why he should have perished at the same time as his patient, like the captain and his ship.

MRS. SMITH. Ah! I hadn't thought of that . . . Perhaps it is true . . . And then, what conclusion do you draw from this?

MR. SMITH. All doctors are quacks. And all patients too. Only the Royal Navy is honest in England.

MRS. SMITH. But not sailors.

MR. SMITH. Naturally. (*A pause. Still reading his paper.*) Here's a thing I don't understand. In the newspaper they always give the age of deceased persons but never the age of the newly born. That doesn't make sense.

MRS. SMITH. I never thought of that!

Another moment of silence. The clock strikes seven times. Silence. The clock strikes three times. Silence. The clock doesn't strike.

MR. SMITH (*still reading his paper*). Tsk, it says here that Bobby Watson died.

MRS. SMITH. My God, the poor man! When did he die?

MR. SMITH. Why do you pretend to be astonished? You know very well that he'd been dead these past two years. Surely you remember that we attended his funeral a year and a half ago.

MRS. SMITH. Oh yes, of course I do remember. I remembered it right away, but I don't understand why you yourself were so surprised to see it in the paper.

MR. SMITH. It wasn't in the paper. It's been three years since his death was announced. I remembered it through an association of ideas.

MRS. SMITH. What a pity! He was so well preserved.

MR. SMITH. He was the handsomest corpse in Great Britain. He didn't look his age. Poor Bobby, he'd been dead for four years and he was still warm. A veritable living corpse. And how cheerful he was!

MRS. SMITH. Poor Bobby.

MR. SMITH. Which poor Bobby do you mean?

MRS. SMITH. It is his wife that I mean. She is called Bobby too, Bobby Watson. Since they both had the same name, you could never tell one from the other when you saw them together. It was only after his death that you could really tell which was which. And there are still people today who confuse her with the deceased and offer their condolences to him. Do you know her?

MR. SMITH. I only met her once, by chance, at Bobby's burial.

MRS. SMITH. I've never seen her. Is she pretty?

MR. SMITH. She has regular features and yet one cannot say that say that

The Bald Soprano

she is pretty. She is too big and stout. Her features are not regular but still one can say that she is very pretty. She is a little too small and too thin. She's a voice teacher.

The clock strikes five times. A long silence.

MRS. SMITH. And when do they plan to be married, those two?

MR. SMITH. Next spring, at the latest.

MRS. SMITH. We shall have to go to their wedding, I suppose.

MR. SMITH. We shall have to give them a wedding present. I wonder what?

MRS. SMITH. Why don't we give them one of the seven silver salvers that were given us for our wedding and which have never been of any use to us? (*Silence.*)

MRS. SMITH. How sad for her to be left a widow so young.

MR. SMITH. Fortunately, they had no children.

MRS. SMITH. That was all they needed! Children! Poor woman, how could she have managed!

MR. SMITH. She's still young. She might very well remarry. She looks so well in mourning.

MRS. SMITH. But who would take care of the children? You know very well that they have a boy and a girl. What are their names?

MR. SMITH. Bobby and Bobby like their parents. Bobby Watson's uncle, old Bobby Watson, is a rich man and very fond of the boy. He might very well pay for Bobby's education.

MRS. SMITH. That would be proper. And Bobby Watson's aunt, old Bobby Watson, might very well, in her turn, pay for the education of Bobby Watson, Bobby Watson's daughter. That way Bobby, Bobby Watson's mother, could remarry. Has she anyone in mind?

MR. SMITH. Yes, a cousin of Bobby Watson's.

MRS. SMITH. Who? Bobby Watson?

MR. SMITH. Which Bobby Watson do you mean?

MRS. SMITH. Why, Bobby Watson, the son of old Bobby Watson, the late Bobby Watson's other uncle.

MR. SMITH. No, it's not that one, it's someone else. It's Bobby Watson, the son of old Bobby Watson, the late Bobby Watson's aunt.

MRS. SMITH. Are you referring to Bobby Watson the commercial traveler?

MR. SMITH. All the Bobby Watsons are commercial travelers.

MRS. SMITH. What a difficult trade! However, they do well at it.

MR. SMITH. Yes, when there's no competition.

MRS. SMITH. And when is there no competition?

MR. SMITH. On Tuesdays, Thursdays, and Tuesdays.

MRS. SMITH. Ah! Three days a week? And what does Bobby Watson do on those days?

MR. SMITH. He rests, he sleeps.

MRS. SMITH. But why doesn't he work those three days if there's no competition?

MR. SMITH. I don't know everything. I can't answer all your idiotic questions!

MRS. SMITH (*offended*). Oh! Are you trying to humiliate me?

MR. SMITH (*all smiles*). You know very well that I'm not.

MRS. SMITH. Men are all alike! You sit there all day long, a cigarette in your mouth, or you powder your nose and rouge your lips, fifty times a day, or else you drink like a fish.

MR. SMITH. But what would you say if you saw men acting like women do, smoking all day long, powdering, rouging their lips, drinking whisky?

MRS. SMITH. It's nothing to me! But if you're only saying that to annoy me . . . I don't care for that kind of joking, you know that very well!

She hurls the socks across the stage and shows her teeth. She gets up.[1]

MR. SMITH (*also getting up and going towards his wife, tenderly*). Oh, my little ducky daddles, what a little spitfire you are! You know that I only said it as a joke! (*He takes her by the waist and kisses her.*) What a ridiculous pair of old lovers we are! Come, let's put out the lights and go bye-byes.

MARY (*entering*). I'm the maid. I have spent a very pleasant afternoon. I've been to the cinema with a man and I've seen a film with some women. After the cinema, we went to drink some brandy and milk and then read the newspaper.

MRS. SMITH. I hope that you've spent a pleasant afternoon, that you went to the cinema with a man and that you drank some brandy and milk.

MR. SMITH. And the newspaper.

MARY. Mr. and Mrs. Martin, your guests, are at the door. They were waiting for me. They didn't dare come in by themselves. They were supposed to have dinner with you this evening.

MRS. SMITH. Oh, yes. We were expecting them. And we were hungry. Since they didn't put in an appearance, we were going to start dinner without them. We've had nothing to eat all day. You should not have gone out!

MARY. But it was you who gave me permission.

MR. SMITH. We didn't do it on purpose.

MARY (*bursts into laughter, then she bursts into tears. Then she smiles*). I bought me a chamber pot.

MRS. SMITH. My dear Mary, please open the door and ask Mr. and Mrs. Martin to step in. We will change quickly.

MR. AND MRS. SMITH exit right. MARY opens the door at the left by which MR. AND MRS. MARTIN enter.

MARY. Why have you come so late! You are not very polite. People should be punctual. Do you understand? But sit down there, anyway, and wait now that you're here.

She exits. MR. AND MRS. MARTIN sit facing each other, without speaking. They smile timidly at each other. The dialogue which follows must be

---

[1] In Nicolas Bataille's production, Mrs. Smith did not show her teeth, nor did she throw the socks very far.

spoken in voices that are drawling, monotonous, a little singsong, without nuances.[2]

MR. MARTIN. Excuse me, madam, but it seems to me, unless I'm mistaken, that I've met you somewhere before.

MRS. MARTIN. I, too, sir. It seems to me that I've met you somewhere before.

MR. MARTIN. Was it, by any chance, at Manchester that I caught a glimpse of you, madam?

MRS. MARTIN. That is very possible. I am originally from the city of Manchester. But I do not have a good memory, sir. I cannot say whether it was there that I caught a glimpse of you or not!

MR. MARTIN. Good God, that's curious! I, too, am originally from the city of Manchester, madam!

MRS. MARTIN. That is curious!

MR. MARTIN. Isn't that curious! Only, I, madam, I left the city of Manchester about five weeks ago.

MRS. MARTIN. That is curious! What a bizarre coincidence! I, too, sir, I left the city of Manchester about five weeks ago.

MR. MARTIN. Madam, I took the 8:30 morning train which arrives in London at 4:45.

MRS. MARTIN. That is curious! How very bizarre! And what a coincidence! I took the same train, sir, I too.

MR. MARTIN. Good Lord, how curious! Perhaps then, madam, it was on the train that I saw you?

MRS. MARTIN. It is indeed possible; that is, not unlikely. It is plausible and, after all, why not! — But I don't recall it, sir!

MR. MARTIN. I traveled second class, madam. There is no second class in England, but I always travel second class.

MRS. MARTIN. That is curious! How very bizarre! And what a coincidence! I, too, sir, I traveled second class.

MR. MARTIN. How curious that is! Perhaps we did meet in second class, my dear lady!

MRS. MARTIN. That is certainly possible, and it is not at all unlikely. But I do not remember very well, my dear sir!

MR. MARTIN. My seat was in coach No. 8, compartment 6, my dear lady.

MRS. MARTIN. How curious that is! My seat was also in coach No. 8, compartment 6, my dear sir!

MR. MARTIN. How curious that is and what a bizarre coincidence! Perhaps we met in compartment 6, my dear lady?

MRS. MARTIN. It is indeed possible, after all! But I do not recall it, my dear sir!

MR. MARTIN. To tell the truth, my dear lady, I do not remember it either,

---

[2] In Nicolas Bataille's production, this dialogue was spoken in a tone and played in a style sincerely tragic.

but it is possible that we caught a glimpse of each other there, and as I think of it, it seems to me even very likely.

MRS. MARTIN. Oh! truly, of course, truly, sir!

MR. MARTIN. How curious it is! I had seat No. 3, next to the window, my dear lady.

MRS. MARTIN. Oh, good Lord, how curious and bizarre! I had seat No. 6, next to the window, across from you, my dear sir.

MR. MARTIN. Good God, how curious that is and what a coincidence! We were then seated facing each other, my dear lady! It is there that we must have seen each other!

MRS. MARTIN. How curious it is! It is possible, but I do not recall it, sir!

MR. MARTIN. To tell the truth, my dear lady, I do not remember it either. However, it is very possible that we saw each other on that occasion.

MRS. MARTIN. It is true, but I am not at all sure of it, sir.

MR. MARTIN. Dear madam, were you not the lady who asked me to place her suitcase in the luggage rack and who thanked me and gave me permission to smoke?

MRS. MARTIN. But of course, that must have been I, sir. How curious it is, how curious it is, and what a coincidence!

MR. MARTIN. How curious it is, how bizarre, what a coincidence! And well, well, it was perhaps at that moment that we came to know each other, madam?

MRS. MARTIN. How curious it is and what a coincidence! It is indeed possible, my dear sir! However, I do not believe that I recall it.

MR. MARTIN. Nor do I, madam. (*A moment of silence. The clock strikes twice, then once.*) Since coming to London, I have resided in Bromfield Street, my dear lady.

MRS. MARTIN. How curious that is, how bizarre! I, too, since coming to London, I have resided in Bromfield Street, my dear sir.

MR. MARTIN. How curious that is, well then, well then, perhaps we have seen each other in Bromfield Street, my dear lady.

MRS. MARTIN. How curious that is, how bizarre! It is indeed possible, after all! But I do not recall it, my dear sir.

MR. MARTIN. I reside at No. 19, my dear lady.

MRS. MARTIN. How curious that is. I also reside at No. 19, my dear sir.

MR. MARTIN. Well then, well then, well then, well then, perhaps we have seen each other in that house, dear lady?

MRS. MARTIN. It is indeed possible but I do not recall it, dear sir.

MR. MARTIN. My flat is on the fifth floor, No. 8, my dear lady.

MRS. MARTIN. How curious it is, good Lord, how bizarre! And what a coincidence! I too reside on the fifth floor, in flat No. 8, dear sir!

MR. MARTIN (*musing*). How curious it is, how curious it is, how curious it is, and what a coincidence! You know, in my bedroom there is a bed, and it is covered with a green eiderdown. This room, with the bed and the green eiderdown, is at the end of the corridor between the w.c. and the bookcase, dear lady!

MRS. MARTIN. What a coincidence, good Lord, what a coincidence! My bedroom, too, has a bed with a green eiderdown and is at the end of the corridor, between the w.c., dear sir, and the bookcase!

MR. MARTIN. How bizarre, curious, strange! Then, madam, we live in the same room and we sleep in the same bed, dear lady. It is perhaps there that we have met!

MRS. MARTIN. How curious it is and what a coincidence! It is indeed possible that we have met there, and perhaps even last night. But I do not recall it, dear sir!

MR. MARTIN. I have a little girl, my little daughter, she lives with me, dear lady. She is two years old, she's blonde, she has a white eye and a red eye, she is very pretty, her name is Alice, dear lady.

MRS. MARTIN. What a bizarre coincidence! I, too, have a little girl. She is two years old, has a white eye and a red eye, she is very pretty, and her name is Alice, too, dear sir!

MR. MARTIN (*in the same drawling, monotonous voice*). How curious it is and what a coincidence! And bizarre! Perhaps they are the same, dear lady!

MRS. MARTIN. How curious it is! It is indeed possible, dear sir. (A *rather long moment of silence. The clock strikes 29 times.*)

MR. MARTIN (*after having reflected at length, gets up slowly and, unhurriedly, moves toward* MRS. MARTIN, *who, surprised by his solemn air, has also gotten up very quietly.* MR. MARTIN, *in the same flat monotonous voice, slightly sing-song*). Then, dear lady, I believe that there can be no doubt about it, we have seen each other before and you are my own wife . . . Elizabeth, I have found you again!

MRS. MARTIN *approaches* MR. MARTIN *without haste. They embrace without expression. The clock strikes once, very loud. This striking of the clock must be so loud that it makes the audience jump. The* MARTINS *do not hear it.*

MRS. MARTIN. Donald, it's you, darling!

They sit together in the same armchair, their arms around each other, and fall asleep. The clock strikes several more times. MARY, *on tiptoe, a finger to her lips, enters quietly and addresses the audience.*

MARY. Elizabeth and Donald are now too happy to be able to hear me. I can therefore let you in on a secret. Elizabeth is not Elizabeth, Donald is not Donald. And here is the proof: the child that Donald spoke of is not Elizabeth's daughter, they are not the same person. Donald's daughter has one white eye and one red eye like Elizabeth's daughter. Whereas Donald's child has a white right eye and a red left eye, Elizabeth's child has a red right eye and a white left eye! Thus all of Donald's system of deduction collapses when it comes up against this last obstacle which destroys his whole theory. In spite of the extraordinary coincidences which seem to be definitive proofs, Donald and Elizabeth, not being the parents of the same child, are not Donald and Elizabeth. It is in vain that he thinks he is Donald, it is in vain that she thinks she is Elizabeth. He believes in vain that she is Elizabeth. She believes in vain that he is Donald — they are sadly deceived. But who is the true Donald? Who is the true Elizabeth? Who has any interest in prolonging this confusion? I don't know. Let's not try to know. Let's leave things as they are. (*She takes several steps toward the door, then returns and says to the audience:*) My real name is Sherlock Holmes. (*She exits.*)

The clock strikes as much as it likes. After several seconds, MR. *and* MRS. MARTIN *separate and take the chairs they had at the beginning.*

MR. MARTIN. Darling, let's forget all that has not passed between us, and, now that we have found each other again, let's try not to lose each other any more, and live as before.

MRS. MARTIN. Yes, darling.

MR. *and* MRS. SMITH *enter from the right, wearing the same clothes.*

MRS. SMITH. Good evening, dear friends! Please forgive us for having made you wait so long. We thought that we should extend you the courtesy to which you are entitled and as soon as we learned that you had been kind enough to give us the pleasure of coming to see us without prior notice we hurried to dress for the occasion.

MR. SMITH (*furious*). We've had nothing to eat all day. And we've been waiting four whole hours for you. Why have you come so late?

MR. *and* MRS. SMITH *sit facing their guests. The striking of the clock underlines the speeches, more or less strongly, according to the case. The* MARTINS, *particularly* MRS. MARTIN, *seem embarrassed and timid. For this reason the conversation begins with difficulty and the words are uttered, at the beginning, awkwardly. A long embarrassed silence at first, then other silences and hesitations follow.*

MR. SMITH. Hm. (*Silence.*)
MRS. SMITH. Hm, hm. (*Silence.*)
MRS. MARTIN. Hm, hm, hm. (*Silence.*)
MR. MARTIN. Hm, hm, hm, hm. (*Silence.*)
MRS. MARTIN. Oh, but definitely. (*Silence.*)
MR. MARTIN. We all have colds. (*Silence.*)
MR. SMITH. Nevertheless, it's not chilly. (*Silence.*)
MRS. SMITH. There's no draft. (*Silence.*)
MR. MARTIN. Oh, no, fortunately. (*Silence.*)
MR. SMITH. Oh dear, oh dear, oh dear. (*Silence.*)
MR. MARTIN. Don't you feel well? (*Silence.*)
MRS. SMITH. No, he's wet his pants. (*Silence.*)
MRS. MARTIN. Oh, sir, at your age, you shouldn't. (*Silence.*)
MR. SMITH. The heart is ageless. (*Silence.*)
MR. MARTIN. That's true. (*Silence.*)

The Bald Soprano

MRS. SMITH. So they say. (*Silence.*)

MRS. MARTIN. They also say the opposite. (*Silence.*)

MR. SMITH. The truth lies somewhere between the two. (*Silence.*)

MR. MARTIN. That's true. (*Silence.*)

MRS. SMITH (*to the* MARTINS). Since you travel so much, you must have many interesting things to tell us.

MR. MARTIN (*to his wife*). My dear, tell us what you've seen today.

MRS. MARTIN. It's scarcely worth the trouble, for no one would believe me.

MR. SMITH. We're not going to question your sincerity!

MRS. SMITH. You will offend us if you think that.

MR. MARTIN (*to his wife*). You will offend them, my dear, if you think that . . .

MRS. MARTIN (*graciously*). Oh well, today I witnessed something extraordinary. Something really incredible.

MR. MARTIN. Tell us quickly, my dear.

MR. SMITH. Oh, this is going to be amusing.

MRS. SMITH. At last.

MRS. MARTIN. Well, today, when I went shopping to buy some vegetables, which are getting to be dearer and dearer . . .

MRS. SMITH. Where is it all going to end!

MR. SMITH. You shouldn't interrupt, my dear, it's very rude.

MRS. MARTIN. In the street, near a café, I saw a man, properly dressed, about fifty years old, or not even that, who . . .

MR. SMITH. Who, what?

MRS. SMITH. Who, what?

MR. SMITH (*to his wife*). Don't interrupt, my dear, you're disgusting.

MRS. SMITH. My dear, it is you who interrupted first, you boor.

MR. SMITH (*to his wife*). Hush. (*To* MRS. MARTIN.) What was this man doing?

MRS. MARTIN. Well, I'm sure you'll say that I'm making it up — he was down on one knee and he was bent over.

MR. MARTIN, MR. SMITH, MRS. SMITH. Oh!

MRS. MARTIN. Yes, bent over.

MR. SMITH. Not possible.

MRS. MARTIN. Yes, bent over. I went near him to see what he was doing . . .

MR. SMITH. And?

MRS. MARTIN. He was tying his shoe lace which had come undone.

MR. MARTIN, MR. SMITH, MRS. SMITH. Fantastic!

MR. SMITH. If someone else had told me this, I'd not believe it.

MR. MARTIN. Why not? One sees things even more extraordinary every day, when one walks around. For instance, today in the Underground I myself saw a man, quietly sitting on a seat, reading his newspaper.

MRS. SMITH. What a character!

MR. SMITH. Perhaps it was the same man!

The doorbell rings.

MR. SMITH. Goodness, someone is ringing.

MRS. SMITH. There must be somebody there. I'll go and see. (*She goes to see, she opens the door and closes it, and comes back.*) Nobody. (*She sits down again.*)

MR. MARTIN. I'm going to give you another example . . .

Doorbell rings again.

MR. SMITH. Goodness, someone is ringing.

MRS. SMITH. There must be somebody there. I'll go and see. (*She goes to see, opens the door, and comes back.*) No one. (*She sits down again.*)

MR. MARTIN (*who has forgotten where he was*). Uh . . .

MRS. MARTIN. You were saying that you were going to give us another example.

MR. MARTIN. Oh, yes . . .

Doorbell rings again.

MR. SMITH. Goodness, someone is ringing.

MRS. SMITH. I'm not going to open the door again.

MR. SMITH. Yes, but there must be someone there!

MRS. SMITH. The first time there was no one. The second time, no one. Why do you think that there is someone there now?

MR. SMITH. Because someone has rung!

MRS. MARTIN. That's no reason.

MR. MARTIN. What? When one hears the doorbell ring, that means someone is at the door ringing to have the door opened.

MRS. MARTIN. Not always. You've just seen otherwise!

MR. MARTIN. In most cases, yes.

MR. SMITH. As for me, when I go to visit someone, I ring in order to be admitted. I think that everyone does the same thing and that each time there is a ring there must be someone there.

MRS. SMITH. That is true in theory. But in reality things happen differently. You have just seen otherwise.

MRS. MARTIN. Your wife is right.

MR. MARTIN. Oh! You women! You always stand up for each other.

MRS. SMITH. Well, I'll go and see. You can't say that I am obstinate, but you will see that there's no one there! (*She goes to look, opens the door and closes it.*) You see, there's no one there. (*She returns to her seat.*)

MRS. SMITH. Oh, these men who always think they're right and who're always wrong!

The doorbell rings again.

MR. SMITH. Goodness, someone is ringing. There must be someone there.

MRS. SMITH (*in a fit of anger*). Don't send me to open the door again. You've seen that it was useless. Experience teaches us that when one hears the doorbell ring it is because there is never anyone there.

MRS. MARTIN. Never.

The Bald Soprano

MR. MARTIN. That's not entirely accurate.

MR. SMITH. In fact it's false. When one hears the doorbell ring it is because there is someone there.

MRS. SMITH. He won't admit he's wrong.

MRS. MARTIN. My husband is very obstinate, too.

MR. SMITH. There's someone there.

MR. MARTIN. That's not impossible.

MRS. SMITH (*to her husband*). No.

MR. SMITH. Yes.

MRS. SMITH. I tell you *no*. In any case you are not going to disturb me again for nothing. If you wish to know, go and look yourself!

MR. SMITH. I'll go.

MRS. SMITH *shrugs her shoulders*. MRS. MARTIN *tosses her head*.

MR. SMITH (*opening the door*). Oh! how do you do. (*He glances at* MRS. SMITH *and the* MARTINS, *who are all surprise*.) It's the Fire Chief!

FIRE CHIEF (*he is of course in uniform and is wearing an enormous shining helmet*). Good evening, ladies and gentlemen. (*The* SMITHS *and the* MARTINS *are still slightly astonished*. MRS. SMITH *turns her head away, in a temper, and does not reply to his greeting*.) Good evening, Mrs. Smith. You appear to be angry.

MRS. SMITH. Oh!

MR. SMITH. You see it's because my wife is a little chagrined at having been proved wrong.

MR. MARTIN. There's been an argument between Mr. and Mrs. Smith, Mr. Fire Chief.

MRS. SMITH (*to* MR. MARTIN). This is no business of yours! (*To* MR. SMITH.) I beg you not to involve outsiders in our family arguments.

MR. SMITH. Oh, my dear, this is not so serious. The Fire Chief is an old friend of the family. His mother courted me, and I knew his father. He asked me to give him my daughter in marriage if ever I had one. And he died waiting.

MR. MARTIN. That's neither his fault, nor yours.

FIRE CHIEF. Well, what is it all about?

MRS. SMITH. My husband was claiming . . .

MR. SMITH. No, it was you who was claiming.

MR. MARTIN. Yes, it was she.

MRS. MARTIN. No, it was he.

FIRE CHIEF. Don't get excited. You tell me, Mrs. Smith.

MRS. SMITH. Well, this is how it was. It is difficult for me to speak openly to you, but a fireman is also a confessor.

FIRE CHIEF. Well then?

MRS. SMITH. We were arguing because my husband said that each time the doorbell rings there is always someone there.

MR. MARTIN. It is plausible.

MRS. SMITH. And I was saying that each time the doorbell rings there is never anyone there.

MRS. MARTIN. It might seem strange.

MRS. SMITH. But it has been proved, not by theoretical demonstrations, but by facts.

MR. SMITH. That's false, since the Fire Chief is here. He rang the bell, I opened the door, and there he was.

MRS. MARTIN. When?

MR. MARTIN. But just now.

MRS. SMITH. Yes, but it was only when you heard the doorbell ring the fourth time that there was someone there. And the fourth time does not count.

MRS. MARTIN. Never. It is only the first three times that count.

MR. SMITH. Mr. Fire Chief, permit me in my turn to ask you several questions.

FIRE CHIEF. Go right ahead.

MR. SMITH. When I opened the door and saw you, it was really you who had rung the bell?

FIRE CHIEF. Yes, it was I.

MR. MARTIN. You were at the door? And you rang in order to be admitted?

FIRE CHIEF. I do not deny it.

MR. SMITH (*to his wife, triumphantly*). You see? I was right. When you hear the doorbell ring, that means someone rang it. You certainly cannot say that the Fire Chief is not someone.

MRS. SMITH. Certainly not. I repeat to you that I was speaking of only the first three times, since the fourth time does not count.

MRS. MARTIN. And when the doorbell rang the first time, was it you?

FIRE CHIEF. No, it was not I.

MRS. MARTIN. You see? The doorbell rang and there was no one there.

MR. MARTIN. Perhaps it was someone else?

MR. SMITH. Were you standing at the door for a long time?

FIRE CHIEF. Three-quarters of an hour.

MR. SMITH. And you saw no one?

FIRE CHIEF. No one. I am sure of that.

MRS. MARTIN. And did you hear the bell when it rang the second time?

FIRE CHIEF. Yes, and that wasn't I either. And there was still no one there.

MRS. SMITH. Victory! I was right.

MR. SMITH (*to his wife*). Not so fast. (*To the* FIRE CHIEF.) And what were you doing at the door?

FIRE CHIEF. Nothing. I was just standing there. I was thinking of many things.

MR. MARTIN (*to the* FIRE CHIEF). But the third time — it was not you who rang?

FIRE CHIEF. Yes, it was I.

The Bald Soprano

MR. SMITH. But when the door was opened nobody was in sight.

FIRE CHIEF. That was because I had hidden myself — as a joke.

MRS. SMITH. Don't make jokes, Mr. Fire Chief. This business is too sad.

MR. MARTIN. In short, we still do not know whether, when the doorbell rings, there is someone there or not!

MRS. SMITH. Never anyone.

MR. SMITH. Always someone.

FIRE CHIEF. I am going to reconcile you. You both are partly right. When the doorbell rings, sometimes there is someone, other times there is no one.

MR. MARTIN. This seems logical to me.

MRS. MARTIN. I think so too.

FIRE CHIEF. Life is very simple, really. (*To the* SMITHS.) Go on and kiss each other.

MRS. SMITH. We just kissed each other a little while ago.

MR. MARTIN. They'll kiss each other tomorrow. They have plenty of time.

MRS. SMITH. Mr. Fire Chief, since you helped us settle this, please make yourself comfortable, take off your helmet and sit down for a moment.

FIRE CHIEF. Excuse me, but I can't stay long. I should like to remove my helmet, but I haven't time to sit down. (*He sits down, without removing his helmet.*) I must admit that I have come to see you for another reason. I am on official business.

MRS. SMITH. And what can we do for you, Mr. Fire Chief?

FIRE CHIEF. I must beg you to excuse my indiscretion (*terribly embarrassed*) . . . uhm (*He points a finger at the* MARTINS.) . . . you don't mind . . . in front of them . . .

MRS. MARTIN. Say whatever you like.

MR. MARTIN. We're old friends. They tell us everything.

MR. SMITH. Speak.

FIRE CHIEF. Eh, well — is there a fire here?

MRS. SMITH. Why do you ask us that?

FIRE CHIEF. It's because — pardon me — I have orders to extinguish all the fires in the city.

MRS. MARTIN. All?

FIRE CHIEF. Yes, all.

MRS. SMITH (*confused*). I don't know . . . I don't think so. Do you want me to go and look?

MR. SMITH (*sniffing*). There can't be one here. There's no smell of anything burning.[3]

FIRE CHIEF (*aggrieved*). None at all? You don't have a little fire in the chimney, something burning in the attic or in the cellar? A little fire just starting, at least?

MRS. SMITH. I am sorry to disappoint you but I do not believe there's any-

---

[3] In Nicolas Bataille's production Mr. and Mrs. Martin sniffed too.

thing here at the moment. I promise that I will notify you when we do have something.

FIRE CHIEF. Please don't forget, it would be a great help.

MRS. SMITH. That's a promise.

FIRE CHIEF (*to the* MARTINS). And there's nothing burning at your house either?

MRS. MARTIN. No, unfortunately.

MR. MARTIN (*to the* FIRE CHIEF). Things aren't going so well just now.

FIRE CHIEF. Very poorly. There's been almost nothing, a few trifles — a chimney, a barn. Nothing important. It doesn't bring in much. And since there are no returns, the profits on output are very meager.

MR. SMITH. Times are bad. That's true all over. It's the same this year with business and agriculture as it is with fires, nothing is prospering.

MR. MARTIN. No wheat, no fires.

FIRE CHIEF. No floods either.

MRS. SMITH. But there is some sugar.

MR. SMITH. That's because it is imported.

MRS. MARTIN. It's harder in the case of fires. The tariffs are too high!

FIRE CHIEF. All the same, there's an occasional asphyxiation by gas, but that's unusual too. For instance, a young woman asphyxiated herself last week — she had left the gas on.

MRS. MARTIN. Had she forgotten it?

FIRE CHIEF. No, but she thought it was her comb.

MR. SMITH. These confusions are always dangerous!

MRS. SMITH. Did you go to see the match dealer?

FIRE CHIEF. There's nothing doing there. He is insured against fires.

MR. MARTIN. Why don't you go see the Vicar of Wakefield, and use my name?

FIRE CHIEF. I don't have the right to extinguish clergymen's fires. The Bishop would get angry. Besides they extinguish their fires themselves, or else they have them put out by vestal virgins.

MR. SMITH. Go see the Durands.

FIRE CHIEF. I can't do that either. He's not English. He's only been naturalized. And naturalized citizens have the right to have houses, but not the right to have them put out if they're burning.

MRS. SMITH. Nevertheless, when they set fire to it last year, it was put out just the same.

FIRE CHIEF. He did that all by himself. Clandestinely. But it's not I who would report him.

MR. SMITH. Neither would I.

MRS. SMITH. Mr. Fire Chief, since you are not too pressed, stay a little while longer. You would be doing us a favor.

FIRE CHIEF. Shall I tell you some stories?

MRS. SMITH. Oh, by all means, how charming of you. (*She kisses him.*)

MR. SMITH, MRS. MARTIN, MR. MARTIN. Yes, yes, some stories, hurrah!
They applaud.

MR. SMITH. And what is even more interesting is the fact that firemen's stories are all true, and they're based on experience.

FIRE CHIEF. I speak from my own experience. Truth, nothing but the truth. No fiction.

MR. MARTIN. That's right. Truth is never found in books, only in life.

MRS. SMITH. Begin!

MR. MARTIN. Begin!

MRS. MARTIN. Be quiet, he is beginning.

FIRE CHIEF (*coughs slightly several times*). Excuse me, don't look at me that way. You embarrass me. You know that I am shy.

MRS. SMITH. Isn't he charming! (*She kisses him.*)

FIRE CHIEF. I'm going to try to begin anyhow. But promise me that you won't listen.

MRS. MARTIN. But if we don't listen to you we won't hear you.

FIRE CHIEF. I didn't think of that!

MRS. SMITH. I told you, he's just a boy.

MR. MARTIN, MR. SMITH. Oh, the sweet child! (*They kiss him.*[4])

MRS. MARTIN. Chin up!

FIRE CHIEF. Well, then! (*He coughs again in a voice shaken by emotions.*) "The Dog and the Cow," an experimental fable. Once upon a time another cow asked another dog: "Why have you not swallowed your trunk?" "Pardon me," replied the dog, "it is because I thought that I was an elephant."

MRS. MARTIN. What is the moral?

FIRE CHIEF. That's for you to find out.

MR. SMITH. He's right.

MRS. SMITH (*furious*). Tell us another.

FIRE CHIEF. A young calf had eaten too much ground glass. As a result, it was obliged to give birth. It brought forth a cow into the world. However, since the calf was male, the cow could not call him Mamma. Nor could she call him Papa, because the calf was too little. The calf was then obliged to get married and the registry office carried out all the details completely à la mode.

MR. SMITH. À la mode de Caen.

MR. MARTIN. Like tripes.

FIRE CHIEF. You've heard that one?

MRS. SMITH. It was in all the papers.

MRS. MARTIN. It happened not far from our house.

FIRE CHIEF. I'll tell you another: "The Cock." Once upon a time, a cock wished to play the dog. But he had no luck because everyone recognized him right away.

---

[4] In Nicolas Bataille's production, they did not kiss the Fire Chief.

MRS. SMITH. On the other hand, the dog that wished to play the cock was never recognized.

MR. SMITH. I'll tell you one: "The Snake and the Fox." Once upon a time, a snake came up to a fox and said: "It seems to me that I know you!" The fox replied to him: "Me too." "Then," said the snake, "give me some money." "A fox doesn't give money," replied the tricky animal, who, in order to escape, jumped down into a deep ravine full of strawberries and chicken honey. But the snake was there waiting for him with a Mephistophelean laugh. The fox pulled out his knife, shouting: "I'm going to teach you how to live!" Then he took to flight, turning his back. But he had no luck. The snake was quicker. With a well-chosen blow of his fist, he struck the fox in the middle of his forehead which broke into a thousand pieces, while he cried: "No! No! Four times no! I'm not your daughter."[5]

MRS. MARTIN. It's interesting.

MRS. SMITH. It's not bad.

MR. MARTIN (*shaking* MR. SMITH's *hand*). My congratulations.

FIRE CHIEF (*jealous*). Not so good. And anyway, I've heard it before.

MR. SMITH. It's terrible.

MRS. SMITH. But it wasn't even true.

MRS. MARTIN. Yes, unfortunately.

MR. MARTIN (*to* MRS. SMITH). It's your turn, dear lady.

MRS. SMITH. I only know one. I'm going to tell it to you. It's called "The Bouquet."

MR. SMITH. My wife has always been romantic.

MR. MARTIN. She's a true Englishwoman.[6]

MRS. SMITH. Here it is: Once upon a time, a fiancé gave a bouquet of flowers to his fiancée, who said, "Thanks"; but before she had said, "Thanks," he, without saying a single word, took back the flowers he had given her in order to teach her a good lesson, and he said, "I take them back." He said, "Goodbye," and took them back and went off in all directions.

MR. MARTIN. Oh, charming! (*He either kisses or does not kiss* MRS. SMITH.)

MRS. MARTIN. You have a wife, Mr. Smith, of whom all the world is jealous.

MR. SMITH. It's true. My wife is intelligence personified. She's even more intelligent than I. In any case, she is much more feminine, everyone says so.

MRS. SMITH (*to the* FIRE CHIEF). Let's have another, Mr. Fire Chief.

FIRE CHIEF. Oh, no, it's too late.

MR. MARTIN. Tell us one, anyway.

FIRE CHIEF. I'm too tired.

MR. SMITH. Please do us a favor.

MR. MARTIN. I beg you.

---

[5] This story was deleted in Nicolas Bataille's production. Mr. Smith went through the gestures only, without making a sound.

[6] These two speeches were repeated three times in the original production.

FIRE CHIEF. No.

MRS. MARTIN. You have a heart of ice. We're sitting on hot coals.

MRS. SMITH (*falls on her knees sobbing, or else she does not do this*). I implore you!

FIRE CHIEF. Righto.

MR. SMITH (*in* MRS. MARTIN's *ear*). He agrees! He's going to bore us again.

MRS. MARTIN. Shh.

MRS. SMITH. No luck. I was too polite.

FIRE CHIEF. "The Headcold." My brother-in-law had, on the paternal side, a first cousin whose maternal uncle had a father-in-law whose paternal grandfather had married as his second wife a young native whose brother he had met on one of his travels, a girl of whom he was enamored and by whom he had a son who married an intrepid lady pharmacist who was none other than the neice of an unknown fourth-class petty officer of the Royal Navy and whose adopted father had an aunt who spoke Spanish fluently and who was, perhaps, one of the granddaughters of an engineer who died young, himself the grandson of the owner of a vineyard which produced mediocre wine, but who had a second cousin, a stay-at-home, a sergeant-major, whose son had married a very pretty young woman, a divorcée, whose first husband was the son of a loyal patriot who, in the hope of making his fortune, had managed to bring up one of his daughters so that she could marry a footman who had known Rothschild, and whose brother, after having changed his trade several times, married and had a daughter whose stunted great-grandfather wore spectacles which had been given him by a cousin of his, the brother-in-law of a man from Portugal, natural son of a miller, not too badly off, whose foster-brother had married the daughter of a former country doctor, who was himself a foster-brother of the son of a forester, himself the natural son of another country doctor, married three times in a row, whose third wife . . .

MR. MARTIN. I knew that third wife, if I'm not mistaken. She ate chicken sitting on a hornet's nest.

FIRE CHIEF. It's not the same one.

MRS. SMITH. Shh!

FIRE CHIEF. As I was saying . . . whose third wife was the daughter of the best midwife in the region and who, early left a widow . . .

MR. SMITH. Like my wife.

FIRE CHIEF. . . . Had married a glazier who was full of life and who had had, by the daughter of a station master, a child who had burned his bridges . . .

MRS. SMITH. His britches?

MR. MARTIN. No, his bridge game.

FIRE CHIEF. And had married an oyster woman, whose father had a brother, mayor of a small town, who had taken as his wife a blonde schoolteacher, whose cousin, a fly fisherman . . .

MR. MARTIN. A fly by night?

FIRE CHIEF. . . . Had married another blonde schoolteacher, named Marie, too, whose brother was married to another Marie, also a blonde schoolteacher . . .

MR. SMITH. Since she's blonde, she must be Marie.

FIRE CHIEF. . . . And whose father had been reared in Canada by an old woman who was the niece of a priest whose grandmother, occasionally in the winter, like everyone else, caught a cold.

MRS. SMITH. A curious story. Almost unbelievable.

MR. MARTIN. If you catch a cold, you should get yourself a colt.

MR. SMITH. It's a useless precaution, but absolutely necessary.

MRS. MARTIN. Excuse me, Mr. Fire Chief, but I did not follow your story very well. At the end, when we got to the grandmother of the priest, I got mixed up.

MR. SMITH. One always gets mixed up in the hands of a priest.

MRS. SMITH. Oh yes, Mr. Fire Chief, begin again. Everyone wants to hear.

FIRE CHIEF. Ah, I don't know whether I'll be able to. I'm on official business. It depends on what time it is.

MRS. SMITH. We don't have the time, here.

FIRE CHIEF. But the clock?

MR. SMITH. It runs badly. It is contradictory, and always indicates the opposite of what the hour really is.

Enter MARY.

MARY. Madam . . . sir . . .

MRS. SMITH. What do you want?

MR. SMITH. What have you come in here for?

MARY. I hope, madam and sir will excuse me . . . and these ladies and gentlemen too . . . I would like . . . I would like . . . to tell you a story, myself.

MRS. MARTIN. What is she saying?

MR. MARTIN. I believe that our friends' maid is going crazy . . . she wants to tell us a story, too.

FIRE CHIEF. Who does she think she is? (*He looks at her.*) Oh!

MRS. SMITH. Why are you butting in?

MR. SMITH. This is really uncalled for, Mary . . .

FIRE CHIEF. Oh! But it is she! Incredible!

MR. SMITH. And you?

MARY. Incredible! Here!

MRS. SMITH. What does all this mean?

MR. SMITH. You know each other?

FIRE CHIEF. And how!

MARY *throws herself on the neck of the* FIRE CHIEF.

MARY. I'm so glad to see you again . . . at last!

MR. *and* MRS. SMITH. Oh!

MR. SMITH. This is too much, here, in our home, in the suburbs of London.

MRS. SMITH. It's not proper! . . .

FIRE CHIEF. It was she who extinguished my first fires.

MARY. I'm your little firehose.

MR. MARTIN. If that is the case . . . dear friends . . . these emotions are understandable, human, honorable . . .

MRS. MARTIN. All that is human is honorable.

MRS. SMITH. Even so, I don't like to see it . . . here among us . . .

MR. SMITH. She's not been properly brought up . . .

FIRE CHIEF. Oh, you have too many prejudices.

MRS. MARTIN. What I think is that a maid, after all — even though it's none of my business — is never anything but a maid . . .

MR. MARTIN. Even if she can sometimes be a rather good detective.

FIRE CHIEF. Let me go.

MARY. Don't be upset! . . . They're not so bad really.

MR. SMITH. Hm . . . hm . . . you two are very touching, but at the same time, a little . . . a little . . .

MR. MARTIN. Yes, that's exactly the word.

MR. SMITH. . . . A little too exhibitionistic . . .

MR. MARTIN. There is a native British modesty — forgive me for attempting, yet again, to define my thought — not understood by foreigners, even by specialists, thanks to which, if I may thus express myself . . . of course, I don't mean to refer to you . . .

MARY. I was going to tell you . . .

MR. SMITH. Don't tell us anything . . .

MARY. Oh yes!

MRS. SMITH. Go, my little Mary, go quietly to the kitchen and read your poems before the mirror . . .

MR. MARTIN. You know, even though I'm not a maid, I also read poems before the mirror.

MRS. MARTIN. This morning when you looked at yourself in the mirror you didn't see yourself.

MR. MARTIN. That's because I wasn't there yet . . .

MARY. All the same, I could, perhaps, recite a little poem for you.

MRS. SMITH. My little Mary, you are frightfully obstinate.

MARY. I'm going to recite a poem, then, is that agreed? It is a poem entitled "The Fire" in honor of the Fire Chief:

>   The Fire
>   The polypoids were burning in the wood
>   A stone caught fire
>   The castle caught fire
>   The forest caught fire
>   The men caught fire
>   The women caught fire
>   The birds caught fire
>   The fish caught fire
>   The water caught fire
>   The sky caught fire

> The ashes caught fire
> The smoke caught fire
> The fire caught fire
> Everything caught fire
> Caught fire, caught fire.

She recites the poem while the SMITHS *are pushing her offstage.*

MRS. MARTIN. That sent chills up my spine . . .

MR. MARTIN. And yet there's a certain warmth in those lines . . .

FIRE CHIEF. I thought it was marvelous.

MRS. SMITH. All the same . . .

MR. SMITH. You're exaggerating . . .

FIRE CHIEF. Just a minute . . . I admit . . . all this is very subjective . . . but this is my conception of the world. My world. My dream. My ideal . . . And now this reminds me that I must leave. Since you don't have the time here, I must tell you that in exactly three-quarters of an hour and sixteen minutes, I'm having a fire at the other end of the city. Consequently, I must hurry. Even though it will be quite unimportant.

MRS. SMITH. What will it be? A little chimney fire?

FIRE CHIEF. Oh, not even that. A straw fire and a little heartburn.

MR. SMITH. Well, we're sorry to see you go.

MRS. SMITH. You have been very entertaining.

MRS. MARTIN. Thanks to you, we have passed a truly Cartesian quarter of an hour.

FIRE CHIEF (*moving towards the door, then stopping*). Speaking of that—the bald soprano? (*General silence, embarrassment.*)

MRS. SMITH. She always wears her hair in the same style.

FIRE CHIEF. Ah! Then goodbye, ladies and gentlemen.

MR. MARTIN. Good luck, and a good fire!

FIRE CHIEF. Let's hope so. For everybody.

> FIRE CHIEF *exits. All accompany him to the door and then return to their seats.*

MRS. MARTIN. I can buy a pocketknife for my brother, but you can't buy Ireland for your grandfather.

MR. SMITH. One walks on his feet, but one heats with electricity or coal.

MR. MARTIN. He who sells an ox today, will have an egg tomorrow.

MRS. SMITH. In real life, one must look out of the window.

MRS. MARTIN. One can sit down on a chair, when the chair doesn't have any.

MR. SMITH. One must always think of everything.

MR. MARTIN. The ceiling is above, the floor below.

MRS. SMITH. When I say yes, it's only a manner of speaking.

MRS. MARTIN. To each his own.

MR. SMITH. Take a circle, caress it, and it will turn vicious.

MRS. SMITH. A schoolmaster teaches his pupils to read, but the cat suckles her young when they are small.

MRS. MARTIN. Nevertheless, it was the cow that gave us tails.
MR. SMITH. When I'm in the country, I love the solitude and the quiet.
MR. MARTIN. You are not old enough yet for that.
MRS. SMITH. Benjamin Franklin was right; you are more nervous than he.
MRS. MARTIN. What are the seven days of the week?
MR. SMITH. Monday, Tuesday, Wednesday, Thursday, Friday, Saturday, Sunday.[7]
MR. MARTIN. Edward is a clerk; his sister Nancy is a typist, and his brother William a shop-assistant.[7]
MRS. SMITH. An odd family!
MRS. MARTIN. I prefer a bird in the bush to a sparrow in a barrow.
MR. SMITH. Rather a steak in a chalet than gristle in a castle.
MR. MARTIN. An Englishman's home is truly his castle.
MRS. SMITH. I don't know enough Spanish to make myself understood.
MRS. MARTIN. I'll give you my mother-in-law's slippers if you'll give me your husband's coffin.
MR. SMITH. I'm looking for a monophysite priest to marry to our maid.
MR. MARTIN. Bread is a staff, whereas bread is also a staff, and an oak springs from an oak every morning at dawn.
MRS. SMITH. My uncle lives in the country, but that's none of the midwife's business.
MR. MARTIN. Paper is for writing, the cat's for the rat. Cheese is for scratching.
MRS. SMITH. The car goes very fast, but the cook beats batter better.
MR. SMITH. Don't be turkeys; rather kiss the conspirator.
MR. MARTIN. Charity begins at home.[8]
MRS. SMITH. I'm waiting for the aqueduct to come and see me at my windmill.
MR. MARTIN. One can prove that social progress is definitely better with sugar.
MR. SMITH. To hell with polishing!

Following this last speech of MR. SMITH'S, *the others are silent for a moment, stupefied. We sense that there is a certain nervous irritation. The strokes of the clock are more nervous too. The speeches which follow must be said, at first, in a glacial, hostile tone. The hostility and the nervousness increase. At the end of this scene, the four characters must be standing very close to each other, screaming their speeches, raising their fists, ready to throw themselves upon each other.*

MR. MARTIN. One doesn't polish spectacles with black wax.
MRS. SMITH. Yes, but with money one can buy anything.
MR. MARTIN. I'd rather kill a rabbit than sing in the garden.
MR. SMITH. Cockatoos, cockatoos, cockatoos, cockatoos, cockatoos, cockatoos, cockatoos, cockatoos, cockatoos, cockatoos.

[7] In English in the original.
[8] In English in the original.

MRS. SMITH. Such caca, such caca, such caca, such caca, such caca, such caca, such caca, such caca, such caca.

MR. MARTIN. Such cascades of cacas, such cascades of cacas, such cascades of cacas, such cascades of cacas, such cascades of cacas, such cascades of cacas, such cascades of cacas, such cascades of cacas.

MR. SMITH. Dogs have fleas, dogs have fleas.

MRS. MARTIN. Cactus, coccyx! crocus! cockaded! cockroach!

MRS. SMITH. Incasker, you incask us.

MR. MARTIN. I'd rather lay an egg in a box than go and steal an ox.

MRS. MARTIN (*opening her mouth very wide*). Ah! oh! ah! oh! Let me gnash my teeth.

MR. SMITH. Crocodile!

MR. MARTIN. Let's go and slap Ulysses.

MR. SMITH. I'm going to live in my cabana among my cacao trees.

MRS. MARTIN. Cacao trees on cacao farms don't bear coconuts, they yield cocoa! Cacao trees on cacao farms don't bear coconuts, they yield cocoa! Cacao trees on cacao farms don't bear coconuts, they yield cocoa.

MRS. SMITH. Mice have lice, lice haven't mice.

MRS. MARTIN. Don't ruche my brooch!

MR. MARTIN. Don't smooch the brooch!

MR. SMITH. Groom the goose, don't goose the groom.

MRS. MARTIN. The goose grooms.

MRS. SMITH. Groom your tooth.

MR. MARTIN. Groom the bridegroom, groom the bridegroom.

MR. SMITH. Seducer seduced!

MRS. MARTIN. Scaramouche!

MRS. SMITH. Sainte-Nitouche!

MR. MARTIN. Go take a douche.

MR. SMITH. I've been goosed.

MRS. MARTIN. Sainte-Nitouche stoops to my cartouche.

MRS. SMITH. "Who'd stoop to blame? . . . and I never choose to stoop."

MR. MARTIN. Robert!

MR. SMITH. Browning!

MRS. MARTIN, MR. SMITH. Rudyard.

MRS. SMITH, MR. MARTIN. Kipling.

MRS. MARTIN, MR. SMITH. Robert Kipling!

MRS. SMITH, MR. MARTIN. Rudyard Browning.[9]

[9] In the French text these speeches read as follows:
MME SMITH. — N'y touchez pas, elle est brisée.
M. MARTIN. — Sully!
M. SMITH. — Prudhomme!
MME MARTIN, M. SMITH. — François.
MME SMITH, M. MARTIN. — Coppée.
MME MARTIN, M. SMITH. — Coppée Sully!
MME SMITH, M. MARTIN. — Prudhomme François.

MRS. MARTIN. Silly gobblegobblers, silly gobblegobblers.
MR. MARTIN. Marietta, spot the pot!
MRS. SMITH. Krishnamurti, Krishnamurti, Krishnamurti!
MR. SMITH. The pope elopes! The pope's got no horoscope. The horoscope's bespoke.
MRS. MARTIN. Bazaar, Balzac, bazooka!
MR. MARTIN. Bizarre, beaux-arts, brassieres!
MR. SMITH. A, e, i, o, u, a, e, i, o, u, a, e, i, o, u, i!
MRS. MARTIN. B, c, d, f, g, l, m, n, p, r, s, t, v, w, x, z!
MR. MARTIN. From sage to stooge, from stage to serge!
MRS. SMITH (*imitating a train*). Choo, choo, choo, choo, choo, choo, choo, choo, choo, choo!
MR. SMITH. It's!
MRS. MARTIN. Not!
MR. MARTIN. That!
MRS. SMITH. Way!
MR. SMITH. It's!
MRS. MARTIN. O!
MR. MARTIN. Ver!
MRS. SMITH. Here!

All together, completely infuriated, screaming in each other's ears. The light is extinguished. In the darkness we hear, in an increasingly rapid rhythm:

ALL TOGETHER. It's not that way, it's over here, it's not that way, it's over here, it's not that way, it's over here, it's not that way, it's over here![10]

The words cease abruptly. Again, the lights come on. MR. AND MRS. MARTIN *are seated like the* SMITHS *at the beginning of the play. The play begins again with the* MARTINS, *who say exactly the same lines as the* SMITHS *in the first scene, while the curtain softly falls.*

[10] When produced, some of the speeches in this last scene were cut or shuffled. Moreover, the final beginning again, if one can call it that, still involved the Smiths, since the author did not have the inspired idea of substituting the Martins for the Smiths until after the hundredth performance.

Selected General Reading List

Bentley, Eric. *In Search of Theater.* 1953.
———. *The Playwright as Thinker.* 1946.
Chandler, Frank. *Modern Continental Playwrights.* 1931.
Clark, Barrett, ed. *European Theories of the Drama.* 1947.
———, and Freedley, George, eds. *A History of Modern Drama.* 1947.
Cole, Toby, ed. *Playwrights on Playwriting.* 1960.
Downer, Alan. *Fifty Years of American Drama: 1900–1950.* 1951.
Drew, Elizabeth. *Discovering Drama.* 1937.
Fergusson, Francis. *The Idea of a Theater.* 1949.
Gassner, John. *Form and Idea in Modern Theatre.* 1956.
———. *Masters of the Drama.* 1954.
———. *The Theatre in Our Times.* 1954.
———. *Theatre at the Crossroads.* 1960.
Jones, Robert Edmond. *The Dramatic Imagination.* 1956.
Krutch, Joseph Wood. *The American Drama Since 1918.* 1957.
———. *"Modernism" in Modern Drama.* 1953.
Lumley, Frederick. *Trends in Twentieth Century Drama.* 1956.
Modern Drama, 1958 —.
Nicoll, Allardyce. *World Drama.* 1950.
O'Hara, Frank, and Bro, Marguerite. *Invitation to the Theatre.* 1951.
Peacock, Ronald. *The Art of Drama.* 1957.
———. *The Poet in the Theatre.* 1960.
Steiner, George. *The Death of Tragedy.* 1961.
The Tulane Drama Review, 1956 —.
Whiting, Frank. *An Introduction to the Theatre.* 1954.
Williams, Raymond. *Drama from Ibsen to Eliot.* 1952.
Young, Stark. *The Theatre.* 1927.

Selected Criticism

Henrik Ibsen

Downs, Brian. *Ibsen: The Intellectual Background.* 1946.
———. *A Study of Six Plays by Ibsen.* 1950.
Koht, Halvdan. *The Life of Ibsen.* 1931.
Northam, John. *Ibsen's Dramatic Method.* 1953.
Shaw, Bernard. *The Quintessence of Ibsenism.* 1913.
Tennant, P. F. *Ibsen's Dramatic Technique.* 1948.
Weigand, Hermann. *The Modern Ibsen.* 1925.

August Strindberg

Dahlström, C. E. W. L. *Strindberg's Dramatic Expressionism.* 1930.
Huneker, James. *Iconoclasts.* 1928.
McGill, V. J. *August Strindberg, the Bedeviled Viking.* 1930.
Modern Drama, December, 1962 (Strindberg number).
Mortensen, Brita, and Downs, Brian. *Strindberg.* 1949.
Sprigge, Elizabeth. *The Strange Life of August Strindberg.* 1949.

Maurice Maeterlinck

Bailly, A. *Maeterlinck.* 1931.
Bithell, Jethro. *Life and Works of Maurice Maeterlinck.* 1930.
Huneker, James. *Iconoclasts.* 1928.
Symons, Arthur. *The Symbolist Movement in Literature.* 1919.
Taylor, Una. *Maurice Maeterlinck.* 1915.

George Bernard Shaw

Bentley, Eric. *Bernard Shaw.* 1947.
Chesterton, G. K. *George Bernard Shaw.* 1909.
Ervine, St. John. *Bernard Shaw, His Life, Work, and Friends.* 1956.
Henderson, Archibald. *Bernard Shaw, Man of the Century.* 1956.
Kronenberger, Louis, ed. *George Bernard Shaw: A Critical Survey.* 1953.
Mander, Raymond, and Mitchenson, Joe. *Theatrical Companion to Shaw.* 1954.
Nethercot, Arthur. *Men and Supermen: The Shavian Portrait Gallery.* 1954.
Pearson, Hesketh. *G.B.S.: A Full-length Portrait.* 1942.
Shaw, Bernard. *Sixteen Self Sketches.* 1949.

William Butler Yeats

Bentley, Eric. "Yeats as a Playwright," *Kenyon Review,* Spring, 1948.
Ellmann, Richard. *Yeats: The Man and the Masks.* 1948.

Selected Criticism

Hall, James, and Steinmann, Martin, eds. *The Permanence of Yeats.* 1950.
Hone, Joseph. *W. B. Yeats.* 1943.
Popkin, Henry. "Yeats as Dramatist," *The Tulane Drama Review,* March, 1959.

JOHN MILLINGTON SYNGE

Bickley, Francis. *J. M. Synge and the Irish Dramatic Movement.* 1912.
Bourgeois, Maurice. *John Millington Synge and the Irish Theatre.* 1913.
Ellis-Fermor, Una. *The Irish Dramatic Movement.* 1939.
Greene, David, and Stephens, Edward. *J. M. Synge.* 1959.
Howe, P. P. *John Millington Synge.* 1912.
Yeats, W. B. *Synge and the Ireland of His Time.* 1911.

LUIGI PIRANDELLO

Bishop, Thomas. *Pirandello and the French Theater.* 1960.
MacClintock, Lander. *The Age of Pirandello.* 1951.
Starkie, Walter. *Luigi Pirandello.* 1937.
Vittorini, Domenico. *The Drama of Luigi Pirandello.* 1935.

BERTOLT BRECHT

Esslin, Martin. *Brecht, A Choice of Evils.* 1959.
Garten, H. F. *Modern German Drama.* 1959.
Gorelik, Mordecai. "An Epic Theatre Catechism," *The Tulane Drama Review,* September, 1959.
Gray, Ronald. *Bertolt Brecht.* 1961.
The Tulane Drama Review, September, 1961 (Brecht number).
Willett, John. *The Theatre of Bertolt Brecht.* 1959.

ARTHUR MILLER

Bentley, Eric. *The Dramatic Event.* 1954.
———, ed. *The Play: A Critical Anthology.* 1951.
Clurman, Harold. *Lies Like Truth.* 1959.
Sievers, W. David. *Freud on Broadway.* 1955.
Welland, Dennis. *Arthur Miller.* 1961.

EUGENE IONESCO

Coe, Richard. *Eugene Ionesco.* 1961.
Esslin, Martin. *The Theatre of the Absurd.* 1961.
Fowlie, Wallace. *Dionysus in Paris.* 1960.
Grossvogel, David. *The Self-Conscious Stage in Modern French Drama.* 1958.
Guicharnaud, Jacques, with Beckelman, June. *Modern French Theatre.* 1961.

Glossary of Terms

NOTE: These definitions in their brevity are often open to further qualification. As Eric Bentley has aptly said in *The Playwright as Thinker*, "The trouble with literary terms is that in proportion as they become impressive they become useless, in proportion as they become exact they become inapplicable."

antagonist   The character who is opposed to the protagonist, or main character.

climax   The point of greatest tension in a play.

comedy   A relatively light form of drama which aims primarily to amuse and which ends happily. Comedy may be earnest and serious, but it is not likely to be sober.

conflict   The chief principle of most plays; it is the struggle which comes from the interplay of opposing forces.

curtain scene   The last moments preceding a curtain.

denouement   The resolution or final settlement of the plot.

dialogue   The conversation of two or more characters.

discussion drama   Drama in which discussion of ideas tends to overshadow overt action.

dramatic conventions   Those conventions which are accepted by both dramatist and audience on the basis of their usefulness. For example, in the fourth wall convention the actors normally address their remarks and face toward the audience, which is supposedly beyond an imaginary fourth wall.

dramatic irony   Irony which exists when the audience is aware of a meaning or a significance of which a character is ignorant.

epic theater   Extensively narrative, non-Aristotelian, overtly didactic drama; it utilizes the "stage-as-machine" concept.

epilogue   A closing section added to a play, providing further comment, interpretation, or information.

exposition   That part of a play which provides an audience with background information.

Glossary of Terms

expressionism The dramatic presentation of a subjective state of mind through physical stage devices such as lighting, sound, scenery, or properties. The subjectivity may be in the mind of either the playwright or the protagonist.

farce An exaggerated kind of comedy using improbable situations, gross incongruities, or horseplay.

folk drama Regional drama portraying the quality of life of an unsophisticated time or place.

foreshadowing The process of giving the audience an intimation of some event to follow.

melodrama Portrayal of recognizable character types involved in usually sensational circumstances which emphasize suspense and action.

monologue A speech by one person; a soliloquy. Today, often interior monologue, a person thinking aloud.

motivation The reason or cause for an action.

naturalism An extreme form of realism which emphasizes literal and unselective fidelity to fact. Often there is an apparent objectivity of presentation and often environment is a strong force in the action. The term applies to both form and content.

pathos The quality in a play which arouses feelings of pity, sorrow, compassion, or sympathy (sympathy is feeling *with* someone).

plot The ordered arrangement of actions in a play. The sub-plot is of secondary importance but usually reinforces the significance of the main plot.

prologue A section preceding the main body of a play.

props, properties Movable objects used on stage; separate from the set.

protagonist The main, or chief, character.

raisonneur The reasoner, or the playwright's mouthpiece or interpreter.

realism A faithful but selective representation of the objective world. Realism imposes a pattern upon its material and usually criticizes the action which it portrays.

romanticism The literary style in which life is heightened or idealized. Often grand characters, distant times and places, or the mysterious or supernatural characterize romanticism. A broad and often vague term, describing both content and form.

symbol, symbolism A symbol is something which stands for something else. Symbolism employs concrete objects to represent such things as ideas, mental states, or abstractions. *Symbolism* has both a general and a narrow meaning (as in the Symbolist movement).

symbolist drama Drama in which symbols carry the burden of the (often vague) theme and in which the unexpressed is often of more importance than what is stated directly.

theater of the grotesque Drama which emphasizes the nonrational, ridiculous, incongruous elements in man's experience.

theater of the absurd Drama which goes beyond the grotesque drama in its theatricalist presentation of life as an absurd, irrational experience; in general, the form expresses the meaning.

theatricalism An inclusive term, describing several nonrealistic dramatic modes which emphasize the use of the physical theater (e.g., lights, sounds, sets).

theme The main idea of a play; not the subject matter.

tragedy Drama in which the conflict results in disaster for the protagonist. Usually universal standards or truths are involved. A difficult term to define or delimit.

verse drama Drama written chiefly or wholly in verse, and therefore nonrealistic to some degree.